Bo

*A Practical
Approach to
Evidence*

# A Practical Approach to Evidence

*Second Edition*

*Peter Murphy*

First published in Great Britain 1980 by Financial Training Publications Limited,
Avenue House, 131 Holland Park Avenue, London W11 4UT

© Financial Training Publications Limited 1980
  Reprinted 1982
  Second edition 1985

ISBN: 0 906322 69 3

Typeset by Kerrypress Ltd, Luton
Printed by Livesey Ltd, Shrewsbury

# Contents

A: Fundamentals of evidence  1.1 What evidence is  1.2 The varieties of
evidence  1.3 Facts which may be proved  1.4 Admissibility and weight  1.5
Tribunals of law and fact: judicial discretion  1.6 Evidence illegally or unfairly
obtained  1.7 The best-evidence rule

A: *The Queen* v *Coke; The Queen* v *Littleton*  2.1 Brief for the prosecution  2.2
Brief for the defence  B: *Blackstone* v *Coke*  2.3 Brief for the plaintiff  2.4 Brief
for the defendant

A: The burden of proof  3.1 Introduction  3.2 The two burdens  3.3 Presumptions and the burden of proof  3.4 Where the legal burden lies  3.5 Where
the evidential burden lies  B: The standard of proof  3.6 Introduction
3.7 Criminal cases  3.8 Civil cases  3.9 Matrimonial causes  3.10 Questions
for discussion

4.1 Uses of the word 'character'  4.2 Uses of character evidence  A: Character as
a fact in issue  4.3 Introduction  4.4 Civil cases  4.5 Criminal cases  B:
Relevant evidence which involves character  4.6 Introduction  4.7 Cross-
examination as to evidence involving character  4.8 Admissible evidence
involving bad character  4.9 Evidence of good character in criminal cases 4.10 *R*
v *Coke; R* v *Littleton*  C: Impeachment of the defendant in criminal cases —the

# Preface

The production of the second edition of *A Practical Approach to Evidence* has been no easy task. The law never remains static for long. But most observers would attest to some feeling of surprise at the extent of change, some of it subtle, some not so subtle, that has occurred since publication of the first edition. As suggested in the preface to the first edition, the exclusion of evidence on public policy grounds has continued in vogue. The courts have probably still not spoken the final words, even on the general principles of that subject. There have been important decisions in the areas of character evidence, similar-fact evidence and corroboration, to name just a few.

All these are recorded in this new edition. They have, however, been overshadowed by the radical impact of the Police and Criminal Evidence Act 1984, which is destined to change the way in which we think about some of the most significant subjects within the law of evidence. In one statute, Parliament has provided for much wider use of documentary hearsay evidence in criminal cases, reversed the rule in *Hollington* v *Hewthorn* in criminal cases, provided an entirely new code of statutory law dealing with confessions, the discretionary exclusion of prosecution evidence and the competence and compellability of the spouse of the accused. The Act does, of course, accomplish much more. It has ushered in a new era in the history of the relationship between the police and suspected persons, in particular in relation to their treatment and interrogation while in custody. While much of this is procedural in nature, it will undoubtedly have a profound once-removed effect on the law of evidence, as the courts learn to do justice in a world without the Judges' Rules. There is hardly a subsection of the Act which will not, in some subtle way, affect the rules of evidence as they are applied in criminal courts. Those parts of the Act which have had a direct impact on the law of evidence are fully dealt with, and reference is made to other potentially significant sections. Because the most important of the Act's provisions take effect only on 1 January 1986, and because the replaced rules of common law and statutory provisions will probably be used to guide the courts for some time to come, they also are stated in abbreviated form wherever appropriate in this edition.

The format of the book, which has proved popular with many teachers, has been kept much the same. Not long after the first edition appeared, a number of requests from teachers led to the publication of a companion case-book, *Evidence: Cases and Argument* written by John Beaumont and the present author. In that work, a companion civil case arising from Margaret Blackstone's adventure with Henry Coke was introduced. In retrospect, this seems so obvious an idea that its omission from the first edition of this work mystifies even the author. It has, therefore, been added in this edition. Certain areas have been re-written simply to reflect further experience of seeking to present the subject to students. The process of refining has led to the omission of some material which appeared in the first edition. The subject of res judicata was felt, on reflection, to be unnecessary to an introductory evidence text, and has been removed. The remainder of the former Chapter 10, dealing with the rule in *Hollington* v *Hewthorn* and its statutory modifications, has been incorporated into the present Chapter 9 where it has been made at home with the subject of opinion evidence.

One grievous blow to the law of evidence was struck, not by the courts but by death, which befell Professor Sir Rupert Cross in 1980. Although denied the use of his eyes, Rupert Cross had vision of a different order, not only in his mastery of the law, but in the kindness and humanity with which he interpreted it and showed it to his students. He was the greatest scholar and teacher of the common-law rules of evidence of his generation, and ranks among the greatest of any generation. His loss is premature and irreparable.

My thanks are again most sincerely expressed to my publishers, especially to Alistair MacQueen and Heather Saward. Few authors can have had such delightful and tolerant friends with whom to work. My thanks are also due to Pat Brown who edited the manuscript, Isabel Morgan, Barrister-at-law and Brian Glover, Barrister-at-law and lecturer at the Inns of Court School of Law, and to many members of the Bar, law teachers and students for their helpful suggestions and encouragement. They have all played a part in this edition. My wife, Hilary Pearson, now herself the author of a major text on computer law, added her own experience of authorship to her love and unfailing good humour, to help and encourage me in this work.

Houston, Texas
1 May 1985

# Preface to the First Edition

The law of evidence underlies the whole practice of law in every field capable of leading in litigation. Not only a thorough understanding of the rules of admissibility, but also a mature feel for the weight and tactical significance of evidence should be a part of the foundation of every practice. Cases are probably won and lost more often for reasons of evidential acumen, or the lack of it, than for reasons of any other sort. At the same time, evidential problems have a habit of arising, to quote a celebrated rule to be found in Chapter 14 of this book, '*ex improviso*, which no human ingenuity could foresee'. Law and practice can almost always be made the subject of prior research; as often as not, evidence presents problems without warning calling for immediate reaction. Failure to object at the right time, or the making of an unfounded objection may in some cases have serious consequences for the fate of the piece of evidence concerned, or the case as a whole. One's opponent's objections, whether well or ill founded must be dealt with. A colleague at the Bar once said to the author that there was, in his opinion, only one rule of evidence, namely a reaction of instinct on hearing any words spoken in court, which said either, 'Yes, that's all right', or 'No, we can't have that'. That sort of instinct exists and very often works even before the witness speaks at all; it takes time to develop; time, and a thorough knowledge of the rules; but it is of incalculable importance.

Given all this, it is somewhat surprising to survey the textbooks on the subject and to find that they are prone to two distinct tendencies. There are those which treat the subject in a highly academic way, divorced from the realities of practice. There are those which treat the subject as a mass of apparently unrelated minutiae, divorced from any discernible theme. There is also, happily, the matchless but demanding work of Professor Cross, comparisons of which are vain. The present work is intended simply to meet the long-felt need of students for the Bar examinations, now joined by students for the Law Society's examinations, and those on degree courses, for a book soundly based around the considerations of practice in the courts. It is hoped that those concerned professionally with the law of evidence may also find it useful. There are, no doubt, many matters of great interest in academic terms which will not be found here; but equally, the important, recurring issues are dealt with in the context of their practical operation, and of the rules of practice which apply to them.

The book is constructed around the facts of a fictitious, but not unrealistic case. All the characters and events in it are fictitious, and any resemblance to persons living or dead entirely coincidental. But the issues which it raises will be familiar to every criminal practitioner. The papers in the case occupy the whole of Chapter 2. It should not be thought that civil evidence is neglected. It is impossible, without an unacceptable sacrifice of realism, to incorporate into one case every important rule of evidence. But in every chapter subsequent to Chapter 2, the reader will find references back to the case of *The*

*Queen* v *Coke and Littleton*, and the reader should familiarise himself with the papers at the outset and return to them time and time again to gain some insight into the practical implications of the rules dealt with in the text. At the end of each chapter, there are questions which counsel acting might have to solve, and these also should be considered. One of the peculiar problems of evidence is that evidential questions rarely come in ones. Cases like *R* v *Christie* [1914] AC 545 sometimes seem to be authority for almost everything that matters. It will be found that throughout the book, reference to rules outside the scope of the chapter under consideration will be made, simply because rules of evidence can rarely be dealt with in isolation from each other. The reader might do very much worse than to read the book from cover to cover, quite quickly and superficially, before beginning serious study.

An attempt has been made to state the law as at 30 June 1980. Evidence is a subject prone to fashion, and at present, after the recent popularity of evidence illegally and unfairly obtained, public policy and confidentiality are in vogue. At the time of writing, the House of Lords has not yet given its reasons for its decision in *British Steel Corporation* v *Granada Television Ltd* (see 11.5) and whether some new twist will emerge remains to be seen.

My thanks are due to my publishers, who have displayed a quite remarkable cheerfulness and tolerance, to Mr Derek French for preparing the indexes of cases and statutes; without their professional skills, this book would never have seen the light of day. It is also a pleasure to thank Miss Diana Bailey MSc and Mr Brian Parkin MSc, MPhil, MI Biol (the former an old forensic friend and adversary) for their help with the forensic evidence in Coke and Littleton; my colleagues and students at the Inns of Court School of Law for their inspiration over the last two years; and above all my wife, Hilary Pearson MA(Oxon), LLB(Lond), Barrister-at-Law, who brought to bear upon the project of writing this book not only her greater experience in the teaching of evidence, but also the considerable volume of love and understanding necessary to sustain me through its darkest hours.

Islington
1 July 1980

# Table of Cases

# Table of Statutes

*Dedication*


This second edition is dedicated to the memory of my father William Joseph Murphy (1916–1984) and to that of Professor Sir Rupert Cross (1912–1980).

# 1    Evidence: The Science of Proof

## A: FUNDAMENTALS OF EVIDENCE

### 1.1   What evidence is

The story is told of an irascible county court judge who was constantly interrupting a litigant in person as the latter tried, evidently commanding an insufficient degree of credibility, to give his evidence in the case in which he was concerned. At length, the exasperated litigant exclaimed: 'Your Honour, I'm telling the truth!' only to receive the reply: 'That may very well be so, but I don't believe you.' Whether or not this story is, as it well may be, apocryphal, it neatly illustrates the selfsame truth as does the following exchange between Bench and Bar, witnessed by the present author: counsel having objected to the tendering by his opponent of a piece of documentary evidence, which appeared to be relevant to the case but inadmissible in law, the judge asked: 'Am I not to hear the truth?', an enquiry which sounds reasonable enough, but which attracted the somewhat startling answer: 'No, Your Lordship is to hear the evidence.'

The moral of these stories is that in any form of litigation, whatever the actual truth or merits of the case (if indeed, these can ever be ascertained) they are worthless unless they can be demonstrated in such a way that the court or tribunal seised of the litigation is prepared to accept and act on them. In any litigation, criminal or civil, one party or the other sets out to demonstrate to the court that his assertions are true (or, at least, probably true) and that accordingly he is entitled to succeed. The plaintiff in a civil case, the prosecutor in a criminal case, each sets out to prove the essential elements of the claim or charge, as ascertained from the relevant rules of the substantive law and reflected in the pleadings or indictment. It must be demonstrated to the court that those rules of substantive law, so reflected, apply to the facts of the case which has been brought, and consequently the plaintiff or prosecutor must find some way of first establishing to the court's satisfaction what the facts actually are.[1] If the defendant disputes those facts, or even if he is not prepared to concede them to be as the plaintiff or prosecutor asserts them to be, then the latter must demonstrate them to the court as being either true or sufficiently probable for the court to act on them, to afford relief or to convict the defendant, as the case may be.

This basic analysis of the process of litigation expresses the need for, and offers some definition of, 'evidence'. Evidence may be defined as any material which tends to persuade the court of the truth or probability of some fact asserted before it. The word 'tends' in this

---

[1]    What facts a particular party must prove, and the standard to which he must prove them in any given case, are in themselves often difficult questions and are considered under the head of Burden and Standard of Proof in Chapter 3, post.

definition is used to emphasise the unhappy truth, brought home so cogently to the litigant in the county court described above, that evidence will persuade a court of the truth or probability of the facts asserted only if it is regarded as truthful, reliable and sufficiently cogent. The definition is necessarily silent about the quality of the material offered. Any material that, if accepted as truthful, reliable and sufficiently cogent, would be capable of persuading the court as desired, may properly be described as evidence.

The innocent, or naive, might reasonably assume from this that once it is shown that material is available which, if accepted in this way, would be capable of having the desired persuasive effect, and which may therefore be described as evidence, it is only necessary to consider the mechanics by which such material may be placed before the court. Indeed, an important part of the law of evidence does concern the ways in which the material is to be presented, and later chapters of this book are concerned with that very topic. But the critical areas of the law of evidence concern the large number of different rules which exclude from consideration by a court, or which limit the power of a court to consider, material of certain kinds, even though that material undoubtedly satisfies our definition of evidence. In other words, evidence is subject to various exclusionary rules, often resembling in their operation some forensic game of chess, by which it is ordained that litigants shall prove the facts necessary to their case. It must be emphasised that the exclusionary rules are by no means necessarily based upon the persuasive value which the material might enjoy if placed before the court. Much evidence is excluded which is clearly capable of impressing as truthful, reliable and cogent, although, with the exception of material which is excluded on the simple ground of some overriding policy of the law, some reason, however historical and however tenuous, can usually be found to provide some measures of justification for the rule.

Given that it must be desirable for a court to decide a case on the basis of the fullest information available, it is at first sight strange that English law has what has been termed an 'exclusionary' attitude towards evidence, that is to say that the law requires a party who seeks to tender evidence to be prepared to show, if called upon to do so, that the evidence does not offend against any of the exclusionary rules. It might be thought a more satisfactory approach would be a generally inclusionary rule that evidence should be put before the court unless some real and obvious injustice or prejudice might be caused to an opponent out of all proporion to the probative value of the evidence in question. Some common-law evidence systems, notably the American Federal Rules, have moved noticeably in this direction. Nothing in such a rule would imply any element of quality in the evidence so admitted, but would leave the court free to make the most informed judgment possible on the evidence as a whole given in the case. There is some sign in recent legislative measures concerned with the law of evidence that the possibilities of the inclusionary approach are beginning to be realised. The Civil Evidence Acts 1968 and 1972 have sought, in civil proceedings, to draw the emphasis of the rules of law away from the possibilities of exclusion, and towards the idea of a norm of inclusion, combined with a vigilant scrutiny of the true value of evidence and its potential, if any, for prejudice. A similar trend may have begun in criminal cases with the passage of the Police and Criminal Evidence Act 1984, although its evidential provisions fall far short of the liberalisation advocated by most commentators and by the Criminal Law Revision Committee in its celebrated 11th Report. But much of the law of evidence has not yet been viewed in this light.

Historically, it is possible to identify a number of major factors in the development of the law, dating from the late eighteenth century, which have influenced the present state of the rules of evidence. It is important to notice these factors now, because, as Maitland said of the forms of action, though dead, they rule us from their graves, and they crop up time and time again in the examination of the rules of admissibility. Without some understanding of these factors, certain parts of the law of evidence are virtually incomprehensible.

### 1.1.1 The prevalence of trial by jury

Commenting on the rule against hearsay, the distinguished American Professor Morgan of Harvard once observed that: 'while distrust of the jury had nothing to do with the origin of the hearsay rule, it has exerted a strong influence in preventing or delaying its liberalisation.' (*Some Problems of Proof under the Anglo-American System of Litigation*, p. 117). The common law was closely bound up with the peculiar exigencies of jury trial, and because any evidence admitted had to be considered by a body of laymen, the law took a protectionist stand against permitting anything which might influence a jury to give effect to an unsound approach to the case, or which might impose on them the need for unreasonable analytical skills. Thus, it was feared that to require juries to weigh up the value of hearsay evidence, or evidence of character, would be to impose too great a burden, and a burden which, if not faithfully borne, might result in an irretrievable prejudice to a party against whom such evidence was tendered. There is, of course, a risk that a jury may, despite careful direction, act upon the wrong principles and it is no doubt necessary to regulate to some extent the material placed before juries. But whether the rules which have developed to keep certain types of evidence from them really operate to prevent them acting misguidedly is open to question. It will become apparent, from the rules discussed later in this book, that juries are habitually called upon to perform considerable feats of analysis, not to say of mental gymnastics. Nonetheless, no major rule of evidence has developed without unmistakable signs of tailoring to the supposed needs of juries, and without doubt it is the comparative rarity of jury trial in civil cases, in modern practice, which has prompted the willingness to experiment with the inclusionary approach in such cases. The Civil Evidence Acts 1968 and 1972 have effectively reversed some two centuries of painstaking jurisprudence concerning the circumstances in which hearsay evidence may be adduced, and this has been almost entirely because it has been felt so much safer to trust the trained mind of the judge sitting alone with the task of weighing and sifting such evidence, than it ever was to entrust the same task to a jury. The conduct of criminal cases is still regulated by that same painstaking jurisprudence of the common law. The few antiseptic traces of hearsay permitted by the Police and Criminal Evidence Act 1984 and its predecessor, the Criminal Evidence Act 1965, have had little impact on this state of the law. It is of some interest to note that despite the entrenched constitutional right to jury trial in American Federal Courts, guaranteed in both criminal and civil cases by the Sixth and Seventh Amendments to the Constitution respectively, those courts have shown a far greater tendency towards liberalisation than have their English counterparts.

### 1.1.2 The dread of manufactured evidence

The common law lived in constant fear of perjury, fabrication and attempts to abuse or pervert the course of justice. The fear had far-reaching consequences, not only in the rejection of specific kinds of evidence which were thought to be particularly prone to abuse (hearsay, again, was a principal offender) but also in the wholesale rejection as witnesses of interested parties or their spouses, in any circumstances. The rule that the parties and their spouses were incompetent to give evidence began to be relaxed in civil cases as late as 1851, and it was not until the Criminal Evidence Act 1898 that the accused in a criminal case became competent to give evidence in his own defence. As a result, provision had often to be made for the proof of facts without recourse to the evidence of those best able to testify about them. The rule was also responsible for many quirks of what is now the law of privilege, not to mention the now abolished procedure of making an unsworn statement from the dock. And the modern law of competence and compellability has yet to recover from some of the complications deriving from its history. Closely bound up with the fear of fabrication is the rule requiring sworn testimony. The solemnity and sanctity of sworn evidence, and the rule that at common law, evidence might not be given except on oath, has invested the law of competence (including the process of being sworn, which has been updated at last by the Oaths Act 1978) with a number of curious features, in particular with respect to the evidence of children of tender years.

### 1.1.3  The harshness of the criminal law in the late eighteenth and nineteenth centuries
Most of the major common-law rules of evidence owe much of their force to judicial attempts, during the formative years of the modern law of evidence, to mitigate some of the harshness of criminal law and procedure towards the accused. Faced with a system in which death was the sentence prescribed for many (at some periods all) felonies, but which denied to the accused the right of representation by counsel in such cases until 1836,[2] and the right to give evidence in his defence until 1898, the judges took seriously their role as the defendant's guardian, and developed many exclusionary rules with a view to redressing the balance. The general exclusion of character evidence, the stringent conditions of admissibility of confessions, the preservation of the defendant's right to remain silent without risk of an adverse inference being drawn against him, the right, only recently abrogated, to make an unsworn statement from the dock, the very burden and standard of proof in criminal cases, all owe much to that period of legal development and have, to a very large extent, retained the characteristics which they then took on; indeed, such characteristics have in most cases remained virtually unchanged, despite the radical changes in criminal process which have since taken place.

'Evidence' must, therefore, be seen not only in the context of the mechanics by which it is to be presented, but first and foremost, in the context of what evidence the law allows to be presented. 'Judicial evidence', as evidence to be presented to a court is sometimes rather unnecessarily called, must not only tend to persuade the court of the truth or probability of the fact in support of which it is tendered, but must also comply with the rules of admissibility; if it does not, the adversary system of litigation dictates that a party shall not be permitted to adduce it. Much of the remainder of this book is concerned with the application of those rules in particular cases. To return to the stories with which this chapter began, it may be pertinent to observe that no case, however compelling in law, can be any stronger than the legally admissible evidence available to prove it to a court. It is not the truth that counts in any piece of controverted litigation, but the evidence, and on that cynical note, we must pass to consider evidence in a little more detail.

---

[2]   The accused was allowed counsel in cases of treason as early as 1695, and appears to have enjoyed the right in the case of misdemeanours from early times.

## 1.2 The varieties of evidence

No subject has suffered more from a hopeless diversity and inconsistency of terminology than evidence. It is impossible to reconcile the various usages, judicial and extra-judicial, which have been made of the terms employed to identify and separate different kinds of evidence. Attempts to make some scientific categorisation of evidence have occasioned endless academic wrangling, and have all failed to at least some extent, simply because evidence has not developed in a scientific way. It is the most pragmatic of subjects, having been developed not by any desire to create a scientific or consistent code, but by the necessities and realities of practice. Evidence underlies the whole practice of law in every field of litigation. It does not lend itself easily to academic classifications. In this book, the use of technical terms will be avoided, or at least simplified, wherever this can be done. But some form of sign convention is needed, and this will be achieved by adopting the following use of terminology.

Before proceeding to classify evidence itself, one or two ancillary terms of some usefulness should be noted. A party who seeks to put evidence before the court is said to 'tender' that evidence, and is described as the 'proponent' of the evidence. Any party who is adverse to the proponent of evidence is referred to as an 'opponent'. A judge, jury or bench of magistrates, having the duty to decide the facts of a case, is referred to as the 'tribunal of fact'. When the judge or the bench decides questions of law, including the admissibility of evidence, the judge or bench is referred to as the 'tribunal of law'. Tribunals of fact and law are treated in more detail in 1.5 post.

### 1.2.1 Substantive definitions

In classifying evidence substantively, the following terminology will suffice for all practical purposes.

### 1.2.1.1 Direct versus circumstantial evidence.

Direct evidence is evidence which requires no mental process on the part of the tribunal of fact in order to draw the conclusion sought by the proponent of the evidence, other than acceptance of the evidence itself. Circumstantial evidence is evidence from which the desired conclusion may be drawn, but which requires the tribunal of fact not only to accept the evidence presented, but also to draw an inference from it. For example, if D is charged with robbery of a bank, and is seen by W running from the bank clutching a wad of banknotes, W's evidence is direct evidence that D was running away from the bank, and circumstantial evidence that D committed the robbery. To arrive at the latter conclusion, the jury must draw certain inferences from the facts perceived by W. This example also shows that circumstantial evidence is not necessarily inferior to direct evidence, if the inference required is obvious and compelling.

### 1.2.1.2 Direct or percipient versus hearsay evidence.

The term direct evidence has a second meaning in the usage of many writers. The alternative term percipient evidence not only avoids any possibility of confusion, but is also more appropriate to describe the opposite of hearsay evidence. Hearsay is a complex subject, occupying in its own right three chapters of this book, and only a brief distinction can be made here. Percipient evidence is evidence of facts which a witness personally perceives using any of his senses. Hearsay evidence is given when a witness recounts a statement made (orally, in a document or otherwise) by another person and where the proponent of the evidence asserts that what the person who made the statement said was true. Thus, the evidence of W that he saw D rob the bank is percipient evidence, whereas the evidence of H (who was not present at the scene of the robbery) that W told H that D robbed the bank is hearsay, if tendered to prove that D robbed the bank. Hearsay is inadmissible unless it falls under an exception recognised by the law.

*1.2.1.3   Primary versus secondary evidence.*   In proving the contents of a document, resort may be had to either primary or secondary evidence. Primary evidence consists of the production of the original document or an admission as to what its contents are or were. Secondary evidence consists of a copy of the document, however produced, or oral evidence about what its contents are or were. Primary evidence is generally required to prove the contents of a document, but in certain circumstances, secondary evidence is admissible for that purpose.[3]

*1.2.1.4   Presumptive or prima facie versus conclusive evidence.*   Presumptive or prima facie evidence is evidence which is declared (usually by statute) to be sufficient evidence of a fact, unless and until an opponent adduces contradictory evidence, in which case the tribunal of fact must weigh all the evidence tendered by all parties, in order to decide whether the fact has been proved. Conclusive evidence, which is rare,[4] is tantamount to a rule of law, since it is evidence which no party is permitted to contradict by evidence. Conclusive evidence, therefore, is inaptly named, and it would be preferable to state the fact so proved as a rule of law. An example of conclusive evidence is the rule that a child under the age of 10 years is to be taken as incapable of committing a criminal offence. By way of contrast, the rule that a child aged between 10 and 14 is presumed to be *doli incapax* is presumptive or prima facie evidence, since evidence to contradict the lack of capacity may be introduced by the prosecution.

### 1.2.2   Definitions of form
Evidence which falls into any of the above categories in its substance or contents must, of course, have or be put into a form in which it can be presented to the court. Evidence is received by a court in the following forms:

*1.2.2.1   Oral evidence.*   Evidence consisting of what is said by any witness in the course of testifying in the instant proceedings. Oral evidence must, with very few exceptions, be given on oath or affirmation[5] and in court, though if a witness is unable to attend court, his evidence may in some cases be taken out of court on commission or, in criminal cases, by a justice of the peace. There are also in some important instances provisions for evidence to be given on affidavit[6] and, in criminal cases, by written statement in a prescribed form.[7] These instances, where they occur, may be regarded the equivalent of oral evidence and indeed, evidence so given has in law the same effect as oral evidence given in court. Oral

---

[3]   In the case of documents requiring enrolment, there is a further kind of primary evidence. See generally, 16.2 post. Where a document is permitted to be proved as hearsay evidence of its contents, the strict rules are relaxed, to some extent. See, for example, Civil Evidence Act 1968, s. 6(1).

[4]   For a statutory example, see Civil Evidence Act 1968, s. 13(1).

[5]   See Chapter 11, Section B, post.

[6]   An affidavit is a written statement of the evidence of the deponent, made on oath or affirmation. See generally RSC, Ord. 38, r. 2; Ord. 41.

[7]   See, e.g., Criminal Justice Act 1967, s. 9(1); Magistrates' Courts Act 1980, s. 102.

evidence is frequently referred to as 'testimony', and this usage is almost invariable in the United States.

*1.2.2.2 Documentary evidence.* Evidence afforded by any document produced for the inspection of the court, whether as direct or hearsay evidence of its contents. A document may also be produced as a piece of real evidence as defined in 1.2.2.3 below. The normal sense of the word 'document' is of some writing or other inscription by which information may be communicated, but modern technology has opened up new possibilities in the form of tape, film and the like, so that the range of materials which may be so described has expanded somewhat the more traditional understanding of the word.[8]

*1.2.2.3 Real evidence.* A term employed to denote any material from which the court may draw conclusions or inferences by using its own senses. The genus includes material objects produced to the court for its inspection, the presentation of the physical characteristics of any person or animal, the demeanour of witnesses (which may or may not be offered or presented to the court by design), views of the *locus in quo* or of any object incapable of being brought to court without undue difficulty and such items as tapes, films and photographs, the physical appearance of which may be significant over and above the sum total of their contents as such. These are all considered in Chapter 16, Section B, post. What is of importance in each case is the visual, aural or other sensory impression which the evidence, by its own characteristics, produces on the court, and on which the court may act to find the truth or probability of any fact which seems to follow from it.

## 1.3 Facts which may be proved

The purpose of evidence being to demonstrate to the court the truth or probability of the facts upon which the success of a party's case depends in law, it follows that evidence must be confined to the proof of facts which are required for that purpose. The proof of supernumerary or unrelated facts will not assist the court, and may in certain cases prejudice the court against a party, while having no probative value on the issues actually before it. It is by no means always easy to determine what facts are required and what are supernumerary, especially in relation to matters said to form part of the 'res gestae', or to be relevant to the facts in issue. These are considered in their proper place, together with the problems which may arise. The facts which a party is permitted to prove are: (a) facts in issue in the case; (b) facts constituting part of, or accompanying and explaining a fact in issue, described as part of the 'res gestae'; (c) facts relevant to a fact in issue: and (d), where appropriate, standards of comparison.

### 1.3.1 Facts in issue

The facts in issue in a case, sometimes called ultimate facts, are the facts which a party to litigation (including the prosecution in a criminal case) must prove in order to succeed in his claim or defence and to show his entitlement to relief (or to obtain a conviction). What these facts may be are not really the concern of the law of evidence, but may be derived from the substantive law applicable to the cause of action, charge or defence in each case.

---

[8] The meaning of the term is considered further in 16.1 post. For certain purposes, the word has been given particular connotations by statute: see, e.g., Police and Criminal Evidence Act 1984, s. 118(1); cf. Criminal Evidence Act 1965, s. 1(4); Civil Evidence Act 1968, s. 10(1).

In procedural terms, they are to be found in the pleadings, indictment or charge, as the case may be.

In a civil case, any fact is in issue if, having regard to the pleadings and the substantive law, it is a fact necessary to the success of any claim or defence disclosed on the pleadings. In respect of the facts that a party must prove in order to establish his claim or defence, the party is said to bear the legal burden of proof.[9]

The number of facts in issue will depend entirely on the nature of the case. In a typical action for negligence, the facts in issue will be those which, if proved, will establish that the defendant owed a duty of care to the plaintiff, that the defendant was in breach of that duty of care and that such breach caused to the plaintiff loss and damage for which he is entitled in law to recover; together with any further facts raised by an affirmative defence, which goes beyond a mere denial of those pleaded by the plaintiff,[10] for example such facts as may establish contributory negligence, volenti non fit injuria or act of God.

In a typical action for breach of contract, the facts in issue will be those which, if proved, would establish a binding and enforceable contract between the plaintiff and the defendant, the due performance of any conditions precedent, a breach by the defendant of the contract and that such breach caused loss to the plaintiff for which he is entitled in law to recover; together with any further facts raised by an affirmative defence which goes beyond a mere denial of the plaintiff's case, such as fraud, illegality, infancy or accord and satisfaction.

The pleadings in a civil action are of cardinal importance in determining what the facts in issue are, in that their object is precisely that the court should be informed what the issues are. By RSC, Ord. 18, r. 7(1):

> ... every pleading must contain, and contain only, a statement in a summary form of the material facts on which the party pleading relies for his claim or defence, as the case may be, but not the evidence by which those facts are to be proved, and the statement must be as brief as the nature of the case admits.

Although RSC, Ord. 20 provides for pleadings to be amended, the court will at trial, adjudicate on the pleaded issues only and will require the evidence to be directed to the facts in issue as ascertained from the pleadings.[11] The court will not (at least without giving leave to amend, on such terms as may be just) adjudicate on other issues or allow evidence directed to other issues.

In criminal cases, the facts in issue are ascertained by reference to the essential elements of the offence as charged in the indictment or summons. The position here is rendered somewhat simpler by the fact that a plea of not guilty puts in issue all the facts necessary to establish the commission by the defendant of the offence charged, and the prosecution bear the legal burden of proving every such element of the offence.[12] There are, however, exceptional cases where the defendant bears the burden of proving some element of his defence, for example insanity within the M'Naghten Rules. In yet other cases the defendant has a lesser burden of raising by evidence certain facts which go beyond a mere

---

[9]  This should be read with Chapter 3, where the legal and evidential burdens of proof are discussed. A fact will be in issue if any party must prove it as a necessary part of his claim or defence.

[10]  See RSC, Ord. 18, r. 8(1).

[11]  See *Esso Petroleum Co. Ltd* v *Southport Corporation* (HL) [1956] AC 218.

[12]  *Woolmington* v *DPP* (HL) [1935] AC 462; *R* v *Sims* (CCA) [1946] KB 531, per Lord Goddard CJ at 539.

denial of his guilt as alleged by the prosecution, for example provocation, before the prosecution are required to rebut those facts in the discharge of their overall burden of proving his guilt.[13] In such cases, the issues raised by the defence are just as much proper subjects of evidence as those raised by the prosecution. The indictment is subject to amendment,[14] but the evidence must be directed towards the essential elements of the offence charged in the indictment, as amended if at all. In summary trial, no point can be taken on formal defects of the process or any variance of the evidence from the actual wording of a summons.[15] But the evidence in a summary trial too must be directed only to the elements of the offence charged. The facts in issue in a criminal case will be the commission by the defendant of the actus reus, the presence of any necessary general or specific intent, and any defence, going beyond a mere denial of the prosecution case, which the defence must or may raise.

Also treated as facts in issue in any case, are facts which affect either the credibility of a witness, or the admissibility of any evidence. Such facts are known as 'secondary' or 'collateral' facts in issue. Evidence may be called, for example, tending to show that a witness for the other side is biased or partial, or suffers from some medical condition which renders his evidence unworthy of belief; or to show that a confession is admissible inasmuch as it was made without oppression, or that secondary evidence of the contents of a document may be adduced because the original cannot be found after due search. These are facts which go to the admissibility or weight of evidence called in support of or to prove the 'primary' facts in issue.

### 1.3.2 Facts forming part of the res gestae

It is not always obvious where a fact begins and ends. To state a fact or event in isolation, without reference to its antecedents in time, place or surrounding circumstances, may render the fact, so stated, difficult or even impossible to comprehend. Other facts or circumstances may be so closely connected with the fact in issue as to be, in reality, part and parcel of the same transaction.[16] Such ancillary facts are described, rather unhappily, as forming part of the res gestae of the fact in issue, and may be proved. The witness is permitted to state facts, not in meaningless isolation, but with such reasonable fullness and in such reasonable context as will make them comprehensible and useful. The rule is not confined by any strict limits of time or place. In the Australian case of *O'Leary v R* (1946) 73 CLR 566, a number of men employed at a timber camp went on a drunken orgy lasting several hours, during which a number of serious assaults were committed, and after which one of their number was found dying, having himself been savagely assaulted. On the prosecution of another of them for his murder, it was held that the episode should be looked at as a whole, including the occurrence of the previous assaults. Dixon J said:

> The evidence disclosed that, under the influence of the beer and wine he had drunk and continued to drink, he engaged in repeated acts of violence which might be regarded as amounting to a connected course of conduct. Without evidence of what, during that time, was done by those men who took any significant part in the matter and especially

[13]  As to these cases, see 3.4.2 and 3.5.2, post.
[14]  Indictments Act 1915, s. 5.
[15]  Magistrates' Courts Act 1980, s. 123.
[16]  This way of describing evidence admissible under the res gestae principle has been held not to be the most accurate when the evidence is hearsay, but remains, it is submitted, a sound statement of the rule for general purposes: *Ratten v R* (PC, Victoria) [1972] AC 378 at 389, per Lord Wilberforce.

evidence of the behaviour of the prisoner, the transaction of which the alleged murder formed an integral part could not be truly understood and isolated from it, could only be presented as an unreal and not very intelligible event. The prisoner's generally violent and hostile conduct might well serve to explain his mind and attitude and, therefore, to implicate him in the resulting homicide.

This rather flexible principle habitually involves admitting evidence, at least in criminal cases, as an exception to the rule against hearsay, since it is likely to consist of statements made by those involved in or witnessing a fact or event, which are tendered with a view to showing that the facts stated by them are true.[17]

For example, in *R* v *Nye and Loan* (CA) (1977) 66 CR App R 252, the Court of Appeal held that a statement made to a police officer by the victim of an assault identifying his assailant, some minutes after the assault, and after the victim had been sitting in his car recovering from the combined effects of the assault and the road traffic accident which preceded it, was admissible under the rule as accompanying and explaining the fact in issue, namely whether the assailant had assaulted the victim.

Almost all the crucial decisions are of this kind, rather than of the kind in *O'Leary*, and the subject is accordingly dealt with fully in the context of common-law exceptions to the rule against hearsay in 6.6, post. In all probability, the reason why there are fewer decisions where no element of hearsay is involved is simply that the rule causes no real difficulty unless the extension into surrounding circumstances is as marked as it was in *O'Leary*. In almost all cases, some matter is admitted as part of the res gestae: be it the manner in which a blow was struck, the appearance of the victim afterwards, the tone of voice in which words were spoken, or many other circumstances of obvious probative value which are immediately connected with a fact in issue.

### 1.3.3 Facts relevant to facts in issue

In *DPP* v *Kilbourne* (HL) [1973] AC 729 at 756 Lord Simon of Glaisdale said:

> Evidence is relevant if it is logically probative or disprobative of some matter which requires proof. It is sufficient to say, even at the risk of etymological tautology, that relevant (i.e., logically probative or disprobative) evidence is evidence which makes the matter which requires proof more or less probable.

This is, perhaps, a simpler and more satisfactory, if less comprehensive definition of relevance, than the classic formulation in Stephen's *Digest*, according to which the word signified that[18]:

> any two facts to which it is applied are so related to each other that according to the common course of events one either taken by itself or in connection with other facts proves or renders probable the past, present or future existence or non-existence of the other.

---

[17]   In civil cases, such evidence would now be admissible, if hearsay, under s. 2 of the Civil Evidence Act 1968.

[18]   *Digest of the Law of Evidence,* 12th ed., art. 1. The definition was somewhat different in earlier editions, but this seems to be the author's mature view.

Neither attains the appealing simplicity of Federal Rule of Evidence 401, whereby in a United States federal court, the phrase 'relevant evidence'

means evidence having any tendency to make the existence of any fact that is of consequence to the determination of the action more probable or less probable than it would be without the evidence.

It is a fundamental rule of the law of evidence that evidence must be relevant in order to be admissible. The converse, however, is not true, since much relevant evidence is made inadmissible by the specific rules of evidence affecting admissibility. This will be further explored in 1.4.1 post.

The need for the proof of facts relevant (within the terms of these or similar definitions) to facts in issue is an obvious one. In some cases, the fact in issue can be proved by the direct evidence of someone who perceived it, as where the witness saw the defendant shoot the deceased. But in very many cases, no such evidence is available, or such direct evidence as there is may be of little weight. Clearly, any facts related to the commission of an offence by the relationship of relevance may be proved so as to demonstrate the truth or probability of the fact in issue (that the defendant murdered the deceased). Thus, if the defendant was later found in possession of some article of the deceased's property which would ordinarily have been about his person at the time of the shooting, this fact is relevant to the fact in issue because it makes it more probable (if accepted) that the fact in issue is true. Equally, if the shooting took place in London, proof of the fact that, at the time of the shooting, the defendant was in Manchester would be relevant as disprovative of the fact in issue. Each of these pieces of relevant evidence involves the drawing of an inference, in order to reach the conclusion that the fact in issue is true or untrue, more probable or less probable, and may therefore be described as 'circumstantial'.[19]

Relevant facts are easier to identify than to describe in the abstract.[20] Provided that the relationship between the allegedly relevant fact and the fact in issue is probative or disprovative, the former may be proved in support of or in contradiction of the latter. *Joy v Phillips, Mills & Co Ltd* (CA) [1916] 1 KB 849, was an action concerning the death of a stable-boy, who had been kicked by a horse. Evidence was admitted to prove that the boy had previously been in the habit of teasing horses, and that, when found, he was holding a halter which he had no occasion to be using at the time. The possession of the halter bore directly on the cause of the boy's death, which was a fact in issue. In this case, the relevant fact was proved by evidence of acts earlier in time than the fact in issue, but it is equally permissible to call evidence proving relevant facts which were contemporaneous with, or subsequent to the fact in issue. In *Woolf v Woolf* (CA) [1931] P 134, it was held that proof of the fact that a couple, who were not married to each other, occupied the same bedroom was clearly probative of an allegation that they had committed adultery, and of the existence at that time of an adulterous relationship. In *R v Dalloz* (CCA) (1908) 1 Cr App R 258, the fact that a driver was proved to have been speeding at a given point was held to be relevant to prove that he had been speeding some short time and distance before.

Some facts may be relevant to more than one issue, and of these no more need be said.

---

[19] See 1.2.1 ante. The word 'circumstantial' has sometimes been accorded a derogatory sense, as if such evidence could have little weight. But, as the illustrations in the text may show, it is often more cogent than indifferent direct evidence, such as a hesitant or uncertain identification.

[20] An invaluable analysis of the cases is given in Cross, *Evidence*, 5th ed. p. 38 et seq.

But irrelevant evidence will be rejected. Like relevance, irrelevance is a matter of degree, and easier to identify than to describe. It has been held irrelevant to an allegation of negligence that after an accident allegedly caused by such negligence, the defendants altered the practice on which the allegation was based.[21] The fact was perfectly consistent with an intention, in the light of fresh information, to improve an existing practice, whereas negligence is to be judged in the light of the state of knowledge at the time of the act or omission complained of. And where a brewer brought an action against a publican for breach of covenant to buy beer from the brewer, the brewer was not permitted to prove, in reply to a defence that the beer previously supplied by him was bad, that he had supplied good beer to other publicans.[22] It is obvious from these illustrations that irrelevant evidence, in addition to its lack of probative value on the facts in issue, carries with it the risk of prejudice against the party affected by it, and paves the way for the opening up of numerous collateral inquiries which can have no value to the proper decision of the case.

*1.3.3.1   Conditional relevance.*   It sometimes happens that the relevance of a particular fact is not immediately clear upon its being introduced in evidence. This is usually because of the simple truth that evidence must be called in order and by one witness at a time. The trial judge is entitled to insist that the relevance of a fact be demonstrated to him, before permitting evidence of that fact to be given. But the practice is to allow proof of the fact 'de bene esse', at least where counsel undertakes to demonstrate the relevance of the evidence in due course by introducing further evidence. If it does not appear, later, that its relevance has been established, the jury must be directed to ignore it, and in some cases, it may be necessary to discharge them if the fact is highly prejudicial. An illustration is where counsel seeks to put in a document in cross-examination, strict proof of which and the relevance of which to the defence must await the presentation of the defence case. Such evidence is described as 'conditionally relevant', because its actual relevance may stand or fall by reference to other evidence.

### 1.3.4   Standards of comparison

Wherever it is necessary to judge the conduct of a party against an objective standard, it may be proved what such objective standard is, or was at the material time and in the material circumstances. Negligence is a common example. The standard of the reasonable man demands that evidence may be given to show how others might reasonably have behaved in similar circumstances, and this fact, if established, is relevant to the necessary assessment of how the party accused in fact behaved. Where the objective standard is one which involves conduct in a situation outside the everyday experience of the court, the standard may be proved by expert evidence of the conduct in such circumstances, for

---

[21]   *Hart* v *Lancashire & Yorkshire Railway Co.* (1869) 21 LT 261. American jurisdictions generally exclude such evidence of 'subsequent remedial measures'. This is not, however, because it is thought to be irrelevant but because, although thought to be relevant, it would be contrary to public policy to admit the evidence. The theory is that the taking of proper remedial measures would be discouraged if evidence of the measures were admissible against the party taking them as evidence of negligence or culpable conduct. The evidence is, however, admissible to prove other facts, if controverted; for example, ownership or control of premises or the feasibility of the measures. See, e.g., Federal Rule of Evidence 407.

[22]   *Holcombe* v *Hewson* (NP) (1810) 2 Camp 391.

example of a reasonable member of a trade or a profession,[23] or of the accepted practice of commercial men.[24] In a common situation of everyday life, it may be a matter of which the judge could take judicial notice, or find proved by the totality of the evidence given in the case.

## 1.4 Admissibility and weight

### 1.4.1 Admissibility

Evidence is said to be admissible, or receivable, if it may be received by the court for the purpose of proving facts before the court, when judged by the law of evidence. As we have seen, although evidence must be relevant in order to be admissible the converse proposition is not valid: not all relevant evidence is admissible.

Unlike relevance, admissibility has nothing to do with the relationship between the evidence tendered and the fact to be proved. Admissibility involves exclusively a determination of whether the law of evidence permits relevant evidence to be received by the court. Some evidence, such as hearsay, is excluded, even though relevant, because of the danger of unreliability inherent in repeated statements and because it cannot be cross-examined on effectively. Some evidence, such as evidence of the previous bad character of the defendant in a criminal case, is excluded, even though relevant, because of considerations of fairness to the defendant and the danger of prejudice flowing from the jury's becoming aware of his record. Some evidence, for example privileged materials and materials which may be withheld on the ground of public policy, are excluded, even though relevant, for reasons of policy that override the interest of the court and the parties in having access to all available evidence. Some witnesses (for example young children) are held to be incompetent to testify at all, and others to be incompetent to testify in certain ways (for example, the rule excluding non-expert opinion testimony in most cases) despite the relevance of the testimony which might otherwise be given. The rules of admissibility are, therefore, unconcerned with the extent to which the tendered evidence might be probative or disprobative of a fact in issue. They proceed from considerations other than relevance. It is this that gives to the law of evidence its exclusionary aspect to which reference was made earlier in this chapter. Inadmissible evidence cannot be entertained by the court, whatever its relevance, and indeed however cogent it might have been.

The question of admissibility is one of law, and is determined by the lex fori, that is the law of England, even when the question is one of the admissibility of evidence originating abroad, or where the facts in issue arose abroad or have some foreign aspect.

### 1.4.1.1 Limited admissibility.
Evidence may, of course, be admissible for more than one purpose, and such evidence causes no problems. However, evidence that is admissible for one purpose, but not for another, referred to as evidence of limited admissibility, causes great difficulty, particularly for juries and other lay tribunals of fact. If evidence is relevant and admissible for one purpose but inadmissible for another purpose, its proponent is entitled to have that evidence admitted. The opponent is, however, entitled

[23]  *Chapman* v *Walton* (1833) 10 Bing 57. The evidence must show what the generally accepted conduct would be, not merely what the witness himself would have done, and as to the limitations on the province of expert evidence, see generally 9.4, post. Such evidence is very common in, e.g., medical and legal negligence cases.
[24]  *Noble* v *Kennoway* (1780) 2 Doug KB 510; *Fleet* v *Murton* (1871) LR 7 QB 126.

to require that the judge direct the jury that they may consider the evidence only for the purpose for which it is admissible, and not for any other purpose. The impact of the evidence on the jury usually outweighs even a scrupulously careful direction. Thus, where defendants D1 and D2 are jointly charged with an offence, the prosecution may adduce evidence of a confession made by D1 implicating both himself and D2. D2 is entitled to have the jury directed that the confession is evidence against D1 only, and not against D2. But an obvious potential for prejudice remains.

   In other cases, the jury may be forgiven for thinking that the law takes unnecessarily curious positions which make their task no easier. It would be interesting to know what juries make of the direction that a previous inconsistent statement, introduced to impeach a witness in cross-examination, is evidence of the inconsistency of the witness but not evidence of the truth of the facts stated therein; or of a direction that a recent complaint made by the complainant in a rape case is evidence confirming her testimony, but not evidence of the facts complained of, and cannot provide the corroboration for which the jury must look.

   In some cases, the risk of prejudice may be so great that a problem posed by a confession admissible against one defendant but not another must be solved by ordering separate trials. But in most cases, the balancing of interests between the proponent and the opponent requires that evidence of limited admissibility be admitted, and the tribunal of fact cautioned not to use it for any purpose for which it is not admissible.

### 1.4.2   Weight

The weight of evidence is a qualitative assessment of the probative value which admissible evidence has in relation to the facts in issue. To say that evidence is relevant and admissible concludes the issue of law, that a party is entitled to bring that evidence before a court. Such evidence then has the potential to persuade the court of the truth or probability of the facts towards which it is directed. But its actual persuasive value in relation to those facts depends upon the view taken by the tribunal of fact of the truthfulness, reliability and cogency of the evidence. Depending upon such a view, evidence may be of virtually no weight at all, or may rest on one of an infinite number of points on the upwards sliding scale, ending with evidence which is so weighty as almost to conclude the case in itself.[25] Although the weight of evidence is a question of fact, and strictly cannot arise until the evidence is first shown to be relevant and admissible, it is not always possible to segregate these qualities of law and fact altogether. The relevance of evidence is closely bound up with its weight and to say that evidence is insufficiently relevant to be admitted, necessarily involves some judgment on its weight. And where the judge has a discretion whether to admit or exclude evidence (as to which see 1.5, post) it is both usual and legitimate for him to take into account the likely weight of the evidence and to compare this with its likely prejudicial effect.

   The assessment of weight depends upon a multiplicity of factors, which would be almost impossible to define, but which may certainly include matters extraneous to the evidence itself, for example other evidence given in the case, or the demeanour of the

---

[25]   The use of the word 'conclude' to express very weighty evidence should not be confused with its use to describe evidence which as a matter of law may not be contradicted, and so 'concludes' an issue: see 1.2.1, ante.

witness who gives the evidence. In cases where hearsay evidence is admissible by virtue of the provisions of Part VII of the Police and Criminal Evidence Act 1984, or, until superseded, of the Criminal Evidence Act 1965 or by virtue of Part 1 of the Civil Evidence Act 1968, Parliament has provided a statement of the matters to be considered in assessing the weight of evidence so admitted.[26] The various factors so enumerated would appear to be those which any reasonable tribunal would in any event take into account, and it is submitted that their elaboration may well be unnecessary.

To say that evidence lacks weight does not mean that such evidence is perjured or dishonestly motivated, or even exaggerated. It is true that evidence having these characteristics will lack weight, but equally, so will evidence which is unreliable because the witness's recollection has failed him, or because he had no adequate opportunity to perceive the facts of which he speaks, or because his knowledge of the facts is insufficient, or, in the case of an expert witness, because his expertise or experience or opportunity to investigate is too limited. So, too, will any evidence which is for any reason unable to afford the court the assistance it needs in relation to the facts in issue.

### 1.5 Tribunals of law and fact: judicial discretion

#### 1.5.1 Tribunals of law and fact
Any process of trial of litigation must provide for the determination of both issues of law and issues of fact. Broadly speaking, in any case tried by a judge sitting with a jury, questions of law arising in the case fall to be determined by the judge and questions of fact by the jury. Jury trial is now rare in civil cases,[27] and the functions of the jury will be considered principally in relation to criminal trials on indictment, in which they are always employed. Where a judge sits alone to consider a civil case, he is himself the tribunal of law and fact and determines all issues of both kinds. In the case of magistrates' courts and tribunals, the court or tribunal is entitled to decide all matters of law and fact canvassed before it, but on matters of law should seek and accept the advice of their clerk or legally qualified chairman.[28]

Questions of law comprise matters relating to the substantive law governing the claim or charge, the admissibility of evidence, any rules of law or practice governing the production or effect of evidence and the question whether there is sufficient evidence to warrant consideration by the tribunal of fact at all. The judicial function also includes the determination of necessary questions ancillary to the trial itself, such as whether cause has been shown in the challenge of a juror, whether the jury, or a particular member of the jury should be discharged, and matters concerning the administration of the trial, for example bail.

Questions of fact comprise the decision of all matters concerning the truth or probability of all facts in issue as derived from the substantive law, pleadings, indictment

---

[26] Police and Criminal Evidence Act 1984, sch. III, ss. 7, 11; Criminal Evidence Act 1965, s. 1(3); Civil Evidence Act 1968, s. 6(3).

[27] Juries are employed in civil cases to try actions for defamation, malicious prosecution, false imprisonment and cases in which fraud is alleged. But their use is not mandatory in such cases, and is not excluded in other cases. See RSC, Ord. 33, r. 5.

[28] As to the proper advisory role of the clerk, see Practice Direction of 2 July 1981 [1981] 2 All ER 831. Stipendiary magistrates are in theory in the same position as lay justices, but the clerk's advice may be less crucial in practice. At courts martial, the tribunal must accept the advice of their judge-advocate on matters of law.

or charge (seen in the light of the burden and standard of proof applicable to the issues) and the weight of any evidence admitted for the purpose of proving or disproving the facts in issue. In a criminal trial, a jury also decide, if necessary, whether the defendant stands mute of malice or by visitation of God, and the question of fitness to plead; but if the defendant is found fit to plead, another jury must be empanelled to try him.

Many issues involve in part a question of law and in part (if the question of law be answered in a way which does not preclude it) a question of fact. Thus, in defamation actions, it is a question of law whether the words complained of are capable of bearing defamatory meaning, and a question of fact whether they are defamatory of the plaintiff. Where corroboration is required as a matter of law, or is to be looked for as a matter of practice, it is a question of law what evidence given, if any, is capable of constituting corroboration, and a question of fact whether such evidence does afford corroboration of the evidence requiring it. There are very many similar matters which consist of mixed issues of law and fact, and in a jury trial, the judge must decide the issue of law, direct the jury accordingly, and then leave the jury to consider any issue of fact permitted or called for by his ruling.

There are cases in which the distinction between matters of law and fact is not entirely clear, and in case of doubt, reference must be made to the appropriate substantive law to establish what matters are to be determined by the judge, and what by the jury. To take just one example, in an action for malicious prosecution, it is a question of fact for the jury to determine what steps the defendant took to inform himself of the truth of the charge, and whether the defendant honestly believed in the truth of the charge; it is for the judge to rule as a matter of law whether the defendant had, in the light of the facts found, any reasonable and probable cause. But in other cases, what is reasonable is a question of fact, for example, whether allegedly provocative words or conduct would have led a reasonable man to react as the defendant did. Moreover, some questions of substantive fact, for instance the proper interpretation of foreign law, are decided by the judge.[29]

The functions of the trial judge in relation to matters involving the law of evidence are concerned with questions of admissibility and the rules governing the production and effect of evidence. A judge sitting alone in a civil case must direct his mind to questions of weight also, but the critical area concerns the functions of the judge and jury in a criminal trial, and the necessary demarcation between those functions.

*1.5.1.1  Admissibility.*  Questions of the admissibility of evidence are matters of law for the judge, with which the jury are not concerned. Counsel should inform each other of any questions of admissibility which are to be referred to the judge, and the controverted evidence should not be opened to or referred to in the presence of the jury, unless and until it is ruled to be admissible. Questions of admissibility are properly decided at the stage when they naturally arise in the course of the case, but where the prosecution (or in some cases the defence) cannot coherently open or begin to present their case without reference to the controverted evidence, the judge should be invited to rule on it as a preliminary issue. Such a case would be where the only evidence against a defendant is a confession, the admissibility of which is disputed.

*1.5.1.2  Procedure for determining admissibility.*  It is as well to put this subject into

---

[29]   Questions of foreign law are questions of fact, and should be proved by expert evidence: see 9.9.5, post.

perspective by noting that most pieces of evidence tendered in most cases are agreed by the parties to be admissible, and are admitted without objection. In such a case, the judge has no role to play until he considers the weight of the evidence (if sitting without a jury) or directs the jury about the evidence. However, where an objection is made to the admissibility of evidence, the judge must rule on the issue in his capacity as the tribunal of law. Where the judge sits with a jury, there is a convenient separation of the tribunals of law and fact, and the procedure for dealing with evidential objections is simple and satisfactory. Where the judge sits alone, or where the magistrates or tribunal are the judges of the law as well as the facts, substantial problems arise. Both situations must be considered.

(a) *Procedure in jury trial.* In a trial before judge and jury, all questions of admissibility, including any questions of foundation affecting the authenticity or originality of a questioned exhibit, are decided by the judge in the absence of the jury. The jury is not concerned with evidence until its admissibility has been established. The judge may, if necessary, hear evidence of secondary facts that affect the admissibility of the tendered evidence, for example the circumstances in which a confession was made. Such a procedure is known as a 'trial within a trial' or proceedings on the 'voir dire' — a name taken from the form of oath prescribed at common law for testimony given on secondary issues. In other cases, the judge will hear only legal argument on the basis of agreed or assumed facts. In any event, the jury will not be exposed to evidence unless and until it is ruled to be admissible. The jury should, however, be present when the judge determines the competence as a witness of a child of tender years or a person subject to disability of mind,[30] because the inquiry affects the weight of the evidence to be given, without exposing the jury to the substance of that evidence. See 11.8, post.

(b) *Procedure in non-jury trial.* The convenient separation between the tribunals of law and fact cannot be reproduced when the judge sits alone, or where the trial is before the magistrates or a tribunal. The voir dire procedure is, therefore, not available to prevent the exposure of the tribunal of fact, during an argument or evidence affecting admissibility, to potentially inadmissible evidence. In some cases, an effective argument can be made without exposing the tribunal of fact to the detail of the evidence, by indicating generally the nature of the disputed evidence. This should be done wherever possible, and is most likely to be effective when the question of admissibility is entirely one of law, and does not involve a question of secondary fact. But in some cases, especially where the tribunal of law must determine secondary facts, there is no alternative but to expose that tribunal to the disputed evidence, and, if the evidence is held to be inadmissible, to request the tribunal to put the evidence out of their minds. There is no doubt that most tribunals make a conscientious effort to do this, but there can also be no doubt that the opponent who successfully objects to evidence is in an unenviable position.

In *F (An infant)* v *Chief Constable of Kent* [1982] Crim LR 682, the Divisional Court held that since the voir dire procedure was inappropriate to summary trial, the magistrates need hear evidence of secondary facts only once, and that such a hearing would suffice to enable the bench both to rule on admissibility and to weigh the evidence tendered, if held to be admissible. In a jury trial, of course, evidence ruled to be admissible is presented and, if necessary, repeated in the presence of the jury. The report of the case is short and yields no indication that the Divisional Court offered any solution to the problem, which will

---

[30] See *R* v *Reynolds* (CCA) [1950] 1 KB 606.

arise also before a tribunal and (with less adverse effect) before a judge sitting alone.[31]

(c)   *Importance of objections.*   In the United States, all jurisdictions concur that unless an evidential error is made part of the record of the trial, an appellate court will not consider the point on appeal, unless the error is one of a very few considered to be so fundamental as to require intervention regardless of objection. Although the appellate courts of this country are less strict, and will often consider points not taken below, this will not always be the case, and a specific objection to a ruling for or against the admissibility of evidence should always be made and argued. The Divisional Court in *F (An infant)* v *Chief Constable of Kent* (ante) noted the importance of obtaining a specific ruling on the question of admissibility from the magistrates, notwithstanding that no separate 'trial within a trial' can take place. In *The Tasmania* (1890) 15 App Cas 223 at 225,[32] Lord Herschell observed that:

> A point not taken at the trial, and presented for the first time in the Court of Appeal . . . ought to be most jealously scrutinised . . . A Court of Appeal ought only to decide in favour of an appellant on a ground there put forward for the first time, if it be satisfied beyond doubt, first that it had before it all the facts bearing upon the new contention as completely as would have been the case if the controversy had arisen at the trial; and next, that no satisfactory explanation could have been offered by those whose conduct is impugned if an opportunity for explanation had been afforded them in the witness box.

In criminal cases, the Court of Appeal (Criminal Division) may be more disposed than its civil counterpart to hear an appeal based on a point of evidence not taken below, if there is a risk of injustice, But it is safer and better not to have to argue that it should do so. An objection should always be made to what appears to be the wrongful admission or exclusion of evidence.

A somewhat different situation prevails where the error is contained in the summing up. Here, there is authority that prosecuting counsel (who cannot appeal against a verdict of not guilty) has a duty to invite the judge to correct any apparent error of law. But the better view is that defence counsel owes a duty to his client, and has no duty to correct what may be an appealable error: *R* v *Cocks* (1976) 63 Cr App R 79, 82 per James LJ. In this event, no criticism should attach to counsel appearing below, and the appellate courts should not hesitate to entertain such grounds of appeal. Although this principle should be, and at present seems to be, well established, it has not proved to be entirely immune from attack.[33]

*1.5.1.3   Production and effect.*   The judge must direct the jury with regard to all matters which arise concerning the production, significance and effect of the evidence given, and the use which they are entitled to make of that evidence. This duty includes the explanation of the burden and standard of proof, the limited use that may be made of evidence of limited admissibility, the operation of any presumptions, the nature of, and

---

[31]   For some practical suggestions, see Murphy & Barnard, *Evidence and Advocacy* (1984) 10–14.

[32]   More leniency is likely to be shown only if the point not raised below is essentially 'procedural' in nature: see, e.g., *Davis* v *Galmoye* (1888) 39 Ch D 322. This should not apply to substantive questions of admissibility of evidence.

[33]   See, e.g., *R* v *Edwards* [1983] Crim LR 484; *R* v *Southgate* (1963) 47 Cr App R 252.

any requirement for, corroboration and where, if at all, it may be found, the rules regarding the evidential value of confessions, the significance of any character evidence, the position of the defendant as a witness in his own defence, and any other such matters of law which may arise.

The judge is entitled to comment on the weight or credibility of any evidence given, provided that he impresses upon the jury that they are the judges of the facts, and it is their view which counts. In some cases, stronger comment is permissible than in others,[34] and in certain cases, some observation on the weight of evidence may be essential if the jury are to be properly informed about their task.[35]

*1.5.1.4 Withdrawing the case from the jury.* It is the judge's duty to consider whether there is sufficient evidence, at the close of the prosecution's case in a criminal trial, to warrant leaving the case to the jury at all. This is a matter of law, and the judge may decide the question at any time after the close of the prosecution case, and whether or not a submission of no case to answer is made by the defence. The judge should withdraw the case from the jury if either there is no evidence that the defendant committed the offence charged, or the evidence to that effect is so tenuous, because of inherent weakness, vagueness or inconsistency, that a properly directed jury could not properly convict on the basis of it. In all other cases, the judge should leave the case to the jury, whose responsibility it is to act as the judges of the facts: see *R v Galbraith* [1981] 1 WLR 1039.[36] The jury may stop the case in favour of the defence at any time after the close of the prosecution case, but may convict only after the completion of the summing up. Submissions of no case to answer may also be made in civil cases, whether or not tried with a jury, though other rules then come into play which are outside the scope of the present work, and for which reference should be made to the *Supreme Court Practice*.

*1.5.2 Judicial discretion*
The categorisation of evidence as either admissible or inadmissible is one well suited to the adversary system of litigation, in the sense that the parties should be free to approach the presentation of their case in the confidence that the rules will be consistently observed. But the question also arises whether the judge, in addition to deciding questions of admissibility, may by virtue of his function of conducting the trial fairly in the interests of all the parties, superimpose upon the questions of admissibility some discretionary decision, either to admit evidence which is technically inadmissible (inclusionary discretion) or to exclude evidence which is technically admissible (exclusionary discretion) so as to meet the justice of any particular case. It must be said that in general, the common law has not accorded judges any substantial degree of discretion, and the only discretion which can safely be regarded as established is a limited exclusionary discretion relating to evidence tendered for the prosecution in criminal cases.

[34] The cases are carefully and fully analysed in Archbold, *Criminal Pleading, Evidence and Practice*, 41st ed., para. 4–430 et seq.
[35] For example, in identification cases: see *R v Turnbull* (CA) [1977] QB 224, and generally 13.3.3.2 post. In general, American judges are not permitted to comment on the facts. Federal judges are permitted to do so, but rarely do because of the strong possibility of reversal on appeal. In Texas, the judge actually gives the jury the charge (sums up) before the closing arguments of counsel, so that counsel argue the case knowing how the jury has been directed.
[36] Cf. *R v Young* (CCA) [1964] 1 WLR 717: Practice Direction [1962] 1 All ER 448. The judge must not usurp the function of the jury — weak cases, like strong ones, are to be considered by the jury: see *R v Barker* (CA) (1975) 65 Cr App R 287 n.

*1.5.2.1  Inclusionary discretion.*  There appears to be no common law discretion to admit inadmissible evidence, either in criminal or civil cases. In *Sparks v R* [1964] AC 964, the appellant was charged with indecently assaulting a young girl. The girl had told her mother that her attacker was 'a coloured boy', whereas the appellant was white. At trial, the girl was not called to give evidence, doubtless because of her young age. It was argued that the description given by the girl should have been admitted because it was 'manifestly unjust' for the jury to be left in ignorance of the fact that the girl had made a statement which tended to exculpate the defendant. The statement was, however, hearsay and inadmissible. The Privy Council rejected arguments that the evidence might be admissible as part of the res gestae or as evidence of a previous identification. This concluded any possibility of this highly relevant evidence being admitted. Lord Morris of Borth-y-Gest said (ibid at 978):

> It was said that it was 'manifestly unjust for the jury to be left throughout the whole trial with the impression that the child could not give any clue to the identity of her assailant'. The cause of justice is, however, best served by adherence to rules which have long been recognised and settled.

Although the appeal was allowed for other reasons, the obvious relevance and cogency of the excluded evidence suggests that, if any general inclusionary discretion had existed, it would have been employed in *Sparks*. No other authority supports such a discretion.

There are, however, some statutory powers to override formal defects or to admit evidence notwithstanding failure to observe applicable procedural requirements, such as that conferred by s. 8(3)(a) of the Civil Evidence Act 1968 (effected by RSC, Ord. 38, r. 29) to permit the admission of hearsay statements technically admissible under ss. 2, 4 or 5 of that Act, notwithstanding the failure of a party to comply with the mandatory rules of court governing their admission.

*1.5.2.2  Exclusionary discretion: civil cases.*  No well defined exclusionary discretion can be demonstrated which applies to civil cases. But it may be that by some process akin to that of the mathematical prediction of a new planet, some discretion must be taken to exist because of the provision of s. 18(5) of the Civil Evidence Act 1968 (echoed in s. 5(3) of the Civil Evidence Act 1972, except that the latter refers to 'civil proceedings' instead of 'legal proceedings') that:

> Nothing in this Act shall prejudice—
> (a)  any power of a court in any legal proceedings, to exclude evidence (whether by preventing questions from being put or otherwise) at its discretion.[37]

There are undoubtedly certain cases where the assessment of relevance or the balancing of competing interests bears a superficial resemblance to the process of the exercise of discretion.[38] But these are, in reality, a function of the decision of the question of admissibility, and the separate existence of an exclusionary discretion cannot be inferred solely from this particular judicial exercise. The existence of such a discretion appears

[37]   To the same effect are Police and Criminal Evidence Act 1984, ss. 72(2), 82(3), although there is no doubt that an exclusionary discretion exists in criminal cases.

[38]   As Professor Cross points out in relation to his treatment of inclusionary discretion: *Evidence*, 5th ed. p. 37.

never to have been canvassed except in the context of the cases dealing with confidential information. It is quite clear as a matter of law that confidentiality is, in itself, no ground for preventing the asking of questions or the operation of discovery designed to elicit information imparted to a witness 'in confidence', or the contents of any 'confidential' document.[39] But it has been suggested that the court may, nonetheless, exercise some discretion to prevent the compelling of disclosure, where the confidence is serious and one which in the public interest generally ought to be respected, and where the relevance and weight of the information in terms of the proceedings as a whole would be relatively small.[40] But in *D* v *NSPCC* (HL) [1978] AC 171 at 239, Lord Simon of Glaisdale appears to have regarded the matter as one based on no foundation more secure than that of the comity between Bench and Bar and the professional judgment of advocates. One might perhaps add to that the obvious forensic reluctance to insist upon pressing a matter to the extent of alienating the tribunal, unless that matter is one which can hardly be avoided. Lord Simon's view was that 'if it comes to the forensic crunch . . . it must be law, not discretion, which is in command', and that the particular question of confidence was one more suited to review by Parliament as a matter of law.

In *ITC Film Distributors* v *Video Exchange Ltd* [1982] Ch 436, Warner J refused to permit a defendant to introduce into evidence certain papers which he had obtained from the plaintiffs and their solicitors by a trick, after the papers had been brought into court for use during the trial. Although the evidence could not have been excluded as a matter of law, simply because it had been obtained illegally or unfairly (see 1.6, post), the learned judge held that the defendant's action amounted to a contempt of court, and that the court 'should not countenance it by admitting such documents in evidence'. It is unclear whether Warner J regarded his decision as an act of discretion. It seems rather that he regarded himself as acceding to an argument addressed to him by counsel for the plaintiffs, according to which the public interest in the freedom of litigants to bring their papers into court without fear that they might be filched by opponents outweighed the public interest that all available evidence should be usable as a vehicle for discovery of the truth. In all probability, the decision cannot be regarded as extending beyond its own unusual facts, and it certainly appears to offer no authority for any general exclusionary discretion.

*1.5.2.3 Exclusionary discretion: criminal cases.* In criminal cases, there is no doubt that the trial judge has a discretion at common law to exclude admissible evidence tendered by the prosecution, on the ground that the probative value of such evidence is substantially outweighed by its likely effect of prejudicing the minds of the tribunal of fact against the defendant. It should be noted that the discretion relates only to evidence tendered by the prosecution, and not to evidence tendered by a co-defendant. The exclusionary discretion is given statutory force by s. 78 of the Police and Criminal Evidence Act 1984, which provides:

(1) In any proceedings the court may refuse to allow evidence on which the prosecution proposes to rely to be given if it appears to the court that, having regard to all the circumstances, including the circumstances in which the evidence was obtained,

---

[39]  Such matter is admissible in law, unless it must be excluded for some reason of public policy, or is also the subject of a specific private privilege: see Chapter 10, post.

[40]  See, e.g., *Attorney-General* v *Mulholland; Attorney-General* v *Foster* (CA) [1963] 2 QB 477, per Donovan LJ at 492.

the admission of the evidence would have such an adverse effect on the fairness of the proceedings that the court ought not to admit it.

(2)   Nothing in this section shall prejudice any rule of law requiring a court to exclude evidence.

By s. 82(1) of the Act, the word 'proceedings' as it applies to s. 78 is confined to criminal proceedings, but includes summary trial and committal proceedings.

The scope of the statutory discretion under s. 78 may call for some judicial clarification. In one respect, the section gives the court a wider discretion than did the common law as declared by the House of Lords in *R* v *Sang* [1980] AC 402. In *Sang*, the House of Lords held that there was no discretion to exclude admissible prosecution evidence, other than admissions, confessions and other evidence obtained from the defendant after the commission of the offence, on the ground that that evidence had been obtained illegally or unfairly. Under s. 78, however, the court may consider, in addition to all other circumstances, the circumstances in which the evidence was obtained. This will be dealt with further in 1.6, post.

A second issue raised by s. 78 is the meaning of the phrase 'such an adverse effect on the fairness of the proceedings that the court ought not to admit it'. At common law, the authorities (including *Sang*) appeared to have established that the judge was required to weigh the probative value of the evidence tendered against its potential prejudice to the defendant. That balancing process determined whether the admissible evidence tendered should be excluded as a matter of discretion. It may well be that Parliament intended the judge to apply substantially the same test in asking himself, for the purposes of s. 78, whether the evidence tendered ought not to be admitted. Certainly, the courts which have considered the discretion at common law have proved generally consistent in calling for the balancing process, and there is no obvious reason to change an approach that has worked well. It is submitted that the 'probative value versus prejudice' test remains adequate to enable the judge to decide whether evidence ought to be admitted for the purposes of s. 78.

How, then, is the balancing process to be further defined? In *Noor Mohamed* v *R* [1949] AC 182,[41] Lord du Parcq delivering the advice of the Privy Council said:

. . . in all such cases the judge ought to consider whether the evidence is sufficiently substantial, having regard to the purpose to which it is professedly directed, to make it desirable in the interest of justice that it should be admitted. If, so far as that purpose is concerned, it can in the circumstances have only trifling weight, the judge will be right to exclude it. To say this is not to confuse weight with admissibility. The distinction is plain, but cases must occur in which it would be unjust to admit evidence of a character gravely prejudicial to the accused even though there may be some tenuous ground for holding it technically admissible. The decision must then be left to the discretion and sense of fairness of the judge.

In *R* v *List* [1966] 1 WLR 9, at 12 Roskill J said:

A trial judge always has an overriding duty in every case to secure a fair trial, and if in any particular case he comes to the conclusion that, even though certain evidence is

---

[41]   At 192. See also *R* v *Christie* [1914] AC 545, per Lord Moulton at 559.

strictly admissible, yet its prejudicial effect once admitted is such as to make it virtually impossible for a dispassionate view of the crucial facts of the case to be thereafter taken by the jury, then the trial judge, in my judgment, should exclude that evidence.

This more modern definition of the discretion is probably somewhat broader than that suggested by Lord du Parcq's words, in the sense that the extremes of the balance, 'trifling weight' and 'gravely prejudicial', would now not be insisted upon, so long as the prejudicial value can be shown to outweigh any realistic probative value. In *R* v *Sang* (HL) [1980] AC 402, at 434 Lord Diplock, having considered the authorities, summed up the position by saying:

> So I would hold that there has now developed a general rule of practice whereby in a trial by jury the judge has a discretion to exclude evidence which, though technically admissible, would probably have a prejudicial influence on the minds of the jury, which would be out of proportion to its true evidential value.

Viscount Dilhorne (ibid at 438) employed the same phrase. Lords Salmon and Fraser of Tullybelton (ibid at 444, 446–7) held that the discretion lay to exclude evidence, where to do so is necessary to ensure a fair trial. Lord Scarman (ibid at 452) adopting the words of Lord Reid in *Myers* v *DPP* held that the discretion lay to exclude, 'if justice so requires', adding that it was not confined to cases in which the prejudicial effect outweighs the probative value, but was confined to cases in which there can be said to be an 'unfair use of evidence'. It is doubtful whether these slightly different statements of the rule, culled from a considerable body of case-law, create any real doubt concerning the court's task, which is to weigh the probative value to the prosecution against the prejudicial effect on the defendant, as far as both can be gauged, and to take the course which seems calculated to produce a fair trial.

The balancing test is now well recognised in other jurisdictions, and has probably attained the status of a general rule of the common law. For example, in the United States, Federal Rule of Evidence 403 provides that: '[A]lthough relevant, evidence may be excluded if its probative value is substantially outweighed by the danger of unfair prejudice, confusion of the issues, or misleading the jury, or by considerations of undue delay, waste of time, or needless presentation of cumulative evidence'. It is to be hoped that judges will continue to tread the familiar paths in applying the new statutory exclusionary discretion provided by s. 78.

Prior to *R* v *Sang* there had been some doubt whether the exclusionary discretion in criminal cases might apply to any type of evidence tendered by the prosecution, or only to certain specified categories of evidence. Section 78 seems to make it clear that the discretion may apply to any prosecution evidence, regardless of its type. It is true, nonetheless, that in practical terms some types of evidence have a greater propensity than others to attract arguments for discretionary exclusion. The most commonly recurring situations in which a trial judge is asked to exercise the discretion are as follows. They are dealt with more fully in their proper places in this book, but to state them here will serve to illustrate how the discretion often works in practice:

(a)   Where evidence is admissible under the similar fact rule, the court is invited to permit the jury to be exposed to very specific aspects of the defendant's previous bad character which are held to have a peculiar relevance to the offence charged because of a striking similarity to the offence charged. Whatever its probative value, such evidence obviously has a very marked potential for prejudice which may often make it effectively impossible for the jury to take a dispassionate view of the offence charged. A trial judge should always bear the balancing test in mind in such a case.[42]

(b)   Where the prosecution propose, on a charge of handling stolen goods, to tender evidence of other occasions on which the defendant has been instrumental in the handling of stolen goods, or has previously been convicted of theft or handling stolen goods, with a view to proving that he knew or believed the goods to be stolen, as permitted by s. 27(3) of the Theft Act 1968. Here, the probative value may not be very great but there is a substantial likelihood of prejudice to the defendant, who may be made to look like a general villain.[43] For this reason, if such evidence would offer the jury no more than minimal assistance, it should certainly be excluded: *R* v *Perry* [1984] Crim LR 680.

(c)   Where the defendant has become liable to be cross-examined as to his character, by virtue of s. 1(*e*) or (*f*) of the Criminal Evidence Act 1898, for similar reasons, the judge may exercise his discretion to exclude such cross-examination altogether, or to confine it to those aspects of the defendant's character which appear to be likely to assist the jury in their assessment of the case or of the defendant's credibility.[44] The present trend favours liberal use of the discretion: *R* v *Watts* [1983] 3 All ER 101; *R* v *Britzmann; R* v *Hall* [1983] 1 All ER 369.

(d)   Prior to the coming into effect of the Police and Criminal Evidence Act 1984, a trial judge who found that a confession tendered by the prosecution was admissible as a matter of law, but had been obtained by means of a breach of the Judges' Rules might exercise his discretion to exclude the confession: *R* v *May* (1952) 36 Cr App R 91. However, the test for admissibility of a confession at common law was whether it had been made voluntarily and in the absence of oppression. Under the Act, the admissibility of confessions is governed by s. 76 which provides for the exclusion of the confession as a matter of law if it was, or may have been obtained either by oppression or in consequence of anything said or done which was likely, in the circumstances existing at the time, to render unreliable any confession that might be made in consequence thereof. The distinction between the common law 'voluntariness' test and the statutory 'reliability' test probably removes confessions from the area of discretion. Although nothing in s. 78 indicates that that section cannot apply to a confession, the reality is that if a judge feels that a confession was obtained in such a manner that it ought not to be admitted by virtue of s. 78, he is surely required to exclude it as a matter of law by virtue of s. 76. This view seems to be confirmed by s. 78(2). This subject is further explored in Chapter 7.

That the above cases are only examples of the working of the exclusionary discretion applicable to evidence generally, and not select categories to which alone the discretion can apply, seems clear not only from the wording of s. 78 but also from the speech of Lord Salmon in *R* v *Sang*. Dealing with the common law discretion, Lord Salmon observed ([1980] AC at 445):

I recognise that there may have been no categories of cases, other than those to which I have referred, in which technically admissible evidence proferred by the Crown has

[42]   *Noor Mohamed* v *R* (PC, British Guiana) [1949] AC 182. See also 5.1 and 5.2, post.
[43]   *R* v *Herron* (CCA) [1967] 1 QB 107, decided under the corresponding provisions of the Larceny Act 1916; see also *R* v *Knott* (CA) [1973] Crim LR 36, and 4.5, post.
[44]   *Selvey* v *DPP* (HL) [1970] AC 304. See also 4.14.3.3, post.

been rejected by the court on the ground that it would make the trial unfair. I cannot, however, accept that a judge's undoubted duty to ensure that the accused has a fair trial is confined to such cases. In my opinion the category of cases is not and never can be closed except by statute.

In fact, statute appears to have opened, rather than closed the categories to include any and all evidence, subject only to the position of confessions discussed above. Not only may the discretion be exercised so as to exclude legally admissible evidence which falls into certain generic categories, such as similar-fact evidence or character evidence, but it may also be exercised so as to exclude specific pieces of evidence whose individual characteristics create an undue risk of prejudice which outweighs their actual probative value. It would surely be legitimate, for example, for a court to exclude certain particularly gruesome photographs of the deceased in a murder case, where precisely the same evidential value might be obtained by the introduction of more dispassionate forensic evidence. Such attacks upon individual pieces of evidence appear to be much more common in American than in English practice, perhaps because of the greater American affinity for graphic demonstrative evidence. However, even in England it should not be overlooked that it is relatively easy for a jury to be swayed or even inflamed by such evidence, when the jurors have not experienced the hardening effect that frequent exposure to such materials may have on lawyers. There is also surely something to be said for the concern of Federal Rule of Evidence 403 to prevent the introduction not only of unduly prejudicial evidence, but also of evidence capable of confusing the issues, misleading the jury or resulting in waste of time or the needless presentation of cumulative evidence, at least where evidence is available that lacks these vices.

As Lord Fraser of Tullybelton recognised in *Sang* [1980] AC 402 at 450, the exercise of the discretion is a subjective matter, and much will turn on the facts of each individual case. As has been said of the concept of 'unfairness to the accused' in another context,[45] it may be an amalgam of many relevant factors, and not least will be the extent to which the evidence would assist the jury in their task of deciding the facts in issue. In one sense, all relevant evidence is 'prejudicial' to the defendant, quite legitimately, the more so if its probative value is high. But evidence may be admissible as a matter of law, if it is relevant to the charge, even though coincidentally it may introduce material which could 'prejudice' him (in the unfair sense) in the eyes of the jury, and evidence is often admitted on that basis. It is when that balance is upset to a real degree in favour of prejudice (in the unfair sense) that discretion may be exercised. It does not follow that discretion must be exercised in any particular case—such is not the nature of discretion, and it is difficult to construct grounds of appeal on the basis of a refusal to exercise an exclusionary discretion, because the trial judge is usually far better placed to assess the matter than an appellate court. Although the appellate courts will sometimes intervene in a case of obvious prejudice arising, for example, from the admission of probatively weak similar-fact evidence, intervention must usually be based on some argument against admissibility in law. In *Selvey* v *DPP* (HL) [1970] AC 304, the House of Lords counselled that, while there was a discretion to prevent cross-examination concerning character, in a case where the defendant had made imputations against the character of a witness for the prosecution,

---

[45] In *King* v *R* (PC, Jamaica) [1969] 1 AC 304 at 318–19, per Lord Hodson delivering the advice of the Privy Council.

within the meaning of s. 1(*f*)(ii) of the Criminal Evidence Act 1898, that discretion would not always be exercised in favour of the defendant merely because the making of such imputations was a necessary part of his defence. Many cases are to be found where relevant evidence has been admitted as probative of the offence charged, even though, coincidentally, such evidence exposes to the jury some damaging aspect of the defendant's character.[46] It is, therefore, of no avail to seek to lay down further definitive guidelines. The question is essentially one of fact, bearing in mind the extent of the discretion as defined by the cases we have considered: the overriding duty of the judge being to ensure that there is a fair trial.

It should be emphasised that the discretion to exclude refers only to evidence tendered by the prosecution. There is no discretion to exclude, at the instance of one defendant, evidence sought to be called by another. Thus, although the prosecution may be restrained from cross-examination concerning character where such a course is technically justified under s. 1(*f*)(ii) of the Criminal Evidence Act 1898, there is no power to prevent a co-defendant from cross-examining to the same effect when he is entitled to do so by virtue of s. 1(*f*)(iii) of the Act.[47] The requirement of a fair trial of persons jointly accused demands that each defendant be free to present his case within the limits of relevance and admissibility.

### 1.6    Evidence illegally or unfairly obtained

Whether the courts should refuse to entertain evidence because it has been obtained by the party tendering it in an illegal or improper manner is a question principally of policy, to which no answer is to be found in the law of evidence as such. Given that the evidence is relevant and does not offend against any of the substantive rules of admissibility, the question resolves itself into whether the courts should admit the evidence as admissible to prove the offence charged, or the claim, and leave the party aggrieved to his civil remedy in respect of any actionable wrong indulged in to obtain it, or whether the courts should act as 'watchdogs' and should decline to allow a party guilty of such wrongdoing to profit by it. A secondary issue is whether, if the evidence so obtained is admissible in law as being relevant and not contrary to the substantive rules, the judge may exclude it in the exercise of some discretion.

These issues are of primary, though not exclusive, importance in criminal cases, and we shall consider how they are resolved in both criminal and civil cases.

In the United States, the constitutionally entrenched rights of the defendant in a criminal case require the exclusion of evidence obtained in violation of any of the defendant's fundamental constitutional rights. Thus, if evidence is seized during an unlawful search of the person or property contrary to the Fourth Amendment right to be protected against unlawful search and seizure, or if evidence is discovered following a compelled statement contrary to the Fifth Amendment privilege against self-incrimination, or if evidence was obtained by means of depriving the defendant of the Sixth Amendment right to counsel, the court must as a matter of law exclude the evidence so obtained. This so-called 'Exclusionary Rule', though subject to periodic attempts to whittle it down, is regarded as one of the pillars of the constitutional protection offered to

---

[46]    See generally 4.1.3 and Chapter 5, *post*, and, on a similar point, *Turner* v *Underwood* (DC) [1948] 2 KB 284.

[47]    *Murdoch* v *Taylor* (HL) [1965] AC 574. See generally 4.15, *post*.

the defendant in a criminal case, and transcends the rules of evidence. American courts have traditionally regarded it as an important part of their constitutional duty to assume the role of watchdog over the conduct of those charged with the investigation of crime, and have been prepared to fulfil this role by excluding from evidence the fruits of wrongful conduct, as well as by offering subsequent civil remedies for such conduct.

In England, it is quite clear that evidence is not rendered inadmissible merely by the manner in which it is obtained. Following the decision of the House of Lords in *R* v *Sang* [1980] AC 402, it also appeared that the common law recognised no discretion to exclude evidence because of the manner in which it has been obtained. The House confirmed the existence of the discretion discussed in 1.5.2.3 ante, to exclude in a criminal case evidence whose prejudicial effect might result in a denial of a fair trial to the defendant. This, however, is a discretion based upon the prejudicial nature of the evidence, and not upon the manner in which it was obtained. Efforts to include in the Police and Criminal Evidence Act 1984 a provision that illegally or unfairly obtained evidence should be inadmissible or excludable as a matter of discretion failed, but by virtue of s. 78 of the Act, the manner in which prosecution evidence is obtained is one matter which the court may take into account in deciding in the exercise of its discretion whether that evidence should be excluded pursuant to the section. This will be discussed further below.

### 1.6.1  Criminal cases

*1.6.1.1  Admissibility.*  The courts have, from an early stage, rejected the concept that evidence should be held to be inadmissible merely on the ground of the manner in which it is obtained. In *Jones* v *Owens* (1870) 34 JP 759, where a constable, in the course of an unlawful search of the defendant, found a quantity of young salmon, which became the subject of a charge, Mellor J said that if such evidence could not be used against him, it would be 'a dangerous obstacle to the administration of justice'. And in *R* v *Leatham*[48] referring to a letter which had been found only because of inadmissible confessions made by the defendant, Crompton J went so far as to say that 'if you steal it even, it would be admissible'. In more recent times, the rule was restated in the leading case of *Kuruma Son of Kaniu* v *R* (PC, Eastern Africa) [1955] AC 197 at 203, in which the defendant was charged with the unlawful possession of ammunition during a period of emergency in Kenya. The ammunition was found during an unlawful search, and it was contended on appeal to the Privy Council that the evidence of the finding was inadmissible because of the manner in which it had been obtained. In delivering the advice of the Privy Council, Lord Goddard CJ rejected the argument decisively, saying:

> In their Lordships' opinion the test to be applied in considering whether the evidence is admissible is whether it is relevant to the matters in issue. If it is, it is admissible and the court is not concerned with how the evidence was obtained. While this proposition may not have been stated in so many words in any English case there are decisions which support it, and in their Lordships' opinion it is plainly right in principle.

The rule has been reaffirmed on several occasions since then, and in *Jeffrey* v *Black*

---

[48]  (1861) 8 Cox CC 498. But see also Police and Criminal Evidence Act 1984, s. 76(4) and 7.7, post.

(DC) [1978] QB 490, the Divisional Court had no doubt that the decision should be accepted. It is relevant to note that this principle of admissibility applies even to cases of 'entrapment' and where evidence is obtained as a result of the activities of an *'agent provocateur'*. Both terms refer to cases in which the defendant is lured into or encouraged in the commission of an offence, for which he is subsequently prosecuted. Two distinct situations may be identified: the first where the *agent provocateur* infiltrates himself into the performance of an offence already under way, for example by posing as a receiver of stolen goods; the second where the agent himself initiates the commission of the offence. and where but for such initiation the offence might not have been committed. It has been held that the distinction may be relevant for the purpose of deciding with what offence the defendant should be charged[49] and for the purpose of mitigation of sentence in certain cases.[50] But entrapment is not a defence in English law, and accordingly it has been held that evidence obtained through the agency of an *agent provocateur*, or during entrapment, is not inadmissible, even though the courts have sometimes deprecated the use of such methods, especially those falling within the second kind of situation referred to above. However, in *R* v *Mealy and Sheridan*[51] the Court of Appeal rejected the very argument that evidence had been obtained in any way unfairly, saying that it was the commission of the offence, and not the evidence, which had been so obtained. This extraordinary view is granted by the learned editors of Archbold[52] the accolade that: 'once stated this point is self-evident', and was much stressed in the argument in the 40th edition of that work. But since in any event, the evidence would be admissible, whether obtained unfairly or not, the point seems to be moot.

*1.6.1.2   Discretion.*   In *R* v *Sang* [1980] AC 402, the defendant was charged with conspiracy to utter counterfeit United States banknotes. He alleged by counsel that he had been induced by an informer, acting on the instructions of the police, to commit an offence that he would not have committed otherwise. As it was then clear law that the existence of entrapment, even if established, would not have been a ground to exclude evidence of the offence as a matter of law, counsel sought to investigate the issue in a trial within a trial, with a view to persuading the trial judge to exclude that evidence in his discretion. The trial judge, taking the view that he had no such discretion to exclude admissible prosecution evidence, ruled accordingly after hearing argument on the hypothetical basis that the defendant's allegations were true.[53] The Court of Appeal subsequently dismissed an appeal against conviction, and the defendant appealed to the House of Lords. The House of Lords held that:

(a)   The judge had a general discretion to exclude admissible prosecution evidence on

---

[49]   See *R* v *Macro* (CA) [1969] Crim LR 205. Generally, the second (but not the first) kind of entrapment mentioned in the text is regarded as a defence in American jurisdictions.

[50]   *R* v *Birtles* (CA) [1969] 1 WLR 1047.

[51]   (1974) 60 Cr App R 59. In *R* v *McEvilly; R* v *Lee* (1973) 60 Cr App R 150, a differently constituted Court of Appeal appears to have assumed (obiter) that if the commission of an offence had been induced, which offence would not otherwise have been committed, the evidence should be rejected as unfairly obtained. This can no longer be regarded as sound.

[52]   41st ed., para. 15–74.

[53]   The judge's view was supported by some authority; for example, the decision of the Court of Appeal in *R* v *Willis* [1976] Crim LR 127, though for the reasons given below in the text, the greater weight of authority supported the existence of the discretion.

the ground that its prejudicial nature might result in the defendant's being denied a fair trial. (This is the general exclusionary discretion now enshrined in s. 78 of the Police and Criminal Evidence Act 1984 and discussed in 1.5.2.3, ante).

(b)   With the exception of admissions, confessions and other evidence obtained from the defendant after commission of the offence (for example, documentary evidence) the judge had no discretion to exclude evidence obtained by improper or unfair means, the court being concerned with the relevance of the evidence in question, not with its source. (At common law, the judge had a discretion to exclude confessions obtained unfairly, in the sense of a breach of the Judges' Rules. The admissibility of confessions under the Police and Criminal Evidence Act 1984 is a question of law rather than discretion: see s. 76 and Chapter 7, post.)

The decision in *Sang* probably represents the nadir of the concern of English courts with the protection of the defendant in criminal cases, and shows how vulnerable a defendant is in the absence of entrenched constitutional safeguards. Although the United States Supreme Court attempts to narrow the effect of the Exclusionary Rule from time to time, a decision such as that in *Sang* would be unthinkable in the United States.

One of the more disturbing aspects of *Sang* is that it was in no way dictated by earlier authority. Indeed, such authority as there was indicated that the manner in which evidence was obtained was a proper subject for consideration by a judge in deciding whether or not to exercise his general exclusionary discretion. For example, in *R* v *Payne* [1963] 1 WLR 637, the defendant's conviction for driving while unfit through drink was quashed by the Court of Criminal Appeal, where it appeared that the defendant's consent to a medical examination at the police station had been obtained by an express assurance that the doctor would not be asked to testify as to whether the defendant was unfit to drive a motor vehicle through drink and where in violation of this assurance, the prosecution nonetheless called the doctor at trial for precisely that purpose. The Court of Criminal Appeal held that, while the doctor's evidence was obviously admissible in law, the trial judge should have excluded it in the exercise of his discretion. This was entirely in accord with the earlier view of Lord Goddard CJ in *Kuruma*. Lord Goddard had said ([1955] AC 197, 204):

> No doubt in a criminal case the judge always has a discretion to disallow evidence if the strict rules of admissibility would operate unfairly against an accused. This was emphasised in the case before this Board of *Noor Mohamed* v *R*, and in the recent case in the House of Lords, *Harris* v *DPP* [(HL) [1952] AC 694]. If, for instance, some admission of some piece of evidence, e.g., a document, had been obtained from a defendant by a trick, no doubt the judge might properly rule it out.

Following this pronouncement, the existence of such a discretion was reaffirmed by many courts, almost always while declining to accept that it should be, or have been, applied on the facts before them. In *Callis* v *Gunn* (DC) [1964] 1 QB 495 at 502, Lord Parker CJ dealing with the question of the admissibility of fingerprint evidence, said:

> In my judgment fingerprint evidence taken in these circumstances is admissible in law subject to this overriding discretion. That discretion, as I understand it, would certainly be exercised by excluding the evidence if there was any suggestion of it having been obtained oppressively, by false representations, by a trick, by threats, by bribes, anything of that sort.

More recently, the Divisional Court in *Jeffrey* v *Black* [1978] QB 490, had once again confirmed the existence of a discretionary power of exclusion. The defendant was charged with the theft of a sandwich from a public house. Before he was charged, police officers took the defendant to his home, stating that they intended to search it. The justices found as a fact that a search of the defendant's room was conducted without his consent, and refused to admit evidence of the discovery of cannabis and cannabis resin in the room. On appeal by the prosecutor, the Divisional Court held that, although the justices had erred in exercising their discretion to exclude the evidence merely because of the irregularity of the search, a discretion to exclude did exist. Lord Widgery CJ pointed out that the discretion was not confined to any particular case, but was '. . . a discretion which every judge has all the time in respect of all the evidence which is tendered by the prosecution'. It appears that Lord Widgery anticipated the statutory position under s. 78 of the Police and Criminal Evidence Act 1984, since his judgment indicates quite clearly both that there exists a general discretion to exclude any evidence tendered by the prosecution, and that one aspect of that discretion is concerned with the manner in which evidence has been obtained. The Lord Chief Justice stressed that the exercise of the discretion would be comparatively rare[54] but added:

> But if the case is exceptional, if the case is such that not only have the police officers entered without authority, but they have been guilty of trickery or they have misled someone, or they have been oppressive or they have been unfair, or in other respects they have behaved in a manner which is morally reprehensible, then it is open to the justices to apply their discretion and decline to allow the particular evidence to be let in as part of the trial.

That the members of the House of Lords in *Sang* recognised the force of these earlier authorities appears clearly from the avenues taken by their Lordships in an effort to escape from them. The most confident approach was that of Lord Diplock, who treated the question essentially as one of first impression for the House. Dealing with Lord Goddard's words in *Kuruma* cited above, Lord Diplock said ([1980] AC 402, 436):

> That statement was not, in my view, ever intended to acknowledge the existence of any wider discretion than to exclude (1) admissible evidence which would probably have a prejudicial influence on the minds of the jury that would be out of proportion to its true evidential value; and (2) evidence tantamount to a self-incriminatory admission which was obtained from the defendant, after the offence had been committed, by means which would justify a judge in excluding an actual confession which had the like self-incriminating effect. As a matter of language, although not as a matter of application, the subsequent dicta go much further than this; but in so far as they do so they have never yet been considered by this House.

---

[54]   At 498. Lord Widgery CJ said: 'I cannot stress the point too strongly that it is a very exceptional situation, and the simple, unvarnished fact that evidence was obtained by police officers who had gone in without bothering to get a search warrant is not enough to justify the magistrates in exercising their discretion to keep the evidence out'. Lord Widgery did not indicate what would be enough. It is possible that the Lord Chief Justice was concerned to avoid any suggestion that the exclusionary discretion should be an object of frequent use in the magistrates' courts in view of the somewhat greater danger that the guidelines might be misunderstood.

Other members of the House sought refuge in arguments which are, with respect, considerably less persuasive. Viscount Dilhorne, dealing with the observations made in *Callis* v *Gunn* and *Jeffrey* v *Black*, said ([1980] AC 402, 441):

> With great respect I do not think that these observations were correct. I have not been able to find any authority for the general principle enunciated by Lord Parker or for these statements by him and by Lord Widgery. If there is any authority for it, it conflicts with Lord Goddard's statement in *Kuruma* v *The Queen* [1955] AC 197 that the court is not concerned with how evidence is obtained.

It may be that Viscount Dilhorne did not have in mind that part of Lord Goddard's judgment in *Kuruma* cited above. It is clear that *Sang* in fact represented a significant change in the law, which surely did not justify the opening remark of Lord Salmon's speech, 'My Lords, this is a strange appeal which plainly has no hope of succeeding', or his later statement that he did 'not propose to comment upon the *obiter dicta* in *Callis* v *Gunn* or in *Jeffrey* v *Black*' ([1980] AC 402, 442, 444, emphasis added). None of the speeches in the House of Lords in *Sang* can conceal the fact that the House was, for the first time, holding that the manner in which prosecution evidence is obtained in a criminal case could not be considered in relation to the exclusionary discretion.

The holding in *Sang* has, happily, been modified by statute: s. 78 of the Police and Criminal Evidence Act 1984. Lord Widgery's judgment in *Jeffrey* v *Black* probably represented the closest approach to the statutory compromise of s. 78 between *Sang* and the earlier authorities. It is true that there is no separate discretion to exclude evidence because of the manner in which it is obtained. Equally, however, it is now clear that the manner in which evidence is obtained is one of the factors to be considered by the judge in deciding whether or not to exercise his general exclusionary discretion. Section 78(1) of the Police and Criminal Evidence Act 1984 provides that:

> In any proceedings the court may refuse to allow evidence on which the prosecution proposes to rely to be given if it appears to the court that, having regard to all the circumstances, *including the circumstances in which the evidence was obtained*, the admission of the evidence would have such an adverse effect on the fairness of the proceedings that the court ought not to admit it. [Emphasis added.]

Section 78 does not indicate what specific matters the court is to consider significant in assessing the circumstances in which the evidence was obtained, and it would seem that, as in the area of the exclusionary discretion in other respects, the guidance provided by earlier authority will remain helpful. Such earlier authority usually concentrated upon the apparent gravity of the illegal or unfair act by means of which the evidence was obtained, the gravity of the charges against the defendant and the likely probative value of the evidence. What may be a justifiable method of obtaining evidence in a case involving a grave breach of national security may not be a justifiable method of obtaining evidence in a case involving the theft of a sandwich from a public house. The court may also consider whether the same or equivalent evidence could have been obtained in a regular manner without any danger of injury or loss. It is clear that a distinction may and should be drawn between cases where little is at stake such as *Jeffrey* v *Black* in which it is surely permissible to sympathise with the view taken by the justices, and cases where much is at stake, such as *R* v *Murphy*.

In *R* v *Murphy* [1965] NI 138, in a powerfully reasoned judgment, the Courts Martial Appeal Court for Northern Ireland went so far as to analyse the matters which should be taken into account in the exercise of discretion in such cases. The court was dealing with an extremely grave case, in which a serving soldier was charged with disclosing information which might be useful to an enemy. In relation to methods of obtaining evidence, the court said: 'A trick is a method as old as the constable in plain clothes . . . and the day has not come when it would be safe to say that the law could be enforced without resort to it.'

The court went on to hold that the proper test for the exercise of the discretion was one of balancing the gravity of the charge, the position of the defendant, and the methods used. In words subsequently adopted by the Privy Council,[55] Lord McDermott said that unfairness to an accused was not susceptible of close definition, but:

> . . . must be judged of in the light of all the material facts and findings and all the surrounding circumstances. The position of the accused, the nature of the investigation, and the gravity or otherwise of the suspected offence may all be relevant. That is not to say that the standard of fairness must bear some sort of inverse proportion to the extent to which the public interest may be involved, but different offences may pose different problems for the police and justify different methods.

Once again, a balancing process proves to be the key to exclusionary discretion.

### 1.6.2   Civil cases

The rule governing the admissibility of illegally or unfairly obtained evidence in civil cases is the same as that in criminal cases, namely that relevant evidence is admissible regardless of the manner in which it is obtained. The court is concerned with the relevance, not the source of evidence and will leave the parties to other remedies for any wrongful acts indulged in to obtain evidence. And just as no general exclusionary discretion can be demonstrated in civil cases corresponding to that which exists in criminal cases, so the judge in a civil case has no discretion to exclude evidence illegally or unfairly obtained. These observations must now be read subject to the decision of Warner J in *ITC Film Distributors* v *Video Exchange Ltd and Others* [1982] Ch 436, which is dealt with below, but, it is submitted, they remain sound. Since, in almost every civil case, the judge sits without a jury, the judge must be made aware, in the course of any application to exclude, that there has been an irregularity in the obtaining of the evidence. The judge may, where necessary, caution himself about the weight of evidence so obtained or draw any appropriate adverse inferences against the proponent of the evidence. Consequently, as with other rules of evidence, the potential for prejudice to the opponent is less in many cases than it would be before a jury.

In *Helliwell* v *Piggott-Sims*[56] the plaintiff obtained documentary and other evidence pursuant to an Anton Piller order made at the end of 1977. Subsequently, in *Rank Film Distributors Ltd* v *Video Information Centre* [1982] AC 380, the House of Lords held that it was open to a defendant in such circumstances to refuse to answer interrogatories which might expose the defendant to possible criminal prosecution under the Copyright Act

---

[55]   In *King* v *R* [1969] 1 AC 304 at 319.
[56]   [1980] FSR 356. See also *Universal City Studios Inc. and Others* v *Hubbard and Others* [1983] 2 All ER 596.

1956 or for conspiracy to defraud, relying upon the privilege against self-incrimination.[57] In the light of this decision, the defendants applied to the trial judge to exclude the evidence obtained by the plaintiffs, on the ground that it had been obtained in violation of the defendants' privilege against self-incrimination. The trial judge refused to exclude the evidence, and the defendants renewed their application in the Court of Appeal. Upholding the decision of the trial judge, Lord Denning MR said ([1980] FSR 356, 357):

> It seems to me that there is a very short answer to it. Assuming for a moment that the full order ought not to have been made in the first place in 1977, nevertheless it has been implemented. The evidence is available in the hands of the plaintiffs for them to give in evidence. I do not think that the judge has any discretion to refuse to admit it in evidence. I know that in criminal cases the judge may have a discretion. That is shown by *Kuruma* v *The Queen* ([1955] AC 197 . . .). But so far as civil cases are concerned, it seems to me that the judge has no discretion. The evidence is relevant and admissible. The judge cannot refuse it on the ground that it may have been unlawfully obtained in the beginning. I do not say that it was unlawfully obtained. It was obtained under an Anton Piller order which was not appealed against. But, even if it was unlawfully obtained, nevertheless the judge is right to admit it in evidence and to go on with the case as he proposes to do.

Bridge and Oliver LJJ agreed with the judgment of Lord Denning MR.

Standing alone in the field is the decision of Warner J in *ITC Film Distributors* v *Video Exchange Ltd and Others* [1982] Ch 436, to which reference was made in 1.5.2.2 ante and which is in all probability confined to its own unusual facts. The defendant, during the trial of an action for breach of copyright, obtained by a trick certain papers which the plaintiffs and their solicitors had brought to court for the purposes of the trial. Since the papers were undoubtedly relevant and apparently admissible, the defendant sought to tender them in evidence. The learned judge held that, despite the general rule that the court had no power to exclude relevant evidence in a civil case, the public interest in the due administration of justice required that parties be free to bring their papers to court without fear that they might be filched during trial, and that this consideration outweighed even the competing public interest that the court should receive all available evidence as a means of ascertaining the truth. He regarded the matter as one of public interest. Warner J cited the following passage from the judgment of Waller LJ in *Riddick* v *Thames Board Mills Ltd* [1977] QB 881, 911–912, a case which held that a party was entitled to be protected against the use of materials disclosed on discovery for purposes other than the litigation in which they were disclosed:

> In *D* v *National Society for the Prevention of Cruelty to Children* [1977] 2 WLR 201, Lord Simon of Glaisdale sets out a number of examples of evidence which as a matter of public policy should be excluded from forensic scrutiny. He instances legal professional privilege, 'without prejudice' communications and others and says, at p.221:

---

[57] The actual decision in *Rank Film Distributors Ltd* v *Video Information Centre* was one which the House of Lords felt reluctantly compelled to reach, and on their prompting was reversed by s. 72 of the Supreme Court Act 1981. This section removes the privilege against self-incrimination in such situations. See generally 10.8.2, post. Since the evidence obtained by the plaintiffs in *Helliwell* v *Piggott-Sims* was, in any event, seized pursuant to a valid order of the court, the defendants' argument seems tenuous at best.

'. . . without attempting to be exhaustive I have tried to show that there is a continuum of relevant evidence which may be excluded from the forensic scrutiny. This extends from that excluded in the interest of the forensic process itself as an instrument of justice (e.g. evidence of propensity to commit crime) through that excluded for such and also for cognate interests (e.g. legal professional privilege), through again that excluded in order to facilitate the avoidance of forensic contestation (e.g. 'without prejudice' communications), to evidence excluded because its adduction might imperil the security of that civil society which the administration of justice itself also subserves (e.g. sources of police information or state secrets)'. I would add the present case to this number. The interests of the proper administration of justice require that there should be no disincentive to full and frank discovery.

Warner J continued ([1982] Ch at 441):

[Counsel for the plaintiffs] submits that I should in my turn add the present case to the list. I think that the interests of the proper administration of justice require that I should do so. I do not overlook that for a party to litigation to take possession by stealth or by a trick of documents belonging to the other side within the precincts of the court is probably contempt of court, so that there may be another sanction. But it seems to me that, if it is contempt of court, then the court should not countenance it by admitting such documents in evidence.

Despite the emphasis placed by Warner J on the policy aspects of his decision, it may be doubted whether any real distinction may be made, in the context of methods employed to obtain evidence, between unlawful or unfair acts which amount to a contempt of court, and those which do not. Nor is it clear whether the learned judge perceived himself to be holding the evidence concerned to be inadmissible (which it almost certainly was not) or whether he was excluding the evidence in the exercise of an assumed discretion, since the judgment does not explore these issues. Although there is a passing reference to *Helliwell* v *Piggott-Sims*, there is no discussion of authorities dealing with improperly obtained evidence, except for an inapposite criminal decision in which the evidence was arguably not obtained improperly. As a decision dealing with the admissibility or discretionary exclusion of illegally or unfairly obtained evidence, the case is probably best regarded as being confined to its own unusual facts, and as no more than an extension of the court's powers to prevent parties from profiting from contempts committed within the precincts of the court. Certainly, it cannot be taken as laying down any more general principle affecting the admissibility or discretionary exclusion of illegally or unfairly obtained evidence in civil cases.

However, Warner J's decision is more easily reconciled with earlier authority as an illustration of the court's undoubted power to restore to an entitled party and prevent improper use of illegally or unfairly obtained evidence. The question of the admissibility of illegally and unfairly obtained evidence should not be confused with the principle that if documentary or other tangible evidence is obtained by illegal or unfair means, the court may order such evidence to be restored to the party entitled to it, and may restrain its use by the obtaining party, provided that proceedings are commenced claiming that relief. In *Calcraft* v *Guest* [1898] 1 QB 759, it was held that a party was entitled to make use as evidence of an improperly obtained copy of a privileged document. However, in *Lord Ashburton* v *Pape* [1913] 2 Ch 469, the Court of Appeal pointed out that that undoubtedly valid rule of evidence did not preclude the court from granting a remedy against illegal methods of obtaining evidence. Cozens Hardy MR said, at 473:

> The rule of evidence as explained in *Calcraft* v *Guest* . . . merely amounts to this, that if a litigant wants to prove a particular document which by reason of privilege or some circumstance he cannot furnish by the production of the original, he may produce a copy as secondary evidence although that copy had been obtained by improper means, and even, it may be, by criminal means. The court in such an action is not really trying the circumstances under which the document was produced. That is not an issue in the case and the court simply says 'Here is a copy of a document which cannot be produced: it may have been stolen, it may have been picked up in the street, it may have improperly got into the possession of the person who proposes to produce it, but that is not a matter which the court in the trial of the action can go into.' But that does not seem to me to have any bearing upon a case where the whole subject-matter of the action is the right to retain the originals or copies of certain documents which are privileged.

The mere fact that a party has obtained evidence improperly does not mean that he is entitled to retain that evidence; however, if he does in fact retain the evidence without protest, then there is no objection to the use of the evidence at trial. The decision in *ITC* v *Video Exchange* is perfectly consistent with this principle, since Warner J excluded the improperly obtained evidence on the plaintiff's motion with the exception of some documents which he had already seen, as to which the plaintiffs' motion was too late.

### 1.7 The best-evidence rule

The 'best-evidence' rule is one of the ghosts of the law of evidence. It has never enjoyed any really certain existence, having originated at some time during the eighteenth century and having since made ephemeral appearances, usually when least expected. The rule itself is a relatively straightforward one, which was stated by Lord Hardwicke LC in *Omychund* v *Barker* (1745) 1 Atk 21 at 49, to be that: 'The judges and sages of the law have laid it down that there is but one general rule of evidence, the best that the nature of the case will admit.'

The rule is in any case a sound one in terms of weight, but the main problem presented is its effect on admissibility. Lord Hardwicke's dictum was given in the context of allowing to be admitted the evidence of a witness who, under then existing rules of common law, was incompetent to take the oath and so to give evidence. But apart from cases of necessity, such as those where a material witness was dead, or the original of a document lost, the rule was never employed to justify the admission of evidence on the ground that a party need do no more than produce the best evidence available in the circumstances of the case. And even the cases of necessity were developed by the courts simply as exceptions to the rule against hearsay, or the rule requiring strict proof of the contents of documents, without reference to a general best-evidence rule. What is more significant is that, had the rule been one of general application, it might have justified the admission of a good deal of hearsay evidence which could be fairly described as the best evidence available, but which was in fact never allowed to be admitted at common law, even in the absence of other evidence.

The history of the rule therefore suggests that evidence has always been held admissible or inadmissible by reference to specific rules of law, and not in accordance with any general theory that the best available evidence must be accepted, whatever form it may take. But the rule was used during the eighteenth and nineteenth centuries to justify the exclusion of evidence tendered of a fact, when 'better' evidence might have been called. Thus, oral evidence of the condition of material objects was rejected on the ground that such objects might have been produced,[58] and circumstantial evidence of an event on the ground that direct evidence might have been called.[59] But the exclusion was never absolute, and was gradually repudiated. Today it can be said with some certainty that the best-evidence rule is extinct, save in one respect, and that any relevant evidence which otherwise satisfies the individual rules of admissibility will be admitted. In *Garton* v *Hunter* [1969] 2 QB 37, Lord Denning MR, referring to an earlier decision excluding indirect evidence that a hereditament was let at a rack rent, on the ground that it was not the best evidence of that fact (*Robinson Brothers (Brewers) Ltd* v *Houghton and Chester-Le-Street Assessment Committee* [1937] 2 KB 445, 468–9 per Scott LJ), said (at 44):

> It is plain that Scott LJ had in mind the old rule that a party must produce the best evidence that the nature of the case will allow, and that any less good evidence is to be excluded. That old rule has gone by the board long ago. The only remaining instance of it that I know is that if an original document is available in one's hands, one must produce it. One cannot give secondary evidence by producing a copy. Nowadays we do not confine ourselves to the best evidence. We admit all relevant evidence. The goodness or badness of it goes only to weight, and not to admissibility. So I fear that Scott LJ was in error.

The rule requiring production of an original (primary evidence) when it is sought to prove as evidence the contents of a document, and that a copy or oral evidence of the contents (secondary evidence) is not admissible save in exceptional cases, remains an important principle of documentary evidence, and is considered in 15.2 post. This rule is also the only remaining refuge of the best-evidence rule.

Cases subsequent to *Garton* v *Hunter* have confirmed that the rule will be confined to the requirement for primary evidence of the contents of documents, and will be construed narrowly, so as to favour the admission of relevant evidence. In *Kajala* v *Noble* (1982) 75 Cr App R 149, the defendant was charged with using threatening behaviour whereby a breach of the peace was likely to be occasioned. This offence was alleged to have been committed during a public disturbance at which a large crowd hurled missiles at the police. A BBC newsteam had filmed the incident, and a prosecution witness identified the defendant by viewing the film. The BBC had a policy of not allowing their films to leave their premises, and in these circumstances, the justices admitted in evidence a video cassette recording, which the court was satisfied was an authentic copy of the film. The defendant appealed against his conviction on the ground that the cassette was not the best evidence and should have been excluded, since the film was, for this purpose, a document. Dismissing the appeal, the Divisional Court held, following *Garton* v *Hunter*, that since the original film was not in the hands of the prosecution, the copy had been rightly

---

[58]   *Chenie* v *Watson* (NP) (1797) Peake Add Cas 123.
[59]   *Williams* v *East India Co*. (1802) 3 East 192.

admitted.[60] The court added:

> In our judgment, the old rule is limited to written documents in the strict sense of the term, and has no relevance to tapes or films.

The best-evidence rule has made ghostly efforts to resuscitate itself from time to time. It arose intriguingly in *R* v *Quinn*; *R* v *Bloom*,[61] in which the defendants were charged with keeping a disorderly house. The Court of Criminal Appeal rejected an argument that the trial judge ought to have permitted the showing to the jury of a film depicting strip-tease acts, which had been prepared by the defence as a deliberate reconstruction of the acts which the defence contended had taken place in the premises concerned, and which was supported by some evidence indicating its accuracy as such. The easiest way to dispose of the appeal might have been to treat the question as one of relevance, since the film was a deliberate reconstruction, but the court chose to decide the issue using the best-evidence rule. Ashworth J said:

> Indeed, in this case, it was admitted that some of the movements in the film (for instance, that of a snake used in one scene) could not be said with any certainty to be the same movements as were made at the material time. In our judgment, this objection goes not only to weight, as was argued, but to admissibility; it is not the best evidence.

Of course, *R* v *Quinn*; *R* v *Bloom* was decided prior to *Garton* v *Hunter*, and if these or similar facts were to recur today, a court might well hold, without reaching the best-evidence rule, that the evidence in question was irrelevant for much the same reasons as those relied upon by Ashworth J in his judgment. It is unlikely that there will be any significant resurgence of the best-evidence rule.

Before parting with the best-evidence rule, it is also worth noting that, quite apart from any question of admissibility, it is clearly desirable that the best evidence be produced which is available, from the point of view of weight, and that the absence of more satisfactory evidence be accounted for, if possible. It is a legitimate matter for comment that more persuasive evidence, or more reliable evidence of a fact, has been ignored in favour of evidence which is demonstrably less so.

---

[60] Apparently, it was not argued that the copy might not be admissible if production of the original by the BBC could be compelled, although it is undoubtedly true that possession of an original by a third party allows proof by secondary evidence only where the third party cannot be compelled to produce the original. Whether this rule might have applied does not appear from the report. See generally 16.3.2, post. See on a similar point *R* v *Wayte* (1982) 76 Cr App R 110.

[61] [1962] 2 QB 245. It is interesting to speculate what the best evidence would have been.

# 2 The Queen v Coke; The Queen v Littleton; Blackstone v Coke

## A: THE QUEEN V COKE; THE QUEEN V LITTLETON

### 2.1 BRIEF FOR THE PROSECUTION

**Instructions to Counsel**

Counsel is instructed in the prosecution of these two defendants, who are due to stand trial at the Oxbridge Crown Court upon the indictment sent with these papers. Counsel also has the statements of witnesses tendered in the committal proceedings on behalf of the prosecution, and a letter from solicitors representing the defendant Littleton, giving notice of alibi as required by s. 11 of the Criminal Justice Act 1967.

There are a number of matters of evidence which Counsel will no doubt wish to consider. Both complainants are under the age of eighteen. The elder sister, Margaret, has been in trouble for shoplifting. On the other hand, the defendant Coke has a previous conviction for rape, said to have been committed under very similar circumstances. In the case of Littleton, the evidence of identification will be of crucial importance, especially in view of his defence of alibi.

The fact of sexual intercourse between Coke and Margaret Blackstone seems to be undisputed, but is in any event supported by the forensic evidence suggesting that the girl had had recent sexual intercourse. There is also the fact which appears to be strongly disputed, that the same defendant was probably the author of the questioned written exhibit, which may assist in the question of his state of mind at the relevant time. Counsel will no doubt wish to consider the state of the expert evidence.

Certain issues arise from the evidence of the police officers, in respect of the search of Coke's flat, apparently without a search warrant, and from the circumstances in which Coke subsequently made his incriminating statement under caution. Counsel's attention is also drawn to the admission of guilt said to be contained in the tape-recorded conversation at the police station between Littleton and his wife.

Counsel is instructed to consider and advise on these and any other points of evidence which may arise.

**Indictment**

IN THE CROWN COURT AT OXBRIDGE

THE QUEEN v HENRY EDWARD COKE and
          MARTIN STEPHEN LITTLETON

Charged as follows:

### COUNT 1

#### Statement of Offence

Rape contrary to section 1(1) of the Sexual Offences Act 1956.

#### Particulars of Offence

Henry Edward Coke on the 8th day of July 1984 raped Margaret Ann Blackstone.

### COUNT 2

#### Statement of Offence

Indecent Assault contrary to section 14(1) of the Sexual Offences Act 1956.

#### Particulars of Offence

Martin Stephen Littleton on the 8th day of July 1984 indecently assaulted Angela Hazel Blackstone.

W. RUSSELL COX

Officer of the Court

**Depositions**

## STATEMENT OF WITNESS

(Criminal Justice Act 1967, s. 9; Magistrates' Courts Act 1980, s. 102; Magistrates' Courts Rules 1981, r. 70)

<u>Statement of:</u>   Margaret Ann Blackstone

<u>Age of Witness</u>   17 (born 3 May 1967)

<u>Occupation of Witness</u>   Schoolgirl

<u>Address of Witness</u>   4 The Hyde, Oxbridge.

   This statement, consisting of 2 pages, each signed by me, is true to the best of my knowledge and belief, and I make it knowing that if it is tendered in evidence, I shall be liable to prosecution if I have wilfully stated in it anything which I know to be false or do not believe to be true.

   <u>Dated the</u> 12th day of July 1984.

<u>Signed:</u>   M.A. Blackstone

<u>Witnessed:</u>   Dennis Bracton D/S

Helen Blackstone (mother)

I am a schoolgirl aged seventeen and live with my parents and my sister Angela at the above address. I have known Henry Coke for quite a long time, because he goes to a youth club which my friends and I go to at weekends. I think he lives in Plowden Drive in Oxbridge. From time to time he has approached me at the club and asked me to go to bed with him, but I have always refused.

   On Sunday, 8 July, I was walking after lunch in the park with Angela, when I saw Henry Coke coming towards us with another man who looked rather older, whom I did not know. We all started talking, and Henry said he had a new album by a band we liked and invited us to his flat to listen to it. I did not really want to go, but Angela was very excited about the idea and so we did. When we got there, Henry put the record on and made us all some coffee. I was sitting on the divan and Henry came and sat next to me. Angela was sitting on the window-ledge next to a large armchair where the other man was sitting.

   After a while, Henry started making suggestions to me that we should have sexual intercourse. I told him to stop and that I did not want him even saying such things while my sister was around. At first he seemed to accept this, but then he got very persistent and started trying to hold my hand and put his arm round my shoulder. I pushed him away. All of a sudden, he pushed me backwards very hard, so that I fell on my back on the divan. I was so taken by surprise that I did not try to get up straight away, and then Henry put his hand up my skirt and pulled my pants down to my ankles. I was very frightened and just lay there. It was only when I saw that he was unzipping his trousers that I started to scream and fight. I was expecting the other man to stop him, but he did nothing. Henry was far too strong for me and he had sexual intercourse with me. I understand what this means, and that is what happened. I did not consent to it, and did nothing to lead Henry to think that I might consent.

When it was over, I got up quickly. I was terribly distressed. To my horror, I saw that Angela was sitting on the other man's lap and that he had his hand up her skirt. I shouted at her to come with me, and we both ran out of the flat and home. Neither of them made any effort to stop us.

When we got home, I could not bring myself to say anything to my mother, and ran straight upstairs, but Angela said something, and shortly afterwards, my mother came up and asked me what had happened. I didn't want to say anything, but after some time my mother more or less dragged the truth out of me, and then called the police. I then went to bed until a bit later, when a lady doctor came and examined me.

I didn't see what was happening to Angela while Henry was having intercourse with me. It was only afterwards that I noticed that she was sitting with the other man. I think I would recognise the other man if I saw him again.

<u>Signed</u>:    M.A. Blackstone         <u>Witnessed</u>:    Dennis Bracton D/S
                                                         Helen Blackstone (mother)

## STATEMENT OF WITNESS

(Criminal Justice Act 1967, s. 9; Magistrates' Courts Act 1980, s. 102; Magistrates' Courts Rules 1981, r. 70)

Statement of:   Angela Hazel Blackstone

Age of Witness   13 (born 4 June 1971)

Occupation of Witness   Schoolgirl

Address of Witness   4 The Hyde, Oxbridge.

This statement, consisting of 2 pages, each signed by me, is true to the best of my knowledge and belief, and I make it knowing that if it is tendered in evidence, I shall be liable to prosecution if I have wilfully stated in it anything which I know to be false or do not believe to be true.

Dated the 12th day of July 1984.

Signed:   Angela H. Blackstone

Witnessed:   Dennis Bracton D/S

Helen Blackstone (mother)

I am a schoolgirl aged thirteen and live with my parents and my sister Margaret at 4 The Hyde, Oxbridge. On Sunday after lunch, Margaret and I went for a walk in the park. We quite often do that. While we were walking, we met two men who I didn't know. One was a bit older than Margaret, and the other was even older, about the same as my uncle Paul, who is about thirty, I think. The older man didn't say much, but the younger one said he had the Least's new album and said we could listen to it. So we went home with him, and the older man came as well.

When we got there, I sat on the window ledge drinking some coffee and listening to the record, which was great. The younger man was sitting next to Margaret on the sofa. They were talking and messing about. Then they seemed to be having an argument and I saw Margaret fall backwards and the man fall on top of her. Margaret was shouting to the man to stop. I didn't understand what was going on, and I was frightened. The older man who was sitting in an armchair by the window told me not to worry, they were only playing. He lifted me off the window-ledge and sat me on his lap. He didn't want me to watch Margaret, and asked me if I liked boys. I wanted to listen to the music, which was very good. Then he put his hand up my skirt and asked me if I liked it. I said I didn't, but he still kept on, and he was rubbing his leg against me.

After one or two minutes, Margaret got up off the sofa. She was crying a lot and shouted to me to come home with her, which I did. Margaret was crying all the way home but she wouldn't tell me what was the matter, and she went straight to her room when we got home. I thought I had better tell mummy in case anything was the matter with Margaret, so I told her everything that had happened.

Later on Sunday afternoon, a policeman came round with a lady police officer and I told them what had happened. Then we went out in the police car, and drove round the streets near the park. While we were doing this, I saw the older man walking along. I am sure it was the same man. We got out and went up with the police to the man, and I pointed at him and said it was the same man who had been sitting in the armchair. Then mummy took me back home while the police spoke to the man. Later on, a lady doctor came and examined me.

Signed:   Angela H. Blackstone         Witnessed:   Dennis Bracton D/S
                                                             Helen Blackstone (mother)

## STATEMENT OF WITNESS

(Criminal Justice Act 1967, s. 9; Magistrates' Courts Act 1980, s. 102; Magistrates' Courts Rules 1981, r. 70)

Statement of:   Helen Blackstone

Age of Witness   Over 21

Occupation of Witness   Housewife

Address of Witness   4 The Hyde, Oxbridge.

This statement, consisting of 1 page, signed by me, is true to the best of my knowledge and belief, and I make it knowing that if it is tendered in evidence, I shall be liable to prosecution if I have wilfully stated in it anything which I know to be false or do not believe to be true.

Dated the 12th day of July 1984.

Signed:   Helen Blackstone        Witnessed:   Dennis Bracton D/S

I live with my husband and two children, Margaret Ann (aged seventeen, born on 3 May 1967) and Angela Hazel (aged thirteen, born on 4 June 1971) at the above address. I now produce copies of the certificates of birth of both my children, marked 'HB1' and 'HB2' respectively.

On Sunday, 8th July, the children went for a walk together after lunch round the park, as they quite often do. They left the house at about 2 o'clock. They are usually back by 3 o'clock to half past, and on this occasion, I noticed that it was a little after 4 o'clock. I heard Margaret running upstairs, and Angela went into the kitchen very quietly, which is unusual. I went into the kitchen and asked Angela if everything was all right. She told me that she and Margaret had been with two men at a flat, and that one of the men had done something to Margaret which upset her. They seemed to be fighting. Angela also said that the other man had sat her on his lap and put his hand up her skirt and kept rubbing his leg against her. She said she didn't like it.

I was very alarmed by all this, and I went up to Margaret's bedroom, where I found her on the bed sobbing violently. She did not want to talk about it, but being sure by now that something terrible had just happened, I shouted at her and slapped her. She then told me that she had been raped by Henry Coke at his flat. I at once went and called the police, and when they came some time later, they talked to both children. They said that Margaret should go to bed until a doctor came to look at her. Angela and I were asked to go out in the police car with them to have a look around.

As we were driving in Plowden Drive, which is not far from the park, Angela suddenly pointed to a man walking towards the police car, and said that it was the man who had touched her while they were sitting in the chair. The car stopped, and the officers and I and Angela approached the man. Angela pointed to the man and said: 'That's him.' The man said he didn't know what she was talking about, or words to that effect, and the officers told me to take Angela home, which I did.

Shortly after we got back home, a doctor arrived from the police and examined both children in my presence.

Signed:   Helen Blackstone        Witnessed:   Dennis Bracton D/S

## STATEMENT OF WITNESS

(Criminal Justice Act 1967, s. 9; Magistrates' Courts Act 1980, s. 102; Magistrates' Courts Rules 1981, r. 70)

Statement of:   Dr Susan Geraldine Vesey

Age of Witness   Over 21

Occupation of Witness   Medical Practitioner

Address of Witness   27 Random Cuttings, Oxbridge.

This statement, consisting of 1 page, signed by me, is true to the best of my knowledge and belief, and I make it knowing that if it is tendered in evidence, I shall be liable to prosecution if I have wilfully stated in it anything which I know to be false or do not believe to be true.

Dated the 16th day of July 1984.

Signed:   Susan Vesey

Witnessed:   Dennis Bracton D/S

I am a medical practitioner in general practice at the above address. I also act as one of the surgeons to the Oxbridge Constabulary. On Sunday 8 July 1984, I was on call as duty police surgeon when as a result of a call from D/I Glanvil, I went to 4 The Hyde, Oxbridge, where I examined Margaret Ann Blackstone (D.O.B. 3 May 1967) and Angela Hazel Blackstone (D.O.B. 4 June 1971) who were identified to me by their mother, Mrs Helen Blackstone.

## RESULTS OF EXAMINATION

Margaret Ann Blackstone

This girl was evidently distressed and crying at the time of my visit, though not hysterical. She was generally in excellent health. Examination of the genital area showed signs of recent sexual intercourse. There were traces of what appeared to be semen, and some reddening of the vaginal region. There were no bruising of or damage to the genitals. I took a vaginal swab which I placed in a sealed polythene bag and labelled 'SGV1 . I later handed this to D/S Bracton.

Angela Hazel Blackstone

This girl was composed and able to tell me what had happened to her. She was in excellent general health and examination revealed nothing of relevance to the inquiry.

Signed:   Susan Vesey          Witnessed:   Dennis Bracton D/S

## STATEMENT OF WITNESS

(Criminal Justice Act 1967, s. 9; Magistrates' Courts Act 1980, s. 102; Magistrates' Courts Rules 1981, r. 70)

Statement of:   Geoffrey Glanvil

Age of Witness   Over 21

Occupation of Witness   Detective Inspector

Address of Witness   Oxbridge Police Station

This statement, consisting of 2 pages, each signed by me, is true to the best of my knowledge and belief, and I make it knowing that if it is tendered in evidence, I shall be liable to prosecution if I have wilfully stated in it anything which I know to be false or do not believe to be true.

Dated the 16th day of July 1984.

Signed:   Geoffrey Glanvil D/I

Witnessed:   Dennis Bracton D/S

On Sunday 8 July 1984, at about 4.15 p.m., I was on duty in plain clothes when as a result of information received, I went in an unmarked police car with D/S Bracton and WPC Raymond to 4 The Hyde, Oxbridge. I there saw a Mrs Helen Blackstone and her two daughters, Miss Margaret Ann Blackstone aged seventeen and Miss Angela Hazel Blackstone aged thirteen. As a result of what they told me, I advised Margaret Blackstone to go to bed at once and I called for the duty police surgeon to attend. WPC Raymond remained with Margaret at my request.

Together with D/S Bracton, Mrs Blackstone and Angela I then drove the police car slowly through a number of streets around the public park near The Hyde. As we were driving along Plowden Drive, I noticed a man walking towards us, tall, slightly built, about thirty to thirty-five, dark hair, wearing a light shirt and blue jeans. Angela pointed out this man at once as the man who had assaulted her. I stopped the car, and with the other occupants got out and approached the man. Angela looked at him, pointed at him and said: 'That's him.' The man replied: 'What on earth is she talking about?' I then asked Mrs Blackstone to take Angela home.

I said to the man: 'What is your name?' He said: 'Martin Littleton. Why?' I said: 'We are police officers. It is alleged that earlier this afternoon you assaulted that girl indecently.' He said: 'Rubbish. I've never seen her before in my life.' I said: 'Have you been at Henry Coke's flat today?' Littleton said: 'I know Henry Coke, but I haven't been there today. I've been at home on my own. In fact, I've only just got up. This must be some sort of mistake.' I said: 'Where do you live?' Littleton said: 'Eldon Villas, number 17.' I then arrested Littleton for indecent assault and cautioned him, and he replied: 'You've got the wrong man, I tell you.' We then conveyed him to Oxbridge police station where he was detained.

At about 5.30 p.m. the same afternoon with D/S Bracton, I went to a first floor flat at 52 Plowden Drive, where the door was opened by a youth of about eighteen years of age, medium build, fair hair and casually dressed. I said: 'Henry Edward Coke?' He said: 'Yes.' I said: 'We are police officers. You are under arrest for raping Margaret Blackstone earlier this afternoon,' and cautioned Coke, who replied: 'Yes, all right, I was expecting you.' While D/S Bracton sat with Coke, I then searched the flat. In a drawer of the bedside cabinet I found several sheets of notepaper upon which were written in ink references to Margaret Blackstone. I took possession of these sheets, which I now produce marked 'GG1'. We then conveyed Coke to Oxbridge Police Station, where he too was detained.

Later, at 7 p.m. the same day, with D/S Bracton, I interviewed Littleton at the police station in the CID office. I reminded him of the caution, and said: 'Now, what about it, Mr Littleton?' Littleton said: 'I'm not answering any questions. I want to see my solicitor.' I said: 'You can see a solicitor at a time convenient to me. I am investigating a serious offence.' Littleton said: 'Nothing to say.' I said: 'Very well, you will be detained over night and I will see you in the morning.' Littleton said: 'No. Please give me bail. My wife will be so worried.' I said: 'Bail is not on at the moment, but I will make sure your wife knows where you are.'

At 7.20 p.m. the same day, with D/S Bracton, I interviewed Henry Coke in the CID office. I said: 'You are still under caution. Do you want to tell me about it?' Coke said: 'Yes, I may as well. With form for the same thing, I reckon I'm going down for a while. Will you write a statement for me?' I said: 'Certainly.' I then wrote at Coke's dictation a statement under caution, between 7.30 and 8 p.m. without any break. I now produce this statement marked 'GG2'. After completing this statement, I said to Coke: 'You have not mentioned the sheets of paper referring to Margaret which I found in your room.' Coke said: 'No. Actually, those are not mine. Lots of my mates fancy Margaret.' I said: 'How do they come to be in your room on this particular day when you rape her?' Coke said: 'They may have been there for months.' I said: 'Will you supply me with specimens of your handwriting so that I can have a scientific comparison made?' He said: 'Yes, all right.' Coke then wrote at my dictation on a piece of paper which I now produce marked 'GG3'. I then handed exhibits 'GG1' and 'GG3' to D/S Bracton for transmission to the forensic science laboratory.

At about 8.45 p.m. the same day, Mrs Davina Littleton arrived at the police station, and was allowed to see her husband in a cell. I positioned myself nearby, so that I could hear clearly what was said, and recorded the conversation using a pocket cassette recorder. After some general conversation, Mrs Littleton asked: 'Martin, tell me the truth. Is there any truth in what the police say?' Littleton replied: 'Yes, I'm afraid so. I don't know what came over me. I just felt her up. I couldn't help myself. I can't explain it.' I now produce the cassette as exhibit 'GG4'.

The next morning at about 9 a.m. I formally charged Coke with rape and Littleton with indecent assault. They were cautioned and neither made any reply.

**Signed:**   Geoffrey Glanvil D/I    **Witnessed:**   Dennis Bracton D/S

## STATEMENT UNDER CAUTION

GG2

Oxbridge Police Station

Date:   8 July 1984

Time:   7.30 p.m.

**Statement of:**   Henry Edward Coke

**Address:**   52 Plowden Drive, Oxbridge

**Age:**   18

**Occupation:**   Apprentice Tailor.

  I, Henry Edward Coke, wish to make a statement. I want someone to write down what I say. I have been told that I need not say anything unless I wish to do so and that whatever I say may be given in evidence.

**Signed:**   H.E. Coke

**Witnessed:**   Geoffrey Glanvil D/I

It's difficult to know where to start really. I've known Margaret for years from the club and seeing her around. I've always fancied her. She's really lovely. I saw her down the club last night wearing one of those see-through blouses. I went home and thought about it a lot, and decided to do something about it. My mate Martin Littleton came round this morning and he had a couple of drinks with me at lunchtime. I told him that Margaret and her sister always went for a stroll in the park after lunch and I was telling him how much I fancied Margaret. We agreed we would meet them if we could and find some reason to take them back to my place. I was really only going to chat Margaret up a bit. Martin said he would look after the little girl for me. So we went up the park, and it went all right. They said they would come back with us to listen to a new record which is very popular down the club at the moment. I put the record on and started chatting Margaret up, while Martin talked to the little girl. Margaret didn't want to know. She was giving me no joy at all. I suddenly came over all funny. I felt I had to have her at all costs. It wasn't difficult. She was sitting next to me on my divan bed. I pushed her backwards on to the bed. She looked rather surprised more than anything else. She had taken her shoes off and she wasn't wearing tights, so I had her pants off quite easily. It was only then she started struggling. It was no trouble. I had it off with her. Then she started crying, which was a bit silly, because she would have enjoyed it if she'd thought about it. She called over to her sister and dragged her off. She was carrying her shoes. I don't think she remembered her pants. I threw them out afterwards.

    After she went I was worried. Obviously, I knew you would probably come for me, but actually, I was more worried about Martin. It was only when I had finished with Margaret that I saw what he was up to with the little girl. He was touching her up and fondling her. I know I was a bit forceful with Margaret, but at least she is old enough. Doing that to a kiddy is really sick. No way was I involved with that. I want to make that clear. That is down to Martin on his own. Once I discovered what was going on, I gave Martin a mouthful. We had quite an argument and I threw him out. I don't know what happened to him after that.

I would like to say I'm sorry for what happened. I really like Margaret and I didn't want to hurt her. It's all very silly. Why can't girls say yes sometimes and just enjoy it?

Signed:    H.E. Coke

Witnessed:    Geoffrey Glanvil D/I

I have read the above statement and I have been told that I can correct, alter or add anything I wish. This statement is true. I have made it of my own free will.

Signed:    H.E. Coke

Witnessed:    Geoffrey Glanvil D/I

Statement taken by me Geoffrey Glanvil between 7.30 p.m. and 8 p.m. No breaks for refreshments.

Signed:    Geoffrey Glanvil D/I

## STATEMENT OF WITNESS

(Criminal Justice Act 1967, s. 9; Magistrates' Courts Act 1980, s. 102; Magistrates' Courts Rules 1981, r. 70)

Statement of:  Dennis Bracton

Age of Witness  Over 21

Occupation of Witness  Detective Sergeant

Address of Witness  Oxbridge Police Station.

This statement, consisting of 2 pages, each signed by me, is true to the best of my knowledge and belief, and I make it knowing that if it is tendered in evidence, I shall be liable to prosecution if I have wilfully stated in it anything which I know to be false or do not believe to be true.

Dated the 16th day of July 1984.

Signed:  Dennis Bracton D/S

Witnessed:  Geoffrey Glanvil D/I

On Sunday 8 July 1984 at about 4.15 p.m. I was on duty in plain clothes when as a result of information received, I went in an unmarked police car with D/I Glanvil and WPC Raymond to 4 The Hyde, Oxbridge. I there saw a Mrs Helen Blackstone and her two daughters, Miss Margaret Blackstone aged seventeen and Miss Angela Blackstone aged thirteen. As a result of what they said, D/I Glanvil advised Margaret Blackstone to go to bed and await the arrival of a doctor. D/I Glanvil then called for the duty police surgeon, Dr Vesey, to attend. WPC Raymond remained at the house with Margaret.

Together with D/I Glanvil, Mrs Blackstone and Angela, I then drove in the police car slowly around various streets near the park just by The Hyde. As we were driving along Plowden Drive, I saw Angela point to a man walking towards us, tall, slightly built, about thirty to thirty-five, dark hair, wearing a light shirt and blue jeans. D/I Glanvil stopped the car, and we all got out and approached the man. Angela looked at him, pointed to him and said: 'That's him.' The man replied: 'What on earth is she talking about?' D/I Glanvil then asked Mrs Blackstone to take Angela home.

D/I Glanvil said to the man: 'What is your name?' He said: 'Martin Littleton. Why?' D/I Glanvil said: 'We are police officers. It is alleged that earlier this afternoon you assaulted that girl indecently.' He said: 'Rubbish. I've never seen her before in my life.' D/I Glanvil said: 'Have you been at Henry Coke's flat today?' Littleton said: 'I know Henry Coke, but I haven't been there today. I've been at home on my own. In fact, I've only just got up. This must be some sort of mistake.' D/I Glanvil said: 'Where do you live?' Littleton said: 'Eldon Villas. Number 17.' D/I Glanvil then arrested Littleton for indecent assault and cautioned him, and Littleton replied: 'You've got the wrong man, I tell you.' We then conveyed Littleton to Oxbridge police station where he was detained.

At about 5.30 p.m. the same day, with D/I Glanvil, I went to a first-floor flat at 52 Plowden Drive, where the door was opened by a youth of about eighteen years, medium build, fair hair and casually dressed. D/I Glanvil said: 'Henry Edward Coke?' He said: 'Yes'. D/I Glanvil said: 'We are police officers. You are under arrest for raping Margaret Blackstone earlier this afternoon' and cautioned Coke, who said: 'Yes, all right, I was expecting you.' I then sat with Coke while D/I Glanvil searched the flat. In a drawer in a bedside cabinet I saw D/I Glanvil find a number of sheets of notepaper, of which he took possession. Coke was then detained at Oxbridge police station.

Later the same day at 7 p.m. with D/I Glanvil I interviewed Littleton in the CID office at Oxbridge police station. D/I Glanvil reminded Littleton of the caution and said: 'Now, what about it, Mr Littleton?' Littleton said: 'I'm not answering any questions. I want to see my solicitor.' D/I Glanvil said: 'You can see a solicitor at a time convenient to me. I am investigating a serious offence.' Littleton said: 'Nothing to say.' D/I Glanvil said: 'Very well, you will be detained overnight and I will see you in the morning.' Littleton said: 'No. Please give me bail. My wife will be so worried.' D/I Glanvil said: 'Bail is not on at the moment, but I will make sure your wife knows where you are.'

At 7.20 p.m. the same day, with D/I Glanvil I interviewed Henry Coke in the CID office. D/I Glanvil said: 'You are still under caution. Do you want to tell me about it?' Coke said: 'Yes, I may as well. With form for the same thing, I reckon I'm going down for a while. Will you write a statement for me?' D/I Glanvil said: 'Certainly.' D/I Glanvil then took a statement under caution from Coke, and while this was being done, I left the room to attend to other matters.

The next morning at about 9 a.m. I was present when D/I Glanvil formally charged Coke and Littleton with rape and indecent assault respectively. They were cautioned and made no reply.

During the evening of 8 July, I had taken possession from D/I Glanvil of exhibits GG1 and GG3. After the defendants had been charged, I took these exhibits from the police station to the surgery of Dr Susan Vesey at 27 Random Cuttings, Oxbridge. I there collected from the doctor a swab contained in a polythene bag marked 'SGV1'. I then conveyed these exhibits personally to the appropriate departments of the Oxbridge forensic science laboratory.

Signed:  Dennis Bracton D/S     Witnessed:  Geoffrey Glanvil D/I

## STATEMENT OF WITNESS

(Criminal Justice Act 1967, s. 9; Magistrates' Courts Act 1980, s. 102; Magistrates' Courts Rules 1981, r. 70)

<u>Statement of:</u>   Lorraine Raymond

<u>Age of Witness</u>   Over 21

<u>Occupation of Witness</u>   Police Constable 24

<u>Address of Witness</u>   Oxbridge Police Station.

This statement, consisting of 1 page, signed by me, is true to the best of my knowledge and belief, and I make it knowing that if it is tendered in evidence, I shall be liable to prosecution if I have wilfully stated in it anything which I know to be false or do not believe to be true.

<u>Dated the</u> 16th day of July 1984.

<u>Signed:</u>   Lorraine Raymond WPC24

<u>Witnessed:</u>   Dennis Bracton D/S

On Sunday 8 July 1984, at about 4.15 p.m. I was on duty in uniform at Oxbridge Police Station, when as a result of information received, I went with D/I Glanvil and D/S Bracton, to 4 The Hyde, Oxbridge, where I saw a Mrs Helen Blackstone and her two daughters, Miss Margaret Blackstone aged seventeen and Miss Angela Blackstone aged thirteen. As a result of what they said, D/I Glanvil advised Margaret Blackstone to go to bed and await the arrival of the police surgeon. At D/I Glanvil's request, I remained in the bedroom with Margaret while the other officers went out in the police car with Mrs Blackstone and Angela.

While we were together, Margaret was initially upset but recovered her composure rapidly. I asked her various questions, in reply to which she gave me an account of her having been raped by a young man known to her called Henry Coke.

At about 5.40 p.m. just after Mrs Blackstone and Angela had returned to the house, the duty police surgeon, Dr Susan Vesey, arrived and I then left and returned to the police station.

<u>Signed:</u>   Lorraine Raymond WCP24   <u>Witnessed:</u>   Dennis Bracton D/S

## STATEMENT OF WITNESS

(Criminal Justice Act 1967, s. 9; Magistrates' Courts Act 1980, s. 102; Magistrates' Courts Rules 1981, r. 70)

<u>Statement of:</u>   Philip Hale BSc

<u>Age of Witness</u>   Over 21

<u>Occupation of Witness</u>   Higher Scientific Officer

<u>Address of Witness</u>   Forensic Science Laboratory, Portland Road, Oxbridge.

This statement, consisting of 1 page, signed by me, is true to the best of my knowledge and belief, and I make it knowing that if it is tendered in evidence, I shall be liable to prosecution if I have wilfully stated in it anything which I know to be false or do not believe to be true.

<u>Dated the</u> 20th day of July 1984.

<u>Signed:</u>   Philip Hale

<u>Witnessed:</u>   Dennis Bracton D/S

I have specialised for the last seven years in the scientific examination of documents and comparison of handwriting. On Monday, 9 July 1984, I received from D/S Bracton exhibits GG1 and GG3 which were identified by means of labels.

Exhibit GG1

This was a bundle of four sheets of lined white notepaper containing various short passages in cursive handwriting in blue ball-point ink. The passages contained references in a sexual context to someone called Margaret Blackstone. I took this to be questioned writing.

Exhibit GG3

This was a single sheet of plain notepaper containing the following words in cursive handwriting in blue ball-point ink: 'Margaret. Margaret Blackstone. I want you. I need you. I must have you. I think about Margaret all the time.'

I took this to be the known handwriting of Henry Edward Coke.

I examined and compared these exhibits.

RESULTS OF EXAMINATION

I found a high probability that the writer of exhibit GG3 also wrote the text of exhibit GG1. I cannot wholly exclude the possibility that the writer of GG1 was a different person from the writer of GG3 but in my opinion this is unlikely.

After examination, I returned the exhibits to Oxbridge police station where I handed them to D/S Bracton.

I have prepared a chart of comparison of the two exhibits which I can use to illustrate my conclusions if necessary.

<u>Signed:</u>   Philip Hale          <u>Witnessed:</u>   Dennis Bracton D/S

## STATEMENT OF WITNESS

(Criminal Justice Act 1967, s. 9; Magistrates' Courts Act 1980, s. 102; Magistrates' Courts Rules 1981, r. 70)

Statement of:   Ernest Espinasse MSc PhD

Age of Witness   Over 21

Occupation of Witness   Higher Scientific Officer

Address of Witness   Forensic Science Laboratory, Portland Road, Oxbridge

This statement, consisting of 1 page, signed by me, is true to the best of my knowledge and belief, and I make it knowing that if it is tendered in evidence, I shall be liable to prosecution if I have wilfully stated in it anything which I know to be false or do not believe to be true.

Dated the 16th day of July 1984.

Signed:   Ernest Espinasse

Witnessed:   Dennis Bracton D/S

On Monday 9 July 1984, I received from D/S Bracton a polythene bag bearing an identifying label marked 'SGV1' and containing a sterilised cotton swab.

I specialise in the detection and identification of traces of blood, semen and other biological matter and in the scientific examination of specimens and exhibits within these fields. I examined exhibit SGV1.

RESULTS OF EXAMINATION

This exhibit yielded positive and readily detectable evidence of human spermatozoa, seminal acid phosphatase and seminal blood-group antigens. From the presence of these factors and the high level at which they were detected, I am able to say that the subject of the swab had had sexual intercourse within a recent time of the taking of the swab. I can say that such intercourse definitely occurred within forty-eight hours of the taking of the swab, and in all probability, within a very much shorter time. I can illustrate and support my conclusions if necessary.

After examination, I resealed the exhibit in sterile material and placed it in a safe place in the laboratory.

Signed:   Ernest Espinasse        Witnessed:   Dennis Bracton D/S

**Previous convictions of defendants and witness**

CONVICTIONS RECORDED AGAINST:   Henry Edward Coke

CONVICTED IN NAME OF:   (As above)

C.R.O. No:   HEC 3421         D.O.B.: 4/3/66

| DATE | COURT | OFFENCE | SENTENCE |
|------|-------|---------|----------|
| 16/4/81 | Oxbridge Crown | Rape (M/O Induced girl to visit him to listen to records and raped her) | Borstal training (released on 14/10/82) |

CONVICTIONS RECORDED AGAINST:   Martin Stephen Littleton

CONVICTED IN NAME OF:

C.R.O. No:                D.O.B.: 11/2/51

| DATE | COURT | OFFENCE | SENTENCE |
|------|-------|---------|----------|
| | | NONE RECORDED | |

CONVICTIONS RECORDED AGAINST:   Margaret Ann Blackstone

CONVICTED IN NAME OF:   (As above)

C.R.O. No:                D.O.B.: 3/5/67

| DATE | COURT | OFFENCE | SENTENCE |
|------|-------|---------|----------|
| 28/11/83 | Oxbridge Juvenile | Theft (shoplifting) | Conditional discharge 2 years |

**Notice of alibi**

## THOMAS, WATSON & CO

| | | |
|---|---|---|
| Solicitors and | 19 College Row | A. Hughes-Thompson |
| Commissioners for | Oxbridge | R. Simms LLB |
| Oaths | Oxshire XX5 3BR | |
| | Tel: Oxbridge 7541 | |

Our Ref: RS/MSL
Your Ref:

The Prosecuting Solicitor
Oxbridge Constabulary
Police Headquarters
Oxbridge

23 July 1984

Dear Sir,

*The Queen v Coke and Littleton*

We act in the above matter for the defendant Martin Stephen Littleton, who is charged with indecent assault.

We are instructed by our client to supply you now, at the first practicable opportunity, with details of our client's alibi, which will be his defence at trial.

On 8 July 1984, a Sunday, our client was asleep in bed until about 2 o'clock that afternoon, having retired to bed after a heavy day's work on the Saturday, shortly before midnight. He got up between about 2.30 and 3 p.m., had something to eat, and feeling slightly unwell, went out for a walk at about 4.15 p.m. or a little after. This was the first time our client had left his house at 17 Eldon Villas, Oxbridge, on that day. It was in the course of that walk that he was stopped by police and arrested.

There are no witnesses in support of the alibi. Our client was alone at home at all material times.

Yours faithfully

Thomas, Watson & Co

## 2.2   BRIEF FOR THE DEFENCE

### Instructions to Counsel on behalf of the defendant Coke

Counsel is instructed on behalf of the defendant Coke, who is charged with rape, as appears from the indictment and statements of the prosecution witnesses sent herewith. The defendant wishes to plead not guilty to this charge, and Counsel will see from his proof of evidence which follows, that he does not deny having sexual intercourse with Margaret Blackstone on the relevant occasion, but says that such intercourse took place with her consent. Counsel will please consider the implications of this defence, and of the fact that according to Coke, the girl is somewhat promiscuous, in the light of the defendant's previous conviction for rape.

The defendant Littleton is of course separately represented, because of the clear conflict of interest between the two, and it is not known what he may say about Coke. It is believed that he may be putting forward a defence of alibi, which would result in a direct conflict of evidence between the defendants. Littleton is apparently a man of previous good character.

Counsel will see that Coke has some serious challenges to the police evidence, both with regard to the search of his flat and his arrest, and his subsequent treatment at the police station. It may be that these matters will affect the admissibility of Coke's alleged oral and written admissions to the police, which on the face of it are very damaging to his case. There is also concern about the written notes found by the police. Coke is adamant that he did not write these, and Counsel will no doubt wish to consider carefully the evidence of the handwriting expert.

Counsel will please consider these matters and the evidence in general.

### Proof of evidence of Coke

*HENRY EDWARD COKE* of 52 Plowden Drive, Oxbridge, will state as follows:

I have been charged with raping a girl called Margaret Blackstone at my flat on 8 July 1984. To this charge I wish to plead not guilty. I admit that I had sexual intercourse with her, but it was with her consent. What happened was as follows.

I have known Margaret for quite a long time, because we both go to the same youth club at weekends. Margaret is a really good-looking girl, and all my mates fancy her as well. I have never made any secret of that fact that I do. I have tried chatting her up at the club on various occasions, and although she was usually with someone else, she gave me the impression that I would be all right if I played my cards right. I decided to try my luck. By this, I mean that I was going to try to have sexual intercourse with her, but not by force or against her will. I saw Margaret the night before the alleged rape, Saturday the 7th at the club, and I made up my mind to meet her 'accidentally' the next afternoon when she was walking with her sister in the park, as she usually does.

In fact, the next morning, my mate Martin Littleton came round. He is a fair bit older than my crowd, and is married, but he helps out at the pub I use as my local and we get on very well. I told him about what I had in mind while we were having a drink at lunchtime. Martin agreed to talk to the little girl while I made my number with Margaret, if we could persuade them to come back to my place with us. We went round the park, and there they were, so we asked them back to listen to a new album from the Least, which all the kids like at the moment, and they came. Margaret seemed quite happy about it. She came and sat next to me on the divan bed and we drank coffee while we listened to the album. She took her shoes off. We were getting on really well. Martin was laughing and talking to the little girl the other side of the room near the window.

Margaret and I then lay down on the sofa, and she made it clear that she wanted to have sexual intercourse with me. She took off her pants, and we had intercourse. This was entirely with her consent. The story she has told to her mother and the police is quite untrue. I think she has made this up because she is embarrassed about doing it with her sister there, and because obviously she was going to be asked how her younger sister came to be interfered with while Margaret was with her. Also, Margaret was not a virgin at the time. Several of my mates have had it off with her. She will do it with anyone. Apparently she threatened to complain that my mate Kevin had raped her last year, when he hadn't at all. She was convicted of shoplifting last year, and it seems she is rather dishonest.

I want to make it clear that I had nothing to do with Martin interfering with the little girl. All I saw was that he was touching her up, when Margaret and I had finished. Margaret must have seen that as well, because she dragged the little girl off pretty quickly. She didn't even wait to put on her shoes, which she carried, and she left her pants behind. I threw them away later on. I was disgusted with Martin. We had a big row, and I threw him out.

I thought then that the police would be round, but there was nothing I could do. Mr Glanvil and Mr Bracton came round at about 5.30 that afternoon. They did not say anything to me, as they say. They rushed in without a word, and started searching the room. I knew who they were. I did say: 'I was expecting you,' which was true, but this was while they were searching the room. I also asked them if they had a search warrant, and was told to shut up. Glanvil found some pieces of paper with a few bawdy remarks about Margaret on them. I think they had been there for ages. My mates used to come round and we would talk about girls and so on, and I think one of them must have written it for a laugh. I certainly did not. I did give the police specimens of my handwriting later, and I am surprised at the conclusions reached by the expert. I definitely did not write those remarks, and I note that he cannot say for certain that I did.

After they had finished the search, Glanvil just said: 'Right, come on.' They took me to the police station. I was not told I was being arrested, and I was not cautioned. Later that day, the officers came to see me in an office and questioned me. It is true that I signed a statement under caution, but this was only because the officers shouted at me and threatened me that if I did not admit raping Margaret, they would do me for interfering with the little girl as well, and Glanvil said they would 'lock me up and throw away the key' for that. I believed this, because I was really horrified by the idea of touching up children, and I could see that they could make it look bad for me. So I made up the statement and dictated it to them. Some of it was of course true, but not the bit about how the intercourse came about. I did not say before making the statement: 'Yes, I may as well. With form for the same thing, I reckon I'm going down for a while.' I just agreed at the end of a session of threats to make one.

It is true that, unfortunately, I have been convicted of rape before. This was in April 1981. I was sent to Borstal, and was there until October 1982. On this occasion, I was guilty and pleaded guilty. I did intend to persuade the girl to make love but I went too far. However, I learned my lesson from this, and I would not have done this again. I have never been in trouble apart from this, and am now apprentice to a tailor. I started this after a course we had in Borstal, and I want to get on with it and lead a useful life.

### Instructions to Counsel on behalf of the defendant Littleton

Counsel is instructed on behalf of the defendant Littleton, a man of good character who has been charged with indecently assaulting a girl of thirteen, as appears from the indictment and statements of the witnesses for the prosecution. Littleton wishes to plead not guilty to this charge, and sets out his defence in the proof of evidence which follows. A proof of evidence from Mrs Littleton is also available, which supports what the defendant has to say in certain important respects.

Counsel will appreciate that in view of the defence of alibi, the issue of identification is crucial to the case. The admissibility and quality of the evidence for the prosecution must be questionable in this respect. Unfortunately, no witness is available to support the alibi itself. It will be particularly important to ensure that the jury hear the whole of the tape of the conversation between the defendant and his wife if it is used in evidence at all, but Counsel will no doubt be anxious to exclude it if this can be done.

Unfortunately, it is believed that the defendant Coke will say that Littleton was at his flat on the day in question and may say that Littleton did in some way assault the girl. In this connection, it is worth observing that Coke has a previous conviction for rape, and it may be that he is protecting the man who was actually there.

Counsel will please consider the matters of evidence which arise in this case.

### Proof of evidence of Littleton

*MARTIN STEPHEN LITTLETON* of 17 Eldon Villas, Oxbridge, will state as follows:

I have been charged with indecently assaulting a girl of thirteen called Angela Blackstone. I wish to plead not guilty. I am a man of thirty-three years of age, married, and I am of good character.

I have a number of part-time occupations, one of which is helping out at a public house called the Turk's Head in Oxbridge. I have come across a youth called Henry Coke there, and I have been to his place in Plowden Drive once or twice. On Sunday, 8 July 1984, the day of the alleged assault, I got up late, about 2.30 or 3 o'clock, as far as I can remember. My wife had been at her sister's over the previous night. I had a bite to eat. Then, because I felt a bit headachy, I went out for a walk in the direction of the park.

I started walking down Plowden Drive in the course of my walk, as this road is on the way from my house to the park. I noticed that there was a car coming towards me rather slowly, but I thought nothing of it until it stopped, and a small girl whom I have never seen before in my life got out with a woman and two men, and came up to me. The girl said something like: 'That's him' and pointed at me. I had no idea what was going on. The police officers then told me what was alleged, and they have correctly recorded my answers, which were to the effect that there had been a mistake over the identity of the attacker. I am sure the girl is genuinely convinced that I assaulted her, but I was not at Coke's flat that day and have no idea what happened. The police did not believe me, and I was arrested and taken to the police station.

Later on, the officers wanted to ask me some more questions, but I refused to answer until I had seen my solicitor, and I was not allowed to see him. Because of this, I was kept in overnight, which really upset me. My wife was due back that afternoon and would have been worried. In fact, the police contacted her, and she arrived at the station to see me later that evening. It now appears that the police recorded what we said to each other during the

few minutes we were allowed in my cell. It is true that we had the conversation to which
D/I Glanvil refers in his statement, but as should appear from the cassette, my wife's
question was asked under the great stress which she felt at what had happened. I very
foolishly lost my temper and answered in an ironical vein, intended to convey nothing
more than anger that she should even have asked the question. I had in fact told her the
truth already, exactly as it appears in this statement, and I hope this is also recorded on the
cassette. I was not making any sort of admission that I had committed the offence.

I see that Henry Coke has told the police that I was at his flat and somehow helped him
in his plan to rape Margaret Blackstone, and then myself molested her sister. This is quite
untrue. I cannot think why he should have said this, as I have never offended him as far as I
know, except that he is obviously trying to shield whoever was there, to cover up his own
guilt. Coke has been in trouble of this sort before. He has been to Borstal for some offence
involving a different girl, although I do not know the details of this.

### Proof of evidence of Mrs Littleton

*DAVINA MARY LITTLETON* of 17 Eldon Villas, Oxbridge, will state as follows:

I am the wife of Martin Stephen Littleton and live with him at the above address.

On Saturday, 7 July 1984, I went for the day to my sister who lives at Winchelham,
because it was her little boy's birthday. Martin was working all day on that Saturday, so he
remained at home, and I arranged to stay the night and return the next day.

On Sunday, 8 July, I arrived home at about 6 o'clock in the evening to find the house
empty. This was rather unusual, as Martin usually stays in if he is not working. By 8
o'clock, I was getting worried. Just about then, I had a telephone call from the Oxbridge
police saying that Martin had been arrested. They wouldn't tell me why over the phone. I
was frantic. I got to the police station as quickly as I could and I saw Inspector Glanvil,
who told me what they said had happened. I told him it was absurd, and said I wanted to
see my husband. After some discussion, I was granted permission to do this, and after
some delay, I was shown into a cell, where he was.

It appears that our conversation was recorded by the police, and I have done my best to
recall it. Unfortunately, I was in such a state that only two things stand out clearly. Firstly,
Martin told me that there must have been a mistake because he had been at home when the
offence was supposed to have been committed. Then, a bit later, I very foolishly begged
him to tell me whether there was any truth in what was said about him. I only did this
because of the state I was in. It caused Martin to lose his temper, and he did reply in the
words recorded by the police. However, it was quite clear that he was speaking in a bitter,
sarcastic tone, and he did not mean that he was really guilty. If he had meant that, I think I
would have had complete hysteria on the spot, and it would have shown in the recording. I
would have been very angry and distressed.

From my knowledge of Martin, which goes back about nine years, six of them as his
wife, the suggestion that he would interfere with children sexually is ludicrous. I have
often seen him with children of friends and relatives, and his attitude towards them has
always been quite normal. He is very popular with everyone who knows him, and has a
good reputation for honesty and helpfulness.

## B: BLACKSTONE v COKE

### 2.3 BRIEF FOR THE PLAINTIFF

**Instructions to Counsel**

Counsel is instructed on behalf of the plaintiff in this action, which arises from the rape of the plaintiff by the defendant in July 1984. Counsel will observe that the plaintiff is assisted by the defendant's conviction of this offence in the Crown Court on 10 January 1985. The defendant asserts that he was wrongly convicted, and counsel will no doubt consider how the matter should be presented, in the light of s. 11 of the Civil Evidence Act 1968. The defendant has never, so far as is known to your instructing solicitors, attempted to deny his paternity of the child until these proceedings, but it is thought that he may try to impute this to one Henneky, who is in the United States at the present time. No notice has been given on behalf of the defendant of an intention to adduce his hearsay evidence, but counsel will find interesting the letter from Henneky's American lawyer.

The plaintiff has available expert evidence from Dr Gray dealing with the plaintiff's psychological sufferings, and from Dr Vesey, who saw her just after the rape and subsequently, dealing with the reasons why the pregnancy was not terminated. Both will be available as witnesses. On instructing solicitors' advice, the plaintiff has declined to submit herself or the child to blood tests. Frankly, we regard the evidence as very strong, and were not prepared to risk exacerbating her suffering. The other side may seek to make some capital out of this.

The defendant's solicitors have issued a subpoena duces tecum against the Director of the Oxbridge City Children's Department apparently in the belief that Miss Blackstone made some damaging admission to him about paternity when consulting the Department on the subject of long-term fostering. The Director has refused to answer enquiries from either side, claiming that public policy prevents this, and it seems that the issue may have to be determined by the court. Miss Blackstone states that she said nothing inconsistent with her case. For our part, we have issued a subpoena to a Fr. Wigmore, a Roman Catholic priest consulted by Mr Coke. It is thought that the defendant may well have said something incriminating to Fr. Wigmore, who, subject to counsel's advice, seems to us to be compellable to repeat it to the court. This information was gleaned from a letter which the defendant's solicitors inadvertently enclosed with a letter to instructing solicitors, and a copy of which counsel will find herewith. The original was returned to Mansfield & Co. in accordance with counsel's advice, but it is hoped that the copy may be useful in evidence.

Counsel will please consider the evidence and advise generally, and appear for the plaintiff.

**Pleadings**

IN THE HIGH COURT OF JUSTICE                  1985 B No: 123
QUEEN'S BENCH DIVISION
OXBRIDGE DISTRICT REGISTRY
Writ issued the 20th day of May 1985
BETWEEN:

MARGARET ANN BLACKSTONE       PLAINTIFF

and

HENRY EDWARD COKE       DEFENDANT

STATEMENT OF CLAIM

1.   On or about the 8th day of July 1984 the Defendant lured the Plaintiff to his flat at 52 Plowden Drive in the City and County of Oxbridge under pretence of a social occasion for listening to music and drinking coffee and there assaulted and beat the Plaintiff by having sexual intercourse with her by force and without her consent.

2.   Further and alternatively the Defendant falsely and against her will imprisoned the Plaintiff in his said flat by force despite the Plaintiff's repeated requests that she be allowed to leave.

3.   Pursuant to the provisions of section 11 of the Civil Evidence Act 1968 the Plaintiff will rely upon the conviction of the Defendant on indictment on the 10th day of January 1985 at the Oxbridge Crown Court before the Honourable Mr Justice Holt and a jury of having raped the Plaintiff on the 8th day of July 1984. Such conviction is relevant in this suit to the Plaintiff's allegations herein that the Defendant had sexual intercourse with the Plaintiff on the said date, that he did so without the Plaintiff's consent and that the Defendant is the father of the Plaintiff's child referred to in the particulars under paragraph 4 hereof.

4.   By reason of the Defendant's assault and battery and/or false imprisonment of the Plaintiff as aforesaid the Plaintiff has suffered personal injury, loss and damage.

PARTICULARS OF PERSONAL INJURY

(i)   Severe pain and irritation of the genital region;
(ii)   Unwanted pregnancy resulting in the confinement of the Plaintiff and the birth to her on the 22nd day of April 1985 of a male child, Kenneth Arthur Blackstone;
(iii)   Post-natal complications and depression;
(iv)   Continuing depression, emotional distress, fear of social ostracism, anxiety over normal social contact with others and lack of self-confidence, all requiring psychiatric treatment.

PARTICULARS OF LOSS AND DAMAGE

| | |
|---|---|
| Expenses of confinement and birth: | £1,000.00 |
| Psychiatrist's fees: | £2,500.00 |
| (and continuing) | |
| | £3,500.00 |

AND THE PLAINTIFF CLAIMS:        (i)   The said sum of £3,500.00

(ii)   Damages.

ALEXANDER NOY

Served this 19th day of May 1985 by Eldon & Co., 12, The Low, Oxbridge, Solicitors for the Plaintiff.

IN THE HIGH COURT OF JUSTICE                    1985 B No: 123
QUEEN'S BENCH DIVISION
OXBRIDGE DISTRICT REGISTRY
BETWEEN:


### MARGARET ANN BLACKSTONE                    PLAINTIFF

— and —

### HENRY EDWARD COKE                    DEFENDANT

## DEFENCE

1.   With reference to paragraph 1 of the Statement of Claim the Defendant admits only that on the 8th day of July 1984 at his said flat he had sexual intercourse with the Plaintiff. The Plaintiff consented to such intercourse. The Defendant denies that he used any force or assaulted or beat the Plaintiff as alleged or at all. Save as expressly admitted above the Defendant denies each and every allegation contained in the said paragraph 1.

2.   With reference to paragraph 2 of the Statement of Claim the Defendant denies that he falsely imprisoned the Plaintiff as alleged or at all. At all material times the Plaintiff was a willing visitor to the Defendant's flat and was free to leave as she wished.

3.   With reference to paragraph 3 of the Statement of Claim the Defendant admits that he was in fact convicted of rape as alleged but denies that he was guilty of the said or any offence. The Defendant will seek to show that he was wrongly convicted and will invite this Honourable Court so to find.

4.   The Defendant admits that the Plaintiff gave birth to a child on the date alleged but denies that he is the father of the said child.

5.   The Defendant makes no admissions with regard to the alleged or any personal injury, loss or damage. If (which is not admitted) the Plaintiff suffered any personal injury, loss or damage the Defendant denies that such injury, loss or damage was caused or contributed to by his said sexual intercourse with the Plaintiff or that he is in any manner responsible therefor.

6.   Further and alternatively such injury, loss or damage as the Plaintiff may prove flowing from her said pregnancy, confinement or giving birth (which is not admitted) was caused by or contributed to by the Plaintiff's refusal or failure to undergo an abortion at the proper time after conception.

7.   In the premises the Defendant denies that the Plaintiff is entitled to the relief claimed or any relief.


                                        HORACE ATKYN


Served this 13th day of June 1985 by Mansfield & Co, Oldschool Buildings, Oxbridge, Solicitor for the Defendant.

**Correspondence**

| | | |
|---|---|---|
| Solicitors | ELDON & Co | 12, The Low, |
| Commissioners for Oaths | | Oxbridge XX5 2BR |
| | | Tel: Oxbridge 62847 |

Geoffrey J. Eldon LL.B
Paul Birch
Stephen M. Paynter B.A.
Mary L. Driver LL.B
Kenneth Stacey
Geraldine C. Eldon M.A.

Messrs. Mansfield & Co.,
Oldschool Bldgs.,
Oxbridge.

Our ref: GJE/MAB
Your ref: SPM/HEC

5 February 1985

Dear Sirs,

   *Re*:

Miss Margaret Blackstone

We act for Miss Blackstone in matters arising from the rape committed on her by your client Mr Henry Coke on the 8 July, 1984, an offence of which he was convicted by a jury at the Oxbridge Crown Court on the 10 January of this year. As a result of this act, our client is now pregnant with Mr Coke's child, and is expected to give birth in April.

We are advised by Counsel that our client is entitled to substantial damages against Mr Coke in respect of the birth, and her severe psychological injury and distress. Your client may consider himself fortunate that our client wishes no more to do with him and is prepared to maintain the child herself with the help of her family. Unless we hear from you within 14 days of this letter with your proposals for settlement of our client's claim, we shall have no alternative but to instruct Counsel to settle proceedings in the High Court.

Yours Faithfully,

Eldon & Co.

## MANSFIELD & Co.

Stanley P. Mansfield
Philip Garrity LL.B
Solicitors and Commissioners for Oaths        Heather L. Morris
Peter G. Bullimore

Oldschool Buildings,
Oxbridge
Tel: 0411

Messrs. Eldon & Co.
12, The Low,
Oxbridge.

Our ref: SPM/HEC
Your ref: GJE/MAB

8 February 1985

Dear Sirs,

   Re:

### Miss Blackstone and Mr Coke

We are in receipt of your letter of the 5th, inst. and confirm that we act for Mr Coke in this matter. If your client does not require maintenance for the child, we are unable to see what damages your client may be entitled to. Our client instructs us that Miss Blackstone was offered the opportunity of an abortion, but declined it. In those circumstances, her damages are no more than nominal. Mr Coke is prepared to pay her the sum of £500 to avoid this unnecessary litigation, provided that it is understood that this is to end the matter once and for all.

Yours Faithfully,

Mansfield & Co.

ELDON & Co.

Solicitors                                      12, The Low,
Commissioners for Oaths                          Oxbridge XX5 2BR
                                                Tel: Oxbridge 6284

Geoffrey J. Eldon LL.B
Paul Birch
Stephen M. Paynter B.A.
Mary L. Driver LL.B
Kenneth Stacey
Geraldine C. Eldon M.A.


Mansfield & Co.,
Oldschool Bldgs.,
Oxbridge.


Our ref: GJE/MAB
Your ref: SPM/HEC


14 February 1985


Dear Sirs,

   Re:


Miss Margaret Blackstone

   We are in receipt of your letter of the 8 February, which both we and our client
consider to be outrageous. In our view, an unwelcomed pregnancy induced by
forcible sexual intercourse, and the inevitable mental and emotional complications
which this must entail in one so young can hardly be written off as 'nominal'. Your
client's offer is rejected.
   In view of your client's attitude, we see no purpose in discussing this matter with
you any further, and we are sending our papers to Counsel.

                    Yours Faithfully,



                    Eldon & Co.

MANSFIELD & Co.

Stanley P. Mansfield
Philip Garrity LL.B
Solicitors and Commissioners for Oaths          Heather L. Morris
Peter G. Bullimore

Oldschool Buildilngs,
Oxbridge
Tel: 0411

Messrs. Eldon & Co.,
12, The Low,
Oxbridge.

Our ref: SPM/HEC
Your ref: GJE/MAB

20 February 1985

Dear Sirs,

Re:

### Miss Blackstone and Mr Coke

Thank you for your letter of the 14th inst. We regret that this matter cannot be concluded without resort to the courts. We have instructions to accept service. We shall of course have to apply for Legal Aid on our client's behalf, and you may in due course like to let us know what kind of 'substantial damages' you feel our client, who is an apprentice tailor approaching his 19th birthday, should be in a position to pay.

We wish to advise you that our client continues to maintain his innocence, and will if necessary seek to prove that the verdict of the jury was wrong. He instructs us that both Miss Blackstone and himself know who the father of her child is, and we hope to have evidence available to confirm what he tells us. You may take this letter as notice to your client to submit herself and the child, when it is born, to a suitable blood test.

If in these circumstances, you wish to proceed, so be it.

Yours Faithfully,

Mansfield & Co.

## ELDON & Co.

Solicitors
Commissioners for Oaths

12, The Low,
Oxbridge XX5 2BR
Tel: Oxbridge 6284

Geoffrey J. Eldon LL.B
Paul Birch
Stephen M. Paynter B.A.
Mary L. Driver LL.B
Kenneth Stacey
Geraldine C. Eldon M.A.

Messrs. Mansfield & Co.,
Oldschool Bldgs.,
Oxbridge.

Our ref: GJE/MAB
Your ref: SPM/HEC

4 March 1985

Dears Sirs,

    Re:           Miss Blackstone and Mr Coke

Thank you for your letter of the 20 February. We too regret that proceedings should be necessary, but your client's attitude leaves us no alternative. It seems to us extraordinary that a man convicted of the offence of rape after a full trial should respond in this way.

We are instructed to reply particularly to your observations as to the paternity of the child with which Miss Blackstone is pregnant. Firstly, while there may be no reason why Miss Blackstone should not have undergone an abortion, we find it incredible that your client should have the temerity, having impregnated ours by force, to dictate to Miss Blackstone what she should or should not do in this regard. If our client had wished to terminate the pregnancy, she was perfectly free to do so, but it was and is for her to decide on these matters and not for your client. Nor is our client prepared to submit herself or her child to any blood test. Our client has indeed no doubt as to the identity of the father, and we have advised her that in view of the available evidence, no further proof is called for.

We take this opportunity of enclosing a letter which, no doubt by inadvertence, you enclosed with your letter to us of the 20 February. On the advice of Counsel, we apprehend that you are entitled to have the original back, but we wish to make it clear that we have copied it for our own use and will in due course tender it as evidence, unless the original is produced or admitted.

               Yours Faithfully,

               Eldon & Co.

MANSFIELD & Co.

Stanley P. Mansfield
Philip Garrity LL.B
Solicitors and Commissioners for Oaths          Heather L. Morris
Peter G. Bullimore

Oldschool Buildings,
Oxbridge
Tel: 0411

H.E. Coke Esq.,
52, Plowden Drive,
Oxbridge.

STRICTLY PERSONAL AND CONFIDENTIAL

Our ref: SPM/HEC
Your ref: GJE/MAB

20 February, 1985

Dear Henry,

Re:

Yourself and Miss Blackstone

As we discussed yesterday, I have written to the otherside in fairly strong terms. As I explained when you telephoned this morning, the court will look at the matter from a strictly legal point of view, although you may see it in other terms too. Certainly, I would not object to your seeking personal advice from Fr. Wigmore about your moral position, but I shall continue, as your solicitor, to uphold your legal rights, subject of course to your instructions.

I have noted what you said about the possibility that Margaret may have given a quite different account of the paternity to the Local Authority Children's Department, and of course I shall look into it.

With my best wishes,

Yours Sincerely,

Stanley P. Mansfield

WARREN B. WITKIN
Attorney at Law

3251 Wontshire Blvd.,
Suite 3400,
Los Angeles, Ca. 90064
Tel: (213) 500 5000

Ms. Margaret A. Blackstone
4, The Hyde,
Oxbridge, England.

8 November 1984

Re: Mr Anthony F. Henneky

Dear Ms. Blackstone:

Mr Anthony F. Henneky has asked me to reply to your recent letter, which hinted obliquely that he might be the father of a child with which you are pregnant at this point in time.

My client tells me that nothing could be further from the truth, and that you are both aware that the father is a Mr Henry E. Coke. Mr Henneky and I hope that this will be the end of the matter, and that you will not repeat such allegations.

If this was not the intent of your letter, please forgive the presumption of this letter.

Very Truly Yours,

Warren B. Witkin

Attorney for Anthony F. Henneky

## 2.4  BRIEF FOR THE DEFENDANT

**Instructions to Counsel**

Counsel will be familiar with this case, having appeared for Mr Coke at his criminal trial, and having settled the pleadings and advised throughout. There is little to add to what counsel already knows. The plaintiff's solicitors have not disclosed any expert medical evidence apart from Dr Gray, and have never responded to our request for blood tests.

Mr Henneky refuses to return from the United States to give evidence, and it seems that we shall have to rely on his written statement under the Civil Evidence Act 1968. Unfortunately, the plaintiff's solicitors have issued a subpoena against Fr. Wigmore, of whom they learnt when regrettably, your instructing solicitors sent astray a letter to Mr Coke. It is hoped that counsel will be able to rely on some privilege for Mr Coke's confidence in Fr. Wigmore, who is minded to refuse to answer any questions on the subject and will no doubt be held in contempt unless some privilege can be found.

The Director of the Children's Department continues to object to revealing any communications passing between his department and the plaintiff, and counsel is asked to ask the judge to rule on this matter, as it may be of some significance to the defence.

As counsel requested, a transcript of the evidence given at the criminal trial has been agreed with the other side and will be available at court for the judge's use.

Counsel will please advise as may be necessary and appear for Mr Coke.

**Proof of evidence of Anthony Filbert Henneky**

1245, Robert E. Lee Boulevard, Gilroy, California USA
5 June 1985.
I am now 32 years of age and reside at the above address. Between 1981 and 1984 I was a student at Oxbridge College of Technology, studying Botany and the technical and economic aspects of market gardening. I came to college rather later in life compared to most of the students, because I worked in market gardening for some years after leaving school. A paper I wrote on the California garlic industry while at college attracted the attention of Mr Jefferson T. Budweiser III, the President of Budweiser Garlic, of Gilroy, California. Mr Budweiser wrote to me and offered me an executive position with his company in Gilroy, which is the major garlic production center in the world. I accepted, and having obtained permission to reside and work in the United States, I moved here in September 1984.

During my stay in Oxbridge, I met a girl called Margaret Blackstone. I think this would be early in 1982. I can only describe Margaret as somewhat promiscuous. She was attracted to me as a rather older person than her other friends. We started to have sexual intercourse on a regular basis. On legal advice, I am not prepared to state when this intercourse began. We had sexual intercourse during 1984, and quite frequently during May and June 1984, when my course was ending and I was preparing to move to the States. I recall specifically the weekend when Margaret states that she was raped by Henry Coke. To my certain recollection, Margaret and I had sexual intercourse on the Friday and Saturday nights in the back of my car after attending the youth club. We might well have seen each other on the Sunday night as well, had it not been for what happened with Coke. After this, we had sexual intercourse once or twice two or three weeks after the Coke incident, and that was the end of our relationship.

After I arrived in the United States, I received a letter from Margaret, to the effect that she was pregnant. She asked me to destroy the letter after reading it which unfortunately I did. I cannot now remember the date on which I received the letter, but it must have been sometime in October 1984. Although the letter did not say so expressly, I formed the impression that Margaret was hinting that the child was mine. This is possible, as we were rather lax over contraception, and often took risks. I took legal advice, and did not reply. I was told by someone I know in England that Henry Coke had been charged with raping Margaret, and it was suggested to me that I might return to give evidence for him. I know nothing of what happened between Coke and Margaret, except that I had the impression that she wasn't interested in him, but I must say that it would not surprise me to hear that she consented to have sex with him, or anyone, for that matter. In any event, I was not then and am not now prepared to return to England to give evidence, as my attorney has advised me not to do so. If this statement is of any use, I am happy for Coke to make use of it, but I am not prepared to leave the United States or to give evidence.

# 3 The Burden and Standard of Proof; Presumptions

## A: THE BURDEN OF PROOF

### 3.1 Introduction

The term 'burden of proof' refers to the general rule that in any legal proceedings, a party who asserts any fact for the purpose of establishing his claim or defence bears the burden of proving that fact to the required degree of proof. It is incumbent on the party making an assertion against his opponent to justify that which he asserts. The reasons for the existence of such a burden are reasons of practical good sense in regulating the conduct of litigation, and it has been said judicially that the principle is 'an ancient rule founded on considerations of good sense and it should not be departed from without strong reasons'.[1]

Every charge, claim or defence, whether in a criminal or a civil case, has certain essential elements, the proof of which is necessary to the success of the party asserting the charge, claim or defence. These essential elements depend on the applicable substantive law, and are known as 'facts in issue' or sometimes as 'ultimate facts' (see 1.3.1, ante). The proof of facts in issue depends in turn upon the ability of a party to prove certain underlying 'evidential facts'. Evidential facts are the facts of the individual case, and are relevant to and probative of the facts in issue (see 1.3.3, ante). For example, the evidential facts that the defendant was driving too fast and on the wrong side of the road may be sufficient to prove the fact in issue, that the defendant was guilty of negligence.

The term 'burden of proof', standing alone, is therefore somewhat ambiguous. It may refer to the obligation of a party to prove a fact in issue, or to the obligation of a party to adduce enough evidence to prove necessary evidential facts. The two are not always the same. For example, although one party may bear the burden of proving the facts in issue, some of the underlying facts may be presumed in his favour (see 3.3 and 17.4) or may be unnecessary unless and until the opponent adduces some evidence to contradict his case. The law recognises two burdens of proof, which correspond to these two different concepts, and which must be considered separately.[2] They may be named and defined as follows.

---

[1]   *Joseph Constantine Steamship Line* v *Imperial Smelting Corporation Ltd* (HL) [1942] AC 154 per Viscount Maugham at 174.
[2]   Some writers point out that there may be more than two burdens, but this analysis is of little, if any, practical significance.

## 3.2 The two burdens

### 3.2.1 The legal or persuasive burden

This is the burden which lies upon a party to convince the tribunal of fact[3] of the truth or probability of any fact that is in issue in the case and is vital to the success of his case. It follows that failure to discharge this burden to the required standard of proof is fatal to the case. Whether this burden has been discharged is a matter for the tribunal of fact to consider on the whole of the evidence given in the case.

### 3.2.2 The evidential burden

This is the burden of adducing sufficient evidence to justify a favourable finding on a given fact. Obviously, failure to present evidence of any relevant fact involves the risk of an adverse finding. Unlike failure ultimately to prove a fact in issue, an adverse finding as to an evidential fact does not inevitably result in failure of the charge, claim or defence. The evidential fact may not be sufficiently important for this; the opponent may offer no contradictory evidence, or his evidence regarding the fact in issue may not be believed. Successful discharge of the evidential burden, therefore, requires no more than proving evidential facts sufficient to justify the tribunal of fact in making a favourable finding as to the facts in issue, while not requiring it to do so. This involves adducing evidence on the basis of which the tribunal of fact would, as a matter of law, be entitled (but not obliged) to find in favour of the party adducing the evidence as to the facts in issue with which the evidence was concerned. This prevents the possibility of the charge, claim or defence being defeated by a submission of no case to answer, or on the basis that there is no issue to leave to the tribunal of fact. A party who achieves this, with respect to any fact in issue, is said to have established a 'prima facie case' with respect to that fact in issue. Establishing a prima facie case as to any fact in issue creates an evidential burden on the opponent, since the opponent's failure to adduce evidence may now result in an unfavourable finding to him. However, the legal burden remains on the proponent of the charge, claim or defence throughout, and is not affected by the discharge of evidential burdens. This is why a discharge of an evidential burden does not compel, though it justifies, a favourable finding. We shall examine this concept further in our discussion of where the evidential burden lies: see 3.5, post.

### 3.2.3 The burden of proof diagram

The diagram overleaf illustrates the operation of the legal and evidential burdens of proof. The continuous line represents the legal burden of proof, and the broken line the evidential burden.

It can be seen that in order to prove his claim, the plaintiff (P) must discharge the legal burden of proof — the continuous line must be extended right up to the point of judgment for P. However, a prima facie case is established by extending the broken line only as far as the prima facie case for P point. The distance between this latter point and the point of judgment for P may be described as the area of risk for the defendant (D), since he bears an evidential burden of proof, once P establishes a prima facie case. The same principles, of course, apply mutatis mutandis to an issue arising from an affirmative defence, as to which D has the legal burden of proof (see 3.4.1, post).

---

[3] See 1.5.1, ante.

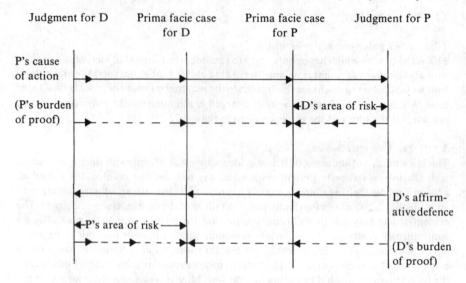

### 3.3  Presumptions and the burden of proof

We shall see in Chapter 17 that in cases where presumptions apply a rule of law provides that on proof of certain facts (the primary facts) certain further facts (the presumed facts) may be taken as proved, even in the absence of further evidence, because of the operation of the presumptions. The detailed working of the more important presumptions will there be considered. A moment's reflection will suffice to perceive that presumptions must inevitably produce some effect on the burden of proof. On this, all writers are agreed. The precise effect produced, however, has been the subject of wide and fundamental disagreements. Two major theories can be identified, and because each probably applies in some cases, depending upon the nature of the presumption, we must look briefly at each. As a preface, it is worth observing an important contrast of approach between English and American writers on the subject of presumptions. English writers have generally assumed that there are different kinds of presumption, which are governed respectively by the two theories about to be discussed.[4] American writers, on the other hand, have sought a theory of universal application to all presumptions, but have found themselves divided on the question of which theory to apply.[5]

According to the first theory, proof of the primary fact creates an evidential burden of proof on the opponent with regard to the presumed fact. Therefore, the presumed fact will be taken as proved unless the opponent adduces evidence sufficient to justify a finding (i.e. establishes a prima facie case) that the presumed fact is disproved. If the opponent succeeds in establishing such a prima facie case, the presumption is rebutted and disappears, with the result that the question of whether the presumed fact has or has not been proved is decided according to the applicable legal burden of proof, without regard

---

[4]  Glanville Williams, *Criminal Law (The General Part)*, 2nd ed., p. 877 et seq, cited and criticised by Professor Cross, *Evidence*, 5th ed., pp. 126–7.

[5]  Thayer, *Preliminary Treatise on Evidence*, 314, 336; 9 Wigmore, Evidence s. 2491(2) (Chadbourn Rev 1981); Morgan and Maguire, 50 *Harv LR* 909 (1937).

to the presumption. This theory is known to American writers as the 'bursting bubble' theory, because of the sudden disappearance of the presumption on the establishment of a prima facie case against the presumed fact. It is also widely known as the Thayer Theory, in honour of Professor Thayer, one of its leading proponents. For English law, Professor Glanville Willliams has described presumptions governed by this theory as 'evidential presumptions'.[6]

According to the second theory, proof of the primary fact operates to shift the legal burden of proof with regard to the presumed fact to the opponent, so that the presumed fact will be taken as proved unless the opponent discharges the legal burden of proof of disproving the presumed fact. Disproof of the presumed fact (as opposed to establishing a prima facie case against it) is therefore required under this theory to rebut the presumption. American writers usually refer to this theory as the Morgan theory, again in honour of a leading proponent. Professor Glanville Williams refers to presumptions governed by this theory as 'persuasive presumptions'.

The distinction is applicable only to civil cases. In a criminal case, the defendant is not called upon to bear the legal burden of proof, save in exceptional cases where such a burden may properly be imposed by law (see 3.4.2, post). No such exceptional case arises merely because of the existence of an applicable presumption. To the extent that a presumption applies against the defendant in a criminal case, it can operate only to create an evidential burden on the defendant, and to the extent that a presumption applies against the prosecution, it probably does not alter the nature of the legal burden of proof which the prosecution bear on the issue of guilt throughout the case.[7]

Which theory applies to any given presumption can be determined only by analysing the wording in which the presumption is couched, or the cases that have interpreted it. There is clear authority that the presumption of the formal validity of a marriage can be rebutted only by evidence sufficient to disprove the presumed fact — the Morgan Theory (*Piers and Another* v *Piers* (1849) 2 HL Cas 331,362) and in the case of the presumption of legitimacy, the same theory is made to apply by statute (s. 26 of the Family Law Reform Act 1969). Conversely, the presumption of regularity and statutory presumptions whereby a primary fact is expressly said to be prima facie evidence of a presumed fact have generally been interpreted as being evidential presumptions, subject to the 'bursting bubble' approach.

### 3.3.1 The presumption diagram
The following diagram illustrates the effect of a presumption on the burden of proof, and

---

[6] Although much criticised as lending too little weight to presumptions, and rendering them 'slight and evanescent' (Morgan and Maguire, op. cit. at 913) the Thayer theory has found wide acceptance as a theory applicable to presumptions generally in the United States. Federal Rule of Evidence 301 provides: 'In all civil actions and proceedings not otherwise provided for by Act of Congress or by these rules, a presumption imposes on the party against whom it is directed the burden of going forward with evidence to rebut or meet the presumption, but does not shift to such party the burden of proof in the sense of the risk of nonpersuasion, which remains throughout the trial upon the party on whom it was originally cast.'

[7] In the United States, there was at one time some doubt whether a presumption could ever apply against the defendant in a criminal case, at least to establish an essential element of the charge, since the burden of proof on the prosecution is entrenched by the Fifth Amendment to the Constitution. It now seems settled that a presumption may operate against the defendant, but that (in contrast to a civil case) the judge may not instruct the jury that they are bound to find the presumed fact proved, even if the defendant offers no evidence.

is similar in form to the burden of proof diagram (3.2.3, ante). As before, the continuous line represents the legal burden of proof, and the broken line the evidential burden. Note the dramatically expanded area of risk to D, compared with that shown on the burden of proof diagram. In fact, on the Morgan theory, D has nothing but an area of risk, since he now bears the legal burden of proof of the presumed fact.

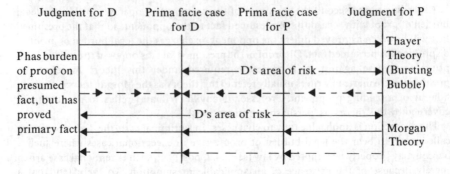

We must now consider in a little more detail where the two burdens of proof lie. The question of where a burden lies may be of importance in any of the following situations:

(a)   Where the right to begin (i.e. to open the case and call evidence first) is disputed or unclear.

(b)   Where a defendant submits, at the close of the case for the prosecution, or the case for the plaintiff, that there is no case to answer.

(c)   Where the tribunal of fact is left in doubt on the whole of the evidence.

(d)   Where an appellate court is called upon to consider the correctness of a summing-up or judgment dealing with the burden of proof.

### 3.4   Where the legal burden lies

#### 3.4.1   Civil cases

The legal burden of proof as to any fact in issue lies upon the party who affirmatively asserts that fact in issue, and to whose claim or defence proof of the fact in issue is essential. The essential elements of a claim or defence are determined by reference to the substantive law. If the plaintiff fails to prove any essential element of his claim, the defendant will be entitled to judgment. The position of the defendant is somewhat different. Since the plaintiff affirmatively asserts his claim, the plaintiff bears the burden of proving the claim, and the defendant assumes no legal burden of proof by merely denying the claim. However, if the defendant asserts a defence which goes beyond a mere denial (sometimes referred to as an 'affirmative defence') the defendant must assume the legal burden of proving such defence. An affirmative defence is most easily recognised by the fact that it raises facts in issue which do not form part of the plaintiff's claim. If, for example the plaintiff claims that the defendant injured him by a negligent act, the defendant may deny negligence without assuming any legal burden of proof. However, if the defendant goes on to assert that the plaintiff was injured through his own negligence, he asserts an affirmative defence not raised as a fact in issue by the plaintiff's claim, and must bear the legal burden of proof of that defence.

It is a sound rule, therefore, that every party must prove each necessary element of his claim or defence. There are cases, however, where it is not easy to determine to whose case a fact in issue is essential, and who should be held to fail if the fact in issue is not proved. In such cases, the courts have inclined to require proof of the party to whom the least difficulty or embarrassment will be caused by the burden, and in deciding this, a sound rule of thumb is to require proof of a positive rather than a negative proposition. In *Joseph Constantine Steamship Line* v *Imperial Smelting Corporation Ltd*[8] charterers claimed damages from the shipowners for breach of charterparty. The defendants claimed that the contract had been frustrated by the destruction of the ship by an explosion, the cause of which was unclear. Such frustration would have concluded the case in favour of the defendants in the absence of any fault on their part. In view of the unsatisfactory state of the evidence, the question of who bore the burden of proving or disproving fault was of crucial importance. The House of Lords held that to require the defendants to prove a negative (the absence of fault) would be unduly onerous. The reality was that the plaintiffs asserted the existence of fault and should be required to prove it. Similarly, in *Levison and Another* v *Patent Steam Carpet Cleaning Ltd* [1978] QB 69, the defendants were guilty of the unexplained loss of the plaintiffs' Chinese carpet, which had been delivered to them for cleaning. A clause in the contract signed by the plaintiffs would have exempted the defendants from liability for negligence, but not for any fundamental breach of contract. It was necessary to determine where the burden of proof on the latter issue lay. The Court of Appeal held that the defendants would find the burden far less onerous, the circumstances of the loss being within their presumed sphere of competence, and accordingly they bore the burden of proof. This is in accord with the rule in cases of bailment that it is for the defendant to show that the loss or damage was not caused by want of reasonable care on his part.

Any question of which party relies on a fact in issue as an essential part of his case, or of who asserts a positive proposition, can in most cases be resolved by reference to the pleadings. The pleadings should make clear in what way the case or defence is put, and fix the legal burden accordingly. The art of pleading enables any assertion to be made in more than one way, and care must be taken to look at the reality and not the language of the pleading. The mere use of negative language should not be allowed to obscure the fact that a positive claim or defence is being asserted, and the substance not the form of the pleading is the true guide. Thus, an assertion that a tenant has failed to repair premises pursuant to his covenant is an affirmative allegation, the proof of which lies on the asserting landlord, even though couched in language in negative form.[9]

The above rules will suffice to pin-point the incidence of the legal burden in civil cases. The specific examples which follow, taken from common kinds of action, follow from the essential elements of the cause of action or defence, would be reflected in the pleadings, and are in no way exceptional.

(a) *Contract.* The plaintiff bears the burden of proving the contract, the due performance of conditions precedent, breach of contract by the defendant and consequent loss to the plaintiff; the defendant of proving any facts going beyond a mere denial of the plaintiff's case, upon which his defence is founded, such as infancy, fraud, or accord and

---

[8] [1942] AC 154. See also *Munro Brice & Co.* v *War Risks Association* [1918] 2 KB 78.
[9] *Soward* v *Leggatt* (1836) 7 C & P 613; see also *Osborn and Another* v *Thompson* (NP) (1839) 9 C & P 337 (assertion that horse unsound, contrary to warranty).

satisfaction. A party relying on an exceptive clause in the contract will usually bear the burden of proving that he falls within its ambit. Thus, where the plaintiff alleged failure to deliver goods, the defendant bore the burden of proving that he fell within an exceptive clause exempting him where the ship and goods were lost by the perils of the sea. The plaintiff would then have to prove any negligence on the part of the defendant disentitling the defendant to the protection of the clause.[10]

(b)  *Negligence.*  The plaintiff bears the burden of proving the duty of care, breach by the defendant of such duty and consequential loss to the plaintiff; the defendant of proving any facts going beyond a mere denial of the plaintiff's case, upon which his defence is founded, such as Act of God, volenti non fit injuria, or contributory negligence.

(c)  *Malicious prosecution.*  The plaintiff bears the burden of proving not only the unsuccessful prosecution of him by the defendant, but also the absence of any reasonable and probable cause for the prosecution, this being an essential element of the plaintiff's case, even though expressed as a negative.[11] By way of contrast, in an action for false imprisonment, where the plaintiff proves the fact of restraint, restraint being prima facie tortious, it is for the defendant to prove lawful justification for his act.[12]

(d)  *Bailment.*  Once the plaintiff proves the fact of the bailment, the burden lies on the defendant to show that the loss of or damage to the goods was not caused by any want of reasonable care on his part.[13]

*3.4.1.1  Blackstone v Coke.*  As a further example, let us consider the facts in issue as stated in the pleadings in *Blackstone v Coke.* Margaret Blackstone's statement of claim states two causes of action, the first for assault and battery, the second for false imprisonment. Clearly, she bears the burden of proving each essential element of each cause of action: on the first cause of action, that Coke's act of sexual intercourse with her was an unlawful application of force to her person; on the second, that Coke deprived her of her liberty for a time without lawful cause. She must also prove any resulting injury, loss or damage for which she claims to be entitled to recover.

In order to ascertain whether Coke as defendant bears any legal burden of proof, we must examine the defence. Although paragraphs 1, 2, 4 and 5 contain some language couched in affirmative terms, that Margaret consented to the sexual intercourse, and that she was free to leave the flat, the essence of these paragraphs is denial. Coke is doing no more than to deny or contradict the plaintiff's claim, and assumes no legal burden of proof. Paragraph 6, however, undoubtedly raises issues of Margaret's own conduct, apparently intended either as a substantive defence to the allegation of loss and damage, or as an allegation of failure to mitigate damage. Neither of these matters was raised by the claim, and each goes beyond a mere denial of the claim. Accordingly, Coke must bear the legal burden of proving these facts in issue, assuming that they would provide him with some partial defence under the substantive law of tort.

The incidence of the legal burden may in civil cases be varied by agreement between the

[10]  *The Glendarroch* (CA) [1894] P 226.
[11]  *Abrath* v *North Eastern Railway Co.* (CA) (1883) 11 QBD 440; affirmed (HL) (1886) 11 App Cas 247.
[12]  *Hicks* v *Faulkner* (DC) (1881) 8 QBD 167.
[13]  *Brook's Wharf & Bull Wharf Ltd* v *Goodman Brothers* (CA) [1937] 1 KB 534: *Port Swettenham Authority* v *T.W. Wu & Co. (M) Sdn Bhd* (PC, Malaysia) [1979] AC 580.

parties.[14] It may also be provided for expressly by some rule of law, for example the provision that in cases of unfair dismissal, the fact of dismissal being proved, the respondent employer bears the burden of showing that the dismissal was fair, notwithstanding that the applicant relies on the contrary assertion for his cause of action.[15]

### 3.4.2 Criminal cases

In criminal cases, the tests appropriate to civil cases based on the allegations set forth in the pleadings and on identifying the party making the affirmative assertion, would offer little assistance. Pleadings in criminal cases are deliberately rudimentary. This is soon apparent on a perusal of the papers in *R* v *Coke*; *R* v *Littleton*. The Indictment Rules require brevity and simplicity in the drafting of indictments, and the indictment reflects this. Apart from Littleton's notice of alibi, the defendants will not plead except for their oral plea of guilty or not guilty at the time of trial. Moreover, although Coke and Littleton will each make assertions of an apparently affirmative nature when giving evidence — Coke that Margaret Blackstone consented to sexual intercourse, Littleton that he was not present at the scene — the prosecution must in fact assert the negative of these propositions. It would be difficult to formulate a general rule for criminal cases by such methods. But in fact, for quite other reasons, reasons of policy connected with fairness to defendants in criminal cases, an entirely distinct rule applies to the legal burden of proof in criminal cases.

In criminal cases the rule is that the legal burden of proving every element of the offence charged, and therefore the guilt of the defendant, lies from first to last on the prosecution. This means that the prosecution must disprove any defence or explanation properly raised by the defendant, even if it appears 'affirmative' in nature. Although now subject to important exceptions, and although the evidential burden does not always coincide with the legal, this principle is undoubtedly of general application. In *Woolmington* v *DPP* [1935] AC 462, the defendant was charged with the murder of his wife. His defence was that the gun had gone off accidentally. The jury were directed that once the prosecution proved that the deceased was killed by the defendant, it was for the defendant to show that the killing was not murder. This was held by the House of Lords to be a misdirection. Viscount Sankey LC expressed the rule in striking words which have become justly celebrated (ibid at 481–2):

> Throughout the web of the English criminal law one golden thread is always to be seen, that it is the duty of the prosecution to prove the prisoner's guilt. . . . If, at the end of and on the whole of the case, there is a reasonable doubt, created by the evidence given by either the prosecution or the prisoner, as to whether the prisoner killed the deceased with a malicious intention, the prosecution has not made out the case and the prisoner is entitled to an acquittal. No matter what the charge or where the trial, the principle that the prosecution must prove the guilt of the prisoner is part of the common law of England and no attempt to whittle it down can be entertained.

The rule applies in general even where part of the case for the prosecution involves a negative, e.g. that Coke had sexual intercourse with Margaret Blackstone without her

---

[14]  See, e.g., *Levy* v *Assicurazioni Generali* (PC, Palestine) [1940] AC 791.
[15]  Employment Protection (Consolidation) Act 1978, s. 57(1).

consent. Lack of consent is an integral part of the prosecution's case on a charge of rape, and the burden of proving that element of the offence lies consequently on the prosecution. The defendant bears no legal burden of proving even affirmative facts in support of his defence. Thus, Littleton need not prove that he was at home when he is alleged to have been indecently assaulting Angela Blackstone, any more than Coke need prove that his sexual intercourse with Margaret Blackstone was consensual. Of course, these statements only concern the incidence of the legal burden; the situation is not necessarily so simple when one considers the evidential burden and tactical matters.

The rule with regard to the legal burden in criminal cases is subject to three important classes of exception:

(a)   Where the burden is put on the defendant by statute.

(b)   Where the defendant has to prove that he is entitled or authorised to do something that is generally proscribed.

(c)   Where the defendant pleads insanity.

*3.4.2.1  Statutory exceptions.*   There are a number of instances where statute expressly puts a legal burden of proving some issue in a criminal case upon the defendant. It should be noted that the burden relates only to the issue dealt with by the statute, and that subject to the issue so dealt with, the prosecution must still prove the guilt of the defendant. Three examples of some importance will suffice:

(a)   *Diminished responsibility.*   'On a charge of murder, it shall be for the defence to prove that the person charged is by virtue of this section not liable to be convicted of murder' (Homicide Act 1957, s. 2(2)). See also *R v Dunbar*.[16]

(b)   *Offensive weapons.*   'Any person who without lawful authority or reasonable excuse, the proof whereof shall lie on him, has with him in any public place any offensive weapon shall be guilty of an offence. . .' (Prevention of Crime Act 1953, s. 1(1)).

(c)   *Corruption.*   'Where in any proceedings against a person for an offence under the Prevention of Corruption Act 1906 or the Public Bodies Corrupt Practices Act 1889 it is proved that any money, gift or other consideration has been paid or given to or received by [certain specified persons] the money, gift, or consideration shall be deemed to have been paid or given and received corruptly as such inducement or reward as is mentioned in such Act unless the contrary is proved.' (Prevention of Corruption Act 1916, s. 2) See also *R v Carr-Briant*.[17]

*3.4.2.2  Statutory offences made subject to exceptions, etc.*   It was said above in relation to civil cases that it is a sound rule that the burden of proof should fall upon the party asserting the affirmative proposition. Although this rule is not of general application in criminal cases, it is now settled that in one type of case, the defendant should bear the burden of proving an affirmative. This is in cases where the offence charged is made by the enactment creating it to be subject to limited exceptions, permitting the behaviour proscribed when committed by persons of a certain class, possessing certain qualifications

---

[16]   (CCA) [1958] 1 QB 1. The law in cases where the prosecution seek to establish diminished responsibility is considered under the heading of insanity (3.4.2.3, post).

[17]   [1943] KB 607. A defendant may be required to prove lack of knowledge. See, e.g., Misuse of Drugs Act 1971, s. 28(2); *R v Champ* [1982] Crim LR 108.

or holding certain licences. Clearly it is a light burden to a defendant to prove that he falls within the excepted class, compared to that which would have to be borne by the prosecution in proving that the defendant is not a member of the class, particularly where the members of the class are numerous or difficult to trace.

Curiously, the position was for a long time clearer in relation to offences tried summarily in the magistrates' courts than in relation to more serious offences tried on indictment. In a summary trial, such cases are governed by s. 101 of the Magistrates' Courts Act 1980 which provides that:

Where the defendant to an information or complaint relies for his defence on any exception, exemption, proviso, excuse or qualification, whether or not it accompanies the description of the offence or matter of complaint in the enactment creating the offence or on which the complaint is founded, the burden of proving the exception, exemption, proviso, excuse or qualification shall be on him; and this notwithstanding that the information or complaint contains an allegation negativing the exception, exemption, proviso, excuse or qualification.

This section applies to a very large number of common summary offences, of which driving a motor vehicle on a road without being the holder of a current driving licence may be cited as an example.[18]

A more general rule was established in *R* v *Edwards* [1975] QB 27. The defendant was charged on indictment with selling liquor without a licence. The sale of liquor was proved, but the prosecution did not call evidence to show that the defendant was not the holder of a licence. It was argued on his behalf that the prosecution had failed to discharge the legal burden of proof on them in this respect. For the prosecution, it was contended that even though in this intance, it was comparatively simple to consult the records of the licensing justices to establish the status of the defendant, the burden of proving that he was the holder of a licence lay on the defendant; that the identically worded predecessor of s. 101 (s. 81 of the Magistrates' Courts Act 1952) was a statutory enactment of a general rule of the common law; and that it was undesirable that the burden of proof on such an issue should be held to vary according to the procedural factor of mode of trial.[19] The Court of Appeal accepted the arguments put forward for the prosecution. The prosecution need not make out a prima facie case that the defendant falls within the exception, whether the exception is expressed as such or as a proviso or in any other language having the same effect, and this applies whether or not the facts in issue are for any reason within the peculiar knowledge of the defendant (hence irrespective of the difficulty or ease with which the prosecution could have proved the negative).[20] The legal burden on the issue lies upon the defendant in such a case.

### 3.4.2.3 *Insanity.*

The defence of insanity has lost much of its former significance since the abolition of the death penalty, and its formulation has been much criticised both on

---

[18]  For examples of the working of the section, see *John* v *Humphreys* (DC) [1955] 1 WLR 325; *R* v *Ewens* (CCA) [1967] 1 QB 322.

[19]  This argument is supported by the fact that in drafting an indictment, the prosecution are not required to negative an exception, proviso, excuse or qualification: Indictment Rules 1971, r. 6(c).

[20]  At common law, a distinction, now obsolete, was to be found between provisos and exceptions, see *R* v *Jarvis* (1756) 1 East 643n. In wider terms, it was thought that a party who asserted the affirmative of a matter peculiarly within his own knowledge bore the burden of proof on the matter; see *R* v *Turner* (1816), 5 M & S 206 at 211 per Bayley J.

legal and medical grounds. Nonetheless, it remains the subject of an exception to the rule on burden of proof. The position is set out clearly in the answers given by the judges to the House of Lords in consequence of *Daniel M'Naghten's Case* (1843) 10 Cl & F 200 at 209–10 as the following extract will show, and the rule has been recognised and followed in subsequent cases.[21]

> Question 2: 'What are the proper questions to be submitted to the jury, where a person alleged to be afflicted with insane delusion respecting one or more particular subjects or persons, is charged with the commission of a crime (murder, for example), and insanity is set up as a defence?'
>
> Question 3: 'In what terms ought the question to be left to the jury as to the prisoner's state of mind at the time when the act was committed?'
>
> Answers (to the second and third questions): 'That the jurors ought to be told in all cases that every man is to be presumed to be sane, and to possess a sufficient degree of reason to be responsible for his crimes, until the contrary be proved to their satisfaction; and that to establish a defence on the ground of insanity, it must be clearly proved that, at the time of the committing of the act, the party accused was labouring under such a defect of reason, from disease of the mind, as not to know the nature and quality of the act he was doing; or, if he did know it, that he did not know he was doing what was wrong.'

It will be observed that question 2 postulates the setting up of insanity as a defence; that is to say, the issue of insanity is raised by the defence for the purpose of obtaining a verdict of not guilty by reason of insanity. It should not be forgotten that, by virtue of s. 6 of the Criminal Procedure (Insanity) Act 1964, where the defendant in a trial for murder contends either that he is insane or that he is suffering from diminished responsibility, the court shall allow the prosecution to adduce or elicit evidence tending to prove the other of those contentions. In this event, the prosecution bear the burden of proving the contention which they make.[22] The burden of proving either defence is therefore borne by the defence in so far as they raise the issue, by way of defence, and the prosecution bear no burden unless and until they go beyond mere denial of the defence and affirmatively assert that the defendant was suffering from the 'other' disability, i.e. that which the defendant himself has not raised by way of defence.

The rule in cases of insanity causes difficulties for juries in cases where the defence is put forward as an alternative to some other defence, for example non-insane automatism, where the prosecution bear the legal burden in all respects and must therefore rebut the defence raised. The jury must then be directed to consider two quite separate burdens of proof in relation to these two defences, even though on the facts the defences may be closely interrelated.[23]

[21]   *R* v *Smith* (CCA) (1910) 6 Cr App R 19 and see *R* v *Carr-Briant* (CCA) [1943] KB 607 for useful general observations on defence burdens.

[22]   And in contrast to the position where the defence bear the burden, it seems that the prosecution must prove the contention beyond reasonable doubt: see *R* v *Grant* [1960] Crim LR 424 and Section B, post. The burden and standard of proof on an issue of fitness to plead depend similarly on the question of who raises it: *R* v *Podola* (CCA) [1960] 1 QB 325; *R* v *Robertson* (CA) [1968] 1 WLR 1767. There is no authority that the prosecution may raise the issue of insanity other than when expressly permitted by statute. Semble, the judge may do so of his own motion: *R* v *Dickie* [1984] 3 All ER 173. The effect of this on the burden of proof is unclear.

[23]   See, e.g., *Bratty* v *Attorney-General for N. Ireland* (HL) [1963] AC 386.

In all the exceptional cases in which the defence bear some legal burden, the burden is confined to that of proving the issue to which it specifically relates. In all other respects, the prosecution bear the overall burden of proving the guilt of the defendant, according to the general rule of *Woolmington's* case. Thus, where insanity or diminished responsibility is raised, the prosecution must first prove that the defendant committed the actus reus of the offence; failing this, the defendant would have no case to answer, and no question of his raising a defence would arise. Equally, in a case of conduct proscribed subject to an exception, the prosecution must first prove that the defendant behaved in the way proscribed, or no question of proof of any exception can arise. In other words, the burden on the defence relates to a specific issue only; in no other respect is the defendant called upon to prove his case.

### 3.5 Where the evidential burden lies

#### 3.5.1 Criminal cases

*3.5.1.1 Generally.* As we saw in 3.3, ante, the evidential burden of proof involves the obligation to adduce evidence legally sufficient to justify, but not compel, a favourable finding as to a given fact in issue. At the outset of a case, it is clear that the evidential burden of proof coincides with the legal burden, since there can be no discharge of the legal burden of proof without discharge of the evidential burden. However, this situation does not necessarily remain unaltered as the trial proceeds. Let us assume that the prosecution succeed in establishing a prima facie case of guilt against the defendant. In a criminal case, the result of this is that the defendant will not succeed on a submission of no case to answer, thereby having the case against him withdrawn from the jury.[24] But neither has the prosecution proved its case. The legal burden can be discharged only on the whole of the evidence, and the defendant's evidence may cast the prosecution's evidence in a different light. What then has the discharge of the evidential burden done? It has created an evidential burden on the defendant, for the defendant now faces the risk that if he fails to offer evidence, there may be an adverse finding as to the facts in issue. Some writers refer to this as a 'shift' in the evidential burden, though in reality, it is more the discharge of one burden and the creation of another in the opponent. What is important to note is that, although the prosecution discharge one evidential burden and the defendant incurs another, the legal burden of proof is not affected in any way. Consistently with the rule in *Woolmington*, the legal burden remains on the prosecution throughout. This is why the defendant faces only a risk, and not the certainty, of conviction if he fails to adduce evidence to contradict the prosecution's case. Thus, although the legal and evidential burdens coincide at the outset of a case, they do not always continue to coincide.

These principles may conveniently be illustrated by the possible course of *R* v *Coke; R* v *Littleton*. The prosecution can only discharge their legal burden of proof by proving to the required standard (beyond reasonable doubt) that Coke had sexual intercourse with Margaret Blackstone without her consent, and that Littleton assaulted Angela Blackstone in an indecent fashion. This is a matter for the jury to consider on the whole of the evidence called for both sides. However, the evidential burden of proving the necessary facts in support of those propositions may be discharged by the prosecution's adducing evidence sufficient to show a prima facie case. This means evidence on which a jury, properly

---

[24] As to the principles applicable to the withdrawal of a criminal case from the jury, see *R* v *Galbraith* [1981] 1 WLR 1039.

directed, could but need not convict. This burden having been discharged, the prosecution have prevented the case from being withdrawn from the jury on a submission of no case to answer; but have done no more.

At this stage, since this is not one of the exceptional cases in which Coke or Littleton bears any legal burden of proof, neither is under any obligation to give or call evidence in his defence. If they take this course, the jury must decide the case on the prosecution's evidence alone and assess whether the prosecution's legal burden has been discharged. In taking this course, however, Coke and Littleton run the clear risk that the evidence for the prosecution will be believed and that the jury will accordingly make adverse findings of facts which may be serious enough to result in conviction. It follows, therefore, that even though the defendants bear no legal burden, the fact that the prosecution successfully establish a prima facie case puts an evidential burden on the defendants.

Precisely the same considerations prevail where the prosecution prove facts which would entitle, but do not oblige, the jury to infer some guilty state of mind which is necessary to proof of the offence charged. Instances are where the prosecution prove recent possession of stolen goods, or lead evidence of a previous conviction for theft or handling stolen goods in the circumtances permitted by s. 27(3) of the Theft Act 1968. The evidence led for the prosecution creates an evidential burden on the defendant, in the sense that in the absence of some explanation consistent with innocence which the jury accept, the jury may infer guilty knowledge. The legal burden of proving guilty knowledge nonetheless remains on the prosecution.

*3.5.1.2  Defences involving new issues.*  In the context of civil cases, we have already noted the distinction between denials and 'affirmative defences' which raise new issues (see 3.4.1, ante). The same distinction is recognised in criminal cases, but because of *Woolmington*, must be treated somewhat differently. Neither the legal nor the evidential burden resting on the prosecution obliges them to anticipate defences which may or may not be raised, or explanations consistent with innocence which may or may not be proffered by the defence. As Hale CJ put it aptly, this would be 'like leaping before one come to the stile'.[25] Thus, while the prosecution must of course offer evidence sufficient to establish a prima facie case as to each element of the offence charged, no burden lies on them to deal with any further issues unless these are expressly raised by the defence. If, therefore, the defendant wishes to rely on some defence or explanation which goes beyond a mere denial of or challenge to the prosecution's evidence and which was not raised by the prosecution, he bears an evidential burden of raising the issue by evidence sufficient to justify a finding in his favour on the issue involved.[26]

The burden on the defendant has been variously described in the cases, and it is frequently said that he must 'lay a proper foundation' for the issue. It is submitted that this must mean only that he bears no more than an evidential burden. Once he discharges this burden by adducing sufficient evidence to make the issue a proper one for the jury to consider, it follows from the incidence of the legal burden that the prosecution must then rebut his case beyond reasonable doubt in order to prove guilt. If, however, the defendant

---

[25]  *Sir Ralph Bovy's Case* (1684) 1 Vent 217.
[26]  The issue must be raised by evidence, not e.g. by a mere assertion by defence counsel: *Parker* v *Smith* (DC) [1974] RTR 500. But whether the evidence is elicited by cross-examination of the prosecution witnesses or is called by the defence is immaterial: *Bullard* v *R* (PC, Trinidad & Tobago) [1957] AC 635.

fails to discharge the evidential burden, the issue will not be left to the jury and the prosecution need not deal with it.

It is of vital importance to distinguish cases where the defence bear this evidential burden of raising the issue from the exceptional cases discussed previously in which the legal burden of proving some issue is cast on the defence. Indeed, in the cases where the evidential burden only is involved, for example provocation or self-defence, the use of the word 'defence' has been rightly criticised as tending to suggest a legal burden of proof which the defence do not bear; it would be preferable to refer to them as 'explanations involving new issues', so as to stress that like any other explanation offered, the prosecution must rebut them in order to prove guilt; nonetheless, they are almost always referred to as defences.

The most common cases in which the defendant raises a new issue which was not a part of the prosecution case, are as follows — the list is not intended to be exhaustive: non-insane automatism[27]; provocation[28]; self-defence or prevention of crime[29]; drunkenness[30]; duress[31]; mechanical defect[32]; reasonable excuse for failing to supply a specimen for a laboratory test in excess-alcohol cases[33]; impossibility of carrying out conspiracy at common law.[34]

*3.5.1.3 Secondary facts.* An evidential burden lies also upon the asserter of a secondary fact, that is to say, a fact which affects the admissibility of evidence or the construction of a document, and consistently with the general rule, the burden so imposed lies on the party who asserts the affirmative proposition.

Thus, a party who asserts that a witness is competent or that secondary evidence is admissible of a lost document, or that the deceased was under a settled, hopeless expectation of death so as to render admissible a statement as a dying declaration, or that the relationship between his opponent and a witness is such as to give rise to bias in the witness's evidence, bears in each case the burden of adducing evidence to support the assertion.[35] The same applies to a party who wishes to adduced parol evidence to complete a written contract, or who asserts a certain interpretation of an ambiguous document.[36]

Evidence bearing on secondary facts is adduced, in a criminal case, in the absence of the jury. Two different kinds of case may require the presentation of secondary evidence, and although both are spoken of loosely as being questions of 'admissibility', they are analytically quite distinct. These may be referred to respectively as questions of admissibility properly so called and questions of authenticity and originality.

---

[27]  *Hill* v *Baxter* (DC) [1958] 1 QB 277; *Bratty* v *Attorney-General for N. Ireland* (HL) [1963] AC 386.

[28]  *Bullard* v *R* (PC, Trinidad & Tobago) [1957] AC 635; *R* v *McPherson* (CCA) (1957) 41 Cr App R 213.

[29]  Criminal Law Act 1967, s. 3, now governs the law. See also on the question of the burden *R* v *Lobell* (CCA) [1957] 1 QB 547; *R* v *Abraham* (CA) [1973] 1 WLR 1270.

[30]  *Kennedy* v *HM Advocate* 1944 JC 171.

[31]  *R* v *Gill* (CCA) [1963] 1 WLR 841.

[32]  *R* v *Spurge* (CCA) [1961] 2 QB 205.

[33]  *R* v *Clarke* (CA) [1969] 1 WLR 1109.

[34]  *R* v *Bennett and Others* (1979) 68 Cr App R 168.

[35]  E.g., *R* v *Thompson* (CCR) [1893] 2 QB 12 (confession); *R* v *Jenkins* (CCR) (1869) LR 1 CCR 187 (dying declaration); *R* v *Yacoob* (1981) 72 Cr App R 313 (competence).

[36]  *Tucker* v *Bennett* (CA) (1887) 38 ChD 1 (parol evidence); *Falck* v *Williams* (PC, New South Wales) [1900] AC 176 (construction).

Questions of admissibility properly so called are those cases in which the judge has to decide whether a proffered piece of evidence is admissible as a matter of law, having regard to the rules of evidence. In order to decide this, the judge may have to receive evidence of secondary facts. For example, in *R* v *Coke; R* v *Littleton* the admissibility of the written statement made by Coke (exhibit GG2) may depend upon the circumstances in which it was made, since the prosecution may have to prove that it was not made under circumstances which were oppressive or which render the confession unreliable. The judge would, therefore, hear evidence about the circumstances in which the confession was made. The admissibility of confessions is dealt with in Chapter 7, post.

Questions of authenticity and originality, on the other hand, are those cases in which there is no question that the evidence tendered is admissible from a legal standpoint, but there is a question whether the piece of evidence tendered is what it purports to be, that it is an original piece of evidence and that it has not been tampered with. These cases concern tangible exhibits, such as photographs and tape-recordings. There is no doubt that such evidence may be admitted, but there must be some foundational showing that the actual exhibit proffered is what it is represented to be. An example from *R* v *Coke; R* v *Littleton* would be the tape-recording of the conversation between Littleton and his wife (exhibit GG4). The judge would therefore receive evidence of the secondary facts necessary to demonstrate that the proffered exhibit is authentic and original, that is to say that it was made in the manner described by D/I Glanvil, that it recorded faithfully the actual conversation between Littleton and his wife, and that it has not since been altered or tampered with.[37]

Although the party proffering the evidence has the burden of proof in either case, the distinction between these two kinds of case has, or should have, important consequences in terms of the applicable standard of proof, and as we shall see in 3.7.3, post, some courts have created problems in this area by ignoring it.

Again, it will be observed that although the form of an assertion may be positive (arguing for admissibility) or negative (arguing for inadmissibility) the burden lies upon the party who in effect asserts the affirmative of the issue. More detailed rules of evidence relating to individual questions of admissibility will be dealt with elsewhere as they occur.

### 3.5.2 Civil cases
Although most of the examples given of the working of the evidential burden have been drawn from criminal cases, the position is the same in civil cases. Thus, if the plaintiff in an action for possession for unauthorised sub-letting makes out a prima facie case by showing that a person other than the lessee is in possession, apparently as a tenant, an evidential burden lies upon the defendant to prove that the occupier is there in some other capacity.[38] Where a landlord shows a prima facie case of title by proving payment of rent by the tenant, the evidential burden lies on the tenant to prove mistake or ignorance of the facts.[39] Where it was proved that statutory precautions had not been observed in relation to a mine, the owner of the mine bore the evidential burden of proving that an explosion, which might have occurred because of the lack of precautions, had not been caused by his lack of care for the safety of those working at the mine.[40] And where it was shown that assurances were given to a residential housekeeper that she would be permitted to reside in

[37]   *R* v *Robson; R* v *Harris* [1972] 1 WLR 651; *R* v *Stevenson and Others* [1971] 1 WLR 1.
[38]   *Doe* d *Hindly* v *Rickarby* (1803) 5 Esp 4.
[39]   *Hindle and Another* v *Hick Brothers Manufacturing Co. Ltd* (CA) [1947] 2 All ER 825.
[40]   *Britannic Merthyr Coal Co. Ltd* v *David* (HL) [1910] AC 74.

a house at her pleasure, and there was accordingly a prima facie case that she had remained in the house in reliance on such assurances, the burden of proof lay on the party giving the assurances to prove that she had not so acted in reliance on them.[41]

The rules as to the burden of proof as to secondary facts apply to civil just as to criminal cases, though the standard of proof varies (see 3.7.3., post).

## B: THE STANDARD OF PROOF

### 3.6 Introduction

The term 'standard of proof' refers to the extent or degree to which the burden of proof must be discharged. It is the measurement of the degree of certainty or probability which the evidence must generate in the mind of the tribunal of fact; the standard to which the tribunal of fact must be convinced by the evidence before the party bearing the burden of proof becomes entitled to succeed in the case, or to have a favourable finding of fact on some issue which he has set out to prove. It is a measurement therefore of the quality and cogency required of evidence tendered with a view to discharging the burden of proof. The standard of proof demanded sometimes varies according to the nature of the issue to be proved, but the fundamental divergence is that between criminal and civil cases.

### 3.6.1 The standard of proof diagram

In a civil case, the standard of proof required is no more than proof on a balance or a preponderance of probabilities, that is to say, sufficient to show that the case of the party having the legal burden of proof is more likely than not to be true. In a criminal case, however, the prosecution must prove the guilt of the defendant to a high standard, usually articulated as proof beyond reasonable doubt.

The diagram overleaf represents the standard of proof in civil and criminal cases, using the analogy of the scales. In a civil case, any tipping of the scales, however slight, in favour of the plaintiff (or party bearing the legal burden of proof) is sufficient to win. If the scales are tipped the other way, then it is clear that D wins. But what is sometimes overlooked is that if the scales remain evenly balanced (i.e. the tribunal of fact is unable to decide) D must also win because the burden of proof has not been discharged on the preponderance of probabilities. In a criminal case, the standard required by the 'beyond reasonable doubt' test on the issue of guilt cannot be precisely measured as a percentage. All that can be said is that the scales must be tipped substantially in favour of the prosecution. If the scales go no further down than the preponderance of probabilities, or remain balanced, D must win.

### 3.7 Criminal cases

### 3.7.1 Prosecution

The standard of proof required of the prosecution in the discharge of the legal burden of proving the guilt of the defendant is a high one. The judge has a duty in all cases to direct the jury in such a way as to impress upon them, by means of an appropriate formulation, how high the standard is.[42] There are two classic formulations of the standard required.

---

[41]   *Greasley* v *Cooke* [1980] 1 WLR 1306.
[42]   Failure to give such a direction is a serious error which should be fatal to a conviction unless the prosecution evidence is overwhelming; cf. *R* v *Edwards* [1983] Crim LR 484.

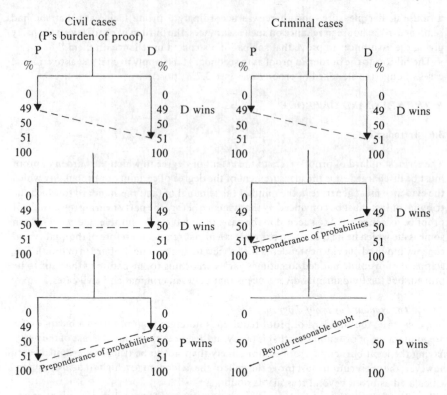

(a)  'Beyond reasonable doubt'. This formulation has been approved on more than one occasion by the House of Lords[43] and has become part of the English language. In *Miller v Minister of Pensions* [1947] 2 All ER 372 at 373, Denning J elaborated on the nature of proof beyond reasonable doubt in these terms:

> It need not reach certainty, but it must carry a high degree of probability. Proof beyond reasonable doubt does not mean proof beyond the shadow of a doubt. The law would fail to protect the community if it admitted fanciful possibilities to deflect the course of justice. If the evidence is so strong against a man as to leave only a remote possibility in his favour which can be dismissed with the sentence 'of course it is possible, but not in the least probable,' the case is proved beyond reasonable doubt, but nothing short of that will suffice.

This formulation fell into some disfavour for a time because of supposed difficulties of explaining to juries the nature of reasonable doubt, if they experienced problems of understanding. Expressions intended to be helpful, but of questionable value, such as, 'a reasonable doubt is one for which you could give reasons if asked' found disfavour in the higher courts and led to some successful appeals against conviction. As a result, a second formulation gained wide favour.

---

[43]  *Woolmington v DPP* (HL) [1935] AC 462 at 481; *Mancini v DPP* (HL) [1942] AC 1 at 11; see also *McGreevy v DPP* [1973] 1 WLR 276.

(b) 'Satisfied so that they feel sure' (or more simply 'sure of guilt'). This formulation was advocated by Lord Goddard CJ in *R* v *Summers*,[44] when he said:

If a jury is told that it is their duty to regard the evidence and see that it satisfies them so that they can feel sure when they return a verdict of guilty, that is much better than using the expression 'reasonable doubt' and I hope in future that that will be done.

In modern practice, much more emphasis is placed on the substance of the direction to the jury as a whole than on the adoption of any particular formula. As long as the judge successfully conveys the high degree of probability required, the direction will be proper. In *R* v *Hepworth and Fearnley* (CCA) [1955] 2 QB 600, Lord Goddard himself observed that a judge would be 'on safe ground' if he directed a jury that 'You must be satisfied beyond reasonable doubt', and added: 'and one could also say: "You must feel sure of the prisoner's guilt."' The matter was cogently expressed by Lord Diplock in *Walters* v *R* (PC Jamaica) [1969] 2 AC 26 at 30, when he pointed out that the judge has the opportunity of assessing the jury during a trial, and can select whatever formula he feels will best assist that jury, avoiding all gloss upon the formula which he uses, as far as possible.

Against this background, the question is simply whether the judge has succeeded overall in stressing the high standard for which the jury should look. In *Ferguson* v *R*[45] the composite formulation 'satisfied beyond reasonable doubt so that you feel sure of the defendant's guilt' was upheld as 'generally safe and sufficient', the Privy Council stressing that there is no set form of words and the test is one of successful communication of the standard in whatever words may be employed. In the ordinary case, of course, use of a time-honoured phrase is wise and above criticism. By way of contrast, the appellate courts have found wanting a number of less emphatic expressions which do not adequately convey the standard, for example: 'satisfied' (standing alone)[46]; 'pretty certain'[47]; 'reasonably sure'.[48]

In cases where the formula 'beyond reasonable doubt' is used, the use of further comment by way of elucidation still causes problems from time to time. It is submitted that the use of such phrases and analogies should be resorted to only when the jury seem in danger of failing to understand what is required of them, and that the judge must ensure that his language, taken as a whole, does not tend to diminish the standard of proof. In *R* v *Ching* (1976) 63 Cr App R 7 at 11, the Court of Appeal said: 'We point out and emphasise that if judges stopped trying to define that which is almost impossible to define there would be fewer appeals.' The court nonetheless recognised that exceptional cases would remain where some further assistance to the jury would be called for. While endorsing earlier criticisms of efforts to define a reasonable doubt as one for which a reason could be given,[49] the court upheld the direction given by the trial judge that a reasonable doubt was: 'something to which you can assign a reason. The sort of matter which might influence you if you were to consider some business matter . . . a matter for example, concerning a

---

[44]  (CCA) [1952] 1 All ER 1059. The passage quoted is taken from the report in 36 Cr App R 14 at 15. The All ER report reads a little differently, albeit to the same effect.
[45]  (PC, Grenada) [1979] 1 WLR 94. See also *R* v *Kritz* (CCA) [1950] 1 KB 82 per Lord Goddard CJ at 89.
[46]  *R* v *Hepworth and Fearnley* (CCA) [1955] 2 QB 600; *R* v *Quinn* [1983] Crim LR 474.
[47]  *R* v *Law* (CA) [1961] Crim LR 52.
[48]  *R* v *Head and Warrener* (CCA) (1961) 45 Cr App R 225.
[49]  See, e.g., *R* v *Stafford; R* v *Luvaglio* [1968] 3 All ER 752n.

mortgage of your house,' The reference to matters related to the personal affairs of the jurors was also approved in *Walters*, but subject to the qualification that the comparison must be with affairs of importance in their lives; and in *R v Gray* (1973) 58 Cr App R 177, it was held by the Court of Appeal to be a misdirection to compare the standard of proof with the degree of care which the jury might exercise in their 'everyday affairs'.

There may, of course, be problems in the use of any formula, and the strongest safeguard still seems to be that of judicial flexibility to meet the needs of individual juries. Nonetheless, it is submitted that the traditional formula 'beyond reasonable doubt' is to be preferred to that of 'feeling sure of guilt'. The latter may in many cases actually suggest too high a standard, and will sometimes tend to confuse legal with scientific certainty.[50] On the other hand, experience has shown that the phrase 'beyond reasonable doubt' has passed into the language by dint of long usage, is understood by juries and can if necessary be elaborated on without confusion.

### 3.7.2 Defence
In the exceptional cases where the defence bear some legal burden of proof on an issue affecting guilt (see 3.4, ante) it is not necessary for the issue to be proved beyond reasonable doubt. The standard of proof required of the defence has been defined as 'not higher than the burden which rests upon a plaintiff or a defendant in civil proceedings'.[51] The standard required in such cases is always the same, regardless of the issue to be proved. The civil standard of proof is that on the balance of probabilities (see post, 3.8).

### 3.7.3 Secondary facts
We have already seen in 3.5.1.3, ante, that there are two distinct kinds of case in which proof of secondary facts may be required, that is to say questions of admissibility properly so called, and questions of authenticity and originality. In relation to questions of admissibility, the standard required for the proof of secondary facts is the same as that required as to the facts in issue. Therefore, in a criminal case, where the prosecution must prove secondary facts in order to demonstrate the admissibility of a piece of evidence, the standard required is that beyond reasonable doubt.[52]

Where the question is one of authenticity or originality, it appeared until recently to have been settled (and, it is submitted, should be the law) that the party proffering the evidence should be required to do no more than establish a prima facie case of authenticity or originality. The reason for this is simply that authenticity and originality are ultimately matters affecting the weight of the evidence, and there is no doubt that the evidence is legally admissible. Questions as to its weight, including any questions of whether the evidence is shown to be authentic or original, are matters for the tribunal of fact. Conversely, where the question is one of whether evidence is legally admissible or not, the tribunal of fact cannot consider the evidence unless it is first ruled to be admissible.

In *R v Robson: R v Harris* [1972] 1 WLR 651,[53] the prosecution sought to introduce into evidence certain tape-recordings. The defence objected to this course, on the grounds that the recordings had not been shown to be the originals, or at least true copies thereof, and

---

[50]   See for example *R v Bracewell* (CA) (1978) 68 Cr App R 44.
[51]   *R v Carr-Briant* (CCA) [1943] KB 607 at 610.
[52]   See e.g., *DPP v Ping Lin* (HL) [1976] AC 574; *R v Yacoob* (1981) 72 Cr App R 313. Presumably, if the defence make the contention, the standard is the balance of probabilities: Cross, *Evidence*, 5th ed., p. 75; Phipson, *Evidence*, 13th ed., para. 4–34.
[53]   See also *R v Stevenson and Others* [1971] 1 WLR 1.

that they were prejudicially unreliable and misleading because of their poor quality. Holding the tape-recordings to be admissible, Shaw J considered the contention that the standard to be applied was that beyond reasonable doubt, and continued:

> This is, of course, right if and when the issue does come before the jury as a matter they have to decide as going to weight and cogency. In the first stage, when the question is solely that of admissibility — i.e. is the evidence competent to be considered by the jury at all? — the judge, it seems to me, would be usurping their function if he purported to deal with not merely the primary issue of admissibility but with what is the ultimate issue of cogency. My own view is that in considering that limited question the judge is required to do no more than to satisfy himself that a prima facie case of originality has been made out by evidence which defines and describes the provenance and history of the recordings up to the moment of production in court. If that evidence appears to remain intact after cross-examination it is not incumbent on him to hear and weigh other evidence which might controvert the prima facie case. To embark on such an enquiry seems to me to trespass on the ultimate function of the jury.

It is noteworthy that Shaw J felt that the judge should not receive evidence from the opponent to controvert the prima facie case of authenticity or originality. This is, of course, in marked contrast to the case where evidence is received on an issue of legal admissibility, where there is no risk of trespassing on the function of the jury and where both sides must be allowed the opportunity to adduce evidence of the relevant secondary facts.

More recently, however, there have been indications that the distinction between admissibility properly so called and authenticity and originality is in danger of being overlooked.[54] In *R v Angeli* [1979] 1 WLR 26, the question was whether disputed writings had rightly been admitted into evidence for the purpose of being compared with samples of the known writings of the appellant. By s. 8 of the Criminal Procedure Act 1865:

> Comparison of the disputed writing with any writing proved to the satisfaction of the judge to be genuine shall be permitted to be made by witnesses, and such writings, and the evidence of witnesses respecting the same, may be submitted to the court and jury as evidence of the genuineness or otherwise of the writing in dispute.

The Court of Appeal held that the words 'proved to the satisfaction of the judge' in the section indicated that Parliament intended the civil standard of proof, on a balance of probabilities, to be applied to proof of the secondary fact of the genuineness of the writing to be used for comparison with the disputed writing. The court professed itself ready to assume that at common law, the standard of proof in a criminal case on questions of admissibility was that beyond reasonable doubt, but found that the matter was governed by an express statutory provision in the instant case.

In *R v Ewing* [1983] QB 1039, however, the decision in *Angeli* was expressly disapproved

---

[54] The distinction is well recognised and preserved in the United States. For example, Federal Rule of Evidence 901, headed 'Requirement of Authentication or Identification' provides in part: '(1) General Provision. The requirement of authentication or identification as a condition precedent to admissibility is satisfied by evidence sufficient to support a finding that the matter in question is what its proponent claims.' In other words, by a prima facie case.

by a differently constituted Court of Appeal, which held that the standard beyond reasonable doubt should have been applied to the same question. In so holding, the Court found that *Angeli* had been decided *per incuriam*, in that the *Angeli* court had not been referred to the decision of the House of Lords in *Blyth* v *Blyth* [1966] AC 643. *Blyth* v *Blyth* was concerned with the very different question of the appropriate standard of proof of a fact in issue, namely whether adultery, relied upon as a ground in a petition for divorce, had been condoned (condonation then being a bar to the grant of a decree of divorce). The relevant statutory provision also contained the word 'satisfied' in the context of condonation, and the issue was what standard this was intended to represent. The House of Lords held that, since divorce was a civil proceeding, the civil standard of proof was appropriate to the issue. This was, however, an application of the general rule of common law that the standard on a secondary issue of admissibility should be the same as that on the facts in issue. The House of Lords held that the word 'satisfied' was not intended to indicate a standard of proof (which was a matter for the common-law rule) but only where the burden of proof on the issue should lie.[55]

The Court of Appeal in *Ewing*, purporting to follow or apply *Blyth* held that the use of the word 'satisfied' in s. 8 of the Criminal Procedure Act 1865, was likewise intended to indicate only the burden of proof, and not the standard. O'Connor LJ said ([1983] 1 QB at 1046–7):

> In our judgment, the words in s. 8 [of the 1865 Act], 'any writing proved to the satisfaction of the judge to be genuine', do not say anything about the standard of proof to be used, but direct that it is the judge, and not the jury, who is to decide, and the standard of proof is governed by common law: see the passage from Lord Pearce's speech in *Blyth* v *Blyth* [1966] AC 643, 672. It follows that when the section is applied in civil cases, the civil standard of proof is used, and when it is applied in criminal cases, the criminal standard should be used. Were it otherwise, the situation created would be unacceptable, where conviction depends on proof that disputed handwriting is that of the accused person and where that proof depends on comparison of the disputed writing with samples alleged to be genuine writings of the accused; we cannot see how this case can be said to be proved beyond reasonable doubt, if the Crown only satisfy the judge, on a balance of probabilities, that the allegedly genuine samples were in fact genuine. The jury may be satisfied beyond a reasonable doubt that the crucial handwriting is by the same hand as the allegedly genuine writings, but if there is a reasonable doubt about the genuineness of such writings, then that must remain a reasonable doubt about the fact that the disputed writing was that of the accused and the case is not proved.

It is submitted that this reasoning is unconvincing. Firstly, *Blyth* v *Blyth* was concerned with a then highly contentious question as to the appropriate standard of proof of facts in issue in divorce cases, at a time when findings of matrimonial offences were thought to carry a stigma of a quasi-criminal nature. It was not concerned (in that part of the decision of the House of Lords) with the admissibility of evidence. To describe *Angeli* as having been decided '*per incuriam*' because the court was not referred to *Blyth* is therefore at least somewhat questionable. Secondly, conceding that the use of the word 'satisfied' in the two very different statutory provisions with which *Blyth* and *Ewing* were concerned was

---

[55]   See the speeches of Lord Pearce, ibid at 672–3 and Lord Denning, ibid at 667.

intended to indicate only the incidence and not the standard of proof, and that the standard applicable depends on common-law principles, it is arguable that both *Ewing* and *Angeli* were wrongly decided. The question of the genuineness of the samples of handwriting used for comparison with the disputed writing is one of fact for the jury, a question of authenticity. Section 8 of the 1865 Act does no more than permit disputed writing to be compared with genuine writing by witnesses, and that evidence submitted to the tribunal of fact. In other words, the section provides for legal admissibility, subject to a foundation of authenticity. The legal admissibility of the writing was not in question. For the reasons set forth by Shaw J in *R v Robson; R v Harris*, the judge risks usurping the function of the jury by investigating the weight of the evidence. His function, arguably, is the same as in relation to the tape-recordings in *Robson*, namely to be satisfied that a prima facie case of authenticity or originality has been established, and then to leave the questions of weight to the jury. It seems that the courts have for the time being rather lost sight of the distinction between admissibility and authenticity.

### 3.8   Civil cases

The standard of proof required of any party to civil proceedings for the discharge of the legal burden of proof is proof on the balance of probabilities. This means no more than that the tribunal of fact must be able to say, on the whole of the evidence, that the case for the asserting party has been shown to be more probable than not. If the probabilities are equal, i.e. the tribunal of fact is wholly undecided, the party bearing the burden of proof will fail.[56]

That this standard is clearly lower than that required of the prosecution in a criminal case has given rise to the difficult problem of defining the proper standard where allegations are made in a civil case which amount to conduct by the opponent of a criminal or quasi-criminal nature. The proof of matrimonial offences, which at one time bore a quasi-criminal stigma, has also caused formidable problems which are considered in 3.9, post.[57]

It now seems clear that the standard of proof where criminal or quasi-criminal conduct is alleged in a civil suit is the normal balance of probabilities. Unfortunately, however, the issue has been clouded more than somewhat by the tendency of judges to stress that the more grave the allegation, the clearer should be the evidence adduced to prove it. There are dicta which suggest (wrongly, it is submitted) that there is some sort of sliding scale of standards of proof between the ordinary balance of probabilities, used in cases where no criminal or quasi-criminal stigma attaches to the allegations made, and some higher degree of proof (though falling short of the criminal standard) used in the cases now being considered.

In *Bater* v *Bater* [1951] P 35 at 37, the issue before the Court of Appeal was the proper standard of proof of a matrimonial cause, but in the course of his judgment, Denning LJ said in more general terms:

As Best CJ and many other great judges have said, 'in proportion as the crime is

---

[56]   *Miller* v *Minister of Pensions* [1947] 2 All ER 372.

[57]   Contempt of court is criminal in nature, and accordingly, the criminal standard of proof applies to contempt proceedings, even if the contempt arises from a civil case, or is contempt of a court having purely civil jurisdiction: *Re Bramblevale Ltd* [1970] Ch 128.

enormous, so ought the proof to be clear'. So also in civil cases, the case may be proved by a preponderance of probability, but there may be degrees of probability within that standard. The degree depends on the subject-matter. A civil court, when considering a charge of fraud, will naturally require for itself a higher degree of probability than that which it would require when asking if negligence is established. It does not adopt so high a degree as a criminal court, even when it is considering a charge of a criminal nature; but still it does require a degree of probability which is commensurate with the occasion.

This passage was considered by the Court of Appeal (of which Denning LJ was a member) in *Hornal* v *Neuberger Products Ltd* [1957] 1 QB 247, an action for damages for breach of warranty and fraudulent misrepresentation. Hodson LJ pointed out that no responsible counsel or judge would make or consider any serious allegation without admitting that cogent evidence was called for to prove it. There is a necessary distinction between the balance of probabilities and the quantity and cogency of the evidence needed to tilt the balance in favour of the allegation; the latter may legitimately be held to vary with the subject-matter, while the former remains constant. In most cases, the result will be the same, whatever the mental processes involved, and as Denning LJ said in *Bater*, the difference of opinion about standard of proof may be no more than a matter of words. Nonetheless, problems can be avoided by precision of words, and it is submitted that the language of Morris LJ in *Hornal* correctly represents the position (ibid at 266):

But in truth no real mischief results from an acceptance of the fact that there is some difference of approach in civil actions. Particularly is this so if the words which are used to define that approach are the servants but not the masters of meaning. Though no court and no jury would give less careful attention to issues lacking gravity than to those marked by it, the very elements of gravity become a part of the whole range of circumstances which have to be weighed in the scale when deciding as to the balance of probabilities.

The law was stated with equal clarity by Ungoed-Thomas J in *Re Dellow's Will Trusts*[58] where a wife was the general legatee under the will of her husband. They had died on the same occasion, the wife being deemed the survivor under s. 184 of the Law of Property Act 1925. The question arose whether the wife had feloniously killed the husband. The learned judge, observing that 'there can hardly be a more grave issue than that' went on to hold that he was satisfied that the allegation was proved. He said, referring to the passage cited above from the judgment of Morris LJ in *Hornal*:

It seems to me that in civil cases it is not so much that a different standard of proof is required in different circumstances varying according to the gravity of the issue, but, as Morris LJ says, the gravity of the issue becomes part of the circumstances which the court has to take into consideration in deciding whether or not the burden of proof has been discharged. The more serious the allegation the more cogent is the evidence required to overcome the unlikelihood of what is alleged and thus to prove it.

---

[58] [1964] 1 WLR 451 at 454–5. And see *Post Office* v *Estuary Radio Ltd* (CA) [1968] 2 QB 740 (offence against Wireless Telegraphy Act 1949); *S & M Carpets (London) Ltd* v *Cornhill Insurance Co. Ltd* [1981] 1 Lloyd's Rep 667 (arson by plaintiff's manager).

## 3.9 Matrimonial causes

In modern practice, there seems to be little reason to differentiate between matrimonial causes and civil cases in general, and for most purposes of evidence, any distinctions are unimportant. However, in relation to the standard of proof, the position is far from clear. Professor Cross once observed that 'it would be rash to essay a general statement with regard to the standard of proof in matrimonial causes'.[59] And in *Bastable* v *Bastable and Sanders* [1968] 1 WLR 1684 at 1685, Willmer LJ was driven to observe: 'If I may say so with all possible respect, sitting in this court I do not find it altogether easy to follow the directions contained in various statements made by members of the House of Lords'.

The source of the trouble is that until the wholesale change in the philosophy of matrimonial law embodied in the stream of reforming legislation beginning with the Divorce Reform Act 1969 (now replaced by the Matrimonial Causes Act 1973) and continuing to the Domestic Proceedings and Magistrates' Courts Act 1978, the law was governed by the concept inherited from the ecclesiastical courts that the 'matrimonial offence' was a grave charge having quasi-criminal character, a concept reinforced by the stigma which proof of such an offence commonly involved. This led naturally to the view that a high standard of proof was required for the proof of such an offence. In *Bater* v *Bater* [1951] P 35, the question arose in relation to a petition on the ground of cruelty whether the trial judge had directed himself correctly that such an offence had to be proved beyond reasonable doubt. The Court of Appeal unanimously held that he had been correct. The decision corresponded to that in *Ginesi* v *Ginesi* (CA) [1948] P 179, in which the same standard was held to be applicable to allegations of adultery, and the proposition was assumed in *Preston-Jones* v *Preston-Jones* (HL) [1951] AC 391, where the issue was whether the standard of proof should be higher rather than lower than beyond reasonable doubt, in a case where the only evidence of adultery was that the husband proved continuous non-access to the wife during the period of 186 to 360 days before the birth of the wife's child.

Some encroachment on the rule was made in *Blyth* v *Blyth* (HL) [1966] AC 643, in which Lord Denning, in a passage with which Lord Pearce concurred, suggested that the grounds for divorce, like any other allegation made in a civil case, might be proved by a preponderance of probability.[60] The issue in *Blyth*, however, was limited to the standard of proof required on the question whether the petitioner had condoned his wife's adultery and, in so far as wider propositions were concerned, any assertions must have been obiter. Nonetheless, they left the way clear for further consideration, and in *Bastable* the Court of Appeal seized the opportunity to apply to an allegation of adultery the standard which Denning LJ had laid down in *Hornal* v *Neuberger Products Ltd* (CA) [1957] 1 QB 247, for civil cases in general, namely proof on the balance of probabilities subject to the requirement of evidence of cogency proportionate to the nature of the charge.

The divergence of authority has never been resolved. It is submitted, however, that the appropriate standard is that applicable to any other civil litigation. The concept of the matrimonial offence has now disappeared[61] and the sole ground for divorce is that the

---

[59]   Cross, *Evidence*, 4th ed., p. 103. In the 5th edition of his work at p. 118 Cross mollified his comment, stating that the law was still unsettled. However, he seems to have adopted the view, shared by the present author, that the normal civil standard now applies to matrimonial causes.

[60]   Subject to the observation made by Lord Denning on other occasions that the degree of proof should be commensurate with the gravity of the charge.

[61]   See, e.g., *Wachtel* v *Wachtel* [1973] Fam 72.

marriage has broken down irretrievably. It cannot now be argued that the consequences of divorce demand any higher standard of proof, as once they did. It is perhaps unfortunate that Parliament did not take the opportunity of making the matter clear once and for all, but some indication of its intention may be gleaned from the provision in s. 26 of the Family Law Reform Act 1969 that: 'Any presumption of law as to the legitimacy or illegitimacy of any person may in any civil proceedings be rebutted by evidence which shows that it is more probable than not that that person is illegitimate or legitimate, as the case may be, and it shall not be necessary to prove that fact beyond reasonable doubt in order to rebut the presumption.' The presumption of legitimacy weighed heavily in many adultery cases in former times, and it is difficult to suppose that a higher standard would now be required to prove adultery as such, or indeed any other fact material to matrimonial causes.[62] Indeed, it may be confidently asserted that the imposition of any higher standard of proof would be contrary to the spirit of the new matrimonial law, and to the policy of the courts, expressed by procedural and substantive emphasis, of diverting the mainstream of litigation away from detailed investigations of the causes of the breakdown and into the fields of proper provision for the affected members of the family.

### 3.10   Questions for discussion

#### 3.10.1   *R* v *Coke; R* v *Littleton*

1   Who bears the burden of proof on the issue of guilt or innocence of Coke and Littleton?

2   Compose directions to the jury which adequately explain both the incidence of the legal burden of proof and the standard of proof required on the issue of guilt or innocence.

3   Are there any issues in the case as to which Coke or Littleton bears any legal burden of proof?

4   Are there any issues in the case as to which Coke or Littleton bears any evidential burden or proof?

5   What must the prosecution do in order to establish a prima facie case as to the charges against Coke and Littleton respectively? What effect would this have on the further conduct of the defence by each defendant?

6   Discuss the burden and standard of proof as to any secondary facts bearing upon the admissibility of the following pieces of evidence: (i) exhibits GG1 and GG3 and the related evidence of Mr Hale; (ii) Coke's written statement under caution, exhibit GG2; (iii) the tape-recording of the conversation between Littleton and Mrs Littleton, exhibit GG4.

#### 3.10.2   *Blackstone* v *Coke*

1   Review the pleadings. On what facts in issue do Margaret Blackstone and Coke respectively bear the legal burden of proof?

2   At the outset of the case, who bears the evidential burden of proof as to the underlying evidential facts? How may this change as the case proceeds?

3   Margaret wishes to introduce into evidence the letter written to Coke by his solicitors dated 20 February 1985. Coke wishes to exclude this evidence, on the ground that it is a privileged communication. Who bears the burden of proof?

---

[62]   This suggestion is intended to encompass not only the facts available to prove irretrievable breakdown, but also the wide variety of other issues which may arise, e.g. the presumption of a valid marriage following a ceremony and cohabitation, see *Mahadervan* v *Mahadervan* [1964] P 233.

4   Assume that Coke was never charged with an offence against Margaret Blackstone, but that Margaret has brought the present action in the same form, but omitting paragraph 3 of the statement of claim. What standard of proof would be required of the plaintiff in proving her claim?

# 4  Evidence of Character

## 4.1  Uses of the word 'character'

The word 'character' bears at least three distinct meanings in the context of the law of evidence. Firstly, it may refer to the reputation in which a person is held in his community, among those by whom he is known; secondly, it may refer to the disposition of a person to behave in a certain way; thirdly, it may refer to specific incidents in the personal history of the subject, for example previous convictions for criminal offences.

Each of these meanings of the word 'character' may also be regarded as a possible method of proving the character of a person, and since a person's character may be an amalgam of each of these factors, it would be reasonable to assume that the law of evidence would permit proof of each. At common law, however, the actual position was very different. Only the reputation of a person in his community, good or bad, was regarded as competent evidence of character. Evidence of the opinion of a witness (as opposed to evidence of reputation) was excluded. So also were evidence of disposition to behave in a certain way and evidence of prior acts on the part of the subject. It should be added, however, that the law may not have been truly settled on this point until the landmark case of *R* v *Rowton* (1865) Le & Ca 520, and that even then, the restriction to evidence of general reputation produced powerful dissent. In the light of the statutory developments that occurred shortly after *Rowton*, the chronology is not unimportant. In an age of limited social mobility, evidence of general reputation in a community was probably a good deal more reliable in determining the true character of a person than it would be today, and it had the further advantage of being untainted by the possible bias of an individual opinion and the prejudicial effect of evidence of disposition or prior conduct.

However, many social changes weakened the cogency of evidence of general reputation and increased the cogency of informed individual opinion. Increasingly systematic records enabled previous convictions and other incidents of a person's life to be proved more readily and accurately. The rules laid down by the Criminal Evidence Act 1898, upon which all the most critical aspects of character evidence now depend, seem to demand and have been construed consistently as demanding broader terms of reference. The common-law rule as set forth in *Rowton* has never formally been abrogated, yet despite the short time which elapsed between the decision in that case and the passage of the 1898 Act, it is now established that for the purposes of the Act, evidence of character is not confined as at common law. Various authorities have drawn attention to the incongruity of this position, some grumbling rather half-heartedly about a transition which actually makes a good deal of sense.[1] The fact of the matter is, as we shall see in succeeding sections of this chapter, that the wording of the Act will not support restriction of character evidence to evidence of general reputation, and the Act would be unworkable if read so as to attempt to impose that restriction on it.

The test which is emerging in the modern authorities is one of relevance. Different situations demand different approaches to character evidence. If a witness has a series of previous convictions for cruelty to animals using a specific form of conduct, his disposition to behave in such a way may be relevant on a subsequent prosecution for an offence based on exactly the same conduct. But if the same person appears as a prosecution witness to a murder committed by another, should those convictions lead a jury to take a less favourable view of his credibility as a witness? If the same person had a previous conviction for perjury, the scene changes again. The law is probably still not finally settled, though it may be said with some certainty that there is a strong trend towards admitting relevant character evidence, and excluding irrelevant character evidence in whatever form, rather than judging such evidence by its form. Evidence of prior, specific, creditable acts tendered as evidence of good character is still excluded for the reasons propounded in *Rowton*, but other forms of character evidence, including opinion evidence, evidence of disposition and evidence of previous convictions, are now habitually admitted when relevant.

## 4.2 Uses of character evidence

Character evidence may be relevant either to some fact in issue or to the credibility of a witness. The rules of evidence governing character evidence in these two situations are quite distinct, and will be considered separately. In addition, there are certain limited cases in which the character of a person is itself a fact in issue in the case and may therefore be proved as such.

### 4.2.1 Character as a fact in issue

In an action for defamation and certain other cases, civil and criminal, one or more aspects of the character of a party may be a fact in issue to be determined by the tribunal of fact, like any other fact in issue. Such cases are exceptional, and will be dealt with briefly in section A of this chapter.

### 4.2.2 Relevant evidence which involves character

Good or bad character may be relevant to one or more facts in issue in the case. This subject will occupy section B of this chapter. There are two very different kinds of case to be considered. In some cases, relevant evidence happens, coincidentally, to reveal some aspect of character and the evidence cannot be presented without that revelation. In others, the character revealed is itself relevant and is introduced for its own sake, and not just as an inevitable by-product of the adduction of relevant evidence. The most significant and difficult species of evidence of the second kind is similar-fact evidence, which warrants a chapter of its own and is dealt with in Chapter 5. In the case of the bad character of the defendant in a criminal case, it is a fundamental rule of English law that the relevance must be other than to prove merely that the defendant acted in conformity with his character in relation to the offence charged.

[1] See, e.g., *R v Dunkley* [1927] 1 KB 323; *Jones v DPP* [1962] AC 635, per Lord Devlin at 699 et seq.

### 4.2.3   Character evidence used for impeachment

Impeachment is the process of attacking the credibility of a witness, with a view to showing that the witness is unworthy of belief, or at least unreliable. Witnesses generally may be impeached by being cross-examined about their character, and the use of cross-examination and extrinsic evidence for this purpose is considered in Chapter 14. In the case of the defendant in a criminal case, however, special rules apply and these are dealt with in section C of this chapter. These rules were introduced and are still governed by the Criminal Evidence Act 1898, which made the defendant a competent witness in his own defence for the first time.

## A: CHARACTER AS A FACT IN ISSUE

### 4.3   Introduction

Where the character of a person is actually a fact in issue in a case, it may be proved or disproved like any other fact in issue. In such a case, evidence of character is admitted, not because of its relevance to some other fact in issue, but because the tribunal of fact must decide the issue of character itself. Such cases are exceptional, and can only arise when at least some aspect of a party's character is an element of a claim, charge or defence. Where only a limited aspect of character is a fact in issue, all other aspects can be admitted only if relevant or for the purposes of impeachment. Although exceptional, examples of character as a fact in issue occur both in civil and criminal cases.

### 4.4   Civil cases

The obvious example in civil cases is an action for defamation. The extent to which the plaintiff's character will be a fact in issue affecting liablity will depend upon the pleaded particulars and defences. If the defence is one of justification, the issue will not be the same as if it were fair comment on a matter of public interest.[2] But depending on the issues raised by the pleadings, the plaintiff's character may prove to be in issue in its widest sense, including general reputation, disposition to behave in certain ways and specific prior conduct. On the issue of damages, it will be the general reputation of the plaintiff that is in issue, since the action is brought to recover damages for injury to reputation. What must be decided is the plaintiff's reputation prior to publication of the defamatory matter, and the extent to which that reputation has been injured or diminished. Evidence of specific prior conduct would be excluded because it would tend to show what the plaintiff's reputation ought to have been, and not what it in fact was.[3]

---

[2]   See generally *Gatley on Libel and Slander,* 7th ed., paras 351, 1235, 1243, 1313; *Fountain v Boodle* (1842) 3 QB 5. The principle is by no means confined to defamation cases. See *Hurst v Evans* [1917] 1 KB 352, where the defence to an action against an insurance company was that the loss was sustained by the dishonesty of the plaintiff's servant; it was admissible to prove that the servant was a known associate of burglars and had entered the plaintiff's service on a forged reference: (general and specific character).

[3]   See *Plato Films Ltd v Speidel* (HL) [1961] AC 1090. Lord Radcliffe suggested that specific acts might be relevant as part of the picture of general reputation, provided that they were sufficiently notorious. Ibid at 1131. See also *Scott v Sampson* (DC) (1882) 8 QBD 491 per Cave J at 503.

### 4.5   Criminal cases

In criminal cases, the obvious prejudice to a defendant likely to result from any exposure of his character has led to a considerable reluctance to entertain offences which make a man's bad character part of the case against him. However, there are cases, limited in number as are their civil counterparts, where character is itself in issue. In criminal cases, this is almost always because some aspect of character is an essential element of the offence (hence, in issue in the case) and so may be proved by evidence like any other fact in issue. These cases are various, and little useful purpose would be served by an attempt at classification, but the following examples will illustrate the genus.

In certain cases, the offence may be committed only by persons who have been sentenced on a previous occasion. By virtue of the Firearms Act 1968, s. 21 as amended, it is an offence for a person who has been sentenced to custody for life or to imprisonment for a term of three years or more or to youth custody for such a term to have a firearm or ammunition in his possession at any time. The jury must be sure, before they can convict, of each element of the offence; one of the elements is that the defendant is a person who has, on a previous occasion, been sentenced to such a term of imprisonment. No other aspect of his character is relevant to guilt, and the jury must be directed to ignore the implications of the evidence for the defendant's character generally, in considering that issue. At a somewhat lower level, the offence of driving a motor vehicle on a road while disqualified from holding or obtaining a driving licence, contrary to s. 99 of the Road Traffic Act 1972, involves proof that the defendant was, on the material date, a person so disqualified. The fact of disqualification alone is in issue, the defendant's character otherwise being irrelevant to guilt. These cases do, nonetheless, provide a stark instance of the risk of prejudice, against which the tribunal of fact must warn itself.

Many summary offences, especially those relating to behaviour in public, involve more general aspects of character. Thus, the offence of loitering or soliciting for the purpose of prostitution, contrary to s. 1 of the Street Offences Act 1959, can be committed only by a 'common prostitute', a fact which may be proved by previous convictions or other evidence of the defendant's way of life generally, and is frequently proved by the assertion of the arresting officer in evidence, unless expressly disputed. The notorious former offence of frequenting or loitering with intent to commit an arrestable offence, contrary to s. 4 of the Vagrancy Act 1824 as amended, was committed by a 'suspected person or reputed thief', a fact often proved by the officer's observation immediately prior to the arrest of the defendant. Furthermore, the required intent might be proved by the 'known character' of the defendant, in conjunction with the circumstances of the case (Prevention of Crimes Act 1871, s. 15).

## B: RELEVANT EVIDENCE WHICH INVOLVES CHARACTER

### 4.6   Introduction

In the cases described in the previous section, which must be regarded as exceptional, evidence of the character of a party is to a greater or lesser extent admissible, not because it is evidence of probative value in relation to some other fact in issue, but because character is itself in issue in the case. In the great majority of cases, both civil and criminal, character is not itself in issue and evidence of character must therefore be judged solely according to its probative value, if any, in relation to the facts in issue. One of the clearest statements of the rule governing the admissibility of evidence of character is that of Lord Herschell in *Makin and Makin* v *Attorney-General for New South Wales* [1894] AC 57, 65:

> It is undoubtedly not competent for the prosecution to adduce evidence tending to show that the accused has been guilty of criminal acts other than those covered by the indictment, for the purposes of leading to the conclusion that the accused is a person likely from his criminal conduct or character to have committed the offence for which he is being tried. On the other hand, the mere fact that the evidence adduced tends to show the commission of other crimes does not render it inadmissible if it be relevant to an issue before the jury . . .

In this passage from his speech, Lord Herschell stated a fundamental rule of English criminal law, namely that the prosecution may not use the defendant's previous bad character to suggest to the jury that he acted in conformity therewith in relation to the offence charged, or in other words that a defendant of known bad character is more likely to have committed the offence charged, simply by reason of his previous character. The law will not 'give a dog a bad name and hang it'.[4] It is certainly arguable that evidence of previous bad character is irrelevant to the issue of guilt if it suggests only that the defendant acted in conformity with his character on the occasion of the offence charged. Some writers take the position that evidence of character tendered to show conforming conduct and no more is relevant to the issue of guilt, because it is reasonably inferable that a person of previous bad character would have acted in a criminal way again. But all agree that evidence of previous bad character is inadmissible if offered for this purpose only. If guilt could be proved by past record, the defence of an innocent person of previous bad character would become difficult, if not impossible. Evidence of bad character always carries an in-built potential for prejudice in the mind of the tribunal of fact, which may preclude a dispassionate view of the evidence as a whole. Of course, by the same analysis, if the dog happens to have a good name, the law will not for that reason alone acquit it. But as we shall see, a rule which owes more to fairness than logic permits the dog to make use of its good name to show conformity with good character on the relevant occasion.

Although Lord Herschell's observations were made in the context of previous criminal acts, it is clear that the same rule applies to evidence of bad character that consists of general reputation or a disposition to behave in a certain way.

It follows that, with the sole exception of evidence of good character tendered by the defendant in a criminal case, evidence involving character is admissible only if it is relevant to a fact in issue for a purpose other than showing that a person acted in conformity with his character on the occasion in question.

### 4.7   Cross-examination as to evidence involving character

The usual course is for the prosecution to prove as part of their case all relevant evidence which they intend to call. This does not mean, however, that this is the only way in which relevant evidence involving character may be introduced. Where the defendant elects to give evidence in his own defence, he may be cross-examined about any matter relevant to the issue of guilt. If the defendant testifies about a relevant matter which the prosecution

---

[4]   As an American court once put it: 'A very bad man may have a very righteous cause': *Thompson* v *Church* (1791) 1 Root (Conn) 312.

did not lead in evidence, and which incidentally involves character, it follows that the defendant may be cross-examined about that matter. The Criminal Evidence Act 1898 made the defendant in a criminal case a competent witness in his own defence for the first time. Similar legislation which had earlier removed the incompetence as witnesses of the parties to civil cases offered those party-witnesses no protection against cross-examination about their character, so that like any other witness, they were liable to such an attack. Parliament determined, however, that a criminal defendant should be afforded protection against revelation of his character in cross-examination, because the common-law prohibition against the introduction of character evidence to prove that the defendant acted in conformity therewith in relation to the offence charged would otherwise be emasculated, and the defendant's right to give evidence undermined.

We shall deal in section C of this chapter with the statutory protection afforded the defendant, and with the cases in which that protection may be lost. Here, however, we shall observe that the Act did not in any way prevent cross-examination as to relevant facts, even where character is incidentally revealed. The statutory code therefore mirrors the common-law distinction between relevant evidence involving character and mere evidence of previous bad character. The pertinent provisions of the Act are s. 1(e) and (f)(i), which provide:

(e) A person charged and being a witness in pursuance of this Act may be asked any question in cross-examination notwithstanding that it would tend to criminate him as to the offence charged:

(f) A person charged and called as a witness in pursuance of this Act shall not be asked, and if asked shall not be required to answer, any question tending to show that he has committed or been convicted of or been charged with any offence other than that wherewith he is then charged, or is of bad character, unless—

(i) the proof that he has committed or been convicted of such other offence is admissible evidence to show that he is guilty of the offence wherewith he is then charged; . . .

Despite the apparently clear wording of these provisions, enacted not long after the decision in *Makin*, some authorities held that some distinction could be drawn between the admissibility of relevant evidence called as part of the prosecution's case and similar evidence adduced in cross-examination of a defendant who elects to give evidence in his defence. The distinction is unrealistic, and overlooks the fact that, even where the defendant introduces some relevant matter for the first time during his evidence, the prosecution would have been entitled to introduce it as part of their case, had they chosen to do so. In relation to similar-fact evidence, the distinction has long been abandoned. In *R v Sims* [1946] 1 KB 531, 539, Lord Goddard CJ pointed out that since similar-fact evidence is a form of character evidence admissible because it is relevant to guilt, it may be introduced as part of the prosecution case, and need not await the presentation of the defence or be limited to cross-examination of the defendant.

An interesting reinforcement of this view is offered by the corresponding American rule. The defendant in a criminal case has a constitutional privilege, under the Fifth Amendment to the United States Constitution, against self-incrimination. This includes the right not to testify in his own defence and the right to have no comment on his absence from the witness-box made to the jury. If, however, the defendant elects to testify, the rule is that he waives the privilege with respect to the offence charged, but not with respect to any other offence. The defendant may be cross-examined about any matter relevant to his guilt as charged. Thus, in *Johnson* v *US* 318 US 189 (1983) the defendant was charged with tax evasion with respect to his federal income tax returns for a number of years prior to 1938. In order to prove the source of his income over a period of time, the prosecution were permitted to show that the defendant's income for the year 1938 derived from protection and gambling operations. It was held that, even though the defendant was not charged with respect to his 1938 income, he could also be cross-examined about that income. Since it was relevant to his guilt as charged, the privilege against self-incrimination as to 1938 was waived when the defendant elected to testify.

In *Jones* v *DPP* [1962] AC 635, 701, Lord Devlin said simply:

In short, the rule in *Makin's* case covers both evidence led against the accused and evidence sought to be obtained from him in cross-examination; proviso (f) shuts out nothing that is relevant to the issue but gives complete protection to the accused against attacks on his reputation and credit unless he throws his hat into the ring.

In the same case, Lord Morris of Borth-y-Gest said at 685:

It was submitted on behalf of the appellant that in cases in which proof of the commission of or the conviction of an offence other than that charged would, within the first permitting provision of proviso (f) be 'admissible evidence' to show that the accused is guilty of the offence wherewith he is then charged, questions could only be put to the accused if, as part of the case for the prosecution, substantive evidence in regard to such other offence had already been given. I cannot agree. The admission of the accused when asked questions in cross-examination would be proof and there is no essential requirement that proof should be given in any other way or at any earlier stage.

Lord Morris went on to point out that it would be desirable that such relevant evidence be presented as part of the prosecution case, though it is submitted that there must be cases in which this will not be possible, or where the prosecution feel that it would be unfair to deal with certain matters unless raised by the defendant. However this may be, it now seems clear that relevant evidence involving character may be presented in either or both ways.

### 4.8 Admissible evidence involving bad character

Cases in which evidence involving character may be relevant fall into two quite distinct groups. In the first group of cases, the relevance arises from the nature of the character itself. In the second group of cases, the relevance lies in a fact unrelated to character, but this fact incidentally reveals at least some aspect of character that is not relevant in itself. Put another way, the distinction is that in the first group, the evidence will be relevant precisely because of the revelation of a specific aspect of character that is in some way probative of the fact in issue, while in the second, the evidence is admissible as relevant despite the fact that it also reveals some aspect of character.

### 4.8.1  Character relevant by its own nature
This subject will be dealt with only briefly here, since it mainly concerns similar-fact evidence (see Chapter 5). Similar-fact evidence is evidence of prior conduct on the part of a

party (usually the defendant in a criminal case, though the principle applies equally to civil cases) which is relevant to guilt as charged or liability because the prior conduct bears such a striking similarity to the facts of the offence or wrong now in question, that the tribunal of fact should be driven to the conclusion that the latter must be the work or act of the person who committed the prior conduct. Such evidence is admitted not despite the fact that it reveals character, but because it does so. This is probably the most critical area of character evidence, since the line between evidence relevant as probative because of its striking similarity to the offence or wrong charged, and evidence which amounts to no more than evidence that a party acted in conformity with his character, is always difficult to discern. But that the line must be drawn is clear from the conclusion of the passage from the speech of Lord Herschell in *Makin* cited above. Immediately following the words cited, Lord Herschell continued:

> ... and it may be so relevant if it bears upon the question whether the acts alleged to constitute the crime charged in the indictment were designed or accidental, or to rebut a defence which would otherwise be open to the accused.

Similar-fact evidence finds its primary use in rebutting defences such as accident, lack of intent and lack of knowledge, and tends to prove the opposite facts of intent, preparation and system. Its use for this purpose is well expressed, and the vital distinction well illustrated, by American Federal Rule of Evidence 404(b). This rule, expressing a principle akin to that declared by Lord Herschell in *Makin*, provides:

> Other crimes, wrongs or acts. Evidence of other crimes, wrongs or acts is not admissible to prove the character of a person in order to show that he acted in conformity therewith. It may, however, be admissible for other purposes, such as proof of motive, opportunity, intent, preparation, plan, knowledge, identity or absence of mistake or accident.

### 4.8.2 Relevant evidence which incidentally reveals character

As Lord Herschell pointed out, relevant evidence is admissible, notwithstanding that it may incidentally reveal some aspect of character, where that evidence is relevant for a purpose other than showing that a party acted in conformity with his character. In this case, however, the relevance must be found outside the revelation of character. The jury will be directed, not that they may find the defendant guilty because the relevant character evidence points unambiguously to his authorship of the offence charged, but that they must not under any circumstances consider the incidentally revealed character as evidence of guilt.

In some cases, the revelation of character will be no more than a background or setting to an offence charged. For example, if would be difficult to prosecute an offence committed by a serving prisoner without telling the jury where and in what circumstances the offence took place. The reason why the defendant was incarcerated at the time is, of course, irrelevant and the jury should be directed not to speculate about it, much less hold it against the defendant in any way.

Usually, however, the revealed character plays a far more significant role in the decision of the issue of guilt than mere background. In the leading case of *Jones v DPP* [1962] AC 635, the defendant was convicted of the murder of a young girl guide in October 1960. He had previously been convicted of raping another girl guide during September 1960.

Although the earlier conviction would have been relevant to the offence charged, in that both involved attacks on girl guides, the prosecution did not lead evidence of it because of a desire to spare the victim of the earlier crime the ordeal of giving evidence again. In statements to the police about the murder charged, the defendant gave an alibi which was false. Subsequently, he admitted that this alibi was false and put forward a second alibi. The second alibi was almost identical to an alibi which the defendant had advanced at his trial on the earlier rape charge. The similarity extended to details of conversations that the defendant alleged he had had with his wife, which were almost word-for-word the same. At trial, the defendant sought to explain his giving of the first, false alibi by giving evidence that he had been 'in trouble' with the police. He was cross-examined about the suspicious similarity of his second alibi for the murder to his alibi on what was referred to as 'another occasion' — no details of the previous conviction being revealed to the jury. The defendant appealed on the ground that the cross-examination should not have been permitted.

The House of Lords unanimously dismissed the appeal. The members of the House were not unanimous as to their reasons, though all those advanced appear very sound. Viscount Simonds and Lords Reid and Morris of Borth-y-Gest based their decision on the wording of s. 1(*f*) of the Criminal Evidence Act 1898, and this aspect of the decision is considered in 4.12.2 post. Lords Denning and Devlin, more simply, viewed the case as presenting no more than a case of relevant evidence, about which the prosecution were entitled to cross-examine by virtue of s. 1(*e*) of the Act. Lord Devlin explained the purpose of the cross-examination as follows ([1962] AC 635, 690):

> My Lords, I would dismiss this appeal on the short ground that the questions objected to were relevant to an issue in the case on which the appellant had testified in chief. It is not disputed that the issue to which the questions related was a relevant one. It concerned the identification of the appellant as being at the material time at the scene of the crime. He testified that at the material time he was with a prostitute in the West End and he supported this alibi by giving evidence of a conversation which he had had with his wife about it a day or two later. The purpose of the questions objected to was to obtain from the appellant an admission (which was given) that when he was being questioned about his movements in relation to another incident some weeks earlier he had set up the same alibi and had supported it with an account of a conversation with his wife in almost identical terms; the prosecution suggested that these similarities showed the whole story of the alibi to be an invented one.

The similarity of the alibis was clearly relevant to the issue of guilt, as it tended to suggest that the alibi was concocted. The prosecution were, therefore, entitled to cross-examine even though the jury must be made aware of 'another occasion'. In *Jones*, the defendant had himself revealed this to the jury during his evidence in chief, but on the basis of the reasoning of Lords Denning and Devlin, the cross-examination would have been proper even had this not been the case, and it is submitted that this reasoning is correct. Note that the prosecution did not introduce any details of the other occasion; this would have been irrelevant to the attack on the veracity of the second alibi. No doubt the prosecution could have argued that it might be relevant to the issue of guilt as a form of similar-fact evidence, but unless this could be established, the detail of the rape would have been inadmissible as tending to show no more than that the defendant acted in conformity with his disposition to attack girl guides.

The House of Lords considered a number of earlier authorities. One of the most interesting is *R* v *Chitson* [1909] 2 KB 945. The defendant was charged with carnal knowledge of a girl under 14, who stated during examination in chief that on the day after the alleged offence, the defendant had told her that he had previously done the same thing to another girl. The trial judge allowed the prosecution to cross-examine the defendant about this statement. Upholding the conviction, the Court of Criminal Appeal said (ibid at 947):

> Although the latter line of questions did no doubt tend to prove that he was of bad character, still they also in our opinion tended to show that he was guilty of the offence with which he was charged, for if he had made that statement to the prosecutrix at the time alleged by her, that fact would strongly corroborate her evidence that the prisoner was the person who had had connexion with her. We are therefore of the opinion that the learned judge rightly admitted the questions . . . because the evidence was material as tending to show that the statement was one likely to have been made to the prosecutrix by the prisoner, and was not invented by her or learnt from someone else, and it was therefore material to the issue as to whether the prisoner did commit the offence for which he was then being tried.

In *Jones*, Lord Reid criticised the reasoning in *Chitson*, holding that the questions would have violated the prohibition in s. 1(*f*) of the Criminal Evidence Act 1898, except for the fact that the girl's evidence about the defendant's statement had already been adduced without objection, so that the jury were already aware of it. Lord Reid concluded that the decision in *Chitson* was correct on the facts and need not be overruled, despite the reasoning which he criticised.[5] It is submitted, with respect, that the decision can be defended on the grounds advanced by the Court of Criminal Appeal, since the making of the statement tended to confirm the evidence of the prosecutrix that it was the defendant who committed the offence.

Moreover, *Chitson* is by no means an isolated decision of its kind. In *R* v *Kurasch* [1915] 2 KB 749 (which Lord Devlin said was not cited to the House of Lords in *Jones*, but was nonetheless 'relevant') the defendant was charged with conspiracy to cheat by means of a mock auction. In evidence in chief, the defendant stated that he was only the servant of a Mrs Dyas, the owner of the business. The Court of Criminal Appeal upheld the decision of the trial judge to allow the prosecution to cross-examine the defendant to show that, in fact, the defendant and Mrs Dyas were living together as man and wife. The propriety of the cross-examination was assailed as violating the prohibition of s. 1(*f*), but the Court regarded the matter as one solely of relevance to the issue of guilt. In *R* v *Kennaway* [1917] 1 KB 25, the defendant was charged with forgery of a will, and two accomplices were called as prosecution witnesses. The accomplices testified that the defendant had told them that he had forged a different will some years previously under similar circumstances, and the defendant was cross-examined both about this statement and about his alleged forgery of the earlier will. The Court of Criminal Appeal upheld the conviction, since the evidence was relevant as tending to corroborate the testimony of the

---

[5] [1962] AC 635, 665. Interestingly, there was no evidence in *Chitson* that the second girl was under the age of consent, so that although the statement reflected badly on the defendant in a general sense, it did not amount to a suggestion of a specific criminal offence.

accomplices. It is submitted that these cases were rightly decided, and are not inconsistent with the decision in *Jones*.

The rule that relevant evidence of character may be admitted has many applications. In *R v B; R v A* [1979] 1 WLR 1185, it was held that evidence of character including previous findings of guilt was admissible for the purpose of rebutting the presumption of *doli incapax* in the case of a child offender between the ages of 10 and 14. By s. 27(3) of the Theft Act 1968, Parliament gave a form of statutory relevance to certain evidence of previous involvement with stolen goods and previous convictions for theft or handling stolen goods, by declaring such evidence to be admissible, in certain narrowly defined circumstances, on a charge of handling stolen goods for the purpose of proving that the defendant knew or believed the goods to be stolen.[6] The relevance of such evidence lies in the likelihood that a person with such a background will have an increased awareness of being in the presence of stolen goods.

The rule under discussion applies equally to civil cases, with the sole difference that a party may not, in a civil case, give evidence of his general good character in order to show that it is more likely that he acted in conformity with that character in relation to the claim or defence in question. Thus, the defendant to a civil action for keeping false weights[7] or for the impeachment of a will on the ground of fraud[8] will not be allowed to assert his good character for the purpose of disproving the claim. Nor, in an old divorce case, was the husband permitted to prove his 'general humanity' in answer to the wife's specific charges of cruelty.[9]

### 4.9    Evidence of good character in criminal cases

#### 4.9.1    Admissibility
Out of the conspicuous concern of the common law to offer as much latitude as possible to a defendant, in view of the procedural and evidential incapacities from which he suffered before the gradual reforms of the nineteenth century, emerged a rule peculiar to criminal trials, that the defendant might in every case prove his general good character. Before the Criminal Evidence Act 1898 rendered the defendant a competent witness in his own defence, this could be achieved only by cross-examination of witnesses for the prosecution, or by calling character witnesses for the defence, and, as will be discussed in 4.14, post, s. 1(*f*)(ii) of the Act had to make provision for the giving of such evidence by the defendant himself.

#### 4.9.2    Method of proof
There was much discussion at common law about the kind of evidence which was permitted by the rule. In the end, it seemed to be settled that it was confined to evidence of general reputation. In *R v Rowton* (CCR) (1865) Le & Ca 520, the defendant was charged

---

[6]    This section must be very narrowly construed, because of the obvious risk of prejudice to the defendant: *R v Bradley* (1980) 70 Cr App R 200. The judge may, of course, exclude the evidence in his discretion, and it has been held that he should do so if it offers 'no more than minimal assistance' to the jury: *R v Perry* [1984] Crim LR 680. See also *R v Knott* [1973] Crim LR 36; *R v Herron* [1967] 1 QB 107 (decided under the corresponding provisions of the Larceny Act 1916).

[7]    *Attorney-General v Bowman* (1791) 2 Bos & P 532n.

[8]    *Goodright, ex dem Faro v Hicks* (1789) Bull NP 296.

[9]    *Narracott v Narracott and Hesketh* (Court for Divorce & Matrimonial Causes) (1864) 3 Sw & Tr 408.

with indecent assault on a boy of 14. The defendant was a schoolmaster. The question arose of the limits of admissible evidence of character offered by a witness, and it was held that the evidence was confined to that of the general reputation of the defendant in the community, and therefore excluded both evidence of specific acts on other occasions, and the witness's own opinion of the defendant. *Rowton* itself was the subject of powerful dissent, and the ink was scarcely dry on the judgments before it was doubted. Although the case has never been specifically reversed, the practice in modern times is to allow the defendant to state his character more widely. This more lenient view may be justified on several grounds: that reputation in a neighbourhood is an ephemeral and largely meaningless concept in days of widespread social mobility, and may well give a positively misleading appraisal of the defendant's true character; that in any case reputation is often undeserved; and that the consistent interpretation of the Criminal Evidence Act 1898 has been favourable to a wider view[10] and it is surely undesirable that two such different meanings should be assigned to the word 'character'.

In modern practice, the defendant is invariably permitted to state that he has no previous convictions. There is also no doubt that the defendant may now call a character witness to state that witness's opinion of the defendant. To that extent, the decision in *Rowton* is no longer applied in practice. However, there is no doubt that *Rowton* continues to preclude the defendant from adducing evidence of prior creditable specific acts. Whether the defendant's evidence of good character may include evidence of his disposition to behave in a certain way is still not absolutely certain after the decision of the Court of Appeal in *R v Redgrave* (1981) 74 Cr App R 10. The defendant was charged with persistently importuning for immoral purposes, by masturbating in a public lavatory while staring at the (male) arresting officers. At the first trial, at which the jury had disagreed, the defendant had been permitted to adduce documents which were described as love letters and photographs of himself in the company of women, said to indicate a familiar relationship with the women, in order to show that his sexual tendency was heterosexual rather than homosexual. At his re-trial, the defendant sought to adduce a selection of the documents, including letters, Valentine cards and photographs, and to testify about his relationship with the women concerned. The trial judge ruled this evidence to be inadmissible, relying on *Rowton*, and the defendant appealed against his conviction on this ground.

It was argued that if the prosecution may adduce relevant evidence of the defendant's homosexual tendencies (a subject discussed in Chapter 5, post) it must be open to the defendant to adduce evidence of his heterosexual disposition for the purpose of suggesting that it is less likely that he committed such an offence. This argument is somewhat, though not greatly, weakened on the facts of the case by the fact that homosexual intent is not an essential element of the offence charged, but there seems no doubt that the evidence tendered was relevant to rebut the clear suggestion of homosexual intent made by the prosecution. The argument is certainly cogent and sympathetic, but the Court of Appeal held that *Rowton* must be followed, and that such evidence of disposition must be excluded. The Court appears to have based itself in part on the proposition that the prosecution could not have adduced evidence of homosexual disposition as relevant to the

[10]    *R v Dunkley* (CCA) [1927] 1 KB 323; *Stirland v DPP* (HL) [1944] AC 315 per Lord Simon LC at 325; *Jones v DPP* (HL) [1962] AC 635 per Lord Denning at 671; and see also the speech of Lord Devlin at 694 et seq.

offence charged, though there is authority which suggests that this is not necessarily the case.[11]

The invitation given to the Court to refuse to follow *Rowton* was too great a step of faith. That the Court had some consciousness of disallowing relevant defence evidence seems clear, and the court adverted with some justification to possible difficulties of calling evidence from a defendant's sexual partners under subpoena. However, it is submitted that *Redgrave* is an unsatisfactory decision which fails to take into account the realities of modern criminal practice. The Court's dilemma seems evident from a passage near the end of the judgment of Lawton LJ (ibid at 15), in which the learned Lord Justice said:

> It was brought to our attention by [counsel for the prosecution] that nowadays, as a matter of practice in this class of case, defendants are often allowed to say that they are happily married and having a normal sexual relationship with their wives. We are not seeking to stop defending counsel putting that kind of information before a jury. It has long been the practice for judges to allow some relaxation of the law of evidence on behalf of defendants. Had this young man been a married man, or alternatively, had he confined his relationship to one girl, it might not have been all that objectionable for him to have given evidence in general terms that his relationship with his wife or the girl was satisfactory. That would have been an indulgence on the part of the court. It would not have been his right to have it said. Until such time as Parliament amends the law of evidence, it is the duty of this Court, and of judges, to keep to the rules, and the rules are clear.

If this is the position, it is submitted that it should be modified as a matter of some urgency. Can the defence in such cases be reduced to depending not only on the indulgence of the court, but also on the fortuitous facts of the defendant's marital status or the number of his girlfriends, to be permitted to adduce evidence that is not only apparently relevant but also potentially cogent? If a strict reading of *Rowton* requires such a result, the time may have come to consign the case to history, and it is to be regretted that the House of Lords refused leave to appeal in *Redgrave*.

The corresponding American Federal Rule of Evidence 405, contains the following far more liberal provision:

> (a)  Reputation or opinion. In all cases in which evidence of character or a trait of character of a person is admissible, proof may be made by testimony as to reputation or by testimony in the form of an opinion. On cross-examination, inquiry is allowable into relevant specific instances of conduct.
>
> (b)  Specific instances of conduct. In cases in which character or a trait of character of a person is an essential element of a charge, claim or defense, proof may also be made of specific instances of his conduct.

Federal Rules of Evidence 404, 608 and 609 contain fairly restrictive provisions

---

[11]    See *R* v *King* [1967] 2 QB 338; *R* v *Horwood* [1970] 1 QB 133; and generally 5.3.1, post. The prosecution may not adduce such evidence merely to show that the defendant acted in conformity with his sexual character in relation to the offence charged, but may do so where it is otherwise relevant to the issue of guilt. They would surely be at liberty to adduce such evidence to rebut evidence of disposition given by the defendant, so that no prejudice to the prosecution would occur by allowing the defendant to do so.

governing the admissibility of character evidence, and cannot be described as liberal in terms of admissibility. The test is essentially one of relevance, whether the evidence is tendered as part of a party's case or for purposes of impeachment of a witness. Rule 405 does not affect admissibility, but only the method of proof where the evidence is admissible. It was not felt necessary to be restrictive as to the method of proof, and indeed the restriction is only a partial restriction on the use of evidence of specific conduct. It is submitted that a similar rule would work satisfactorily in English law also.

A defendant who gives evidence of his good character, or elicits his good character in cross-examination of the witnesses for the prosecution, may now be cross-examined about his character, both general and specific, under the provisions of the Criminal Evidence Act 1898 s. 1(*f*)(ii) (see 4.14, post). Any witness called on behalf of the defendant to speak about his character may be cross-examined on that subject and, like any other witness, may be cross-examined as to his own credit. Furthermore, the prosecution are entitled to call evidence in rebuttal of the evidence called for the defence,[12] and this includes, in modern law, the right to prove the previous convictions of the defendant, if they are not admitted.[13] The outer limits of the rules are perhaps drawn by cases such as *R v Wood and Parker* (1841) 5 Jur 225, where it was held that it was permissible to cross-examine character witnesses to show that the defendant was rumoured to have participated in offences other than that charged. The rule makes perfect sense, to the extent that general reputation must take account of rumour as well as other intangibles, of which it is largely composed. Nonetheless, it is submitted that the decision would be unlikely to be followed today unless a defendant rested his evidence specifically upon general reputation within the meaning of the common-law rule.

It must also be stressed that, for the purposes under consideration, character is indivisible; the defendant cannot assert part of his character, which he believes to be good and therefore favourable to him, without opening up to scrutiny his character as a whole.[14] The rule is one of obvious justice, in so far as the court should not be misled. On the other hand, Professor Nokes has drawn attention to the fact that, if a man is charged with forgery, cross-examination about his conviction for cruelty to animals 'can have no purpose but prejudice'.[15] In *R v Winfield* [1939] 4 All ER 164, the defendant was charged with indecent assault on a woman and produced a character witness who, in cross-examination, revealed the defendant's previous conviction for dishonesty. The Court of Criminal Appeal accepted this as proper, though it is not apparent that the jury were really assisted by, or that they would have been misled in any material sense by being denied access to, that information. It may be that the answer lies in the power of the trial judge to limit cross-examination, even where permitted in law, in the interests of ensuring a fair trial, and there are instances of the opening up of character being limited for this reason.[16]

[12] The same was formerly true where an assertion of good character was made in an unsworn statement from the dock: *R v Campbell; R v Lear; R v Nicholls* (CA) (1979) 69 Cr App R 221. But contrast the position as to rebuttal where the defendant does not raise his good character, but loses his shield in the other circumstances envisaged by s. 1(*f*)(ii): *R v Butterwasser* (CCA) [1948] 1 KB 1; 4.11, post.

[13] *R v Redd* (CCA) [1923] 1 KB 104.

[14] *Stirland v DPP* (HL) [1944] AC 315 per Lord Simon LC at 326.

[15] *Introduction to Evidence*, 4th ed., 140.

[16] An argument can be made, in cases where character becomes admissible because of the conduct of the defence, that only character evidence relevant to the jury's assessment of credibility should be permitted; cf. *Selvey v DPP* [1970] AC 304; *R v Watts* [1983] 3 All ER 101. But where a defendant voluntarily raises the issue of his own good character, there is a strong basis for refusing to allow him to withhold selected areas of his character from the jury.

*4.9.3  Evidential value*

There are in theory two possible views on the use which may be made by the jury of evidence of good character called by the defence. On one view, it might go only to the credit of the defendant as a witness. On the other, it might go further than that, and cast doubt on the case for the prosecution, by showing that the defendant is less likely, because of his character, to have committed the offence charged. Only in recent times does a clear judicial preference appear to have emerged for the latter view. There were earlier pronouncements in its favour[17] but these were taken as having been supplanted by the decision in *R* v *Falconer-Atlee* (CA) (1973) 58 Cr App R 348, in which the 'credit only' direction was strongly affirmed. The logical result of *Falconer-Atlee* was that, if the defendant chose not to give evidence in his defence, then evidence of good character elicited in cross-examination, or given by character witnesses, would not be relevant for any purpose, and the jury should be directed to disregard it. This consequence arose, and was squarely faced by the trial judge, in *R* v *Bryant; R* v *Oxley* [1979] QB 108, 119. The Court of Appeal, while dismissing the appeal against conviction, held that the judge had been wrong to direct the jury that since the defendant's credit was not in issue, the evidence of his good character could have no value. This approach was said by the Court of Appeal to be 'too restrictive'. The court added:

> The possession of a good character is a matter which does go primarily to the issue of credibility. This has been made clear in a number of recent cases. But juries should be directed that it is capable of bearing a more general significance which is best illustrated by what was said by Williams J in *R* v *Stannard and Others* [(1837) C & P 673, 675]: 'I have no doubt. . . that evidence to character must be considered as evidence in the cause. It is evidence, as my brother Patteson has said, to be submitted to the jury, to induce them to say whether they think it likely that a person with such a character would have committed the offence.'

**4.10   *R* v *Coke: R* v *Littleton***

The result of these rules, as applied to the cases of Coke and Littleton, may be summarised as follows. In neither case is character a fact in issue. Therefore, Coke's previous conviction for rape could be proved by the prosecution only if it is relevant for a purpose other than showing that Coke has a disposition to commit rape, and that he acted in conformity with that disposition on the occasion of the incident involving Margaret Blackstone. In other words, the prosecution cannot adduce evidence of the prior rape and, in effect, say to the jury 'look at his record; do you not think it likely that he committed rape on the occasion charged?' There appears to be no relevance other than this in the prior rape, unless the facts of that case prove to be strikingly similar, so that it becomes admissible as relevant to the present offence charged. This we will consider further in Chapter 5. Subject to this, and to any statements made by Coke while giving evidence at trial, which might make the prior rape relevant, Coke should be able to forestall any attempt by the prosecution to adduce such evidence against him, or to cross-examine him about it. Littleton may assert his good character, by way of defence, in any of the following ways: (a) by cross-examination of a witness for the prosecution (in this case, D/I Glanvil as the officer in charge of the case would be preferable) to show that he has not

---

[17]   *R* v *Stannard and Others* (1837) 7 C & P 673; *R* v *Bellis* (CCA) [1966] 1 WLR 234.

previously been convicted of any offence and that nothing is known adverse to his character; (b) by himself giving evidence of his general character, lack of previous convictions and sexual disposition; (c) by calling character witnesses to any of these matters, for which purpose his wife would seem a likely choice in view of the matters in her proof of evidence concerning Littleton's disposition in sexual matters and towards children generally. The jury would be entitled to regard such evidence as relevant to the issue of his guilt or innocence, and on a charge of this sort, the evidence may well carry considerable weight, but it is subject to challenge by the prosecution in cross-examination and by rebutting evidence.

It is usually a safe principle that a defendant with bad character, conscious of the risk of prejudice, would wish always to keep the record from the jury, and this would certainly be sound here, where Coke's offence is liable to be particularly prejudicial to the mind of the jury, because of its similarity to that charged. But in some cases, a defendant may take a different view, and assert his 'limited good character'. The idea is becoming more prevalent as it is recognised that juries are increasingly well informed, both by the administrative process under which they are summoned, and less formally, by realistic presentation by the media, and that they are increasingly disinclined to hold a man's past against him. There is a school of thought among many advocates that the jury should be trusted with the defendant's record as an alternative to taking the risk that silence on the subject will prompt speculation. Most jurors now serve in a number of cases during their term of service, and are not slow to appreciate why no reference to character is made in one case, when in the previous case, the defendant's good character was loudly proclaimed. In many cases, the jury will give credit to a defendant who is frank with them. This is particularly useful where the defendant's previous record is for offences quite different in nature from that now charged, or where he states that in the past he has always recognised his guilt by pleading guilty, but is now contesting the case because he is innocent. If this line is taken, it is tactically essential to bring out the whole of the defendant's character in chief. If it is (and it will be) dragged out in cross-examination, after a partial revelation, all hope of credit for frankness will be lost, and the jury will be rightly suspicious. It must be stressed that, though the ploy is often valid, it would be dicing with death in a case such as Coke's, because of the nature of his previous conviction.

## C: IMPEACHMENT OF THE DEFENDANT IN CRIMINAL CASES — THE CRIMINAL EVIDENCE ACT 1898

### 4.11 Introduction

Before the Criminal Evidence Act 1898 came into effect, the defendant in a criminal case was not a competent witness in his own defence. Section 1 of the Act rendered him competent (though not compellable) as a witness for the defence at every stage of the proceedings.[18] This would have meant, in the absence of further provision, that like any other witness, the defendant would be open to attacks on his credit by cross-examination

---

[18]   The competence of the defendant is considered generally in Chapter 11, post. Until earlier in the nineteenth century, the parties to civil cases had likewise been incompetent on their own behalf, but their emancipation as witnesses was not accompanied by protection of the sort offered by the 1898 Act in criminal cases. Indeed, they also became compellable.

concerning his character. Because of the risk of prejudice peculiarly associated with character in criminal cases. Parliament determined to afford the defendant a substantial, albeit not unlimited, protection against such attack, in the no doubt justified belief that the right to give evidence might otherwise be rarely exercised.

The protection was achieved by building into the Act a complete code regulating the cross-examination of a defendant who chooses to give evidence as permitted by the statute. The code, as enacted by s. 1 provisos (e) and (f), stands in full force today, subject only to one amendment to s. 1(f)(iii) by the Criminal Evidence Act 1979 designed to restore the original intention of Parliament. It is worth reading the code as a whole, before considering it in more detail.

Provided as follows:—. . .

(e)   A person charged and being a witness in pursuance of this Act may be asked any question in cross-examination notwithstanding that it would tend to criminate him as to the offence charged:

(f)   A person charged and called as a witness in pursuance of this Act shall not be asked, and if asked shall not be required to answer, any question tending to show that he has committed or been convicted of or been charged with any offence other than that wherewith he is then charged, or is of bad character, unless—

(i)   the proof that he has committed or been convicted of such other offence is admissible evidence to show that he is guilty of the offence wherewith he is then charged; or

(ii)   he has personally or by his advocate asked questions of the witnesses for the prosecution with a view to establish his own good character, or has given evidence of his own good character, or the nature or conduct of the defence is such as to involve imputations on the character of the prosecutor or the witnesses for the prosecution; or

(iii)   he has given evidence against any other person charged in the same proceedings.

The pattern of the code is that, although of course the cross-examination of the defendant may freely seek to convict him of the offence charged, he is invested with what is usually referred to as a 'shield' in respect of other offences and of his bad character. This shield may be 'lost' in any of the circumstances envisaged by s. 1(f)(i), (ii), or (iii), the consequence of which is that the defendant becomes liable to be cross-examined about the matters otherwise prohibited, and then stands in effect in the same position as witnesses generally. It is important to note that the Act is only dealing with cross-examination, which is obviously available only where the defendant chooses to give evidence. Thus, in *R v Butterwasser* (CCA) [1948] 1 KB1, the nature or conduct of the defence involved imputations on the character of the witnesses for the prosecution, so that the defendant lost his shield, by virtue of s. 1(f)(ii). He declined to give evidence, and called no witnesses to his character. The prosecution were allowed to call evidence of the defendant's bad character. An appeal against conviction was allowed, because that evidence was wrongly admitted. The Act referred only to cross-examination, and gave no right to the prosecution to adduce evidence.[19] The position is, as we have seen, different where·the

[19]   See also *R v De Vere* [1981] 3 All ER 473. On the duty of counsel representing a defendant who does not give evidence, but who wishes allegations to be put to witnesses for the prosecution amounting to imputations on character, see 13.4.

defendant by whatever means asserts his good character, in which case the prosecution are entitled at common law to rebut, in addition to cross-examining under s. 1(*f*)(ii).

It is important to note also that the right to cross-examine about character is governed exclusively by the Act. There is no common-law right to do so, nor does the trial judge have any discretion to permit such cross-examination where it would not be permissible under the Act: *R* v *Weekes* (1983) 77 Cr App R 207.

Perhaps the most significant feature of the code, however, is one not so readily apparent on the face of it, namely that the effect of any evidence elicited by cross-examination under proviso (*e*) and (*f*)(i) is one of relevance to the offence charged (i.e. going to the issue in the case); whereas the effect of similar evidence elicited under proviso (*f*)(ii) and (iii) is to go only to the credit of the defendant as a witness. This reflects the two possible uses of character evidence, with which this chapter began. It will be convenient to consider the provisions under those headings, but before doing so, we must examine some general questions about the prohibition in s. 1(*f*).

## 4.12 Section 1(f): the prohibition

'A person charged and called as a witness in pursuance of this Act shall not be asked, and if asked shall not be required to answer, any question tending to show that he has committed or been convicted of or been charged with any offence other than that wherewith he is then charged, or is of bad character ...'

### 4.12.1 'If asked shall not be required to answer'
The wording of the Act is clearly designed and intended to apply to cross-examination, and the reference to 'being required' shows that it is not intended to inhibit the evidence given by the defendant in chief, so he is at that stage free to deal with the matters referred to.[20] Of course, if he does so, then his character is opened up to cross-examination.

### 4.12.2 'Any questions tending to show'
The words quoted mean 'tending to reveal to the jury'. As we saw in *Jones* v *DPP* (HL) [1962] AC 635 (see 4.8, ante), the defendant sought to explain his giving of an alibi, which he later admitted to be false, on the basis that he had 'been in trouble with the police before' and did not want to be in trouble again. After admitting the alibi to be false, the defendant had given a second alibi, which was so completely identical to one given by him in relation to another case, that the prosecution sought and obtained leave to cross-examine him with regard to what his alibi had been on 'another occasion'. No details of the nature of the previous 'trouble' were introduced. On appeal, it was argued that the cross-examination contravened the prohibition in s. 1(*f*). A majority of the House of Lords held that it was proper, in that the defendant, by the way in which his defence was conducted, had already told the jury that he had been involved in 'trouble', so that the questioning did not reveal to the jury anything which they did not already know, and did

---

[20] *Jones* v *DPP* (HL) [1962] AC 635 per Lord Reid at 663. But questions by the judge or counsel for a co-defendant would be caught by the Act: *R* v *Ratcliffe* (CCA) (1919) 14 Cr App R 95; *R* v *Roberts* (CCA) [1936] 1 All ER 23.

not, therefore, 'tend to show' any prohibited matter which the defence had not already introduced.[21]

It is the effect of the questions put that must be considered. If a question in fact has the effect of revealing prohibited matter, if truthfully answered, it is improper — for example, a question which, if answered truthfully, would oblige the defendant to say that he had been in prison at a certain time.[22] Often the effect of a line of cross-examination must be looked at: the whole line may contravene the prohibition, even though individual questions may be perfectly proper in themselves. The prohibition is not limited to questions taken individually.

### 4.12.3  'Committed or been convicted of or been charged with'
The prohibition is not limited to actual convictions, and even questions tending to show the commission of an offence not charged must be disallowed, for example, questions tending to show acts of dishonesty concurrent with, but other than those charged.[23]

The word 'charged' refers to a formal charge of an offence, not merely to suspicion, so that in *Stirland* v *DPP* (HL) [1944] AC 315, where the defendant, charged with forgery, gave evidence that he had never before been charged with any offence, it was held to be improper to cross-examine him to the effect that he had previously been dismissed from his employment with a bank because of suspected forgery: the defendant's evidence was accurate. He had not been charged. The cross-examination as framed was irrelevant and did nothing to rebut it. The wording would be wide enough, however, to include previous offences with which the defendant had been charged, but of which he had been acquitted, though questions of relevance often arise in relation to previous acquittals.

### 4.12.4  'Any offence'
The absence of limitation shows that the prohibition extends to offences committed after, as well as those committed before, the offence charged.[24] Where the shield is lost, it is therefore proper to cross-examine about such offences, and it has been held to be within the judge's discretion, in such a case, to allow cross-examination of a defendant, otherwise of good character, about offences committed some 10 months after the offence charged.[25]

### 4.12.5  'Or is of bad character'
There has been much speculation about the meaning which Parliament intended to give to the word 'character' when enacting the 1898 Act. It is variously argued that Parliament intended either to maintain the narrow definition, insisted upon in *R* v *Rowton* (CCR) (1865) Le & Ca 520 (see 4.9.2, ante), of general reputation only, or, by the reference to previous specific incidents, to open up the subject of character to a more comprehensive definition. Whatever Parliament actually intended, it is now settled that the word has acquired a wide connotation, for the purposes of the Act, and that the disposition of a

---

[21]   The minority held the line of cross-examination to be proper for equally cogent reasons, Lord Denning because it was admissible under proviso (e) and Lord Devlin because it was relevant to an issue of fact raised by the defendant in evidence in chief, namely his identification as having been at the scene of the crime at a material time. See 4.8, ante.

[22]   *R* v *Haslam* (CCA) (1916) 12 Cr App R 10. The intent of the questioner matters not. The actual effect of the question is what counts: *R* v *Ellis* [1910] 2 KB 746, 757; *Jones* v *DPP* [1962] AC 635.

[23]   *R* v *Wilson* (CCA) (1915) 11 Cr App R 251.

[24]   *R* v *Wood* (CCA) [1920] 2 KB 179.

[25]   *R* v *Coltress* (CA) (1978) 68 Cr App R 193.

defendant is included in his 'character' for this purpose.[26] Since previous convictions and offences, and sometimes previous charges, are added by the specific words, it follows that the Act is broad enough to incorporate each of the three possible meanings of the word 'character' set out in 4.1, ante. It is submitted that this is sensible and satisfactory for the practical working of the Act, and deserves more enthusiastic support than the grudging status of 'too late to argue the contrary' which has sometimes been accorded to it. Indeed, the facts of *R v Dunkley*, in which Lord Hewart CJ employed exactly that epithet,[27] seem to show that much of the 'code', in particular the operation of the part of s. 1(*f*)(ii) dealing with 'imputations on the character of the prosecutor or the witnesses for the prosecution', would be meaningless on a *Rowton* view. It is difficult to see how there can be an 'imputation' on a general reputation; it may be that the sub-section is intended to mean: 'If the nature or conduct of the defence is such as to involve an assertion that the prosecutor is or the witnesses for the prosecution are of bad general reputation', but the actual line of defence envisaged by the section is that the witness does not have a good reputation, but that the witness is not entitled to a good reputation. It would only be in rare cases, and for few and unimportant purposes, that the Act would come into effect, if read in such a way. It surely cannot be argued that a defendant may not allege the fabrication of evidence against him by a prosecution witness, because to do so would attack, not the witness's actual reputation, but his entitlement to a good reputation: Equally artificial would seem any similar limitation on the extent of cross-examination of the defendant, where permitted by the section.

### 4.13 Cross-examination relevant to guilt as charged: s. 1(e) and s. 1(f)(i)

(*e*)   A person charged and being a witness in pursuance of this Act may be asked any question in cross-examination notwithstanding that it would tend to criminate him as to the offence charged:

(*f*)   A person charged and called as a witness in pursuance of this Act shall not be asked, and if asked shall not be required to answer, any question tending to show that he has committed or been convicted of or been charged with any offence other than that wherewith he is then charged, or is of bad character, unless—

   (i)   the proof that he has committed or been convicted of such other offence is admissible evidence to show that he is guilty of the offence wherewith he is then charged; . . .

It cannot be emphasised sufficiently that cross-examination permitted by virtue of s. 1(*e*) or (*f*)(i) is permitted because of its relevance to the issue of guilt. In this respect, it differs fundamentally from that permitted by virtue of s. 1(*f*)(ii) or (iii), which affects only the credit of the defendant as a witness.

The essential test, therefore, under s. 1(*e*) or (*f*)(i) is that of relevance to the issue of guilt, and as we have seen previously (4.6–4.8, ante) that test is the same as that which governs the question of whether the prosecution may adduce evidence of character as part of their case against the defendant. We have already examined *Jones v DPP* and other authorities that illustrate this principle of relevance.

---

[26]   See *R v Dunkley* (CCA) [1927] 1 KB 323 and the rather eccentric decision in *Malindi v R* (PC, Rhodesia & Nyasaland) [1967] 1 AC 439.

[27]   See [1927] 1 KB 323 at 329. In *Jones v DPP* [1962] AC 635, Lord Devlin was equally unenthusiastic, ibid at 709–711.

**4.14    Cross-examination relevant to credit: s. 1(f)(ii)**

... unless—...

(ii) he has personally or by his advocate asked questions of the witnesses for the prosecution with a view to establish his own good character, or has given evidence of his good character, or the nature or conduct of the defence is such as to involve imputations on the character of the prosecutor or the witnesses for the prosecution; ...

Under this exception and under s. 1(f)(iii), where cross-examination is permitted by the section, it goes to the credit of the defendant only, and not to his guilt as charged. This will be considered in more detail in 4.16, after the detailed working of the two exceptions has been described.

*4.14.1  'Good character'*
It is envisaged that the defendant may attempt to establish his good character by either of the two methods described in the section, or by both together; in any such case, the shield is lost. However, what amounts to an assertion of good character may not always be easy to determine. It may be assumed that the rule will cover any evidence adduced by the defence which is not otherwise relevant to the issue of guilt and which in fact has the effect of inviting the jury to infer that the defendant is a man less likely, from whatever considerations of character, to have committed the offence charged than would otherwise have appeared to them to be the case. The most obvious case is where the defendant asserts that he has no previous convictions, or that he is a man above suspicion or of good moral character, in whatever terms, or that the offence charged is contrary to his disposition. But the assertion may be less direct, as where the defendant asserts that he is married with a family and in regular employment,[28] or that he is a religious person,[29] or that he is a member of a generally respected profession, institution, society or club[30] or that he has other attributes which people in general would be likely to think creditable.

However, it is submitted that where any such attributes are of direct relevance to the defence, apart from any assertion of good character, the defendant would not be within the scope of the exception. Thus, if a defendant charged with going equipped for burglary or theft, sought to explain his possession of certain implements by reference to his trade as a builder, it is submitted that he would not thereby 'give evidence of his good character' for this purpose, though if he went on to say that he earned his living honestly by building and had no inclination to steal, he would have exceeded his necessary assertion of his defence and put his character in issue. On a not dissimilar point, it was held in *R v Thomson* (CCA) [1966] 1 WLR 405, that where a defendant explained his running away from a police officer by saying that he had been fined, and thought that he would be arrested for non-payment of the fine, he did not assert his character, but merely accounted for an otherwise incriminating piece of evidence against him. He had not in any way misled the court, or sought to assert his character as such, and it was wrong of the trial judge to

[28]   *R v Baker* (CCA) (1912) 7 Cr App R 252; *R v Coulman* (CCA) (1927) Cr App R 106.
[29]   *R v Ferguson* (CCA) (1909) 2 Cr App R 250.
[30]   Presumably this may be impliedly asserted by appearance or dress, e.g., a school tie. It is a moot and interesting question how far a defendant may safely appear respectably or tidily dressed in court, without risking making an implied assertion of good character. Occasionally, the appellate courts have had to intervene to prevent absurd results, as in *R v Hamilton* (CA) [1969] Crim LR 486, where the trial judge wrongly ordered the defendant to remove his regimental blazer before giving evidence.

compel him to say for what offence he had been fined, and to allow cross-examination concerning his previous convictions.

### 4.14.2 'The nature or conduct of the defence'

Quite independently of the assertion of the defendant's good character, the shield will be lost if 'the nature or conduct of the defence is such as to involve imputations on the character of the prosecutor or the witnesses for the prosecution'. Such imputation may be made by cross-examination of the prosecutor or his witness or in evidence by the defendant. The use of the two words 'nature' and 'conduct' implies that the very assertion of certain lines of defence may in itself lead to the loss of the shield, as opposed to a deliberate decision to present the case in certain ways. Indeed, it has been held that even where the making of such imputations is an indispensable part of the defence, and is regretted, the shield will be lost. In *Selvey* v *DPP* (HL) [1970] AC 304, the defendant was charged with buggery with M. In addition to the allegation that no such act had ever occurred, it was suggested to M in cross-examination (inevitably, since it was the defence) that M had offered to commit buggery with the defendant in return for money, and had falsely accused the defendant when the offer was refused. It was held that the defendant had lost his shield. And in *R* v *Bishop* (CA) [1975] QB 274, where, on a charge of burglary, the defendant sought to explain his presence in a room where his fingerprints were found by alleging that he had had a homosexual relationship with the occupier, who was a witness for the prosecution, it was held that the shield was lost, even though the allegation was directed, not at discrediting the witness, but at refuting an essential element of the offence, namely that the defendant had been a trespasser in the room.

It has been recognised, however, that the strict application of s. 1(*f*)(ii) may in some cases cause the defendant a degree of prejudice out of proportion to the assistance that the jury would receive from hearing cross-examination. In *Selvey* v *DPP* the House of Lords accepted that the trial judge has a discretion to exclude or restrict cross-examination which is technically proper by virtue of s. 1(*f*)(ii). More recently, the Court of Appeal in *R* v *Britzman; R* v *Hall* [1983] 1 All ER 369, laid down guidelines to be followed in the exercise of the discretion. This is dealt with in 4.16.3.3, post.

### 4.14.3 'Imputations on the character'

It seems that any charge of faults or vices, reputed or real, will amount to an imputation on character. The classic case is, of course, the stark attribution to the prosecutor or his witness of the actual offence charged,[31] but precisely the same result will follow where the charge made involves some other offence, or, as in *R* v *Bishop*, behaviour which is not criminal, but might be thought morally discreditable, in the light of current public opinion. Consequently, the evaluation of 'imputations' should be expected to be fluid and not static. It is an open question whether, had the relationship in *R* v *Bishop* been a heterosexual one, the same result would have obtained, and whether it would have mattered whether the relationship was or was not adulterous. But where the charge is of a trivial or inconsequential nature, and involves nothing seriously discreditable, it is wrong to hold that the shield has been lost, so that the judge erred in permitting a defendant charged with assault to be cross-examined about a previous conviction for assault, merely because a prosecution witness, who admitted having been drunk on the relevant occasion,

---

[31] See e.g. *R* v *Hudson* (CCA) [1912] 2 KB 464.

was asked in cross-examination whether he had also sworn.[32]

It seems that an allegation, however expressed, which amounts to an accusation of malicious prosecution or fabrication of evidence, must constitute an imputation on character. Such charges are found in a variety of forms, such as allegations that a confession has been obtained by bribes or threats,[33] or has been fabricated,[34] or that unnecessary remands have been asked for to enable false evidence to be obtained.[35] The judge will look at the actual effect of the defence, and the loss of the shield cannot be avoided by the phrasing of questions so as to make what is in reality a clear allegation of fabrication appear to be no more than a suggestion of some innocent error.[36] It is suggested that where such serious allegations must be made in the course of the defence, the best course for counsel is to make them in unambiguous terms, and to put in the defendant's character in chief, thereby avoiding at least the unpleasant process of having it dragged out in cross-examination.[37]

By s. 66 of the Police and Criminal Evidence Act 1984, the Secretary of State is directed to issue codes of practice in connection with the exercise by the police of their statutory powers of search and seizure, detention, questioning and identification. If the law develops as it did in respect of the Judges' Rules governing those matters prior to the coming into force of the Act and the introduction of the codes of practice, it should be held that an allegation of a breach of the code of practice should not, without more, amount to an imputation on the character of the person allegedly committing the breach. Some breaches are technical in nature, and others, while affecting the rights of the defendant in a substantial way, nonetheless do not involve dishonest or immoral conduct. The nature of the breach alleged may, of course, leave no doubt that an imputation on character is being made. A failure to record in written form some peripheral details of a custodial interrogation is clearly different in degree from fabrication or falsification of a written confession. Section 66(11) makes the codes admissible in evidence in any proceedings, and they may be considered whenever relevant, but the test of an imputation should, it is submitted, remain as stated above. Section 66(10) provides that a breach of the code shall not, without more, render the person committing the breach liable to any criminal or civil proceedings, and it seems that an allegation of a breach should be construed accordingly for the purposes of deciding whether an imputation on character has been made.

Two distinctions are well established. Firstly, the mere assertion by a defendant of his innocence of the offence charged will not amount to an imputation on the character of the prosecutor or his witnesses, whereas an assertion which goes beyond what is necessary for the denial of guilt is capable of being so regarded, if in other respects it appears to amount to one.[38] If the rule were otherwise, then in many cases, the mere entering of a plea of not guilty would in itself amount to an imputation on character, because the very contesting of

---

[32]    *R v McLean* (CA) [1978] Crim LR 430. But what if the witness had been said to be, not drunk, but under the influence of drugs?

[33]    *R v Wright* (CCA) (1910) 5 Cr App R 131.

[34]    *R v Clark* (CCA) [1955] 2 QB 469.

[35]    *R v Jones* (CCA) (1923) 17 Cr App R 117.

[36]    *R v Britzman; R v Hall* (CA) [1983] 1 All ER 369; *R v Tanner* (CA) (1977) 66 Cr App R 56. The test is whether it follows from the cross-examination that the evidence has been 'made up' rather than wrongly recorded.

[37]    For the duty of counsel where he is instructed to make imputations on character, see 13.4 post.

[38]    The rule is sometimes charmingly illustrated by comparing *R v Rouse* (CCR) [1904] 1 KB 184 ('liar' held to be merely an emphatic denial of guilt) with *R v Rappolt* (CCA) (1911) 6 Cr App R 156 ('such a horrible liar that his brother would not speak to him' held an imputation).

a charge is often of necessity an assertion, at least by implication, that the witnesses on the other side are prepared to, and do in due course, commit perjury, or that they have fabricated evidence against the defendant. The rule is, therefore, necessary to the proper administration of justice, to avoid defences being inhibited by the intrusion of character in many cases. And even if the denial is couched in strong terms, the shield will remain intact if that is all it is.[39] Secondly, on a charge of rape, the defendant may assert consent on the part of the complainant to the act complained of, without losing his shield.[40]

### 4.14.4   R v Coke; R v Littleton

The rule is not always easy to apply, and there is a very fine line in some cases between denial and imputation on character. If Coke alleges that Margaret Blackstone consented to have sexual intercourse with him, that is an allegation which operates to deny an essential element of the offence charged, that is to say, that he had sexual intercourse with her without her consent. But as noted above, an allegation of consent in rape cases is considered a denial of guilt, and no more, so that Coke may challenge this part of the case without losing his shield. Of course, quite a different position would emerge if Coke went beyond that, and with leave[41] cross-examined Margaret to the effect that she was promiscuous, or had 'had it off with several of his mates' or that she had threatened dishonestly to accuse his mate Kevin of raping her the previous year. These questions would not be of direct relevance to the question of consent on the material occasion and would, in effect go only to credit. They would, therefore, bring s. 1(*f*)(ii) into play.[42] Of course, Coke would also lose his shield by bringing out Margaret's conviction for shoplifting, which would be an obvious imputation on character. It would seem, in view of the nature of Coke's previous conviction, and the unlikelihood of Margaret's credibility being affected adversely on this matter solely by her conviction for shoplifting, that any cross-examination concerned with credit would have to be directed boldly to sexual matters. In particular, the false allegation about Kevin may justify the loss of the shield, if the jury might take a very different view of Margaret as a witness, but it must be emphasised that the choice facing a defence advocate in such a case is a difficult one calling for mature judgment.

An imputation may be made, not only by cross-examination of the prosecutor or his witness, but by the defendant himself in evidence. Normally, the defendant would, in order to lend credibility to his imputation, wish to go into the witness-box and support on oath the matters which have been put on his behalf in cross-examination. If he does not, the judge is likely to comment in his summing-up, even though the prosecution may not do so in a closing speech; in any case, his absence from the box in such circumstances is unlikely to pass unnoticed by the jury. If Coke goes into the witness-box to support the allegations made against Margaret, he may be cross-examined about them. Even if no

---

[39]   *Selvey* v *DPP* (HL) [1970] AC 304.

[40]   *R* v *Turner* (CCA) [1944] KB 463; *R* v *Cook* (CCA) [1959] 2 QB 340 in which Devlin J at 347 considered rape cases to be *sui generis*. The more usual view is that an allegation of consent is mere denial of guilt: *Selvey* v *DPP* (HL) [1970] AC 304.

[41]   Leave is required to cross-examine the complainant about her sexual experience with other men: Sexual Offences (Amendment) Act 1976, s. 2

[42]   Like other cross-examination concerned with credit, Margaret's answers would be final, subject to the exceptions discussed in 13.7 post. It may be that her denial of a wrongful threat to Kevin could be contradicted. On the other hand, answers relevant to consent are not collateral, and may be contradicted by rebutting evidence: *R* v *Riley* (CCR) (1887) 18 QBD 481. They are relevant to guilt, not to credit, and this includes the complainant's voluntary sexual association with the defendant.

imputation were made on Margaret's character in cross-examination of her, or by Coke in chief, he may be drawn to make some imputation in the course of cross-examination by the prosecution. His answers in cross-examination are strictly part of the prosecution case, and not an aspect of the 'nature or conduct of the defence'[43] and it would seem to be wrong to hold that s. 1(*f*)(ii) is brought into play if he is drawn for the first time to make some involuntary remark amounting to an imputation. To that extent, Coke would be protected against remarks made by him in answer to hostile questioning. However, if in cross-examination, he merely reinforces imputations already made by him or on his behalf, and expressly repeats them, then his shield will be lost.

### 4.14.5 *'The prosecutor or the witnesses for the prosecution'*
Imputations, of whatever nature, do not fall within the terms of the section unless they relate to the character of the prosecutor or a witness for the prosecution. Thus, in *R* v *Lee* (CA) (1975) 62 Cr App R 33, the defence were entitled to cross-examine the witnesses for the prosecution with a view to showing that two men, not called as witnesses, might have been guilty of the offence charged, and did not thereby invoke s. 1(*f*)(ii). And in *R* v *Biggin* (CCA) [1920] KB 213, a murder case, it was held that the deceased, against whom allegations of improper advances were made by the defendant with a view to establishing provocation, was not 'the prosecutor' within the meaning of the section. It is, of course, only in cases of these kinds that it is likely to be of interest to the defence to make allegations against persons not called as witnesses for the prosecution, but it seems that when they arise, the imputations may be made with impunity.

### 4.15   Cross-examination relevant to credit: s. 1(f)(iii)

. . . unless — . . .
  (iii)   he has given evidence against any other person charged in the same proceedings.

### 4.15.1   *'Has given evidence against'*
What has to be considered is the effect of the defendant's evidence on the case for the co-defendant. The expression 'given evidence against' does not connote any hostile intent by the defendant towards the co-defendant. As Lord Morris of Borth-y-Gest put it in *Murdoch* v *Taylor*[44] it is irrelevant whether the evidence is 'the product of pained reluctance or of malevolent eagerness'. It is, therefore, the impact of the evidence, not the motive with which it was given, which is material; an objective assessment must be made of the effect likely to be produced on the jury.
  Lord Morris went on to say: 'If, while ignoring anything trivial or casual, the positive evidence given by the witness would rationally have to be included in any survey or summary of the evidence in the case which, if accepted, would warrant the conviction of the "other person charged . . ." then the witness would have given evidence against such other person.'
  A defendant will have given evidence against a co-defendant if his evidence either supports the prosecution case against the co-defendant in a material respect, or undermines the case for the co-defendant, thereby making it more likely that the co-

---

[43]   *R* v *Jones* (CCA) (1909) 3 Cr App R 67.
[44]   (HL) [1965] AC 574 at 584. The likelihood of one defendant 'giving evidence against' another is not by itself a ground for ordering separate trials: *R* v *Hoggins* (CA) [1967] 1 WLR 1223.

defendant will be convicted. So much was confirmed by the House of Lords in *Murdoch* v *Taylor* [1965] AC 574. In *R* v *Varley* [1981] 2 All ER 519, the Court of Appeal added guidance for trial judges called upon to determine whether a defendant is entitled to cross-examine another as to his character. Defendants A and B were jointly charged with robbery. At trial, A admitted that both he and B had participated in the robbery, but stated that he had been forced to do so by threats on his life made by B. B gave evidence that he had taken no part in the robbery and that A's evidence was untrue. The trial judge permitted counsel for A to cross-examine B as to his previous convictions, on the ground that B had given evidence against A. B appealed against his conviction on the ground that the cross-examination had been improperly allowed. Dismissing the appeal, the Court of Appeal reviewed the leading authorities, including *Murdoch* v *Taylor* and laid down the following guidelines ([1982] 2 All ER 519, 522):

> Now, putting all the reported cases together, are there established principles which might serve as guidance to trial judges when called on to give rulings in this very difficult area of the law? We venture to think that they are these . . . (1) If it is established that a person jointly charged has given evidence against the co-defendant that defendant has a right to cross-examine the other as to previous convictions and the trial judge has no discretion to refuse an application. (2) Such evidence may be given either in chief or during cross-examination. (3) It has to be objectively decided whether the evidence either supports the prosecution case in a material respect or undermines the defence of the co-accused. A hostile intent is irrelevant. (4) If consideration has to be given to the undermining of the other's defence care must be taken to see that the evidence clearly undermines the defence. Inconvenience to or inconsistency with the other's defence is not of itself sufficient. (5) Mere denial of participation in a joint venture is not of itself sufficient to rank as evidence against the co-defendant. For the proviso to apply, such denial must lead to the conclusion that if the witness did not participate then it must have been the other who did. (6) Where the one defendant asserts or in due course would assert one view of the joint venture which is directly contradicted by the other, such contradiction may be evidence against the co-defendant.

If evidence designed to assist the case of the witness also has the effect of supporting a material part of the prosecution's case against the co-defendant, which the co-defendant denies, and so does more to undermine the case for the co-defendant than that of the prosection, s. 1(*f*)(iii) will be brought into play.[45] But the subsection has produced some curious, if strictly logical results. In *R* v *Bruce and Others* [1975] 1 WLR 1252, Bruce, McGuiness and others were charged jointly with robbery, by surrounding and robbing the victim. They were convicted by the jury of theft. McGuiness's defence was that there had been a plan to rob, but that he had not been a party to it. Bruce's defence was that there had never been a plan to rob at all. The Court of Appeal held that Bruce had not 'given evidence against' McGuiness, within the meaning of the section. Although his evidence contradicted that of McGuiness, its effect, if believed, was to render it more likely that McGuiness would be acquitted, there having been no plan to commit the offence charged. It was a mere denial by Bruce of a part of the prosecution case, which McGuinesss admitted.

---

[45] *R* v *Hatton* (CA) (1976) 64 Cr App R 88.

### 4.15.2  'Any other person charged in the same proceedings'

The words 'in the same proceedings' were substituted by the Criminal Evidence Act 1979 for the original 'with the same offence', which had given rise to many problems and had, in the end, been interpreted very narrowly.[46] The new wording restores the intention of the Act, and is wide enough to cover any case where the defendants are being tried before the same court on the same occasion, and not only where they are jointly charged, in the sense that a joint enterprise in respect of one offence is alleged against them.

#### 4.15.2.1  *R v Coke; R v Littleton.*

It follows that if Coke gives evidence in his defence that he was with Littleton on 8 July 1979 and that Littleton was present in his flat during the afternoon, while he was having sexual intercourse with Margaret Blackstone, he would seriously undermine Littleton's defence of alibi and would 'give evidence against him' for the purposes of s. 1(*f*)(iii). This would entitle counsel for Littleton to cross-examine Coke about his character, under the exception.

### 4.16  Section 1(e) and (f): some general considerations

#### 4.16.1  *Evidential effect of cross-examination*

It has already been observed that an important distinction must be made between answers elicited in cross-examination under s. 1(*e*) and s. 1(*f*)(i), which deal with matters relevant to guilt, and those elicited under s. 1(*f*)(ii) or (iii), which are relevant to credit only. When summing up evidence given under s. 1(*e*) and (*f*)(i), therefore, it is appropriate to direct the jury that they may regard the evidence as part of the case against the defendant, which may go to establish some element of the offence charged, or to corroborate other evidence against him. The same direction, given in respect of evidence elicited under s. 1(*f*)(ii) or (iii) would be a serious misdirection, resulting almost certainly in the conviction being quashed.[47] The proper direction in such cases is that the evidence is relevant to the assessment of the defendant's evidence of good character, or of the likely truth or force of his imputations on character or his evidence against the co-defendant.[48] Where the jury reject evidence of good character, or find groundless some imputation on character, it is also probable and proper that they should draw some adverse inference about the defendant's general credit as a witness.[49]

#### 4.16.2  *Scope of permitted cross-examination*

Although the effect of cross-examination differs as between s. 1(*e*) and (*f*)(i) on the one hand, and s. 1(*f*)(ii) and (iii) on the other, it should not be overlooked that relevance is always a factor in defining what questions are proper cross-examination. We saw that in *Jones* v *DPP* for example (4.8, ante) the prosecution cross-examined the defendant about his giving an alibi on 'another occasion', because that was relevant to the likely falsehood of his alibi in relation to the offence charged, but did not inform the jury of the nature of that other occasion. That was a case where the cross-examination was relevant to guilt as charged. But in cases where the cross-examination is confined to the issue of the defendant's credit, relevance is, it is submitted, also the true test.

---

[46]  See, e.g., *Commissioner of Police of the Metropolis* v *Hills* [1978] 3 WLR 423; *R* v *Rockman* (CA) (1977) 67 Cr App R 171.

[47]  *R* v *Watts* (CA) [1983] 3 All ER 101; *R* v *Vickers* (CA) [1972] Crim LR 101.

[48]  *R* v *Watts* [1983] 3 All ER 101; *Maxwell* v *DPP* [1935] AC 309; *R* v *Cook* (CCA) [1959] 2 QB 340.

[49]  *R* v *Richardson; R* v *Longman* [1969] 1 QB 299.

Even where the defendant puts his own character in issue by an assertion of good character, and even though character is indivisible in such a case, the cross-examination must be relevant in the sense that it tends to rebut the defendant's character evidence. In *Maxwell v DPP* [1935] AC 309, a defendant charged with manslaughter by performing an illegal abortion that resulted in the death of the patient, testified that he was of 'good, clean moral character'. He was cross-examined to show that on a previous occasion, he had been charged with, but acquitted of a similar offence committed in similar circumstances. It was held that the questioning was improper. Although the defendant had undoubtedly put his character in issue, and although the fact that he had been charged was within the terms of s. 1 of the 1898 Act, the evidence involved no more than a previous acquittal, which did not rebut the statement made by the defendant about his character. The point is not that the defendant was being permitted to divide or conceal some aspect of his character, but that since the cross-examination did not in fact reveal anything that the jury was entitled to find discreditable to the defendant, it was simply irrelevant and obviously highly prejudicial. This does not mean that evidence of previous acquittals can never be relevant to a defendant's credit. Relevance depends upon the actual evidence given by the defendant, and it is not sufficient to assert merely that the defendant has put his character in issue in order to justify any form of cross-examination.

In the course of his speech, Viscount Sankey LC said ([1935] AC at 318–9):

As has already been pointed out, the prisoner in the present case threw away his shield and therefore, the learned counsel for the prosecution was entitled to ask him, and he could be required to answer, any question tending to show that he had committed or been convicted of or been charged with an offence, but subject to the consideration that the question asked him must be one which was relevant and admissible in the case of an ordinary witness . . .

. . . When it is sought to justify a question, it must not only be brought within the terms of the permission, but also must be capable of justification according to the general rules of evidence and in particular must satisfy the test of relevance.

In *R v Waldman*[50] the cross-examination of the defendant about both a previous conviction and a previous acquittal was upheld, where the defendant's evidence was that he had a 'good reputation for honesty'. Since reputations are affected by charges and acquittals as well as convictions, and always depend to some extent on mere rumour, the cross-examination was relevant and proper, and *Maxwell* was clearly distinguishable.

Similarly, in *Stirland v DPP* [1944] AC 315, the defendant, who was charged with forgery, gave evidence that he had never been charged with any offence whatever. He was cross-examined by means of questions which insinuated that he had left a previous employment under suspicion, whether well or ill-founded being unclear, of a different forgery. The House of Lords held that the cross-examination was improper. The defendant must fairly be understood to have meant that he had never formally been charged before a court, in which he had been truthful. The cross-examination was, therefore, irrelevant. In the course of his speech, Viscount Simon LC formulated six propositions concerning cross-examination about character, two of which, pertinent to our present discussion, the Lord Chancellor stated as follows ([1944] AC at 326–7):

[50]    (1934) 24 Cr App R 204. See also *R v Meehan and Meehan* [1978] Crim LR 690.

(2) [the defendant] may, however, be cross-examined as to any of the evidence he has given in chief including statements concerning his good record, with a view to testing his veracity or accuracy or to showing that he is not to be believed on his oath . . . . (5) It is no disproof of good character that a man has been suspected or accused of a previous crime. Such questions as 'Were you suspected?' or 'Were you accused?' are inadmissible because they are irrelevant to the issue of character, and can only be asked if the accused has sworn expressly to the contrary: see r. 2 above.

Viscount Simon had already clearly held that the questions asked of the defendant were irrelevant when judged by this test. At 324, he said:

Questions whether his former employer had suspected him of forgery were not, therefore, any challenge to the veracity of what he had said. Neither were they relevant as going to disprove good character. The most virtuous may be suspected, and an unproved accusation proves nothing against the accused, but the questions, while irrelevant both to the charge which was being tried and to the issue of good character, were calculated to injure the appellant in the eyes of the jury by suggesting that he had been in trouble before, and were, therefore, not fair to him. They should not have been put, and, if put, should have been disallowed.

The requirement of relevance applies also to cases in which the defendant does not assert his own character, but becomes liable to cross-examination about it because he has made imputations on the character of the prosecutor or his witnesses or has given evidence against a person charged in the same proceedings. The question is, about what facts may the prosecution cross-examine? In cases where the cross-examination is relevant to guilt, or where the defendant has volunteered evidence of his good character, the prosecution may appropriately cross-examine as to as much detail as is necessary to demonstrate guilt or to rebut the defendant's evidence. But in cases where the defendant has made imputations or has given evidence against a co-defendant, the sole issue should be the credit of the defendant as the author of the imputations or evidence. In order to demonstrate this, it should be necessary only to show that the defendant is, in fact, of bad character, and this is normally achieved by cross-examination as to previous convictions.

In *R v France and France* [1979] Crim LR 48, the defendants were charged with theft from a jeweller's shop, by the distinctive method of taking property while the shopkeeper's attention was distracted. The defence involved imputations on the character of the witnesses for the prosecution, and accordingly the prosecution were permitted to cross-examine one defendant as to previous convictions for offences of dishonesty. The defendant was asked, despite objection, about the method of committing a previous offence which also involved the deliberate distraction of attention in order to facilitate theft. The prosecution did not contend that the previous offence was relevant to guilt because of its similarity to the offence charged, so that the cross-examination was clearly proper only in so far as it went to the issue of credit. The conviction was quashed by the Court of Appeal, since the evidence of the detail (as opposed to the existence) of the previous conviction exceeded the bounds of relevance to credit, and would have been proper only had the prosecution been entitled to adduce it as relevant to the issue of guilt. The jury need know only that the defendant is a person of bad character, in order to assess his credit as the author of the imputations as to credit.

The report of *France* in the *Criminal Law Review* was criticised by the Court of Appeal in

*R* v *Watts* [1983] 3 All ER 101, as being corrupt when compared to the original transcript, and that Court viewed *France* with suspicion. But the Court of Appeal which decided *Watts* did not have to consider the question of the degree of detail which would have been proper, since the appeal was allowed on a more compelling ground (see 4.16.3.3, post). Even before *Watts*, *France* was distinguished by a differently constituted Court of Appeal in *R* v *Duncalf* [1979] 1 WLR 918, which, as if to suggest that some terrible curse hovers above this branch of the law, also suffers from a problem of an apparently corrupt report. Five defendants visited eleven shops in the course of a period of under an hour, and were charged with conspiracy to steal. The defence involved imputations on the character of prosecution witnesses, but the report does not clearly indicate the precise ground on which the resulting cross-examination was permitted. The court appears to have held that cross-examination was proper as to the detail, as well as the existence of the previous convictions, because they were so similar to the offence charged that the detail would in any event have been admissible as relevant to guilt as charged. This was the point of distinction of *France*. Unfortunately, the subsection referred to as justifying this in at least one report of the case ([1979] 2 All ER 1116, 1122) is s. 1(*f*)(ii), which surely must be incorrect. The report at [1979] 1 WLR 918, 924 refers to s. 1(*f*)(i) which is consistent with relevance to guilt as charged.[51]

So understood, there seems to be nothing in the curse of the corrupt reports to suggest that *France* and *Duncalf* were not correctly decided on their own facts, and they demonstrate the difference in the scope of permissible cross-examination in the different situations to which they apply.

The courts have only just begun to feel their way towards a recognition of the principle of relevance in relation to the cross-examination as to character of a defendant who has made imputations on the character of prosecution witnesses or given evidence against a co-defendant. There have, it is true, been cases where the irrelevance of certain kinds of previous convictions to the question of whether the defendant should be believed on his oath (which is the real issue in such cases) has been held to justify, or even require the exercise of a discretion by the trial judge to exclude or limit the cross-examination in order to prevent or limit prejudice. Such cases are *R* v *Watts* [1983] 3 All ER 101 and *Selvey* v *DPP* [1970] AC 304, which are examined in 16.3.3, post. It is submitted, however, that the problem could best be solved by a relevance test. If the issue is whether the defendant is worthy of belief when he contends that prosecution witnesses fabricated evidence against him, his previous conviction for perjury or an offence of dishonesty may well be relevant, but a previous conviction for indecent assault probably has nothing to do with it. If the defendant happens to be charged with indecent assault, the latter is not only irrelevant but gravely prejudicial. Yet as the law now stands, only judicial discretion stands in the way of the exclusion of that conviction. There is authority upon which a rule of relevance could be developed in such cases, which are unlike those in which the defendant asserts his good character or where the previous conviction is relevant to guilt as charged, and it is submitted that it would be highly desirable.

An attempt to formulate a rule of relevance has been made in American jurisdictions. For example, Federal Rule of Evidence 609(a), headed 'Impeachment by evidence of conviction of crime', which applies equally to a defendant called as a witness, provides:

---

[51] An interesting exegesis of the heterodoxy of the various reports of the judgment of the Court of Appeal in *Duncalf* is undertaken by Pattenden [1982] Crim LR 707, 714–717.

(a)   General rule. For the purpose of attacking the credibility of a witness, evidence
that he has been convicted of a crime shall be admitted if elicited from him or
established by public record during cross-examination but only if the crime (1) was
punishable by death or imprisonment in excess of one year under the law under which
he was convicted, and the court determines that the probative value of admitting this
evidence outweighs its prejudicial effect to the defendant, or (2) involved dishonesty or
false statement, regardless of the punishment.

Relevance under this rule is predicated either on the nature of the offence (dishonesty or
false statement) or the gravity of the offence as indicated by the possible (not the actual)
sentence, the minimum requirement as to punishment being that generally used in
American jurisdictions to distinguish felonies from misdemeanours. It is noteworthy that
in cases where the gravity of the offence is the test, the court is required to weigh the
possibility of prejudice against the probative value of the evidence, before permitting the
cross-examination. Even previous convictions for serious offences do not necessarily
indicate that the defendant should not be believed on his oath as a witness.[52]

It appears to be the practice, where evidence is relevant to credit, to permit the
defendant to be asked how he pleaded on a previous occasion on which he was convicted.
It is submitted that although some objection in terms of theory can be made to the practice
(in that it appears to admit, in the case of a plea of not guilty and subsequent conviction,
some evidence of opinion short of general reputation), the question ought to be allowed as
tending to show that the defendant's evidence must be seen, in terms of credit, as that of a
man who on a previous occasion, has unsuccessfully denied his guilt and, perhaps, been
disbelieved on his oath.

It is improper for the prosecution to cross-examine a defendant as to the legal aid
application submitted by him in relation to his legal representation at a trial, where that
application is not itself in evidence in the case. In *R* v *Stubbs*[53] the Court of Appeal allowed
an appeal against conviction where the prosecution had cross-examined a defendant to
suggest that a statement made by him in the application concerning his wife's capital was
incorrect. The defendant had put his good character in issue, and had testified that he had
no motive to commit the offence of dishonesty with which he was charged, which involved
a comparatively small sum of money, because of his wife's capital. The Court of Appeal
regarded the practice of making use of a legal aid application in this way as wrong,
pointing out that the defendant should in any event have been warned that he was not
obliged to incriminate himself by his answer, since making a false statement in a legal aid
application may amount to an offence. The careful direction of the judge that the jury
should not regard the cross-examination as affecting any issue other than credit was held
to be insufficient to cure the error.

### 4.16.3   Role of judge
All matters concerning the admissibility of cross-examination under s. 1(*e*) and (*f*) are
matters of law for the judge, who should be invited to give a ruling on the matter in the
absence of the jury before such cross-examination proceeds. The following are questions
and considerations within the province of the judge.

---

[52]   In a similar way, Federal Rule of Evidence 608, dealing with evidence of character other than
previous convictions, used to impeach a witness (including the defendant) limits such evidence to
evidence relevant to truthfulness or untruthfulness.
[53]   [1982] 1 All ER 424. See also *R* v *Winter* [1980] Crim LR 659.

*4.16.3.1 Warning.* Where a defendant proceeds in such a way as to risk exposing his character under s. 1(*f*)(ii), it is desirable that the judge should warn the defendant in good time of the possible consequences of his defence or evidence. This applies even where the defendant is represented, when the warning should be addressed to counsel.[54] For this purpose, it is desirable that the judge should be aware that the defendant is of previous bad character. The judge should be provided with a copy of the defendant's record and antecedents: *R* v *Ewing* (CA) [1983] 2 All ER 645, 649.

*4.16.3.2 Leave.* In all but the clearest cases, leave of the judge should be sought before proceeding to cross-examine under s. 1(*e*) or (*f*). Even if there is no dispute about the operation of the section, it is a matter of law for the judge whether an imputation on character has been made, or whether one defendant has given evidence against another. Of course, if the judge has already ruled previous offences admissible as similar fact, where previous matters are in issue in the case, or where the defendant has given evidence of his good character, then no leave need be asked, as there is then no question of law for the judge to determine.

*4.16.3.3 Discretion.* At common law, it was well established that the discretion of the trial judge in a criminal case to exclude admissible evidence tendered by the prosecution, on the ground that its probative value was substantially outweighed by its prejudicial effect, might be exercised so as to disallow cross-examination of a defendant as to character, even where proper as a matter of law under s. 1(*e*) or (*f*) of the Criminal Evidence Act 1898.[55] This applies only to cross-examination by the prosecution, since, as we saw in 4.15.1, ante, there is no discretion to restrain cross-examination by a co-defendant where proper under s. 1(*f*)(iii).

The discretion is particularly crucial under s. 1(*f*)(ii), in cases where the sole issue is the credit of the defendant as the author of an imputation. As Singleton J pointed out in *R* v *Jenkins* (1945) 31 Cr App R 1 at 15, there are cases in which such cross-examination 'may be fraught with results which immeasurably outweigh the result of the questions put by the defence and make a fair trial almost impossible'.

At common law, there existed one discretion that applied to prosecution evidence generally, and of which restraint of cross-examination as to character was only one example. It is probable that the discretion should in future be exercised under s. 78(1) of the Police and Criminal Evidence Act 1984, the provisions of which are set forth and discussed in 1.5.2.3, ante. This will make no difference to the guiding principles by which the discretion should be exercised.

These principles were discussed in general terms by the House of Lords in the leading case of *Selvey* v *DPP* [1970] AC 304, cited in 4.14.2, ante, for the proposition that the mere fact that the making of imputations on prosecution witnesses is an essential part of the defence does not mean that the right to cross-examine under s. 1(*f*)(ii) does not arise. The House of Lords also held that this fact does not mean that the discretion to exclude the cross-examination should automatically be exercised in favour of the defendant in such a

---

[54]   *R* v *Cook* (CCA) [1959] 2 QB 340, emphasised in *Selvey* v *DPP* (HL) [1970] AC 304. For the practice in magistrates' courts, see *R* v *Weston-super-Mare Justices, ex parte Townsend* (DC) [1968] 3 All ER 225n.
[55]   As to the exclusionary discretion in criminal cases generally at common law and under the Police and Criminal Evidence Act 1984, see 1.5.2.3, ante.

case. It would seem, however, that it is a matter which the judge should consider as part of the overall picture. Lord Guest said ([1970] AC 304, 352):

I find it unnecessary to say more on the principles on which discretion should be exercised. This guiding star should be fairness to the accused. This idea is best expressed by Devlin J in *R* v *Cook* [[1959] 2 QB 340 at 347]. In following this star the fact that the imputation was a necessary part of the accused's defence is a consideration which will no doubt be taken into account by the trial judge. If, however, the accused or his counsel goes beyond developing his defence in order to blacken the character of a prosecution witness, this no doubt will be another factor to be taken into account. If it is suggested that the exercise of this discretion may be whimsical and depend on the individual idiosyncrasies of the judge, this is inevitable where it is a question of discretion, but I am satisfied that this is a lesser risk than attempting to shackle the judge's power within a strait-jacket.

The consideration of whether what is necessary for the conduct of the defence has been exceeded will be weighed together with such other matters as the gravity of the previous offences, the prejudice that may arise if they are superficially similar to the offence charged, the length of time that has elapsed since the commission of the previous offences and the strength of the prosecution case. More specific guidelines were provided by the Court of Appeal in *R* v *Britzman; R* v *Hall* [1983] 1 All ER 369, 373. Lawton LJ said:

We hope that it will be helpful for both judges and counsel if we set out some guidelines for the exercise of discretion in favour of defendants. First, it should be used if there is nothing more than a denial, however emphatic or offensively made, of an act or even a short series of acts amounting to one incident or in what was said to have been a short interview. Examples are provided by the kind of evidence given in pickpocket cases and where the defendant is alleged to have said: 'who grassed on me this time?' The position would be different, however, if there were a denial of evidence of a long period of detailed observation extending over hours, and, just as in this case and in *R* v *Tanner* [(CA) (1977) 66 Cr App R 56], where there were denials of long conversations.

Second, cross-examination should only be allowed if the judge is sure that there is no possibility of mistake, misunderstanding or confusion and that the jury will inevitably have to decide whether the prosecution witnesses have fabricated evidence. Defendants sometimes make wild allegations when giving evidence. Allowance should be made for the strain of being in the witness-box and the exaggerated use of language which sometimes results from such strain or lack of education or mental instability. Particular care should be used when a defendant is led into making allegations during cross-examination. The defendant who, during cross-examination, is driven to explaining away the evidence by saying it has been made up or planted on him usually convicts himself without having his previous convictions brought out. Finally, there is no need for the prosecution to rely on s. 1(*f*)(ii) if the evidence against a defendant is overwhelming.

In *R* v *Watts* [1983] 3 All ER 101, a defendant of low intelligence was charged with indecent assault on a housewife, which was by no means a serious offence of its kind. At trial, he asserted, in effect though not in so many words, that the police officers had fabricated alleged oral admissions and had written a statement for the defendant in words that he had not spoken. These allegations were undoubtedly imputations on the character of the officers, and the prosecution were permitted to cross-examine the defendant to show that he had previous convictions for indecent assault on young girls. The trial judge gave the jury an essentially correct direction as to the evidential effect of the cross-examination. The Court of Appeal nonetheless allowed an appeal against conviction for reasons stated by Lord Lane CJ in the following terms ([1983] 3 All ER at 105):

> The direction was, of itself, sound in law but in the circumstances of this case it would have been extremely difficult, if not practically impossible, for the jury to have done what the judge was suggesting. The prejudice which the appellant must have suffered in the eyes of the jury when it was disclosed that he had previous convictions for offences against young children could hardly have been greater. The probative value of the convictions, on the sole issue on which they were admissible, was, at best, slight. The previous offences did not involve dishonesty. Nor were they so similar to the offence which the jury were trying that they could have been admitted as evidence of similar facts on the issue of identity . . . We cannot help feeling that if the matter had been argued before [the judge] in the absence of the jury and in the same care as that with which we have examined the case today, he would have exercised his discretion differently.
>
> There is a passage in the opinion of their Lordships in *Maxwell* v *DPP* [1935] AC 309 at 321 which seems to us to be appropriate. It is in the speech of Viscount Sankey LC. It relates, inter alia, to the exercise of the judge's discretion, and reads as follows: '. . . the question whether a man has been convicted . . . ought not to be admitted . . . if there is any risk of the jury being misled into thinking that it goes not to credibility but to the probability of his having committed the offence of which he is charged'.
>
> That exactly fits the present circumstances, and for the reasons which we have endeavoured to indicate, this grave risk was overlooked by the judge.

It is submitted that the observations of the Court of Appeal in *Watts* are capable of application to many cases in which the prosecution assume that the right to cross-examine as to character should be automatic once an imputation has been made. As suggested in 4.16.2, ante, it might be preferable to exclude some such cross-examination as a matter of law as being irrelevant. But the kind of cross-examination employed in *Watts* should surely be restrained.

### 4.16.4 Who may cross-examine

It has been assumed, thus far, that the prosecution has an interest in cross-examining under s. 1(*f*)(ii) and the co-defendant under s. 1(*f*)(iii), and this is almost invariably the case. However, nothing in the Act prevents cross-examination by the prosecution under s. 1(*f*)(iii) or by the co-defendant under s. 1(*f*)(ii), and it must be taken that these courses are possible in some cases.[56] It was specifically envisaged in *Murdoch* v *Taylor*[57] that the former course might be taken and postulated that the prosecution would be subject to the judge's discretion. Presumably, this would arise where defendant A had for any reason

---

[56] See *R* v *Russell* (CA) [1971] 1 QB 151; *R* v *Lovett* (CA) [1973] 1 WLR 241. The present decisions must be read with care, as they often turn on the now replaced wording 'charged with the same offence' in s. 1(*f*)(iii) which inhibited much cross-examination which would now be permitted under that exception.

[57] [1965] AC 574 per Lord Donovan at 593.

neglected to avail himself of the Act and where the prosecution had an interest in contesting the evidence given against him by defendant B, as being contrary to their own case against defendant B, whom they seek to cross-examine. In the latter case, presumably defendant A would wish to cross-examine to dissociate himself forcibly from some attack made upon the prosecution witnesses by defendant B, but there are obvious dangers in doing that, and it seems that the court would have a discretion to prevent such cross-examination, in a case where defendant A could not have been adversely affected by the course taken by the defence of defendant B.[58] Where defendant A gives evidence of his good character, it is submitted that he may be cross-examined on the subject on behalf of defendant B.

### 4.17  Introduction of character by co-defendant outside the Act

Although the defence must be given the fullest possible freedom to conduct the case as they see fit, the judge must hold the balance between defendants charged in the same proceedings. Evidence of character is, of course, in general irrelevant to prove guilt, and where this is so, it cannot acquire relevance to that issue merely because it is elicited for the co-defendant instead of the prosecution. It appears, therefore, that only where, exceptionally, the character of defendant A is relevant directly to the question of the guilt or innocence of defendant B is defendant B entitled to introduce it and then subject to the discretion of the judge. In *R* v *Miller and Others* (1952) 36 Cr App R 169, Devlin J allowed defendant B, who was jointly charged with defendant A with evading import duties on certain goods, to establish by cross-examination of a witness for the prosecution that defendant A had been in prison on certain dates, when the importations had come to an end. The relevance of this evidence was that it tended to show that defendant A had been principally responsible for the importations, and so strengthened the case of defendant B. This decision was approved in *R* v *Neale* (1977) 65 Cr App R 304, by the Court of Appeal. On the facts, the evidence sought to be elicited by defendant B concerning defendant A's known propensity to commit arson, was held to be irrelevant to defendant B's defence of alibi, on a joint charge of arson. Had the jury had to decide which of the two had committed arson, both being present, the result would, it seems, have been different.[59]

In all cases where the character of one defendant is not relevant to the guilt of the co-defendant, the co-defendant is not at liberty to introduce it, any more than the prosecution, unless the case falls within the exceptions provided by s. 1 of the Criminal Evidence Act 1898.

### 4.18  Inadvertent references to character

It happens not infrequently that, because of some inadvertent reference in the witness-box, or the wrongful exposure to the jury of some document, part of the bad character of a defendant is unintentionally exposed to the jury, when it is not admissible for any purpose. In such a case, the judge has power to discharge the jury and order a new trial, if application is made to him on behalf of the defendant affected, or presumably of his own motion. The question of discharge of the jury is in all cases one within the discretion of the judge. It by no means follows that the jury must in every case be discharged. The judge

---

[58]   *R* v *Lovett* (CA) [1973] 1 WLR 241.
[59]   Cf. *Lowery* v *R* (PC, Victoria) [1974] AC 85.

must weigh the gravity of the revelation to the case for the defence, and must take into account the prejudice and inconvenience which a retrial may cause to any co-defendants. If the slip is inconsequential, or occurs in the course of a long trial and is likely to be forgotten by the jury,[60] or where the matter can be dealt with by a firm direction, it will be proper to continue. It would also be manifestly right to continue where the defendant, seeing the trial go against him, 'inadvertently' lets slip something of his past record. But in general, it is submitted that the interests of justice require the discharge of the jury, the appearance of a fair trial being as important as the reality. It is difficult wholly to exclude the possibility that the jury will be influenced wrongly against the defendant.

The same principle applies where character is revealed, not directly, but by necessary implication through the adduction of other evidence. In *R v Lamb* (1980) 71 Cr App R 198, it was held that production by the prosecution of Criminal Record Office photographs from which witnesses had identified the defendant was improper, in a case where the defendant had co-operated in participating in an identification parade, and where at trial the defence had not done or said anything to provide any reason for their production. Delivering the judgment of the Court of Appeal, Lawton LJ said (ibid at 203):

> In our judgment, the production of the photographs as part of the prosecution's case and without anything being said or done by the defence, calling for or justifying the production of these photographs, was an irregularity which should not have occurred. It is not, I think, overstating the case to say that it was equivalent to the prosecution leading, as part of their case, the fact that the accused had a criminal record.

### 4.19 Spent convictions

The Rehabilitation of Offenders Act 1974 provides that in certain cases, convictions recorded against an offender shall become 'spent', and that the offender shall be treated in law as if he had not committed the offence: see s. 4(1). The section does not apply in various situations, of which one is the use of previous convictions in the course of criminal proceedings. Where, therefore, it is permissible to introduce evidence of previous convictions, the fact that a conviction is spent does not prevent its being referred to, as a matter of law. However, unless clearly cogent as similar-fact evidence or of particular relevance to credit, convictions old enough to be spent will be unlikely to carry much weight, and may often create in the mind of the jury a sense of unfairness to the defendant. Quite apart from this, it is obviously desirable that the spirit of the Act should be observed, and for this purpose, an important practice direction was issued by the Lord Chief Justice on 30 June 1975 [1975] 1 WLR 1065. The most significant provisions for present purposes are para. 4, which indicates that no reference should be made to a spent conviction 'when such reference can be reasonably avoided', and para. 6, which provides: 'No one should refer in open court to a spent conviction without the authority of the judge, which authority should not be given unless the interests of justice so require.' In *R v*

---

[60] As in *R v Coughlan and Young* (CA)(1976) 63 Cr App R 33, where the slip was 'sensibly' ignored by all concerned, and mentioned later to the judge. In the context of the trial as a whole, the error had no significance. It must always be right to approach the matter calmly, to allow a lapse of time before raising the matter, so that the significance to the jury will be minimised. It must be remembered that such questions loom larger in the minds of lawyers than of laymen and, if played down, the reference is often, in the long run, unimportant.

*Nye* (CA) (1982) 75 Cr App R 247, it was held to be wrong in principle for the prosecution to be allowed to cross-examine about convictions that are minor or remote in time.

It is also of importance to observe the provisions of s. 16(2) of the Children and Young Persons Act 1963:

> In any proceedings for an offence committed or alleged to have been committed by a person of or over the age of twenty-one, any offence of which he was found guilty while under the age of fourteen shall be disregarded for the purposes of any evidence relating to his previous convictions; and he shall not be asked, and if asked shall not be required to answer, any question relating to such an offence, notwithstanding that the question would otherwise be admissible under section 1 of the Crimi... ' Evidence Act 1898.

### 4.20 Questions for discussion

#### 4.20.1 *R* v *Coke; R* v *Littleton*

1    May the prosecution make use of Coke's previous conviction for rape, in order to assist in proving his guilt on the charge of raping Margaret Blackstone?

2    May Littleton seek to establish his good character, by way of defence? If so:

(a)    What matters may be canvassed, by way of 'character evidence' for this purpose?

(b)    By what means may Littleton establish his good character?

(c)    If Littleton were not of good character, what steps might the prosecution take to deal with a false or misleading assertion of good character by him?

(d)    What will be the evidential value of Littleton's good character, if established?

3    What advice would you give to Coke about the voluntary exposure of his character to the jury, if it were contemplated?

4    Assuming that Coke gives evidence in his defence, what would be the effect of the following:

(a)    Coke's counsel has cross-examined Margaret, seeking to show that she consented to have sexual intercourse with him on the occasion of the alleged rape?

(b)    Coke's counsel has cross-examined Margaret seeking to show that (i) she is promiscuous; and (ii) that last year, she falsely accused Kevin of raping her?

(c)    Coke's counsel has suggested to Margaret in cross-examination that she is dishonest, as evidenced by her conviction for shoplifting, and is given to telling lies?

(d)    Coke has given evidence in chief that he went to a good school and is honest and hard-working?

5    What would be the effect of the matters raised in question 4(a) (b) and (c) if Coke declined to give evidence?

6    What would be the effect of Coke's giving evidence in chief that Littleton was with him throughout the relevant Sunday, and in particular while Margaret and Angela were at his flat?

#### 4.20.2 *Blackstone* v *Coke*

1    May Margaret Blackstone give evidence at trial that she is a young woman of virtuous character, with a view to showing that it is likely that she did not consent to have sexual intercourse with Coke on the occasion in question?

2   May Coke call witnesses at trial to state that they had previously had sexual relations with Margaret, with a view to showing that it is likely that she did consent on the occasion in question?

3   May Coke introduce evidence that Margaret had sexual intercourse with Anthony Henneky, in order to show that Henneky may be the father of her child?

# 5　Similar-fact Evidence

## A: CRIMINAL CASES

### 5.1　Introduction

We saw in 4.7, ante, that evidence of bad character, while inadmissible to prove that the defendant acted in conformity therewith in relation to the offence charged, may be admissible in certain cases because it is relevant to the issue of the defendant's guilt as charged. Further, that while in some cases such evidence may be admissible notwithstanding that some aspect of the defendant's character is incidentally revealed thereby, in other cases the relevance lies in the very character evidence itself. The defendant's character is revealed, not as incidental to some other piece of relevant evidence, but because it is itself the relevant evidence. It is this latter kind of case which we shall consider in this chapter.

Cases in which the relevance of character evidence lies within the nature of the character itself are usually those involving what is termed 'similar-fact evidence', and it is with these cases that this chapter is primarily concerned. However, there are also cases in which incriminating evidence is found on the defendant or in a place or vehicle under his control, and where that incriminating evidence, while relevant by its very nature to the offence charged, suggests some aspect of bad character. These examples have usually been treated together in the authorities, rightly so, inasmuch as they are all authorities which depend on relevance, and we shall follow this practice.

In cases of similar-fact evidence, the relevance to the issue of guilt is to be found in specific and detailed aspects of the character or disposition of a person, reflected in past conduct, which is similar to the conduct now complained of to such a degree that its very similarity creates a relevance to the issue of guilt of the offence now charged. This will be the case where the prosecution can point to a previous offence which, because of its nature or the method or circumstances of its commission, bears an unmistakable resemblance to the offence charged; a similarity which transcends any matter of mere curiosity or coincidence, and which drives the jury to say 'these two offences, the previous offence and that now charged, can only be the work of one and the same person'. The features of the previous offence, when compared to those of the offence charged, reveal clearly and distinctly what is sometimes called the 'hallmark' of a particular offender. This conclusion, as opposed to the forbidden conclusion that a person merely acted in conformity with known previous character, is reached only when the features are very remarkable and the similarity very striking.

The most important use of similar-fact evidence is to rebut defences such as mistake, accident, innocent association and lack of knowledge, by proving affirmatively system, plan, knowledge or intent or identification. But despite some contrary dicta in the older cases, similar-fact evidence is not confined to such uses. Like any other relevant evidence, similar-fact evidence may be presented as part of the prosecution case, and need not await an indication of the nature of the defence. If the defendant gives evidence, he may be cross-examined about the similar-fact evidence by virtue of s. 1(*e*) and (*f*)(i) of the Criminal Evidence Act 1898, since it is evidence relevant to his guilt of the offence charged. Similar-fact evidence may also be tendered by the defence in a criminal case, and by any party in a civil case, and these matters are considered later in this chapter. However, most of the cases are concerned with the admissibility of similar-fact evidence tendered by the prosecution in criminal cases, and the principles of admissibility will, for convenience, be dealt with in that context.

It cannot be stressed too highly that, despite the variety of expressions found in the cases to describe the test of the admissibility of similar-fact evidence, some of these being helpful and some unhelpful, the ultimate and only true test is one of relevance to the issue of guilt. Indeed, it will be readily perceived that the admission of mere evidence of conformity under the guise of similar-fact evidence carries a greater potential for unfair prejudice to the defendant than any other kind of evidence. This is simply because the improper admission of evidence of similar offences or acts, while lacking real probative value, will probably so affect the jury that they may be unable thereafter to take an unbiased and dispassionate view of the case. The admissibility of similar-fact evidence and the necessary assessment of its relevance are among the most crucial of all decisions that a trial judge can be asked to make in a criminal trial. The principles must always be kept at the forefront of the discussion.

In *Makin and Makin* v *Attorney-General for New South Wales*[1] the defendants were charged with the murder of a child, whose skeleton was found in their back garden and whom they had 'adopted' from its mother in return for a sum of money, inadequate for its maintenance. The facts were consistent with the allegation that the defendants had killed the child for the maintenance, but equally were consistent with natural death followed by an irregular burial. It was held that evidence of the finding of other remains of children similarly 'adopted' by the defendants, which had been buried in the garden of a previous residence of the defendants, was rightly admitted to show the nature of the defendants' practice and so to prove the fate of the child in question. The effect of the evidence was to render any suggestion of accident or coincidence incredible by any reasonable tribunal, and thus it went far beyond mere evidence of disposition to behave in a certain way. Viewed from a positive standpoint, the evidence went to prove a systematic course of conduct characteristic of those particular defendants, which supported the allegation of their conduct in relation to the offence charged. Lord Herschell LC expressed the rule of admissibility in clear and cogent terms which have never been surpassed, saying:[2]

It is undoubtedly not competent for the prosecution to adduce evidence tending to show that the accused has been guilty of criminal acts other than those covered by the indictment, for the purpose of leading to the conclusion that the accused is a person likely from his criminal conduct or character to have committed the offence for which he is being tried. On the other hand, the mere fact that the evidence adduced tends to show the commission of other crimes does not render it inadmissible if it be relevant to

---

[1]   (PC, New South Wales) [1894] AC 57.
[2]   Ibid at 65.

an issue before the jury, and it may be so relevant if it bears upon the question whether the acts alleged to constitute the crime charged in the indictment were designed or accidental, or to rebut a defence which would otherwise be open to the accused.

## 5.2 Relevance and striking similarity

The test of admissibility of evidence of similar facts is one of relevance to the offence charged. While such probative value is found in the element of 'striking similarity' often referred to in the cases, the latter phrase has been described as no more than a convenient label, which must not be allowed to obscure the true test.[3] It remains true, nonetheless, that it is to the degree of similarity that reference must be made in order to determine the probative value of the evidence in question.

Thus, in the celebrated case of *R* v *Smith*[4], where the defendant was charged with the murder of a woman with whom he had gone through a ceremony of marriage, evidence of the deaths of two other women with whom the defendant had gone through a ceremony of marriage was held to have been rightly admitted. In each case, the deceased woman was found drowned in her bath; in each case, the door of the bathroom would not lock; in each case, the defendant had informed a medical practitioner that the woman suffered from epileptic fits; and in each case, the woman's life was insured for the benefit of the defendant. The devastating degree of similarity was relevant to the issue of the guilt of the defendant of the offence charged. Conversely, in *Noor Mohamed* v *R* [1949] AC 182, the Privy Council rejected an attempt to shore up an otherwise unpromising case by the introduction of tenuous evidence bearing only a superficial similarity to the circumstances of the offence charged. The defendant was charged with the murder of a woman with whom he lived by causing her to take cyanide — a substance which the defendant had in his possession lawfully in the course of his trade as goldsmith. There was no direct evidence that the defendant caused the deceased to take the cyanide, and there was some evidence that she might have committed suicide. Weak evidence tending to suggest that the defendant had previously killed his wife by causing her to take cyanide on the pretence that it was a cure for toothache, was held to have been wrongly admitted. There was no showing of relevance where the evidence was not strikingly similar and, indeed, tenuous in itself.

The question of admissibility is one of law for the judge, who must rule on the relevance and probative value of the evidence. If the judge decides in law in favour of admitting the evidence, he may nonetheless refuse in his discretion to admit it, if, in his opinion, its prejudicial effect would substantially outweigh its probative value. Similar fact is necessarily prejudicial to the defendant, exposing as it does a sensitive aspect of his character or disposition, and in some cases the risk of the jury being wrongly influenced by the sheer damning of the defendant's character cannot be justified by the degree of probative quality offered. If, however, the evidence is admitted, the jury must consider it

---

[3]   *R* v *Scarrott* (CA) [1978] QB 1016 at 1021–2 per Scarman LJ. *R* v *Rance, R* v *Herron* (CA) (1975) 62 Cr App R 118.
[4]   (CCA) (1915) 11 Cr App R 229. This extraordinary case may perhaps be best explained by misquoting Lady Bracknell (Wilde, *The Importance of Being Earnest*). To lose one 'wife' under such circumstances may be regarded as a misfortune; to lose a second looks like carelessness; to lose a third looks like murder. It would be hard to think of better evidence of system than that offered by the facts of the case.

in the light of the evidence as a whole.[5] The authorities seem to suggest that the requisite relevance and degree of probative value can be found if the proposed similar-fact evidence: (a) goes to the offence itself and not merely to peripheral circumstances; and (b) exhibits strikingly similar features which are not so commonplace as to be evidentially insignificant.

### 5.2.1 Similarity going to the offence itself

The similarity must relate to the offence itself, and evidence which does no more than suggest similar behaviour in other or peripheral respects should not be admitted. Thus, in *R v Rodley* [1913] 3 KB 468, the defendant was charged with housebreaking with intent to rape. It was proved that he had climbed down the chimney of a house, and was then surprised by the girl's father. His defence was that he intended only to court the girl with her consent. Evidence was held to have been wrongly admitted that an hour later, and some three miles away, he entered another house by the chimney and had sexual intercourse with a different girl with her consent. The evidence disclosed nothing of real probative value in relation to the offence charged and, in particular, nothing of relevance to the alleged intent, even though it drew attention to the defendant's somewhat individual approach to entering houses. The point was also made forcibly in the more recent decision in *R v Tricoglus* (1976) 65 Cr App R 16, in which the defendant was charged with the rape of A. A's evidence was that she had accepted a lift from a bearded man driving a Mini. Evidence was rightly admitted from G to the effect that, some twelve days before the rape of A, she (G) had been raped in the same cul-de-sac as A by a bearded man from whom she had accepted a lift. G identified the defendant's car when shown it, after some uncertainty about its make. On the other hand, evidence was wrongly admitted from M and C, who had been offered, but had refused lifts from a bearded man driving a Mini, even though there was a close connection in time and place and even though C had recorded, correctly save for one figure, the registration number of the defendant's car. The relevance lay in the commission of another offence, not merely in repeated circumstances.

However, where similar conduct is relevant to the circumstances surrounding the commission of an offence, but may not in itself amount to an offence, such evidence may be admissible if it relates not to peripheral circumstances, but to surrounding circumstances which clearly indicate an intent to commit an offence similar to that charged. Where the circumstances indicate such an intent, they may be relevant to the offence charged, even though the contemplated offence was not committed or completed on the other occasion. In *R v Barrington* [1981] 1 WLR 419, the defendant was charged with indecently assaulting three girls in the house of a woman with whom he was living, and who was alleged to have assisted in procuring the girls for him, and in some instances to have participated in the offences. The evidence revealed six distinctive features. The girls were all lured to the house as babysitters. It was represented to them that the woman with whom the defendant lived was a professional photographer. The girls were told that they could win a cash prize for posing for nude photographs. The girls were shown pornographic photographs. The defendant described himself falsely as a well-known script-writer and 'a friend of the stars'. Finally, similar efforts were made to persuade the girls to pose for nude photographs. The defence suggested that the evidence of the complainants was totally untrue. The prosecution were permitted to call three other girls to give evidence that they had visited the house in the same circumstances, and had been

---

[5]   See *DPP v Boardman* (HL) [1975] AC 421 per Lord Salmon at 463.

treated in a manner identical to the complainants, except that no indecent assault had actually been committed against them.[6] The defendant appealed against his conviction on the ground that the similar evidence did not disclose the commission of any offence on the other occasions, related to the surrounding circumstances only and should not have been admitted. The Court of Appeal upheld the conviction. Dunn LJ said:

> It is well established that, although evidence of a disposition or propensity to commit the offence with which the accused is charged is not admissible, evidence may in certain circumstances be led of similar facts tending to show that the accused is guilty of the offence charged. Such evidence has, it appears, hitherto only been admitted where it has disclosed the commission of similar offences although it has also included the surrounding circumstances. In some cases the similarity of the surrounding circumstances has been stressed more than the similarity of the mode of commission of the offences themselves. Surrounding circumstances include the preliminaries leading up to the offence, such as the mode and place of the initial approach and the inducement offered or words used.
>
> The various facts recited by the judge in this case as constituting similar facts were so similar to the facts of the surrounding circumstances in the evidence of the complainants that they can properly be described as 'striking'. That they did not include evidence of the commission of offences similar to those with which the appellant was charged does not mean that they are not logically probative in determining the guilt of the appellant. Indeed, we are of opinion that taken as a whole they are inexplicable on the basis of coincidence and that they are of positive probative value in assisting to determine the truth of the charges against the appellant, in that they tended to show that he was guilty of the offences with which he was charged.

### 5.2.2  Striking similarity in significant features

A high degree of similarity, and a similarity in features which are themselves striking and not commonplace, are essential if any probative value is to be extracted from similar-fact evidence.

Even before any question of the degree of similarity arises, the question whether the facts themselves are striking or commonplace must be examined. If they are commonplace, their similarity will have little or no significance; similarity of commonplace matters is only to be expected and has no special evidential significance. In this respect, it is particularly important to bear in mind the warning given by Scarman LJ in *Scarrott* that it is probative value, and not mere similarity, which matters. In the same judgment, Scarman LJ went on to say ([1978] QB 1016, 1022):

> Positive probative value is what the law requires, if similar-fact evidence is to be admissible. Such probative value is not provided by the mere repetition of similar facts; there has to be some feature or features in the evidence sought to be adduced which provides a link — an underlying link as it has been called in some of the cases. The existence of such a link is not to be inferred from mere similarity of facts which are

---

[6]  So, at least, it was argued and apparently accepted by the Court of Appeal. But since the 'similar-fact girls' were accosted to pose for nude photographs and at least one did so, it is not beyond argument that an indecent assault may have been committed, at any rate against the two girls who were under sixteen years of age.

themselves so commonplace that they can provide no sure ground for saying that they point to the commission by the accused of the offence under consideration.

It must also be self-evident that, unless the degree of similarity is striking, no inference can safely be drawn so as to connect the defendant with the offence charged. Anything less than striking similarity to the extent of the hallmark of a particular offender is evidence of mere disposition, and must be rejected.

## 5.3 Application of the rule

These principles are easy enough to state, but have caused some difficulty in practice in relation to sexual cases, which were for some long time viewed as being subject to special rules. Although the House of Lords has decisively rejected any special categorisation of these offences,[7] it remains desirable to examine separately the application to them of the rule, and then to look at the more straightforward history of other offences.

### 5.3.1 Sexual cases
Although now discredited, the 'special category' view was firmly held in many of the older cases, and has made one or two surprising reappearances in cases after *Boardman*. The older view probably originated in cases dealing with the discovery of incriminating evidence, the nature of which revealed some aspect of bad character, usually by suggesting a disposition towards deviant sexual conduct. In the ages in which such cases as *R v Thompson* [1918] AC 221 and *R v Sims* [1946] KB 531, were decided, it seemed, no doubt, natural enough to the appellate courts to hold that certain forms of sexual conduct were, in and of themselves, so far deviant that any repetition of them would be strikingly similar enough to be relevant to an offence charged which consisted of such conduct. As will appear from the cases cited below, this thinking spilled over from relevant incriminating evidence into evidence of similar facts, and indeed into what appears to be little more than judicially sanctioned evidence of sexual disposition ('Are you a homosexual?' and like questions).

The view can be traced back at least as far as *Thompson* v *R* [1918] AC 221, in which the defendant was charged with acts of gross indecency with boys on 16 March. The evidence was that the man who had committed the acts had made an appointment to meet the same boys at the same place and for the same purpose on 19 March. On the latter date, the defendant was arrested at the meeting-place, and said: 'You've got the wrong man.' The issue from the first to last was identification. The House of Lords upheld the admission of evidence of finding in the defendant's room photographs of naked boys, and finding on the defendant himself, when he was arrested, a powder puff. Various grounds were advanced to justify the reception of this evidence. Lord Finlay LC thought that the defendant's possession of these articles showed that he had the same 'abnormal propensities' as the man who had committed the acts on 16 March. Lord Atkinson and Lord Parker of Waddington both considered (the latter with 'some hesitation') that it was relevant to the issue of identification. But it was Lord Sumner who in the following words paved the way for an unfortunate segregation of sexual (specifically, it seems, homosexual) offences, so far as the reception of similar fact evidence is concerned (ibid at 235):

---

[7] In *DPP* v *Boardman* [1975] AC 421 at 430.

A thief, a cheat, a coiner, or housebreaker is only a particular specimen of the genus rogue, and, though no doubt each tends to keep to his own line of business, they all alike possess the by no means extraordinary mental characteristic that they propose somehow to get their living dishonestly. So common a characteristic is not a recognisable mark of the individual. Persons, however, who commit the offences now under consideration seek the habitual gratification of a particular perverted lust, which not only takes them out of the class of ordinary men gone wrong, but stamps them with the hallmark of a specialised and extraordinary class as much as if they carried on their bodies some physical peculiarity.

Although Lord Sumner's observations may have been intended to apply to specific sexual offences having relatively unusual features, there is no doubt that they were interpreted to mean that sexual offences, at least if committed against children or if involving some form of homosexual behaviour, were in themselves so distinctive as to justify the admission of evidence which on strict analysis proved no more than a fairly general sexual propensity. This interpretation had two consequences. The first was that evidence that the defendant was a homosexual became admissible to show that he committed the homosexual offence charged. The second was that evidence of homosexual behaviour on other occasions became admissible for the same purpose. Happily, both consequences have been mitigated by subsequent authority, at least to some degree.

In *R* v *King* [1967] 2 QB 338, the defendant was charged with various offences relating to gross indecency, attempted buggery and indecent assault. It was held that the answer 'Yes' given by the defendant in cross-examination to the question, 'Are you a homosexual?' was admissible, in a case where the defendant denied committing the acts alleged. The Court of Appeal held that the evidence came 'plainly within the principle' in *Thompson*. Lord Parker CJ said: 'It is no different putting to a man the question "Are you a homosexual?" from putting to him certain indecent photographs of a homosexual nature found in his possession and saying to him: "Are these yours?" ' (ibid at 346). The jury were, however, rightly directed that such evidence did not of itself mean that the defendant had committed any offence, In *R* v *Horwood* [1970] 1QB 133, some inroad was made on *King's* case. It was held that, asuming that the admission of homosexuality did not mean that the defendant had committed any offence, it was only in:

. . . very exceptional circumstances that evidence of this nature can be admitted to rebut innocent association. *R* v *King* was an exceptional case; the admitted facts were such that the admission that the defendant was a homosexual could properly be said to be relevant to the issue before the jury. In our judgment that decision cannot be taken as authority for the proposition that in all cases where a man is charged with a homosexual offence he may be asked either by the police or in the witness-box the question: 'Are you a homosexual?'[8]

In fact, it is submitted, assuming that the evidence does not mean that the defendant has

---

[8]   Ibid per O'Connor J at 139. It is not clear why the court regarded *King* as exceptional, as the principle in *Thompson* was never confined to cases where identity was in issue: see *R* v *Twiss* (CCA) [1918] 2 KB 853, and *DPP* v *Boardman* (HL) [1975] AC 421 per Lord Hailsham of St Marylebone at 452 and Lord Cross of Chelsea at 458. The answer given in *Horwood* was such as to be of no real evidential value in any event. It was: 'I used to be; I'm cured now. The doctor's given me some pills to take when the urge comes on. I go out with girls now like anyone else.'

committed the offence charged, it is difficult to see why the evidence should ever be admitted, unless the defendant denies being a homosexual or having ever committed homosexual acts and makes such denial a part of his defence. If this proposition be accepted, it must have been equally valid at the time of the decision in *Thompson*, because of the statement of principle enunciated by Lord Herschell LC in *Makin* (see 5.1).

The second consequence has proved somewhat more resilient. The cry of Lord Sumner was taken up in a number of subsequent cases, notably by Lord Goddard CJ in *R v Sims* [1946] KB 531. Sims was charged with offences of sodomy and gross indecency with four different men on different occasions. Application was made for the separate trial of these charges. The refusal of the application was upheld, on the ground that the evidence on each was relevant to and probative of each other charge. The relevant feature in such cases, it was said, lay in 'the abnormal and perverted propensity which stamps the individual as clearly as if marked by a physical deformity'. The Court of Criminal Appeal added, significantly (ibid at 540): 'Sodomy is a crime in a special category . . . On this account, in regard to this crime we think that the repetition of the acts is itself a specific feature connecting the accused with the crime.'

The court would have been prepared to extend the same rule to offences against children. In *R v Southern* (1930) 22 Cr App R 6, where the defendant was charged with one offence against a boy of thirteen and one offence some four months later against a girl of five, the Court of Criminal Appeal held that the two should have been tried separately because, '. . . although they were offences of the same class, arising from filthy lust, they were not the same in law, nor were they in fact connected except by the circumstance that the same man was accused of both'. Of this decision the court in *Sims* said: 'If the court in *Southern's* case intended to go to the length of saying that because one count related to a little boy and another to a little girl separate trials should have been granted, we are not disposed to follow the decision' ([1946] KB 531, 543–4).

The state of the law in consequence of *Thompson* was reviewed in *DPP v Boardman* [1975] AC 421. The defendant, the headmaster of a boarding school, was charged with committing buggery with S, a boy of sixteen (as to which he was convicted of an attempt) and with inciting H, a boy of seventeen, to commit buggery with him. The similarity of these offences was said to lie in the facts that both boys were pupils at the school; that the defendant disturbed both in a dormitory; that he used similar words in order to induce their participation; and that he preferred to play the passive role in the act of buggery. While both Lords Wilberforce and Cross of Chelsea described the case as 'borderline', the House of Lords held that the evidence on each charge was relevant to and probative of both that charge and the other, so that in considering each charge evidence relating to the other was admissible as similar fact.[9] Counsel for the prosecution expressly disavowed any desire to argue that the mere fact of homosexuality in itself could ever be sufficient to justify the reception of similar fact, so that the House was in effect invited to consign the basis of *Thompson* and *Sims* to the past. The House took up the challenge, holding that homosexual cases were not to be placed in any special category. As Lord Wilberforce observed (ibid at 444): 'In matters of experience it is for the judge to keep close to current mores. What is striking in one age is normal in another: the perversions of yesterday may be the routine or the fashions of tomorrow'. Lord Salmon said: 'It is plain . . . that the

---

[9] The effect of such a ruling is of course that the jury may regard the evidence on each charge as evidence in relation to both, as opposed to keeping the two separate, as in other cases of joint trial, and in the light of *DPP v Kilbourne* (HL) [1973] AC 729, the evidence may be mutually corroborative.

principles stated by Lord Herschell [in *Makin*] are of universal application and that homosexual offences are not exempt from them as at one time seems to have been supposed: see *Thompson* v *R . . . and R* v *Sims'* (ibid at 461). Accordingly, the law is that in any criminal case, evidence of similar facts may be admitted as probative of the offence charged if such probative value can be demonstrated from the striking similarity of the facts to the offence charged. The point was also made by Lords Hailsham of St Marylebone and Cross of Chelsea that no logical distinction could be drawn between cases where the defendant advanced the defence of 'innocent association' and cases of complete denial of the offence charged.

The emphasis on the relevant features, rather than the nature of the offence charged was neatly expressed by Lord Hailsham as follows (ibid at 454):

> . . . whilst it would certainly not be enough to identify the culprit in a series of burglaries that he climbed in through a ground-floor window, the fact that he left the same humorous limerick on the walls of the sitting room, or an esoteric symbol written in lipstick on the mirror, might well be enough. In a sex case, to adopt an example given in argument in the Court of Appeal, whilst a repeated homosexual act by itself might be quite insufficient to admit the evidence as confirmatory of identity or design, the fact that it was alleged to have been performed wearing the ceremonial head-dress of a Red Indian chief or other eccentric garb might well in appropriate circumstances suffice.

The application of these apparently clear principles since *Boardman* has, however, proved unexpectedly erratic; unexpectedly because of the promising start made by *R* v *Novac and Others*.[10] One defendant had on various occasions met boys in places of amusement, had offered them money to play gambling machines and then shelter at his home. The defendant then committed acts of buggery and attempted buggery while sharing a bed with the boys. Of this evidence, Bridge LJ said (ibid at 112):

> We cannot think that two or more alleged offences of buggery or attempted buggery committed in bed at the residence of the alleged offender with boys to whom he had offered shelter can be said to have been committed in a uniquely or strikingly similar manner. If a man is going to commit buggery with a boy he picks up, it must surely be a commonplace feature of such an encounter that he will take the boy home with him and commit the offence in bed. The fact that the boys may in each case have been picked up by [the defendant] in the first instance at amusement arcades may be a feature more nearly approximating to a 'unique or striking similarity' within the ambit of Lord Salmon's principle [in *Boardman*]. It is not, however, a similarity in the commission of the crime. It is a similarity in the surrounding circumstances and is not, in our judgment, sufficiently proximate to the commission of the crime itself to lead to the conclusion that the repetition of this feature would make the boys' stories inexplicable on the basis of coincidence.

The sex offender in the Red Indian head-dress was referred to by the trial judge in *Novac* in his summing-up, without disapproval by the Court of Appeal. Nonetheless, his war cry went unheeded in *R* v *Johannsen*,[11] in which, although the facts were virtually

---

[10]   (1976) 65 Cr App R 107 (CA, Bridge LJ, Wien and Kenneth Jones JJ).
[11]   (1977) 65 Cr App R 101 (CA, Lawton LJ, Nield and Boreham JJ).

indistinguishable from those of *Novac*, the decision in *Novac* appears not to have been cited to the court. The result was a regression to the *Thompson/Sims* approach. The court dealt with the argument for the appellant that there was no striking similarity sufficient to admit similar fact, in these terms (ibid at 103):

> We do not find it necessary to set out in much detail the sordid evidence given in this case . . . The prosecution's case was that between May and December 1975 he made a practice of accosting boys in amusement arcades and similar places, offering them money or a meal or treating them to a game, taking them to his accommodation or on to the beach, and there committing the offences charged. His particular homosexual propensities were to handle the boys' penises and getting them to do the same with his, fellatio and buggery . . . We have no hesitation in deciding that there were striking similarities about what happened to each of the boys — the accostings in the same kind of places, the enticements, the visits to his accommodation, his homosexual propensities and his ways of gratifying them.

Faced with this outright conflict of approach, yet another Court of Appeal in *R v Scarrott*[12] made it plain that each case must be looked at on its own facts, and that no general rule could be laid down so as to be given the status of a rule of law, except the need to find in any case, as a condition of admissibility, that the similar-fact evidence became, on the facts of the case considered as a whole, probative of the offence charged. Both *Novac* and *Johannsen* were cited to the court. Scarman LJ, referring to, 'I hesitate to say a striking similarity, but certainly a remarkable similarity between the salient facts' of the two, observed that 'it is very difficult to determine why or how the court reached the decision that it did in these cases'. This difficulty arose not because of any error in either the decisions or the reports of them, but because each had been determined after a proper investigation of its own facts, and by the drawing of a line on the basis of those facts.

It is submitted that the Court of Appeal, differently constituted, has varied in its approach to the law, and while each case must indeed turn on its own facts, *Johannsen* is irreconcilable with the principles laid down in *Boardman* and should not be followed. There is some sign that the Court will prefer the approach in *Novac*. In *R v Inder* (1977) 67 Cr App R 143, a conviction was quashed where the features said by the prosecution to display a 'uniquely or strikingly similar' quality, were in fact no more than the 'stock in trade of the seducer of small boys' and were such as 'appear in the vast majority of cases that come before the courts'. And in *R v Clarke* (1977) 67 Cr App R 398, the court held that three counts alleging attempted buggery and indecent assault on the defendant's stepson should have been severed from four counts of sexual offences against his stepdaughter, not because the sexes of the children differed, but because no sufficient similarity was shown by the evidence. It is submitted that the difference in sex must be one factor to be taken into account in applying the test, but clearly need not be the only nor even the dominant factor.

### 5.3.2 Cases other than sexual cases
Outside the sphere of sexual cases, the application of the relevance test has been rather less difficult to follow. The examples which follow are offered for the purpose of illustrating the application in certain specific types of case.

---

[12] [1978] QB 1016 (CA, Roskill and Scarman LJJ and Wien J). Wien J had been a member of the court in *Novac*.

In *R* v *Straffen*[13] the defendant was charged with the murder of a girl, a murder committed during a fairly short period of time when he was an absconder from Broadmoor. Evidence was rightly admitted that the defendant had twice previously killed small girls by the same method (strangulation) and had left their bodies in a substantially similar condition, i.e. unconcealed and sexually unmolested. In *R* v *Morris* (1969) 54 Cr App R 69, indecent photographs taken of a girl by the defendant, who had pleaded guilty to the indecent assault of that girl, were admitted on a charge of the murder of a different girl, where the photographs bore a striking resemblance to the appearance of the dead body of the murdered girl on its discovery.

In *R* v *Mansfield* [1978] 1 WLR 1102, the defendant was charged, *inter alia*, with three counts of arson. The fires were started within a period of three weeks, the first in an hotel where the defendant lived, the second and third in an hotel where he worked as a kitchen porter. In each case, the method of starting the fire was distinctive; in each the defendant had an opportunity to start the fire; in each case, he was seen nearby acting suspiciously, and lied to the police when questioned; and in the case of the third fire, a waste-paper bin from the defendant's room was found near the site of the fire. It was held that evidence of each fire was admissible in relation to each count, and accordingly that the trial judge had rightly refused to sever the indictment.

In *R* v *Rance; R* v *Herron* (1975) 62 Cr App R 118, Rance, the managing director of a building company, was convicted of corruptly procuring the payment of money to Herron, a local councillor (who was convicted of corruptly receiving the money). This payment had been procured by means including the signature by Rance of a false certificate describing Herron as a 'subcontractor'. Rance said that he must have been deceived into signing the certificate. Evidence was rightly admitted of similar payments to other councillors supported by other false certificates. It is noteworthy that the Court of Appeal held that the mere existence of some dispute about the similar-fact evidence (in this case, the defendant said that he believed the other certificates to be genuine) did not prevent the evidence from being admitted. This factor does, of course, set one additional problem for the jury to solve. It would seem that even a dispute about the facts themselves, as opposed to the defendant's state of mind, would not prevent similar-fact evidence from being adduced. Naturally, if the jury did not find the similar facts proved, they would be irrelevant and of no evidential value.

It may be seen from *R* v *Mustafa* (1976) 65 Cr App R 26, and from *R* v *Seaman* (1978) 67 Cr App R 234, that even in offences of a much more common type, such as theft, evidence of similar facts may be admissible to show system or identification, where the degree of distinctiveness is high. In a commonplace offence, however, it seems that only a peculiarly distinctive *modus operandi* would suffice to distinguish the particular characteristics of the offence from the multitude of necessarily similar offences committed by others under the like circumstances. In a common offence, it must always be proportionately harder to argue in favour of relevance based on any hallmark of a particular individual offender, and the risk of prejudice is obviously very considerable.[14]

---

[13]   (CCA) [1952] 2 QB 911. See also *R* v *Evans* (CCA) [1950] 1 All ER 610.
[14]   One of the arguments on appeal in *Mustafa* related to prejudicial effect, it being undisputed that the evidence had probative value because of a high degree of similarity. The decision in *Seaman*, which amounted to no more than successive shoplifting exhibitions, must surely be open to grave question.

## 5.4    Similar-fact evidence called for defence

The defence may, of course, adduce any relevant evidence in the same way as may the prosecution. This may include similar-fact evidence. The difficulty arises when, as is usually the case, that evidence is tendered in order to produce an adverse effect on the case for a co-defendant. As we saw in Chapter 4, one defendant is permitted to cross-examine a co-defendant about his character only when permitted by s. 1(*f*)(iii) of the Criminal Evidence Act 1898, in cases where the co-defendant has given evidence against the cross-examining defendant. The character of the co-defendant is otherwise protected by the shield. It follows that a defendant may adduce evidence revealing the character of a co-defendant only when that evidence is relevant. It is submitted that, in these circumstances, relevance must mean not only that the evidence tends to support the prosecution case against the co-defendant (which may be irrelevant to the issue of the guilt of the defendant), but also that the guilt of the co-defendant is relevant to the issue of guilt of the defendant, for example because the offence charged must have been committed by one or other, but not both of them.

There can be little doubt that similar-fact evidence, or other relevant evidence of character or disposition, will rarely be admissible for this purpose, since only in comparatively unusual cases will the guilt of one defendant necessarily point to the innocence of another. It is submitted that it would not be enough that two defendants are seeking to blame each other for the offence, unless the guilt of one must lead to the inescapable conclusion that the other must be innocent, so that the guilt of one is plainly relevant to the innocence of the other. In many cases, although defendants blame each other, the evidence is perfectly consistent with the guilt of all, so that evidence adduced by one defendant which incriminates another may be evidence of the other's guilt but may also be irrelevant to the issue of the innocence of the defendant adducing the evidence. It may be arguable in some situations that a defendant may be entitled to adduce evidence tending to show that a co-defendant played a major role in the offence charged. But the unusual nature of the circumstances in which similar-fact evidence is admissible for the defence when it has the effect of revealing the character of a co-defendant may be illustrated by *Lowery* v *R*[15].

The facts were that one of two defendants, and no one else, had undoubtedly murdered a girl for no reason other than the sadistic pleasure of the killing. Evidence was adduced by one defendant from a psychologist, who testified that it was more likely that the co-defendant had committed the offence, because the co-defendant had an aggressive personality and limited self-control. The Privy Council held that the evidence had been rightly admitted, in that it showed not just that the co-defendant acted in conformity with his known disposition in relation to the offence charged, but was relevant to the issue of the guilt of the defendant adducing the evidence in a case where the jury had to decide specifically which of the two defendants had committed the offence. The evidence tendered in *Lowery* was, of course, evidence of disposition rather than similar-fact evidence, but there is no reason why the principle should not apply to any relevant evidence.

Mindful of the unusual facts of *Lowery*, the courts have scrutinised such evidence with great care, and have applied the test of relevance strictly. In *R* v *Neale* (1977) 65 Cr App R

---

[15]    (PC Victoria) [1974] AC 85. See also *R* v *Rimmer and Beech* [1983] Crim LR 250; *R* v *Bracewell* (1978) 68 Cr App R 44.

304, the defendants were charged with arson. The defence of defendant A was that he was not present when the fire was set. The trial judge rejected evidence tendered by defendant A tending to show that defendant B had previously set fires in similar circumstances. On appeal, the trial judge was upheld. Although such evidence would undoubtedly assist in the conviction of defendant B, it had no relevance to the innocence of defendant A, which was based entirely on his alibi. So far as the defence of alibi was concerned, the question of who set the fire was irrelevant. Had A's defence been that he was present, but that B had set the fire, the result might well have been different.[16]

## B: CIVIL CASES

### 5.5  Application to civil cases

Although it has been said that in civil cases, even where similar-fact evidence is technically admissible, the court has a discretion, and should refuse to admit it unless it would not only 'afford a reasonable presumption as to the matter in dispute, but would be reasonably conclusive, and would not raise a difficult and doubtful controversy of precisely the same kind as that which the jury have to determine',[17] the rule in modern times is almost certainly the same as that in criminal cases. Now that jury trial is comparatively rare in civil cases, the judge has ample power to reject evidence which will not assist him in the determination of the pleaded issues, and can deal with the likelihood of prejudice in the same way.

The position was stated by the Court of Appeal in *Mood Music Publishing Co. Ltd v De Wolfe Ltd* [1976] Ch 119. The plaintiffs were the owners of the copyright in a musical work called 'Sogno Nostalgico'. They alleged that the defendants had infringed such copyright by supplying for broadcasting a work called 'Girl in the Dark'. It was not disputed that the works were similar, but the defendants contended that the similarity was accidental, and denied copying, even though 'Sogno Nostalgico' was composed prior to 'Girl in the Dark'. It was held that evidence was relevant and admissible to show that on other occasions the defendants had reproduced works subject to copyright; one of the three relevant occasions being a reproduction by the defendants as a result of an 'entrapment' set up by the plaintiffs for the express purpose of obtaining evidence against the defendants. Lord Denning MR said (ibid at 127):

> The criminal courts have been very careful not to admit such evidence unless its probative value is so strong that it should be received in the interests of justice: and its admission will not operate unfairly to the accused. In civil cases the courts have followed a similar line but have not been so chary of admitting it. In civil cases the courts will admit evidence of similar facts if it is logically probative, that is, if it is logically relevant in determining the matter which is in issue: provided that it is not oppressive or unfair to the other side: and also that the other side has fair notice of it and is able to deal with it.

No better contrast could be provided than that in a sequel to the *Mood Music* case,

---

[16]  For a case in which evidence was rejected because of insufficient probative value, see *R v Nightingale* [1977] Crim LR 744.
[17]  *Managers of Metropolitan Asylum District v Hill and Others (Appeal No. 1)* (HL) (1882) 47 LT 29 at 35 per Lord Watson. See also *Attorney-General v Nottingham Corporation* [1904] 1 Ch 673.

namely *E. G. Music* v *S.F. (Film) Distributors* [1978] FSR 121, in which the third defendants had been the defendants in the *Mood Music* case. The plaintiffs sought discovery of all the infringements alleged in *Mood Music* with a view to their admission as similar-fact evidence in relation to the infringement alleged in the instant case. Whitford J rejected the application on the ground that such evidence was relevant only to the credit of the third defendants and was not relevant to any issue on the pleadings.

Other examples of the same principles are given below, the rule of admissibility being the same.

Where it is relevant, to prove the behaviour of an animal, in addition to the conduct of the animal on the relevant occasion, its conduct of a similar nature on other occasions may be admitted.[18]

In cases of libel, prior libels of the plaintiff written by the defendant are admissible to prove actual malice or deliberate publication, as are the circumstances surrounding publication of such prior libels.[19]

In *Sattin* v *National Union Bank* (1978) 122 SJ 367, a plaintiff who claimed in respect of the loss by the defendant bank of a diamond which he deposited with them as security for an overdraft, was held to be entitled to adduce evidence of another occasion when jewellery so deposited had been found to be missing. The Court of Appeal's decision was based on the relevance of the evidence to rebut the defence that the defendants had used reasonable safeguards in securing the property deposited with them by customers.

## C: GENERAL CONSIDERATIONS

### 5.6 Uses of similar-fact evidence

In the older cases, great importance was attached to the purpose for which similar-fact evidence was sought to be admitted, and in particular, it was held that it could be admitted only for the purpose of rebutting a defence actually raised by the defendant, such as mistaken identity, coincidence, innocent association and the like, which defences were clearly open to attack by evidence of strikingly similar behaviour on other occasions. As Lord Sumner said in *Thompson* v *R* [1918] AC at 232: 'The mere theory that a plea of not guilty puts everything material in issue is not enough for this purpose. The prosecution cannot credit the accused with fancy defences in order to rebut them at the outset with some damning piece of prejudice.'

However, once it is accepted that the test of admissibility is one of relevance and probative value in relation to the offence charged, there can be no logical basis for forbidding the prosecution to adduce similar-fact evidence unless and until some specific defence is raised. If the evidence is no more than 'prejudice' then it should not be admitted in any event. And in more recent authorities, a more consistent approach has been adopted which has now replaced the older rule. In *R* v *Sims* Lord Goddard CJ put the matter very clearly [1946] 1 KB 531, 539:

It has often been said that the admissibility of evidence of this kind depends on the nature of the defence raised by the accused . . . If one starts with the assumption that all evidence tending to show a disposition towards a particular crime must be excluded

---

[18] *Osborne* v *Chocqueel* (DC) [1896] 2 QB 109 (a bulldog).
[19] *Barrett* v *Long* (HL) (1856) 3 HL Cas 395.

unless justified, then the justification of evidence of this kind is that it tends to rebut a defence otherwise open to the accused; but if one starts with the general proposition that all evidence that is logically probative is admissible unless excluded, then evidence of this kind does not have to seek a justification but is admissible irrespective of the issues raised by the defence, and this we think is the correct view.

Although this statement met some criticism as going rather too far,[20] it is undoubtedly the basis of the present law. The position was confirmed in the case of *Harris* v *DPP* [1952] AC 694, in which it was held that the words 'logically probative' do not open the door to unlimited evidence of disposition, but are apt to mean that the prosecution are not required to wait until the defendant has actually raised a specific defence. Indeed, in the absence of the evidence of similar facts, he may never be called upon to raise any defence because of lack of evidence against him. The prosecution are entitled to present as part of their case any evidence which is relevant and admissible to prove the charge on the facts given, including any issue necessarily raised by the facts or which may properly be anticipated on the facts. To do so, observed Viscount Simon, at p.709, 'involve[s] no extension of the principle in *Makin'*, and as was observed in *Noor Mohamed*, could hardly be described as "credit[ing] the accused with fancy defences"' ([1949] AC 182 at 191). Thus, once an issue is fairly before the court on a plea of not guilty, the evidence of similar facts, if admissible at all, is admissible at the outset. As long as this rule is understood, there can be little harm in cataloguing the issues to which similar-fact evidence can be said to go, but it would be a mistake to suppose that the catalogue can ever be a closed one.

One of the areas which has caused problems is that of the complete denial by the defendant that the act complained of ever took place at all. In *R* v *Chandor* [1959] 1 QB 545, where the defendant was charged with offences against one boy in Croydon and against another in the Lake District, to which the defence was a complete denial, it was held that a succession of incidents was irrelevant to determine whether the incident had ever occurred, though such evidence might have been highly relevant on an issue of identity, intent or innocent association. The decision was followed in *R* v *Flack* [1969] 2 All ER 784, where the defendant was charged with three offences of incest with three different sisters, which he completely denied. It was held that the evidence on each charge was relevant to and admissible as evidence on that charge only. These cases drew comment in *DPP* v *Boardman* both from Lord Hailsham of St Marylebone and Lord Cross of Chelsea. Lord Hailsham failed to see the logical distinction between cases of innocent association or the like and complete denial, 'since the permutations are too various to admit of universally appropriate labels' ([1975] AC 421, 452). Lord Cross said, perhaps more helpfully (ibid at 458):

> If I am charged with a sexual offence why should it make any difference to the admissibility or non-admissibility of similar-fact evidence whether my case is that the meeting at which the offence is said to have been committed never took place or that I committed no offence in the course of it? In each case I am saying that my accuser is lying . . . In *R* v *Chandor* and *R* v *Flack* the Court of Appeal approved the distinction between the two types of defence for the purposes of the admission of similar-fact evidence. But though the decisions in these two cases may well have been correct, I cannot, as at present advised, agree with that part of the reasoning in them.

[20]   See, e.g., *Noor Mohamed* v *R* (PC, British Guiana) [1949] AC 182 at 194, and by Lord Goddard CJ himself in *R* v *Hall* (CCA) [1952] 1 KB 302 at 306.

Professor Elliott [1983] Crim LR 284, 293, draws attention to the interesting New Zealand case of *Holloway* [1980] 1 NZLR 315. The defendant was charged with rape. The complainant stated that she answered an advertisement in a newspaper for a live-in housekeeper; that when she arrived at the defendant's house, the defendant was drinking and violent; that he made her take a bath and then raped her. The prosecution proposed to call seven other women whose treatment at the hands of the defendant was strikingly similar, including the detail of the compulsory bath, save that the nature of the sexual impropriety varied. However, the defendant intimated to the court by counsel that the defence would be one of consent, and on this basis, the trial judge rejected the evidence tendered as irrelevant to the issue of consent. Had the defendant denied that the incident had ever taken place, the relevance of the similar-fact evidence would perhaps have been more readily apparent, but it is submitted that even on the issue of consent, it could be argued that the evidence showed a degree of planning and intent on the part of the defendant, which might have led the jury to view any evidence given by the complainant and the defendant in a very different light.

It is submitted that the view of Lord Cross in *Boardman* is to be preferred, although the nature of the defence may well influence the judge in the exercise of his discretion in any case where the probative value is less than extremely cogent. The risk of prejudice in the case of literal total denial, is obvious and serious.[21]

The other problem lies in the admissibility of incriminating articles found in the possession of the accused. The decision in the case of *Thompson* v *R* [1918] AC 221, is clearly open to criticism in the light of the more modern approach to evidence of disposition and similar facts, but has never been abrogated. It has indeed been followed in a number of cases. The justification in *Thompson's* case was principally that the finding of the articles went to rebut the defence of mistaken identity, but it may be that if the rule is still in force, such evidence has now become generally admissible from the outset. In *R* v *Reading and Others* [1966] 1 WLR 836, the articles were such as to connect the defendant with a certain robbery, and there was admitted evidence of possession of articles stolen in the course of such robbery, which clearly linked the defendant with the robbery. And more recently, in *R* v *Mustafa* (1976) 65 Cr App R 26, the principle was used to justify the reception of evidence that a stolen Access card had been found (in a Barclaycard holder) at the defendant's home, a week after two successful thefts which it was alleged the defendant had committed by using a stolen Barclaycard and forging the signature of its holder.

The rationale of *Reading* and *Mustafa* is no doubt the specific probative value afforded by evidence of the possession of the articles in question. The real criticism of *Thompson* may be, not the time at which the evidence would now become admissible, but the likelihood that the evidence itself might now be regarded as doing no more than showing a fairly general disposition. It is submitted that the case should not now be followed.

### 5.7   Forms of similar-fact evidence

The admissibility of similar-fact evidence does not depend on whether the defendant has previously been charged with an offence in relation to the similar conduct, or on what the verdict may have been, if he has been charged and tried. Of course, the jury are free to accept or reject the evidence tendered, as they are free to accept or reject any other evidence in the case. If the defendant was charged and tried, but acquitted in respect of the

---

[21]   This view is also held by the editors of Phipson, 13th ed., para. 12–24.

similar conduct, it may be that its weight would be very seriously compromised, although the circumstances of the previous conduct might remain relevant to the offence charged. As we have already observed (see *R* v *Rance and Herron* (1975) 62 Cr App R 118 and 5.3.2, ante), the fact that the defendant disputes the similar-fact evidence does not render it inadmissible. In civil cases, it is more likely that the previous conduct will not amount to a criminal offence, but may constitute tortious or other wrongful conduct. This does not affect the admissibility of the evidence, if relevant.

An important question is whether, if the defendant has been convicted of an offence in relation to the previous conduct, the prosecution may prove the fact of the conviction, in addition to proving the conduct itself. As a matter of common sense, it would seem appropriate for the jury to know that they are not dealing with mere unproved allegations, particuarly if the defendant seeks to dispute the facts of the previous conduct. Moreover, the wording of s. 1(*f*)(i) of the Criminal Evidence Act 1898 would seem to indicate that the fact of conviction may be cross-examined to where relevant to the issue of guilt, and in keeping with the general rule the prosecution should be able to adduce as part of their case matters as to which they would be entitled to cross-examine the defendant. Nonetheless, it has been argued that, since the conviction represents no more than the opinion of another court, it should be inadmissible. Both from a theoretical and a practical standpoint, there are substantial reasons in favour of allowing the fact of the conviction to be proved, and this has commonly been the practice in criminal courts.

Some doubt was cast on this practice by the decision of the Court of Appeal in *R* v *Shepherd and Shepherd* (1980) 71 Cr App R 120. The defendants were charged with harrassment of a tenant and his family who lived in their house. The same tenant gave similar-fact evidence about other acts of harrassment not covered by the indictment, the purpose of the evidence being to prove intent on the part of the defendants. When the defendants disputed this evidence, the prosecution proved that the defendants had previously been convicted of harrassment, based upon the same testimony by the tenant. Despite the fact that the trial judge clearly directed the jury that assessment of the similar-fact evidence was entirely a matter for their decision, the Court of Appeal held that, assuming that the similar-fact evidence was in itself admissible, the fact of the conviction should not have been adduced. The conviction was quashed. The judgment of the Court is, with respect, very far from clear in its reasoning. It appears that the basis of the decision was that the conviction showed that the word of the tenant had been preferred to that of the defendants on another occasion, which might predispose the jury against the defendant, and which in any case amounted to the inadmissible opinion evidence of the previous convicting court.

It may be that *Shepherd* can be explained as a case on its own facts. It is certainly significant that the similar-fact evidence came from the same tenant, though this is not an unknown situation in similar-fact cases, and has never previously been thought to alter the court's approach to the admissibility of relevant evidence. It may also be argued that harrassment of tenants is an unusual offence, in that it involves evidence as to occurrences over a period of time, and in that the question of intent is very important. The purpose of the similar-fact evidence was, of course, to show intent and there is nothing in the report to suggest that it was not admissible for this purpose.[22]

---

[22]   The Court did not consider whether the previous conduct, in itself, was admissible as similar-fact evidence, finding that it was unnecessary to do so in the light of its decision as to the admission of the conviction.

Of particular interest is the court's reference to the dictum of Lord Sankey LC in *Maxwell* v *DPP* [1935] AC 309 at 321, that '. . . the question whether a man has been convicted, charged or acquitted ought not to be admitted, even if it goes to credibility, if there is any risk of the jury being misled into thinking that it goes not to credibility but to the probability of his having committed the offence of which he is charged' (71 Cr App R at 124). It seems, with respect, that the Court failed to appreciate that *Maxwell* was a case concerned only with credibility, and in which the evidence of character could not have been admissible as relevant to the issue of guilt. The dictum of Lord Sankey LC cannot, therefore, be taken as referring to cases where similar-fact evidence is admitted as relevant to the issue of guilt. Indeed, if so understood, it would nullify the admissibility of such evidence entirely. *Maxwell* appears, from the report in the Criminal Appeal Reports, to be the only case dealing with character evidence referred to by the Court in giving judgment.

Although the common-law position has been confused by *Shepherd*, it is submitted that statute has now provided a solution. By s. 74(3) of the Police and Criminal Evidence Act 1984, where relevant, proof that a defendant was convicted of a previous offence is now admissible to show that the defendant did in fact commit that offence, and he shall be taken to have committed that offence unless the contrary is proved. Since similar-fact evidence is admitted because of its relevance to guilt as charged, there would seem to be no reason why this section should not apply to offences admitted as similar-fact evidence. This section is considered further in 9.15.2 post.

The test of admissibility being one of relevance, evidence of facts which occurred subsequent to those forming the subject-matter of the instant charge are equally capable of having a probative value, and may accordingly be admitted. Thus in *R* v *Geering* (1849) 18 LJMC 215, on a charge of murder by the defendant of her husband using arsenic, evidence was rightly admitted of the subsequent death by arsenic poisoning of two of the defendant's sons and the illness of a third from the same cause, the defendant being responsible for the food of all the victims during the relevant period.

The similar-fact evidence can and should be proved as part of the prosecution case. If the defendant gives evidence, he may be cross-examined as provided by s. 1 of the Criminal Evidence Act 1898 (proviso) (*e*) and (*f*)(i).

### 5.8 Questions for discussion: *R* v *Coke*; *R* v *Littleton*

1  Is there some striking similarity in Coke's previous conviction for rape, which would give rise to probative value on the present charge?

2  If so, of what does it consist?

3  Is it of importance for any purpose that Coke's defence is one of consent?

4  Is the judge likely to exercise his discretion to exclude the evidence?

5  At what stage would the prosecution be entitled to lead the evidence, and would it make any difference that Coke would be shown to have a previous conviction?

6  If Margaret Blackstone had previously had sexual intercourse with Coke, but denied this in cross-examination, could Coke adduce evidence of such acts as part of his case?

7  Can Coke prove as part of his case that last year, Margaret threatened to complain falsely that she had been raped by his mate, Kevin?

# 6   *The Rule Against Hearsay–I*

## A: THE RULE AGAINST HEARSAY

### 6.1   Theory and development of the rule

The rule against hearsay is one of the most important and commonly applied rules of the law of evidence, and yet at the same time, the least understood by students, the profession and the judiciary. The rule against hearsay may be stated simply and comprehensibly, even if not with complete immunity from academic attack, in the following terms: evidence by any witness of what another person stated (whether verbally, in writing or otherwise) on any prior occasion is inadmissible for the purpose of proving that any fact stated by that other person on that prior occasion is true. Much of the difficulty which the rule seems to cause is the result of forgetting that the rule against hearsay does not exclude statements made by others on prior occasions for all purposes, but only when tendered for the purpose of proving that some fact so stated is true. For any other relevant purpose, for example to prove that the statement was in fact made, was made on a given occasion or in a certain way, or had a certain legal effect, such evidence may be freely admitted, if necessary with a limited admissibility direction to the jury. We shall have much to say about the importance of distinguishing the purpose of the evidence later in this chapter. In its simplest terms, the rule means that if you wish to prove that a fact is true, you can call A to state, basing himself upon his own knowledge or observation, that the fact is true, but you cannot call B to state that A told him that the fact is true.

Similarly, American Federal Rule of Evidence 801(c) provides that 'hearsay'

. . . is a statement, other than one made by the declarant while testifying at the trial or hearing, offered in evidence to prove the truth of the matter asserted.

The rule derives from an awareness that hearsay, if admitted, would carry with it at least two formidable difficulties: first, that evidence consisting of a communication made to the witness by someone else has the inherent danger of unreliability through repetition, the danger increasing in proportion to the number of communications involved before the ultimate recipient gives evidence; second, that hearsay evidence cannot be challenged in cross-examination, except on the inadequate basis of the veracity or reliability of the source of the communication, and therefore the court cannot see and hear the evidence of a person who actually witnessed the fact in question directly tested. Both difficulties arise from the lack of percipient evidence. Neither of these objections is theoretically fatal to the actual reception of hearsay evidence, because the view might equally well be taken that hearsay should be admitted, but should ordinarily be given little weight, or should not be acted upon in the absence of corroboration. Not all hearsay is unreliable. Frequently, it comes from an unimpeachable source, and is manifestly cogent, and it may be the best or the only available evidence of the fact to be proved. In such cases, there is no reason of theory why it should not be admitted and accorded full weight. This is often true in the case of documentary hearsay statements.

When there is added to these objections, however, the risk of concoction—which Professor Cross has described as 'one aspect of the great pathological dread of manufactured evidence which beset English lawyers of the late eighteenth and early nineteenth centuries'[1]—one can see why the common law set its face firmly against the admission of hearsay evidence. Had matters stopped there, the consideration of the rule would be a short and relatively simple matter. But even at common law, it was recognised that the sheer indispensability of hearsay to the determination of the truth in many cases meant that there had to be some exceptions. Where necessary witnesses were dead, where acts were hopelessly ambiguous without some contemporary explanation by those who performed them, where facts otherwise incapable of proof were stated in records kept, for the express purpose of future reference, by public officials acting under a duty, the law allowed hearsay to be admitted, subject to exacting and sometimes excessively rigorous safeguards. In recent times, important exceptions applicable to criminal trials began to be enacted by statute, to supplement the rules at common law. By far the most significant was the Criminal Evidence Act 1965, passed in panic, after the House of Lords in *Myers v DPP* (HC) [1965] AC 1001 had shrunk from the prospect of legislating judicially for a wholesale exception in favour of the admission of hearsay commercial records, in the absence of which prosecutions for offences of serious dishonesty might have come to an abrupt end.

*Myers* illustrated the fact that the development of common-law exceptions to the rule against hearsay was too piecemeal and too narrow to satisfy the demands of modern practice. But 20 years after this truth could no longer be concealed, the common-law exceptions remain of considerable importance in criminal cases, and statutory reform of the rule is as yet far from comprehensive. Certain limited reforms, in the sense of statutory exceptions, were introduced in civil cases by the Evidence Act 1938 and in criminal cases by the Criminal Evidence Act 1965. Reform in the sense of a new approach to hearsay evidence as a whole began only later and remains incomplete. In civil proceedings, the Civil Evidence Act 1968, within certain limits and with extensive safeguards, adopted the view that hearsay should be a question of weight, rather than a question of admissibility. Although the Act is often spoken of as an 'exception' to the rule against hearsay and arguably is so, it is more realistic to say that it has created a wholly new rule for civil proceedings in favour of the admission of hearsay evidence, while maintaining a sceptical vigilance over the weight of evidence so admitted. The Act has also given statutory force, for civil cases, to certain of the common-law exceptions referred to above. The reason, undoubtedly, why this step was first taken in civil cases and not in criminal, was that it was felt safer to entrust the sifting and weighing of hearsay evidence to the trained, critical mind of a judge sitting alone, than to a jury of laymen who may be accustomed in their daily lives to acting uncritically on what they are told by others. But many doubted whether such a task, though admittedly difficult, is any more so than that of applying the rule that an out-of-court confession made by A implicating both himself and B is evidence against A but not against B, or the rule that a recent complaint in a sexual case is evidence confirming the complainant's story, but not evidence of the facts stated in it, and is

---

[1] *Evidence*, 5th ed., p.479.

incapable of affording corroboration of the complainant's evidence, or for that matter any more difficult than many other feats which juries are commonly called on to perform. Both the Law Reform Committee and the Criminal Law Revision Committee[2] recommended corresponding reforms in criminal cases. At length, the Police and Criminal Evidence Act 1984 recognised that hearsay evidence contained in documentary records or produced by computers should, with adequate safeguards, be admissible in criminal proceedings. Though less comprehensive than the Civil Evidence Act 1968, the 1984 Act represents a major change in the philosophy of criminal evidence and allows juries to be confronted with the most reliable kinds of hearsay evidence. It will be surprising if it is not the thin end of the wedge. The Act also made sweeping changes in the law governing confessions (perhaps the most crucial exception to the rule against hearsay in criminal cases), which are dealt with in Chapter 7.

The rule against hearsay will, therefore, occupy a great deal of space. The remainder of this chapter is taken up by consideration in this section of the scope of the common-law rule itself, and in section B of the minor common-law exceptions applicable to criminal cases. Chapter 7 is concerned with the major common-law exceptions of admissions and confessions and statements made by and in the presence of defendants. Chapter 8 deals with the statutory exceptions, principally the Civil Evidence Act 1968 and the Police and Criminal Evidence Act 1984.

### 6.2 Application of the rule

The common-law rule against hearsay (as modified by statute) applies to all adversarial proceedings in any court and in any other tribunal to whose proceedings the rules of evidence apply. There is sometimes a tendency in criminal cases to permit limited relaxations of the rule in relation to evidence tendered by the defence, but the practice is contrary to authority and has been deprecated. In *R v Turner and Others* (1975) 61 Cr App R 67, the trial judge was held to have been correct in refusing to admit evidence to the effect that a person not called as a witness had admitted having committed the offence charged. The person concerned had withdrawn the admission after making it, but this should not have affected the admissibility of what he had said. Only by calling him as a witness (when their difficulties would have included his privilege against self-incrimination) could the defence have properly put the evidence before the court. And in *Sparks v R* [1964] AC 964, where the defendant was charged with indecently assaulting a girl aged just under four years, who did not give evidence and was presumably incompetent to do so, the Privy Council held that the evidence of the girl's mother to the effect that the girl had told her that the attacker was coloured (the defendant being white) had been rightly rejected. Dealing with this point, Lord Morris of Borth-y-Gest, giving the reasons for the committee's advice, said (ibid at 978):

> It was said that 'it was manifestly unjust for the jury to be left throughout the whole trial with the impression that the child could not give any clue to the identity of her assailant'. The cause of justice is, however, best served by adherence to rules which have long been recognised and settled. If the girl had made a remark to her mother (not in the presence of the appellant) to the effect that it was the appellant who had assaulted her

---

[2]   Law Reform Committee, 13th report, paras. 48–52; Criminal Law Revision Committee, 11th report, paras. 229–48.

and if the girl was not to be a witness at the trial, evidence as to what she had said would be the merest hearsay. In such circumstances it would be the defence who would wish to challenge a contention, if advanced, that it would be 'manifestly unjust' for the jury not to know that the girl had given a clue to the identity of her assailant.

Later, after rejecting a contention that the evidence was admissible under the res gestae exception to the hearsay rule (section B, post), Lord Morris pointed out that, if the evidence had been of an incriminating statement which had been admitted for the prosecution as part of a recent complaint, it would not have been evidence of the truth of what the girl had said. He added:

> Their Lordships can see no basis upon which evidence concerning a remark made by her to her mother could be admitted. Even if any basis for its admission could be found the evidence of the making of the remark would not be any evidence of the truth of the remark. Evidence of the making of the remark could not in any event possess a higher probative value than would attach to evidence of the making of a complaint in a case where the complainant gives evidence or to evidence of an accusation made to or in the presence of an accused. Nor can the principle of the matter vary according as to whether a remark is helpful to or hurtful to an accused person.

Happily, the appeal was allowed for other reasons, but the result of the application of the rule in such cases, though logically impeccable, is to say the least disturbing.

It is important to note that the rule against hearsay is not appropriate to non-adversarial proceedings, where the purpose of the proceedings is not to determine a dispute between parties but to investigate questions such as the welfare of children on an inquisitorial basis. Hence in *Humberside County Council* v *R* (DC) [1977] 1 WLR 1251, where evidence existed that the guardian of a child, who was not a party to proceedings to determine whether a care order should be made, had made admissions of his ill-treatment of the child, such statements were admissible when related by other witnesses, despite their apparently hearsay character, because they were relevant to the object of the court's inquiry. The ratio of the decision appears to be a relatively narrow one, in that the court was faced with a statutory duty under s.1(2) of the Children and Young Persons Act 1969, not to decide a dispute between parties, but to determine whether it was satisfied that certain conditions were shown to exist. Lord Widgery CJ emphasised that the rule against hearsay is of general application to proceedings in juvenile courts, which are of an adversarial nature, and the same would be true of contested custody proceedings, which involve a dispute between parties, notwithstanding that the court must first and foremost consider what is in the best interests of the child. And in *R* v *Commission for Racial Equality, ex parte Cottrell & Rothon* [1980] 1 WLR 1580, it was held that the Commission was entitled to act, in its role of investigating and adjudicating upon complaints of racial discrimination (an essentially inquisitorial function) on the admittedly hearsay reports produced by its employees, to whom the Commission properly delegated the task of investigation.

## 6.3 The two questions

At the outset of this chapter, we saw that the rule against hearsay excludes evidence of statements made by others on prior occasions if tendered for the purpose of proving that some fact so stated on such a prior occasion is true, but not for any other relevant purpose. We further noted that the forgetting of this principle is the source of most errors and misunderstandings surrounding the rule against hearsay. It is essential to remember that evidence of a statement made on a prior occasion is not necessarily hearsay. It may, depending on the purpose for which it is tendered, be admissible evidence of the fact that the statement was made, or that it was made on a certain occasion or in a certain way, or that it had a certain legal effect. Whether such evidence may be admissible for one or more of these purposes will depend upon whether any such issue falls to be decided, or in other words whether it is relevant. If there is no relevance in any of these issues in the context of the case, then it will probably be apparent that the only relevance of the statement is the proof of the truth of some fact stated on the prior occasion, for which purpose it is inadmissible.

The terminology generally employed to distinguish these two uses of prior statements is confusing. Traditionally, prior statements tendered as relevant for a purpose other than that of proving the truth of a fact stated have been described as 'direct' evidence, and for this purpose 'direct' means only the opposite of hearsay. However, 'direct' as a term of art in the law of evidence also means the opposite of 'circumstantial' (see 1.2.1, ante). Admissible evidence of prior statements may either be 'direct' (non-circumstantial) or circumstantial evidence of a fact. For example, the making of a statement may be 'direct' evidence that the statement was in fact made, and circumstantial evidence of the state of mind of the maker of the statement and may be admissible to prove both facts. To describe evidence as 'direct' in the sense of not being hearsay is, therefore, not infrequently ambiguous. In order to avoid confusion, we shall simply describe statements which are not hearsay as 'non-hearsay', adapting slightly the helpful usage of the American Federal Rules of Evidence.[3]

To distinguish hearsay from non-hearsay statements, it is necessary to answer two questions, and not just one. The first question is 'how and when was the statement made?' The point of asking it is to establish whether the statement was made on a prior occasion. This is generally very straightforward, since unless the statement was made from the witness-box in the trial or proceeding in which the suspected hearsay itself is being tendered, it was made on a prior occasion. The second question, frequently overlooked or wrongly answered, is 'for what purpose is the prior statement tendered?' The point of asking it is to establish whether there is any relevance in the statement other than to prove the truth of some fact stated. Both questions must be asked if hearsay is to be identified correctly.

### 6.3.1   The hearsay diagrams

*Hearsay diagram 1*
    Fact 1:
    D robbed the bank ...................................... PW .................................... HW

As an aid to answering the second question, consider hearsay diagram 1, which illustrates the formation of hearsay. A witness, PW, perceives a fact which will later become relevant to a case, namely that D took part in the robbery of a bank. Obviously, PW is able to give

---

[3]   The ambiguity can also be avoided by the use of the term 'percipient evidence' to mean non-hearsay, as suggested in 1.2.1, ante.

non-hearsay, percipient evidence of this fact for the purpose of proving that D robbed the bank. Hence the name PW for percipient witness. But now suppose that PW related to another person, whom we shall call HW as shorthand for hearsay witness, what he saw and that PW thereafter became unavailable as a witness at D's trial because of disability, absence or for some other sufficient reason. HW was not present at the robbery and has no knowledge of D's involvement in the robbery, if any, except in terms of what PW told him. Could the prosecution call HW as a witness at D's trial to tell the court what PW had told him?

As usual, the first question is not difficult to answer. PW's statement was clearly made on a prior occasion, in the sense that it was not made while testifying at D's trial. The second question, however, is crucial to our understanding. For what purpose could the prosecution wish to place evidence of PW's statement to HW before the jury? There is no relevance in the mere fact that the statement was made, or in how it was made. The prosecution's object, and the only relevance of the statement is to prove that D was involved in the robbery of the bank. In other words, it would be tendered for the purpose of proving that what PW stated to HW was true. For this purpose, the evidence is inadmissible hearsay.

Contrast this with the position illustrated by hearsay diagram 2.

*Hearsay diagram 2*
Fact 1:
D robbed the bank ...................................... PW ...................................... HW
  [Fact 1]                                   Fact 2:
                          PW told HW that D robbed the bank ............................ HW
                                                                (Alias PW2)

Assume now that D has been able to establish that he was not involved in the robbery of the bank. D sues PW for defamation, relying on the false statement made by PW to HW. This has changed the facts of the case and the potential relevance of PW's statement, but not the rule against hearsay. The fact that PW made the statement at all is now highly relevant, since unless D proves this, his action is bound to fail. The statement is now relevant for a purpose other than proving that D robbed the bank, and is admissible non-hearsay evidence for that purpose. If D calls HW to prove that PW made the statement to him, HW is giving non-hearsay, direct (non-circumstantial) evidence that the statement was in fact made in the form complained of (we should now probably change HW's name to PW2), and is relevant to show that PW defamed D. This demonstrates that whether a prior statement has a relevance which makes it non-hearsay depends on the issues before the court.

Finally, hearsay diagram 3 illustrates that even in D's suit for defamation, we could imagine the formation of hearsay evidence just by changing the facts slightly.

*Hearsay diagram 3*
Fact 1:
D robbed the bank ...................................... PW ...................................... HW
  [Fact 1]                                    Fact 2:
                          PW told HW that D robbed the bank ............HW............ HW2
                                                          (Alias PW2)

Now we have postulated that HW told HW2 about the statement made by PW. If HW gives evidence that PW made the statement to him, that evidence would, of course, be non-hearsay evidence that the statement was made. But if D wished to call HW2 to prove that same fact, the evidence of HW2 would be hearsay for that purpose, since it would consist entirely of what HW had told HW2. HW2 was not present when the statement was made, and has no knowledge of it except in terms of what HW told him.

The distinction between hearsay and non-hearsay has probably never been more charmingly illustrated than by the late Professor Cross, who used to teach that if W1 proposed to testify that W2 had told him that he (W2) had seen pink elephants coming across his lawn, the testimony would be inadmissible to prove that pink elephants had crossed the lawn, but admissible to prove that on the relevant occasion W2 had had too much to drink.

The identification of hearsay becomes natural with practice, but does depend crucially upon remembering to ask and answer not just the first, but both questions. The two questions must now be explored in more detail.

## 6.4   Question 1: when and how made?

### 6.4.1   When
The rule against hearsay applies to all statements made by a person, other than while giving evidence in the actual proceedings in which the suspected hearsay is tendered. Such prior statements are sometimes referred to as 'out-of-court' statements, but the phrase can be misleading because the rule excludes statements even when made in court in the course of giving evidence in other proceedings.[4] Even where the two proceedings are closely related, a prior sworn statement is hearsay. For example, a deposition taken at old-style committal proceedings is hearsay for the purpose of the trial and may be admitted as evidence at trial only where a statutory exception to the rule against hearsay applies. The same applies where a witness makes a written witness statement, even though it is made expressly subject to the penalty of perjury. The rule against hearsay also applies to prior statements made by the witness himself, repeated by the witness at trial. These statements, however, are the subject of separate rules, which depend on whether the prior statement is consistent or inconsistent with the testimony of the witness at trial, and are considered in their appropriate places in Chapters 12 and 13.

### 6.4.2   How
It matters not whether the statement was made orally, in a document, by gesture or by any other medium of communication. At common law, the rule against hearsay applies to statements made or produced by any means, as long as the statement was intended by the maker to communicate information.[5] Cases involving statements not intended to communicate a fact, but which nonetheless have that effect, have caused problems which are discussed in 6.8, post. The principle, however, is simple enough. It is the effect of a statement, not the means by which it is made, which is most significant. The rule against hearsay is designed to prevent a party from proving facts through the mouth of someone who is not before the court to give evidence and to be cross-examined. It is logical that the rule should also prevent attempts to prove the facts through that someone's pen, his

---

[4]   *R v Eriswell (Inhabitants)* (1790) 3 TR 707; *Haines v Guthrie* (1884) 13 QBD 818.
[5]   Cf. *Chandrasekera v R* (PC Ceylon) [1937] AC 220.

camera, his computer, his bodily movements or any other means of expression.

Documents are the most important source of hearsay statements, and it must be emphasised that documentary statements are subject to the rule against hearsay as they are to the rules of evidence generally. The point was brought home in alarming circumstances in *Myers v DPP* (HL) [1965] AC 1001. In this case, the defendant was convicted of offences of dishonesty in relation to motor vehicles. His practice was to buy up wrecked cars with their log books, to disguise stolen cars so that they corresponded as nearly as possible with the wrecks and their log-books, and to sell the stolen cars as if they were the wrecks, repaired by him. In order to prove their case, the prosecution adduced evidence from a witness in charge of records which were kept on microfilm, containing details of every car made at the works of a certain manufacturer. The microfilm was prepared from records compiled by workmen on cards, which were destroyed after being filmed, and which recorded the cylinder-block number of each car. Since the cylinder-block number was stamped indelibly on the engine of each vehicle, the evidence was of some value to the prosecution in proving the true identity of the cars in question. The House of Lords was unanimous in holding that the evidence contained in the records was hearsay, and that it could not be admitted under any recognised exception to the rule. Their Lordships also held that it would be eminently reasonable and convenient that it should be admitted if possible. But while the minority (Lords Pearce and Donovan) were prepared to extend the range of exceptions to deal with the admissibility of some records, the majority (Lords Reid, Morris of Borth-y-Gest and Hodson) held that such a change was one to be made, if at all, by the legislature.

The implications of the decision were at once compelling and horrific. Many prosecutions for offences of dishonesty depend upon trade or business records being admitted as evidence of the facts recorded in them, which may have been compiled, as were those in *Myers*, by large numbers of persons, who may be dead, unavailable or unable to remember their contents; they may extend over a long period of time. It would be by the sheerest good fortune only that any relevant facts could be proved from them by admissible evidence. The legislature, as has been noted, responded by introducing a statutory basis for the admission of trade or business records under certain circumstances in the form of the hastily drafted Criminal Evidence Act 1965.

But the principle of *Myers v DPP* has survived the reversal of the actual result in terms of admissibility on the facts of that case. Many documents could not be brought within the terms of the Criminal Evidence Act 1965 and many escape the wider nets of the Police and Criminal Evidence Act 1984 and the Civil Evidence Act 1968. There remain many cases where private documents containing statements which are highly relevant and obviously reliable evidence, must be excluded for the purposes of proving the truth of the facts stated in them.[6]

## 6.5 Question 2: for what purpose tendered?

It has already been pointed out that the source of the statement alone does not determine whether or not it is hearsay. The crucial second question must also be asked and answered. Failure to do so has led to the wrongful exclusion of perfectly admissible non-hearsay evidence. Such errors are a result of what Professor Cross called the 'superstitious awe . . . about having any truck with evidence which involves A's telling the court what B

---

[6]  Private documents were, of course, not admissible under the common-law exception in favour of the contents of public documents (see 6.13, post), and may not be 'records'.

said'.[7] In analysing the second question, the consideration of relevance must be borne in mind. Could the statement be relevant for a purpose other than proving the truth of some fact asserted in it? We shall look at examples of both hearsay and non-hearsay statements. The hearsay statements, which will be examined first, are those cases in which the statement has no relevance except proving the truth of some fact stated. The non-hearsay statements, although probably impossible to classify comprehensively, are relevant for the most part for one or more of the following reasons, and will be examined in those categories:

(a)  statements having legal effect or significance;

(b)  statements as direct evidence that the statement was made, or was made on a particular occasion or in a certain way;

(c)  statements as circumstantial evidence of the state of mind of the maker or recipient of the statement;

(d)  statements as circumstantial evidence of other relevant facts.

We shall also examine three particularly problematical areas on the borderline between hearsay and non-hearsay—unintended communications, evidence of the absence of records or information where its presence would have been significant, and the relationship between hearsay and real evidence (especially in relation to evidence produced by computers and other mechanical devices).

It must be borne in mind in considering the existing case-law that many of the hearsay problems discussed in this chapter would now be avoided by applying one of the modern statutory rules, notably under the Civil Evidence Act 1968 or the Police and Criminal Evidence Act 1984. Detailed discussions of this topic must await Chapter 8. We are presently considering only the common-law rule against hearsay, which will remain of great importance in criminal cases until the law is further reformed. The problems posed by the older cases can and do recur in analogous situations.

### 6.6  Hearsay statements

In *R* v *Gibson* (CCR) (1887) 18 QBD 537, an unidentified woman had said to the prosecutor at the scene of the wounding charged, 'The man who threw the stone went in there,' indicating a house in which the defendant was found. The woman's statement to the prosecutor was not made while giving evidence in the proceedings, and was obviously tendered for the purpose of suggesting that the person found in the house was the culprit, i.e. that the fact stated was true. The statement was inadmissible hearsay; evidence of the identity of the defendant should have been given by calling the woman. Cases where statements are tendered for the purpose of proving identity, and which plainly cannot be justified as having relevance to any other issue, are a good example of the working of rule at the common law. In *Jones* v *Metcalfe* [1967] 1 WLR 1286, an eyewitness to a road traffic accident took the registration number of a lorry, the bad driving of which was said to have caused a collision between two other vehicles. The eyewitness reported the number to the police, who as a result interviewed the defendant, and obtained his admission that he had been driving a lorry of that number on the relevant day. He denied, however, that his driving had been such as to cause any accident. By the time the defendant was tried by the magistrates for driving without due care and attention, the eyewitness was unable to remember what the number of the lorry was. The police officer's evidence, which included an account of what he had been told by the eyewitness, was hearsay and inadmissible on the issue of the identity of the lorry, because it consisted of a statement made by the eyewitness other than while giving evidence at the trial and was clearly relevant only to the issue of identity, the Bench being invited to accept the truth of what the eyewitness had said to the officer about what the registration number was. The conviction was quashed by the Divisional Court, on the ground that there was no evidence upon which the justices were entitled to find that a lorry of the number recorded was that responsible for the accident.

It will be noticed that at common law it made no difference that, in *Gibson*, the woman was unable to be called to give evidence at all, whereas in *Jones* v *Metcalfe* the eyewitness was called, but was unable to deal with the question of identity. Yet, there is obviously a considerable qualitative difference between the pieces of evidence in the two cases, in that the eyewitness in *Jones* v *Metcalfe* afforded evidence of everything except the actual link of the number, and that he would have been able to give evidence even of this, by refreshing his memory from the police officer's note, had he verified it contemporaneously.[8] The artificiality of this position produced expressions of reluctance in the decision of the Divisional Court, on the part of all three members. In particular, Diplock LJ said (ibid at 1290–1):

I reluctantly agree. Like [Lord Parker CJ] I have every sympathy with the magistrates because the inference of fact that the appellant was the driver of the lorry at the time of the accident is irresistible as a matter of common sense. But this is a branch of the law which has little to do with common sense. The inference that the appellant was the driver of the lorry was really an inference of what the independent witness said to the police when he gave them the lorry number, and since what he had said to the police would have been inadmissible as hearsay, to infer what he said to the police is inadmissible also. What makes it even more absurd is, as [Lord Parker CJ] pointed out, that if when the independent witness gave the number of the lorry to the police officer, the latter had written it down in his presence, then the police officer's note could have been shown to the independent witness and he could have used it, not to tell the justices what he told the police officer, but to refresh his memory. This case does illustrate . . . the need to reform the law of evidence.

Another interesting distinction between *R* v *Gibson* and *Jones* v *Metcalfe* is that while the evidence of the police officer in the latter might now be admissible by virtue of s.68 of the Police and Criminal Evidence Act 1984, as being part of a record compiled by the officer acting under a duty from information supplied by a person with personal knowledge of the facts supplied, the statement of the woman in the former would still be inadmissible in a criminal case. The common-law principle in the two cases is identical; only the extent of the statutory reform differs.

The identity cases are only one example of the working of the rule excluding hearsay statements at common law. In *R* v *Attard*,[9] for instance, the prosecution sought to prove

8   As to refreshing the memory from contemporaneous notes, see 12.2, post.
9   (1958) 43 Cr App R 90. This decision led to the universal practice of calling the interpreter as a witness in such cases.

the substance of an interview which had taken place between the defendant and a police officer, relating to the offence charged. The interview had been conducted through the medium of an interpreter, because the defendant, who was Maltese, was unable to speak English. All would have been well, had the interpreter been called to prove the conversation, but the officer purported to give evidence of what had been said between the defendant and himself. It was held that his evidence as to what had been said was hearsay. Whatever was said in English by the officer (which could not be understood by the defendant) was in any case inadmissible to prove the truth of facts stated by the officer, but more importantly, the officer could not give percipient evidence of the substance of what had been said in Maltese by the defendant or the interpreter; he was relating what the interpreter had said the conversation had been, with a view to proving what it had in fact been.

Where hearsay evidence would be inadmissible to prove the truth of a fact, it would seem to follow, and has been held, that any admission made by a party against his interest, based solely upon that hearsay and not upon matters within his own knowledge, should be rejected as having no more evidential value than the hearsay on which it was based.[10] Thus, in *Surujpaul* v *R*[11] the defendant was charged with murder as an accessory before the fact. He made an admission that the murder in question had in fact been committed. It was held that this admission should not have been received in evidence, because the defendant had not been present at the murder, had no personal knowledge of the facts which he was purporting to admit and was relying entirely upon what he had been told by another. In *Comptroller of Customs* v *Western Lectric Co. Ltd* [1966] AC 367, the respondents were charged with making a false declaration on a customs import entry produced to a customs officer, the false declaration relating to the country of origin of certain goods. The articles were entered as having their origin either in Australia or the United Kingdom, and if this was true, they would have been subject to a preferential tariff. Inspection of the goods by a customs officer revealed that the articles were labelled respectively, 'Denmark' and 'Made in USA', and in the light of this, the respondents' agent filed a further entry stating the origin of the goods to be Denmark and the United States. This further entry was subsequently relied on as an admission by the respondents of the true origin of the goods. The Privy Council held that a conviction could not be based upon an admission so clearly made solely in reliance on the hearsay markings of the goods.[12] Lord Hodson, delivering the judgment of their Lordships, observed that:

> If a man admits something of which he knows nothing it is of no real evidential value. The admission made by the respondents' agent was an admission made upon reading the marks and labels on those goods and was of no more evidential value than those marks and labels themselves.

For very similar reasons, in *R* v *Marshall*[13] the trial judge accepted a submission of no

---

[10]   For the admissibility of admissions against interest, see Chapter 7.

[11]   (PC, British Guiana) [1958] 1 WLR 1050, but see *R* v *Chatwood* [1980] 1 WLR 874, *R* v *Korniak* [1983] Crim LR 109 and 7.3, post.

[12]   As to which see *Patel* v *Comptroller of Customs* (PC, Fiji) [1966] AC 356. *Quaere* whether the marks and labels would be admissible by virtue of the Police and Criminal Evidence Act 1984: see Chapter 8, post. Where the defendant has some personal knowledge of the facts which he admits, his admission may be prima facie evidence of the facts admitted even though based solely upon his past experience: see *R* v *Chatwood* [1980] 1 WLR 874.

[13]   [1977] Crim LR 106, but see also *R* v *Korniak* [1983] Crim LR 109.

case to answer where, on a charge of handling stolen goods, the only evidence from which the jury could infer that the goods were stolen was an admission made to the police by the defendant that this was the case. This admission was based solely on what the defendant had been told by a man who sold him the goods. The decision is an excellent illustration of the extent of the hearsay rule, because although the admission was not evidence that the goods were stolen, it would have been admissible and cogent evidence that the defendant knew or believed them to be stolen, i.e. of his state of mind at the time when he received them.

## 6.7 Non-hearsay statements

Statements made on prior occasions will be non-hearsay and admissible where they enjoy a relevance independent of the proof of the truth of facts stated therein. It is impossible to categorise definitively the cases in which evidence of prior statements will be admissible as non-hearsay evidence. But the most important examples can be classified into four categories, which may be regarded as typical.

### 6.7.1 Statement having legal effect or significance

A statement may be admitted as non-hearsay evidence, if it is tendered for the purpose of proving a transaction having legal effect or significance which the statement itself constitutes. For example, if P alleges that he entered into an oral contract with D, P may testify as to the words spoken by D which are alleged to constitute D's offer or acceptance, or the consideration which D agreed to accept and provide. In a criminal context, a police officer may give evidence that he heard D1, D2 and D3 have a conversation which amounted to a conspiracy, or that he found a letter written by D1 to D2 containing the terms of a conspiracy. Such statements, known to some American writers as 'verbal acts', themselves have legal effect or significance in creating a legally effective relationship. There is no relevant issue of the truth or otherwise of any fact stated by the parties. The only issue is what statement was made, and whether the statement was sufficient in law to bring about the claimed legal consequences. On these issues, evidence of the making of the statement is clearly non-hearsay and direct evidence that the legal effect was created.

In some cases, the making of a statement must be proved, not because the statement itself gives rise directly to legal consequences, but because the making of the statement is a necessary preliminary to other steps having legal consequences. In *R v Chapman* [1969] 2 QB 436, the defendant was charged with driving with excess alcohol, following a road traffic accident which had resulted in his being taken to hospital. Under those circumstances, the Road Safety Act 1967 provided that before he was required to supply a specimen of breath, the police officer should ascertain from the doctor in charge of the defendant that the former had no objection to such specimen being required. The officer gave evidence that he had asked the doctor, who had offered no objection. It was argued on appeal that the doctor should have been called to state that he had had no objection, but the Court of Appeal rejected the suggestion that the officer's evidence was hearsay. The only issue was whether the doctor had or had not in fact given his consent to the sample being required. Whether what the doctor said was true or not was not in issue. The giving of consent created the legal consequence that the defendant was required to supply the sample.

### 6.7.2 Statement admissible to prove that it was made, or was made on a particular occasion or in a certain way

The fact that a statement was made, was made on a particular occasion or was made in a certain way may itself be an essential element of a claim, charge or defence, and so be a fact in issue in the case. For example, where a plaintiff sues for defamation, or a prosecution is brought for threatening words, the fact that the statement complained of was made, and made on the occasion and in the manner alleged may be proved as part of the case. If the defendant to the claim for defamation raises a defence of privilege, he may give evidence that the form or occasion of the statement were such as entitle him to claim the privilege. Although the tribunal of fact will have to decide on the defamatory or threatening nature of the statements, there is no question of tendering the statements to prove the truth of any facts stated in them; the only issues are whether they were made, and if so, in what circumstances. Evidence of the statements will be non-hearsay and admissible on those issues. As in the case of statements having legal effect or significance, the statements themselves produce certain legal consequences, which in this instance are in terms of creating or negating a claim, charge or defence. A statement may constitute a criminal or tortious act, just as a physical act may.

### 6.7.3 Statement as circumstantial evidence of state of mind

A statement may be non-hearsay, circumstantial evidence of the state of mind of the maker or the recipient of the statement. Since a person's state of mind cannot be proved by direct evidence, it is always a proper subject of circumstantial evidence. The state of mind is affected by statements received, and reflected by statements made, and both may be relevant where the state of mind of a person is in issue. The circumstances in which state of mind is relevant are many and varied. Intent, whether guilty or innocent, knowledge or belief and motive may all be proved by circumstantial evidence of statements made or received by the subject, and for this purpose, such statements are non-hearsay.

In *Subramaniam* v *Public Prosecutor* (PC Malaya) [1956] 1 WLR 965, the defendant was charged with unlawful possession of firearms, contrary to certain emergency regulations. It would have been a defence for the defendant to show that he had a lawful excuse for the possession, and he sought to give evidence that he had been threatened by terrorists, and possessed the weapons only while in a state of duress induced by the threats made by the terrorists. The defendant was prevented from giving this evidence on the ground that it was hearsay—a classic example of error resulting from failure to ask the second question to which we have referred in our hearsay analysis. On appeal, the Privy Council held that the defendant had been entitled to give evidence of what the terrorists had said to him, since this was clearly relevant to his claimed state of mind. The statements received by the defendant could be taken as having affected his mind in relation to his possession of the firearms, and so were circumstantial evidence of the defence of duress.

Evidence of state of mind is frequently important in cases of criminal offences involving a mental element, and may be relevant to the prosecution's case as showing a guilty mind, or (as in *Subramaniam*) to the defence case as showing the absence of a guilty state of mind. In cases where the charge is one of handling stolen goods, statements made to the defendant by the thief are admissible, non-hearsay evidence for the purpose of showing knowledge or belief on the part of the defendant that the goods were stolen, or the absence of that knowledge or belief (though they would, of course, be hearsay if tendered only to show that the goods were or were not in fact stolen). In *R* v *Willis* [1960] 1 WLR 55, where the defendant was charged with larceny of a drum of metal cable, and had given answers to the police about it which might have appeared incriminating, the defendant sought to give in evidence a conversation between his employee and himself, the content of which might have put his answers to the police in a very different light by suggesting an innocent state of mind. It was held on appeal that the refusal of the trial judge to allow the evidence to be admitted was incorrect. There was no question of the conversation being tendered to prove the truth of anything said by the defendant or his employee. The issue was simply what had been said, and the effect of what had been said on the defendant's state of mind.

A guilty state of mind may sometimes be shown by false statements made by a defendant, irrespective of the actual content of the statement. In *Jones* v *DPP* [1962] AC 635, the fact that the defendant had given a false alibi, almost identical to that used by him in relation to an earlier charge, showed a guilty state of mind. In such a case, the prosecution would not wish to tender the statement made by the defendant as a confession (in which case it would be admissible as an exception to the rule against hearsay: see Chapter 7), because by so doing, the prosecution would assert that the content of the statement was true. But the prosecution may assert that the very falsity of the statement is non-hearsay, circumstantial evidence of the guilty state of mind of the defendant. The fact that the defendant made a false statement, or made a statement false in a particular respect which is revealing, is what is relevant, and not the truth of any particular fact stated therein.

An interesting example is *Mawaz Khan and Amanat Khan* v *R* [1967] 1 AC 454. The defendants were charged with the murder of another man on a certain day, and it was alleged that they had been injured in the course of the murder. Each made a statement to the police, independently of the other, giving an identical alibi according to which they had been together at a club and had sustained their injuries in the course of fighting each other there. Neither defendant gave evidence at the trial, and they subsequently appealed on the ground that the trial judge had invited the jury to view the statements as evidence against both of them, if satisfied that they were fabrications. This would have been a clearly erroneous direction if the prosecution had tendered the statements as confessions, asserting and relying on their truth, since in such a case a statement is evidence only against the maker, and not against anyone else affected by its contents.[14] If the statements in this case were hearsay and admissible only as confessions, therefore, the trial judge was guilty of a serious misdirection. The Privy Council, upholding the majority view of the Supreme Court of Hong Kong, held that the statements were not hearsay. The trial judge had directed the jury as follows:

> The Crown's case here is not that these statements are true and that what one says ought to be considered as evidence of what actually happened. What the Crown say is that these statements have been shown to be a tissue of lies and that they disclose an attempt to fabricate a joint story. Now . . . if you come to that conclusion then the fabrication of a joint story would be evidence against both. It would be evidence that they had co-operated after the alleged crime.

Holding this direction to be a proper one, Lord Hodson said (ibid at 462):

[14] The statements could be said to be evidence 'against' the defendants only in so far as the jury rejected them as statements of truth. As they were entirely self-serving, they could otherwise have no evidential value in a case where the makers did not give evidence. Where a jury conclude that a defendant has deliberately lied in order to seek to exculpate himself, they are entitled to draw adverse inferences from that conclusion: see 7.10.3 and 7.11, post.

Their Lordships agree with Hogan CJ and Rigby AJ in accepting the generality of the proposition maintained by the text writers and to be found in *Subramaniam's* case that a statement is not hearsay and is admissible when it is proposed to establish by the evidence, not the truth of the statement, but the fact that it was made. Not only therefore can the statements of each appellant be used against each appellant individually . . . but they can without any breach of the hearsay rule be used, not for the purpose of establishing the truth of the assertions contained therein, but for the purpose of asking the jury to hold the assertions false and to draw inferences from their falsity.

The statements were relevant as tending to show that the makers were acting in concert and that such action indicated a common guilt.

What was of relevance to the issue was not the truth of any fact actually contained in either statement, but the fact that two statements had been made, apparently independently of each other, but asserting in detail the same innocent account of the matter. If the jury rejected this account, having heard the whole of the evidence, then it was relevant for them to consider the implications of having before them two statements, obviously fabricated as part of a prearranged plan, and to draw inferences about the guilt of the defendants. The relevance of the statements lay in the very fact that they had been made in the form they were, as showing the defendants' guilty state of mind.

Intent is a state of mind which may readily be shown by reference to statements made by the subject, and non-hearsay evidence of statements made by the subject is often employed both in civil and criminal cases to show intent. The intent of a testator or a debtor or a tortfeasor may be shown in this way. Note in the following cases the rather close distinction made by the courts between the acceptable non-hearsay purpose of the evidence admitted, and the rejected hearsay purposes. In *Attorney-General* v *Good* (1825) M'Cle 2 Yo 286, the demonstrably untrue statement of the wife of a debtor, to the effect that her husband was away from home, was admitted to show the husband's intention of defrauding his creditors. The statement was not evidence of the fact that the husband was, or was not at home, but was evidence tending to support the allegation that he was setting up a false story as to his whereabouts. Similarly, in *Hayslep* v *Gymer* (1834) 1 A & E 162, where the housekeeper of the deceased was able to produce a written note stating that she had received certain goods as a gift from her late employer, the statement was admitted to qualify and explain her act of handing the goods over to another, and so to rebut the apparent significance of that act as an admission that she was not entitled to them. It was not, however, evidence that the goods were a gift. The occasion or manner of the making of a statement may also be admitted as non-hearsay evidence to show the time at which or the circumstances in which a state of mind was acquired. For example, if it is relevant to show the date on which a person became aware of a fact, evidence that a statement was made to him on or before that date, from which he should have known of the fact, is admissible, non-hearsay evidence that he knew of the fact on or before that date. And a statement may similarly be non-hearsay evidence of what detail the recipient should have known of the facts dealt with in the statement.

### 6.7.4   Statement as circumstantial evidence of other relevant facts
By far the most difficult problems in distinguishing between hearsay and non-hearsay evidence are to be found in cases in which the statement is said to be relevant to a fact in issue other than state of mind. Some very close disinctions have been made by the courts, which are by no means beyond criticism. It is necessary, by way of introduction, to

appreciate that the courts have been anxious to limit the exclusionary effects of the common-law rule against hearsay. It was not until the decision in *Myers* v *DPP* in 1965 that the true scale of the need for legislative reform became fully apparent. Before that time, the courts had wrestled valiantly with the common-law exceptions to the rule against hearsay, and had attempted to use the concept of circumstantial evidence to circumvent the most restrictive effects of the rule. In many cases, the courts admitted statements as circumstantial evidence of facts, to which the state of mind of the maker of the statement bore no obvious relevance. In such cases, it was difficult to see how the statement could have any relevance to the facts in issue, except on the basis of at least a tacit assumption that some facts stated were true. In many cases, the need for such artificial reasoning has now been removed by statutory reform, principally under the Civil Evidence Act 1968 and the Police and Criminal Evidence 1984, but once again, the common-law position remains of importance in criminal cases while statutory reform is incomplete.

Not all cases where a statement is offered as circumstantial evidence present difficulties. Just as there are cases in which a statement may itself constitute a criminal or tortious act, so a statement may be clear circumstantial evidence that such an act has occurred or is occurring. An excellent illustration is *Woodhouse* v *Hall* (1980) 72 Cr App R 39, in which the Divisional Court held that evidence of conversations that allegedly took place between police officers and women working in a massage parlour, in which details of the availability and cost of sexual services were discussed, was admissible as non-hearsay, circumstantial evidence that the premises were being operated as a brothel. The very fact that such statements were made was evidence from which the justices could draw that inference—and there was no question of the statements being used to prove the truth of facts stated.

Delivering the judgment of the court, Donaldson LJ said (ibid at 42):

We have been referred to *Ratten* v *R* . . . [1972] AC 378, a Privy Council case, but one which reflects English law. For my part I think it is sufficient to refer to a short passage in the opinion of the Board which was delivered by Lord Wilberforce . . . : 'The mere fact that evidence of a witness includes evidence as to words spoken by another person who is not called, is no objection to its admissibility. Words spoken are facts just as much as any other action by a human being. If the speaking of words is a relevant fact, a witness may give evidence that they were spoken. A question of hearsay only arises when the words spoken are relied on "testimonially", i.e. as establishing some fact narrated by the words . . .'
     There is no question here of the hearsay rule arising at all. The relevant issue was, did these ladies make these offers? The offers were oral and the police officers were entitled to give evidence of them. The evidence, in my judgment, was wrongly excluded and should have been admitted.[15]

The proper use of statements as circumstantial evidence is very well illustrated by this decision. But difficulties have arisen in cases where the courts have sought to justify as circumstantial evidence statements which appear to be relied upon by their proponents, at least indirectly, to prove the truth of facts stated. Typically, the courts have achieved their object by permitting the evidence to be admitted for the purpose of 'supporting' or 'confirming' other admissible evidence, even though it is difficult to see how such support or confirmation is offered unless some facts stated are taken to be true.

In *Lloyd* v *Powell Duffryn Steam Coal Co. Ltd* [1914] AC 733 it was sought to show that the plaintiff and her child were dependants of a workman who had been killed, it was alleged, through the fault of the defendants. In order to show this, the plaintiff had to prove that the deceased was the father of her child, and had promised and intended to marry her. The House of Lords held that the plaintiff's evidence of paternity and of the deceased's intentions towards her could be supported by evidence of statements made by the deceased during his lifetime, which were to the effect that he regarded the plaintiff as his fiancée and the child as his. The words were a form of treatment of the plaintiff and the child as such, and could only have been spoken on the basis that the deceased believed himself to be the father of the child and that he intended to support the plaintiff and the child as his dependants. Since the deceased's statements were rejected as statements by a person, since deceased, against his interest (which would have rendered them admissible, exceptionally, even if hearsay: see section B of this chapter, post) they could not be evidence that the child was his, and their admissibility was, therefore, confined to support of what the plaintiff had said. But the distinction is plainly tenuous. It surely cannot be realistically maintained that the belief or statement of the deceased could support the evidence of the plaintiff, unless at least some assumption were made that such belief or statement was the truth; the fact that the belief was held, or the statement made, taken alone, assists not at all. The same reasoning, however, was employed in *Re Jenion, Jenion* v *Wynne* [1952] Ch 454 where, the declarations of a deceased mother being admissible at common law (as an exception to the hearsay rule) for the purpose of proving that her children were illegitimate, the statements of the putative father that the children were his, were held admissible for the purpose, not of proving the illegitimacy, but of supporting the declarations of the mother.

These admittedly ingenious efforts to invest apparently hearsay evidence with the character of non-hearsay evidence, have caused considerable confusion about the extent of the common-law rule against hearsay. Nowhere is this confusion better exemplified than in the decision of the Court of Criminal Appeal in *R* v *Rice and Others* [1963] 1 QB 857. On a charge of conspiracy, part of the prosecution case against Rice was that he had taken a flight to Manchester on or about a certain date, in the company of a co-defendant, Hoather. This was denied. The prosecution produced an airline ticket to Manchester in respect of a date at about the relevant time, affording two seats in the names of Rice and Moore (another co-defendant). The prosecution suggested that Hoather flew in place of Moore. The ticket was put to Rice in cross-examination, and, he having denied all knowledge of it, it was exhibited and shown to the jury. On appeal it was argued, understandably, that the ticket could have been tendered for no purpose except that of suggesting to the jury that it was evidence of the fact that Rice had flown to Manchester on the day shown, and that it was accordingly hearsay and had been wrongly admitted. The Court rejected the argument on the basis that the ticket was relevant and admissible circumstantial evidence on the issue of whether Rice had flown to Manchester. The following extraordinary passages are taken from the judgment of the court delivered by Winn J[16]:

---

[16]  Ibid at 872–3; cf. the more reasonable earlier decision in *R* v *Podmore* (1930) 22 Cr App R 36. (Finding of documents partly in handwriting of deceased admissible to prove dishonest relationship between defendant and deceased, precise nature of which was immaterial).

The court thinks that it would have been more accurate had the recorder said that the production of the ticket from the place where used tickets would properly be kept was a fact from which the jury might infer that probably two people had flown on the particular flight and that it might or might not seem to them by applying their common knowledge of such matters that the passengers bore the surnames which were written on the ticket.

It is plain that the latter inference was not one to be readily accepted in a case where it was not suggested that [the appellant] Moore, whose name was on the ticket, had actually flown; indeed it is obvious that pro tanto the potential inference was excluded. Nevertheless it remained open for partial acceptance in respect of [the appellant] Rice . . . .

So far as Rice was concerned the ticket was treated differently and assumed importance from the direction given that the jury might, if they saw fit, regard it as corroboration of Hoather's evidence that Rice flew with him to Manchester and that Rice booked the ticket . . . .

The court finds no misdirection in that passage . . . .

The court doubts whether the air ticket could constitute admissible evidence that the booking was effected either by Rice or even by any man of that name but it does not think that for relevant purposes the distinction between the booking of the ticket and the use of it was material with regard either to the case against Rice or to his defence.

It may be that the explanation of this judgment is that the Court of Criminal Appeal appreciated and shied away from the awful truth which was finally conceded by the House of Lords in *Myers* v *DPP*, that the exclusion of such apparently reliable business records would pave the way for a coach and four to be driven through the whole process of prosecution for many offences. The court's reasoning found some support from the Court of Appeal, and the minority of the House of Lords, in *Myers*,[17] but the terms of that support lack conviction. It is submitted that it is indefensible and nonsensical to tell a jury that they can consider whether 'the passengers bore the surnames which were written on the ticket', while also telling them that they are not to consider the ticket as evidence of any fact stated in it. Hopefully, the Police and Criminal Evidence Act 1984 has prevented many similar counsels of desperation, but it has not removed the problem altogether.

Better reasoned is the decision of the Privy Council in *Ratten* v *R* (PC, Victoria [1972] AC 378). The defendant was charged with the murder of his wife by shooting. His defence was that the gun had gone off accidentally while he was cleaning it. A telephone operator gave evidence that about five minutes before the time when the wife was known to be dead, she received a call from a hysterical woman, made from the defendant's telephone number, in which the woman said, 'Get me the police', and gave the defendant's address. The question was whether the detail of this call was admissible. The Privy Council held that the evidence was not hearsay, despite the nature of the words spoken by (as it must have been) the wife, because the call was relevant to prove that the wife had made such a

---

[17]  See [1965] AC 1001, per Widgery J at 1007–8; Lord Pearce at 1044–5; Lord Donovan at 1048, all of whom saw *Rice* and *Myers* as involving the same problem. The argument makes the ticket into a piece of 'real evidence', and so seeks to circumvent the rule against hearsay: see the very similar reasoning of Sir Jocelyn Simon P in *The Statue of Liberty* [1968] 1 WLR 739, considered in 15.5.5. See also *US* v *Snow* 517 F2d 441 (9th Circ 1975) (tag on briefcase seized at airport which bore name of defendant 'Bill Snow' admitted as circumstantial evidence of defendant's possession or ownership of briefcase).

call shortly before her death, and, if the jury wished to draw the inference, that she was at that time in a state of emotion or fear. These matters tended to refute the defendant's account of the episode and in particular his defence of accident.[18] It is perhaps arguable that this object could have been achieved without giving in evidence what had been said by the wife during the call, a point which may be emphasised by considering what the position should have been if the wife had instead said, 'My husband is trying to kill me' or something else directly incriminating of that kind. But Lord Wilberforce regarded the words as a part of the 'composite act' of a telephone call, and held that to confine evidence to part only of the call 'would be to deprive the act of most of its significance' (ibid at 388). It is certainly quite tenable to contend that the circumstances prevailing immediately before the wife's death were of great relevance to the defence raised by the defendant, and to that extent there was clearly a perfectly legitimate use to be made of the evidence as a piece of direct evidence on that issue. Its hearsay character is of far less importance than in a case such as *Rice*.

## 6.8   Three hearsay problems

Three areas of particular difficulty were identified at common law with regard to the distinction between hearsay and non-hearsay evidence. These were unintended communications, evidence of the absence of records or information where their presence would have been of significance, and the relationship between hearsay and real evidence, with special reference to evidence produced by computers and other mechanical devices. Although statute has now provided partial solutions to the problems posed, these problems cannot be regarded as having been solved entirely. They must still be examined briefly.

### 6.8.1   Unintended communications
In the context of the rule against hearsay, unintended communications are statements not intended to communicate a fact, and which do not express the fact directly, but which nonetheless do suggest the fact by necessary implication. In the classic case of *Wright* v *Doe* d *Tatham* (Exch) (1837) 7 A & E 313, the question arose whether, on the issue of the testamentary capacity of a testator, evidence could be admitted of letters written to the testator by businessmen during the relevant period of his life, which were said to be of such a nature that they would have been written only to a person in command of his mental faculties. In deciding this question, Parke B had two options. It was open to him to regard the evidence as hearsay, because the letters were tendered as being, in effect, statements that the testator was of sound mind, and for the purpose of proving that fact. It was also open to him to admit the letters as circumstantial evidence of the testator's testamentary capacity, because the letters might be seen as no more than a piece of evidence that the testator was, at the time he received them, conducting normal business affairs.

Parke B preferred the former option, and excluded the letters on the ground that they were hearsay if tendered for the purpose of proving the testamentary capacity of the testator.[19] He likened the case to one in which a sea captain, having inspected a vessel,

---

[18]   It was held alternatively that even if the statement by the wife were hearsay, it was admissible under the res gestae principle (see 6.11, post).
[19]   A further objection to the evidence was that the letters represented inadmissible opinion evidence by the authors on the issue of the testator's testamentary capacity.

embarked on it with his family, which evidence the learned Baron thought would be inadmissible on the issue of the seaworthiness of the vessel. The principle derived from this and other cases is that a statement which by implication conveys facts which it was not intended to communicate may be hearsay, if tendered for the purpose of proving the truth of those facts. In *Teper* v *R* [1952] AC 480, the Privy Council quashed the conviction of the defendant on a charge of arson of his shop, where the prosecution had been permitted, in order to contradict the defendant's alibi, to adduce evidence that a woman at the scene of the blaze had been heard to shout to a passing motorist (who resembled the defendant) 'your place burning down and you going away from the fire'. Although not intended as a statement of identification, the statement in fact offered evidence of identification to the tribunal of fact, and was therefore hearsay when tendered to prove that the person driving away from the scene had been the defendant.

In civil cases, the problem of unintended communications has been solved by s.2 of the Civil Evidence Act 1968, which as we shall see in Chapter 8, renders admissible many hearsay statements that would not have been admissible at common law. In criminal cases, however, the problem has not yet been resolved. It may be that a more modern court would permit at least some unintended communications to be admitted as circumstantial evidence, following the reasoning of such cases as *Rice* and *Ratten*, discussed above. But since it is surely the effect of the statement, rather than the intent of the maker which is significant, it remains arguable that the decision of Parke B should be followed in criminal cases, pending further statutory reform. The distinction between statements intended to convey a fact directly, and statements which suggest the same fact by necessary implication is not a compelling one.

### 6.8.2 *Absence of record or information*

The question posed here is whether a party may adduce evidence of the absence of any record or information of a fact or event, for the purpose of proving that the fact is untrue or the event did not occur, in circumstances where, if the fact were true or the event had occurred, some record or information about it would ordinarily have been compiled and maintained. The concept gives rise to a hearsay problem in the same way as would the adduction of a record to prove that the fact is true or that the event occurred, because in a sense the absence of a record is just as much a statement circumstantially relevant to the issue of the truth of the fact as the presence of a record. In the United States, it is generally recognised that such evidence is hearsay at common law, but many jurisdictions, including the Federal Rules of Evidence, render evidence of the absence of record admissible, if the records themselves would be admissible to prove the truth of the facts recorded, as an exception to the rule against hearsay.

A similar solution would be possible in English law, since statutory reform has rendered certain hearsay records admissible both in civil and criminal cases. But it cannot be said that any solution has so far been adopted. Indeed, it cannot even be said with confidence that the nature of the problem has been fully recognised.

In *R* v *Patel* (1981) 73 Cr App R 117, the defendant was charged with assisting the illegal entry into the United Kingdom of one Ashraf. In order to prove that Ashraf was not a person entitled to enter the United Kingdom, the prosecution called a chief immigration officer, who testified that he had examined Home Office records, which revealed that fact.

---

[20] The same records would be admissible pursuant to s. 68 of the Police and Criminal Evidence Act 1984. However, this would not necessarily resolve the problem—see the comments on the later case of *Shore* in the text.

It was argued on appeal that this evidence was inadmissible, since the Home Office records were inadmissible hearsay and the immigration officer's testimony about the absence of Ashraf's name was likewise hearsay and inadmissible. The Court of Appeal accepted the submission and allowed the appeal. It was conceded that the Home Office records would have been hearsay at common law, in the light of *Myers* v *DPP*, and that they were not admissible under the then applicable Criminal Evidence Act 1965 because that Act applied only to records of a 'trade or business'.[20] This led the court to venture the strange observation that:

> . . . an officer responsible for their compilation and custody should have been called to give evidence that the method of compilation and custody is such that if Ashraf's name is not there, he must be an illegal entrant. It is not suggested that [the officer actually called] is such an officer.

With respect, it is not clear why this would have made any difference, unless the officer called had some actual personal knowledge about Ashraf. Even had such an officer testified about the method of compilation, the conclusion that Ashraf was an illegal entrant could be reached only on the assumption that the absence of his name accurately reflected his status, or in other words that the information suggested by the absence of the record was true. If the court was inclined to treat the evidence as hearsay, rather than as circumstantial evidence, it is submitted that the evidence suggested by the court would not have cured the defect.

However, the court's observation had an effect on the subsequent Court of Appeal which considered *R* v *Shore* (1982) 76 Cr App R 72. The defendant was charged with dishonestly handling stolen goods, namely three vehicle springs. The springs were found on the defendant's premises and were subsequently identified as having been supplied by the manufacturer to the company from which they were stolen. The prosecution called the stock clerk and parts sales manager of the company. The effect of their testimony was that the receipt, sale and use of all parts in the company's possession were recorded in the company's records, and that there was no record of the sale or use of the springs in question. From this evidence, the jury were invited to infer that the springs had left the company's premises through theft. The court dismissed an appeal against conviction, based in part on a submission that the evidence of the absence of records was hearsay. The court noted the comments of the court in *Patel*, and held that the witnesses called by the prosecution had complied with the requirement of testifying about the method of compilation. Since the records in *Shore* were, unlike those in *Patel*, admissible by virtue of the Criminal Evidence Act 1965, the court could presumably have held that the evidence of the absence of a record was admissible despite its hearsay character. However, the court took the different view that the absence of record indicating the sale or use of the springs was non-hearsay, circumstantial evidence, from which the jury were entitled to draw the inference that the springs had been stolen.

At present, therefore, the position of evidence of this kind is unclear. It is arguable that evidence of the absence of record or information, where record or information might have been expected, is non-hearsay, circumstantial evidence proving the absence of the fact which might have been recorded. It would seem that the absence of record, and its significance, must be proved by the testimony of witnesses responsible for the compilation and custody of the record, so that the method of compilation is known, and the significance of the absence of record may be assessed. Equally, however, it may be argued that the evidence of absence of record is hearsay and inadmissible in a case where the records themselves would not be admissible. This argument, however, would involve persuading a future court that the solution favoured by the *Patel* court does not solve the hearsay problem. It would be in accord with the recent trend to regard such evidence as non-hearsay, and despite the considerable theoretical problems, it would appear more realistic to adopt this approach for future cases.

### 6.8.3   Hearsay and real evidence

Real evidence is evidence of a tangible nature from which the tribunal of fact can derive information using its own senses: see generally Chapter 15, part B, post. This information results in direct or circumstantial evidence of relevant facts, for example where the court is presented with a photograph or tape-recording, from which direct evidence can be derived or inferences drawn about relevant facts depicted therein. An uncomfortable interface between real evidence and the rule against hearsay has been identified, particularly where the real evidence is produced by a mechanical device, be that device a clock, an automatic traffic signal, a radar device or a computer. As technology produced ever more efficient machines, the problem intensified. So far as mechanical devices other than computers are concerned, readings and other information produced by a mechanical device are now admitted at common law as real evidence, provided that the device is shown to have been working properly or to have been accurate on the relevant occasion. The proponent of the evidence is aided in this regard by a presumption that the device was functioning correctly. So far as evidence produced by computers is concerned, such evidence may now be admitted by virtue of statute both in civil and criminal cases, as an exception to the rule against hearsay. The detail of these rules is given in 8.5, 8.12 and 15.5, post. In general, it may be said that the useful nature of evidence produced by machines, and our increasing dependence upon machines in all aspects of life have probably made it inevitable and sensible that the hearsay element of such evidence be subordinated. As technology moves forward, such evidence also becomes increasingly reliable, thereby removing (as in the case of many documents) a major justification for its exclusion.

### 6.9   Practical considerations—avoidance and evasion: *R* v *Coke; R* v *Littleton*

Witnesses hardly ever appreciate the demands of the rule against hearsay, unless they are witnesses such as police officers who have some professional acquaintance with the rule. It is therefore of some importance to scrutinise witness statements (and, in less leisurely circumstances, oral evidence as it is given) with a view to testing any evidence which appears to consist of an account of what the witness was told by someone else. When the two questions have been asked, the evidence under scrutiny will emerge as falling into either the category of non-hearsay evidence (in which case it is admissible from the witness) or hearsay (in which case it may not be). If the evidence is hearsay, it must also be further examined with a view to seeing whether it can be brought within some exception, but discussion of this further step must await section B and Chapters 7 and 8.

Most criminal cases abound with examples of each category, and despite the attention given above to the difficult cases, the distinction, though vital, is not usually too difficult. Let us take, for example, the following passages from the depositions in the case of Coke and Littleton:

(a)   Statement of Margaret Blackstone: 'We all started talking and Henry said that he had a new album by a band we liked, and invited us to his flat to listen to it.'

(b)   Statement of WPC Raymond: 'I asked her [Margaret] various questions, in reply to which she gave me an account of her having been raped by a young man known to her called Henry Coke.'

Both pieces of evidence, proposed to be given by the witnesses from whose depositions they are taken, clearly consist of statments made to the witness by others when not giving evidence in these proceedings. Question 1 therefore answers itself. As to question 2, a moment's thought dictates different results in the two instances given. In the first, the purpose and relevance of the evidence has nothing whatsoever to do with the truth of what Coke said. It is to be adduced for the purpose of showing the means by which Coke succeeded in persuading the girls to come to his flat. It is therefore a piece of relevant, circumstantial evidence. The second is quite different. The only possible purpose of adducing evidence of what Margaret said to WPC Raymond is to suggest that what was said was true. The mere making of such a statement can have no relevance in itself, and unless it can be brought within an exception, the statement is hearsay and inadmissible.[21]

The strictures of the rule against hearsay produce, not infrequently, a sense of frustration in practitioners and witnesses at not being able to adduce evidence which would tend to reveal clearly the truth of a case. This frustration has led to the widespread use of devices, some legitimate others less so, designed to minimise the effect of the rule's restrictiveness. The ideal avoidance is, of course, to call percipient evidence of the fact or event to be proved, from a witness who perceived it. But this desirable possibility is not always available. A witness can, of course, be asked to say, answering merely yes or no, whether he had a conversation with someone or looked at some document, but such evidence is usually neither very relevant nor very useful. In practice, devices are habitually tolerated which necessarily involve the tacit assertion by a witness of what he has been told by another, but which give meaning and sequence to his evidence of what he himself saw or did. The classic instance is the evidence of a police officer, beginning with the words, 'acting on information received'. Of course, the jury are bound to realise that there is a connection between what the officer was told, and the inquiries he thereafter made, and in many cases it will inevitably appear that the officer was told something about the defendant. But in practice, there can really be little objection; no jury is likely to think that the officer commenced his inquiries through some telepathy or divine revelation, and in many cases if the information seems to have been inaccurate, it may actually assist the defence. Certainly, the jury are unlikely to give any weight at all to a communication whose details are unknown, made by someone about whom they are told nothing.[22]

There are, however, other devices which are less harmless, which have been deprecated by the appellate courts, but which continue to enjoy a surprising degree of liberty in practice. They may be illustrated by the following examples:

---

[21]   The distinction arose in what appears to be the earliest ever reported criminal case: *Adam and Others* Gen 3: 9–19. The Man, the Woman and the Serpent were charged with eating the fruit of the Tree of the Knowledge of Good and Evil. On being questioned about her part in the offence, the Woman replied, 'The Serpent beguiled me, and I did eat.' This reply would be inadmissible hearsay against the Serpent, charged as a counsellor or procurer; but would be admissible, direct evidence that the Woman was beguiled, if beguilement were her defence. It is noteworthy that the report contains no suggestion that there was any other evidence against the Serpent, and it is difficult to avoid the conclusion that he was wrongly convicted.

[22]   But *quaere* whether the relaxation should be permitted further than really necessary to account for what is subsequently done. Should, for instance, 'as a result of an emergency call' be allowed?

(a)   On a charge of theft:
Q.   Did you have a conversation with X?
A.   Yes.
Q.   Then what did you do?
A.   As a result of that conversation, I arrested the defendant for theft.

(b)   On a charge of obtaining by false pretences (taken from *R* v *Saunders* [1899] 1 QB 490):
Q.   Did you make inquiries as to whether any trade had been done by the prisoners?
A.   I did.
Q.   Did you as the result of such inquiries find that any had been done?
A.   I did not.

Both passages may be thought objectionable because, although neither reveals the exact terms of the conversation or enquiry which took place, each reveals the substance of it by necessary implication. In each case, the first question and answer is undoubtedly admissible, so far as it goes. But at the stage of the second question and answer, it may be that the two diverge. In the first example, the passage may perhaps be justified as a slight extension of the 'acting on information received' sequence, whose dangers are more formidable in theory than in practice; the jury may simply think that the officer should have made further inquiries by questioning the defendant. But in the second, the passage is a naked evasion of the rule, in that the witness is being asked, in effect to relate the substance of what he was told, even though the question is framed so as to seem to ask him what he did. Quite separate problems arise where a witness states that, having spoken to X, he said to the defendant, 'X tells me that you have stolen his property. What do you say?' If the defendant adopts the truth of what X has said, by admitting his guilt, then all is well: his admission will be evidence against him. But if he denies it, or refuses to answer, the admissibility of the passage can be a difficult matter, which is explored in Chapter 7. It is certain, however, that the witness's assertion of what X said is not evidence against the defendant of itself.

The lesson to be learnt from these examples is a sound one in every evidential question, that it is the actual effect and not the form of the question and answer which matters, and that one has to look at the whole passage in order to gauge this, and not just at individual questions and answers. Evidence is not admissible if it in fact consists of hearsay, whether or not a question seems to be framed so as to deal with evidence of what the witness perceived or did. In the analogous context of privilege, the use of such devices was the subject of adverse comment by Lord Devlin in *Glinski* v *McIver* (HL) [1962] AC 726, 780, in the following terms:

> But it was thought . . . that privilege would be claimed . . . . So the customary devices were employed which are popularly supposed, though I do not understand why, to evade objections of inadmissibility based on hearsay or privilege or the like. The first consists in not asking what was said in a conversation or written in a document but in asking what the conversation or document was about; it is apparently thought that what would be objectionable if fully exposed is permissible if decently veiled . . . . The other device is to ask by means of 'Yes' or 'No' questions what was done. (Just answer 'Yes' or 'No': Did you go to see counsel? Do not tell us what he said but as a result of it did you do something? What did you do?) This device is commonly defended on the ground that counsel is asking only about what was done and not about what was said.

But in truth what was done is relevant only because from it there can be inferred something about what was said. Such evidence seems to me to be clearly objectionable. If there is nothing in it, it is irrelevant; if there is something in it, what there is in it is inadmissible.

This deprecation notwithstanding, in practice witnesses continue to be permitted to state that they had conversations with others and that as a result of such conversations, took certain steps or acted in certain ways, and it may be that in most cases, no or little harm can result, while the evidence is made easier for the jury to follow. The judge has, undoubtedly, ample power to exclude in a case where harm may be done. For example, there could be no objection of substance to D/I Glanvil or D/S Bracton stating that he began his inquiries as a result of information received. Nothing is added to the direct evidence given by other witnesses, and of course the jury may and will expect to hear that Mrs Blackstone contacted the police after Margaret's complaint.

## B: COMMON-LAW EXCEPTIONS

### 6.10   Introduction

At the beginning of the preceding section, it was said that the rigidity of the rule against hearsay at common law inevitably gave rise to exceptions. The exceptions were narrowly construed, and by means of such restrictive construction the domain of the rule against hearsay was jealously guarded. For this reason alone, the common-law exceptions failed to meet the needs of contemporary practice. And in more modern times, when a more liberal interpretation might have been expected to prevail, their importance has been overshadowed by the emergence of more general statutory exceptions. Consequently, it is unnecessary to consider them in great detail, and what follows is a reasonably concise account of the working of the three exceptions of general significance, namely (a) the res gestae principle, (b) declarations by persons since deceased and (c) statements contained in public documents. Of these, the last has now more or less been superseded by statute. There were several other small exceptions recognised by the common law, applicable to more specific situations. These were by no means finally settled in their operation and extent, were of importance in relation to civil cases and have now been superseded by the Civil Evidence Act 1968.

It is to be observed that each of the exceptions referred to below has two characteristics. The first is that each is justified by the consideration that, did the exception not exist, the facts to be proved would be difficult, and often impossible to prove at all, and there would be a serious hindrance to the administration of justice. The res gestae principle is called for by the ambiguity of many facts standing alone without contemporary explanation or qualification; declarations by persons since deceased are rendered necessary by the finality of the grave; statements in public documents gained acceptance because of the proliferation of important facts recorded in them, which neither informant nor recorder could be expected to recall, even if available to give evidence. The second, and equally important, characteristic is that each is closely circumscribed by stringent safeguards which severely limit their application in the interests of ensuring, so far as possible, the reliability of the statements admitted. Under the res gestae principle, the safeguard is the spontaneity of the statement, the absence of concoction; in the case of declarations by persons since deceased, it lies in adversity to the interests of the maker, or in his duty or in his certainty of impending death; in the case of public documents, it lies in the orderly and prompt making of a record by a public official pursuant to his duty for the purpose of future public reference. In the nineteenth-century cases, the safeguards were insisted upon to a degree which sometimes threatened the very life of the exception; in more recent times, a more lenient approach is to be seen, though the spirit of the safeguards remains.

It is also important to stress that because the evidence admitted under exceptions to the rule is hearsay in character, where it is admitted, it is admitted as evidence of the truth of the facts contained in the statement, i.e. admitted for the purpose for which, but for the exception, it would be inadmissible. There is no question here of evidence being divested of its hearsay character, and being admitted as relevant non-hearsay evidence on some other issue. As we have seen, non-hearsay evidence has no need of an exception because it is unaffected by the rule.

## 6.11 The res gestae principle

The actual expression 'res gestae' is probably best ignored, save for the amusement it has afforded to writers and judges. It is a piece of grammatical nonsense, in that if the phrase is to be employed at all, it should certainly appear, not in its plural form, but in the singular '*pars rei gestae*'. It has been unkindly but correctly dealt with by Lord Wilberforce, who has said that 'the expression "res gestae", like many Latin phrases, is often used to cover situations insufficiently analysed in clear English terms'.[23] It connotes simply that there are of necessity many facts and events, of which evidence is to be given, of which accompanying, contemporaneous statements are an integral constituent part; so that the fact or event, if narrated without reference to the statement, would be ambiguous, meaningless or misleading. Despite some assertions to the contrary,[24] the accompanying, integral statement may be narrated as evidence of the truth of the facts stated in it, but the essential factor in each case is that of spontaneity or contemporaneity, without which the statement could hardly be described as an integral part of the fact or event to be proved. The cases in which the principle has been applied are various, and various ways of classifying them have been suggested. In any event, the main theme of the res gestae principle runs through them all alike, and classification is not of critical importance. That adopted in producing the three categories below is a slightly truncated version of that used by Professor Cross.[25] The categories themselves are no more than identifiable situations to which the principle has been applied, and whatever their differences of fact, they all alike fall aptly within the words of Grove J in *Howe* v *Malkin* (1878) 40 LT 196, that: 'Though you cannot give in evidence a declaration per se, yet when there is an act accompanied by a statement which is so mixed up with it as to become part of the res gestae, evidence of such a statement may be given.'

### 6.11.1 *Statements accompanying and explaining relevant acts*
Where the true significance of a relevant act falls to be proved, the statement of the actor on that subject may be the best evidence of it, provided that the statement is not a calculated justification, and provided that the statement actually relates and refers to the

---

[23] In *Ratten* v *R* (PC, Victoria) [1972] AC 378 at 388.
[24] For example, by Lord Atkinson in *R* v *Christie* (HL) [1914] AC 545 at 553. Certain statements may, of course, also have some value as non-hearsay evidence, and be admissible also for some other purpose.
[25] *Evidence*, 5th ed., p. 576 et seq.

act which it is said to explain. These provisos dictate the conditions under which such cases may be brought within the rule. Firstly, the statement must be contemporaneous with the act; whether it is so is a question of fact and degree in every case, and the test seems to be whether the statement does in reality accompany and explain the act, as opposed to being no more than a subsequent apologia for it, made after reflection. Where the act is a continuing one, however, the statement may be one made during its continuance, as where the stated intentions of a bankrupt in going or remaining abroad are admitted to show his intention *vis-à-vis* his creditors. His intention may be equivocal at the time of his departure, and may only become apparent by his statements made while abroad.[26] Secondly, the statement must relate to the act; in *R* v *Bliss* (1837) 7 A & E 550, evidence that, when planting a tree, a tenant of land (since deceased) had said that the tree was being planted on the boundary of his estate, was rejected as evidence of the location of the boundary. Had the tree been planted as a deliberate act of demarcation of the boundary, the case might have been different; but the statement as an observation coincidental to any possible question of the boundary's limits at the time when it was made could not be said to explain the planting of the tree. In cases falling under this head, the statement to be admitted must be that of the actor, who can explain his act by direct evidence, and not the (opinion) evidence of someone who witnessed the act.

### 6.11.2   *Spontaneous statements by participants in or observers of events*

The common law recognised that an event might also be explained by some spontaneous statement in the nature of an uncalculated outburst in the heat of the moment, made by someone who either played some part in the event in question or who witnessed it. This application of the rule is known in the United States by the graphic name 'the excited utterance rule'. The obvious need in cases of this kind was for a safeguard against concoction to the advantage of the maker of the statement, and this was achieved by a rule in favour of strict proof of spontaneity. The rule is one of some antiquity, as may be seen from the decision in *Thompson* v *Trevanion* (1693) Skin 402, which was an action by the plaintiff for an assault on his wife. Holt CJ held 'that what the wife said immediately upon the hurt received, and before that she had time to devise or contrive any thing for her own advantage, might be given in evidence'. The dictum struck exactly the right note, in stressing the rationale of the requirement of spontaneity, and it would have been as well if it had been adhered to in the spirit, rather than the letter. But in the nineteenth century, the concept of spontaneity was carried to absurd lengths for its own sake, rather than for the purpose of ensuring the necessary degree of reliability. There is usually cited, as the apotheosis of this trend, the grotesque case of *R* v *Bedingfield* (1879) 14 Cox CC 341, in which evidence that when the victim of an alleged murder stumbled from a room where she had been alone with the defendant, her throat cut by a mortal wound, she said, 'See what Harry has done!', was rejected by Cockburn CJ, on the ground that the statement was insufficiently spontaneous.

The decision in *Bedingfield* was not dictated by earlier authority. Indeed, it was plainly contrary to that in *R* v *Foster* (1834) 6 C & P 325, in which on a charge of manslaughter by the reckless driving of a cabriolet, a statement made by the deceased after the event was admitted to prove the nature of the vehicle which had run him down. The absurdity of the decision in *Bedingfield* has been realised and departed from, and it is almost certain that it

---

[26]   See e.g., *Rouch* v *Great Western Railway Co.* (1841) 1 QB 51.

no longer represents the law. Commenting on *Bedingfield* in *Ratten* v *R*,[27] Lord Wilberforce observed that 'there could hardly be a case where the words uttered carried more clearly the mark of spontaneity and intense involvement.' The facts of *Ratten* have been dealt with in 6.7, ante, when we concentrated on the primary ground of the decision of the Privy Council, that the substance of the telephone call made by the wife very shortly before her death at the hands of the defendant was not hearsay, because it represented circumstantial evidence of the state of affairs then prevailing at the defendant's house, and powerfully contradicted his defence of accident. But as an alternative basis for their decision, the Privy Council held that, even had the evidence of the call been hearsay, it would have been admissible by virtue of the res gestae principle. On a strict application of *Bedingfield*, the evidence must have been rejected, but the Privy Council did not view this approach as the correct one. Lord Wilberforce proposed a quite different test, which, it is submitted, would restore the original common-law position, and indeed the spirit of the rule ([1972] AC 378 at 389):

The possibility of concoction, or fabrication, where it exists, is on the other hand an entirely valid reason for exclusion, and is probably the real test which judges in fact apply. In their Lordships' opinion this should be recognised and applied directly as the relevant test: the test should not be the uncertain one whether the making of the statement was in some sense part of the event or transaction. This may often be difficult to establish: such external matters as the time which elapses between the events and the speaking of the words (or vice versa), and differences in location being relevant factors but not, taken by themselves, decisive criteria. As regards statements made after the event it must be for the judge, by preliminary ruling, to satisfy himself that the statement was so clearly made in circumstances of spontaneity or involvement in the event that the possibility of concoction can be disregarded. Conversely, if he considers that the statement was made by way of narrative of a detached prior event so that the speaker was so disengaged from it as to be able to construct or adapt his account, he should exclude it. And the same must in principle be true of statements made before the event. The test should be not the uncertain one, whether the making of the statement should be regarded as part of the event or transaction. This may often be difficult to show. But if the drama, leading up to the climax, has commenced and assumed such intensity and pressure that the utterance can safely be regarded as a true reflection of what was unrolling or actually happening, it ought to be received. The expression 'res gestae' may conveniently sum up these criteria, but the reality of them must always be kept in mind: it is this that lies behind the best reasoned of the judges' rulings.

The emphasis on the reliability of the statement, rather than on the quest for literal spontaneity, is surely to be welcomed as breathing fresh life into a source of evidence that had almost been strangled by the nineteenth-century cases, but it seems that the pendulum may more recently have swung too far in the opposite direction to *Bedingfield*. In *R* v *Nye and Loan* (1977) 66 Cr App R 252, the driver of a vehicle involved in a road traffic accident was assaulted by a passenger in another vehicle. He then sat in his car, recovering from the effect of the assault, and some minutes later, when the police arrived, identified his assailant to them. The words which he spoke were held to have been properly admitted

---

[27]  (PC, Victoria) [1972] AC 378 at 390. The decision has also been doubted elsewhere: see, e.g., *R* v *Taylor* (Supreme Court of South Africa) 1961 (3) SA 616. American Federal Rule of Evidence 803(1) and (2) provides a more liberal time element.

under the res gestae principle. Although it is true that the *Ratten* test makes it a matter essentially for the judge to determine whether the words are a 'true reflection' of what had happened, spoken under 'intensity and pressure', and although consequently it will be only in comparatively rare cases that their admission will provide the foundation for an appeal, it must be said that the decision is a very difficult one to justify. Whatever the effect of the assault in rendering concoction during a period of recovery less likely, it does not appear that there was any real element of spontaneity which would have excluded the possibility of it in real terms, and it is almost certainly impossible to reconcile this decision with the sound statement of the common law in *Thompson v Trevanion*.

American Federal Rule of Evidence 803(2), dealing with 'excited utterances', seems to capture the common-law spirit well by providing for the admissibility of ' . . . A statement relating to a startling event or condition made while the declarant was under the stress of excitement caused by the event or condition'. This may allow for extended periods of time, for example where the declarant suffers shock and cannot speak for some time after the event.

### 6.11.3   Contemporaneous declarations of the physical or mental state of the speaker

Statements narrating the contemporaneous physical or mental state of the speaker, including his emotions and feelings, 'present sense impressions' in American usage, are admitted as part of the res gestae, on an assumption of spontaniety and involvement. Thus, in *R v Conde* (1868) 10 Cox CC 547, on a charge of neglect of a child by depriving it of food, the child's complaints of feeling hungry were held to be admissible. The rule permits a statement of what the condition was, but not of its cause, unless the cause is itself admissible by virtue of the res gestae principle or some other exception to the hearsay rule, for example, as a dying declaration. In *R v Horsford The Times*, 2 June, 1898, the deceased had made a statement to a doctor in the terms, 'I have taken poison; [the defendant] sent it to me.' On the trial of the defendant for murder, the first part of the statement was admitted, but the second rejected. The same result was reached by the United States Supreme Court in the celebrated case of *Shephard v US* 290 US 96 (1933), rejecting under this rule the statement made by the since deceased wife of the defendant: 'Dr Shephard has poisoned me.' The wife's statement of the symptoms she was experiencing would, however, be admissible.

The statement must concern only the contemporaneous condition of the speaker. In *R v Parker* (1960) 45 Cr App R 1, it was held to be wrong to admit evidence that the defendant's wife (with whose unlawful wounding the defendant was charged) had said to a neighbour, 'He shot me; he said he would.'

### 6.12   Declarations by persons since deceased

The intervention of death between the making of a statement and the trial of proceedings to which facts contained in the statement are relevant, quite obviously produces unique problems, to which the usual rules of hearsay are not altogether appropriate. The rules which grew up at common law to deal with such cases reflect the stark truth that in the absence of some provision it would have been impossible to prove many facts of great importance, which had occurred some fairly long time in the past and which were not the subject of any admissible record. In modern times, there is at least one statutory exception designed to meet the same difficulty. The rules at common law show that declarations made by persons since deceased are admissible, exceptionally, to prove the facts contained in them, in four kinds of case, which may be examined briefly. None of them is of very great contemporary importance, because of the growth of more general exceptions to the rule against hearsay, particularly in civil cases, and, in the case of dying declarations, because of the growing practice (so damaging to one of the common law's most romantic rules) of incapacitating by anaesthesia those who might otherwise be in a state of mind to make dying declarations.[28] In each case considered, the declaration may have been made orally or in writing.

### 6.12.1 Matters of public concern
In order to prove matters of custom, prescriptive rights, public rights, pedigree and the like the declarations of persons since deceased are admissible.[29] Public rights may be those which affect the public at large, for example the right to take tolls on part of a highway, or those which are 'general' rights, which affect the inhabitants of a particular district, or some other class of people, for example rights of common. In civil cases, such declarations would almost always now be admissible under part 1 of the Civil Evidence Act 1968, and in criminal cases their occurrence must now be very rare.

### 6.12.2 Declarations against interest
The fears of the common law regarding manufactured evidence in the context of the rule against hearsay subsided where the statement sought to be admitted was one contrary to the interests of the maker. Indeed, we shall see in the next chapter the extent to which adverse admissions and confessions by the living may be important. Similarly, a declaration made by a person since deceased is admissible to prove the facts it states if its contents were, at the time when the statement was made, against the interests of the maker. It seems that the interests so affected may be either pecuniary, as where the maker acknowledges his indebtedness, or proprietary, as where the maker acknowledges that he is not the owner of property or that he holds property upon certain terms. It would seem, however, that the fact that the statement would have tended to expose the maker to criminal prosecution will not be sufficient.[30] Whether it would be sufficient that the statement would have tended to expose the maker to tortious liability is not clear, but it is certainly possible to regard this as an example of a statement against the pecuniary interest of the maker.[31] The statement must have been against the interests of the maker at the time when it was made; the maker must have known it to be against his interests when he made

---

[28]   For this reason, these exceptions are here described in outline only. For fuller accounts, see Cross, *Evidence*, 5th ed., p. 503 et seq, p. 551 et seq; Phipson, *Evidence*, 13th ed., para. 24–01 et seq.

[29]   Matters of this sort may also be proved at common law by evidence of general reputation and family tradition: see 9.2, post; Civil Evidence Act 1968, s. 9(3) and (4).

[30]   See the *Sussex Peerage Case* (HL) (1844) 11 Cl & F 85. Apart from the difficulty of squeezing such cases within the scope of the rule, there is the formidable practical objection that to do so would produce cases where confessions made by accomplices who died before trial might be admitted as evidence against the defendant, whereas statements of the same kind made by living accomplices are evidence only against the maker. Indeed, this occurs in American practice, in which possible exposure to civil or criminal liability is a sufficient adverse interest: see Federal Rule of Evidence 804(3); *Chambers* v *Mississippi* 410 US 284 (1973). As to the statements tending to show adultery, see *B* v *Attorney-General* [1965] P278. At one time, co-respondents bore a risk of having to pay damages for adultery, as well as costs.

[31]   An acknowledgement of a moral obligation to pay seems to be enough, even if the obligation could not have been enforced: *Coward* v *Motor Insurers' Bureau* (CA) [1963] 1 QB 259. If this is right, there must be a basis for admitting statements of fact which might have rendered the maker liable to an award of damages against him.

the statement; and, although there has been considerable conflict of authority,[32] the better view is that the maker must have had personal knowledge of the facts stated by him. These conditions, of course, seek to ensure that the statement may safely be relied on, so far as possible.

The facts which may be proved by declarations against interest are in no way limited to those which might have been contemplated by the maker when making the statement, and the court may use the statement as evidence of facts which the maker would have regarded as incidental to or even irrelevant to the purpose of the statement. In *Higham* v *Ridgway* (1808) 10 East 109, a statement made by a deceased midwife that he had delivered a child on a certain day and acknowledging payment of his fees, was held to be admissible evidence of the child's date of birth. The importance of the statement to the midwife was that it showed that he had been paid, and being accordingly against his pecuniary interest, it would have been admissible to prove that fact. But it was admitted for a quite different, and incidental purpose, to prove a fact which, while not in itself against the maker's interest, was contained in a statement which, taken as a whole, had that effect.

### 6.12.3  Declarations in the course of duty

Declarations by persons since deceased are admissible if they consist of declarations of the acts of the maker of the statement which he owed a specific duty to record, and if the acts recorded were actually performed by him. The duty must be one owed by the maker to another. It seems that the duty in this context should be a legal or at least professional one,[33] but though the cases point in this direction, moral duties do not seem to have been excluded specifically, and to include them would be in keeping with the scope of duty envisaged by s. 4 of the Civil Evidence Act 1968, and s. 68 of the Police and Criminal Evidence Act 1984, under which such statements are, if contained in a document, now equally admissible. The record must have been made contemporaneously with the performance of the act, but this requirement is not literal and is, as in other contexts,[34] one of fact and degree. The declaration must no doubt be made within a period of time consistent with the proper execution of the duty to record, and it may be supposed, while the facts were fresh in the mind of the recorder. But it appears that there may be no objection where the declaration was made prior to the act being performed, provided that the act was performed and provided that it was performed contemporaneously with the declaration. In *R* v *Buckley*,[35] on a charge of murdering a police constable, an oral declaration by the constable to his superior that he was about to go to keep observation on the defendant was held to be admissible as evidence of what the contable was doing when he met his death, and therefore as evidence, in effect, of the identity of the murderer. The requirements are, again, imposed in the interests of ensuring that the statements admitted are reliable as being made promptly and under a duty, and therefore as presumptively accurate. In *Price* v *Earl of Torrington* (1703) 1 Salk 285, a record made in the evening of the day on which the acts were done was held sufficient, whereas in *The Henry Coxon* (1878) 3 PD 156, the delay of an entry in a ship's log-book made two days after the acts recorded was held fatal. But these times are not absolute. The duty may involve recording

---

[32]  Summarised by Professor Cross, *Evidence*, 5th ed., p. 559.

[33]  *Mills* v *Mills* (1920) 36 TLR 772; *Simon* v *Simon and Others* [1936] P 17.

[34]  Cf. the position with regard to documents used to refresh the memory, where a similar condition is imposed so as to ensure accuracy, so far as possible: see 12.2 post.

[35]  (1873) 13 Cox CC 293. One would think that this decision represents the outer limits of the rule, and might not necessarily be followed today.

at, say, weekly intervals, on a time-sheet or in a book of accounts, and it is submitted that a prompt entry in accordance with that duty would be acceptable. Specific cases dealing with questions of contemporaneity are probably best regarded as examples of the working of the principle and not as laying down hard and fast rules on maximum intervals of time.

### 6.12.4  Dying declarations in homicide cases

On an indictment for murder or manslaughter, the dying declarations of the victim are admissible to prove the cause and circumstances of the death. The rule is a specific one, applying only to the criminal cases stated, and allowing the evidence only for the limited purpose stated. Attempts were at one time made to extend the rule to other offences, for example on a trial for the rape of a deceased person,[36] but these were firmly rejected, even in fairly plausible cases such as *R v Hutchinson*,[37] a charge of using an instrument with intent to procure a miscarriage, where the offence had actually resulted in the death of the deceased. But the true rule may be that the death of the deceased must itself be the subject-matter of the charge, in which case there would seem to be no reason why dying declarations should not be admitted in cases of causing death by reckless driving, or aiding and abetting suicide. As to this, there is as yet no authority. It appears that the declaration is admissible equally whether it is favourable or unfavourable to the defendant, as in *R v Scaife* (1836) 2 Lew CC 150, where the declaration tended to suggest that the deceased had provoked the defendant.

The rationale of the rule is that the reliability of the declaration is assured by the imminence of death, and the consequent lack of motivation to tell anything other than the truth. It is doubtful whether the principle has ever been expressed more forcibly than it was by Eyre CB in the following celebrated exposition in *R v Woodcock*[38]:

> Now the general principle on which this species of evidence is admitted is, that they are declarations made in extremity, when the party is at the point of death, and when every hope of this world has gone: when every motive to falsehood is silenced, and the mind is induced by the most powerful considerations to speak the truth.

The situation gave rise, the Chief Baron added, to an 'obligation equal to a positive oath administered in a court of justice'.

Like the requirement of contemporaneity in the res gestae cases (with which the present rule often overlaps) that of a 'settled, hopeless expectation of death', which developed from the dicta in *Woodcock* and elsewhere, having started as a sensible enough check on the reliability of the declaration, achieved a high degree of artificiality and technicality and was enforced more for its own sake than anything else. What matters is the state of mind in which the maker of the statement was when he made it. If he was under a settled, hopeless expectation of death, the declaration will be admissible, even where the deceased's belief was contradicted by his surgeon,[39] and even where the deceased did not

---

[36]  *R v Newton and Carpenter* (1859) 1 F & F 641.
[37]  (1822) cited in 2 B & C 608n; and see *R v Hind* (CCR) (1860) 8 Cox CC 300 (procuring abortion).
[38]  (1789) 1 Leach 500 at 502. The United States Supreme Court in *Shephard v US* 290 US 96 (1933) came a close second: 'There must be a settled, hopeless expectation that death is near at hand, and what is said must have been spoken in the hush of its impending presence. . . . The patient must have spoken with the consciousness of a swift and certain doom.' And see the dying speech of Melun, Shakespeare, King John, Act 5, Scene IV.
[39]  *R v Peel* (1860) 2 F & F 21.

die for some eleven days after making the declaration, during which time he was repeatedly assured that he would recover.[40] But if the deceased appears from the available evidence to have entertained any hope of recovery at all, and was under no certainty of death, the declaration must be rejected. Thus where the deceased merely thought himself to be in great danger,[41] or said that he had 'no hope of recovery at present',[42] the evidence was rejected on the basis that the expectation of death could not be said to be settled and hopeless.

The proof of statements made by persons since deceased is often a matter of some difficulty if such statements are made orally, and can be so in the case of written statements. It appears that although the evidence tendered will not necessarily be inadmissible merely because the witness from whom it comes cannot remember literally every word of the statement, if the witness cannot at least swear that what he remembers is substantially the complete and accurate statement, it should be rejected. So too where the deceased was incoherent, or died before the statement was finished, as in the dramatic instance of *Waugh* v *R* [1950] AC 203, where the deceased said, referring to the defendant, 'The man has an old grudge for me simply because . . .', and died before he could complete the sentence. The Privy Council held that the declaration, tendered as a dying declaration in a prosecution of the defendant for the murder of the deceased, should not have been admitted. Even where a statement is complete, it must be right for the trial judge to warn the jury of any danger of incoherence or inaccuracy which appears from the face of the evidence.[43] And he must, it is submitted, have some degree of discretion to exclude, even where the statement is admissible in law, where there appears to be an appreciable risk of unreliability arising from the circumstances in which the deceased was at the relevant time.

### 6.13  Facts contained in public documents

Statements made in public documents were, at common law, admissible as prima facie, though not conclusive, evidence of the facts contained in them.[44] This exception to the rule against hearsay is justified by the formidable problems which might otherwise arise of proving a multiplicity of facts of public concern or interest, recorded over considerable periods of time, by a variety of public officials charged with the duty of recording certain matters for the purpose of future public reference, who, even if not dead or unavailable, could not be expected to have any recollection of the matters recorded. The number and types of public documents falling within the rule was of course, immense and continually growing, but the common-law rule diminished considerably in significance because of interventions by statute in favour of the admissibility of specific classes of document. Quite apart from the many specific provisions in particular statutes, the common-law rule has in most cases been superseded by the provisions of the Civil Evidence Act 1968 and the Police and Criminal Evidence Act 1984. Almost all public documents would now fall

---

[40]   *R* v *Mosley and Morrill* (CCR) (1825) 1 Mood CC 97.
[41]   *R* v *Errington and Others* (1838) 2 Lew CC 150.
[42]   *R* v *Jenkins* (CCR) (1869) LR 1 CCR 187.
[43]   See *Nembhard* v *R* [1982] 1 WLR 151: no special warning or corroboration is required, even where the dying declaration is the only evidence against the defendant.
[44]   See generally *Irish Society* v *Bishop of Derry* (HL) (1846) 12 Cl & F 641, *Sturla* v *Freccia* (HL) (1880) 5 App Cas 623. A certified copy is sufficient proof of such a document.

within these provisions dealing with the admissibility of hearsay statements contained in records made by persons acting under a duty to do so. In addition, the effect of s. 9(1) and (2) of the Civil Evidence Act 1968 is that any statements made in public documents which, but for part 1 of the Act, would have been admissible as evidence of the facts contained in them by virtue of the common-law rule, are now admissible for that purpose by virtue of that section.

The safeguard at common law, the equivalent of contemporaneity or the settled, hopeless expectation of death elsewhere, lay in the circumstances in which the document was compiled. The conditions of admissibility under the rule were: (a) that the document must have been made and preserved for public use and must contain matters of public interest; (b) that it must be open to public inspection; (c) that the entry or record sought to be proved must have been made promptly after the events which it purports to record; and (d) that the entry or record sought to be proved must have been made by a person having a duty to inquire into and satisfy himself of the truth of the facts recorded.

The fourth condition gave rise to difficulty in modern times, because of the changing nature of public records. The most important part of the common-law safeguard was the duty to inquire into the facts, which lay upon a public official charged with compiling a document for public reference. But the whole theory of the safeguard depended upon the premise that records made for public use were in earlier times compiled by local officers, who would habitually either officiate at or have personal knowledge of the events which they recorded, or who could at least reasonably be expected to make any necessary inquiries from those immediately concerned. The classic illustration is that of the vicar who kept records of baptism, marriages and burials within the parish. In an uncomplicated and localised society, such records might reasonably be trusted on that basis. But in a complex, more diverse and much larger society, the reality is very different, and public officers are now charged with making many records for public use, the contents of which they could not possibly personally know or verify. This exposed a serious deficiency in the common-law rule, when applied to modern records, a deficiency which was clearly and forcibly demonstrated in *R* v *Halpin* [1975] QB 907. Halpin and others were charged with conspiracy to defraud a local authority, and corruption, arising from the performance of a service contract for the supply and renewal of paving stones for the local authority. It was material for the prosecution to prove that, during the period of the conspiracy, the defendant and his wife were in effect the sole shareholders and directors of the company which had the contract with the local authority, from which the jury might be invited to infer that the defendant was in a position to, and did in fact, exercise control over the transactions which were said to be fraudulent. In order to prove this, the prosecution adduced the contents of the file from the Companies Register containing the annual statutory returns of the company, which were required to be made by the company and submitted to the Registrar by virtue of s. 124 of the Companies Act 1948. Although such returns were required to be made and submitted, there was no statutory provision for the admissibility of the statements contained in them, so that, being hearsay, they could be admitted for the purposes desired by the prosecution only if they were admissible under the public documents rule. It was cogently argued on appeal that the returns offended by failing to satisfy the fourth condition, in that the file was not made by a person having a duty to inquire into and satisfy himself of the truth of the facts recorded. To this argument, there was really no answer, but the Court of Appeal, holding that the common law must, 'move with the times', were content to modify the condition judicially to suit modern conditions. Geoffrey Lane LJ, delivering the judgment of the court, said (ibid at 915):

. . . the common law should move with the times and should recognise the fact that the official charged with recording matters of public import can no longer in this highly complicated world, as like as not, have personal knowledge of their accuracy.

What has happened now is that the function originally performed by one man has had to be shared between two: the first having the knowledge and the statutory duty to record that knowledge and forward it to the Registrar of Companies, the second having the duty to preserve that document and to show it to members of the public under proper conditions as required.

Where a duty is cast upon a limited company by statute to make accurate returns of company matters to the Registrar of Companies, so that those returns can be filed and inspected by members of the public, the necessary conditions, in the judgment of this court, have been fulfilled for that document to have been admissible.

The terms of the judgment in *Halpin* foreshadowed the provisions of s. 68 of the Police and Criminal Evidence Act 1984, by alluding to the separate requirements of compilation under a duty and the supply of information by a person having, or who might reasonably be supposed to have personal knowledge of the facts. In civil cases, public documents may now always be admitted pursuant to the Civil Evidence Act 1968. In criminal cases, it should now be possible to admit public documents under this section in almost every case, as Parliament evidently intended (see 8.11, post). It may be that cases could be imagined where the conditions of admissiblity required by the section could not be satisfied, so that some evidence might still be admissible in a civil case, but not in a criminal case, but such cases would be extremely rare. Section 68(3) provides that nothing in the section shall prejudice the admissibility of any evidence that would be admissible apart from the section, which would seem to indicate that the common-law rule could be invoked in such a case. The rules of admissibility at common law set forth above would then apply.

For the above reasons, it would be an uneconomic use of space to reproduce here the material contained in the first edition of this work dealing with what documents are public. The distinction between private and public documents should now rarely, if ever, be significant. If necessary, reference should be made to the first edition of this work at pp. 150–1 or, for a more detailed description, to Phipson, *Evidence*, 13th ed., paras. 25–01 et seq.

### 6.14   Questions for discussion: *R v Coke; R v Littleton*

1   In the depositions and defence proofs of evidence in the cases of Coke and Littleton, identify and distinguish any examples you can find of statements made on prior occasions:

   (a)   which are admissible, non-hearsay evidence;

   (b)   which are inadmissible hearsay;

   (c)   which are admissible only by virtue of a common-law exception to the rule against hearsay.

2   Consider specifically the admissibility of exhibit GG1 (the suspected handwriting of Coke found at his flat by D/I Glanvil).

# 7    The Rule Against Hearsay–II

## A: ADMISSIONS

### 7.1    Principles of admissibility

In 6.12, ante, it was said that the common law was prepared to allow evidence of a statement by a deceased person to be admitted, despite its hearsay character, if its effect was adverse to the interests of the maker of the statement. The putative absence of risk of concoction and exaggeration in such statements, contrasted with that obviously present in the case of self-serving or previous consistent statements, removes one of the important objections to hearsay evidence. As with the dead, so with the living. At common law, statements adverse to the case of the maker are admissible, as an exception to the rule against hearsay, to prove the truth of the facts admitted. The safeguard inherent in this exception is simply that a party has no motive to admit facts which are prejudicial to his case, unless such facts are true. Admissions have traditionally been regarded as one of the least suspect forms of hearsay, and their use as evidence has long been recognised. Indeed, some American jurisdictions now regard 'admissions by a party opponent' as non-hearsay statements: see e.g. Federal Rule of Evidence 801(d)(2). In English law, however, admissions are still received as an exception to the hearsay rule. Certainly in criminal cases, there can be little doubt that they are the most important of all exceptions to the rule against hearsay.

The admissions dealt with in this chapter are properly referred to as informal admissions. This term serves to distinguish them from formal admissions,[1] which are concessions made *inter partes* for the purpose of the proceedings, having the effect (as if made on the pleadings) of establishing the facts formally admitted without the need for recourse to evidence and which cannot be withdrawn without leave.

Informal admissions are statements made by a party (or by some person by whose admission a party is bound as a matter of law) from which the court would be entitled to, but is not bound to, find facts or draw inferences adverse to the case of that party. An informal admission is, therefore, merely one piece of evidence to which the court may have regard when considering the facts to which it relates. Its weight will depend upon the circumstances in which it is made, and the clarity or ambiguity of the contents of the statement. Evidence may be given to explain away or contradict the admission, or to show that because of the circumstances in which it was made, no or little weight should be

---

[1]    See 16.2, post; and see the subject of judicial confessions, dealt with in 10.8.1, post. Certain admissions may also have effect as estoppels by conduct or *per rem judicatam*, which are outside the scope of this work.

attached to it. An admission may be inferred from a statement in any form, whether oral, in writing or by some conduct which can only be interpreted as an acknowledgement of a weakness or defect in a party's case, such as evidence of a conspiracy between a relative of the party and a solicitor's clerk to suborn false witnesses at the trial[2], or of the deliberate destruction of evidence.

The common-law rule has been much modified by practice, particularly in relation to criminal cases, in which specialised rules of admissibility have been developed. Admissions relevant to the issue of guilt in criminal cases are known as confessions, and are subject to special conditions of admissibility, which are considered in section B of this chapter. In civil cases, the common-law rules prevail, although they now enjoy a statutory basis by virtue of s. 9 of the Civil Evidence Act 1968 which, so far as material, provides that:

(1)   In any civil proceedings, a statement which, if this Part of this Act had not been passed, would by virtue of any rule of law mentioned in subsection (2) below have been admissible as evidence of any fact stated therein shall be admissible as evidence of that fact by virtue of this subsection.

(2)   The rules of law referred to in subsection (1) above are the following, that is to say any rule of law—

(a)   whereby in any civil proceedings an admission adverse to a party to the proceedings, whether made by that party or by another person, may be given in evidence against that party for the purpose of proving any fact stated in the admission . . ..

Because an informal admission is no more than a piece of evidence relevant to the determination of the truth or probability of certain facts, and because consequently its effect and weight (if any) are questions of fact, the proper interpretation of the statement is of great importance. It is, therefore, a fundamental principle that the whole of a statement said to contain an admission adverse to the case of the maker should be looked at by the court. It would be quite wrong to isolate, and perhaps take out of context, some part of a statement which appears on the face of it to constitute an admission. The statement read as a whole may have a quite different effect, which may modify or altogether nullify the appearance of an adverse admission. The evidential value of statements partly favourable and partly adverse to the maker has given rise to considerable problems in criminal cases, in which self-serving statements are inadmissible to prove the truth of any relevant facts stated therein. This is considered further in 7.13, post. But in civil cases, there seems to be no reason why those parts of the statement favourable to the maker should not be admissible to prove the truth of the facts stated, in the same way as those parts which are adverse. Be this as it may, the whole statement must be put before the court.[3]

The important rules at common law concern the circumstances in which a party may be bound by admissions made by other persons, or made by himself while acting in a different capacity, and the extent of the facts which may be proved by adverse admission. These matters will now be considered.

---

[2]   *Moriarty and Another* v *London, Chatham & Dover Railway Co.* (1870) LR 5 QB 314.
[3]   In criminal cases, statements may sometimes be edited, so as to exclude matters which are inadmissible and prejudicial, for example revelations of bad character. See 7.12.2, post.

### 7.2 What admissions may bind a party

In addition to the simple case where a party makes, in his personal capacity, a statement adverse to his interests, an admission made in other circumstances or by other persons may bind the party, in the sense of being admissible evidence of the facts admitted adverse to his case. The admissibility in such cases depends upon the relationship between the party and the maker of the statement, which is sometimes, though not altogether happily, described as one of 'privity'. This imports some identity of interest in the litigation, or in the subject-matter of the litigation, which suggests that an admission from the maker of the statement is tantamount to, or should be regarded as if it were, an admission by the party himself. In some cases, the identity is one imputed by the law rather than having any realistic basis of fact. The cases which call for consideration, from a practical point of view, are those referred to below.

#### 7.2.1 Parties in other capacities

Wherever a party litigates in his personal capacity, either as plaintiff or defendant or otherwise, any admission made by him on another occasion may be proved against him, even though it may have been made by him in a representative or other capacity, such as in proceedings in which he represented a person under disability,[4] or acted on behalf of beneficiaries or dependants.

At common law, however, the converse proposition would not hold good, there being no justification, in the absence of some other relationship of privity, for holding that a party to proceedings in which he is necessarily represented by another, should be prejudiced by any admission made by that representative elsewhere in his personal capacity. Thus, in *Legge* v *Edmonds* (1855) 25 LJ Ch 125, where the issue was the legitimacy or illegitimacy of a child of the plaintiff, who was suing as administratix of her husband's estate, admissions made by the plaintiff tending to show that she had committed adultery were held to be inadmissible, although in any proceedings involving the plaintiff in her personal capacity, they would clearly have been admissible on the same issue. In civil cases, it may be that such statements could now be admitted under s. 2 of the Civil Evidence Act 1968, even if not under s. 9, and there is some authority to suggest that the court might exempt such admissions from the notice procedure in the interests of securing a fair trial, to avoid what might otherwise be the consequence that the party relying on such admissions might be obliged to call an opposite party.[5] Since representative proceedings refer in reality only to civil cases, it may be that the common law has now been wholly superseded by statute to this extent, though the weight of admissions received in such circumstances may not always be very great. The position of private prosecutors in criminal cases may, however, prompt some academic speculation.

#### 7.2.2 Other parties

At common law, an admission made by one party is evidence against the maker of the statement, but not against any other party implicated by it. This principle is of considerable practical importance in relation to confessions in criminal cases, and is further considered in 7.12.3, post. In civil cases, admissions made by other parties may now be rendered admissible under s. 2 of the Civil Evidence Act 1968. The common-law

---

[4]   *Stanton* v *Percival* (HL) (1855) 5 HL Cas 257.
[5]   See *Tremelbye (Selangor) Rubber Co. Ltd* v *Stekel and Others* [1971] 1 WLR 226; 8.7.4, post.

rule has the logical, though curious, result that if A and B are jointly charged with the same offence, for example with conspiring together unlawfully, A may be convicted upon his admission that he and B were guilty of the conspiracy, while B may have to be acquitted because of the lack of admissible evidence against him, A's admission being of no evidential value against B.[6]

This rule must be carefully distinguished from a very different rule, with which it is sometimes confused, according to which, where A and B are jointly charged and the prosecution allege a common design, the acts and declarations of A and B in furtherance of the common design, even though made by one in the absence of the other, are admissible evidence against both to prove the existence and carrying out of the common design.[7] This rule has been beset by serious misconceptions. It is sometimes said, quite wrongly, that it applies only to cases of conspiracy. While the rule clearly does apply to cases of conspiracy, it is by no means limited to cases where conspiracy is charged as such, but extends to all cases where an agreement to engage in a common design is implicit in the charge. Thus, whether a number of defendants are charged with conspiracy, or with a number of substantive offences committed pursuant to a conspiracy, should not affect the principle, and it is submitted that dicta in some cases such as *R* v *Dawson; R* v *Wenlock* [1960] 1 WLR 163, 170, to the effect that charges of conspiracy may work injustice by rendering admissible evidence which would be inadmissible on equivalent substantive charges, are ill-founded. However, it is also submitted that this misconception flows from another and more fundamental misconception, namely that declarations in furtherance of a common design are hearsay in character, and therefore are admitted by virtue of the exception in favour of admissions. In fact, it is submitted, such declarations are non-hearsay direct or circumstantial evidence of the common design. If A and B combine together to rob a bank, and while A waits in the getaway car, B enters the bank and says to the cashier, 'I've got a gun; give me the money', it is absurd to suggest that A can object to a witness relating B's words on the ground that the witness would be giving hearsay evidence. Words can amount to conduct, and B's words are just as much direct evidence of the carrying out of the common design as would be the fact that B actually produced a gun and silently threatened the cashier with it.[8] Of course, once the common design has come to an end, evidence of any declarations made *subsequently* by individual defendants would be hearsay, and admissible only by virtue of an exception, if at all. Thus, if the design is ended by the arrest of the defendants, and A makes admissions to the police implicating both himself and B, what he says can be treated as evidence only against himself and not against B. And even during the continuance of the common design, declarations which are in no way in furtherance of it, and therefore have no value as non-hearsay evidence, may equally be hearsay. In *R* v *Blake and Tye* (1844) 6 QB 126, where Tye made entries in two books which tended to incriminate both himself and Blake in a conspiracy to evade customs duty, the entries in one book, which were part of the mechanics of the conspiracy, were admissible against both Tye and Blake as being declarations in furtherance of it.

---

[6]    Cf. *DPP* v *Shannon* (HL) [1975] AC 717. Before the passing of the Civil Evidence Act 1968, the same result frequently obtained in divorce cases, where A obtained a decree on the ground of adultery by Mrs A and B, on the admission of Mrs A, while B was dismissed from the suit for lack of evidence against him. As to conspiracy see also the Criminal Law Act 1977, s. 5(8) and (9).

[7]    The rule is one of some antiquity at common law, and admits, for example, the individual speeches, placards and printed leaflets of various defendants, made for the purposes of the common design, as evidence against each of them: see e.g., *R* v *Duffield* (1851) 5 Cóx CC 404.

[8]    The declarations may also have legal effect as constituting the unlawful agreement. In any event, they are non-hearsay and admissible: see generally 6.7, ante.

However, those in the second book, which were pure matters of record made for Tye's personal convenience and unrelated to the carrying out of the common design, were admissible against Tye as an admission, but inadmissible hearsay against Blake.

### 7.2.3 Witnesses in other proceedings

At common law there was some controversy over the position of a person who was a party in two successive legal actions. What view should be taken of evidence which such a person had relied on in the first action but which could be taken as an admission on an issue in the second action? It was clear that, in general, unless the same witness would give the same evidence in the second action, it was not possible to use in the second action evidence given only in the first without breaking the rule against hearsay.[9] However, in some cases, the courts permitted reliance upon admissions contained in affidavits of witnesses previously relied upon by a party.[10] Happily, the position has been clarified by s. 2 of the Civil Evidence Act 1968, which expressly provides for the admissibility in civil cases of statements made in evidence in other proceedings. In criminal cases, while it is theoretically possible that recourse might be had to the common-law rules, it is difficult to dispute the view of Professor Cross[11] that it is highly improbable that a criminal court would permit the use against a defendant of admissions contained in affidavits made by third parties, even where the defendant had relied upon them in some earlier proceedings.

### 7.2.4 Agents

Admissions made by an agent acting within the scope of his authority are admissible against his principal. The agent acts within his authority, for this purpose, not only when he is authorised to make such admissions expressly, but also when he is authorised to represent the principal for any purpose and the admissions are made in the proper course of that representation. It is, therefore, unlikely that admissions made by an agent relating to transactions prior to the commencement of the agency will be admissible, but there is no reason why the agent should not be given express authority to deal with them. Similarly, it is unlikely that a servant of the principal should be able to make admissions which may be received against his employer, but it is a question of fact whether he has received any proper authority. In civil cases, statements made by agents or employees may now be admitted under s. 2 of the Civil Evidence Act 1968, thus removing a number of difficult questions concerning the scope of the agency.[12]

The agency must be shown to exist and to extend to authorise the agent sufficiently before the admission made by the agent can be received. The agency may be proved by direct evidence, or in a civil case presumably by the hearsay statement of the agent. But there seems to be no reason why the court should not infer the existence and scope of the agency from the facts before it, for example where a person, in response to a request to see someone able to deal authoritatively with a certain matter, comes forward and purports to deal with the enquirer.[13]

---

[9] See generally *British Thomson-Houston Co. Ltd* v *British Insulated & Helsby Cables Ltd* (CA) [1924] 2 Ch 160. The rule was confused by the possibility of using such admissions to prove knowledge or agency, and by the possibility of estoppel.

[10] *Evans* v *Merthyr Tydfil UDC* (CA) [1899] 1 Ch 241.

[11] *Evidence*, 5th ed., p.523–4.

[12] In civil cases such as *Burr* v *Ware RDC* (CA) [1939] 2 All ER 688, statements made by employees would now be admitted under s. 2. As to the notice procedure applying to such cases, see 7.2.1, ante.

[13] *Edwards* v *Brookes (Milk) Ltd* (DC) [1963] 1 WLR 795. But see also *R* v *Evans* [1981] Crim LR 699 which suggests that at least in a criminal case, the existence of the agency must be proved.

Admissions by agents admissible for present purposes are those made by the agent to third parties, and not those contained in statements made by the agent to the principal. Thus, although the directors of a company may make admissions admissible against the company during the course of proper dealings on the company's behalf with third parties, their statements made, for example, to a meeting of the shareholders, cannot be received as admissions against the company.[14]

It is worth commenting specifically upon two particular instances of the many conceivable forms of agency which may give rise to admissions, namely those of legal representatives and spouses of parties.

*7.2.4.1   Legal representatives.*   In civil cases, a solicitor has an implied authority, arising from his general instructions, to make on behalf of his client either a formal admission dispensing with the need for further proof of the facts admitted, or statements on the client's behalf within the proper scope of his instructions which may subsequently prove to be adverse to the client's case and so become admissible as informal admissions. Such statements may be made in court or in chambers, or in correspondence or documents written in connection with the subject-matter of the proceedings.[15] After, though not before the issue of proceedings, the solicitor may compromise a claim on behalf of the client. But it appears that an admission made by the solicitor to a person other than an adverse party to the proceedings, or outside his proper conduct of the proceedings, or by way of fraud on his client, cannot be received.

In criminal cases, formal admissions may now also be made, by virtue of s. 10 of the Criminal Justice Act 1967, and these have, broadly, the same effect as they would in civil cases. But statements which later prove adverse will be admissible as informal admissions only where they are made upon the express instructions of the client, and not where they are made only upon the basis of a solicitor's general instructions,[16] although by s. 11(5) of the Criminal Justice Act 1967 a notice of alibi given pursuant to that section by a solicitor is deemed to have been given with the authority of the defendant, unless the contrary is proved.

Counsel may likewise make admissions, both formal and informal, which may later be admitted against his client, although his authority is narrower than that of the solicitor, in that he must have been acting within the terms of his brief or instructions in relation to the matter in question. Nonetheless, counsel's authority pursuant to his instructions is that of conducting the case in every respect, and this includes the power, in civil cases, to consent to judgment, call no evidence or to compromise the suit. Statements made in court or in chambers by counsel, or assented to by signing an endorsement on his opponent's brief, may be relied upon by the court as admissions. However, admissions made in such ways will be admissible only for the purposes of the proceedings in which they are made, and admissions made in interlocutory proceedings will, it seems, not bind the client on the hearing of the main suit, at least where there is no estoppel and the other side would not be prejudiced by the rejection of the admission.[17] In criminal cases also, statements made by

---

[14]   *Re Devala Provident Gold Mining Co.* (1883) 22 Ch D 593. Though they might, if relevant, be received as admissions against the directors personally.
[15]   An admission by letter that the client has no defence may be proved with a view to obtaining immediate judgment: *Ellis* v *Allen* [1914] 1 Ch 904. This does not of course apply to without-prejudice communications: see 10.3, post.
[16]   See, e.g., *R* v *Downer* (CCR) (1880) 14 Cox CC 486.
[17]   *H. Clark (Doncaster) Ltd* v *Wilkinson* (CA) [1965] Ch 694. Whether this ought to be the position seems, to say the least, open to question. See also *Langdale* v *Danby* [1982] 3 All ER 129.

counsel in open court may be admitted against the defendant, because of counsel's general authority to speak on his client's behalf and on his instructions. In *R* v *Turner and Others* (1975) 61 Cr App R 67, an admission of an offence made by counsel in the course of mitigation of another offence, was held to be admissible on the prosecution of the defendant for the offence so admitted.

*7.2.4.2 Spouses.* It is also worthy of note that the law does not impute any agency capable of permitting evidence of admissions against the 'principal', merely because of the relationship of husband and wife. There may on the facts of a given case be evidence that one spouse gave sufficient authority to the other, for example to conduct his business, but in the absence of such evidence, admissions made by one spouse will not be evidence against the other. The same principle applies to other relationships, for example that of parent and child.[18]

### 7.3 What may be proved by admission

Informal admissions may be received on matters of fact or law, or on both together. So far as matters of fact are concerned, we have seen[19] that admissions should be founded upon the personal knowledge of the maker of the statement, and will be rejected as evidence of the facts admitted where the admission is based upon pure hearsay as to which the maker has no personal knowledge. But where the maker of the statement is speaking about matters perceived by him, his admission may be prima facie evidence of the facts admitted, even where further evidence, such as expert evidence, ought to be tendered in order to prove the facts more specifically. Thus, in *R* v *Chatwood and Others*,[20] the admission of an experienced drug user was admitted as prima facie evidence that the substance with which he injected himself was a dangerous drug. There would seem to be no conflict between this decision and those in such cases as *Comptroller of Customs* v *Western Lectric Co. Ltd* because in the *Chatwood* case, the identity of the drug was in any event a matter to be proved by evidence of opinion, and although expert opinion might be of more value, that of an experienced user was by no means to be disregarded, and was evidence upon which the jury was entitled to act. And there have been instances where facts within the peculiar competence of the defendant have been proved by his own admission, even though necessarily based upon hearsay, as for example his age.[21] The explanation of these decisions seems to be one of convenience and the unlikelihood of injustice to the defendant. The weight of admissions of fact is, as we have seen, a question of fact depending upon the circumstances and terms of the statement. In some cases, particularly in divorce cases where the maker of the statement may have some interest to serve in making it, the court will scrutinise the admission with care, as it will if there appears to be any doubt about the reliability of the statement, having regard to the maker's state of mind at the time.

Admissions of matters of law, though admissible, are usually of little weight, being founded on (generally uninformed) opinion. Indeed, an admission on a question of

---

[18]   *G(A)* v *G(T)* (CA) [1970] 2 QB 643.

[19]   6.6, ante; *Comptroller of Customs* v *Western Lectric Co. Ltd* (PC, Fiji) [1966] AC 367; *R* v *Marshall* [1977] Crim LR 106.

[20]   (CA) [1980] 1 All ER 467. See also *R* v *Korniak* [1983] Crim LR 109; *R* v *Hulbert* (1979) 69 Cr App R 243.

[21]   *R* v *Walker* (1884) 1 Cox CC 99; *R* v *Turner* (CCA) [1910] 1 KB 346.

foreign law, for instance the validity of a marriage celebrated abroad, where the prosecution is for bigamy, will be rejected altogether.[22] But admissions of the validity of English marriages are admissible,[23] and the cases show a variety of other matters of law which have been established by admission, including the existence of a nuisance.[24] There is no objection to the reception of an admission of law which seems even to conclude the very point which the jury have to decide, for example an admission that the defendant stole the property, the subject of the indictment, though the weight of such admission must still be considered: there may be cases where the defendant's apparently clear admission is nullified by evidence that he did not understand the legal nature of theft, and intended only to admit a perhaps innocent taking of the property. But such admissions, particularly when dealing with non-technical and common offences, are often of very great weight, and may in fact conclude the case against the defendant in themselves. There is, of course, an obvious danger in acting on an admission of a matter of law where the matter is a technical one or may be open to debate, and there will be cases where the only safe course is to reject the admission altogether, as was done in *R* v *Philp* (1830) 1 Mood CC 263, where the defendant's admission of the prosecutor's title to property met precisely that fate.

## B: CONFESSIONS

### 7.4 Admissibility of confessions: introduction

An adverse admission relevant to the issue of guilt in a criminal case is known at common law as a confession, and the same terminology is employed by the Police and Criminal Evidence Act 1984. As indicated above, confessions represent the most important and most frequently encountered exception to the rule against hearsay in criminal cases. Fundamental changes in the law pertaining to confessions have been introduced by the Police and Criminal Evidence Act 1984, but in order to understand these changes, it is necessary to understand the principles of admissibility developed at common law to govern the admissibility of confessions. This introduction will summarise the most important aspects of the common-law rules. We will then proceed to examine the new statutory definition and rules of admissibility of confessions.

### 7.4.1 Confessions at common law

While the common law recognised that a confession might be both reliable and cogent as evidence of guilt, and indeed saw no objection to a conviction in cases where a confession was the only evidence against the defendant,[25] the law also recognised that a confession could be regarded as reliable only when given freely and voluntarily. If coerced or forced, the reliability of the confession might be fatally compromised, and the integrity of the system of administration of justice itself made to suffer. The exclusion of evidence obtained by torture, force or other coercive methods was the means of protection of the defendant developed by the judges during the eighteenth and nineteenth centuries, when the memory of an age when such methods were commonplace still lingered. Its

---

[22]   *R* v *Naguib* (CCA) [1917] 1 KB 359.
[23]   *R* v *Flaherty* (1847) 2 Car & Kir 782; though the admission would not of itself justify a conviction for bigamy.
[24]   *R* v *Neville* (NP) (1791) 1 Peake 91.
[25]   See e.g. *R* v *Baldry* (CCR) (1852) 1 Den CC 430.

significance may be gauged by the fact that in English law, the rule that a confession obtained by oppression or in circumstances likely to render it unreliable must be excluded, is the only instance of the mandatory exclusion of illegally or unfairly obtained evidence.[26]

The classic statement of the common-law rule as to admissibility of confessions was that of Lord Sumner in *Ibrahim v R* [1914] AC 599, 609:

> It has long been established . . . that no statement by an accused is admissible in evidence against him unless it is shown by the prosecution to have been a voluntary statement, in the sense that it has not been obtained from him either by fear of prejudice or hope of advantage exercised[27] or held out by a person in authority.

In common parlance, 'voluntary' meant simply 'of one's own free will'.[28]

The test of voluntariness, as defined by Lord Sumner, was supplemented by Lord Parker CJ in *Callis v Gunn* [1964] 1 QB 495, 501, when he added the requirement that a confession must not have been obtained in 'an oppressive manner'. Whether Lord Parker CJ intended to add to the legal requirements for admissibility is open to some doubt, since his observation was, strictly speaking, obiter—the case involved the admissibility of fingerprint evidence. But when the Judges' Rules appeared in revised form in 1964, the introduction stated that the Rules did not affect the principle, which was 'overriding and applicable in all cases', that:

> . . . it is a fundamental condition of the admissibility in evidence against any person, equally of any oral answer given by that person to a question put by a police officer and of any statement made by that person, that it shall have been voluntary, in the sense that it has not been obtained from him by fear of prejudice or hope of advantage, exercised or held out by a person in authority, *or by oppression* [emphasis added].

Whether the requirement of oppression in fact added anything to that of voluntariness is open to doubt. Oppression was defined judicially only once, by Sachs J in *R v Priestly*[29]:

> . . . to my mind, this word, in the context of the principles under consideration imports something which tends to sap, and has sapped, that free will which must exist before a confession is voluntary . . . . Whether or not there is oppression in an individual case depends upon many elements. I am not going into all of them. They include such things as the length of time of any individual period of questioning, the length of time intervening between periods of questioning, whether the accused person had been given proper refreshment or not, and the characteristics of the person who makes the statement. What may be oppressive as regards a child, an invalid or an old man or somebody inexperienced in the ways of this world may turn out not to be oppressive

---

[26]   See *R v Sang* [1980] AC 402 and 1.6, ante. The trial judge may take the method of obtaining other kinds of evidence into account in deciding whether to exercise his general discretion to exclude legally admissible evidence: see Police and Criminal Evidence Act 1984, s. 78(1) and 1.5.2.3, ante. In the United States, the 'exclusionary rule' applies to any evidence illegally obtained.

[27]   In *DPP v Ping Lin* [1976] AC 574, 597–8, Lord Hailsham of St Marylebone pointed out that the word 'exercised' in this passage is probably a reporter's mis-rendering of 'excited'.

[28]   See *R v Rennie* [1982] 1 All ER 385, per Lord Lane CJ at 389.

[29]   (1965) 51 Cr App R 1; and see Lord MacDermott extra-judicially (1968) 21 *Current Legal Problems* 10.

when one finds that the accused person is of a tough character and an experienced man of the world.

The definition suggests little distinction between voluntariness and an absence of oppression.

Lord Sumner's phrases 'fear of prejudice' and 'hope of advantage' are habitually spoken of as 'threats' and 'inducements' respectively. While this is a useful form of shorthand, it gave rise to some problems in the application of the rules of admissibility at common law. In particular, the suggestion of some deliberate act in the words 'threats' and 'inducements' for a time led the courts to concentrate on the mind of the questioner, rather than on the mind of the suspect. Since the problem may recur, despite the apparently clear wording of the 1984 Act, it is worth pursuing briefly. In *R* v *Isequilla* [1975] 1 WLR 716, 721–2, the Court of Appeal concluded that:

> . . . under the existing law the exclusion of a confession as a matter of law because it is not voluntary is always related to some conduct on the part of authority which is improper or unjustified. Included in the phrase 'improper or unjustified' of course must be the offering of an inducement, because it is improper in this context for those in authority to try to induce a suspect to make a confession.

This view of the law would have left the defendant without recourse in a case where, without any improper intent and perhaps even without realising it, the questioner created some fear of prejudice or hope of advantage in the mind of the suspect. In such a case, the resulting confession might well be involuntary, but under the *Isequilla* rule, would nonetheless be admissible. In *DPP* v *Ping Lin* [1976] AC 574, the House of Lords was called upon to decide whether it was the state of mind of the questioner or that of the suspect which was to control the question of voluntariness. The House firmly held that it was the latter that governed the question of whether or not the confession was voluntary, and that should therefore also control the question of admissibility. Lord Salmon (ibid at 606) said:

> In the context of the question raised by this appeal, it is difficult to understand the relevance of the references to impropriety in some of the cases to which we have been referred. No doubt, for anyone to obtain a confession or statement in breach of the established rule is *ex hypothesi* improper. Indeed, it is impossible to imagine how the rule could be breached with propriety. It would seem, therefore, that the references to impropriety add nothing . . ..
>
> In my opinion, the intention of a person in authority who makes a threat or a promise or offers any inducement prior to an accused making a confession or statement is irrelevant. So is the fact that the threat is gentle or the promise or inducement slight save in so far as this may throw any light on the vital question—was the confession or statement procured by the express or implicit threat, promise or inducement.

It will be noted that at common law the rules of admissibility applied only where the fear of prejudice or hope of advantage was excited or held out, or the oppression created by a 'person in authority'. There was much case-law bearing on the question of what persons were or were not persons in authority.[30] It was, however, settled that a person in authority must have, or reasonably be thought by the suspect to have, some influence over his arrest, detention or prosecution, or in other words, be a person from whom a threat or inducement might appear credible. The limitation of the rule in this way was not of great importance, since the vast majority of confessions are made to police officers and others who are undoubtedly persons in authority, and it has now been abolished expressly by the Police and Criminal Evidence Act 1984. But it remains germane to consider it in the light of the common-law rule that the fear of prejudice or hope of advantage must have been generated by the person in authority, with the consequence that self-generated fears and hopes would not destroy the voluntariness of the confession.[31] We shall see that the result should be different under the new statutory rules, even though the confession is made to a person who would previously have been a person in authority.

In addition to the rules governing admissibility, at common law the trial judge had power to exclude a confession, in the exercise of his discretion, where it had been obtained by means of or following a breach of the Judges' Rules. The Judges' Rules were rules of conduct and procedure for the guidance of police officers and others concerned in the arrest, detention and interrogation of suspects. They were first promulgated by the judges of the then King's Bench Division in 1912, and subsequently revised from time to time. The Rules were not rules of law, and did not affect the principles of admissibility of confessions. However, in *R* v *May* (1952) 36 Cr App R 91, 93, Lord Goddard CJ held that the trial judge might refuse to admit a statement if a breach of the rules occurred. But the main importance of the Rules always lay in the fact that a breach of the rules might provide evidence that the resulting confession was not voluntary. The Rules are superseded by Codes of Practice introduced pursuant to the Police and Criminal Evidence Act 1984, and the effect of the Codes on the exclusionary rules is discussed in 7.9, post.

### 7.4.2   Definition of confession

At common law, a confession was the name given to an adverse admission by the accused relevant to the issue of guilt in a criminal case. Section 82(1) of the Police and Criminal Evidence Act 1984 now provides the following statutory definition:

> 'confession' includes any statement wholly or partly adverse to the person who made it, whether made to a person in authority or not and whether made in words or otherwise.

A confession, like any other admission, may be made orally, in writing, by conduct or in any way from which a proper inference may be drawn adverse to the maker. Usually, confessions are made to police officers or other investigators as a result of interrogation, but may equally be made to the victim of an offence, a friend or relative or any other person. The law regarding confessions is now the same in all cases, and it no longer matters whether the person to whom the confession is made is a person in authority.

Although in common parlance, the word 'confession' connotes a full admission of guilt, it has no such meaning in law, either at common law or under the statutory definition. As

---

[30]   See e.g. *Deokinanan* v *R* [1969] 1 AC 20; *R* v *Wilson; R* v *Marshall-Graham* [1967] 2 QB 406, and generally the first edition of this work, pp.160–162.

[31]   See *R* v *Rennie* [1982] 1 All ER 385; 7.5.3, post.

long as any part of a statement is adverse to the maker, in that it has some relevance to the issue of guilt, it will be deemed a confession for the purpose of the law of evidence. Even an indirect admission will suffice, if some adverse inference can properly be drawn. The question of partly adverse statements, however, raises other difficulties, considered in 7.13, post.

Until the passing of the Police and Criminal Evidence Act 1984 confessions made to police officers were almost always made either orally, or in a written statement under caution signed by the suspect, and if oral, recorded subsequently by the police officer in his notebook without further reference to the suspect. Sometimes, regrettably rarely, oral statements were reduced to writing by means of the making of a contemporaneous note. Disputes arise very frequently as to what was said during interviews, and the circumstances in which it was said, and with regard to the way in which a statement under caution was made. These disputes are aired in the context of trials-within-trials to decide the admissibility of the confessions, and consume considerable amounts of court time. In an effort to curtail these problems, s. 60 of the 1984 Act requires the Home Secretary to issue a Code of Practice dealing with the tape-recording of interviews conducted with suspects at a police station, and to direct that interviews of persons suspected of criminal offences to be designated (and potentially all such offences) shall be tape-recorded in accordance with the Code of Practice. Tape-recording is being introduced experimentally in different parts of the country, so that the practicability of the requirement, and its impact in reducing disputes over the contents of interviews may be assessed. Tape-recording may, in future, become the most significant method of recording confessions, but unrecorded confessions will continue to be admissible in evidence subject to the same rules of admissibility.

### 7.4.3  Admissibility of confessions

At common law, confessions were admissible as an exception to the rule against hearsay, to prove the truth of the matters admitted. This is still the case, but their admissibility is now provided for expressly by statute. Section 76(1) of the Police and Criminal Evidence Act 1984 provides that:

> In any proceedings a confession made by an accused person may be given in evidence against him in so far as it is relevant to any matter in issue in the proceedings and is not excluded by the court in pursuance of this section.

'Proceedings' means criminal proceedings, including courts martial: s. 82(1). This subsection is intended to govern the admissibility of confessions in all such proceedings, and is unaffected by the specific provisions of Part VII of the Act dealing with the admissibility of certain other documentary hearsay evidence in criminal proceedings (dealt with in part B of Chapter 8, post). The circumstances in which a confession may be excluded by the court are considered below.

### 7.5  Exclusion of confessions

We have seen that a confession is to be admissible if relevant to any issue in the proceedings, and unless excluded by the court. As to the latter, s. 76 further provides:

> (2)  If, in any proceedings where the prosecution proposes to give in evidence a

confession made by an accused person, it is represented to the court that the confession was or may have been obtained—

(*a*)   by oppression of the person who made it; or

(*b*)   in consequence of anything said or done which was likely, in the circumstances existing at the time, to render unreliable any confession which might be made by him in consequence thereof,

the court shall not allow the confession to be given in evidence against him except in so far as the prosecution proves to the court beyond reasonable doubt that the confession (notwithstanding that it may be true) was not obtained as aforesaid.

(3)   In any proceedings where the prosecution proposes to give in evidence a confession made by an accused person, the court may of its own motion require the prosecution, as a condition of allowing it to do so, to prove that the confession was not obtained as mentioned in subsection (2) above.

'Proceedings' refers, once again, to criminal proceedings. It should be noted that exclusion of the confession is mandatory unless the prosecution prove that it was not obtained in either of the ways mentioned in subsection (2)—the court is given no discretion in this respect. Moreover, the court, in its role as protector of the right of the defendant to a fair trial, may of its own motion require the prosecution to demonstrate the admissibility of the confession, even where no objection is made by the defence.

Another important point made clear by subsection (2) and often overlooked at common law, is that the test of admissibility is not whether the confession appears to be true, but the manner in which it was obtained. True or false, the confession must be excluded unless the prosecution prove that it was not obtained in either of the proscribed ways. Whether or not the confession is true is a matter for the jury, which can arise only if it is first determined that it is admissible.

There must, as at common law, be a causative connection between the oppression or the circumstances and the making of the confession. This is made clear by the words 'by oppression' and 'in consequence of anything said or done'. It is not enough that the court conclude that oppression or circumstances may have existed. The court must also conclude that the confession may in fact have been made as a result. This, as Lord Salmon observed in *DPP* v *Ping Lin* (ante) is and will continue to be the 'vital question', and the question which will almost always require the evidence of the defendant himself on the voir dire in support of his application to exclude a confession.

We must now examine the provisions of s. 76(2) in more detail.

### 7.5.1   Burden and standard of proof

Following the rule at common law, the burden lies on the prosecution to prove the admissibility of a confession, if this is disputed by the defendant or if so ordered by the court of its own motion. The standard of proof is that beyond reasonable doubt, which was always recognised as the required standard at common law on the issue of admissibility of a confession, whatever the vagaries of the standard of proof on other secondary issues.[32] It follows that the judge must exclude a confession if he concludes that

---

[32]   See 3.7.3, ante.

it may have been obtained in either of the proscribed ways; he need not conclude that it was so obtained.

### 7.5.2   Statements obtained by oppression

Although the Act has dispensed with the concept of voluntariness, preferring to speak in terms of reliability, it has retained that of oppression, defining it in terms rather different from those suggested at common law. The dual statutory concepts of oppression and reliability appear to reflect the desire of the legislature to allow the courts to inquire both into the conduct of those to whom the confession was made, and into the totality of the circumstances in which it was made, some of which may be altogether independent of those to whom it was made. If the courts interpret s. 76(2) in that way, the subsection will prove to have expanded significantly the common-law grounds for exclusion. For the purposes of s. 76, subsection (8) defines 'oppression' as including:

> . . . torture, inhuman or degrading treatment, and the use or threat of violence (whether or not amounting to torture).

The proper construction of this provision may cause some difficulty. The use of the word 'include' appears apt to suggest that the kinds of treatment listed are not intended to represent an exhaustive catalogue of those which a court may find to be oppressive, but merely to state specifically that which was never doubted at common law, namely that any confession which may have been obtained by such methods must be excluded. If s. 76(8) were intended to be exhaustive, in the sense of providing a complete definition of oppression, it would have two consequences of considerable import.

Firstly, it would confine oppression to conduct of a serious kind and would reject the idea of the many individual circumstances which may sap the free will of the suspect, as postulated by Sachs J in *R* v *Priestly* (ante). Oppression would, in fact, become a rare ground for excluding confessions, given the reluctance of the courts to make findings that the police may have engaged in such conduct. It is submitted that 'oppression' need not be so confined. Oppression is a composite picture of individual circumstances, rather than just the result of a particular kind of treatment. The factors adumbrated by Sachs J, including the length of, and between, periods of questioning, the availability of refreshments and so on, and others such as whether the suspect was kept in isolation, are surely relevant to the question of whether a confession ought to be admitted. If it is the free will of the suspect that is important, the court may surely consider whether that free will may be sapped by methods less extreme than those listed in s. 76(8)—especially in the case of a vulnerable suspect who is elderly, young or simply overawed by his or her first experience of a police station. At common law the cases recognised that extreme treatment is not always required to induce a confession. In *R* v *Smith* [1959] 2 QB 35, 37, Lord Parker CJ said that the court will be 'at pains to hold that even the most gentle . . . threats or slight inducements will taint a confession'. And in *Commissioners of Customs and Excise* v *Harz and Another* [1967] 1 AC 760, 820 Lord Reid said:

> It is true that many of the so-called inducements have been so vague that no reasonable man would have been influenced by them, but one must remember that not all accused are reasonable men or women: they may be very ignorant and terrified by the predicament in which they find themselves. So it may have been right to err on the safe side.

Secondly, such a restrictive interpretation would be an inadequate substitute for the abrogated common-law requirement of voluntariness. Although oppression, thus defined, would to some extent cover Lord Sumner's fear of prejudice element, in so far as the fear was one of violent or inhuman treatment, it would not cover fear of prejudice arising from the threat of denial of bail, of charging other members of the family and the like, except by recourse to the strained interpretation of those threats as being inhuman or degrading treatment. Nor would it cover Lord Sumner's hope of advantage element, as where a confession is induced by the promise of bail or a lenient sentence, or of having offences taken into consideration or being permitted to plead guilty to a reduced charge or a reduced number of charges. Since inducements are just as capable as threats, and arguably more so, of resulting in a confession, this would be a serious omission. It may be that in such circumstances, the court would hold that the confession had been made in circumstances likely to make it unreliable, but such conduct is not inappropriately described as oppressive.

It is to be hoped that the courts will heed the use of the word 'include' in s. 76(8) and will not overlook the variety of individual circumstances and personal characteristics of the suspect which were held to be capable of building up a picture of oppression at common law.

### 7.5.3 Unreliable confessions

The second ground for exclusion is potentially very wide, and represents a welcome extension of the common-law rules. The reference to 'circumstances', the use of the word 'reliable' rather than 'voluntary' and of the phrase 'anything said or done', appear to give the court a broad mandate to inquire thoroughly into the circumstances in which the confession was made.

In particular, the court is no longer confined to considerations of voluntariness as developed by the cases. Although at common law it was said that the categories of threats and inducements which might render a confession involuntary were never closed,[33] so that the court could consider any kind of threat or inducement that might be alleged, the court was nonetheless able to exclude only where there was a fear of prejudice or hope of advantage excited or held out by a person in authority. If a threat of detention or promise of bail was made, a threat of further charges or a promise of reduced charges, a threat to charge the wife or a promise not to charge the husband, the law worked well enough. But it did not provide for cases in which some personal circumstance, perhaps unknown to the police officers and irrelevant to the charge, acted as its own inducement to confess. Under the Act, the court may consider circumstances entirely unconnected with the police officers (which may lead courts to exclude more readily than was the case when some implication of wrongful conduct was almost inevitable). The test is not whether anyone did something wrong, but whether the court feels confident that a jury should be permitted to act on the confession.

The Act contains no definition of 'reliable' or 'unreliable', probably because none is required. Obviously, the court is not to usurp the function of the jury in determining the weight to be accorded to the confession. It is submitted that the role of the court is to consider whether the circumstances, considered as a whole, disclose any reason to doubt that it would be safe to leave the confession to the jury for their consideration. It is to be noted that the Act requires only that that which was said or done may have been likely, in

---

[33] See *R v Middleton* [1975] QB 191, 197 per Edmund Davies LJ.

the light of the circumstances, to render *any* confession which might have been made in consequence thereof, unreliable. The court is not required to find, and should not attempt to find that the confession actually made is, or even that it may, in fact, be unreliable; this is a question of weight for the jury. If what was said or done is such that *any* confession that might have been made in consequence thereof is likely to be unreliable, then the confession actually made in consequence thereof must be excluded.

The Act clarifies two specific and recurring problems of common law under the voluntariness test. Firstly, it confirms the decision of the House of Lords in *DPP* v *Ping Lin* [1976] AC 574 (and see 7.4, ante) that the intent of the police officers or other persons to whom the confession is made, is irrelevant, except as evidence that the confession may have been obtained in such a way that it must be excluded. There is no need to show or suggest any wrongful conduct, whether deliberate or inadvertent, on the part of the officers, unless the sole ground of the application to exclude is deliberate oppression such as that consisting of the conduct specified in s. 76(8). Even in such a case, it is submitted on the basis of *Ping Lin*, that it is the effect on the suspect's mind, and not the wrongful conduct of the officers, that constitutes the ground of the application.

Secondly, since it is no longer necessary to show that the confession may have been induced by a fear of prejudice or hope of advantage excited or held out by a person in authority, it is possible to envisage a case in which the circumstances requiring exclusion are generated by the defendant himself, or may consist solely of the workings of the defendant's mind. In *R* v *Rennie* [1982] 1 All ER 385, the defendant was questioned about various offences of fraud, in which the police suspected that members of his family were also implicated. When a police officer mentioned this latter suspicion, the defendant at once said: 'No, don't bring the rest of the family into this. I admit it was my fault.' At the hearing of the defendant's application to exclude this confession (and further similar statements) a police officer testified that the defendant appeared to fear that the family would be brought into it. The judge rejected this evidence, and admitted the confession on the ground that it was voluntary. On appeal, it was argued that the confession should have been excluded because the evidence showed that the defendant might have made the confession in the hope of protecting other members of his family. Dismissing the appeal, Lord Lane CJ said (ibid at 388):

> Even if it were the fact that the appellant had decided to admit his guilt because he hoped that if he did so the police would cease their inquiries into the part played by his mother, it does not follow the confession should have been excluded.
>
> Very few confessions are inspired solely by remorse. Often the motives of an accused are mixed and include a hope that an early admission may lead to an earlier release or a lighter sentence. If it were the law that the mere presence of such a motive, even if prompted by something said or done by a person in authority, led inexorably to the exclusion of a confession, nearly every confession would be rendered inadmissible. This is not the law. In some cases the hope may be self-generated. If so, it is irrelevant, even if it proves the dominant motive for making the confession. In such a case the confession will not have been obtained by anything said or done by a person in authority . . . .
>
> There can be few prisoners who are being firmly but fairly questioned in a police station to whom it does not occur that they might be able to bring both their interrogation and their detention to an earlier end by confession.

It is submitted that 'self-generated' hopes may not be irrelevant under the Act, as the court in *Rennie* held them to be at common law, because of the abrogation of any requirement of generation by a person in authority. It may be that, should the facts of *Rennie* recur, they would provide a good example of circumstances which might have rendered any confession unreliable, especially if the frank evidence of the officer as to the defendant's apparent fears were accepted. No doubt the same principle may be applied to confessions obtained while the defendant was suffering under the effects of illness, physical or mental, drink or drugs (even if not a deliberate taking advantage of his condition, which might be a breach of the Code of Practice).[34] It is submitted that the decision of Melford Stevenson J in *R v Kwabena Poku* [1978] Crim LR 488 should also be followed if the facts should recur. In that case, the learned judge excluded a confession to attempted rape, made by the defendant when a police officer told him, in good faith but mistakenly, that there was forensic evidence of seminal stains that would incriminate him; no such evidence existed.

As at common law, there may be cases where the oppression or circumstances pass away before the confession is made, so that there is no causative connection between the former and the latter, and in such a case, the confession may be received. An example is *R v Smith* [1959] 2 QB 35. The first confession made by the defendant, a serving soldier, was rejected because it was made to his regimental sergeant-major (a person in authority) who had threatened to keep a number of soldiers on parade until a confession was forthcoming from one of them. However, when that treatment had ended, the defendant made further oral and written confessions to regular investigating officers, who presented no fear of prejudice or hope of advantage. These latter confessions were admitted.

### 7.6 Evidence yielded by inadmissible confessions

Confessions may be useful to the prosecution for more reasons than one. We have so far considered the admissibility of the confession as evidence of the truth of the facts admitted, as an exception to the rule against hearsay. But a confession may also yield other admissible evidence, the discovery of which is made possible or facilitated by what is said in the confession, as where the defendant in his confession tells the police where to find the stolen goods or the body of his victim. If the confession is admissible, no difficulty arises, for the prosecution are then entitled to adduce evidence, not only of the confession itself but also of the evidence discovered as a result. But if the confession is excluded at trial, does other evidence discovered as a result of it become 'tainted' as being 'the fruit of the poisonous tree', and must it therefore be excluded also? In fact, this question contains two distinct sub-questions. Firstly, may the prosecution adduce the discovered evidence without reference to the confession? Secondly, may the prosecution adduce evidence that the other evidence was discovered because of a confession made by the defendant?

At common law, it was held that the discovered evidence might be admitted, even though the confession was excluded, provided that the discovered evidence was capable of being 'fully and satisfactorily proved' without any reference to the confession.[35] It was suggested at one time that that part of the confession necessary to explain the discovery of the other evidence might be admitted for that limited purpose, while the remainder of the confession was excluded, but this unsatisfactory approach was ultimately rejected.[36] In

---

[34]   Cf. *R v Davis* [1979] Crim LR 167. As to confessions made by the mentally handicapped, see also s. 77 of the Act and 7.8, post.

[35]   *R v Warickshall* (1783) 1 Leach 263. Where a confession is excluded, it must not be referred to in the presence of the jury for any purpose: *R v Treacy* [1944] 2 All ER 229. But see the Police and Criminal Evidence Act 1984, s. 76(4)(*b*).

[36]   *R v Gould* (1840) 9 C & P 364; *R v Berriman* (1854) 6 Cox CC 388.

some cases, the discovered evidence was held to be so intimately connected with the inadmissible confession that the former could not be adduced. In *R* v *Barker* [1941] 2 KB 381, confessions made by the defendant were excluded because of inducements made to him by officers of the Inland Revenue. The prosecution sought, nonetheless, to adduce evidence of books produced by the defendant, which were said to contain evidence of fraud. However, as it appeared that the books were part and parcel of the confession, and had been produced as part of and for the purpose of explaining the confession, it was held that they, too, must be rejected.

By s. 76(4), (5) and (6) of the Police and Criminal Evidence Act 1984:

(4)   The fact that a confession is wholly or partly excluded in pursuance of this section shall not affect the admissibility in evidence—

(*a*)   of any facts discovered as a result of the confession . . ..

(5)   Evidence that a fact to which this subsection applies was discovered as a result of a statement made by an accused person shall not be admissible unless evidence of how it was discovered is given by him or on his behalf.

(6)   Subsection (5) above applies—

(*a*)   to any fact discovered as a result of a confession which is wholly excluded in pursuance of this section; and
(*b*)   to any fact discovered as a result of a confession which is partly so excluded, if the fact is discovered as a result of the excluded part of the confession.

Subsection (4) deals with the first of the two sub-questions posed above. The subsection does not appear to alter the common-law rule that an excluded confession, or part, may not be referred to in the presence of the jury for any purpose. It does, however, provide that the discovered evidence shall be admissible, notwithstanding that the confession is excluded. It is unclear what, if anything the legislature intended to happen in future in situations such as that in *R* v *Barker*. It is submitted that, where the discovered evidence cannot be adduced without necessarily referring to the confession, it must be excluded. More frequently, the discovered evidence will appear strange to a jury because of the absence of evidence as to how it was discovered, but where, for example, evidence is discovered because of some inadmissible hearsay communication to the police, the same problem occurs. It is usually not a serious one, and can if necessary be mitigated by a direction to the jury against speculation about the source of the discovered evidence.

Subsections (5) and (6) answer our second sub-question by providing that evidence that the discovered evidence was discovered because of an excluded confession may be introduced only by the defence. Once introduced, however, the prosecution may presumably investigate the matter further, in accordance with the usual rule of evidence that to introduce a subject which might have been excluded opens up the whole to scrutiny. The defence should consider long and hard before opening the door.

### 7.7   Excluded confessions as relevant non-hearsay evidence

By s. 76(4) of the Police and Criminal Evidence Act 1984:

(4)   The fact that a confession is wholly or partly excluded in pursuance of this section shall not affect the admissibility in evidence—

. . .

(*b*)   where the confession is relevant as showing that the accused speaks, writes or expresses himself in a particular way, of so much of the confession as is necessary to show that he does so.

We saw in 6.7, ante that a statement may be admissible as non-hearsay evidence, if relevant for a purpose other than proving the truth of facts stated therein. A statement may be relevant as showing, inter alia, the way in which the maker expresses himself, including his command or lack of command of the English language, his use of idiom, his grammatical ability, his vocabulary and his style of writing. Frequently, these matters are canvassed in the course of an application to exclude a confession, in order to suggest that the defendant could or could not have made, or is or is not likely to have made the alleged confession. But since the subsection is dealing with confessions that have already been excluded, it is clear that the intended relevance lies elsewhere.

The case of *R* v *Treacy* [1944] 2 All ER 229, is authority for the well-known rule of evidence that a confession, or part of a confession which is excluded, must not thereafter be referred to in the presence of the jury for any purpose. It follows that, at common law, even if the confession may have some relevance other than the truth of the facts admitted, it may not be referred to if excluded. There is no reason why this rule should not continue to apply in general when confessions are excluded under s. 76 of the 1984 Act, as it did at common law. Section 76(4)(*b*) creates an exception to the rule in the one kind of case described. An example would be where the defendant denies speaking English, and his ability to speak English is relevant to an issue in the case, for example his ability to complete an allegedly fraudulent loan application; or where a defendant charged with a sophisticated offence of bank fraud claims to be virtually illiterate.

In cases not covered by this subsection, it is submitted that the general rule precluding any use of the confession should apply.

### 7.8   Confessions by the mentally handicapped

By s. 77 of the Police and Criminal Evidence Act 1984:

(1)   Without prejudice to the general duty of the court at a trial on indictment to direct the jury on any matter on which it appears to the court appropriate to do so, where at such a trial—

(*a*)   the case against the accused depends wholly or substantially on a confession by him; and
(*b*)   the court is satisfied—
   (i)   that he is mentally handicapped; and
   (ii)   that the confession was not made in the presence of an independent person,

the court shall warn the jury that there is a special need for caution before convicting the accused in reliance on the confession, and shall explain that the need arises because of the circumstances mentioned in paragraphs (*a*) and (*b*) above.

Section 77(2) makes provision for a magistrates' court conducting a summary trial to treat such cases as requiring special caution. Section 77(3) defines a person as mentally handicapped when 'he is in a state of arrested or incomplete development of mind which includes significant impairment of intelligence and social functioning'. The same subsection defines an 'independent person' as excluding a police officer or a person employed for or engaged on police purposes.

It should be added that it would surely be proper for the court to take into account the circumstances mentioned in this section in determining whether any confession made by a mentally handicapped person under such circumstances may be unreliable, and whether the confession actually made must therefore be excluded. However, the direction called for by the section is mandatory in all such cases, even where the judge considers that no question of unreliability arises. The weight of the confession, if admitted, is of course a question of fact for the jury.

### 7.9  The Code of Practice and the exclusion of confessions

Section 66 of the Police and Criminal Evidence Act 1984 provides that:

The Secretary of State shall issue codes of practice in connection with—

(*a*)   the exercise by police officers of statutory powers—
  (i)   to search a person without first arresting him; or
  (ii)   to search a vehicle without making an arrest;
(*b*)   the detention, treatment, questioning and identification of persons by police officers;
(*c*)   searches of premises by police officers; and
(*d*)   the seizure of property found by police officers on persons or premises.

Section 60 similarly requires the Secretary of State to issue a Code of Practice in connection with the tape-recording of interviews. When these Codes of Practice have been laid before Parliament, as called for by the Act, and are promulgated and take effect, they will constitute a body of procedural rules for the guidance of police officers and other professional investigators, for example investigators employed by the Customs and Excise, the Inland Revenue or the Department of Health and Social Security.[37] The Codes will deal comprehensively with matters affecting the detention, arrest, search and interrogation of suspects. The detail of the rules is outside the scope of this work, but the Codes of Practice must be considered in relation to the possible effect of breaches of the rules on the admissibility of confessions.

The Codes of Practice are designed to supplant the Judges' Rules, which since they were first formulated in 1912 were the rules of practice recognised by the courts for the conduct of police officers and other professional investigators in relation to detention, arrest, search and interrogation. The relationship between breaches of the Judges' Rules and the admissibility of confessions that resulted from or followed such breaches was never satisfactorily defined. The Rules were rules of practice only, and not rules of law. Their preamble made it clear that they did not affect the overriding principle that confessions

---

[37]   As to other investigators, see s. 67(9) of the Act. The Judges' Rules also applied to such investigators: see Rule 6.

must have been voluntary and obtained in the absence of oppression. But it went on to add:

> Within that principle the following rules are put forward as a guide to police officers conducting investigations. Non-conformity with these rules may render answers and statements liable to be excluded from evidence in subsequent criminal proceedings.

In *R* v *May*[38] Lord Goddard CJ said:

> The test of the admissibility of a statement is whether it is a voluntary statement. There are certain rules known as the Judges' Rules which are not rules of law but rules of practice drawn up for the guidance of police officers; and if a statement has been made in circumstances not in accordance with the Rules, in law that statement is not made inadmissible if it is a voluntary statement, although in its discretion the court can always refuse to admit it if the court thinks there has been a breach of the Rules.

In practice, the courts proved reluctant to exclude a confession on account of a 'technical breach' of the Rules, in other words in cases where the breach had no effect on the voluntariness of the statement either because the breach was a relatively minor one, or because the breach was not closely related to the making of the confession. The Rules were generally regarded as an aid to the determination of whether the confession had been made voluntarily, rather than as a basis for exclusion in their own right. This was clearly indicated by the decision of the Court of Appeal in *R* v *Prager* [1972] 1 WLR 260. The defendant, who was charged with serious offences contrary to the Official Secrets Acts, was interrogated without caution in breach of Rule 2 of the Judges' Rules. The decision not to caution was taken deliberately and in advance of the interrogation by the interrogating officers, a decision said to be justified by the serious nature of the case and the possibility of damage to the national interest. The trial judge, Lord Widgery CJ, held that the resulting confession was voluntary and declined to consider separately whether or not it should be excluded on discretionary grounds because of the breach of Rule 2. On appeal, it was argued that this approach was impermissible. However, Edmund Davies LJ, in dismissing the appeal, said (ibid at 265-6):

> [Counsel] submitted before us that it was imperative that Lord Widgery CJ decided first whether Rule 2 had or had not been breached, for, if it had been, the confession should not have been admitted unless there emerged 'some compelling reason why the breach should have been overlooked'. He cited no authority for that proposition, which, he claimed, involved a point of law of very great importance. This 'complete lack of authority' (to use [counsel's] phrase) is not surprising, for in our judgment, the proposition advanced involves no point of law and is manifestly unsound. Its acceptance would exalt the Judges' Rules into rules of law. That they do not purport to be, and there is abundant authority for saying that they are nothing of the kind. Their non-observance may, and at times does, lead to the exclusion of an alleged confession; but ultimately all turns on the judge's decision whether, breach or no breach, it has been

---

[38]   (1952) 36 Cr App R 91, 93. The discretion referred to by Lord Goddard CJ was expressly re-affirmed by the House of Lords in *R* v *Sang* [1980] AC 402, even though the House held that there was no general common law discretion to exclude other evidence obtained illegally or unfairly.

shown to have been made voluntarily. In the present case, Lord Widgery CJ was, without deciding the point, prepared to assume in the accused's favour that there had been a breach of Rule 2, and then proceeded to consider whether its voluntary nature had nevertheless been established. In our judgment, no valid criticism of that approach can be made. On the contrary, it appears to us entirely sound.

Although the common-law test of voluntariness has now been supplanted by the statutory test, discussed above, laid down by s. 76 of the Police and Criminal Evidence Act 1984, the correct approach would appear to be to make similar use of the provisions of the Codes of Practice in determining whether any ground exists for excluding a confession. Indeed, the evidential status of the Codes is provided for expressly by s. 67(11) of the Act:

> In all criminal and civil proceedings any such code shall be admissible in evidence; and if any provision of such a code appears to the court or tribunal conducting the proceedings to be relevant to any question arising in the proceedings it shall be taken into account in determining that question.

A breach of the provisions of the Codes may be relevant as showing oppressive conduct, or the existence of the circumstances likely to render any confession made by a defendant unreliable. Much will depend on the nature and gravity of the breach, as was the case under the Judges' Rules, and there is no basis for supposing that a breach of the Code per se, which has no effect or no more than a minimal effect on the making of a confession, will result in the confession being excluded.

Although the courts expressed their power to exclude on the ground of a breach of the Judges' Rules as discretionary, it does not follow that the same approach must be maintained in relation to the Codes of Practice. Indeed, experience with the Judges' Rules suggests that the discretionary power is relatively unimportant as an independent basis for exclusion, and that the courts have demonstrated a clear preference for the approach of using the Rules as one factor in determining the question of admissibility. Prior to the coming into effect of the 1984 Act, a trial judge was entitled to exercise the common-law discretion to exclude admissible prosecution evidence, on the ground that its probative value was substantially outweighed by the danger of unfair prejudice. There is now a statutory discretion under s. 78(1) of the Act, by which:

> In any proceedings the court may refuse to allow evidence on which the prosecution proposes to rely to be given if it appears to the court that, having regard to all the circumstances, including the circumstances in which the evidence was obtained, the admission of the evidence would have such an adverse effect on the fairness of the proceedings that the court ought not to admit it.

There is no reason to suppose that this discretion cannot apply to evidence of a confession, as well as to any other evidence, and the court is expressly enabled to consider the circumstances in which the evidence was obtained. It is submitted that, if the provisions of the Act are applied consistently, it should be an academic question whether the trial judge determines to exclude a confession because the circumstances give rise to doubt about the reliability of any confession which the defendant might have made, or because of the exercise of the discretion under s. 78. In either case, the prosecution will have failed to prove beyond reasonable doubt that the confession was not obtained in one of the ways proscribed by s. 76. It may be, therefore, that the courts will not be called upon to consider whether breaches of the Codes of Practice have an independent effect on the admissibility of confessions and that such breaches will be considered in their true light as a part of the circumstances in which the confession was obtained. In this way, the Codes will have a role to play, as did the Judges' Rules, in the determination of the admissibility of confessions.

## 7.10 Challenging confessions as a question of fact

Like any other evidence, the circumstances or contents of a confession may be disputed as a question of fact. In other words, as in Coke's case, a defendant may dispute that he made a confession at all, or that what he did say has been properly and accurately recorded;[39] or he may allege that the circumstances in which he made the confession are quite different from those related by the officer. We have already seen that a defendant may dispute, as a matter of law, the admissibility of a confession. This is a matter for the judge to determine in the absence of the jury. The defendant may also invite the judge, similarly a matter of law to be decided in the absence of the jury, to exclude the confession in the exercise of his discretion. If the judge decides that the confession should be admitted, the result is that the confession may be proved in the presence of the jury and becomes evidence in the case for them to consider. But the weight to be attached to the confession is a question of fact for the jury, and although the jury are not concerned with oppression or reliability as such, it is both proper and necessary for the defence to raise in front of the jury the allegations which they make about the confession. Those allegations, having been relevant to the issue of law of admissibility, are equally relevant at a later stage to the weight, if any, to be accorded to the confession. If the jury think that the defendant may not have made the confession at all, or that it is unreliable, then the admissibility of the confession will not matter; the jury will accord it little or no weight, and will not act on it to convict. Another good reason for renewing the defence case in front of the jury is that should further evidence come to light, even at that late stage, from which the judge may infer that his earlier ruling was wrong, he may reconsider it and withdraw the confession from the jury.[40]

### 7.10.1 *R* v *Coke; R* v *Littleton*
Counsel for Coke may make, as it were, a three-pronged attack on the oral and written confessions related by D/I Glanvil. He may (a) dispute admissibility, (b) invite the exercise of the discretion to exclude; and if unsuccessful (c) attack the inspector's evidence as an issue of fact in front of the jury. Each of these prongs of the attack involves putting Coke's case in cross-examination and, probably, his giving evidence of what occurred at the police station. There is nothing inconsistent in his disputing the admissibility of, or

---

[39]   Usually, though not inevitably, such allegations will involve an imputation on the character of the officer concerned, because they suggest fabrication of evidence; this, subject to the judge's discretion, will expose the defendant to cross-examination under s. 1(*f*)(ii) of the Criminal Evidence Act 1898, should he later give evidence before the jury: see 4.14, ante.

[40]   *R* v *Watson* (CA) [1980] 2 All ER 293. Ordinarily, this will result in the discharge of the jury and an order for a new trial, because of the risk of prejudice to the defendant arising from the jury's having been exposed to inadmissible evidence. But in his discretion, the judge may decide to continue and give the jury a strongly worded warning in the summing-up, particularly if the confession would in any event have carried little weight. As to procedure, see 1.5.1.2, ante.

inviting the judge to exclude, the alleged oral confession ('Yes, I may as well . . .') while later maintaining as a question of fact, if it is admitted, that he never said those words. The question of admissibility must be judged on the footing that the confession was made. If the alleged confession is ruled to be admissible, but the jury do not accept that it was made, then they will disregard it. Coke may, with complete consistency, adopt each of the three methods of attack, or any or all of them, and in view of the nature of his case, it seems inevitable that he would take this course. As to the written confession. Coke may raise the circumstances in which he said it was obtained, firstly so as to dispute its admissibility, and secondly, if it is admitted, to suggest to the jury that no weight should be accorded to it.

### 7.11 Practice: proof of confessions

The practice relating to the proof of confessions may be conveniently summarised as follows, bearing in mind the points made in the preceding paragraphs.

(a) If admissibility of the confession is not in dispute, it may be opened to and proved before the jury; its weight is then a matter of fact for them.

(b) If admissibility is disputed, or if the defence intend to invite the judge to exclude the confession in the exercise of his discretion, counsel for the defence should inform counsel for the prosecution of this intention at the outset of the trial, and the confession should not be opened to the jury or referred to in their presence. At the moment when the subject arises naturally for the first time in evidence,[41] the jury should be asked to withdraw, and the questions of law are then resolved by the judge in a 'trial within a trial', properly known as the 'voir dire'.[42]

(c) It is necessary to add one or two words concerning evidence given by the defendant on the voir dire, because of the decision of the Privy Council in *Wong Kam Ming* v *R* [1980] AC 247, which has clarified (albeit not entirely happily) various matters of practice which had previously been obscure. The defendant was charged with murder and malicious wounding arising from a violent attack by a group of men against a massage parlour in Hong Kong, for which the motive was apparently revenge. The only evidence against him was his own confession in writing that he had been present at the scene of the attack, and had 'chopped' someone with a knife. As a result of an objection by the defence, heard on the voir dire, the trial judge held the statement to be inadmissible and excluded it. But in the course of giving evidence on the voir dire, the defendant had been asked in cross-examination whether the contents of his statement were in fact true, and had admitted that he had been present and that he had played some part in the attack. The Crown applied for, and were given, leave to prove before the jury the defendant's admissions on the voir dire, and later, when the defendant gave evidence before the jury, to cross-examine him with regard to discrepancies between his evidence in front of the jury and his evidence on the voir dire. It fell to the Privy Council to answer three principal questions: (a) may the defendant properly be asked, on the voir dire, whether the contents of his confession are true? (b) may the prosecution prove, as part of their case before the jury, incriminating evidence given by the defendant on the voir dire? and (c) may the prosecution cross-examine the defendant in front of the jury with regard to his previous inconsistent evidence on the voir dire? The first two of these questions carried the subsidiary questions,

---

[41] If the opening cannot be made intelligible without the confession, e.g. because it is the only evidence, the matter may be dealt with as a preliminary point.

[42] As to the use of the voir dire to determine admissibility, see 1.5.1.2, ante.

whether, if the answer to the principal question was in the affirmative, any judicial discretion lay to exclude such evidence. To the first two questions, the first by a majority,[43] the second unanimously, the Privy Council gave the answer no; to the third, unanimously, they answered, 'only if the confession has been admitted after the voir dire'. The two subsidiary questions, therefore, did not require an answer.

There are a number of practical criticisms which may be made of the decision. On the first question, while, as the majority held and as is now reflected in s. 76(2) of the Police and Criminal Evidence Act 1984, the trial judge is not concerned on the voir dire with the truth of the confession, but only with its admissibility, it is often relevant to enquire whether the confession is true, simply because this may affect the issue of how it came to be made. Did the defendant involuntarily or while under oppression invent a pack of lies, or blurt out the truth? The voir dire is by no means the only example of the style, language or content of a statement being relevant to issues arising in a criminal case. Indeed, s. 76(4)(*b*) of the Police and Criminal Evidence Act 1984 now provides for the admissibility of such relevant evidence even where a confession has been excluded by the judge: see 7.7, ante. If it is alleged (as it often is) that the words of the confession are those, not of the defendant, but of the officer, does the confession contain some element of truth which the officer could not then have known? In *R* v *Hammond*[44] the Court of Criminal Appeal expressly sanctioned cross-examination of a defendant concerning the truth of a confession alleged not to be voluntary, although it was there put on the less satisfactory basis that such questions went to credit. On the second question, while some rule of policy may be thought to protect the defendant from having exposed to the jury what he has said on the voir dire, it is not entirely clear why the interests of justice may require the jury to be kept in ignorance, and perhaps to acquit in ignorance of the fact that the defendant has admitted an oath during the trial that the whole or part of the case against him is true. Certainly, the position on the voir dire must, if it is the correct position, for some reason be different from that with regard to other forms of judicial confession. The answer to the third question is perhaps the strangest of all. It is not easy to see how the answer can be reconciled with the fact that counsel for the prosecution is entitled by statute[45] to cross-examine the defendant with regard to previous statements made by him inconsistent with his evidence before the jury.

In *R* v *Brophy* [1981] 2 All ER 705, the defendant was charged in Northern Ireland with an offence of being a member of a proscribed organisation, namely the IRA. He was tried by a judge sitting alone pursuant to the Northern Ireland (Emergency Provisions) Act 1978. The defendant successfully applied to the judge to exclude a confession on the ground that the prosecution had failed to prove that it had not been obtained by ill-treatment while in custody. The prosecution then successfully sought leave to prove as part of their case on the issue of guilt a clear admission made by the defendant while testifying on the voir dire, to the effect that he had been a member of the IRA. On the basis of this evidence, the defendant was convicted. The Court of Appeal in Northern Ireland allowed the defendant's appeal against conviction, on the ground that his testimony that

[43] Lords Diplock, Salmon, Edmund, Davies and Keith; Lord Hailsham of St Marylebone dissenting.

[44] (CCA) [1941] 3 All ER 318. The majority view of the Privy Council in *Wong Kam Ming* was that this case should be 'treated as overruled'.

[45] Criminal Procedure Act 1865, s. 4. In *Wong Kam Ming*, the Privy Council was concerned with a provision of the Hong Kong Evidence Ordinance to the same effect. For more detailed criticism of this decision, see Murphy [1979] Crim LR 364.

he had been a member of the IRA was relevant to the issue on the voir dire, and that accordingly the prosecution were not entitled to adduce evidence of the admission made in the course of that testimony. The House of Lords unanimously dismissed the prosecution's appeal. The House agreed with the Court of Appeal that if the testimony was relevant to the issue on the voir dire, the prosecution were not entitled to adduce it on the issue of guilt or to rely on any admission made during such testimony. The House also agreed that the admission was relevant, since the knowledge of the police officers that the defendant had been a member of the IRA might have affected their treatment of the defendant during interrogation.

*Brophy* differed from *Wong Kam Ming* in two respects, namely that in *Brophy*, the trial was without a jury and the admission was volunteered during evidence in chief, not elicited during cross-examination. But Lord Fraser of Tullybelton, with whose speech the other Lords agreed, cited with approval the following passage from the speech of Lord Hailsham in *Wong Kam Ming* ([1979] AC 247, 261):

> It is therefore of very great importance that the courts should continue to insist that before extra-judicial statements can be admitted in evidence the prosecution must be made to prove beyond reasonable doubt that the statement was not obtained in a manner which would be reprobated and was therefore in the truest sense voluntary. For this reason it is necessary that the accused should be able and feel free either by his own testimony or by other means to challenge the voluntary character of the tendered statement. If, as happened in the instant appeal, the prosecution were to be permitted to introduce into the trial the evidence of the accused given in the course of the voir dire when the statement to which it relates has been excluded, whether in order to supplement the evidence otherwise available as part of the prosecution case, or by way of cross-examination of the accused, the important principles of public policy to which I have referred would certainly become eroded, possibly even to vanishing point.

Lord Fraser added that the right of the defendant to give evidence on the voir dire without affecting his right to remain silent at the substantive trial was absolute. However, if the defendant went out of his way on the voir dire to boast of his crimes or to make a political speech, it would be open to the court to hold that such testimony was not relevant to the issues. In this event, the prosecution would be entitled to adduce evidence of what the defendant had said. The law governing the second question posed in *Wong Kam Ming* now seems clearly established.

### 7.12 Practice: use of confessions

#### 7.12.1 Against the maker

A confession, proved as an exception to the rule against hearsay, is admissible as evidence of the truth of the matters adverse to the defendant contained therein, if relevant to any matter in issue: s. 76(1) and (7) of the Police and Criminal Evidence Act 1984. It may, if the jury think it right, be relied upon to convict, even in the absence of other evidence. As Erle J said in *R v Baldry* (CCR) (1852) 1 Den CC 430, a 'confession . . . well proved . . . is the best evidence that can be produced'. Because the weight of a confession is a question of fact, the Court of Appeal will rarely interfere with a conviction based upon such evidence, even where it is unsupported by other evidence.[46] However, where the

---

[46]  But see the observations of Cave J in *R v Thompson* [1893] 2 QB 12 at 18.

terms of the confession are such that no reasonable jury could safely draw the necessary inference of guilt from it, the conviction may be quashed as being unsafe and unsatisfactory; this may occur where the defendant's words are wholly ambiguous, as where he merely says in answer to an allegation 'All right', which may amount to no more than an acknowledgement that it has been made, or as in *R* v *Schofield* (1917) 12 Cr App R 191, 'Just my luck', which may indicate no more than an expression of dismay at being wrongly suspected. The confession should, it is submitted, be clear and compelling before a jury are invited to act on it, unsupported, to convict, but if it is so, then it must be left to them on that basis.

### 7.12.2   Editing of confessions: R v Coke; R v Littleton

Confessions are subject to the rule regarding admissions generally that the whole statement must be put before the court, to be looked at as a whole and in context. This means that where a statement is partly adverse to, and partly favourable to, the defendant, he is entitled to have both parts placed before the jury, although this may cause problems of evidential value which are considered in 7.13, post. But there are occasions when confessions must be placed before the jury in an 'edited' form, in order to prevent the jury from being exposed to prejudicial and inadmissible material. When a confession is made, it is important that it should be recorded in the defendant's words, exactly as it is made. Frequently, confessions contain some allusion to the defendant's bad character. The answer said to have been given by Coke, when invited to tell D/I Glanvil what had happened, 'Yes, I may as well. With form for the same thing, I reckon I'm going down for a while. Will you write a statement for me?' is not an uncommon example. Clearly, the jury are entitled to hear what Coke said to the inspector, but any probative value in the allusion to his previous conviction, in the context of his confession, is more than outweighed by the prejudicial effect which the answer might have in the minds of the jury. The answer should, therefore, be edited to omit the offending passage, provided that this can be done without doing a fatal degree of violence to the sense (in which case the judge may have to exclude altogether). The inspector should, therefore, be asked (before giving evidence) to limit his account of the answer to 'Yes, I may as well . . . Will you write a statement for me?' or, arguably, to those words and 'I reckon I'm going down for a while', but certainly omitting the reference to 'form for the same thing'. If this is not done, and the inadmissible and prejudicial part is given in evidence, the conviction will almost certainly be quashed.[47] With a written confession, the same principle applies, and edited copies of the statement should be produced for the use of the jury, with no marks of editing.[48] No doubt the same practice should be followed if the transcript of a tape-recorded interview is to be placed before the jury.

[47]   However, the rule is one of practice, rather than law. If the defendant makes an incriminating reply to an allegation put to him, it is probably admissible in strict law, even though it would tend to expose some aspect of his character; and in *Turner* v *Underwood* (DC) [1948] 2 KB 284, a reply in terms similar to Coke's was held to have been properly admitted as a matter of law. But the court emphasised that as a matter of almost invariable practice, it should be excluded, at least in jury cases. (*Turner* v *Underwood* was an appeal from a magistrates' court.) In *R* v *Knight and Thompson* (1946) 31 Cr App R 52, a conviction on indictment was quashed because of a failure to edit out details of previous convictions, and it is submitted that this must be correct in almost every case.

[48]   This is sometimes said to involve a degree of deception of the jury, but in reality is no more so than the exclusion of any other evidence on legal grounds. The practice enjoys the clear sanction and approval of the courts: see *R* v *Weaver*; *R* v *Weaver* (CA) [1968] 1 QB 353.

### 7.12.3  Confessions implicating co-defendants

At common law, it is a fundamental principle of the use of admissions and confessions that an admission or confession is evidence against the maker of the confession only, and not against any other person implicated by it. This is a rule applicable to statements made in all circumstances by way of admission, including a plea of guilty in the face of the court. It is sometimes said that the co-defendant may make the statement evidence against him if he is present when it is made, and does not dissent from it, or adopts it as his own. However, this is an apparent exception only, in that if, on the whole of the evidence, the jury think that the co-defendant has adopted what was said, then it is in reality his own confession and no longer merely that of the maker of the statement. The rule has no exception at common law; a confession is inadmissible hearsay against all but the maker of it. This is, of course, in stark contrast to the position when a defendant gives evidence from the witness-box in the course of the trial, when, like any other evidence, what he says is evidence in the case for all purposes, whether or not it implicates the co-defendant. In the light of the reference to Littleton by Coke in his statement under caution, the implications of the rule must be carefully examined in their case.

An excellent example of the rule is *R* v *Spinks* [1982] 1 All ER 587. The defendant was charged with doing an act, namely concealing a knife, with intent to impede the apprehension or prosecution of another, F, who had committed the arrestable offence of wounding. At the defendant's trial, there was no evidence that F had committed a wounding except F's own confession to the police, which had not, of course, been made in the defendant's presence. The trial judge refused to withdraw the case from the jury. The defendant did not give evidence, and was convicted. On appeal, the Court of Appeal re-affirmed that F's confession, though evidence against F, was not evidence against the defendant that F had committed a wounding. Russell J said:

> In the judgment of this court the offence with which the appellant was charged and the means of establishing it do not provide any exception to the universal rule which excludes out of court admissions being used to provide evidence against a co-accused, whether indicted jointly or separately . . . .
>
> In his summing up the recorder left the jury with the clear impression that they could, if they wished, rely on [F's] admissions to prove the wounding, not only against him but against the appellant. In so doing there was a plain misdirection and for the reasons we have indicated we have come to the conclusion that this appeal must be allowed and the conviction quashed.

The rule involves important difficulties of practice. Confessions by one defendant implicating another are one of the hazards of joint trial, which must be accepted. The mere fact that the situation arises is no ground, in itself, for separate trials. Where defendants are jointly charged they should ordinarily be tried together. In *R* v *Lake*[49] the defendant and two others were charged with conspiracy to burgle. Both co-defendants made statements to the police which implicated Lake very seriously in the offence. Despite the risk of prejudice arising from the volume of inadmissible material against Lake, the Court of Appeal declined to interfere with the decision of the trial judge to refuse an application for separate trial. But the Court of Appeal recognised that there would be exceptional

---

[49]  (1976) 64 Cr App R 172; and see the observations of the Court of Appeal in *R* v *Josephs and Christie* (1977) 65 Cr App R 253.

cases, where the probative value of a confession is very considerable against the maker, while the prejudicial effect is equally considerable against the co-defendant, where such an order may be necessary.

Frequently, the problem can be solved, or at least minimised, by editing. This course is not always available, because both the prosecution and the maker of the statement may have reasons for wanting the whole statement to go to the jury. If A says that B was wholly or partly to blame, this may in some cases be cogent evidence against A. But where the reference to B is of little or no significance to the case against A, the judge can and should order A's statement to be edited.[50]

What is vital, in any case where A's statement implicates his co-defendant B, is that the judge should direct the jury that the statement is evidence against A only and not against B. Whether juries succeed in this exercise in mental gymnastics is a moot point, but they are frequently assisted by the observation that it is clearly unfair to hold against B a statement made in his absence by A, who may have his own reasons for implicating B, and to which B had no chance of replying. Be that as it may, the absence of a clear direction on the point will be fatal to B's conviction.[51] The statement cannot be evidence against B for any purpose. In *R v Dibble* (1908) 1 Cr App R 155, this applied even where A offered to give evidence for the prosecution against B, was treated as hostile and cross-examined on his statement. A's statement implicated B, but was evidence going only to A's credit, and the failure of the trial judge to direct the jury not to regard it as evidence against B was fatal to B's conviction.

### 7.13  Partly adverse statements

It happens very frequently that a defendant will make a written or oral statement which, while partly adverse to his case, also contains exculpatory or self-serving passages. We have already seen that the whole of the statement must in general go to the jury, and that the weight of the statement as a confession is a matter of fact for the jury. The latter proposition involves the further conclusion that it is for the jury to say whether the statement tendered amounts to a confession at all. Unless it does, the jury will not act on it as evidence against the defendant. But the undoubtedly proper admission of entire statements also involves a problem of evidential value in criminal cases, in that self-serving statements are not evidence of the truth of the facts contained in them, whereas confessions are so[52]: see 12.3, post.

In *R v Storey; R v Anwar* (1968) 52 Cr App R 334, the defendant was charged with possession of cannabis. The prosecution succeeded in establishing a prima facie case against her, and she did not give evidence. The defendant then sought to rely for her defence on a statement she had made to the police which was exculpatory in content. The trial judge, however, summed up to the jury on the basis that the statement was inadmissible to prove the truth of any facts stated therein. On appeal against conviction, the Court of Appeal held that the summing up was proper. Had the defendant given evidence on oath to the same effect, the jury could have considered her evidence, but not her prior statement, as evidence of the truth of the facts stated.

---

[50]   See, e.g., *R v Rogers and Tarran* [1971] Crim LR 413.

[51]   *R v Gunewardene* (CCA) [1951] 2 KB 600.

[52]   In civil cases, s. 2 of the Civil Evidence Act 1968 is wide enough to admit self-serving statements as evidence of the truth of the facts stated in them, so that, except in relation to weight, the problem is avoided.

No assistance can be derived from the fact that s. 82(1) of the Police and Criminal Evidence Act 1984 defines a 'confession' as 'any statement *wholly or partly adverse to the person who made it*'. Although s. 76(1) renders a confession, thus defined, admissible, it also specifies that it shall be admissible 'against' the accused who made it. No legislative intent to render exculpatory passages admissible in favour of the accused, for the purpose of proving the truth of facts stated therein, can therefore be inferred.[53]

The different evidential effects of adverse and exculpatory passages within the same statement produced substantial problems for juries, and it is doubtful whether juries were completely faithful to the directions they received from judges. In *R* v *Donaldson; R* v *Watson; R* v *Reed* (1976) 64 Cr App R 59, 65, James LJ said:

> In our view there is a clear distinction to be made between statements of admission adduced by the Crown as part of the case against the defendant and statements entirely of a self-serving nature made and sought to be relied upon by a defendant. When the Crown adduce a statement relied upon as an admission it is for the jury to consider the whole statement including any passages that contain qualifications or explanations favourable to the defendant, that bear upon the passages relied upon by the prosecution as an admission, and it is for the jury to decide whether the statement viewed as a whole constitutes an admission. To this extent, the statement may be said to be evidence of the facts stated therein . . . .
>
> When the Crown adduce evidence in the form of a statement by the defendant which is not relied on as an admission of the offence charged, such a statement is evidence in the trial, in that it is evidence that the defendant made the statement and of his reaction, which is part of the general picture which the jury have to consider, but it is not evidence of the facts stated.

This 'clear distinction' was no doubt clear enough to the Court of Appeal, but it was just as clear that some other approach must be devised if juries were to be enabled to look properly at a statement made by a defendant and offered in evidence as a confession. It is true that the exculpatory passages may also have relevance for purposes other than to prove the truth of facts stated, for example to show the defendant's reaction when taxed with the offence, as 'part of the general picture'. Moreover, the defendant is entitled to have the jury read passages which negate or present in a different light passages which might otherwise appear incriminating.[54] But in many cases, the subtlety of the distinction must have been lost on juries, who most probably viewed the statement as a whole and assessed its value accordingly.

In *R* v *Duncan* (1981) 73 Cr App R 359, a differently constituted Court of Appeal proposed a fresh approach, after a review of the authorities. The defendant was charged with murder, and made a statement, part of which appeared to be a confession of guilt as charged and part of which appeared to suggest the defence of provocation. Lord Lane CJ said:

> The issue between the parties here is the extent to which confessions are properly to be

---

[53] To the contrary, it is plain that Parliament did not intend to render exculpatory material admissible, since a clause having exactly that effect (clause 73(4)) appeared in the Bill brought from the House of Commons on 17 May 1984, but was subsequently deleted and does not appear in the Act.

[54] *R* v *McGregor* [1968] 1 QB 371.

regarded as evidence of the truth of the facts which they state. Both parties are agreed that if a statement is adduced as an admission against interest, the whole of the statement must be admitted. Any other course would obviously be unfair.

It is contended on behalf of the Crown that this rule does not, however, make the contents of the statement evidence of the facts contained therein except in so far as those statements are admissions against interest. [Counsel for the appellant] on the other hand . . . contends that the whole statement is evidence of the truth of the facts contained therein. He, however, concedes that the judge is entitled to explain to the jury, if indeed it needs explanation, that the weight to be given to those parts of the statement which contain admissions against interest may be very different from the weight to be given to the parts which are self-exculpatory.

One is bound to observe that if the contentions of the Crown are correct, the judge would be faced with a very difficult task in trying to explain to the jury the difference between those parts of a 'mixed' statement (if we may call it such) which were truly confessions and those parts which were self-exculpatory. It is doubtful if the result would be readily intelligible . . . Judges should not be obliged to give meaningless or unintelligible directions to juries.

The learned Lord Chief Justice then reviewed the authorities, and concluded:

Where a 'mixed' statement is under consideration by the jury in a case where the defendant has not given evidence, it seems to us that the simplest, and therefore the method most likely to produce a just result, is for the jury to be told that the whole statement, both the incriminating parts and the excuses or explanations, must be considered by them in deciding where the truth lies. It is, to say the least, not helpful to try to explain to the jury that the exculpatory parts of a statement are something less than evidence of the facts they state. Equally, where appropriate, as it usually will be, the judge may, and should, point out that the incriminating parts are likely to be true (otherwise why say them?), whereas the excuses do not have the same weight.

It is submitted that this approach is to be preferred to that called for by earlier cases. Since the whole statement is admitted in evidence because it is relied on by the prosecution as a confession, the jury must decide whether, taken as a whole, it is a confession. The theoretical objection that the exculpatory parts are not evidence of the truth of the facts stated therein may be overcome by the fact that the jury have to take the statement as a whole, and give such weight to it as they think fit. It has always been recognised that the exculpatory passages may be relied on by the defence for the purpose of rebutting the apparently incriminating nature of adverse passages, and no real extension of this rule is called for by the approach taken in *Duncan*. No real repudiation of the rule against self-serving statements is involved, since the statement is adduced by the prosecution, and the jury is being directed to do no more than to subject prosecution evidence to proper scrutiny. The situation is obviously very different from that in *R v Storey*; *R v Anwar*, in which the defence sought to rely on a self-serving statement to establish a defence.

It may be doubted whether *Duncan* represents any real departure from established principle. The general practice has in any case been to permit the jury to know what the defendant may have said when taxed with the offence, even if consistent with his defence, if only to show his reaction when confronted. This is largely a consideration of fairness to the defence. However, it should be noted that the court is entitled to exclude a statement made by the defendant which is deliberately self-serving, especially one made after consultation with a solicitor, which may be designed to infiltrate the prosecution case. Although as a general rule the jury should be told what the defendant says in answer to the charge (unless it consists of an inadmissible confession), the prosecution do not have to permit the defendant to make use of a set piece. However, each case must be considered on its own facts, and a statement should not be excluded merely because the defendant had spoken with a solicitor before making it.[55]

## C: STATEMENTS IN THE PRESENCE OF THE DEFENDANT

### 7.14   Principles of admissibility

Where statements relevant to the issues in a case are made in the presence of a party, such statements may be admitted in order to explain the reaction of that party to the statements or, if the party accepts or adopts the truth of the statements, as part of any adverse admission made by him. The rule applies at common law to civil and criminal cases alike, but has lost its identity in civil cases because of the breadth of s. 2 of the Civil Evidence Act 1968. The critical area of the rule, in modern practice, lies in the treatment of statements made by way of taxing the defendant with the offence charged in criminal cases. The practice of interrogation is, of course, based upon putting to the defendant allegations, and therefore the repetition to him of hearsay statements, in order to elicit his reaction to them. If the defendant acknowledges the truth of such allegations, they merge into his confession, and no separate problem of the admissibility of the allegations will arise. But difficulties do present themselves where the defendant denies the allegations, or remains silent.

### 7.14.1   The defendant's denials

Where the defendant denies the allegations put to him, although as a matter of law the statements remain admissible for the limited purpose of showing his reaction, they gain no further force from what the defendant says, and in some cases, because of the risk of prejudice, it may be right to exclude the interrogation altogether. Otherwise, the prosecution may in effect be permitted to put before the jury the substance of their case in a hearsay form, which would plainly be inadmissible in any other circumstances unless the defendant accepted its truth. An interrogation consisting of a series of hearsay allegations, followed by the defendant's denial of each *seriatim* is of no evidential value to the prosecution, but may be prejudicial to the defence. It does not follow that this will always be the case, because it may be that the prosecution are entitled to rely upon the manner of the denial, for example where the defendant gives a demonstrably untrue explanation which, though on the face of it consistent with innocence, becomes incriminating when disproved. The trial judge may in some cases have to hear argument, or decide the question on the voir dire.

There is clear authority that, as a matter of practice, statements made in the defendant's presence should be excluded if, in the opinion of the judge, there is no material on which the jury could properly find that the defendant accepted the truth of what was being put to him, and accordingly adopted the allegations by way of confession. If the jury may

---

[55]   *R v Newsome* (1980) 71 Cr App R 325; *R v McCarthy* (1980) 71 Cr App R 142; *R v Pearce* [1979] Crim LR 658.

properly draw that conclusion, then it must be left to them as a question of fact. In *R v Norton* [1910] 2 KB 946, the conviction was quashed when a hearsay statement was narrated to the jury, there being no evidence that the defendant had in any way accepted it, and the soundness of the general proposition was accepted by the House of Lords in *R v Christie* [1914] AC 545. The defendant was charged with indecent assault on a small boy. The boy was called to give evidence unsworn, but although he described the assault, he did not speak to the fact that shortly afterwards, he had identified the defendant to his mother and a police officer. The mother and the officer were called to give evidence of the identification, and the evidence was that when confronted in this way, the defendant said, 'I am innocent' — an account which he maintained from first to last. One of the matters canvassed on appeal was that the boy's statement should have been excluded in view of the reaction of the defendant to it. Ultimately, the House determined to quash the conviction because of a misdirection on corroboration, but the argument mentioned drew some sympathy. Lord Reading said (ibid at 565):

> In general, such evidence can have little or no value in its direct bearing on the case unless the accused, upon hearing the statement, by conduct and demeanour, or by the answer made by him, or in certain circumstances by the refraining from an answer, acknowledged the truth of the statement either in whole or in part, or did or said something from which the jury could infer such an acknowledgement, for if he acknowledged its truth, he accepted it as his own statement of the facts.

Lord Moulton referred to the rule of exclusion, in the absence of some evidence of acceptance by the defendant, as 'a practice of a very salutary nature', and indicated that the hearsay statement could have no evidential value unless somehow adopted.[56]

As a matter of practice, it will be apparent that in many cases there will be no risk of prejudice simply because there is other, direct evidence of the nature of the prosecution's allegations, and for the jury to hear it repeated with a denial can do no real harm; indeed, the evidence of consistency with the defence offered at trial may actually assist the defendant. But where there is no direct evidence, or no direct evidence of that precise kind, or where the jury may be misled into looking for corroboration where it cannot exist, the risk is very great. Even where this risk is not present, if the allegations are numerous or very grave, there is some danger that the jury may unconsciously adopt them as fact. In all such cases, and where there is any possibility of prejudice, it is submitted that such hearsay evidence is better excluded.[57]

### 7.14.2 The defendant's silence

If statements made in the defendant's presence should be excluded as mere hearsay, unless there is evidence from which it can be inferred that the defendant acknowledged the truth of the allegations contained in them, it would seem to follow that it should only be in exceptional circumstances that the defendant's silence should be held to constitute an acknowledgement of the kind required. The caution that a suspect is not obliged to say anything serves, not to create a right which the defendant did not previously enjoy, but to remind him of the right which he enjoys at every stage of an investigation. The principle was applied in *Hall* v *R* [1971] 1 WLR 298, where the defendant was charged with

---

[56] Ibid at 559–60. See also per Lord Atkinson at 553–4.
[57] For an instance of extreme prejudice, see *R v Taylor* (CA) [1978] Crim LR 92.

possession of a controlled drug. The evidence against him was that, the drug having been found on premises which he occupied jointly with others, but not in his room, he was told by an officer that another defendant had said that the drug belonged to him, and that the defendant made no reply to this allegation. The Privy Council held that the defendant's conviction could not be sustained. Lord Diplock said (ibid at 301):

> It is a clear and widely known principle of the common law . . . that a person is entitled to refrain from answering a question put to him for the purpose of discovering whether he has committed a criminal offence. A fortiori he is under no obligation to comment when he is informed that someone else has accused him of an offence. It may be that in very exceptional circumstances an inference may be drawn from a failure to give an explanation or a disclaimer, but in their Lordships' view silence alone on being informed by a police officer that someone else has made an accusation against him cannot give rise to an inference that the person to whom this information is communicated accepts the truth of the accusation . . . .
>
> The caution merely serves to remind the accused of a right which he already possesses at common law. The fact that in a particular case he has not been reminded of it is no ground for inferring that his silence was not in exercise of that right, but was an acknowledgement of the truth of the accusation.

Lord Diplock's reference to 'very exceptional circumstances', in which silence might be held to constitute some form of admission may have been based on what Cave J had said in R v Mitchell (1892) 17 Cox CC 503, 508, although Mitchell may not have been cited in argument in Hall. It is important to put the dictum of Cave J into context. The defendant in Mitchell was charged with procuring a miscarriage by unlawful means, and so causing the death of the woman concerned. A statement made by the deceased woman was held not to be admissible as a dying declaration, and the taking of her deposition by a magistrate had to be stopped when the deceased became too ill to continue, and before the defendant's solicitor had had any opportunity to cross-examine her; it was accordingly inadmissible in evidence, as it might have been by statute if completed. It was sought to admit what there was of the deposition as a statement made in the presence of the defendant. Cave J rejected the attempt, holding that the defendant, who was legally represented, could not reasonably have been expected to make any reply in the circumstances. Against that background, the learned judge said:

> Now the whole admissibility of statements of this kind rests upon the consideration that if a charge is made against a person in that person's presence, it is reasonable to expect that he or she will immediately deny it, and that the absence of such a denial is some evidence of an admission on the part of the person charged, and of the truth of the charge. Undoubtedly, when persons are speaking on even terms and a charge is made, and the person charged says nothing, and expresses no indignation, and does nothing to repel the charge, that is some evidence to show that he admits the charge to be true.

The important emphases in this dictum are firstly, the circumstance that the defendant and his accuser should have been 'on even terms', and secondly, that it must have been reasonable to expect some reaction, in the way of indignation or refutation of the charge. It seems that what Cave J must have had in mind was a situation where some spontaneous accusation was made, to which some reply was available which, on the basis that the defendant was innocent, might naturally have been expected by way of spontaneous riposte. In such a context, the principle seems unobjectionable, and indeed has been applied in cases where its use could hardly be questioned.[58] But it fits uneasily in more modern times into the context of a formal interview between defendant and police officer, where more mature consideration has supervened upon the heat of the moment. It is tempting to add that the dictum seems to fit especially uneasily where the defendant has been cautioned, but remembering the words of Lord Diplock in *Hall*, that the caution is a reminder, not a creator, of the right of silence, perhaps this should not, of itself, matter. Nonetheless, in *R v Chandler* [1976] 1 WLR 585, the Court of Appeal applied the dictum to just such a case. The 'even terms' were said to result from the fact that the defendant was in the company of his solicitor when interviewed. But even on the basis that this may produce even terms within the meaning of the dictum, it is difficult to see that the situation could have been such that the defendant might reasonably have been expected to seek to rebut the charge. Indeed, the facts of *R v Mitchell* and the decision of Cave J on those facts, seem to suggest exactly the opposite. Lawton LJ said (ibid at 590):

> Some comment on the defendant's lack of frankness before he was cautioned was justified provided the jury's attention was directed to the right issue, which was whether in the circumstances the defendant's silence amount to an acceptance by him of what the detective sergeant had said. If he accepted what had been said, then the next question should have been whether guilt could reasonably be inferred from what he had accepted. To suggest, as the judge did that the defendant's silence could indicate guilt was to short-circuit the intellectual process which has to be followed.

With respect, the intellectual process advocated by Lawton LJ seems to be just as suspect as that advocated by the trial judge. It was apparently pointed out in argument to the Court of Appeal that no distinction could properly be drawn between pre- and post-caution interrogation, if the right of silence was to prevail, and the words of Lord Diplock in *Hall* were drawn to the Court's attention. But these were stigmatised by Lawton LJ as seeming 'to conflict with *R v Christie* and with earlier cases and authorities'. A passage from the speech of Lord Atkinson in *Christie* [1914] AC 545 at 554, was cited to lend weight to this proposition. But the House of Lords in *Christie* was not concerned with such a situation, because the defendant did rebut the charge, and the passage cited bears no obvious relation to the facts which the Privy Council had to consider in *Hall*. If *Chandler* was rightly decided, it would seem to follow that a solicitor who is present when his client is interviewed can no longer safely advise his client to exercise his right of silence. It may be, and indeed it has been strenuously advocated in many quarters, that the position of the defendant at common law is too favourable under modern conditions, and that a jury should be entitled to draw some inference from his silence. But if so, such a step surely requires the intervention of statute.

Some support for *Chandler* is sometimes claimed in the decision of the Privy Council in *Parkes v R* [1976] 1 WLR 1251, in which the advice was delivered by Lord Diplock. *Parkes* was decided after *Chandler*, but the latter case appears not to have been cited. The defendant was charged with the murder of a girl. The girl's mother found her bleeding very shortly after the infliction of the wound, and saw the defendant nearby holding a knife. The mother twice accused the defendant of stabbing her daughter, and to these

---

[58] See e.g., *Bessela v Stern* (CA) (1877) 2 CPD 265.

accusations he made no reply, but when the mother said that she intended to detain him until the police arrived, the defendant attempted to stab her with the knife. Lord Diplock based himself upon the dictum of Cave J in *Mitchell*, and held that the trial judge had been 'perfectly entitled to instruct the jury that the defendant's reactions to the accusations, including his silence, were matters which they could take into account along with other evidence in deciding whether the defendant in fact committed the act with which he was charged'. It is submitted that this must be correct. It was precisely the sort of case which Cave J presumably had in mind. One might perhaps go further, and say that the silence of the defendant was a relatively small part of an obviously guilty reaction, which the jury were entitled to consider, to the mother's accusation. His action in attacking the mother could be considered as some form of admission that there was truth in her accusations. *Parkes* could hardly be further away from *Chandler* on the facts.

It is submitted that the true rule is that unless the defendant's silence can properly be left to the jury as a form of admission of the allegation, in the very exceptional circumstances envisaged in *Mitchell* and exemplified in *Parkes*, the statements made to the defendant ought to be viewed in the same way as if the allegations had been denied.[59]

### 7.15  Questions for discussion

#### 7.15.1  *R* v *Coke; R* v *Littleton*
1  What arguments should be made for and against the admissibility of:
(a)  Coke's alleged reply to D/I Glanvil on being arrested at his flat;
(b)  Coke's oral answers at the police station; and
(c)  Coke's written statement under caution?
2  What factors will affect the weight of these pieces of evidence, if admitted?
3  What steps should be taken at trial to decide the admissibility of these pieces of evidence?
4  How should the judge direct the jury as to how to regard Coke's written statement under caution in considering the guilt or innocence of Littleton?
5  How should the judge direct the jury with regard to Littleton's denials and silence when questioned about the offence charged?
6  Should the judge admit evidence of Angela Blackstone's words 'that's him' when identifying Littleton, in the light of Littleton's reply and his pre-arrest answers to the officers? Would your opinion change if Littleton had made no reply?

#### 7.15.2  *Blackstone* v *Coke*
1  May Coke adduce as an admission:
(a)  Margaret's refusal to undergo a blood test. Does it matter that this refusal was communicated by her solicitors?
(b)  The contents of Margaret's letter to Henneky?
2  May Coke adduce as an admission Henneky's statement that he had sexual intercourse with Margaret at a time consistent with the conception of her child?

---

[59]  As to the significance of a failure to answer letters, see generally *Bessela* v *Stern* (CA) (1877) 2 CPD 265; *Wiedemann* v *Walpole* [1891] 2 QB 534 per Lord Esher MR at 537–8; *R* v *Edwards* [1983] Crim LR 539.

# 8 *The Rule Against Hearsay – III*

## 8.1 Introduction

In Chapter 6, we noted that the exceptions to the rule against hearsay which grew up at common law proved inadequate to deal with demands of modern litigation. Yet statutory reform was slow to come and, until recently, limited in scope. A variety of statutes provided for the admissibility of individual kinds of documentary hearsay. The use of depositions and statements taken out of court before justices of the peace for limited evidential purposes in criminal cases was well recognised, and the Criminal Justice Act 1967 provided for the wider use of witness statements both in committal proceedings and at trial, subject, however, to the absence of objection. In civil cases, the Evidence Act 1938 made some tentative concessions to hearsay. However, these provisions, while useful, were more in the nature of responses to individual needs than systematic attempts to modernise the rules of evidence. They will not be dealt with here.

At length, the decision of the House of Lords in *Myers* v *DPP* [1965] AC 1001, confirmed what many had already sensed, namely that the time had come when the law of evidence must be adapted to fit the needs of litigation in the latter half of the twentieth century. No longer could the courts sensibly be deprived of access to manifestly reliable forms of hearsay evidence, as society's dependence on documentary records and information created by and stored in computers increased. *Myers* made it clear that the courts could or would not take responsibility for such radical changes in the law, and that reform must come from Parliament. The Criminal Evidence Act 1965 was a hastily drafted stop-gap measure which did duty valiantly for 20 years. Yet it was relatively limited in scope, providing only for the admissibility of documentary records of a trade or business, and then only when direct oral evidence of the recorded facts was unavailable for specified reasons. It encountered problems with evidence produced by or stored in machines. More comprehensive reform was advocated by the Law Reform Committee and the Criminal Law Revision Committee.[1]

The Civil Evidence Act 1968 represented a far more radical and thorough-going reform. The fact that jury trial is comparatively rare in civil cases encouraged experimentation with reform. The Act did far more than just provide exceptions to the rule against hearsay. It created a new code of evidence law for civil cases, which rendered much hearsay evidence admissible, not only documentary hearsay contained in records, but also oral and written hearsay statements and statements produced by computers. In many cases, the hearsay evidence is admissible even though the maker of the statement is available as a

---

[1] Law Reform Committee, 13th report, paras 48–52; Criminal Law Revision Committee, 11th report, paras 229–48.

witness. The opponent of a party who proposes to adduce evidence admissible by virtue of the Act is provided with certain safeguards, including mandatory notice provisions. The judge is now more concerned with the weight of hearsay evidence than with its admissibility, and as always when the trial is by the judge alone, the professional judgment of the parties' advisers is as powerful a restraint on the use of unreliable evidence as any rule of admissibility. The Act gave statutory force to the most important common-law exceptions, for example admissions and facts contained in public documents. Only in civil proceedings in the magistrates' courts, to which the Act has not been extended, is the earlier law now of any general importance; in those proceedings, the common law and the Evidence Act 1938 continue to apply. The 1968 Act applies only to hearsay statements of fact. The Civil Evidence Act 1972 extended its principles to hearsay statements of opinion.

The Police and Criminal Evidence Act 1984 repeals the Criminal Evidence Act 1965 and broadens the scope of admissible hearsay evidence in criminal cases. It has not, however, attempted to emulate the Civil Evidence Act 1968. It provides that documentary hearsay contained in records shall be admissible when direct, oral evidence of the facts recorded is not available, with safeguards similar to those provided by s.4 of the Civil Evidence Act 1968. It also provides for the admissibility of evidence produced by computers, again with certain safeguards designed to ensure reliability. There is no provision for the admissibility of hearsay statements of other kinds. The Act extends to hearsay statements of fact only and not to statements of opinion.

English law is still far from a general codified approach to the rule against hearsay. In criminal cases, there is now an interesting mix of new and old legal ideas, common law and statutory. It is probable that, as the new rules prove successful and the fears of misleading juries subside, further modernisations of the rules pertaining to criminal cases will be contemplated. Comfort may be found in the American experience. For example, the Federal Rules of Evidence contain a total of 29 exceptions to the rule against hearsay, and treat as non-hearsay certain statements that would be hearsay in England. Although trial by jury is guaranteed in the federal courts both in criminal and civil cases by the Sixth and Seventh Amendments to the Constitution, the courts have successfully introduced a far more liberal approach to the rule against hearsay.

## A: HEARSAY ADMISSIBLE BY STATUTE IN CIVIL CASES

### 8.2   Civil Evidence Act 1968: introduction

Although the Civil Evidence Act 1968 is often referred to as an 'exception' to the rule against hearsay, and although it too has its limitations on admissibility of hearsay evidence, the reality is that the Act has in effect swept away, so far as civil cases are concerned, the common-law rule against hearsay, and substituted for it a statutory code which provides for the general admissibility of hearsay evidence subject to important evidential and procedural safeguards. The code is contained in Part 1 of the Act, which consists of ss. 1–10 inclusive, and which must be read together with the important related procedural provisions contained in RSC, Ord. 38, rr.21–31, made pursuant to s. 8.

The purpose and effect of the Act is stated in direct terms in s. 1:

(1)   In any civil proceedings a statement other than one made by a person while giving oral evidence in those proceedings shall be admissible as evidence of any fact stated therein to the extent that it is so admissible by virtue of any provision of this part of this

Act or by virtue of any other statutory provision or by agreement of the parties, but not otherwise.

(2)   In this section 'statutory provision' means any provision contained in, or in an instrument made under, this or any other Act, including any Act passed after this Act.

The meaning of 'civil proceedings' is explained by the interpretation section, s. 18, as follows:

(1)   In this Act 'civil proceedings' includes, in addition to civil proceedings in any of the ordinary courts of law—

(a)   civil proceedings before any other tribunal, being proceedings in relation to which the strict rules of evidence apply; and
(b)   an arbitration or reference, whether under an enactment or not, but does not include civil proceedings in relation to which the strict rules of evidence do not apply.

The bulk of the Act was, by s. 20(4), to be brought into effect by statutory instrument made by the Lord Chancellor, and as observed in note 1, the Act does not as yet apply to proceedings within the civil jurisdiction of the magistrates' courts. To these proceedings, the provisions of the Evidence Act 1938 continue to apply where appropriate, and only at such time as the 1968 Act is extended will the 1938 Act be repealed in relation to such proceedings, as it has in relation to the other 'civil proceedings' referred to in s. 18 of the 1968 Act. The exclusion of proceedings to which the strict rules of evidence do not apply reflects the fact that in such proceedings, no authority is needed for the admission of the kinds of evidence for which provision is made by the Act.

It is important to note that s. 1 permits the admission of hearsay evidence only in the three circumstances set out, that is to say, (a) by virtue of one of the provisions of the Act, (b) by virtue of any other statutory provision, or (c) by agreement between the parties. The section expressly excludes any other possibility of admission of hearsay evidence in civil proceedings, and must therefore be taken to have abrogated, in relation to civil proceedings, the common-law exceptions to the rule against hearsay, although as we saw in Chapter 6, certain of the common-law rules have been 'adopted' and given statutory force by s. 9.[2] Whether evidence is admissible by virtue of 'any other statutory provision', in addition to being admissible by virtue of s. 2, s. 4 or s. 5 of the 1968 Act, may be of importance inasmuch as the notice procedure, which applies to evidence admissible under those sections by virtue of RSC, Ord. 38, does not apply to evidence which can be admitted otherwise.[3] It may therefore be avoided in such cases. The power of the parties in civil cases to make an agreement at any time about evidence which is to be admissible, generally or for any particular purpose, in those proceedings, is expressly preserved by s. 18(5)(b) of the 1968 Act.

The only defect of evidence cured by the Act is that of its hearsay character. Nothing in the Act gives any licence to admit evidence which is, for any other reason, inadmissible

---

[2]   See 6.10 et seq, ante; see also 7.1, ante, and 9.2, post.
[3]   For this purpose, s. 9 of the 1968 Act is itself an 'other statutory provision', in the sense that s. 9(5) and Ord. 38, r. 21(2) exclude from the notice procedure evidence admissible under that section, even though it may also be admissible under s. 2, s. 4 or s. 5.

under the general law of evidence. Clearly, a party tendering evidence cannot be in a more favourable position because he proposes to have the evidence admitted in a hearsay form by virtue of the Act than if he proposed to call non-hearsay evidence of the same facts. The major sections providing for admission of specific categories of hearsay statement, that is to say, s. 2, s. 4 and s. 5, each provide expressly that the admissibility shall be of evidence 'of any fact stated therein of which direct oral evidence would be admissible'. These provisions are reinforced by s. 18(5)(*a*), which preserves the power of the court in any case to exclude evidence in the exercise of its discretion; this is of course in addition to the power of the court to exclude evidence as a matter of law, where it is for any reasons inadmissible.

Leaving aside s. 1, which has already been dealt with, it is now proposed to indicate briefly the structure of the remaining sections of Part 1 of the Act, and the places in which they are to be dealt with.

The major provisions within the general framework of s. 1, providing for the admissibility of hearsay evidence in particular cases or of particular kinds are s. 2 (statements made other than while giving evidence in the instant proceedings), s. 4 (statements contained in documents which are, or are parts of, records) and s. 5 (statements produced by computers). These sections are considered further in this chapter.

Section 3 deals with the evidential value of previous consistent or inconsistent statements and of documents used by a witness to refresh his memory while giving evidence, and is dealt with in relation to those matters in 12.2, 12.3, 12.4 and 13.6, post.

Section 6 deals with various questions relating to the determination of admissiblity of, and proof of, statements tendered under the Act, and with the assessment of the weight of statements admitted under certain sections, which matters are dealt with in this chapter, and with the position of hearsay statements in relation to the rules of corroboration, which is dealt with in 14.4, post.

Section 7 provides for the admissibility of evidence tending to discredit evidence given under s. 2 or s. 4, where the maker of a hearsay statement is not called to give evidence, and is dealt with in 13.11, post.

Section 8 requires or gives authority for the making of the various rules of court necessary to give effect to the proposed procedural framework within which Part 1 is to operate. The rules concerned, contained in RSC, Ord. 38, are considered in this chapter, and s. 8 requires no further comment.

Section 9, as we have seen, adopts and gives statutory force to a number of rules of the common law permitting the use of hearsay evidence for various purposes, without changing the substance of the law in those cases. The different rules so adopted are referred to in the context of their operation at common law, in the places where they arise naturally; admissions in 7.1, public documents in 6.13, evidence of reputation in 9.2.

Section 10 deals with a number of important definitions and interpretations relevant to Part 1, and these are considered in this chapter, so far as material.

### 8.3  Statements admissible under s. 2

Section 2 of the Act provides as follows:

(1)  In any civil proceedings a statement made, whether orally or in a document or otherwise, by any person, whether called as a witness in those proceedings or not, shall,

subject to this section and to rules of court, be admissible as evidence of any fact stated therein of which direct oral evidence by him would be admissible.

(2) Where in any civil proceedings a party desiring to give a statement in evidence by virtue of this section has called or intends to call as a witness in the proceedings the person by whom the statement was made, the statement—

(a) shall not be given in evidence by virtue of this section on behalf of that party without the leave of the court; and
(b) without prejudice to paragraph (a) above, shall not be given in evidence by virtue of this section on behalf of that party before the conclusion of the examination-in-chief of the person by whom it was made, except—
(i) where before that person is called the court allows evidence of the making of the statement to be given on behalf of that party by some other person; or
(ii) in so far as the court allows the person by whom the statement was made to narrate it in the course of his examination-in-chief on the ground that to prevent him from doing so would adversely affect the intelligibility of his evidence.

(3) Where in any civil proceedings a statement which was made otherwise than in a document is admissible by virtue of this section, no evidence other than direct oral evidence by the person who made the statement or any person who heard or otherwise perceived it being made shall be admissible for the purpose of proving it:
Provided that if the statement in question was made by a person while giving oral evidence in some other legal proceedings (whether civil or criminal), it may be proved in any manner authorised by the court.

### 8.3.1 Section 2(1)

This subsection provides for the general admissibility of statements made by persons other than while giving evidence in the instant proceedings as evidence of the truth of the facts stated therein—a literal reversal of the rule against hearsay at common law. It should be noted firstly that the subsection permits the admission of such hearsay statements, whether or not the maker of the statement is also called as a witness, though if he is called, the statement is admissible in its own right only with leave and subject to the other conditions laid down by s. 2(2).[4] Secondly, it is to be observed that the section, like the remainder of Part 1 of the 1968 Act, applies only to statements of fact. The principle has been extended to hearsay statements of opinion, where such evidence is admissible under the general law of evidence, by the Civil Evidence Act 1972. This is considered briefly in 8.8 and at greater length in Chapter 9, post. Thirdly, as we have observed, the phrase, 'evidence of any fact stated therein of which direct oral evidence by him would be admissible', makes the obvious limitation that the evidence admitted under the section must be such that it would be unobjectionable by reference to the rules of evidence generally, if it were given orally by the maker of the statement, apart from the consideration of hearsay.

Some question arises as to the limits of the kind of 'statement' which may fall within the subsection. For the purposes of Part I of the Act, s. 10(1) provides that 'Statement'

---

⁴ Where the maker of the statement is also called as a witness, his admissible hearsay statement is incapable in law of corroborating his evidence: Civil Evidence Act 1968, s. 6(4)(a).

includes any representation of fact, whether made in words or otherwise'.

Section 2(1) provides that it should not matter whether the statement is made 'orally or in a document or otherwise', although statements made otherwise than in a document are made subject to further provisions under s. 2(3). It seems fairly clear, therefore, that the subsection includes statements made in the form of conduct, for example that which was rejected under the common-law rules against previous consistent statements in *Corke* v *Corke and Cooke*[5] where the wife and the co-respondent were not permitted to give evidence that, on being discovered in a compromising situation together, they telephoned a doctor with a view to being examined and so disproving the suggestion of adultery. The subsection should also be construed to permit the reception of unintended communications from which the court might be enabled to draw inferences of fact. The shout of the bystander in *Teper* v *R*,[6] 'Your place burning and you going away from the fire', the letters in *Wright* v *Doe d'Tatham* (1837) 7 AE 313, written by businessmen to the testator, indicative of his mental capacity at the time they were written, the action of the mythical sea-captain postulated by Parke B in that case, who, after inspecting a ship for seaworthiness, embarked upon it with his family, were all rejected at common law, and must all be reconsidered in the light of s. 2(1). Professor Cross[7] argues that statements made orally (or, presumably, in writing) may be within the subsection as being implied representations of fact, even if not intended by the maker as communicative of the fact stated, but rejects the idea that statements made by conduct and not intended to be assertive can fall within it. But it may be that the distinction is one of weight rather than admissibility. The use of the word 'representation' in the definition of 'statement' in s. 10(1) is not felicitous to give effect to either case, and it is to be regretted that the Act did not make the point clear.

### 8.3.2   Section 2(2)

The provisions of s. 2(2) refer to cases where the maker of the hearsay statement is to be called or has been called as a witness, and it is proposed to adduce his hearsay statement also, either by way of supplement to his evidence or as a previous consistent statement or both, such courses being specifically envisaged by the wording of s. 2(1). There is no limitation as such on the reasons for what may appear to be a duplication of evidence, but while the weight of a previous consistent statement which has no other function may be very slight, there are cases where it is necessary or desirable for the proper presentation of the case that the oral evidence of the witness should be supplemented by the evidence of a hearsay statement made by him. Such a case would be one where, because of illness, age or the sheer lapse of time, the witness's evidence would be less reliable or even literally unintelligible without the earlier statement. This use of the statutory provisions was grudgingly accepted as almost an unfortunate consequence of the corresponding provisions of the Evidence Act 1938,[8] but is now clearly intended to follow and is to be welcomed. The granting and refusal of leave under s. 2(2) (*a*) will be based on the judge's view of what would be fair to both sides, and it is by no means to be assessed only with

---

[5]   (CA) [1958] P 93; see 12.3, post.

[6]   (PC, British Guiana) [1952] AC 480; the facts are easily translatable into those of a civil case, and may refer to matters other than identification, for example in an action for personal injuries where a bystander shouts in the direction of the plaintiff, 'Don't go in there without a safety helmet'; as to unintended communications see 6.8.1, ante.

[7]   *Evidence*, 5th ed., pp. 495–6.

[8]   See *Harvey* v *Smith-Wood* [1964] 2 QB 171; a proper case, if ever there was one.

regard to the interests of the party seeking to adduce the evidence. There may be cases where the judge deems it unjust to the other side to allow a witness's hearsay statement to be given, having regard to the importance of his evidence to the case, the circumstances of the making of the statement, or its apparent lack of reliability. He will no doubt exercise his powers to allow the evidence in a case where to do so would promote a fair trial by helping the court to discover the truth, and where no injustice can be caused by that course.

The requirement of leave is the most important difference between cases where the maker of the statement is to be called (when leave is needed to adduce the hearsay statement) and cases where the maker is not called (when leave is not needed). The remaining provisions of s. 2(2) are self-explanatory; s. 2(2)(*b*) is designed to ensure that the cross-examiner of a witness, whose hearsay statement is to be adduced in addition to his oral evidence, is enabled, as far as may be possible having regard to the interests of all the parties, to cross-examine the witness on the basis of unprompted oral evidence given before the adduction of the hearsay statement. This is of particular importance where the hearsay statement is in writing, and is not a document from which the witness would be entitled to refresh his memory while giving evidence. The provision is actually of benefit to both sides, inasmuch as if the witness cannot be cross-examined properly on what oral evidence he is able to give, the weight of his evidence may be seriously affected. It would also appear to be proper and appropriate for the judge to delay his decision whether or not to grant leave for the admission of the hearsay statement until the natural moment arrives for it under s. 2(2)(*b*), when he will usually be able to form a more complete view of the matter, in the light of the evidence in chief.

### 8.3.3   Section 2(3)

This part of the section creates a significant distinction between statements made in a document and statements made otherwise. With the exception referred to in the proviso to the subsection, statements made otherwise than in documents must be proved by the direct oral evidence of the maker of the statement or a person who perceived (usually, but not necessarily, heard) the statement being made. The provision accords recognition to the evident truth that statements contained in documents can be proved with greater certainty and accuracy than those made in transient form.

Before expanding on the importance of the distinction, it will be convenient to observe the kinds of statements which will fall into either camp. Section 10(1) provides that, for the purposes of Part 1 of the Act:

'document' includes, in addition to a document in writing—

(*a*)   any map, plan, graph or drawing;

(*b*)   any photograph;

(*c*)   any disc, tape, sound track or other device in which sounds or other data (not being visual images) are embodied so as to be capable (with or without the aid of some other equipment) of being reproduced therefrom; and

(*d*)   any film, negative, tape or other device in which one or more visual images are embodied so as to be capable (as aforesaid) of being reproduced therefrom . . . .

What seems to be intended is a statement made in a form which is permanent, to the extent of being capable of being produced to the court in its original form at the time of trial, either by being produced as such, or by being played back to the court by the use of appropriate equipment, such as a projector or tape-recorder. It would, therefore, seem that the kinds of statement which will fall within the provisions of s. 2(3) are those in transient form, that is to say statements made orally, or by conduct.

It is sometimes said that s. 2(3) limits the contents of statements not made in documents to 'first-hand hearsay', whereas those made in documents are admissible also when they contain 'second-hand hearsay'. By the expressions 'first-hand' and 'second-hand' hearsay, is meant that if A perceives an event and makes a statement about it to B, then evidence from either A or B about what A said in his statement is at one remove only from the direct evidence of the event (first-hand); whereas if B repeats A's statement to C, who was not present when it was made, then coming from C, it is at second remove from the direct evidence (second-hand). At the risk of splitting hairs, the Act does not in fact say that second-hand hearsay is inadmissible, but that in the case of a statement not made in a document, such statement (while admissible) may only be proved by the evidence of the maker or of a person who perceived it being made. It is a question of means of proof and no more. The result is that if A's statement is made orally, A himself or B may give evidence to prove it, but C may not; if A's statement is contained in a document, it may be proved (subject to s. 6(1), see 8.6 post) by C or by anyone who is able to prove that it is A's statement. This is a preferable and more accurate way of expressing the requirement of s. 2(3). The customary use of the terms 'first-hand' and 'second-hand' may occasionally brand as inadmissible a statement which is arguably quite capable of being admitted, as where B makes a contemporaneous note of what A says, or even secretly records it on tape, and later gives the writing or tape to C. It may be an interesting semantic question whether this is first or second-hand, but it seems perfectly arguable that A's statement was made in a document and so may be proved by C. If B merely later writes down his recollection of what A said and gives the writing to C, C cannot prove the statement, not because it is second-hand, but because the Act says that his evidence is inadmissible for that purpose; the statement may be proved quite properly either by A or by B.

Statements made by a person while giving oral evidence in other legal proceedings are admissible under s. 2[9] and are exempted from the evidential requirements of s. 2(3) notwithstanding that they are made otherwise than in a document. Indeed, the proviso to the subsection allows a considerable degree of latitude in the manner of proof. It should be observed that, while the court is free to permit proof of the statement concerned in any manner which seems to be appropriate, the Court of Appeal was prepared to hold in *Taylor* v *Taylor*[10] that with regard to a criminal trial on indictment, the transcript of evidence was admissible under s. 2. It would probably have been more precise to say that the transcript was a proper manner of proving the statements made in the course of giving evidence, which statements were admissible under s.2, but clearly, the practice is the most satisfactory and accurate available to the court. In courts where no such record is taken as will enable an exact transcript to be produced, resort may be had to notes taken by the Bench or the clerk, or even by a legal representative. In view of the wording of the proviso, it would be open to the court, in the last resort, to permit a witness to narrate what evidence he had himself given in other proceedings, or to call another person who heard

---

[9]  Though their admissibility and the conditions on which they are admitted are governed by RSC, Ord. 38, r. 28 (made under the authority of s. 8(3)(*b*) of the Act) which gives the court wide powers to regulate their admission and proof; see 8.7, post.

[10]  [1970] 1 WLR 1148. The court thought that the transcript of the summing-up might have to be admitted under s. 4 of the Act as part of a record compiled by the shorthand writer acting under a duty, as opposed to s. 2.

the former evidence being given. An application for the court to rule on this matter in advance may be made by any party under RSC, Ord.38, r. 28.

### 8.3.4 Blackstone v Coke

That the provisions of s. 2 of the Act represent a radical departure from the common-law position may be seen readily by comparing the availability of a significant piece of evidence in *Blackstone* v *Coke* with that in its criminal counterpart, *R* v *Coke; R* v *Littleton*. In the former, it would now be possible for Coke to adduce evidence of hearsay statements made by Anthony Henneky, who is not available to give evidence, whereas in a criminal case this course would not be open to him. Only so much of the statement as consists of facts of which direct, oral evidence would be admissible, may be admitted. But this would include evidence of Henneky's relationship with Margaret, and possible paternity of her child. Whether the judge would accord great weight to such evidence may be doubted, but its potential for affecting the outcome seems clear. In a criminal case, no exception or statutory rule would permit this evidence to be given, despite its possible exculpatory value.

### 8.4 Statements admissible under s. 4

By s. 4 of the Act:

(1) Without prejudice to section 5 of this Act, in any civil proceedings a statement contained in a document shall, subject to this section and to rules of court, be admissible as evidence of any fact therein of which direct oral evidence would be admissible, if the document is, or forms part of, a record compiled by a person acting under a duty from information which was supplied by a person (whether acting under a duty or not) who had, or may reasonably be supposed to have had, personal knowledge of the matters dealt with in that information and which, if not supplied by that person to the compiler of the record directly, was supplied by him to the compiler of the record indirectly through one or more intermediaries each acting under a duty.

(2) Where in any civil proceedings a party desiring to give a statement in evidence by virtue of this section has called or intends to call as a witness in the proceedings the person who originally supplied the information from which the record containing the statement was compiled, the statement—

(a) shall not be given in evidence by virtue of this section on behalf of that party without the leave of the court; and

(b) without prejudice to paragraph (a) above, shall not without the leave of the court be given in evidence by virtue of this section on behalf of that party before the conclusion of the examination-in-chief of the person who originally supplied the said information.

(3) Any reference in this section to a person acting under a duty includes a reference to a person acting in the course of any trade, business, profession or other occupation in which he is engaged or employed or for the purposes of any paid or unpaid office held by him.

This section, which relates to the admissibility of records, represented a considerable extension of the admissibility permitted by s. 1 of the Criminal Evidence Act 1965 in criminal cases, and both were used as a model for s. 68 of the Police and Criminal Evidence Act 1984. Section 4 applies only to statements contained in 'documents' within the meaning of s. 10(1), which was discussed in 8.3.3, and like s. 2, preserves the requirement of general admissibility under the rules of evidence, by the limitation that the statement may be evidence, 'of any fact stated therein of which direct oral evidence would be admissible'. Various matters require some further consideration.

### 8.4.1 'Record'

The word 'record' appears both in this section of the 1968 Act and in s. 68 of the Police and Criminal Evidence Act 1984. It appeared also in the Criminal Evidence Act 1965. It has never been defined judicially in a comprehensive way, although various courts have considered it in both civil and criminal cases. In *R* v *Tirado* (1974) 59 Cr App R 80, 89, the Court of Appeal, Criminal Division, expressed 'some hesitation' in deciding that a file of correspondence, maintained simply as a repository for letters as and when they came in, could be a 'record' for the purposes of the 1965 Act, although the case turned on another point. There is some force in the objection. Certainly, the words 'compiled . . . from information supplied' suggest an element of deliberation in the making of a source of future reference, though they suggest no necessary minimum quality, which may be a matter affecting only the weight of the evidence. The Act does not require that the information received shall be dealt with in any particular way, except for the record being 'compiled', and no doubt in many cases adding to a file would suffice if no other steps were appropriate or necessary to turn the information into a record. It would be contrary to the spirit of the Act to exclude a source of information deliberately compiled as such, even if the method of compilation, and consequently the weight of the evidence, may be unimpressive. None of this suggests that the evidence proffered in *Tirado*, which consisted of an apparently random collection of letters received from various people, should have been admissible.

In *R* v *Gwilliam* [1968] 1 WLR 1839, the Court of Appeal, Criminal Division, doubted whether a single Home Office consignment note could in itself amount to a record, though the court expressly declined to decide the case on this ground. This and other matters were probably resolved by the later case of *R* v *Jones; R* v *Sullivan* [1978] 1 WLR 195. The defendants were directors of a transport business, and were charged with conspiracy to steal from containers. The containers broken into had been packed in the Far East and shipped to England. It was necessary for the prosecution to prove the original contents of the containers, and for this purpose, they put in evidence bills of lading and other documents. On appeal, it was argued that each set of documents merely dealt with a single shipment of goods and, having a limited life-span, could not be or form part of a record. The court rejected this argument. Geoffrey Lane LJ said (ibid at 199):

> Although it is not an exhaustive definition of the word, 'record' in this context means a history of events in some form which is not evanescent. How long the record is likely to be kept is immaterial: it may be something which is indeed more lasting than bronze, but the degree of permanence does not seem to us to make or mar the fulfilment of the definition of the word 'record'. The record in each individual case will last as long as commercial necessity may demand.

> The documents in the present case seem to us to fall precisely into that category. They are the written records of the particular transaction . . . . They are carefully and

deliberately compiled for the information of those in this country who are going to be the recipients of the goods.

More significant than the quantity or commercial lifetime of the documents is their content. It is important to stress that the Act renders admissible only records compiled from information supplied under defined circumstances, and this is important as an indication of reliability. If the documents are not a primary or original source of information, but a digest or analysis of that information, they do not constitute a 'record' for the purposes of s. 4. In *H* v *Schering Chemicals Ltd* [1983] 1 WLR 143, the plaintiffs brought an action against the defendant pharmaceutical companies, alleging negligence in the manufacture and marketing of a drug used by the plaintiffs. The plaintiffs sought to admit, pursuant to s. 4, voluminous documents which consisted of summaries of medical research and letters to and articles published in medical journals. Bingham J refused to admit the documents as a 'record'. The learned judge said:

Having considered the matter as best I can in the light of the arguments and the authorities, I have come to the conclusion that the documents which form part of the large bundle before me are not records within the meaning of s. 4 of the 1968 Act. The intention of that section was, I believe, to admit in evidence records which a historian would regard as original or primary sources, that is documents which either give effect to a transaction itself or which contain a contemporaneous register of information supplied by those with direct knowledge of the facts . . . .
Judged by the same standard the documents in the present case, I think, are not records and are not primary or original sources. They are a digest or analysis of records which must exist or have existed, but they are not themselves those records. If the plaintiffs' submission were right it would, I think, mean that anyone who wrote a letter to *The Times*, having done research and summarising the result of that research in his letter, would find his letter admissible as evidence of the facts under s. 4. That is not, I think, the intent of the section . . . .

This decision was applied by Peter Gibson J in *Savings and Investment Bank Ltd* v *Gasco Investments (Netherlands) BV and others* [1984] 1 All ER 296 in rejecting the argument that reports made by inspectors appointed pursuant to ss. 165 and 172 of the Companies Act 1948, were admissible as a record under s. 4. Noting that the inspectors had been 'manifestly painstaking in the preparation of their reports', the learned judge held them to be inadmissible. Having considered *H* v *Schering Chemicals Ltd*, he concluded:

. . . I respectfully accept as correct the test propounded by Bingham J. To my mind it is obvious that a report by inspectors and their comments and conclusions thereon, is not a record in any ordinary sense of the word. It falls short of simply compiling the information supplied to them in the sense that some information will not be included in the report, and it goes beyond such a compilation in that it expresses opinions thereon.

### 8.4.2 *'Acting under a duty'*
The records rendered admissible by s. 4 are not confined to those of any particular kind of organisation, but instead, a safeguard is introduced to ensure some degree of accuracy in the records admitted by requiring that the record shall have been made by a person acting

under a 'duty', and thus carrying some measure of personal responsibility for that which he records. The duty requirement does not apply to the person who originally supplied the information from which the record is compiled, though his conduct is subject to the separate safeguard of the requirement of personal knowledge. But the duty requirement does apply to 'intermediaries', that is to say, anyone who acts as a link in the chain of communication or supply of the information from the original supplier to the eventual compiler of the record. This is a sensible provision, which avoided a gap in the corresponding safeguard of the Criminal Evidence Act 1965, a gap now also closed by the Police and Criminal Evidence Act 1984.

The non-exclusive definition of 'duty' provided by s. 4(3) shows that a wide approach is intended. The duty need not relate only to commercial matters, and need not even relate to any function for which the compiler is paid, but would include duties arising from public or even private, honorary offices, and so would appear to cover not only legal duties, but also social or moral ones. The term has not yet given rise to difficulty.

### 8.4.3   The requirement of personal knowledge

The original supplier of the information is subject to the requirement that he had, or may reasonably be supposed to have had, personal knowledge of the matters dealt with in the information which he supplied. The trial judge is entitled, under s. 6(2), in deciding the admissibility of statements tendered under s. 4, to have regard to the circumstances in which the statement was made or to its form and contents and to draw any reasonable inference from those matters. It may be that in many cases, the actual or probable state of personal knowledge of the supplier will be readily apparent. But it appears that the court will be ready to hold that the supplier may reasonably be supposed to have had such knowledge in a case where lapse of time has rendered such a finding necessary, at least where the supplier was carrying out public or official function. In *Knight and Others* v *David and Others* [1971] 1 WLR 1671, a claim by the plaintiffs to certain land depended upon events which occurred in 1886, and for the purpose of establishing that claim, the plaintiffs sought to put in evidence a tithe map and tithe apportionment survey, made under the provisions of the Tithe Act 1836. Goulding J, while holding that these documents were admissible at common law as proving public or general rights,[11] was prepared to infer also that the supplier of the information contained in them, acting as he was in an important public capacity, might reasonably be supposed to have had personal knowledge of the matters dealt with in the information which he supplied with a view to those documents being compiled.

### 8.4.4   Section 4(2)

This subsection makes provision, similar but not exactly identical to that in s. 2(2), for cases where the party tendering admissible evidence contained in a record proposes also to call as a witness the original supplier of the information. The purpose of the provisions is the same as that of s. 2(2) (see 8.3.2,ante). But it is both interesting and important to note that, while the same requirement of leave and the same limitation on the time when the statement may be put in evidence are imposed, the latter is in this section absolute, and is not capable of being relieved by the exceptions provided for in s. 2.

---

[11]   Strictly, this seems to be incorrect, because the rule referred by by Goulding J is one incorporated into the Civil Evidence Act 1968 by s. 9; but this makes no difference of substance in its operation, and the learned judge's view seems plainly right in principle.

### 8.4.5 *Blackstone v Coke*

The admissibility of facts contained in records, as above defined, is a most important source of evidence in modern civil litigation. No doubt every organisation of significance compiles and maintains records of many different kinds, from information supplied by field-workers and representatives of every kind. The section is not confined to commercial organisations, but extends to governmental and private bodies also. A frequent use of s. 4 is in relation to medical records. In *Blackstone* v *Coke*, for example, Margaret Blackstone might well adduce the records maintained by the hospital in which she was confined, if an issue arose as to her medical treatment. Although possibly voluminous and contributed to by a number of different doctors and nurses, the documents in question would be perfectly admissible as evidence of the facts contained in them, about which those doctors and nurses could have given direct, oral evidence.

## 8.5 Statements admissible under s. 5

It is not proposed to consider here the detailed provisions of s. 5, which, though not unimportant and indeed likely to become more so as technology advances, have not yet attracted the attention of the courts. The section provides that in civil proceedings, subject to various safeguards relating to proof of the proper supply of information to, and the proper working of the computer, and to rules of court, statements produced by computers are to be admissible 'as evidence of any fact stated therein of which direct oral evidence would be admissible'. The section was clearly designed to permit the introduction of a certain degree of mechanically and automatically produced evidence, and to avoid the problems which had arisen under the Criminal Evidence Act 1965 with regard to the requirement in that Act that in every case an element of personal knowledge is to be looked for which the operator of an automatic machine may well not have.[12] Again, this section became in part a model for the corresponding s. 69 of the Police and Criminal Evidence Act 1984. The latter, however, is much simplified (8.12, post). It is to be noticed that, in s. 4 of the Civil Evidence Act 1968, the operation of that section (in which there is also a requirement of personal knowledge) is expressly said to be 'without prejudice to s. 5.'

By s. 5(6), for the purposes of Part 1 of the Act: '"computer" means any device for storing and processing information, and any reference to information being derived from other information is a reference to its being derived therefrom by calculation, comparison or any other process.'

## 8.6 Section 6: proof, admissibility, weight

Section 6 deals with matters ancillary to the admission of statements tendered under s. 2, s.4 or s.5 (and, in the case of the provisions for the determination of weight, those tendered under s. 3) of the Act. The provisions of s. 6(4) dealing with such statements in the context of corroboration, are dealt with in 14.4, post. The matters considered here concern the mode of proof of admissible hearsay statements (s. 6(1)), the determination of the admissibility of such statements (s. 6(2)) and their weight when admitted (s. 6(3)).

---

[12] See 8.11.4 and 15.5.5, post.

*8.6.1   Section 6(1)*

This subsection provides for the proof of statements tendered under s. 2, s. 4 or s. 5 of the Act and contained in documents (within the meaning of s. 10(1)). It will be recalled that statements admissible under s. 2 which are not made in documents are subject to the special rule of proof set out in s. 2(3). Section 6(1) provides that:

> Where in any civil proceedings a statement contained in a document is proposed to be given in evidence by virtue of section 2, 4 or 5 of this Act it may, subject to any rules of court, be proved by the production of that document or (whether or not that document is still in existence) by the production of a copy of that document, or of the material part thereof, authenticated in such manner as the court may approve.

The subsection must be read together with s. 10(2), which provides that:

> In this part of this Act any reference to a copy of a document includes—
>
> (a)   in the case of a document falling within paragraph (c) but not (d) of the definition of 'document' in the foregoing subsection, [13] a transcript of the sounds or other data embodied therein;
> (b)   in the case of a document falling within paragraph (d) and not (c) of that definition,[14] a reproduction or still reproduction of the image or images embodied therein, whether enlarged or not;
> (c)   in the case of a document falling within both those paragraphs, such a transcript together with such a still reproduction; and
> (d)   in the case of a document falling within the said paragraph (d) of which a visual image is embodied in a document falling within that paragraph, a reproduction of that image, whether enlarged or not,
>
> and any reference to a copy of the material part of a document shall be construed accordingly.

In the case of documents in written form, including for this purpose the maps, plans, graphs and drawings referred to in s. 10(1)(a) and (b), the absence of any mandatory requirement would appear to indicate that any form of manual, automatic or photographic copy will suffice, provided that it is capable of being properly authenticated. The term 'authenticated' in s. 6(1) presumably means no more than that the copy should be shown to be a true copy of the original, however and whenever made, and the evidence required to prove this is not specified, the matter being one for the court in every case.

This permissive code of proof of admissible hearsay contained in documents contrasts vividly with the strict requirements at common law for the proof of the contents of documents tendered as non-hearsay evidence, in which case the production of the original is required, save in certain exceptional cases; see 15.2, post.

---

[13]   Paragraph (c) is concerned with sounds and aural data capable of being reproduced: see 8.3.3, ante.

[14]   Paragraph (d) is concerned with visual images on film and the like capable of being reproduced: see 8.3.3, ante.

### 8.6.2 Section 6(2)

Section 6(2) relates to the determination of admissibility of a statement under s. 2, s. 4 or s. 5, and provides for reference to the circumstances in which the statement was made and to its form and contents, if made in a document. Clearly, the matters referred to in s. 6(2) are those which are likely to assist the judge in the assessment of the various conditions of admissibility which he may have to consider for the purposes of s. 2, s. 4 or s. 5. A party who disputes the admissibility of such a statement is entitled to have the matter investigated, and as we shall see in 8.7, the rules of court are designed to ensure that this process can be effected at an interlocutory stage of the proceedings, so that the trial itself is not subject to undue interruption because of disputes over admissibility. Nonetheless, there will be unforeseen matters which require and must be given attention, and if necessary decided by the judge, at the trial stage. Section 6(2) provides that:

> For the purpose of deciding whether or not a statement is admissible in evidence by virtue of section 2, 4 or 5 of this Act, the court may draw any reasonable inference from the circumstances in which the statement was made or otherwise came into being or from any other circumstances, including, in the case of a statement contained in a document, the form and contents of that document.

### 8.6.3 Section 6(3)

By this subsection:

> In estimating the weight, if any, to be attached to a statement admissible in evidence by virtue of section 2, 3, 4 or 5 of this Act regard shall be had to all the circumstances from which any inference can reasonably be drawn as to the accuracy or otherwise of the statement and, in particular—
>
> (a)   in the case of a statement falling within section 2(1) or 3(1) or (2) of this Act, to the question whether or not the statement was made contemporaneously with the occurrence or existence of the facts stated, and to the question whether or not the maker of the statement had any incentive to conceal or misrepresent the facts;
>
> (b)   in the case of a statement falling within section 4(1) of this Act, to the question whether or not the person who originally supplied the information from which the record containing the statement was compiled did so contemporaneously with the occurrence or existence of the facts dealt with in that information, and to the question whether or not that person, or any person concerned with compiling or keeping the record containing the statement, had any incentive to conceal or misrepresent the facts; and
>
> (c)   [makes equivalent provision for statements admissible under s. 5].

The subsection does not call for comment, except that the question of weight is much easier to deal with in civil cases (where the judge will inevitably form his own view at an early stage, and where, in some cases, his view of the likely weight may even lead him to refuse leave where leave is required for admission), than in criminal cases, where the trial judge may well be obliged to direct the jury with regard to the weight of evidence admitted under the Police and Criminal Evidence Act 1984. Although it is a ground of appeal in civil cases that a decision was against the weight of the evidence, a judge cannot be tied to the literal wording of s. 6(3), and it is to be noticed that the paragraphs of the subsection are expressed to be merely particular instances of 'all the circumstances from which any inference can reasonably be drawn as to the accuracy or otherwise of the statement', to which the judge is to have regard.

## 8.7 The notice procedure

Section 8 of the Civil Evidence Act 1968 provides statutory authority for the creation of a substantial body of rules of court within the framework of which s. 2, s. 4 and s. 5 shall operate. Section 8(1) provides:

> Provision shall be made by rules of court as to the procedure which, subject to any exceptions provided for in the rules, must be followed and the other conditions which, subject as aforesaid, must be fulfilled before a statement can be given in evidence in civil proceedings by virtue of section 2, 4 or 5 of this Act.

The remainder of the section provides specifically for various kinds of rule, sometimes in mandatory form and sometimes by way of an enabling provision. The resulting rules governing practice in the High Court are to be found in RSC, Ord. 38, rr. 21–31.[15] They will be examined here only so as to highlight the evidential points which they raise. For the more detailed practical working of the rules, reference should be made to the *Supreme Court Practice*. The overriding purpose of the rules is to bring about and enforce a system of notice, that is to say a procedure of general application that, as a requirement of practice, a party wishing to give in evidence a hearsay statement admissible by virtue of s. 2, s. 4 or s. 5 must first give to each other party notice of that intention, indicating the nature and substance of the evidence which is sought to be adduced. The opponent is then enabled, by himself giving notice, to compel the party seeking to adduce the evidence to call as a witness the maker of the statement, unless for one of a number of reasons the maker is not available to be called, or there would be no point in calling him to deal with the evidence in question. In effect, the rules impose a further condition of admissibility upon statements tendered under these sections, albeit a condition of practice rather than law, and albeit that the court is given a general discretion to admit despite non-compliance with the rules. The provisions may be summarised as follows, in a convenient and much abbreviated form, before being considered in more detail.

(a)    By r. 21, a party wishing to adduce hearsay evidence under s. 2, s. 4 or s. 5 must, within certain time-limits, serve notice of his intention to do so, the form of such notice differing with the section applicable to the evidence.

(b)    On receipt of such notice, any other party may serve, under r. 26, a counter-notice requiring the party wishing to adduce the evidence to call as a witness any person named in the original notice as being a person involved in the making or receiving of the hearsay statement in question. Subject to the court's discretion, failure to comply with a counter-notice will result in the hearsay evidence being inadmissible.

(c)    A counter-notice may be ineffective, however, where the party wishing to adduce the evidence states in his notice that for any one of the reasons enumerated in r. 25, it is not

---

[15]    The corresponding practice in the county court is to be found in CCR, Ord. 20, rr. 20–32. These are not considered separately here, but may be found in the *County Court Practice*. RSC, Ord. 38, rr. 30–31, relating to evidence admissible under s. 7 of the Act, are also not considered here.

possible, or is pointless, to call the person in respect of whom the counter-notice was to be given. The opponent must then either accept this position, or invite the court to determine whether the reason alleged does in fact apply to the person concerned, having served a counter-notice indicating that he disputes the applicability of the reason given. The court will then decide whether the counter-notice may take effect so as to require the attendance of that person. If the reason given is held to apply to that person, the hearsay statement is admissible and he need not be called.

(d)   The court has an overriding discretion, by virtue of r. 29, to receive evidence under s. 2, s. 4 or s. 5, notwithstanding any non-compliance with the rules. This discretion must, of course, be exercised judicially so as to do justice between the parties and ensure a fair trial, having regard to all the circumstances.

These provisions must now be considered in a little more detail.

### 8.7.1   Notice of intention
By r. 21:

(1)   Subject to the provisions of this rule, a party to a cause or matter who desires to give in evidence at the trial or hearing of the cause or matter any statement which is admissible in evidence by virtue of section, 2, 4 or 5 of the Act must—

(a)   in the case of a cause or matter which is required to be set down for trial or hearing or adjourned into court, within 21 days after it is set down or so adjourned, or within such other period as the Court may specify, and

(b)   in the case of any other cause or matter, within 21 days after the date on which an appointment for the first hearing of the cause or matter is obtained, or within such other period as the Court may specify,

serve on every other party to the cause or matter notice of his desire to do so, and the notice must comply with the provisions of rule 22, 23 or 24, as the circumstances of the case require.

(2)   Paragraph (1) shall not apply in relation to any statement which is admissible as evidence of any fact stated therein by virtue not only of the said section 2, 4 or 5 but by virtue also of any other statutory provision within the meaning of section 1 of the Act.[16]

The time-limits imposed, within which notice must be given, are intended to ensure that, so far as possible, every other party is given an adequate length of time to determine whether he accepts the admissibility of the statement, or whether he wishes to take any steps to dispute it. It is also important that any such issues as may arise should be considered and dealt with, as far as possible, at the interlocutory stage, so that the smooth and expeditious conduct of the trial is not affected by unnecessary applications relating to the admissibility of evidence.

The form of the notice varies according to which section applies to the statement sought

---

[16]   For self-evident reasons, r. 21(3) provides that no notice need be given where the hearsay statement sought to be admitted is alleged to have been made by a deceased and is to be admitted in a probate action the subject of which is the deceased's estate.

to be admitted. The form is governed in the case of statements admissible under s. 2 by r. 22, in the case of those admissible under s. 4 by r. 23[17] and in the case of those admissible under s. 5 by r. 24. Rule 24 is not considered further in detail. The principal provisions of r. 22 and r. 23 are as follows:

22.—(1)  If the statement is admissible by virtue of section 2 of the Act and was made otherwise than in a document, the notice must contain particulars of—

(a)   the time, place and circumstances at or in which the statement was made;
(b)   the person by whom, and the person to whom, the statement was made; and
(c)   the substance of the statement or, if material, the words used.

(2)   If the statement is admissible by virtue of the said section 2 and was made in a document, a copy or transcript of the document, or of the relevant part thereof, must be annexed to the notice and the notice must contain such (if any) of the particulars mentioned in paragraph (1)(a) and (b) as are not apparent on the face of the document or part . . ..

23.—(1)   In the statement is admissible by virtue of section 4 of the Act, the notice must have annexed to it a copy or transcript of the document containing the statement, or of the relevant part thereof, and must contain—

(a)   particulars of—
    (i)   the person by whom the record containing the statement was compiled; and
    (ii)   the person who originally supplied the information from which the record was compiled; and
    (iii)   any other person through whom that information was supplied to the compiler of that record;
and, in the case of any such person as is referred to in (i) or (iii) above, a description of the duty under which that person was acting when compiling that record or supplying information from which that record was compiled, as the case may be;
(b)   if not apparent on the face of the document annexed to the notice, a description of the nature of the record which, or part of which, contains the statement; and
(c)   particulars of the time, place and circumstances at or in which that record or part was compiled.

In addition, rules 22, 23 and 24 each provide that if the party giving the notice alleges that any person, particulars of whom are contained in the notice, cannot or should not be called as a witness at the trial or hearing, for any of the reasons specified in r. 25, then the notice must contain a statement to that effect specifying the reason relied on. This is to enable other parties to refer such reason to the court under r. 27. The object of having notices in the forms indicated in these rules is, of course, to ensure that the other party's disadvantage in being faced with hearsay evidence is balanced by his knowing in advance as much about the evidence as he can, and by his being enabled, in consequence, to decide

---

[17]   If the statement tendered as admissible by virtue of s. 2 or s. 4 is one consisting of evidence given (orally or in a document) in other legal proceedings, or is contained in a record of direct oral evidence so given, the notice under r. 21 makes available the procedure under r. 28, as an alternative to a r. 26 counter-notice in such cases: see 8.7.2, post.

whether a counter-notice should be served under r. 26. The degree of detail insisted upon by the rules does in fact provide a real measure of compensation for having to accept, if it must be accepted, evidence admissible under one of the sections to which the rules apply. It also illustrates the advantage to a party in being able to justify, if he can, the admission of hearsay statements other than under s. 2, s. 4 or s. 5, for example under s. 9; in such a case, he escapes the notice procedure altogether, and not only avoids giving his hand away before the trial, but also avoids the possibility of a counter-notice. This is made clear by r. 21(2). Hearsay evidence admitted by agreement of the parties, as it may be under s. 1, would present no practical problem in this context, but in order to dispense with notice altogether every party affected must agree to its admission, any party who does not agree being entitled to notice under r. 21.

The provisions of r. 21 are to be enforced assiduously. Any party wishing to adduce hearsay evidence under s. 2, s. 4 or s. 5 must serve a notice in his own right. Thus in *Letraset International Ltd* v *Dymo Ltd*[18] where the plaintiffs served notice of their intention to adduce hearsay statements admissible under s. 2, consisting of evidence given on their behalf at a previous hearing, but later abandoned their intention to adduce them, the defendants were held not to be entitled to adduce such statements as part of their case without first serving notice on the plaintiffs under r. 21 in their own right; they were not entitled to rely for that purpose on the notice given by the plaintiffs because the plaintiffs were not able to infer from their own notice the exact nature and extent of the evidence which the defendants intended to adduce. The rule also applies to a case where a party intends to adduce in evidence hearsay statements made in documents disclosed to him on discovery.[19]

### 8.7.2  Counter-notice

Rule 26 provides that:

(1)  Subject to paragraphs (2) and (3), any party to a cause or matter on whom a notice under rule 21 is served may within 21 days after service of the notice on him serve on the party who gave the notice a counter-notice requiring that party to call as a witness at the trial or hearing of the cause or matter any person (naming him) particulars of whom are contained in the notice . . .

(4)  If the party to a cause or matter by whom a notice under rule 21 is served fails to comply with a counter-notice duly served on him under this rule, then, unless any of the reasons specified in rule 25 applies in relation to the person named in the counter-notice, and without prejudice to the powers of the Court under rule 29, the statement to which the notice under rule 21 relates shall not be admissible at the trial or hearing of the cause or matter as evidence of any fact stated therein by virtue of section 2, 4 or 5 of the Act, as the case may be.

It is important to note the effect of a counter-notice. It does not oblige the party on whom it is served to call the person referred to as a witness. The effect of r. 26(4) is that if such person is not called, the statement, the subject of the r. 21 notice, will not be admissible by virtue of s. 2, s. 4 or s. 5, unless either r. 25 applies or the judge exercises his

---

[18]  [1976] RPC 65. The point was not considered on appeal.
[19]  *Minnesota Mining & Manufacturing Co.* v *Johnson & Johnson Ltd* (CA) [1976] FSR 6.

discretion to admit it under r. 29. It does not necessarily mean that the statement cannot be admitted, and nothing in the rule precludes the admission of the statement under some other statutory provision, or as a piece of non-hearsay evidence for a purpose other than to prove the truth of the facts stated in it. If the witness is called, as required by the counter-notice, the effect is not that his hearsay statement is thereby rendered inadmissible,[20] but that it will be admissible only subject to the requirement of leave, and to the other requirements of s. 2(2) or s. 4(2), as the case may be.

Apart from the cases to which r. 25 applies, counter-notice should be served wherever it is wished to require the attendance of a person referred to in the r. 21 notice, except in cases falling within r. 28. These are cases where the r.21 notice expresses a wish to give in evidence a statement, admissible under s. 2, consisting of evidence given (orally or in a document) in other legal proceedings, or a statement, admissible under s. 4, contained in a record of any direct oral evidence so given. In such cases, r. 28, made under the authority of s. 8(3)(b) of the Act, confers on the court a wide power to permit such evidence to be given, to impose conditions on its admissibility and to give general directions with respect to it. In such cases, r. 26(3) provides that no counter-notice should be served, but instead, an application made to the court for directions under r. 28.

While a party is at liberty to serve a counter-notice in any case except those mentioned above, it is pertinent to observe that the court has ample power to deal by way of costs with unnecessary requirements for witnesses to attend, and with any waste of the court's time. The procedure should, therefore, be used with some discretion, bearing in mind not only the nature but also the likely weight of the evidence to be adduced on the other side, and remembering that there are cases where a witness giving oral evidence may invest part of the case with a force which may be wholly lacking in a hearsay document.

### 8.7.3  *Witnesses who cannot or should not be called*
As we have seen, r. 22, r. 23 and r. 24 provide that r. 21 notices given in the cases to which, they are appropriate may and should contain any allegation made that a person named in the notice cannot or should not be called as a witness, and the reason relied on for that allegation should be set out. The reasons upon which reliance may be placed for this purpose are laid down in r. 25, and no other reasons may be resorted to. Rule 25 provides that:

> The reasons referred to in rules 22(3), 23(2) and 24(3) are that the person in question is dead, or beyond the seas, or unfit by reason of his bodily or mental condition to attend as a witness or that despite the exercise of reasonable diligence it has not been possible to identify or to find him or that he cannot reasonably be expected to have any recollection of matters relevant to the accuracy or otherwise of the statement to which the notice relates.

The inclusion of such an allegation in a r. 21 notice has an immediate effect on the subsequent procedure. Firstly, it imposes restrictions on the service and effect of a counter-notice. By r. 26(2):

> Where any notice under rule 21 contains a statement that any person particulars of

---

[20]   *Pace* the *Supreme Court Practice*, which in the commentary on r. 26 appears to suggest the contrary.

whom are contained in the notice cannot or should not be called as a witness for the reason specified therein, a party shall not be entitled to serve a counter-notice under this rule requiring that person to be called as a witness at the trial or hearing of the cause or matter unless he contends that the person can or, as the case may be, should be called, and in that case he must include in his counter-notice a statement to that effect.

There may, of course, be cases where even the limited use which may be made of a counter-notice in these circumstances is useless, as where it can readily be demonstrated that the person referred to is dead or beyond the seas, but the other reasons may easily give rise to considerable dispute. In such case, any party may refer such dispute to the court under r. 27 for determination of the question whether any of the reasons specified in r. 25 applies to the person in question. The court may, and will if possible, determine this issue before trial, and where this is done, no further application may be made at trial unless fresh evidence comes to light, which could not, with reasonable diligence, have been adduced at the original application: r. 27(3). If the court determines that a r. 25 reason applies, the party seeking to adduce the hearsay evidence is entitled to do so in any event. If no r. 25 reason is found to apply, the counter-notice will take effect in the normal way.

Any one of the r. 25 reasons, standing alone, will suffice if shown to apply. In *Rasool* v *West Midlands Passenger Transport Executive*,[21] the defendant wished to adduce the hearsay statement of a person who, according to their r. 21 notice, had 'left her former address and cannot at present be found. It is understood that she is now beyond the seas and is probably resident in Jamaica'. On the available evidence, this account appeared to be accurate, although the defendants had made no effort to trace the potential witness. It was argued for the plaintiffs that the statement was not admissible, because even if the missing witness was beyond the seas, it was still for the defendants to show that despite the exercise of reasonable diligence, she could not be found. Finer J rejected the plaintiff's argument, holding that the reasons given in r. 25 were disjunctive, and that the provision that the witness could not be found with reasonable diligence was simply one of them. If the defendants established any one reason, as they had, the balance of probabilities being the appropriate standard of proof in the matter, the statement was admissible. This decision was approved by the Court of Appeal in *Piermay Shipping Co. SA and Another* v *Chester*.[22]

### 8.7.4 The court's discretion

By s. 8(3)(*a*) of the Act, the rules of court to be made were empowered to confer on the court a discretion to allow the admission of a statement under s.2, s. 4 or s.5 despite the non-compliance in any particular case with the rules concerning admissibility. The court was not, however, to be given any discretion to exclude admissible evidence, where the rules had been complied with, save in the sole instance of statements falling within what later became r. 28, consisting of evidence given, or the record of oral evidence given, in

---

[21] [1974] 3 All ER 638. Of interest are Finer J's observations at 642 as to the possible consequences to the defendants of not seeking to find the witness.

[22] [1978] 1 WLR 411. Whether this ought to be the position is open to some question. Both Finer J in *Rasool* and Donaldson J at first instance in *Piermay* recognised that the construction left something to be desired. But it was evidently a deliberate step by Parliament, which as Eveleigh LJ pointed out in *Piermay*, departed from the position under the Evidence Act 1938, under which beyond the seas was insufficient unless it was also shown that a person could not be found with reasonable diligence.

other proceedings. The existence of a wide inclusionary discretion was felt to be necessary to prevent the new law from being encumbered or even strangled by excessive technicality. The discretion is conferred by r. 29, which provides that:

(1)  Without prejudice to section 2(2)(*a*) and 4(2)(*a*) of the Act and rule 28, the Court may, if it thinks it just to do so, allow a statement falling within section 2(1), 4(1) or 5(1) of the Act to be given in evidence at the trial or hearing of a cause or matter notwithstanding—

(*a*)  that the statement is one in relation to which rule 21(1) applies and that the party desiring to give the statement in evidence has failed to comply with that rule, or

(*b*)  that that party has failed to comply with any requirement of a counter-notice relating to that statement which was served on him in accordance with rule 26.

(2)  Without prejudice to the generality of paragraph (1), the Court may exercise its power under the paragraph to allow a statement to be given in evidence at the trial or hearing of a cause or matter if a refusal to exercise that power might oblige the party desiring to give the statement in evidence to call as a witness at the trial or hearing an opposite party or a person who is or was at the material time the servant or agent of an opposite party.

The discretion must be exercised judicially, with a view to doing justice between the parties and securing a fair trial. The operation of the general discretion under r. 29(1) may be aptly illustrated by contrasting the cases of *Ford* v *Lewis* [1971] 1 WLR 623 and *Morris* v *Stratford-on-Avon RDC* [1973] 1 WLR 1059. In *Ford* v *Lewis*, the infant plaintiff was struck by a vehicle driven by the defendant. The plaintiff was, at the material time, in the charge of her parents, and the defendant (who by the time of the trial was a mental patient and incapable of giving evidence) wished to put in evidence, *inter alia*, statements made in medical records and in a document which he himself had made, which tended to show that the plaintiff's father was very drunk at the time of the accident. No notices under r. 21 had been served in respect of such statements. The reason for non-compliance with the rule emerged for the first time in the Court of Appeal, and was that notice had been withheld on the advice of counsel, apparently on the purported ground that it was not known how the plaintiff's case was to be put, and whether it would be necessary to use the statements in evidence. The Court of Appeal were, therefore, faced with the situation that the trial judge had been unaware of the true reason why the rules had not been complied with, and had to decide whether the request for exercise of discretion under r. 29 could be upheld. The whole court condemned the course which had been adopted on behalf of the defendant, and while Davies LJ was against the granting of a new trial because of the already considerable delay and because it seemed to him that the ultimate result must be the same, the majority (Edmund Davies and Karminski LJJ) held that the order was inevitable. Edmund Davies LJ said ([1971] 1 WLR at 633):

In these most unfortunate circumstances, it seems to me impossible that the defendant should be permitted to rely upon the judge's purported exercise of his discretion under r. 29. I hold that there can be no valid exercise of such discretion if there has (for any reason) been a deliberate withholding from the court of the reason for non-compliance. Had Veale J known that this was the result of a deliberate decision based upon the tactical value of surprise, I regard it as inconceivable that he would have ruled in favour of admitting the statement. But, with the profoundest respect to Davies LJ, I go so far as to say that, even if he had, such an attitude ought not to be countenanced by this court. A suitor who deliberately flouts the rules has no right to ask the court to exercise in his favour a discretionary indulgence created by those very same rules. Furthermore, a judge who, to his knowledge, finds himself confronted by such a situation would not, as I think, be acting judicially if he nevertheless exercised his discretion in favour of the recalcitrant suitor. The rules are there to be respected, and those who defy them should not be indulged or excused. Slackness is one thing; deliberate disobedience another. The former may be overlooked; the latter never, even though, as here it derives from mistaken zeal on the client's behalf. To tolerate it would be dangerous to justice.

In *Morris* v *Stratford-on-Avon RDC*, on the other hand, the facts were entirely different. At the trial of an action for personal injury some five years after the event, a witness gave evidence for the defendants. At the conclusion of his examination in chief, it became apparent for the first time to counsel for the defendant that it would be desirable that an application should be made to the trial judge to admit, in the exercise of his discretion, a statement made by the witness some nine months after the event. The judge admitted the statement, despite objection on behalf of the plaintiff. No notice had, of course, been served under r. 21. The Court of Appeal upheld the judge's exercise of discretion. Megaw LJ said ([1973] 1 WLR at 1063):

Nothing that I say must be taken in any way as suggesting that non-compliance with the rules as to notices is a matter that can be lightly overlooked. On the other hand, there must be cases in which there is, sensibly and reasonably, no ground for supposing that a statement which is in existence is going to be used by a party. It would perhaps be unfortunate if the matter were to be so interpreted that, in every case, those who are advising a party felt it necessary to advise him that, if there is any possibility, however remote, that as a result of something which may happen hereafter, an application might be sought to be made, then notice should be given in advance. But, quite clearly, if there is reason to suppose, on proper consideration of the evidence, that such an application may be made, then care must be taken that the proper notices should be given.

Megaw LJ then held that no blame whatsoever could attach to counsel in the instant case, considered *Ford* v *Lewis*, and concluded (ibid at 1064–5):

It is perfectly apparent that that is not this case, and that this case bears no conceivable relationship to the matters which motivated the court to take the course that it did in that case. However, it is right that careful consideration should always be given, on an application of this sort, to matters such as those that were stressed before us by counsel for the plaintiff: for example, that the statement was taken as a proof of evidence and that it was not closely contemporary with the time of the accident but was taken some nine months later. Those are matters which of course go to weight; but they can also be relevant on the question of a decision as to the exercise of discretion. Another matter which in my judgment must always be carefully watched, when an application of this sort is made under the Civil Evidence Act 1968 without proper notices having been given, is for the judge to make sure, so far as he can, that no injustice will be done to the other party by reason of the statement being allowed to be put in evidence. If there is ground to suppose that there will be any injustice caused, or that the other party will be materially prejudiced or embarrassed, then the judge should either refuse to allow the document to be admitted or, in his discretion, allow it on terms, such as an adjournment at the cost of the party seeking to put in the statement.

It would be difficult to elaborate usefully on those very clear guidelines offered by the Court of Appeal on the exercise of the discretion under r. 29.

Without prejudice to the general discretion under r. 29(1), there is a more specific discretion under r. 29(2), designed to avoid the possibility that the notice procedure might actually lead to the result that a party who serves a notice under r. 21 might, by reason of the service on him of a counter-notice (or an application under r. 28), be compelled as the price of putting in a hearsay statement, to call as a witness an opposite party or a person who is, or was at a material time, the servant or agent of an opposite party. This is a real danger when it is proposed to use against a party a hearsay statement made by such a person on another occasion. The discretion is there to guard against the possibility, in effect, that a party might be forced to call a foreseeably hostile, or at least foreseeably unreliable, witness. Its proper use is illustrated by the decision of Pennycuick V–C in *Tremelbye (Selangor) Rubber Co. Ltd* v *Stekel and Others* [1971] 1 WLR 226. The plaintiff company brought an action alleging that the various defendants had been party to a dishonest transaction whereby the plaintiff company's money had been used in the purchase of its own shares. One defendant and three employees of another defendant (a bank) had given evidence for the prosecution in criminal proceedings arising from a Board of Trade inquiry in respect of the same matters. The plaintiffs sought to put in evidence the statements of those persons contained in the transcript of the evidence in the criminal proceedings. It was held that the interests of justice required that the plaintiffs be permitted to adduce the transcript. Failing such a direction, the plaintiffs would be placed in the obviously invidious position of having either to call witnesses allied with their opponents, who could not be expected to give favourable evidence, or to forego the use of relevant and perhaps cogent evidence in their favour. The evidence was allowed to be admitted on terms that the defendants should have the opportunity to cross-examine the witnesses, and the plaintiffs to re-examine without the limitation on the questions which could ordinarily be put to 'their own' witnesses. Although the decision turned on an application for leave under r. 28, it would appear that the result must have been the same in the case of a counter-notice. The situation was that contemplated expressly by r. 29(2).

## 8.8   Civil Evidence Act 1972

It will be recalled that the Civil Evidence Act 1968 applies only to statements of fact, a provision that excludes statements of opinion, when contained in hearsay statements, even where such opinion would be admissible by the general law of evidence, if given by means of non-hearsay evidence. The Civil Evidence Act 1972 extended the application of the 1968 Act to statements of opinion by the following words contained in s. 1(1):

Subject to the provisions of this section, part 1 . . . of the Civil Evidence Act 1968, except s. 5, . . . shall apply in relation to statements of opinion as it applies in relation to statements of fact, subject to the necessary modifications and in particular the modification that any reference to a fact stated in a statement shall be construed as a reference to a matter dealt with therein.

This subsection applies alike to statements admissible under s. 2 and those admissible under s. 4 of the 1968 Act but the particular exigencies of the latter section called for more precise definition of the circumstances in which hearsay statements of opinion might properly be admitted as contained in records, and accordingly s. 1(2) of the 1972 Act provides that:

> Section 4 . . . of the Civil Evidence Act 1968, as applied by subsection (1) above, shall not render admissible in any civil proceedings a statement of opinion contained in a record unless that statement would be admissible in those proceedings if made in the course of giving oral evidence by the person who originally supplied the information from which the record was compiled; but where a statement of opinion contained in a record deals with a matter on which the person who originally supplied the information from which the record was compiled is (or would if living be) qualified to give oral expert evidence, the said section 4, as applied by subsesction (1) above, shall have effect in relation to that statement as if so much of subsection (1) of that section as requires personal knowledge on the part of that person were omitted.

This provision achieves two important results. Firstly, it removes what would otherwise have been a serious ambiguity by providing that it is not the opinion evidence of everyone concerned in the making of a record which may be admitted under s. 4. The opinion evidence of the compiler of the record, or of an intermediary by whom the information was transmitted from the original supplier to the compiler, is not admissible even though contained in the record unless, coincidentally, it would also be admissible if given in the course of oral evidence by the original supplier of the information. This must, of course, be looked at by reference to the general law of opinion evidence, dealt with in Chapter 9, post. But it may be worth observing that by s. 3(2) of the 1972 Act, Parliament also provided that:

> It is hereby declared that where a person is called as a witness in any civil proceedings, a statement of opinion by him on any relevant matter on which he is not qualified to give expert evidence, if made as a way of conveying relevant facts personally perceived by him, is admissible as evidence of what he perceived.

Secondly, the subsection removes the requirement of personal knowledge in s. 4, in so far as the supplier of the information is dealing with a matter on which he is, or would have been, qualified to give expert-opinion evidence. The safeguard of personal knowledge, which is apposite to statements of fact, would have no real meaning in relation to statements of opinion. But the competence of the supplier as an expert is in itself some safeguard, and must be established to the court's satisfaction if asserted.

The consequence of the extension of Part 1 of the 1968 Act to statements of opinion is, on the face of it, that such statements should be subject to the notice procedure as if they were statements of fact. In relation to non-expert opinion, this is indeed the result.[23] But, in the case of expert-opinion evidence, the 1972 Act itself provided a separate statutory authority for the making of different rules of court, designed to promote general, early disclosure of such evidence to the other parties as a condition of being permitted to adduce

---

[23] RSC, Ord. 38, r. 34, extends to such cases the provisions of rr. 20–23 and 25–33, 'with such modifications as the court may direct or the circumstances of the case may require'.

it. The rules of court dealing with expert evidence are, accordingly, quite distinct from those relating to statements of fact and non-expert opinion. The rules for expert-opinion evidence are to be found in RSC, Ord. 38, rr. 36–44, and are dealt with in detail in 9.6, post, but it may be observed here that they are not confined to hearsay statements, but deal with the treatment of expert evidence generally in civil proceedings. Where a party calls as a witness the maker of an expert report, such report may be put in evidence at the commencement of the maker's examination in chief or at such other time as the court may direct: Ord. 38, r. 43. This departure from the rule for other witnesses in s. 2(2) and s. 4(2) of the 1968 Act, authorised by s. 2(1) of the 1972 Act, is obviously justified by the nature of the evidence.

### 8.9 Affidavits

It is not possible, within the scope of the present work, to consider in detail the practice relating to affidavits, but it should be noted that by RSC, Ord. 41, r. 5, an affidavit to be used in interlocutory proceedings may state the opinion, information or belief of the deponent, together with the source of that opinion, information or belief. Subject to the operation of that rule, and of Ord. 38, r. 3 (which gives the court wide powers to deal with the proof of relevant matters generally), r. 21(4) provides that the requirement of notice under r. 21 shall not apply to statements which a party to such proceedings desires to have included in his affidavit or an affidavit to be used on his behalf in those proceedings. But where it is proper for evidence to be given on affidavit in any final proceedings, in the sense of proceedings in which the substantive merits of the case are to be determined, Ord. 41, r. 5, does not apply, and the notice procedure under r. 21 then operates in the case of any other admissible hearsay evidence tendered under s. 2, s. 4 or s. 5. The exemption, therefore, applies only to affidavits used in interlocutory proceedings.[24] Moreover, no rule permits the inclusion of hearsay statements without notice in any document exhibited to an affidavit, whether in final or interlocutory proceedings. The rule covers the affidavit itself and no more.[25]

### B: HEARSAY ADMISSIBLE BY STATUTE IN CRIMINAL CASES

### 8.10   Police and Criminal Evidence Act 1984: introduction

The Police and Criminal Evidence Act 1984 repeals the Criminal Evidence Act 1965 and substitutes a new and wider series of provisions governing the admissibility in criminal cases of certain documentary hearsay evidence and hearsay evidence produced by computers. These provisions are to be found in ss. 68 and 69 supplemented by sch. 3 of the Act. Their main features combine certain of those found in the Civil Evidence Act 1968 and the Criminal Evidence Act 1965. Paragraph 15 of sch. 3 provides that ss. 68 and 69 may be further supplemented by rules of court, but at the time of writing, no such rules have been promulgated. The new provisions apply to all criminal proceedings, including courts martial (s. 72(1)).

As in the case of the Civil Evidence Act 1968 the Act cures only the defect of hearsay.

---

24   *Nationwide Building Society v Bateman* [1978] 1 WLR 394.
25   *Re Koscot Interplanetary (UK) Ltd* [1972] 3 All ER 829.

The evidence admitted must be of facts 'of which direct, oral evidence would be admissible', that is to say, unobjectionable apart from the question of hearsay.

## 8.11 Evidence admissible by virtue of s. 68

By s. 68 of the Police and Criminal Evidence Act 1984:

(1)  Subject to section 69 below, a statement in a document shall be admissible in any proceedings as evidence of any fact stated therein of which direct oral evidence would be admissible if—

(*a*)  the document is or forms part of a record compiled by a person acting under a duty from information supplied by a person (whether acting under a duty or not) who had, or may reasonably be supposed to have had, personal knowledge of the matters dealt with in that information; and

(*b*)  any condition relating to the person who supplied the information which is specified in subsection (2) below is satisfied.

(2)  The conditions mentioned in subsection (1)(b) above are—

(*a*)  that the person who supplied the information—
   (i)   is dead or by reason of his bodily or mental condition unfit to attend as a witness;
   (ii)  is outside the United Kingdom and it is not reasonably practicable to secure his attendance; or
   (iii) cannot reasonably be expected (having regard to the time which has elapsed since he supplied or acquired the information and to all the circumstances) to have any recollection of the matters dealt with in that information;
   (*b*)  that all reasonable steps have been taken to identify the person who supplied the information but that he cannot be identified; and
   (*c*)  that, the identity of the person who supplied the information being known, all reasonable steps have been taken to find him, but that he cannot be found.

(3)  Nothing in this section shall prejudice the admissibility of any evidence that would be admissible apart from this section.

### 8.11.1 'Statement in a document'
Sections 72(1) and 118(1) provide that the terms 'statement' and 'document' shall have the same meanings as in Part 1 of the Civil Evidence Act 1968. See 8.3.1 and 8.3.3, ante.

### 8.11.2 'Record'
No statutory definition of the word 'record' is provided. It would seem that the word bears the same basic connotation as in s. 4 of the Civil Evidence Act 1968 and formerly the Criminal Evidence Act 1965. This connotation was developed by a number of cases, both civil and criminal, discussed in 8.4.1, ante. Perhaps the most significant feature of the 1984 Act is that the word 'record' may now be interpreted as widely as in the Civil Evidence Act 1968. The Criminal Evidence Act 1965 permitted documentary evidence to be admitted only where the record was one relating to a trade or business. This inconvenient restriction not only excluded much reliable evidence contained in the records of public and

governmental bodies, but also wastefully consumed judicial time in esoteric debate about what amounted to a trade or business.[26] The new, wider provision is to be welcomed.

However, the Act also contains a further provision that was not included in either the 1965 or the 1968 Act. By para. 2 of sch. 3:

Where—

(a)   a document setting out the evidence which a person could be expected to give as a witness has been prepared for the purpose of any pending or contemplated proceedings; and

(b)   it falls within subsection (1) of section 68 above,

a statement contained in it shall not be given in evidence by virtue of that section without leave of the court, and the court shall not give leave unless it is of the opinion that the statement ought to be admitted in the interests of justice, having regard—

(i)   to the circumstances in which leave is sought and in particular to the contents of the statement; and

(ii)   to any likelihood that the accused will be prejudiced by its admission in the absence of the person who supplied the information on which it is based.

The intention of this provision is apparently to prevent the admission in evidence of documentary hearsay in the form of depositions, witness statements or proofs of evidence, if there is a risk of prejudice to the defendant in a criminal trial. These hearsay statements are prepared routinely in preparation for criminal trials. In many cases, such documents would be inadmissible under s. 68 because they cannot aptly be described as 'records'. The Act has no provision corresponding to that of the Civil Evidence Act 1968 permitting the admission of hearsay statements not contained in records. Moreover, the witness would have to be unavailable for one of the reasons specified in s. 68(2). But it is possible to envisage a case in which a court might legitimately hold that a witness statement is a record compiled by a police officer acting under a duty, from information supplied to him by a witness who has knowledge of the facts. Prior to the Act, a number of statutory provisions existed to permit the use of depositions and witness statements in evidence, and this may always be done if there is no objection.[27] However, s. 68 standing alone would have permitted this to be done in any case where the document was a record and where the witness was unavailable for one of the specified reasons.

A document prepared specifically for the proceedings is potentially prejudicial because, even if unconsciously, it will usually be tailored to serve the interests of the party preparing it. Where the document is admissible under s. 68, the opponent will have no opportunity to counter the effect of this by cross-examination. This paragraph provides the judge with the opportunity to exclude such evidence in any case where the contents of the statement may be prejudicial to the defendant. It is at least arguable that the judge had power to do this in any event, in the exercise of his general discretion under s. 78 (see 1.5.2.3, ante). But this provision is a useful addition, because the requirement of leave ensures that the judge's attention is given to the matter, even if no objection is made, and because the provision that leave shall not be given unless the court forms the positive view that it is in

[26]   See, e.g., *R v Crayden* [1978] 1 WLR 604; and generally the first edition of this work, pp.198–9.

[27]   See, e.g., Magistrates' Courts Act 1980, ss. 102, 103, 105.

the interests of justice to do so is stronger than a mere matter of discretion.

The paragraph assumes, as will usually be the case, that the evidence in question will be a witness statement prepared by the prosecution, but neither the paragraph nor s. 68 is so limited. A court may one day have to decide whether there is power to prevent evidence admissible under s. 68 from being given by one defendant, on the ground of possible prejudice to a co-defendant. In the analogous cases involving the discretionary exclusion of evidence at common law, it has been held that the judge has no such power.[28]

As noted above, this is a problem which Parliament has perceived to affect criminal cases only. There is no such provision in the Civil Evidence Act 1968, even though corresponding American rules of evidence (designed for jury trials) exclude self-serving documents prepared for the purposes of litigation both in civil and criminal proceedings. However, the weight of such evidence, even where admissible under the 1968 Act, may be very slight.

### 8.11.3 'Acting under a duty'
The compiler must have been acting under a duty in compiling the record. As in the Civil Evidence Act 1968, this is an important safeguard designed to ensure reliability. Paragraph 6 of sch. 3 defines 'acting under a duty' in exactly the same way as s. 4(3) of the 1968 Act (see 8.4.2, ante). And, as in the case of evidence admissible under s. 4 of the 1968 Act, the duty requirement applies also to intermediaries through whom the information is passed from the supplier to the compiler: see para. 1 of sch. 3 to the 1984 Act.

### 8.11.4 The requirement of personal knowledge
The person who supplies the information must have, or it must be capable of being supposed reasonably that he has, personal knowledge of the matters dealt with in the information. This wording is also identical to that of s. 4 of the Civil Evidence Act 1968 and will no doubt be interpreted in the same way (see 8.4.3, ante). There is no objection to the supplier of the information and the compiler of the record being one and the same person, providing that both the duty and personal knowledge requirements are met: see para. 1 of sch. 3 to the 1984 Act.

The corresponding requirement of the Criminal Evidence Act 1965 gave rise to considerable problems in relation to evidence produced by computers. In *R v Pettigrew* (1980) 71 Cr App R 39, decided not long before the first edition of this work appeared, the Court of Appeal held that evidence consisting of a computer print-out produced at the Bank of England was inadmissible under the Criminal Evidence Act 1965, to prove that banknotes found in the possession of the defendant came from a sequence of notes bearing certain serial numbers and which had been stolen. The machine which produced the print-out had automatic functions of recording serial numbers and of destroying defective banknotes, and those automatic functions meant that the operator of the machine lacked personal knowledge of the facts stated in the print-out, even though he knew what notes were introduced into the machine. The 1965 Act had no provision corresponding either to s. 5 of the Civil Evidence Act 1968 or s. 69 of the Police and Criminal Evidence Act 1984, permitting the admission of evidence produced by computers. Accordingly, the evidence was admissible, if at all, only under the provision corresponding to s. 68 of the 1984 Act. The first edition of this work predicted further problems, arising from the difficulties of applying the personal knowedge requirement to the operators of computers.[29] Some of

---

[28] See, e.g., *Murdoch v Taylor* [1965] AC 574; 1.5.2.3, ante.
[29] Ibid pp. 199–200.

these problems duly surfaced, and were dealt with by the inelegant recourse of disguising the evidence as real evidence. This is considered in more detail in 15.5.5, post. Such evidence will now generally be admissible under s. 69, where different and more appropriate safeguards of reliability will apply (8.12, post).

### 8.11.5   Conditions relating to the supplier

These conditions, though not identically worded, are in substance the same as those given in the Criminal Evidence Act 1965. The use of the words 'any condition' in s. 68(1)(b) suggests that they are intended to be disjunctive. This would mean that it suffices that any one of the conditions be satisfied, in order to make a piece of evidence admissible. Although the Civil Evidence Act 1968 contains no corresponding provisions, the availability of the maker of a hearsay statement or the supplier of information is relevant to the notice provisions of RSC, Ord.38, r.21 et seq. Where the maker or supplier is unavailable for reasons again broadly similar to those given by s. 68(2), the proponent of the evidence may have it admitted free of any demands made in a counter-notice: see RSC, Ord.38, rr.25 and 26, and 8.7.2, 8.7.3 ante. In this context, it has been held that the presence of any one reason suffices (see 8.7.3, ante) and it is submitted that s. 68 should be interpreted in the same way. It is to be noted that the witness need not be physically unavailable. In many cases, the identity and whereabouts of the witness will be known, but there will be no likelihood of his having any recollection of the matters dealt with in the record. In a world full of organisational records, this reality was a more compelling reason even than death, disability or disappearance to reform the common-law rule against hearsay, in so far as it affected the admissibility of documentary evidence. A short review of the facts of Myers is enough to drive the point home.

### 8.11.6   Determination of admissibility and weight

8.11.6.1   Admissibility.   Where the admissibility of evidence under s. 68 is disputed, the judge must determine the question as one of law, and may if necessary receive secondary evidence on the voir dire, to satisfy himself with regard to any of the conditions of admissibility. Under the Criminal Evidence Act 1965 it was held by the Court of Appeal in R v Nicholls (1976) 63 Cr App R 187, that the defendant was entitled to have such issues resolved before the evidence could be admitted. No doubt this decision would be followed under the 1984 Act.

By para. 14 of sch. 3 to the 1984 Act:

> For the purpose of deciding whether or not a statement is . . . admissible [under either s. 68 or s. 69] the court may draw any reasonable inference—
>
> (a)   from the circumstances in which the statement was made or otherwise came into being; or
> (b)   from any other circumstances, including the form and contents of the document in which the statement is contained.

Paragraph 5 of the schedule provides that in determining for the purpose of s. 68(2)(a)(i) whether a person is unfit to attend court as a witness, the court may act on a certificate purporting to be signed by a registered medical practitioner.

These provisions are primarily designed to aid the judge in assessing whether the reliability safeguards of duty and personal knowledge are satisfied, and in determining whether or not to admit a statement containing the proposed evidence of a person, prepared for the purpose of pending or contemplated proceedings.

*8.11.6.2 Weight.* Paragraph 7 of the schedule lays down factors to be taken into account in assessing the weight of a statement admitted under s. 68. This is in terms substantially similar to those of s. 6(3) of the Civil Evidence Act 1968 and those of s. 1(3) of the Criminal Evidence Act 1965 and provides that:

> In estimating the weight, if any, to be attached to a statement admissible in evidence by virtue of section 68 above regard shall be had to all the circumstances from which any inference can reasonably be drawn as to the accuracy or otherwise of the statement and in particular—

> (*a*) to the question whether or not the person who supplied the information from which the record containing the statement was compiled did so contemporaneously with the occurrence or existence of the facts dealt with in that information; and
> (*b*) to the question whether or not that person, or any other person concerned with compiling or keeping the record containing the statement, had any incentive to conceal or misrepresent the facts.

No doubt the judge should direct the attention of the jury to these factors, insofar as is appropriate on the facts of the case, although no necessarily in the exact words of the paragraph.

**8.12   Evidence admissible under s. 69**

By s. 69 of the Police and Criminal Evidence Act 1984:

> (1)   In any proceedings, a statement in a document produced by a computer shall not be admissible as evidence of any fact stated therein unless it is shown—

> (*a*)   that there are no reasonable grounds for believing that the statement is inaccurate because of improper use of the computer;
> (*b*)   that at all material times the computer was operating properly, or if not, that any respect in which it was not operating properly or was out of operation was not such as to affect the production of the document or the accuracy of its contents; . . .

Subsection (2) provides that rules of court may be made requiring information to be provided in advance about any statement to be tendered as admissible under this section. This is no doubt intended to allow the opponent to investigate whether the conditions of admissibility are satisfied. By subsection 1(*c*) the proponent of the evidence may be required to comply with the rules as a further condition of admissibility. At the time of writing, no such rules have been promulgated.

The Act does not define the word 'computer'. It may be that it should be defined in the same way as for the purposes of the Civil Evidence Act 1968: see s. 5(6) of that Act and 8.5, ante.

Section 69 represents a welcome simplification of s. 5 of the Civil Evidence Act 1968. The sole criterion of admissibility is now that of the absence of any abuse or malfunction of the computer. The proponent of the evidence must affirmatively demonstrate the absence of these factors, in so far as relevant to the production or accuracy of the statement. Paragraphs 8 and 9 of sch. 3 provide that this foundational evidence may be given by a certificate purporting to be signed by 'a person occupying a responsible position in relation to the operation of the computer', unless the court requires oral evidence to be given.[30]

As noted in 8.11.6, ante, para. 14 of sch. 3, dealing with inferences that may be drawn by the court in determining the question of admissibility, applies to evidence tendered as being admissible under s. 69, as well as under s. 68.

Paragraphs 11 and 12 of sch. 3 lay down the factors to be taken into account in assessing the weight of evidence admitted under s. 69. These are similar in scope and intent to those of para. 7 in relation to evidence admitted under s. 68, and need not be reproduced here.

**8.13    Sections 68 and 69: miscellaneous matters**

*8.13.1    Impeachment of hearsay evidence*
Paragraph 3 of sch. 3 provides for the admissibility of evidence designed to discredit evidence admitted under s. 68, by attacking the credibility of the supplier of the information; this is dealt with in 13.11, post.

*8.13.2    Corroboration*
Consistently with s. 6(4) of the Civil Evidence Act 1968, para. 4 of sch. 3 provides that a statement admissible under s. 68 shall not be capable of corroborating evidence given by the person who supplied the information on which the statement is based. This provision is, in general terms, necessary because of the rule that corroborative evidence must come from a source independent of the evidence to be corroborated: see 14.4, post. In the 1968 Act, the provision had an obvious function, in that hearsay statements may be admissible even if the maker of the statement is to be called as a witness, and the provision in the 1984 Act probably derives its inspiration from the earlier statute. However, it may be noted that under the 1984 Act, the statement will not be admissible at all, unless at least one of the conditions set forth in s. 68(2) is satisfied. These seem to envisage that the supplier should not be giving evidence, in which case there is nothing to corroborate. The only case to which the provision appears capable of application is one in which condition (*a*) (iii) is present, and the supplier testifies in addition to his hearsay statement contained in the record. In such a case, the witness will probably do no more (if the condition is really satisfied) than state that whatever he said at the time was accurate, and the intention must be to prevent self-corroboration in such a case. It would seem unlikely to be worth calling the supplier in such circumstances in any event.

*8.13.3    Use of copies*
Following s. 6(1) of the Civil Evidence Act 1968 (see 8.6.1, ante) para. 13 of sch. 3 provides:

Where in any proceedings a statement contained in a document is admissible in

---

[30]    The certificate is to be 'evidence of anything stated in it'. This surely makes it the most comprehensive provision for the admissibility of hearsay in the entire Act, and probably in any Act!

evidence by virtue of section 68 above or in accordance with section 69 above it may be proved—

(*a*) by the production of the document; or

(*b*) (whether or not that document is still in existence) by the production of a copy of that document, or of the material part of it,

authenticated in such manner as the court may approve.

As in the 1968 Act, the strict requirement of original evidence, which at common law generally demands the production of the original to prove documents admitted as non-hearsay evidence in their own right (15.1 and 15.2, post) is dispensed with in the case of documents admitted as hearsay evidence of the truth of facts stated in them.

By s. 72(1), 'copy' has the same meaning as in Part 1 of the Civil Evidence Act 1968 (8.6.1, ante).

Moreover, s. 71 of the 1984 Act provides that:

In any proceedings the contents of a document may (whether or not the document is still in existence) be proved by the production of an enlargement of a microfilm copy of that document or of the material part of it, authenticated in such manner as the court may approve.

### 8.14    Questions for discussion

#### *8.14.1    R* v *Coke; R* v *Littleton*

1    Assume that it is desired to prove the age of Angela Blackstone at the time of the assault on her allegedly committed by Littleton; that both parents are now dead; and that a birth certificate, duly signed and filed, is available. Would the certificate be admissible? What foundation would have to be laid? In what form should it be placed before the court?

2    Assume that Dr Espinasse accomplished his work using a computer, and that the results are available in the form of computer data, a print-out of which can be produced. Would such a print-out be admissible, and if so, admissible evidence of what? What foundation would have to be laid?

#### *8.14.2    Blackstone* v *Coke*

1    Discuss the admissibility of the proof of evidence supplied by Anthony Henneky. What weight is it likely to have? What notice should Coke give of his intention to adduce it? Can Margaret serve an effective counter-notice?

2    Discuss the admissibility of the records of the hospital in which Margaret gave birth to her son. What notice would have to be given? What should Coke's solicitors do in response to such notice?

# 9 Opinion Evidence; Previous Judgments as Evidence

In this chapter, we shall consider two related topics. The first is the extent to which a witness may express an opinion on the facts of a case, as opposed to giving evidence of the facts. It is, of course, the usual function of the witness to establish the facts by giving factual evidence, and the function of the tribunal of fact to form an opinion as to the facts. We shall see, however, that all witnesses may express some opinions and that expert witnesses are called for that very purpose.

The second topic is the use as evidence of previous judgments. When a court of competent jurisdiction decides facts, it gives expression to an opinion about those facts, formed after due judicial consideration. There are obvious reasons of economy and comity for making use of such previous judgments as evidence, where a court has to consider the facts found by a previous court in connection with different issues. The use of previous criminal convictions to prove, in later civil proceedings, that the person convicted committed the offence of which he was convicted, is an important example. The reason why this topic is dealt with in a chapter concerned with opinion evidence is that a previous judgment is a statement of opinion, albeit expressed by a court rather than a witness. The common law decided against the admissibility of previous judgments for several reasons, including the theoretical one that opinion evidence should not ordinarily be admissible to prove facts in issue, but the most important of which was the difficulty of identifying the precise basis of the opinion of the previous court. This was the celebrated rule in *Hollington* v *Hewthorn* [1943] KB 587. But the utility of such evidence has prevailed, and statute permits its use in certain specific instances both in civil and criminal cases. This use of previous judgments must be distinguished from the rules of law pertaining to *res judicata*, which preclude a party from re-litigating or disputing earlier adverse judicial decisions made in litigation between the same parties or their predecessors in interest.

## A: OPINION EVIDENCE

### 9.1 General rule

The general rule of common law was that the opinions, beliefs and inferences of a witness were inadmissible to prove the truth of the matters believed or inferred if such matters were in issue or relevant to facts in issue in the case. Apart from the question of the relevance and reliability of opinion evidence it was held to offend by usurping the function of the court, to form an opinion on the facts in issue, on the basis of the facts proved by the evidence placed before it.

This did not, of course, prevent the admission of such evidence for other purposes, notably for the purpose of proving what the state of mind of the holder of an opinion was, at a certain time, if relevant to do so. Thus, in *Sheen* v *Bumpstead* (1863) 2 HC 193 the belief of a party who represented that a trader was solvent was held admissible on the question, not whether the trader was solvent, but whether the representation was made in good faith. And the belief of a defendant charged with handling stolen goods will be admitted to show that he knew or believed, or did not know or believe, that the goods were stolen, but will be inadmissible to prove that the goods were in fact stolen.[1]

The same rule applied to evidence of general reputation, or public opinion, which is no more than an extended form of opinion evidence. Such evidence will be inadmissible to prove the truth of the matters generally reputed or believed to be true, but will be admissible to prove what the general reputation of a matter, or the state of public opinion on that matter, in fact was at a given time, if relevant to do so.[2]

The common-law rule that opinion evidence is inadmissible to prove the truth of the matter believed is subject to three important exceptions, but otherwise remains in full effect. The exceptions are:

(a)   General reputation will be admissible to prove matters of public concern, which would otherwise be impossible or very difficult to prove.

(b)   Expert-opinion evidence is admissible to prove matters of specialised knowledge, on which the court would be unable properly to reach a conclusion unaided.

(c)   Non-expert-opinion evidence may be received on matters within the competence and experience of lay persons generally.

Before examining the detail of these exceptions, it is worth observing that wherever opinion evidence is admissible in civil cases it may be given in the form of hearsay statements according to and subject to the provisions of Part 1 of the Civil Evidence Act 1968.[3] That Act did not originally apply to statements of opinion, but it was envisaged that it should be extended, and by s. 1 of the Civil Evidence Act 1972:

(1)   Subject to the provisions of this section, Part 1 (hearsay evidence) of the Civil Evidence Act 1968, except s. 5 (statements produced by computers), shall apply in relation to statements of opinion as it applies in relation to statements of fact, subject to the necessary modifications and in particular the modification that any reference to a fact stated in a statement shall be construed as a reference to a matter dealt with therein.

Section 1(2) provides that where the statement of opinion is contained in a record, and it is sought to admit it under s. 4 of the 1968 Act, the statement must be one which would be admissible if made in direct oral evidence by the original supplier of the information from which the record was compiled. But where the statement would be admissible because the original supplier is or was qualified to give expert opinion evidence to that effect, s. 4 of the 1968 Act applies without any requirement of personal knowledge, which would be inapposite to such evidence.

Statements of opinion may, therefore, be admitted under either s. 2 or s. 4 of the 1968 Act, as the circumstances permit. In all cases except that of expert-opinion evidence, for which separate provision is made by s. 2 of the 1972 Act, a party wishing to adduce hearsay

---

[1]   Cf. *R* v *Marshall* [1977] Crim LR106.
[2]   See 9.2(d), post.
[3]   The provisions of Part 1 of the 1968 Act are considered in detail in Chapter 8, ante.

evidence of opinion, must comply with the notice procedure laid down, pursuant to s. 8 of the 1968 Act, by RSC, Ord. 38, rr. 21–31.[4]

No such provision for the admission of hearsay opinion evidence is made by ss. 68–72 of the Police and Criminal Evidence Act 1984, which provide for the admissibility of documentary hearsay evidence in criminal proceedings. Hearsay evidence admitted in criminal proceedings pursuant to these sections is accordingly admissible only as evidence of any facts stated, and not as evidence of statements of opinion made in the documents in question.

## 9.2   General reputation: principles of admissibility

We have already observed that the common law succeeded in overcoming its objections to certain presumptively unreliable forms of evidence in cases where, unless such evidence were admitted, no evidence would be available, or where the relevant facts would be, in practical terms impossible, to prove. It was accordingly accepted that in cases where direct evidence was difficult or impossible to obtain with regard to matters of public concern, such matters might, as a last resort, be proved by evidence of general reputation. At the time when the rule evolved, matters of public concern were often difficult to prove, either because of the difficulty of physically marshalling the necessary volume of evidence, or because relevant witnesses might be dead or unavailable. Happily, the increasing availability and reliability of public records has rendered the task progressively easier, but resort is still had to the common-law in some circumstances.

Evidence of general reputation may be admitted in the following cases:

(a)   To establish matters of pedigree or the existence of a marriage. The contemporary importance of the rule lies in the proof of such questions of some antiquity, as matters of marriage and descent are, increasingly, capable of proof by official records.

(b)   To identify a reference to a person or thing, or to prove the existence of a public or general right. The question of identification of a reference here is one of identification of a reference in the mind of the public generally. Thus, in an action for defamation, it is necessary to show that the matter complained of referred to the plaintiff. This may be proved by evidence that the matter was taken, by the public generally, as referring to the plaintiff, for which purpose evidence, e.g., that the plaintiff was publicly jeered at after publication, may be admitted to prove the reference.[5] And in the rather strange case of *Re Steel, Wappett* v *Robinson* [1903] 1 Ch 135, the extent of a devise of land in a will was proved by evidence that certain fields were known locally as 'customary freeholds', and so corresponded with the words of the devise of 'my freehold lands and hereditaments at Morland Field', although the fields in question were, in fact, privileged copyholds.

(c)   To prove good or bad character. In *R* v *Rowton* (1865) Le & Ca 520, it was held that character should be equated with the general reputation of a person in his locality, so that at common law such evidence was not only admissible, but was the only admissible evidence for this purpose. In modern times, it is generally accepted that 'character' is a wider concept than one of reputation, and indeed the use of evidence of reputation has been criticised as tending to show, not the actual character but merely the generally accepted character of a person. Nonetheless, such evidence is certainly admissible

---

[4]   The notice procedure is considered in detail in 8.7, ante. For s. 2 of the 1972 Act, see 9.4, post.
[5]   See, e.g., *Cook* v *Ward* (1830) 6 Bing 409.

whenever it is relevant to prove character, and is of considerable importance where the defendant in a criminal case seeks to establish his good character.[6]

(d)   To prove the state of public opinion on a mattter. Public opinion may be relevant in cases involving passing off, trademarks and the like, where it may be necessary to show the effect of representations about or the promotion of a product. Frequently, this may be proved by evidence of reputation based on a survey of public opinion, if shown to be prepared by reliable methods and to be based on accurate and representative sources of information: *Customglass Boats Ltd and Another* v *Salthouse Bros Ltd* [1976] RPC 589. Such a survey may be used by an expert as a basis for an expert opinion as to the present or likely future state of public opinion on such an issue: *Sodastream Ltd* v *Thorn Cascade Ltd* [1982] RPC 459; *Lego Systems A/S* v *Lego M. Lemelstrich Ltd* [1983] FSR 155, 173–182.

In all the above cases save the last, the admissibility of evidence of reputation in civil cases is expressly provided for by s. 9(3) of the Civil Evidence Act 1968. The section does not change the rules stated above[7] but provides that the evidence shall be admissible by virtue of the section, where previously it would have been admissible by virtue of any of the common-law rules referred to. The section adds to the idea of reputation that of 'family tradition', which is a more specific and limited version of the idea of reputation and is of particular relevance in cases of pedigree and marriage. The section is additional to the provisions of s. 2 and s. 4, under which some statements might also be admissible as hearsay statements of the matters contained in them, but where evidence is admissible by virtue of s. 9(3) has the advantage that it may be adduced free of the restrictions of law in ss. 2–7 of the 1968 Act, and of the notice procedure laid down by RSC, Ord. 38, rr. 21–31.[8]

## 9.3   Expert-opinion evidence: principles of admissibility

It is an ancient rule of the common law that on a subject requiring special knowledge and competence, evidence is admissible from witnesses who have acquired, by study or practice, the necessary expertise on the subject. Such witnesses are known as 'experts'. The evidence is justified by the fact that the court would be unable, unaided, to draw proper inferences and form proper opinions from such specialised facts as were proved before it, and even perhaps to judge what facts have been satisfactorily proved. As long ago as 1782, Lord Mansfield said in *Folkes* v *Chadd and Others* (1782) 3 Doug 157, that the opinion of scientific men upon proven facts may be given by men of science within their own science. Today, the variety of matters upon which expert evidence is required is constantly growing, and the role of expert witnesses continually expanding. A number of important and common applications of expert evidence in modern practice will be referred to individually in 9.9, post.

### 9.3.1   Competence, admissibility and weight

Qualification to give expert evidence is technically a matter of competence, and the court should investigate the credentials of a proposed witness before permitting him to give expert evidence. No doubt a witness who lacked any apparent qualification should not be

---

[6]   The admissibility of character evidence is dealt with fully in Chapter 4. See in particular 4.1, 4.3 and 4.9.

[7]   Civil Evidence Act 1968, s. 9(6).

[8]   Ibid s. 9(5).

heard, but if the witness has some claim to expertise, the modern practice is to receive his evidence, though its weight may be open to serious adverse comment if the apparent expertise is not translated into reality. The court is concerned with actual expertise, not with the means by which that expertise is acquired. Paper qualifications by themselves may not be a guarantee of actual skills relevant to the questions before the court, and expertise gained by substantial relevant experience certainly renders an expert witness competent, and may invest his evidence with considerable weight. In *R* v *Silverlock*[9] a solicitor, who had made a study of handwriting, was allowed to give evidence as an expert, notwithstanding his lack of formal qualification on the subject, because of his demonstrable actual skill.

An expert witness, if competent, is, like any other witness, also compellable. In *Harmony Shipping Co. SA* v *Saudi Europe Line Ltd and Others* [1979] 1 WLR 1380, a handwriting expert, having been consulted on behalf of the plaintiffs, was later consulted by solicitors for the defendants. After giving them his opinion on certain documents relevant to the action, the expert realised that he had inadvertently advised both sides and, in accordance with his professional rules, declined to accept further instructions from the defendants. The defendants served on him a *subpoena ad testificandum*, which he sought to have set aside. The Court of Appeal held that he was compellable to give evidence for the defendants, and that there was no contractual relationship between the expert and the plaintiff which would (even if enforceable, which must be doubtful[10]) bind the expert not to appear for the defendants. Of course, some of the communications passing between the expert and the plaintiffs would be protected by legal professional privilege, subject to any waiver by the plaintiffs.[11]

Expert opinion evidence may be contradicted and cross-examined, like any other evidence, and the attack may include cross-examination going to credit. The position of an expert is that he must be regarded as any other independent witness, and although he enjoys such weight as may follow from his peculiar ability to assist the court, it will be a misdirection to direct the jury that his evidence should be accepted unless the witness himself betrays reasons for rejecting it.[12] The tribunal of fact must obviously retain control over the findings of fact, which are its ultimate reponsibility. This does not mean that expert evidence of a categorical nature, which is effectively unchallenged, may be disregarded capriciously in favour of unaided lay opinion, and it would be equally wrong to invite the jury to take this course[13] or to content themselves with unaided observation on a matter calling for expert evidence.[14] But there will be occasions where the tribunal of fact will be driven to reject evidence, and occasions where the tribunal will have to choose between conflicting opinions from experts dealing with the same matters. The courts have

⁹   (CCR) [1894] 2 QB 766. Cf. *R* v *Murphy* (CA) [1980] 2 WLR 74, and Federal Rule of Evidence 702: 'If scientific technical or other specialised knowledge will assist the trier of fact to understand the evidence or to determine a fact in issue, a witness qualified as an expert *by knowledge, skill experience, training or education* may testify thereto in the form of an opinion or otherwise.'

¹⁰   As Lord Denning MR pointed out at 1386, such a contract would probably be held to be contrary to public policy. Indeed, if the decision in the case had been otherwise, one party might, by instructing every reputable expert, effectively deprive his opponent of expert advice, and create 'property' in expert witnesses.

¹¹   This would apply to confidential communications between a party, or his legal advisers, and the expert. But not to documents or other tangible evidence on which the expert bases his opinion, or to the opinion itself. See *R* v *King* [1983] 1 All ER 929 and 10.9, post.

¹²   *R* v *Lanfear* (CA) [1968] 2 QB 77.

¹³   *Anderson* v *R* (PC, Jamaica) [1972] AC 100.

¹⁴   *R* v *Tilley; R* v *Tilley* (CCA) [1961] 1 WLR 1309.

not always accorded to expert evidence the recognition it deserves, perhaps because of the risk that a witness who usually receives a fee for his appearance may with less than true scientific objectivity, render an opinion unduly favourable to the party calling him, although there is no greater risk of actual corruption than with other kinds of witness. It seems that the present emphasis on the independent status of experts may have reversed the older preference for direct evidence, which was sometimes taken to unrealistic lengths.[15]

### 9.4 Function of expert evidence

#### 9.4.1 Opinions on an ultimate issue

The function of an expert witness is to assist the court by giving evidence of his opinion on the matters of specialised knowledge on which his assistance is sought. At common law, this was held to mean that the expert might not be asked his opinion on the 'ultimate question', or in other words he might not be asked directly his opinion on an issue in the case. The reason was that he would thereby usurp the function of the court. Thus, the witness might describe to the court the mental condition of the defendant, but might not be asked whether the defendant was insane if that was the issue which the court had to decide.[16] It has not been decided whether the rule precluding expert testimony on an ultimate issue remains in effect at common law, though it has generally been assumed that experts need no longer be so confined. Certainly, in civil cases it would seem to matter little whether or not an expert witness expresses in so many words to a judge who is the tribunal of fact what is obviously the necessary conclusion of his testimony on a relevant issue. In criminal cases, it may be that the trial judge should retain the power to stop the expert short of doing the jury's work for them. This seems to have been the experience in the United States. For some time, the Federal Rules of Evidence permitted experts to testify freely on ultimate issues, both in civil and criminal cases. However, because it appeared that such testimony might be accorded undue weight by juries in criminal cases, particularly in those involving questions of the defendant's mental state, the relevant rule was modified to restore the common-law position in part. Federal Rule of Evidence 704 now provides:

(a) Except as provided in subdivision (b), testimony in the form of an opinion or inference otherwise admissible is not objectionable because it embraces an ultimate issue to be decided by the trier of fact.

(b) No expert witness testifying with respect to the mental state or condition of a defendant in a criminal case may state an opinion or inference as to whether the defendant did or did not have the mental state or condition constituting the element of the crime charged or of a defense thereto. Such ultimate issues are matters for the trier of fact alone.

It is submitted that the English common law should now permit expressions of opinion by experts on ultimate issues, subject to the power of the judge to limit testimony in any case

---

[15] As in *Bowden* v *Bowden* (1917) 62 SJ 105 where the direct evidence of the mother of the paternity of a child born to her 307 days after her last intercourse with her husband was preferred to the opinion of several doctors to the contrary.

[16] *Daniel M'Naghten's Case* (HL) (1843) 10 Cl & F 200.

where there is a danger of the jury according the testimony undue weight, cases involving such defences as insanity, diminished responsibility or automatism providing examples (though not the only examples) of likely areas for judicial restraint. In civil cases, the common-law position has been abrogated, sensibly, by s. 3 of the Civil Evidence Act 1968, which provides:

(1) Subject to any rules of court . . . where a person is called as a witness in any civil proceedings, his opinion on any relevant matter on which he is qualified to give expert evidence, shall be admissible in evidence . . .

(3) In this section 'relevant matter' includes an issue in the proceedings in question.

It is generally considered that the same principle now applies in criminal cases. Certainly, great artificiality was produced by the previously supposed limitation. It is not suggested that the new approach binds the court in any way to accept any evidence given, so there is no good reason why the expert should not be asked to deal with the point which everyone knows he is called to prove or disprove, subject to the discretion of the judge in a criminal jury trial.

### 9.4.2   Subjects of valid lay opinion

Also of great importance is the rule that expert-opinion evidence will not be admitted if it relates only to a question on which the lay opinion of the tribunal of fact is equally valid. This is to state no more than the obvious proposition that expert evidence is confined to those matters on which it is necessary in order to assist the court to determine the issues. Thus, where the question is one of the intent of a defendant, in a case where there is no question of mental illness, the evidence of psychiatrists will not assist the jury to determine that issue, the matter being one within the jury's experience of everyday affairs.[17] And it has been said, with reference to an issue of provocation, that psychiatric evidence 'has not yet become a satisfactory substitute for the common sense of juries or magistrates on matters within their experience of life'.[18] The reaction of the defendant to certain provoking circumstances, and the reasonableness of that reaction, have been held to be issues determinable without expert assistance.[19] On the other hand, defences which fall outside the ordinary experience of jurors, such as insanity and diminished responsibility, are proper subjects of expert medical evidence, and although the jury are not bound to accept such evidence, and must look at all evidence in the case including any conflict in the medical evidence,[20] they should act on the evidence before them. The Court of Appeal will quash a verdict of guilty of murder, where the unchallenged medical evidence suggests that such a verdict is wrong, and is itself uncontradicted by other evidence.[21] Similarly, the defence of automatism is one outside the normal experience of juries, and is a proper subject of expert evidence. In *R* v *Smith* [1979] 1 WLR 1445, the Court of Appeal upheld the admission of expert evidence tending to show that the evidence of the defendant

---

[17]   *R* v *Chard* (CA) (1971) 56 Cr App R 268.
[18]   *R* v *Turner* (CA) [1975] QB 834 per Lawton LJ at 843.
[19]   This rule is said to be unaffected by the decision in *DPP* v *Camplin* (HL) [1978] AC 705, *sed quaere* whether the jury could never be assisted by evidence of the likely reaction of persons with certain abnormal characteristics.
[20]   *Walton* v *R* (PC, Barbados) [1978] AC 788; *R* v *Kiszko* (CA) (1978) 68 Cr App R 62.
[21]   *R* v *Matheson* (CCA) [1958] 1 WLR 474.

consistent with his defence of automatism, that he had killed in his sleep, was scientifically impossible.

In the case of *Lowery* v *R* [1974] AC 85, which is generally thought to turn upon its own facts, two defendants were charged with the murder of a girl, in circumstances from which it was clear that one or other of them, or possibly both, must have been guilty of the murder. There was no motive for the murder except the sheer, sadistic pleasure of committing it. In order to show that his co-defendant was the more likely of the two to have committed the murder, one defendant called evidence from a psychiatrist, tending to show that the co-defendant had a character and disposition which rendered him likely to behave in the way alleged, certainly more so than the defendant. The co-defendant contended on appeal that the evidence had been wrongly admitted. Although on the face of it, the evidence was open to considerable question, because it was an attempt to adduce expert-opinion evidence on the very subject which the jury had to decide and which seemed to be a matter within their competence, the Privy Council dismissed the appeal. It was held that on the specific issue before the jury, which required a decision as to the veracity of the two defendants, the evidence was relevant and admissible and assisted the jury, if they accepted it, to resolve that question. The decision is probably best regarded as applying only to such specific circumstances, and not as any general exception to the usual rule. In *R* v *Turner* [1975] QB 834, the Court of Appeal, in holding that the trial judge had been correct in rejecting the expert evidence of a psychiatrist, the effect of which was to suggest that the defendant's evidence as to how he came to kill his girl-friend was credible in the light of his mental state at the time, specifically treated *Lowery* as having been decided on 'its special facts'. The court added:

> We do not consider that it is an authority for the proposition that in all cases psychologists and psychiatrists can be called to prove the probability of the accused's veracity. If any such rule was applied in our courts trial by psychiatrists would be likely to take the place of trial by jury and magistrates. We do not find that prospect attractive and the law does not at present provide for it.

In *R* v *Rimmer and Beech* [1983] Crim LR 250, a case not dissimilar to *Lowery*, except that the 'either-one-or-the-other' motif was less clear, the Court of Appeal upheld the decision of the trial judge to exclude expert evidence which appeared to affect only veracity, apparently on the ground that such evidence would do no more than explore collateral issues which would be likely to confuse rather than assist the jury.

It should be noted, to avoid confusion, that a specific rule of evidence permits the calling of medical evidence to show that any witness (including a defendant who gives evidence) suffers from a disease, defect or abnormality of mind such as to affect the reliability of his evidence (see *Toohey* v *Commissioner of Police of the Metropolis* [1965] AC 595 and 13.7.4, post). This, however, relates to the state of mind of the witness at the time of testifying at trial, and not to his state of mind at the time when the offence was committed.

## 9.5 Presentation of expert evidence

The presentation of expert evidence may be accomplished by a number of versatile techniques that are not available in the case of a factual, lay witness. This is not only because the expert witness is called upon to present and explain a usually quite detailed and technical opinion, but also because a good expert will have that facility in the witness-box which is gained from familiarity with the process of testifying. It is worth noting that, in contrast to the positon with lay witnesses, it is proper for counsel to confer directly with experts in conference on all matters of expert evidence, though not on unrelated questions of fact.[22] This allows the presentation of the expert's evidence to be co-ordinated so aʋ to have the maximum possible impact on judge or jury.

In planning the presentation of expert testimony, a number of techniques of presentation should always be borne in mind. There appears at one time to have been a rule that an expert might not give reasons for his opinion during examination in chief, though he might be required to do so in cross-examination, and might then develop them further in re-examination. This rule is now obsolete, and the practice is for an expert to develop his testimony in any convenient way, and to explain his opinion fully, even in chief. This greatly assists the presentation of the expert's evidence. An expert may be asked to explain his opinions. He may be asked hypothetical questions, which should be couched in terms of the facts expected to be proved (in cross-examination, they will be based on the facts which the cross-examiner expect to prove). He may be asked to refer to any work of authority on his subject, and may lay a foundation himself by testifying to the authority of the work. The court will consider the work in evaluating the expert's opinion, though the court should not refer to passages not relied upon or referred to by the expert or by the cross-examiners. The expert may relate to the court the results of any pertinent tests or experiments that he has conducted, and may with the permission of the court conduct a demonstration in court, though the latter must be carefully controlled in the interests of fairness to all parties.

The one area which causes problems is the relationship of expert testimony to the primary or underlying data on which an expert opinion may be based, in whole or in part. An expert bases his opinion on many matters derived from his general knowledge, training and education, his professional experience, including experience of other cases and research conducted for the purpose of the case in which he is retained. Much of the material available to the expert from experience and research is material which would be inadmissible as evidence in its own right because it is hearsay. The question is, therefore, to what extent an expert can deal with such material in explaining his opinion.

In *English Exporters (London) Ltd* v *Eldonwall Ltd* [1973] Ch 415, Megarry J, dealing with expert testimony given by a valuer as to comparable leases for the purpose of determining the amount of rent and interim rent which should be assessed to a tenant during the continuation of a tenancy, formulated four propositions as to the relationship between that opinion evidence and the hearsay underlying data on which it was based. The learned judge expressed these as follows:

> Putting matters shortly, and leaving on one side the matters that I have mentioned, such as the Civil Evidence Act 1968 and anything made admissible by questions in cross-examination, in my judgment a valuer giving expert evidence in chief (or in re-examination)—
>
> (a)    may express the opinions that he has formed as to values even though substantial contributions to the formation of those opinions have been made by matters of which he has no first-hand knowledge;

---

[22]    For a more detailed treatment of the practicalities of expert evidence, see Murphy and Barnard, *Evidence and Advocacy*, Chapter 7.

(b) may give evidence as to the details of any transactions within his personal knowledge, in order to establish them as matters of fact; and

(c) may express his opinion as to the significance of any transactions which are or will be proved by admissible evidence (whether or not given by him) in relation to the valuation with which he is concerned; but

(d) may not give hearsay evidence stating the details of any transactions not within his personal knowledge in order to establish them as matters of fact.

To those propositions I would add that for counsel to put in a list of comparables ought to amount to a warranty by him of his intention to tender admissible evidence of all that is shown on the list.

This decision shows that the expert cannot, by using underlying facts as the basis of his opinion, make those facts evidence in the case, unless fortuitously he happens to have personal knowledge of the transactions concerned. Therefore, either the expert or other witnesses, as appropriate, must prove by direct, competent evidence all the facts necessary to establish the elements of the charge, claim or defence. The function of the expert is to give his opinion on independently established facts. This does not mean, however, that the expert cannot base his opinion on other material, which may well be hearsay and inadmissible, and which is not a part of the factual background of the case which the other witnesses are to prove.

In *R v Abadom* [1983] 1 All ER 364, the defendant was charged with robbery. The prosecution relied on the fact that the defendant had broken a window during the robbery, and that fragments of glass adhering to and embedded in a pair of shoes taken from his home subsequently had come from the broken window. An expert witness gave evidence that glass taken from the window and the glass taken from the defendant's shoes had an identical refractive index. The witness further testified that he had consulted statistics compiled by the Home Office Central Research Establishment, which revealed that the refractive index referred to occurred only in 4% of all glass samples investigated by the Establishment. He then gave it as his opinion that there was a very strong likelihood that the glass found on the shoes had come from the broken window. The defendant was convicted and appealed on the ground that the evidence of the statistics was hearsay and inadmissible. Dismissing the appeal, the Court of Appeal held that since the necessary primary facts as to the source of the glass samples had been proved by other competent evidence, the expert had been entitled to make use of statistical material in forming his opinion, in the same way as other work, including unpublished work in the field. Furthermore, the expert should refer to that material during his testimony, so that the court may weigh the cogency and probative value of the opinion. Reliance by an expert on the work of others did not infringe the rule against hearsay. It was conceded that if the same statistical information had been contained in an authoritative reference work, the expert might have relied upon it, and the court saw no reason to preclude reference to unpublished data known to the expert.

It should, of course, be stressed that the testimony of the expert did not make the statistics evidence. The court may, however, refer to such data in assessing the weight of the expert's opinion. In *H and Another v Schering Chemicals Ltd and Another*,[23] an action

---

[23]   [1983] 1 All ER 849. See also *Seyfang v G D Searle & Co.* [1973] QB 148; *R v Turner* [1975] QB 834.

in which it was alleged that the defendants had negligently manufactured and marketed a drug, a question arose as to the admissibility of documents consisting of summaries of the results of research into the drug, and published articles and letters about the drug taken from medical journals. Bingham J held that, although the documents in question were hearsay and were not admissible under the Civil Evidence Act 1968 or otherwise in their own right, the plaintiffs were entitled to have their expert witnesses refer to them, and the court would thereupon consider them for the limited purpose of assessing the weight of that expert evidence. The learned judge also observed that where an expert refers to the results of research published by a reputable authority in a reputable journal, the court will ordinarily regard those results as supporting any inferences fairly to be drawn from them, unless and until some different approach is shown to be correct. It is, therefore, fairly clear that, in an indirect sense, the expert may invest data on which he relies with some limited evidential qualities.

### 9.6   Disclosure of expert evidence in civil cases

As we have seen, with the exception of expert evidence, opinion evidence consisting of hearsay statements, which are sought to be admitted by virtue of s. 2 or s. 4 of the Civil Evidence Act 1968, as extended by the Act of 1972, is subject to the notice procedure contained in RSC, Ord. 38, rr. 21–31.[24] In respect of expert-opinion evidence, Parliament determined to lay down a separate and much more far-reaching code, which in effect requires pre-trial disclosure of expert evidence proposed to be adduced in civil cases. Power to establish the code was given by s. 2 of the Civil Evidence Act 1972 and it has been promulgated in RSC, Ord. 38, rr.36–44. It is vital to stress that the code applies to expert evidence generally and not just to evidence admissible as hearsay by virtue of the Act. The purpose of the code is to save time and costs. It recognises that in the majority of cases there is a wide area of agreement between experts, and if that area can be identified at an early stage then evidence can be shortened and attention concentrated on the areas of disagreement. In many cases, it may lead to complete agreement of all relevant expert evidence before the trial begins.

There is no doubt that the code has been effective in its aim, and there are indications that the courts will insist upon its observation.[25] However, the very extent and nature of the provisions require proper safeguards for the parties affected by them, and there are powers to restrict the evidence which may be ordered to be disclosed, and to admit evidence despite disclosure in a proper case. The court is given power to override the rules by giving leave to adduce evidence, notwithstanding failure to comply. Reference must, however, be made at once to one important matter. Expert reports, which may later form the basis of the evidence called, are very frequently, if not usually, the subject of legal professional privilege. The Act provides that such privilege shall not prevent the operation of the code[26] but does not operate to remove such documents from the protection of privilege, which continues to attach to them within the usual rules.[27] A party is not,

---

[24]   See 8.7 and 9.1, ante. The notice procedure may be applied by the court, as a matter of discretion, in the limited cases dealt with by RSC, Ord. 38, r. 41 (post).

[25]   See *Ollett* v *Bristol Aerojet Ltd* [1979] 1 WLR 1197.

[26]   Civil Evidence Act 1972, s. 2(3).

[27]   *Causton* v *Mann Egerton (Johnsons) Ltd* (CA) [1974] 1 WLR 162. For legal profession privilege, see 10.9, post.

therefore, compellable to disclose privileged expert reports in his possession, but is precluded (subject to safeguards) from adducing in evidence the matters contained in them unless they are disclosed.

### 9.6.1 The statute

Section 2(2) of the Civil Evidence Act 1972 provides that the notice procedure of RSC, Ord. 38, rr.21–31 shall not apply to statements of fact or opinion contained in expert reports[28] that are proposed to be admitted as hearsay under s. 2 of the 1968 Act. In place of the notice procedure, s. 2(3)(*a*) of the 1972 Act permits rules to be made enabling the court to direct disclosure by a party to the other parties, in the form of expert reports, of the expert evidence proposed to be adduced by that party at trial. Section 2(3)(*b*) adds that the rules may prohibit the adducing of evidence, which is the subject of a direction, without leave, if the direction has not been complied with.

In addition to the provisions dealing with admissible hearsay, s. 2(4) provides that enabling rules may be made dealing with oral expert evidence, so as to provide conditions subject to which it may be given. Section 2(5) provides that the rules may prohibit the adducing, without leave, of any oral expert evidence whatsoever, if any direction given under s. 2(3) is not complied with. Where a party calls or intends to call as a witness the maker of a (hearsay) expert report, admissible under s. 2 of the 1968 Act, s. 2(1) of the 1972 Act and RSC, Ord.38, r. 43 exempt that party from the restrictions imposed in respect of other witnesses by s. 2(2) of the 1968 Act, and allow the report to be put in evidence at the commencement of its maker's evidence in chief, or at such other time as the court may direct.

### 9.6.2 The rules

The rules made in pursuance of these wide enabling provisions have taken full advantage of the powers provided. The principal rule is Ord. 38, r. 36, which provides that:

(1) Except with the leave of the court or where all parties agree, no expert evidence may be adduced at the trial or hearing of any cause or matter unless the party seeking to adduce the evidence has applied to the court to determine whether a direction should be given under rule 37, 38 or 41 (whichever is appropriate) and has complied with any direction given on the application.[29]

The existence of three separate rules (37, 38 and 41) under which directions may be given in different cases is authorised by s. 2(6) of the 1972 Act which provides that the rules may make different provisions for different classes of case, for expert reports dealing with matters of different classes and for other different circumstances. Similarly, Ord. 38, r. 39, allows the court to limit a direction given under rr. 37 or 38 (it would be inappropriate under r. 41) to part only of the evidence sought to be adduced. Rule 36 clearly places the onus upon a party wishing to adduce expert-opinion evidence to apply for directions, and to see that the directions are complied with.

The three rules under which directions may be given have somewhat different

[28] An 'expert report' is a 'written report by a person dealing wholly or mainly with matters on which he is (or would if living be) qualified to give expert evidence': Civil Evidence Act 1972, s. 2(7).

[29] R. 36(2) contains an exception for matters which are permitted to be stated in affidavits; see Ord. 41, r.5.

provisions, and apply to different types of evidence, as follows. Rules 37 and 38 apply to proposed oral evidence and r. 41 to proposed evidence contained in statements.

*9.6.2.1   Rule 37: oral medical evidence in actions for personal injuries.*   The emphasis in this type of evidence is in favour of mandatory disclosure, in all but certain exceptional cases. Where an application is made under r. 36, in respect of oral expert evidence relating to medical matters, the court shall direct disclosure in the form of written reports, unless there is 'sufficient reason' for not doing so. By r. 37(2), the court may treat as a sufficient reason the fact that the pleadings contain an allegation of medical negligence[30] or that the expert evidence may express an opinion on the manner in which injuries were sustained, or on the genuineness of symptoms. In these cases, disclosure would effectively force a premature disclosure of the strength of a party's case on the facts directly in issue. The rule does not suggest that these facts are the only ones capable of amounting to sufficient reason, and the matter appears to that extent to be discretionary, subject to the obvious mandatory intention of the rule as a whole.

*9.6.2.2   Rule 38: other oral expert evidence.*   In cases of oral expert evidence to which r. 37 does not apply, the emphasis is rather different. Rule 38 provides in such cases that the court may, if satisfied that it is desirable to do so, direct that the substance of the proposed evidence be disclosed in written reports. Rule 38(2) refers to 'sufficient reason for not giving such a direction', and mentions under that head evidence based upon a version of the facts in dispute between the parties, and upon matters outside the personal observation and professional expertise of the expert.

*9.6.2.3   Rule 41: expert evidence contained in statements.*   This rule provides for cases where the expert evidence, of whatever nature, is contained in an (admissible hearsay) statement and the party seeking to adduce it alleges that the maker of the statement cannot or should not be called as a witness.[31] In such a case, the court may, but evidently need not, direct that the evidence be subject to the notice procedure under rr. 21–31, with any necessary modifications.

It is also necessary to observe one further provision, under which directions are subject to absolute mandatory disclosure. By virtue of Ord. 38, r. 40, where a party intends to apply under r. 36 in an action arising out of an accident on land due to a collision or apprehended collision, in respect of the expert evidence of an engineer in connection with motor vehicles, that party must, before the hearing of the summons for directions make available to all other parties a report by the engineer containing the substance of his evidence.

*9.6.3   Time for application*
Applications under r. 36 should, wherever possible, be dealt with on the summons for directions.[32] The master has power to limit the number of witnesses who may be called on

---

[30]   As to disclosure in cases involving medical malpractice, see generally *Brown v Merton, Sutton and Wandsworth Area Health Authority* [1982] 1 All ER 650; *Rahman v Kirklees Area Health Authority* [1980] 1 WLR 1244.

[31]   This is a muted echo of Ord. 38, r. 25 (see 8.7, ante). It lacks the complication of the mandatory application of the notice procedure, but enables the court to apply that procedure in a proper case, presumably where it would be unjust not to do so, having regard to the nature of the evidence.

[32]   Practice Direction (QBD) [1974] 2 All ER 966.

either side,[33] and the exercise of this power should be considered in the interests of saving time and costs. The task is much simplified if proper disclosure has been made. The master may also direct agreeement of expert reports, but only in a case where this is clearly appropriate.[34]

### 9.6.4 Mutuality and timing of disclosure

In general, the court will seek to achieve fairness through mutuality in the timing of disclosure of expert reports: Practice Direction [1974] 2 All ER 1966. However, as this Direction itself makes clear, this will not be an invariable rule. There are cases in which fairness dictates prior disclosure by one party, for reasons associated with the saving of costs, the avoidance of surprise and the need to avoid amendments at trial. In *Kirkup* v *British Rail Engineering Ltd and other appeals* [1983] 1 All ER 855, where some 3,000 claims for damages alleging industrially-caused deafness had been brought against the defendants arising from employment in 12 different work-places, it was to be anticipated that a number of different expert engineers would be advising the plaintiffs, and that the defendants could not expect to meet their various opinions with a single, standard expert report. It was, therefore, reasonable in the circumstances to require the plaintiffs to disclose expert reports first, so that the defendants' expert might consider and deal with them.

### 9.6.5 Effect of disclosure

The consequences of disclosure of expert reports for the purposes of the proceedings are starkly stated by Ord. 38, r. 42: 'A party to any cause or matter may put in evidence any expert report disclosed to him by any other party in accordance with this part [i.e. rr. 35–44] of this Order.'

It follows, therefore, that once disclosure has been made, the report cannot be kept out, if another party wishes to put it in, merely because the party who produced it has decided not to rely upon it or not to call the evidence in question. It is essential to decide before the application for directions, whether the evidence should be disclosed, or whether the report should be used only for assistance in the conduct and assessment of the case, in which case its privilege can and should be protected.

### 9.7 Disclosure of expert evidence in criminal cases

In accordance with the very different approach to evidence in criminal cases, in which there is no discovery and in which disclosure of evidence before trial, particularly by the defence, has been extremely limited, there was until recently no provision corresponding to those just discussed in civil cases, for the pre-trial disclosure of expert evidence. However, s. 81 of the Police and Criminal Evidence Act 1984, provides:

(1)   Crown Court Rules may make provision for—

(a)   requiring any party to proceedings before the court to disclose to the other party or parties any expert evidence which he proposes to adduce in the proceedings; and

---

[33]   See RSC, Ord. 38, r. 4; Ord. 25, r. 3.
[34]   *Proctor* v *Peebles (Papermakers) Ltd* [1941] 2 All ER 80.

(*b*)    prohibiting a party who fails to comply in respect of any evidence with any requirement imposed by virtue of paragraph (a) above from adducing that evidence without leave of the court.

(2)    Crown Court Rules made by virtue of this section may specify the kinds of expert evidence to which they apply and may exempt facts or matters of any description specified in the rules.

At the time of writing, no such rules have been promulgated. It may be anticipated, in keeping with the practice in cases where the defence are required to supply details of an alibi in advance of trial, that the discretion of the court may be exercised more liberally in criminal cases than in civil, at least in favour of the defence. Courts have so far proved reluctant to compel a defendant to go to trial in a criminal case without being able to make use of crucial evidence, particularly where the failure to disclose is the fault of the defendant's legal advisors.

### 9.8    Expert evidence called by the court

In civil actions in the High Court, the court may, in any non-jury case,[35] and on the application of any party, appoint an independent expert (the 'court expert') to inquire and report upon any question of fact or opinion, where any question for an expert arises.[36] The question may not be one of law or construction. An 'expert' for this purpose is defined as: 'any person who has such knowledge or experience of or in connection with [the] question that his opinion on it would be admissible in evidence' (Ord. 40, r. 1(4)). The expert makes and sends to the court a report. Any party may apply for leave to cross-examine the court expert, and there is limited provision for the parties to call evidence to contradict him (Ord. 40, rr. 4,6). If the report is agreed, it may clearly be treated as evidence in the case, but Ord. 40, r. 2(3) provides, somewhat mysteriously, that: 'Any part of a court expert's report which is not accepted by all the parties . . . shall be treated as information furnished to the Court and be given such weight as the Court thinks fit.'

It has been suggested that the court has an inherent power to appoint an expert, even in the absence of an application, where it is in need of assistance[37] and apparently even where a party objects to such a course.[38]

In certain very limited cases, 'assessors' may sit with the judge.[39] Their function is not that of witnesses; they sit to advise the judge with regard to specialised questions of fact, and are members of the court, although their views may be overruled by the judge. The principal use of assessors is in Admiralty cases.

---

[35]    No such provision exists for criminal cases or in magistrates' courts.
[36]    RSC, Ord. 40, r. 1. See also the corresponding provision of Ord. 32, r. 16 (Judge in chambers) Supreme Court Act 1981, s. 70, and Ord. 103, r. 27 (appointment of scientific advisers in patent actions). The 'question' and the identity of the court expert shall be agreed if possible, or otherwise settled by the court: Ord. 40, r. 1(2), (3).
[37]    *Colls* v *Home & Colonial Stores Ltd* (HL) [1904] AC 179 per Lord MacNaughton at 192; *Badische Anilin und Soda Fabrik v Levinstein* (1883) 24 ChD 156.
[38]    *Attorney-General* v *Birmingham, Tame & Rea District Drainage Board* (HL) [1912] AC 788.
[39]    Supreme Court Act 1981, s. 70; RSC, Ord. 33, r. 6.

**9.9   Common subjects of expert evidence**

Although there is a considerable number of subjects upon which expert-opinion evidence may be admitted, the following are of common occurrence in practice, and merit some individual mention.

*9.9.1   Scientific and technical matters (examples from R v Coke; R v Littleton)*
Reference has already been made to the existence of specific rules of court, which relate to the treatment of medical evidence in personal injury cases and the evidence of engineers in motor-vehicle collision cases. These rules are, perhaps, sufficient testimony in themselves to the everyday importance of such evidence. There are also many other areas of scientific and technological evidence, and the field is an expanding one. In Coke's case, we see an example of the evidence produced by a forensic scientist, Dr Espinasse. Forensic science ranges over a very wide range of matters—of particular though not exclusive significance in criminal cases—matters such as the presence and age of fingerprints and blood stains; the examination of weapons and ammunition; the identification of drugs, poisons and chemicals, fibres and paint. Dr Espinasse's evidence will, no doubt, be agreed in the present case, as Coke does not dispute having had sexual intercourse with Margaret Blackstone. But it is noteworthy how significant the evidence would be, were that matter to be challenged. The witness states his examination of the exhibit, 'SGV1' as a piece of factual evidence, and goes on to give his opinion and his reasons. Of course, no forensic evidence is beyond challenge, and it is a matter for the jury; but the evidence remains formidable, and as we have seen, the judge should not invite the jury to disregard it capriciously. The evidence of Dr Espinasse can, of course, go no further than to indicate the occurrence, within a certain time, of sexual intercourse. The medical evidence of Dr Vesey could go further, by suggesting that such intercourse was forcible, and this too would be a matter of expert opinion by the doctor based upon her observation and examination of Margaret. In fact, Dr Vesey's evidence is far from damning in this respect.
   It is vital, in all cases involving any examination of exhibits that there should be evidence accounting for the safe-keeping and treatment of each exhibit from the moment of its creation or appropriation, until the moment of its examination by the expert, and indeed, if it is to be produced as evidence in court, until trial. It may be noted that there is a 'chain' of possession of exhibit SGV1 from Dr Vesey to D/S Bracton to Dr Espinasse, and it is important that this chain should be unbroken. There is a similar chain in respect of the handwriting exhibits GG1 and GG3 from D/I Glanvil to D/S Bracton to Mr Hale. The safe-keeping is of considerable importance in relation to the tape-recording of the conversation between Littleton and his wife. Before admitting the tape in evidence, the judge will have to satisfy himself that there is a prima facie case that the tape is original and authentic. For this purpose, D/I Glanvil will have to account for his keeping of the cassette, exhibit GG4, from the moment of the recording until its production in court.[40] Should there be any doubt as to its originality, or any question of interference with it, expert evidence may be highly valuable on that issue.

*9.9.2   Documents and handwriting (example from R v Coke; R v Littleton)*
The scientific examination of documents and handwriting is a specialised branch of forensic science. The detailed legal basis for evidence of examination and comparison of

---

[40]   *R v Robson; R v Harris* [1972] 1 WLR 651. See 15.5, post.

documents and handwriting is considered in 15.4, post, to which reference should be made. It will be seen that the first task of the prosecution is to prove the genuineness of the sample of handwriting provided by Coke (exhibit GG3). By genuineness is meant authorship by Coke, and this can be proved by the evidence of D/I Glanvil, if not admitted. Once this is established, evidence of a comparison with the disputed writing (exhibit GG1) becomes admissible[41] and Mr Hale may state both his examination of and comparison of the exhibits, and his consequent opinion. The disputed question of authorship, and its significance, if proved, are of course matters of fact for the jury. It may be seen that Mr Hale's evidence, though not conclusive, is certainly strong, and it may be that cross-examination would have to involve analysis of the chart produced by him, perhaps with the aid of expert advice for the defence on the technical questions raised.

Evidence of this sort is, of course, of great importance in many criminal and civil cases, where the authenticity of a document or signature, or due execution, falls to be proved, and is particularly relevant to cases involving fraud or forgery.

### 9.9.3   Art, literature, learning, etc.

Expert evidence on these subjects may be adduced where matters concerning specialised fields fall to be proved. There may be various uses of it, but one which tends to occur frequently is in relation to the defence of 'public good' under s. 4 of the Obscene Publications Act 1959, as amended. The defence provides that a person shall not be convicted of an offence under s. 2 in relation to an obscene article, 'if it is proved that publication of the article in question is justified as being for the public good on the ground that it is in the interests of science, literature, art or learning, or of other objects of general concern'. The phrase 'other objects of general concern' is restricted to the specific matters alluded to in s. 4 and does not permit of a wider interpretation, for instance the relief of sexual tension in the context of the general pyschiatric health of the community.[42]

Expert evidence is admissible to prove or disprove the defence under s. 4 which is clearly a matter upon which the jury will require guidance, in order to arrive at a proper opinion. However, the defence will only arise on the assumption that the jury consider the article to be obscene which is a question of fact for them, and upon which expert evidence is not admissible.[43]

### 9.9.4   Professional and trade practices and standards

Evidence from members of a profession or trade, either generally or in a particular field of reference or a particular geographical area, will be admissible as expert-opinion evidence to show the practice of the profession or trade, or the standard expected of reasonably competent members thereof. Such evidence is relevant to establish customary terms of contracts of various sorts, the existence of trade practices, the reasonableness of covenants in restraint of trade, the standard of professional competence reasonably expected of a person against whom negligence is alleged in the exercise of his profession, and a variety of other matters.

---

[41]   Criminal Procedure Act 1865, s. 8.

[42]   *DPP* v *Jordan* (HL) [1977] AC 699.

[43]   *Attorney-General's Reference (No. 3 of 1977)* (CA) [1978] 1 WLR 1123. In an exceptional case, a jury may be assisted by expert evidence on the likely effect of material on special classes of reader, e.g. children, in their task of deciding whether the material would be likely to deprave or corrupt: *DPP* v *A & B C Chewing Gum Ltd* (DC) [1968] 1 QB 159.

*9.9.5 Foreign law*

Questions of foreign law, which for this purpose means the law prevailing in any jurisdiction other than England and Wales, are questions of fact, and should, where relevant, be proved by evidence, like any other question of fact.[44] It is obviously desirable, and has always been the practice, that foreign law should be proved by expert evidence from a witness who has knowledge or experience of the law concerned. In relation to civil proceedings, s. 4(1) of the Civil Evidence Act 1972 now provides that:

> It is hereby declared that in civil proceedings a person who is suitably qualified to do so on account of his knowledge or experience is competent to give expert evidence as to the law of any country or territory outside [England and Wales] irrespective of whether he has acted or is entitled to act as a legal practitioner there.

The form of the section as a declaration suggests that it is intended to confirm what was thought to be the position at common law, and indeed, there is authority to support the proposition.[45]

Section 4(2), designed to avoid the embarrassing prospect of different decisions by English courts on identical points of foreign law, provides for proof of such points by reference to reported decisions of superior courts in England in which they have previously been decided. Such evidence, of which notice must be given, may be contradicted, but will otherwise be accepted as proving the point of foreign law concerned.[46]

**9.10 Non-expert opinion evidence: principles of admissibility**

As was observed at the outset of this chapter, opinion evidence was rejected at common law as evidence of the truth of the matters believed, at least partly because it tended to usurp the function of the court. Nowhere is this defect more apparent than in relation to the opinion of persons not qualified as experts on matters directly in issue in the proceedings.

By s. 3(2) of the Civil Evidence Act 1972:

> It is hereby declared that where a person is called as a witness in any civil proceedings, a statement of opinion by him on any relevant matter on which he is not qualified to give expert evidence, if made as a way of conveying relevant facts personally perceived by him, is admissible as evidence of what he perceived.

Much controversy has raged as to whether this declaration accurately represents the state of the common law, and therefore whether it may apply in effect to criminal cases also.[47] It is submitted that this is and should be the case. The admissibility is confined to

---

[44]  However, the jury should not be left to decide it without a definitive direction. The judge may have to decide between conflicting opinions: *Re Duke of Wellington, Glentanar* v *Wellington* [1947] Ch 506; affirmed (CA) [1948] Ch 118.

[45]  *Brailey* v *Rhodesia Consolidated Ltd* [1910] 2 Ch 95 (Reader in Roman-Dutch Law in the Inns of Court).

[46]  Civil Evidence Act 1972, s. 4(2)(*b*)

[47]  The point was apparently not adverted to in *Rasool* v *West Midland Passenger Transport Executive* [1974] 3 All ER 638, where a statement made by the defendants' witness (admissible otherwise under s. 2 of the Civil Evidence Act 1968) contained the words: 'The bus driver was in no way to blame for the accident'. This statement was, it seems, not called into question by the way in which it was expressed, the witness seeking to explain what she had seen, but the decision is hardly satisfactory.

matters of the general competence and experience of people generally, which they are able and accustomed to appreciate by a process of observation of commonplace facts, and which require no process of conscious deduction. They are in reality matters of perception, perceived directly by the witness while using his ordinary senses, so that while in an abstract sense it may be said that the witness is expressing an opinion, he is in fact merely using natural language to convey facts which he perceived, and which would otherwise be difficult, if not impossible, to relate. The American Federal Rule of Evidence 701 expresses the same idea in the following language:

> Opinion testimony by lay witnesses. If the witness is not testifying as an expert, his testimony in the form of opinions or inferences is limited to those opinions or inferences which are (a) rationally based on the perception of the witness and (b) helpful to a clear understanding of his testimony or the determination of a fact in issue.

There can be no final rule on where the line of admissibility may be drawn. In any case tried without a jury, the matter is likely to be resolved by the judge taking a realistic view of what the witness is trying to say. The following cases are examples only of the use of non-expert-opinion evidence.

### 9.10.1 Identity and resemblance

A witness may state that a person, thing or document is the same as, or bears a resemblance to, one that he has seen on a previous occasion. The matter is one of perception, and there would be formidable difficulties of proof in very many cases if this were not permitted.[48] Both the identifying witness and any other person who witnessed a previous identification, may give evidence of what transpired on that occasion.[49] This is subject, in criminal cases, to the safeguards required in the interests of preventing potentially misleading or incorrect evidence being given of identification, and to the various administrative requirements for the proper treatment of evidence of identification.[50] But in general, a witness may give evidence of matters within this category, and may be referred to any photograph or other exhibit necessary to enable him to explain what he perceived.

### 9.10.2 Mental or physical condition

The rule applies to observable conditions, in so far as expert evidence is not required of them. The condition of the witness himself is admissible as well as that of others, and he may state his reaction to events or circumstances, or his reasons for his acts, provided that he does not infringe the rule against previous consistent statements. He may not, however, state his opinion of the intentions of others,[51] which must be objectionable as inadmissible opinion or hearsay, or both. Wherever the condition of a person must be proved with more precision than a lay person can provide, so that the court must have expert evidence of it, the opinion of a witness other than an expert is inadmissible. A good illustration is *R v Davies* [1962] 1 WLR 1111, where it was held that, although a lay witness could state that

---

[48]   See, e.g., *Fryer v Gathercole* (1849) 4 Exch 262 per Pollock CB. The rule also applies to handwriting with which the witness is personally familiar.

[49]   *R v Osbourne; R v Virtue* (CA) [1973] QB 678.

[50]   *R v Turnbull* (CA) [1977] QB 224. See generally 12.3.3.2, post.

[51]   *Townsend v Moore* (CA) [1905] P 66.

a person had been drinking, which was a matter of general competence, he might not state that that person was unfit to drive through drink, which was a matter of expert medical evidence. For the same reason, a lay witness may not be called to prove the sanity of another[52] although his evidence is apparently admissible on the issue of his own sanity.[53]

### 9.10.3 Age, speed, value

These matters are usually assumed to be within ordinary human experience, although evidence can obviously prove them only to a reasonable approximation.[54] The weight of such evidence will depend, *inter alia*, on the apparent experience of the witness, e.g. as a driver or passenger if his evidence relates to speed. It would seem that evidence of value should be admissible only in respect of objects in common use or knowledge, and not where the object is, for example, an antique or otherwise of special value, upon which expert evidence would be required.[55]

## 9.11 Affidavits

Although evidence permitted to be given by affidavit is, like other evidence, subject to the ordinary rules of admissibility, it is provided by RSC, Ord. 41, r. 5(2), that: 'An affidavit sworn for the purpose of being used in interlocutory proceedings may contain statements of information or belief with the sources and grounds thereof'.

The rule is confined to interlocutory proceedings, where the rights and liabilities of the parties are not decided. Thus, in *Nationwide Building Society* v *Bateman* [1978] 1 WLR 394, an affidavit which was permitted to be sworn for the purposes of a mortgage action, and was used in final proceedings, was held to be irregular, where it contained matters which the deponent was unable to prove of his own knowledge.

It is also essential that the affidavit state the sources and grounds of the belief deposed to. Although in practice the requirement appears often to be ignored, the courts occasionally comment strongly on the matter[56] and there is power to strike the affidavit out.

The purpose of the rule is to permit the introduction of admissible hearsay evidence in interlocutory matters, where it might have been given in the course of oral evidence in final proceedings.

### B: PREVIOUS JUDGMENTS AS EVIDENCE

We must now proceed to examine the specific problems of opinion evidence raised by the use of previous judgments of other courts for the purpose of establishing facts in issue. The common law permitted judgments to be admitted for the limited purpose of proving, where relevant to do so, their own existence, contents and legal effect. Judgments of courts of competent jurisdiction are public transactions and are presumed to have been made

---

[52]   *R* v *Neville* (1837) Craw & D Abr C 96; *Greenslade* v *Dare* (1855) 20 Beav 284.
[53]   *Hunter* v *Edney* (1885) 10 PD 93.
[54]   No one is liable to be convicted of speeding on the uncorroborated evidence of opinion of one witness as to speed: Road Traffic Regulation Act 1967, s. 78A(2).
[55]   *R* v *Beckett* (CCA) (1913) 8 Cr App R 204.
[56]   See e.g., *Re J.L. Young Manufacturing Co. Ltd, Young* v *J.L. Young Manufacturing Co. Ltd* (CA) [1900] 2 Ch 753.

and recorded faithfully. But whereas a judgment was evidence, indeed conclusive evidence of its own existence, contents and effect, most common-law authorities held that it was not evidence of the facts on which the judgment was based. Thus, in an action for malicious prosecution, the record of the verdict of the jury acquitting the plaintiff of the criminal charge brought against him was conclusive evidence of the facts that the defendant had brought the charge against the plaintiff and that the plaintiff had been acquitted, but was not admissible to prove that the plaintiff was in fact innocent of the charge, or that the defendant had brought the charge maliciously: *Purcell* v *M'Namara* (1808) 1 Camp 199. The conclusive nature of the contents and legal effect of a judgment also meant that a witness was not permitted to give evidence, the effect of which was to contradict a previous judgment, even though the judgment was not in itself evidence of the facts to which the witness proposed to testify.

The question of greatest significance, and that which will occupy the remainder of this chapter, is whether a previous judgment may be used not merely to prove its own existence, contents and legal effect, but also the facts on which it was based, where those facts are in issue in or relevant to subsequent proceedings.

### 9.12   Generally

At common law there was until relatively recently no fixed view of the admissibility of a judgment as evidence of the facts upon which it was based, for or against strangers to the judgment (i.e. those not parties to the suit in which it was pronounced). There was some authority either way, and it was certainly possible to find examples of cases where, with obviously convenient results, the courts overcame the apparent stumbling blocks of theory and allowed reliance on previous judgments. Thus, in *Re Crippen* [1911] P 108, a husband, who was subsequently executed for the murder of his wife, made a will, and the executrix thereby appointed sought to administer the estate of the murdered wife. Application was made to vest the wife's estate elsewhere, on the ground that the husband's estate should not be permitted to benefit from his crime. It was argued that the conviction of the husband was not admissible to prove that he had murdered his wife. But the court held that, where there was an issue of rights accruing as a result of crime, the conviction was admissible as prima facie evidence of the commission of such crime. And in *Partington* v *Partington and Atkinson* [1925] P 34 a finding of adultery against a husband made in a suit in which the husband was co-respondent, and to which the wife was not a party, was admissible for the wife, in a subsequent suit brought by her against the husband, as prima facie evidence of his adultery.

It seems from these cases that there was a limited recognition of previous judgments as evidence of facts on which they were based but that, unlike the position when only the formal existence or effect of the judgment is relied on, the evidence could be only prima facie, and was certainly not conclusive. The question was further complicated by confusion in some authorities between this question, and the question of the operation of judgments *in rem*, and questions of other exceptional rules of evidence concerned with such matters as custom and public rights, which might sometimes be established by judgments.

### 9.13   The rule in *Hollington* v *Hewthorn*

At length, it was apparent that the balance of authority lay against the admissibility of judgments for or against strangers, to prove the facts on which the judgment was based, and the rule was authoritatively laid down by the Court of Appeal in *Hollington* v *F. Hewthorn & Co. Ltd* [1943] KB 587. In an action for negligence by the plaintiff against an individual defendant and his employer, arising from a road traffic accident, it was held that the conviction of the individual defendant of the offence of driving without due care and attention was not admissible to prove that the individual defendant had been negligent. Despite the superficial attraction of the close similarity of issues in the different proceedings, and of the argument that the plaintiff, although not a party to the prosecution, could hardly be prejudiced by the admission of the conviction, the evidence was rejected for three formidable reasons: that the opinion of the previous tribunal was irrelevant; that findings of fact by the justices, especially in an uncontested case, might be qualitatively different from those which should prevail in a contested action in the High Court; and that it would be extremely difficult, if possible at all, to identify the facts upon which the conviction was based.

### 9.14 Reversal of the rule in civil cases

The first statutory inroad on the rule in *Hollington* v *Hewthorn* was made in civil cases. In civil cases in which several different plaintiffs or defendants may be entitled to recover or may be liable for the consequences of the same wrongful civil act, procedural provisions permit joinder of all necessary parties and consolidation of actions. This means that closely related civil claims can usually be adjudicated together and that the need for reliance upon previous judgments given in civil proceedings can often be avoided. However, problems may still arise with previous criminal convictions and findings of adultery or paternity. Three kinds of case are principally concerned:

(a)   Where the plaintiff wishes to prove the conviction of the defendant of a criminal offence, relevant to the plaintiff's cause of action or to an issue in civil proceedings.

(b)   Where a party to an action for defamation wishes to prove that another has been convicted of a criminal offence, where the commission or otherwise of such offence is relevant to the action.

(c)   Where a party to civil proceedings (e.g. divorce) wishes to rely upon a finding of adultery or paternity made against another in previous proceedings relevant to his cause of action or an issue in the instant proceedings.

In these kinds of cases, Parliament decided that the convenience of permitting proof to be made in the manner described above outweighs even the cogent reservations expressed in *Hollington* v *Hewthorn* and by ss. 11–13 of the Civil Evidence Act 1968 made previous judgments admissible, but in these kinds of case only. The Police and Criminal Evidence Act 1984, ss. 74 and 75 has now made for criminal cases provision similar to s. 11 of the 1968 Act. This is considered in 9.15, post.

#### 9.14.1   Convictions relevant to civil proceedings
Section 11 of the Civil Evidence Act 1968, provides as follows:

(1)   In any civil proceedings the fact that a person has been convicted of an offence by or before any court in the United Kingdom or by a court-martial there or elsewhere

shall . . . be admissible in evidence for the purpose of proving, where to do so is relevant to any issue in those proceedings, that he committed that offence, whether he was so convicted upon a plea of guilty or otherwise and whether or not he is a party to the civil proceedings; but no conviction other than a subsisting one shall be admissible in evidence by virtue of this section.

(2)    In any civil proceedings in which by virtue of this section a person is proved to have been convicted of an offence by or before any court in the United Kingdom or by a court-martial there or elsewhere—

(a)    he shall be taken to have committed that offence unless the contrary is proved; and
(b)    without prejudice to the reception of any other admissible evidence for the purpose of identifying the facts on which the conviction was based, the contents of any document which is admissible as evidence of the conviction, and the contents of the information, complaint, indictment or charge-sheet on which the person in question was convicted, shall be admissible in evidence for that purpose.

So far as s. 11(1) is concerned, the following points should be noted:

(a)    The expression 'civil proceedings' is defined by s. 18(1), for all purposes of the Act, including ss. 11–13 (see 8.2, ante).
(b)    The section has no application to a conviction by a court outside the United Kingdom, other than a court-martial.
(c)    It is irrelevant whether or not the person convicted is a party to the civil proceedings, for example the servant or agent of the defendant for whose acts the defendant is vicariously liable; it is also irrelevant whether or not the criminal proceedings were contested.
(d)    A 'subsisting' conviction means one which has not been quashed on appeal, and will include a conviction substituted by an appellate court for the original conviction. But the mere fact that an appeal is pending against a conviction does not mean that the conviction is not 'subsisting' for the purpose of s. 1; in such a case, any civil proceedings to which the conviction is said to be relevant should be adjourned, if necessary, pending the outcome of the appeal.[57]

The construction of s. 11(2)(a) has given rise to differences of opinion among those judges who have been called upon to consider it. It is generally accepted that where a conviction is proved by virtue of s. 11, it has the effect of reversing the burden of proof, so that the party seeking to assert that the offence was not committed would bear the burden of proving that fact, on the balance of probabilities. Where the commission of the offence is an issue central to the cause of action or defence, the burden of proof so reversed will be the legal burden. Thus in *Wauchope* v *Mordecai* [1970] 1 WLR 317, the plaintiff had been knocked off his bicycle when the defendant opened the door of a car as the plaintiff was passing. The defendant was later convicted of the offence of opening the door so as to cause injury or danger. By an oversight, the trial judge was not referred to s. 11 and found for the defendant, basing his decision on the failure of the plaintiff to discharge the legal burden of proof. The Court of Appeal allowed the plaintiff's appeal. The burden lay on

[57]    *Re Raphael, Raphael* v *d'Antin and Another* [1973] 1 WLR 998.

the defendant to prove that he had not opened the door negligently, and if the judge had considered s. 11, he must have found that that burden had not been discharged.

The decision in *Wauchope* v *Mordecai* left open, however, the question of the weight which should be attached to the conviction, once admitted, as evidence of the commission of the offence. In *Taylor* v *Taylor* [1970] 1 WLR 1148, a wife petitioned for divorce on the ground of her husband's adultery. The adultery complained of was incestuous, in that it had been committed with the daughter of the family. The husband had been convicted of the relevant incest, and his application for leave to appeal against conviction was refused. The wife tendered evidence of the conviction in the divorce proceedings under s. 11, and the husband sought to prove that he had not committed the offence. The trial judge found, on the basis of the depositions used at the trial and on the basis of oral evidence taken before him, which the Court of Appeal found to be unsatisfactory, that the husband had discharged the burden on him and had proved that he had not committed incest. The Court of Appeal allowed an appeal by the wife. In the words of Davies LJ 'it is obvious that, when a man has been convicted by twelve of his fellow countrymen and countrywomen at a criminal trial, the verdict of the jury is a matter which is entitled to very great weight when the convicted person is seeking, in the words of the statute, to prove the contrary' ([1970] 1 WLR at 1152). The trial judge should, accordingly, have obtained a transcript, or otherwise satisfied himself with regard to the evidence and details of the criminal trial and thus embarked upon a full and searching investigation of the husband's case, to see whether the burden of proof was discharged. There was not sufficient evidence upon which his conclusion could have been based.[58]

The Court of Appeal in *Taylor* v *Taylor* were referred to the decision at first instance of Paull J in *Stupple* v *Royal Insurance Co. Ltd; Stupple* v *Same* [1971] 1 QB 50, which had not then reached the Court of Appeal. That case involved a claim and counterclaim in respect of sums of money, said to be the proceeds of a robbery, of which Mr Stupple had been convicted. The issue, in effect, was whether his conviction was correct. Paull J asked himself the question, what his view would have been if he had sat as a juryman on the criminal trial. Though this approach won some support in *Taylor* v *Taylor*, it won none from the differently constituted Court of Appeal that heard the *Stupple* case. But the court upheld the judge's view that the conviction, and its affirmation by the Court of Criminal Appeal, were: 'from a practical point of view . . . conclusive'.[59] The Court of Appeal was, however, unable to agree on the precise effect of s. 11(2)(a) in terms of weight. Lord Denning MR thought that the evidence went further than merely shifting the burden of

---

[58] The limits of the means by which a party may discharge the burden of disproving a conviction cannot be said to be settled. In *Stupple* v *Royal Insurance Co. Ltd; Stupple* v *Same* (CA) [1971] 1 QB 50, Lord Denning MR conceived of a broad range of weapons, by calling fresh evidence, discrediting evidence given at the trial, and even by explaining a plea of guilty or a failure to appeal, to rebut the obvious inference. But it seems, as Paull J held at first instance, that the court is not entitled to consider, as if it were a criminal appellate court, the circumstances of the conduct of the trial; it must confine itself to the evidence and papers, and the formal record. In *Taylor* v *Taylor* the Court postulated that the evidence at the trial would be admissible (presumably as evidence of truth) under either s. 2(1) or s. 4(1) of the Act, though the summing up would more probably be admissible under s. 4(1) as a record made by the shorthand writer acting under a duty.

[59] Lord Denning MR has since said (in *McIlkenny* v *Chief Constable of the West Midlands and Another* [1980] 2 WLR 689 that evidence adduced to disprove a conviction must be decisive. This was doubted in the first edition of this work, and judicially by Lord Diplock on appeal in the same case, sub nom. *Hunter* v *Chief Constable of the West Midlands and Another* [1982] AC 529 at 544. Lord Diplock held that the usual civil standard of proof applied. He conceded, though, that disproof would be an 'uphill task'.

proof, and was 'a weighty piece of evidence in itself'. The conviction 'itself tells in the scale in the civil action'. Conversely Buckley LJ said: 'In my judgment, proof of conviction under this section gives rise to the statutory presumption laid down in s. 11(2)(a), which, like any other presumption, will give way to evidence establishing the contrary on the balance of probability, without itself affording any evidential weight to be taken into account in determining whether that onus has been discharged' ([1971] 1 QB 50 at 76). The third member of the court, Winn LJ expressed no opinion on the point. It is submitted that the intention and wording of the section are alike better served by the view of Lord Denning MR.

Whatever the position, there now seems to be no reason why a conviction, admitted under s. 11, should not corroborate other evidence called for the party tendering it. Such a result had been approved in *Mash* v *Darley* [1914] 1 KB 1, but had necessarily perished under the rule in *Hollington* v *Hewthorn*. The decision was that the conviction of a respondent to affiliation proceedings, for unlawful sexual intercourse with the applicant, was capable of corroborating her evidence, as required in such proceedings. It is submitted that the case is now sound law, once again.

### 9.14.2   *Findings of adultery and paternity relevant to civil proceedings*

Section 12 of the Civil Evidence Act 1968, provides:

(1)   In any civil proceedings—

(*a*)   the fact that a person has been found guilty of adultery in any matrimonial proceedings; and
(*b*)   the fact that a person has been adjudged to be the father of a child in affiliation proceedings before any court in the United Kingdom,

shall . . . be admissible in evidence for the purpose of proving, where to do so is relevant to any issue in those civil proceedings, that he committed the adultery to which the finding relates or, as the case may be, is (or was) the father of that child, whether or not he offered any defence to the allegation of adultery or paternity and whether or not he is a party to the civil proceedings; but no finding or adjudication other than a subsisting one shall be admissible in evidence by virtue of this section.

(2)   In any civil proceedings in which by virtue of this section a person is proved to have been found guilty of adultery as mentioned in subsection (1)(a)above or to have been adjudged to be the father of a child as mentioned in subsection (1)(b)above—

(*a*)   he shall be taken to have committed the adultery to which the finding relates or, as the case may be, to be (or have been) the father of that child, unless the contrary is proved; and
(*b*)   [provides for the admissibility of evidence to show the facts on which the finding or adjudication was based].

It will be observed that the section follows closely the provisions of s. 11, and it would appear that the law relating to s. 11, as set out above, will apply with any necessary modifications to this section also. Certainly, it has been held that the effect of the section is to reverse the burden of proof and to require the party seeking to disprove the finding or adjudication to do so, on a balance of probabilities.[60] The expression 'matrimonial proceedings' does not include matrimonial proceedings in a magistrates' court, and is confined to proceedings in England and Wales (s. 12(5)).

### 9.14.3  Convictions relevant to defamation actions

Section 13 of the Civil Evidence Act 1968 provides:

> (1)   In an action for libel or slander in which the question whether a person did or did not commit a criminal offence is relevant to an issue arising in the action, proof that at the time when that issue falls to be determined, that person stands convicted of that offence shall be conclusive evidence that he committed that offence; and his conviction thereof shall be admissible in evidence accordingly.

The operation of s. 13 differs greatly from that of s. 11, in that the conviction is conclusive evidence of the commission of the offence. The reason for this wording of the section is to prevent the abuse of defamation proceedings for the purpose of attempting to reopen convictions, even when they may have been affirmed on appeal, and also to protect those concerned in writing or publishing justifiable material, relying upon the conviction for the truth of what they write or publish. It must, therefore, follow that a statement of claim, which does no more than complain of a statement, accurate in itself, which asserts and fairly comments upon the fact that a person has committed an offence of which he has been lawfully convicted, must be struck out; though where the statement complained of also alleges matter not covered by s. 13, it may be right to leave the whole statement of claim intact.[61]

By s. 13(3), a person stands convicted of an offence only if there is against him a subsisting conviction of the offence by or before a court in the United Kingdom or a court martial there or elsewhere.

### 9.14.4  Sections 11–13: general considerations

Where any document is admissible to identify the facts upon which a conviction, finding or adjudication is based, a certified or authenticated copy of such document shall be admissible in evidence, and shall be taken to be a true copy, unless the contrary is shown (ss. 11(4), 12(4), 13(4)).

By RSC, Ord. 18, r. 7A, in an action tried with pleadings, a party who wishes to rely on evidence pursuant to s. 11 or s. 12 must plead his intention, specifying the fact relied upon, and must indicate the issue in the case to which it is relevant. The rule does not apply to evidence admissible under s.13, presumably because the evidence is not open to challenge except to deny that there is a subsisting conviction. There would appear to be no reason why such evidence should not be pleaded, in view of its effect in law.

### 9.15  Reversal of the rule in criminal cases

The Police and Criminal Evidence Act 1984, introduced provisions similar to those of s. 11 of the Civil Evidence Act 1968, applicable to criminal proceedings. Section 74 of the 1984

---

[60]   *Sutton* v *Sutton* [1970] 1 WLR 183. For the use of transcripts of previous matrimonial proceedings, see Practice Direction of 13 June 1969 [1969] 1 WLR 1192.

[61]   *Levene* v *Roxhan and Others* (CA) [1970] 1 WLR 1322.

Act makes convictions admissible for the purpose of proving that the person convicted of an offence committed that offence. Section 75(4) limits this to subsisting convictions. Although the Act is silent on the point, it would seem safe to assume that a conviction quashed on appeal or the subject of a free pardon would not be subsisting, but that the mere fact that an appeal is pending would not affect the subsistence of the conviction; cf. *Re Raphael, Raphael* v *d'Antin and Another* [1973] 1 WLR 998 and see 9.14.1, ante. For the purpose of criminal proceedings, we must distinguish two different types of case: those in which a conviction of a person other than the defendant is relevant; and those in which a conviction of the defendant is relevant. These cases are provided for separately by s. 74.

### 9.15.1  Persons other than the defendant

As to these persons, s. 74 provides:

(1)  In any proceedings the fact that a person other than the accused has been convicted of an offence by or before any court in the United Kingdom or by a Service court outside the United Kingdom shall be admissible in evidence for the purpose of proving, where to do so is relevant to any issue in those proceedings, that that person committed that offence, whether or not any other evidence of his having committed that offence is given.

(2)  In any proceedings in which by virtue of this section a person other than the accused is proved to have been convicted of an offence by or before any court in the United Kingdom or by a Service court outside the United Kingdom, he shall be taken to have committed that offence unless the contrary is proved.

As with s. 11 of the Civil Evidence Act 1968 in civil cases, these provisions have the effect of abrogating the rule in *Hollington* v *Hewthorn*, so that not only is the conviction admissible evidence to prove that the person convicted committed the offence, but that person is also taken to have committed the offence unless the contrary is proved. Disproof of the commission of offences in criminal cases is considered in 9.15.3 below.

The section portends the demise of one of the best known rules of the criminal law, namely that which provided that on a charge of handling stolen goods, the conviction of the thief was inadmissible to show that the goods were stolen. The conviction of the thief is now admissible for that very purpose, and establishes the fact unless the contrary is proved. Similarly, in a prosecution for assisting offenders, contrary to s. 4 of the Criminal Law Act 1967, the conviction of the principal offender may be proved as evidence that the person assisted had committed an arrestable offence. This evidence, too would have been inadmissible at common law. In certain cases, it may be envisaged that these provisions may also be useful to the defence. There would now surely be no objection to a defendant proving that another person not being tried on the same occasion was convicted of the offence with which the defendant is now charged, in a case where the commission of the offence by the other was relevant to the issue of guilt or innocence of the defendant now being tried.

### 9.15.2  The defendant

As to the defendant, the section provides:

(3)   In any proceedings where evidence is admissible of the fact that the accused has committed an offence, in so far as that evidence is relevant to any matter in issue in the proceedings for a reason other than a tendency to show in the accused a disposition to commit the kind of offence with which he is charged, if the accused is proved to have been convicted of the offence—

(*a*)   by or before any court in the United Kingdom; or

(*b*)   by a Service court outside the United Kingdom,

he shall be taken to have committed that offence unless the contrary is proved.

It is submitted that this subsection is unfortunately worded. The section is not, apparently, intended to alter the law governing the admissibility of character evidence, but only to provide for proof of convictions to establish, where relevant to do so, that the defendant committed the offences of which he was convicted. This being so, it is difficult to understand the phrase 'for a reason other than a tendency to show in the accused a disposition to commit the kind of offence with which he is charged'. Character evidence in whatever form would anyway be inadmissible for this purpose (see generally Chapters 4 and 5, ante) and the subsection is premised upon the evidence being admissible, which presumably means admissible under the general rules of evidence. Character evidence, including evidence of previous convictions, is admissible only where the previous conviction is itself a fact in issue in the case, or where it is for some reason relevant to prove guilt as charged, for example as similar-fact evidence, or relevant to the credit of the defendant where the defendant has lost the shield provided by s. 1(*f*)of the Criminal Evidence Act 1898. What the section does is to permit the proof of a conviction to stand as evidence that the defendant did commit an offence relevant and properly admissible, such as one relied upon by the prosecution as similar-fact evidence. By rendering the conviction admissible evidence of this fact, and by placing the burden of disproving commission of the offence on the defendant, Parliament has probably simplified the task of jurors in cases where the defendant denies commission of the similar-fact offences despite a conviction, and laid to rest the doubts expressed in *R* v *Shepherd and Shepherd* (1980) 71 Cr App R 121, as to the admissibility of the fact of conviction in similar-fact cases: see 5.7, ante. Section 74(3) also provides a means of proof in cases where the commission of a previous offence is itself a fact in issue in the case, or where the commission of an offence is expressly made admissible by statute, for example under s. 27 (3) of the Theft Act 1968.

It is unfortunate, too, that the section does not make clear whether or not it is intended to affect the admissibility of the facts on which a conviction is based. As we saw in Chapters 4 and 5, whether details of the underlying facts are admissible depends upon the issue to which the conviction is relevant. If it is relevant only to credit, the fact of conviction alone will be admissible, whereas if it is relevant to guilt as charged, the detail of the underlying facts will most probably be the reason why the evidence is relevant. It must be assumed that the subsection is not intended to affect this position. Section 75 of the Act provides a means of proof of the underlying facts,which is considered in 9.15.4, post, but s. 75 does not purport to affect the rules governing the admissibility of the underlying facts.

### 9.15.3   *Disproof of convictions*
As under s. 11 of the Civil Evidence Act 1968, a party who wishes to prove that a convicted

person did not commit the offence of which he was convicted bears the burden of so proving. As we have seen (Chapter 3 and 3.4.2, ante) the defence may be called upon to bear the legal burden of proof on individual issues in a criminal case, without in any way altering the overall burden of proving guilt as charged, which lies on the prosecution throughout. Consistently with the rule in other instances where this occurs, it should be held that the standard of proof to be required of the defence on this issue is not more than that on a preponderance of probabilities: see *R* v *Carr-Briant* [1943] KB 607, 610 and 3.7.2, ante.

However, as with the corresponding provision of s. 11 of the Civil Evidence Act 1968, the section fails to address the question of the weight to be attached to the conviction, once proved. The arguments advanced in this as yet unresolved controversy in *Taylor v Taylor* [1970] 1 WLR 1148, *Stupple* v *Royal Insurance Co. Ltd* [1971] 1 QB 50 and *Hunter* v *Chief Constable of the West Midlands and Another* [1982] AC 529 were fully rehearsed in 9.14.1 and need not be repeated. But it may be that the courts will feel that less weight should be accorded to a conviction in a criminal case, and that the approach of Buckley LJ in *Stupple* should be preferred to that of Lord Denning MR. If so, this will not be because the weight to be accorded to the verdict or finding of a previous criminal court should be less in a later criminal court than in a later civil court, but because of the proper reluctance of criminal courts to put any fact of consequence to the issue of guilt effectively beyond disproof by the defendant. How the courts will in fact deal with the problem remains to be seen. But it should not be forgotten that the conviction will play a different role in the scheme of things in a criminal case than in a civil case, because of the overall burden and standard of proof. It is submitted that it would be proper to direct the jury that, although the defendant is to be taken to have committed the offence in question unless he proves the contrary, proof of that previous conviction should be regarded as evidence of guilt only if the jury feel sure that that is the right conclusion to reach on the basis of all the evidence in the case. It would seem wrong to direct the jury that the commission of the previous offence, or the proof of the previous conviction, carry any especial weight in themselves.

### 9.15.4   *Proof of underlying facts*
Section 75 of the Police and Criminal Evidence Act 1984, provides as follows for the proof of the facts on which a conviction was based:

(1)   Where evidence that a person has been convicted of an offence is admissible by virtue of s. 74 above, then without prejudice to the reception of any other admissible evidence for the purpose of identifying the facts on which the conviction was based—

(*a*)   the contents of any document which is admissible as evidence of the conviction; and
(*b*)   the contents of the information, complaint, indictment or charge-sheet on which the person in question was convicted,

shall be admissible in evidence for that purpose.

Section 75 (2) provides for the admissibility of properly authenticated copies of the documents admissible as proof by virtue of s. 75(1). The phrase 'the contents of any document which is admissible as evidence of the conviction' includes the contents of a certificate of conviction, which by virtue of s. 73(1) is, together with proof of the identity of the person who was convicted as the person now before the court, evidence of the conviction.

For the reason given above, it is to be assumed that this section is not intended to affect the rules governing the admissibility of the underlying facts of a previous offence. It will be noted that the detail of the facts which could be proved by means of evidence admissible under s. 75(1) would in all probability be insufficient to provide the detail necessary for proof of previous convictions as similar-fact evidence, in which cases the calling of witnesses to the previous offences will still be necessary, but will suffice for cases where the commission of the previous offence is a fact in issue or is relevant to guilt for a purpose unconnected with the detail of the offence, for example where proof of the theft of stolen goods is needed but the exact circumstances of the theft are irrelevant. Frequently, the documents made admissible by this section may assist the court in determining whether the previous conviction is relevant or admissible, or perhaps whether its probative value may be substantially outweighed by its potential for prejudice to the defendant.

### 9.15.5 *Sections 73–75: general considerations*
Probably because of the difficulty of proving the effect and facts of foreign convictions, the Act limits its provisions to convictions of courts in the United Kingdom and of service courts elsewhere.

The Act does not require notice to be given of an intention to adduce evidence of previous convictions under s. 74. Ordinarily, the prosecution are, in any event, bound to disclose their evidence in advance of trial, where the trial is to be on indictment. But no provision is made for summary trial, or cases where the defence propose to make use of the section. There is no equivalent of the pleading requirement in civil cases.

By s. 73(1) of the Act, the conviction itself may be proved by a combination of two matters; firstly, a certificate of conviction as defined in the subsection; secondly, proof that the person named in the certificate is the person now before the court and alleged to be the person named therein. This latter requirement is easily overlooked. A certificate proves only that someone of the name stated was convicted of an offence; it must be proved, if disputed, by the evidence of a witness who was present, that the person named in the certificate and the person present in court are one and the same.

Section 74(4) provides that nothing in the section is intended to prejudice the admissibility of any conviction admissible apart from the section, or any enactment which makes a conviction conclusive evidence of any fact.

## 9.16 Questions for discussion

### 9.16.1 *R* v *Coke; R* v *Littleton*
1   What primary facts must be proved as a basis for the expert testimony to be given by: (a) Mr Hale; (b) Dr Vesey; (c) Dr Espinasse? What witnesses should be called to prove these primary facts?

2   Frame a series of questions designed to adduce the evidence in chief of Mr Hale for the prosecution. How would you make use of the chart which he has prepared?

3   Assume that you act for Coke, and that your handwriting expert has advised you that Mr Hale's conclusion can be attacked because a leading work on the scientific examination of documents suggests that he had insufficient known samples of Coke's handwriting to enable a valid comparison to be made. How would you cross-examine Mr Hale, and how would the leading work be treated by the court?

### 9.16.2   *Blackstone* v *Coke*

1   What rules of pre-trial disclosure of expert testimony govern the proposed testimony of Mr Hale, Dr Vesey and Dr Espinasse, if they are to be called on behalf of the plaintiff?

2   If Coke is convicted at his criminal trial of raping Margaret, what use may Margaret make of that conviction as evidence in her action against Coke?

3   Would Coke be entitled to seek to prove that, despite the conviction, he was not guilty of the rape? What proof would be required for this?

4   How would Margaret go about proving the conviction and the facts on which it was based?

5   What difference, if any, would it make if, at the time of trial in the civil action, Coke's conviction was the subject of a pending appeal to the Court of Appeal, Criminal Division?

# 10 Public Policy and Privilege

## 10.1 Public policy and privilege contrasted

One of the major principles recognised by the law in the conduct of litigation is that of disclosure of evidence. By this expression is meant that the parties should disclose, to each other and for the purposes of the proceedings,[1] any and all evidence, relevant to the issues in those proceedings, which is or has been in their possession, custody and power. The object of the principle is simply that all such relevant evidence in the case should be available to be inspected by all parties, and that the parties should be free to place before the court any evidence which will assist it in determining the truth and in doing justice between the parties. The idea of inspection of evidence in the possession of another party is primarily of importance in the field of documentary and real evidence, and most of the battles in the field of public policy and privilege have been fought in relation to such evidence. But the principle of disclosure and its object of enabling the parties to place before the court all relevant and admissible evidence, applies to evidence in whatever form, and the rules of privilege in particular are of considerable significance in relation to certain kinds of oral evidence.

The principle has as a necessary corollary the rule that no party should be entitled to frustrate or hinder the doing of justice in any proceedings by withholding from his opponent or from the court evidence which is relevant and admissible for that purpose. But this cannot be an absolute rule. It may be overridden by some important public interest that certain evidence should not be disclosed to a party because of the likelihood of danger to the national interest or of impairment of the working of some aspect of the public service. In such a case, as Lord Reid pointed out in *Conway* v *Rimmer and Another* (HL) [1968] AC 910, 940, the public interest in the doing of justice as between the parties to litigation has to be balanced against a different but equally demanding public interest:

> It is universally recognised that here there are two kinds of public interest which may clash. There is the public interest that harm shall not be done to the nation or the public service by disclosure of certain documents, and there is the public interest that the administration of justice shall not be frustrated by the withholding of documents which must be produced if justice is to be done. There are many cases where the nature of the injury which would or might be done to the nation or the public service is of so grave a character that no other interest, public or private, can be allowed to prevail over it.

---

[1]   The court will not countenance the abuse of its process, which results from the improper use of evidence ordered to be disclosed, i.e. the use of such evidence for purposes other than the proper conduct of the instant proceedings: *Riddick* v *Thames Board Mills Ltd* (CA) [1977] QB 881; *Church of Scientology* v *DHSS* (CA) [1979] 1 WLR 723; *Home Office* v *Harman* [1983] AC 280.

The result of such considerations may be that facts of undoubted relevance to proceedings, which may indeed sometimes be potentially conclusive of such proceedings, will not be permitted to be proved. Such facts are said to be excluded by public policy. Even outside this sphere, the rule of disclosure has never been an absolute one. The law recognises that other considerations may enter the field, even where they appear to be of a purely private nature. Although most private interests must bow to the requirement of a fair and open trial, some are important enough to override it. Certain rules may prevent evidence being given, for example the rule that no person should be compelled to divulge what has passed between him and his legal advisers in the course of seeking and giving legal advice. Evidence which enjoys a measure of protection for a reason of this kind is said to be privileged. Again, evidence of undoubted relevance, and sometimes potentially conclusive evidence, may be withheld, and the interests of other parties are affected accordingly. Where a privilege is claimed and upheld, no adverse inference may be drawn by the tribunal of fact against the person claiming the privilege, based upon that party's refusal to give or disclose the privileged evidence.[2] The privileges recognised by English law are few and limited. The privileges against self-incrimination and compelled disclosure of confidential communications between lawyer and client are recognised generally in common-law jurisdictions, including England. But in other respects, English law maintains an illiberal attitude to confidential communications. Parliament, it is true, recently created for the first time a limited privilege for journalists with respect to their sources of information (Contempt of Court Act 1981, s. 10: see 10.11, post). But it has also abolished entirely the privilege against compelled matrimonial communications (Police and Criminal Evidence Act 1984, s. 80(9)). The law has failed to accord recognition to other privileges which American common law has always upheld, for example the privileges against compelled disclosure of confidential communications between doctor or psychotherapist and patient, or priest and penitent.

The fact that evidence which is relevant[3] and otherwise admissible may be excluded by public policy or privilege, lends to the two subjects of this chapter an appearance of similarity which is misleading. The rules and their operation are quite distinct, and any superficial identity of result is more than outweighed by substantial and far-reaching differences.[4] The principal differences are worth considering in a little detail before the individual rules themselves are examined.

### 10.1.1 Possibility of waiver

Private privilege has always been a rule against compulsion, and has never prevented the voluntary disclosure or giving of privileged evidence by a person entitled to insist on the privilege. A person who voluntarily discloses in such circumstances is said to waive his privilege. Privilege may, according to the circumstances in which it arises, apply to evidence in the possession of, or capable of being given by, a party to proceedings, or any witness in the proceedings. The privilege is personal to that party or witness, and he alone can waive it.[5] Conversely, the onus of asserting the privilege also rests on the party or

---

[2]   *Wentworth* v *Lloyd* (HL) (1864) 10 HL Cas 589.
[3]   If evidence is not relevant then no question of public policy or privilege will arise: *R* v *Cheltenham Justices, ex parte Secretary of State for Trade* (DC) [1977] 1 WLR 95.
[4]   The distinction is not assisted by the use of the misleading term 'Crown privilege' to describe some aspects of public policy. For criticism of this usage, see *Rogers* v *Home Secretary; Gaming Board for Great Britain* v *Rogers* (HL) [1973] AC 388 per Lord Reid at 400 and Lord Pearson at 406.
[5]   It seems to follow, and has been held, that a party cannot in general found an appeal on the upholding or rejection of a privilege attaching to his witness: *R* v *Kinglake* (1870) 22 LT 335.

witness entitled to it, and evidence disclosed or given other than under unlawful compulsion will be admissible for all purposes, even though privilege might with advice or diligence have been asserted in respect of it.[6]

When a privilege is waived, the result is that the evidence may be given by any party, and is treated like any other evidence in the case. A party may not waive privilege with respect to part of a communication, which he regards as favourable and wishes to adduce in evidence, and claim to maintain the privilege with respect to other parts which he would prefer to withhold, unless the different parts are clearly and readily severable and deal with quite different subjects. In *Great Atlantic Insurance Co* v *Home Insurance Co. and Others* [1981] 2 All ER 485, the Court of Appeal held that by reading into the record two paragraphs of a memorandum received by the plaintiffs from their American attorneys, the whole of which was clearly privileged, counsel for the plaintiffs had waived any privilege in the whole document, since both the part read and the parts withheld dealt with the same subject-matter. Templeman LJ referred to *Churton* v *Frewen* (1865) 2 Drew & Sm 390, in which the court refused disclosure of a privileged report which contained extracts from and references to documents and records kept in a public registry, these latter not being privileged. Although this was a case in which it was sought to obtain disclosure of, rather than withhold a part, the reasoning is equally applicable to both situations. The court said (ibid at 394) that:

> . . . it would be very dangerous, and trench very much upon the principle which protects the report itself, if that were permitted; for it would be hardly possible to seal up and effectually protect from inspection those parts which constitute the report, and which it is admitted there is no right to see. Such a report would most probably (indeed, from its nature, almost necessarily) be not merely a collection of extracts from and copies of ancient records, with a distinct and separate report referring to them; but the extracts and copies would be so interspersed with . . . observations and comments . . . as to render it quite impossible to separate the different portions.

For this reason, it is incumbent on a party to consider carefully before making use of any part of a privileged document or other communication; the remainder should be scrutinised with great care. It is to be noted that in *Great Atlantic*, the plaintiffs did not intend any waiver. Indeed, counsel had mistakenly thought that he had read the whole document into the record. But it is actual disclosure, and not intent, which governs whether a waiver has occurred.

On the other hand, although the waiver operates with respect to the entirety of the communication, it does not extend beyond the transaction dealt with in the communication and cannot be used to defeat privilege in unrelated communications. What is unrelated must be decided by the court as a question of fact in each case.[7]

An objection made on the ground of public policy may be made by any person, and in many cases a governmental entity makes the objection, even though not a party to the case, by means of intervention. The court may even take the objection of its own motion. Because of the nature of the public policy objection, it has been doubted whether it can ever be waived, though the better view would seem to be that it depends on the nature of

---

[6]  See, e.g., *R* v *Noel* (CCA) [1914] 3 KB 848.

[7]  See, e.g., *General Accident Fire and Life Assurance Corp. Ltd and Others* v *Tanter and Others* [1984] 1 All ER 35.

the document. In *Rogers* v *Home Secretary; Gaming Board for Great Britain* v *Rogers*[8]
Lord Simon said:

> It is true that the public interest which demands that evidence be withheld has to be
> weighed against the public interest in the administration of justice that courts should
> have the fullest possible access to all relevant material . . .; but once the former public
> interest is held to outweigh the latter, the evidence cannot in any circumstances be
> admitted. It is not a privilege which may be waived — by the Crown . . . or by anyone
> else.

However, in *Alfred Crompton Amusement Machines Ltd* v *Customs and Excise
Commissioners (No. 2)* [1974] AC 405, 434 Lord Cross indicated that if a person or party
(such as an informer) for whose benefit the objection was made volunteered to testify or
disclose the evidence, then a waiver could be permitted.

The Court of Appeal in *Hehir* v *Commissioner of Police of the Metropolis* [1982] 1 WLR
715, was faced with this conflict of authority. The plaintiff was arrested and charged with a
minor offence under the Vagrancy Act 1824, which was subsequently dismissed. He filed
suit against the Commissioner, claiming damages for alleged false imprisonment and
malicious prosecution on the part of the police officers involved. The plaintiff had made a
statement for the purposes of a police inquiry conducted under s. 49 of the Police Act
1964. All such statements were protected from disclosure because of the need for candid,
confidential statements to be made by police officers and others.[9] At trial, counsel for the
Commissioner sought to cross-examine the plaintiff on his statement, and the plaintiff
objected. A two-judge Court of Appeal, on an interlocutory appeal, reluctantly upheld the
plaintiff's objection. Since the whole of the material compiled during the s. 49 inquiry was
subject to immunity from disclosure in the public interest, so as to encourage future
candour, the Commissioner was not entitled to waive the immunity as to any part, even
for the purpose of cross-examining the plaintiff. Lawton and Brightman LJJ were
unanimous in holding that waiver could not be permitted on the facts presented, though
Brightman LJ left open for future decision the question whether public policy immunity
might not in certain circumstances be waived.

Lord Denning MR has said on more than one occasion that waiver might be permitted
in certain cases. In *Campbell* v *Tameside MBC*[10] he indicated disapproval of the decision in
*Hehir* and added:

> I know that in the days of the old Crown Privilege it was often said that it could not be
> waived. That is still correct when the documents are in the vital category spoken of by
> Lord Reid in *Conway* v *Rimmer* [1968] AC 910 at 940. This category includes all those
> documents which must be kept top secret because the disclosure of them would be
> injurious to national defence or to diplomatic relations or the detection of crime (as the
> names of informers). But not where the documents come within Lord Reid's lower

---

[8]  [1973] AC 388, 407. In *Air Canada and Others* v *Secretary of State for Trade and Another (No. 2)*
[1983] 2 AC 394, 436 Lord Fraser, apparently obiter, seemed to agree with Lord Simon's view that
waiver is precluded in all cases.

[9]  See *Neilson* v *Laugharne* [1981] QB 736 and 10.5, post.

[10]  [1982] QB 1065, where Lord Denning MR was plainly speaking obiter, as he was on the same
subject in *Neilson* v *Laugharne* [1981] QB 736, 747. See also Lord Denning's remarks dissenting in the
Court of Appeal in *Burmah Oil Co. Ltd* v *Bank of England* [1979] 1 WLR 473 at 487.

category. This category includes documents which are kept confidential in order that subordinates should be frank and candid in their reports, or for any other good reason. In those cases, the privilege can be waived by the maker and recipients of the confidential document.

It is submitted that Lord Denning's obiter dicta should be followed as a sensible way of balancing competing interests. Not every document capable of attracting public policy immunity must necessarily be witheld in every case, though no doubt the governmental entity most responsible for the confidential evidence would have to consent. The purported waiver or desire to waive of others should be held insufficient in the absence of such agreement by the responsible authority.

### 10.1.2 Use of secondary evidence

Where facts are excluded by public policy, not only are the documents which are the immediate subject of the exclusion affected, but the result is that the contents of such documents cannot be proved in evidence by secondary means. This excludes copies of such documents, oral evidence of their contents and even their use by a witness to refresh his memory.[11]

On the other hand, privilege attaches only to an original document or communication as such and although secondary evidence of such documents or communications is, in law, confidential, it is nonetheless admissible to prove the facts contained therein. It follows, therefore, that an opponent may prove facts contained in a privileged document by producing a copy of the document or by adducing oral evidence of its contents.[12] Thus, in *Calcraft* v *Guest* (CA) [1889] 1 QB 759, the defendant was held to be entitled to put in evidence copies of proofs of evidence of witnesses of the plaintiff's predecessor in title, relating to a previous action, the originals of these documents (which were plainly privileged under the legal professional privilege rule) having been returned to the plaintiff. The privilege attached only to the original, and did not inhibit the proof of the contents by other means, even though the plaintiff could not be compelled to produce the original or to disclose it to the defendant. In *Rumping* v *DPP* [1964] AC 814, the House of Lords held that a letter written by the defendant to his wife, which amounted to a confession to the murder with which he was charged, could be put in evidence by the prosecution, it having been handed over to the police by a person to whom it had been entrusted for posting. The letter would have been privileged, had it reached the wife's hands, as a matrimonial communication, and the decision illustrates an even wider rule than that in *Calcraft* v *Guest*, namely that privilege attaching to the original can be lost by its actual disclosure, even where no waiver is intended.

The lesson to be learnt from these examples is that privilege must be jealously guarded: it ceases to exist if waived or lost, and is rendered impotent by copying unless prompt

---

[11]   See *Gain* v *Gain* [1961] 1 WLR 1469. Any course which expressly or by necessary implication involves the revelation of the contents seems to be prohibited.

[12]   In accordance with the usual rule (see 1.6, ante, and *R* v *Sang* (HL) [1980] AC 402), the means by which the secondary evidence is obtained, even if improper or illegal, is irrelevant to the question of its admissibility. But an injunction will be granted to restore to proper possession privileged or confidential documents, and to restrain their use by persons not entitled to have them, if proceedings are brought for this purpose: *Lord Ashburton* v *Pape* (CA) [1913] 2 Ch 469. However, no injunction will be granted to restrain the use of relevant evidence by the Crown in a public prosecution: *Butler* v *Board of Trade* [1971] Ch 680. See 1.6.2, ante.

action can be taken to restrain the copier. The lesson was learnt the hard way in *R* v *Tompkins* (1977) 67 Cr App R 181, where, the defendant having given certain evidence in chief, there was put to him during cross-examination a note which he had earlier written to his counsel which contradicted his evidence. The contents of the note were not read out, but on seeing it, the defendant admitted that he had not told the truth in chief and altered his evidence. He was subsequently convicted. The Court of Appeal rejected an argument that the prosecution had not been entitled to make use of the note as, in effect, a previous inconsistent statement. Although originally privileged, as a communication between client and legal adviser, its loss entitled the prosecution to make use of it, once it was in their hands. Ormrod LJ observed, perhaps a little unkindly, that it would require 'a remarkable exercise in moral philosophy' to conclude that perjury should not be exposed where such means came to hand.

### 10.1.3 Taking the objection

Where the Crown is a party to proceedings and proposes to withhold documentary evidence on the ground of public policy, the documents concerned can be included in the part of the list of documents that deals with the items that are subject to an objection to production. The matter will then be dealt with on a summons for discovery. Where the Crown is not a party, and in cases where the process of discovery is not available,[13] the objection should be taken at trial, after notice. In any event, the objection should be supported by evidence, usually given by affidavit, sworn by the relevant minister or a subordinate of sufficient authority and responsibility.[14] The court has power to regulate the manner in which the objection can be made, and may require to be satisfied by further evidence. However, a certificate signed by the minister is habitually accepted, provided that, like an affidavit, it deals with the material matters. The requirements are that the identity and nature of the documents are described with sufficient particularity, that the grounds of the objection are stated and that the affidavit or certificate should state that the maker has personally examined the documents in question, before reaching the conclusion that they should be withheld in the public interest.[15]

The claim on the ground of public policy may legitimately be made either on a 'contents basis' or a 'class basis', that is to say, the objection may relate to specific facts contained in specific documents, or to the entirety of a certain class of documents because of their collective character. The court is more likely to be sympathetic if an objection is based on the specific contents of a document than if it is based only on the document's classification, especially where the class appears to the court to consist of 'routine communications'.[16]

A claim to privilege relating to documentary evidence must be made in the list of documents (RSC, Ord. 24, r. 5(2)), and argued on a summons for discovery, if it relates to documents within the possession or power of the party claiming privilege. In many cases, however, the claim relates solely to oral evidence, and is made at trial in the course of

---

[13]  Discovery is not available in criminal cases, and is not invariably used in actions in the county courts: see RSC, Ord. 24; CCR, Ord. 14. Discovery may be ordered by an industrial tribunal when appropriate. For cases to which the Crown is a party see the Crown Proceedings Act 1947, s. 28. See also RSC, Ord. 24, r. 15.

[14]  *Alfred Crompton Amusement Machines Ltd* v *Commissioners of Customs & Excise (No. 2)* (CA) [1972] 2 QB 102. The point was not considered in the House of Lords.

[15]  See *Re Grosvenor Hotel, London (No. 2)* (CA) [1965] Ch 1210 per Lord Denning MR at 1244.

[16]  See the comments of Lord Reid in *Conway* v *Rimmer and Another* (HL) [1968] AC 910 at 940–1 and 10.4.1 post.

evidence, at the moment when a question is asked to which objection is taken. This course is appropriate, for example, when the privilege claimed is that against self-incrimination, and generally where the privilege is that of a witness, rather than a party. The judge must then rule on the matter before allowing the evidence to proceed. In a criminal case, he should do so in the absence of the jury, and may do so in camera if necessary, for example to test a claim to the privilege against self-incrimination. The ruling may require evidence to support or resist the claim, or legal argument or both.

## A: PUBLIC POLICY

### 10.2   Introduction: the 'affairs of state' cases

Until the decision in *Rogers* v *Home Secretary; Gaming Board for Great Britain* v *Rogers* [1973] AC 388, the expression 'Crown Privilege' was employed to denote the cases in which evidence might be excluded on the ground that an important public interest outweighed the interest of the court and the parties in having access to all relevant evidence. The term was misleading for three reasons, and should no longer be used. Firstly, the Crown need not be the party raising the objection, and need not be, and often is not a party to the case. Secondly, the rule now applies to information in the possession of organs of local, as well as central government and does not have to relate to matters of high national concern, such as affairs of state. Thirdly, for the reasons given above, it is not a privilege in the true sense of that word. The phrase 'public-policy immunity' or some variation thereof is now generally substituted as a name for the rule.

However, the old term 'Crown Privilege' serves to call to mind that much of the law relating to public-policy immunity was developed by the courts in cases concerned with the highest affairs of state, such as national security, state secrets in time of war and matters of great diplomatic importance. The obviously high public interest in conserving the confidentiality of evidence touching on such matters had important consequences in the rules of evidence which the courts developed. Thus, it was at one time held that the court could not question the certificate given by the competent minister, stating that evidence must be withheld in the national interest. The supposed rule that public-policy immunity cannot be waived, which has still not finally been confirmed or rejected (10.1.1, ante) derives from the same concern. The public interest in the administration of justice could not compete with such clearly higher public interests.

In *Asiatic Petroleum Co. Ltd* v *Anglo-Persian Oil Co. Ltd* [1916] 1 KB 822, the court refused to permit disclosure of documents which would have revealed details of military plans during the First World War. And in the celebrated case of *Duncan* v *Cammell Laird & Co Ltd*[17] the plaintiff in an action for damages for personal injury, which arose from his work on the submarine *Thetis*, was refused discovery of the plans and specifications of the submarine for similar reasons of policy. In this case, the First Lord of the Admiralty, on behalf of the government, ordered the defendants to object to the disclosure of the requested documents.

If public-policy immunity was originally confined to such high affairs of state, it is certain that it is no longer so confined, and lesser areas of public interest have been identified, some of which must give way to the public interest in the administration of

---

[17]   (HL) [1942] AC 624. Until a later House of Lords in *Conway* v *Rimmer* [1968] AC 910, departed from it, *Duncan* v *Cammell Laird & Co. Ltd* was the leading authority. None of the strictures cast on it in *Conway* v *Rimmer* appear to cast doubt on the correctness of the decision in *Duncan* on its own facts.

justice which requires disclosure.[18] The law of public-policy immunity now develops in three well-established categories, which are dealt with in detail in 10.5, 10.6 and 10.7, post. These are: (a) governmental and administrative matters (a vast area in which the 'affairs of state' cases are now included); (b) cases involving information given for the detection of crime and other necessary public purposes; and (c) cases involving other confidential information.[19]

The public policy referred to in connection with public-policy immunity is that of the United Kingdom. The law does not recognise 'foreign state privilege'.[20]

It remains to add one more observation about the 'affairs of state' cases. There is still a school of thought that certain documents of high importance should never be disclosed in litigation. An objection to disclosure of documents relating to such matters should almost always be allowed, even on a class basis. Such documents relate to the workings of inner government, the formulation of national policy and similarly high matters. They were dealt with by Lord Reid in his speech in *Conway* v *Rimmer* [1968] AC 910, 952, as follows:

> I do not doubt that there are certain classes of documents which ought not to be disclosed whatever their content may be. Virtually everyone agrees that cabinet minutes and the like ought not to be disclosed until such time as they are only of historical interest.

The most important reason for this was that:

> . . . such disclosure would create or fan ill-informed or captious public or political criticism. The business of government is difficult enough as it is, and no government could contemplate with equanimity the inner workings of the government machine being exposed to the gaze of those ready to criticise without adequate knowledge of the background and perhaps with some axe to grind.

In Lord Reid's view, this would apply to:

> . . . all documents concerned with policy making within departments including, it may be, minutes and the like by quite junior officials and correspondence with outside bodies.

And significantly, Lord Reid added:

> Further it may be that deliberations about a particular case require protection as much as deliberations about policy.

Lord Reid's sentiments were echoed in respect of documents such as cabinet minutes, dispatches from ambassadors and communications between departmental heads, by the

---

[18]   See, e.g., *Campbell* v *Tameside MBC* [1982] QB 1065.
[19]   The better view is probably that public policy develops within these categories, rather than that new categories can be recognised by the courts. In *Fender* v *St John-Mildmay* (HL) [1938] AC 1, Lord Atkin at 10 and Lord Thankerton at 23 saw any extension of the categories as a matter for Parliament, not the courts. The contrary view of Lord Hailsham of St Marylebone expressed in *D* v *NSPCC* (HL) 1978] AC 171 at 230, that the courts may extend the categories as conditions change, has not received universal agreement. However, given the scope for expanding the existing categories, the point may be only of academic interest.
[20]   See *Buttes Gas and Oil Co.* v *Hammer and Others (No. 3)* (CA) [1981] QB 223. The decision of the House of Lords on the substantive issues ([1982] AC 888) rendered the discovery dispute moot, and it was not considered by the House.

other members of the House.[21] For similar reasons the conduct of military affairs,[22] the government's activities in the administration of colonies,[23] the good relations of the United Kingdom with foreign powers[24] and other similar affairs of state in the strictest sense, have generally been protected against disclosure.[25]

However, since the House of Lords in *Conway v Rimmer* was expressly abrogating the rule in the older cases, including *Duncan v Cammell Laird & Co Ltd*, that the minister's certificate could not be questioned by the court, it would seem that no class of documents should be excluded automatically. More recently, in *Burmah Oil Co. Ltd v Bank of England* [1980] AC 1090, 1134, a case in which the House of Lords considered memoranda of meetings attended by government ministers and other documents which would have revealed the inner workings of high-level government, Lord Keith of Kinkel re-stated the position in, it is submitted, a more satisfactory way:

> In my opinion, it would be going too far to lay down that no document in any particular one of the categories mentioned [by the House of Lords in *Conway v Rimmer*] should never in any circumstances be ordered to be produced, and indeed I did not understand counsel for the Attorney-General to pitch his submission that high before this House. . . . [T]he nature of the litigation and the apparent importance to it of the documents in question may in extreme cases demand production even of the most sensitive communications at the highest level. Such a case might fortunately be unlikely to arise in this country, but in circumstances such as those of *Sankey v Whitlam* [(1978) 21 ALR 505] or *Nixon v US* [418 US 683 (1974)] . . . I do not doubt that the principles there expounded would fall to be applied. There can be discerned in modern times a trend towards more open governmental methods than were prevalent in the past. No doubt it is for Parliament and not for courts of law to say how far that trend should go. The courts are, however, concerned with the consideration that it is in the public interest that justice should be done and should be publicly recognised as having been done. This may demand, though no doubt only in a very limited number of cases, that the inner workings of government should be exposed to public gaze, and there may be some who would regard this as likely to lead, not to captious or ill-informed criticism, but to criticism calculated to improve the nature of that working as affecting the individual citizen.

Lord Scarman in the same case (ibid at 1144) thought that it would be inconsistent with *Conway v Rimmer* to hold that the court should not be permitted to consider the issue of disclosure solely because of the apparently 'high level' nature of the documents.

In *Air Canada and Others v Secretary of State for Trade and Another (No. 2)* [1983] 2 AC 394, 432, Lord Fraser of Tullybelton said, referring to the passage from Lord Reid's speech in *Conway v Rimmer* quoted above:

> The latter observation was strictly speaking obiter in *Conway v Rimmer*, where the documents in question were reports on a probationer police constable by his superiors.
> I do not think that even Cabinet minutes are completely immune from disclosure in a

---

[21] See the speeches of Lord Hodson at 973 and Lord Pearce at 987.

[22] *Beatson v Skene* (1860) 5 H & N 838; *HMS Bellerophon* (1874) 44 LJ Adm 5.

[23] *Hennessy v Wright* (DC) (1888) 21 QBD 509.

[24] *R v Governor of Brixton Prison, ex parte Soblen* (CA) [1963] 2 QB 243 at 273–4. See also *Buttes Gas & Oil Co. v Hammer and others (No.3)* (CA) [1981] 1 QB 223.

[25] See the list of examples given in Phipson, *Evidence*, 13th ed., para. 14–04. However, many of the older cases might have been decided differently if they had been heard after *Conway v Rimmer*.

case where, for example, the issue in a litigation involves serious misconduct by a Cabinet minister. Such cases have occurred in Australia (see *Sankey* v *Whitlam*) . . . and in the United States (see *Nixon* v *US*) . . . but fortunately not in the United Kingdom: see also the New Zealand case of *Environmental Defence Society Inc.* v *South Pacific Aluminium Ltd (No. 2)* [1981] 1 NZLR 153. But, while Cabinet documents do not have complete immunity, they are entitled to a high degree of protection against disclosure.

No doubt the occasion would be rare when such documents would in fact be disclosed, but the point made by Lord Fraser, and by Lords Keith and Scarman in *Burmah Oil* appears well taken. The documents which Lord Fraser was considering were such that they did 'not quite enjoy the status of Cabinet minutes, but they approach that level in that they may disclose the reasons for Cabinet decisions and the process by which the decisions were reached'. The case turned on other issues, but Lord Fraser was content to assume that normally, such documents should not be disclosed until they have become of purely historical interest.

If this be right, then the 'affairs of state' cases do not form a separate category, and differ from other cases involving governmental and administrative matters only in degree, that is to say, that the high probability that disclosure will be refused depends upon the facts of the case, the nature of the evidence itself, and not upon a rule of law.

With this in mind, we must now answer two important questions about the operation of public policy immunity in modern law. These questions are:

(a)   Are the courts able or entitled to question the assertion by the minister that documents should be withheld on the ground of public policy?

(b)   If the answer to question (a) be yes, by what criterion should the minister's claim be judged?

**10.3   May the court question the claim to withhold?**

The point of departure from the rules laid down in the 'affairs of state' cases was the decision of the House of Lords in *Conway* v *Rimmer*. The appellant had been a probationer police officer in the Cheshire Constabulary, but had been dismissed as unlikely to become an efficient police officer. During his term of service, he had been charged with, but acquitted of, theft, the allegation being that he had stolen a torch belonging to a colleague. Being dissatisfied with his treatment, he brought an action for malicious prosecution against the chief constable. At the stage of discovery, the Home Secretary claimed that certain reports, relating to the appellant's qualities as a probationer officer and to the decision to prosecute him, should be withheld on the ground of public policy. The reports were undoubtedly relevant to the action, and an interesting facet of the case was that the chief constable had no objection to their disclosure. The ground advanced by the Home Secretary was simply that the production of the documents would be 'injurious to the public interest'. With this encouragement, the House of Lords abrogated the rule developed in the older 'affairs of state' cases, and held that the courts may review and consider the claim made by the government, and were not obliged to accept it as final. The House ordered the documents in question to be produced for their inspection, and it appearing that no real harm to the administration of the Cheshire Constabulary was likely to result, but that the documents would be useful to the plaintiff in his action, their disclosure was ordered.

On the question whether the court had any power to question the view of the minister, the House acknowledged, as it had to, that the minister was far better placed than the court to assess what was in the public interest. This consideration had led an earlier House of Lords, in *Duncan* v *Cammell Laird & Co. Ltd*, to hold that the minister's certificate should be conclusive and binding on the court, so that the trial judge had no power to admit or order disclosure of documents protected, in effect, by executive decision. For a variety of reasons, the later House in *Conway* v *Rimmer* had no compunction about departing from the decision in *Duncan*. The exhaustive review of the authorities undertaken by Lords Reid and Morris of Borth-y-Gest shows that the conclusion reached in *Duncan* v *Cammell Laird & Co. Ltd* was founded in part on an erroneous belief that the law of Scotland regarded ministerial objections as conclusive, and on the related reasoning that in such a respect the law of England ought not to differ from that of Scotland. Given the correctness of the first proposition, the second would surely also be correct, but as Lord Morris was able to show, the first was incorrect. This suggested that the House need not show undue concern in refusing to follow *Duncan* v *Cammell Laird & Co. Ltd*.

Undoubtedly the most cogent reason for the decision in *Conway* v *Rimmer* was the dissatisfaction felt almost universally with the former rule, because of the ease with which it could be used to provide a blanket immunity from production for documents of no more than marginal importance to any identifiable national interest. After *Duncan* v *Cammell Laird & Co. Ltd* there had been a number of cases which had given rise to a strongly expressed judicial disquiet. In *Broome* v *Broome*[26] the minister objected to the admission in divorce proceedings of documents relating to efforts by a Service welfare organisation to reconcile the parties, on the ground that its disclosure might 'prejudice the morale of the armed forces'. The court, scathing in its impotence, commented on the lack of discernible public interest in the matter and remarked that the matter was one which properly fell under the head of private privilege and no more. In *Ellis* v *Home Office* [1953] 2 QB 135, Devlin J, faced with an objection from the Home Office to the disclosure of reports by doctors and prison officers on the mental condition of a prisoner and dealing with his assault on a fellow prisoner, who sought damages against the Home Office, referred to an 'uneasy feeling' that justice had not been done and more than an uneasy feeling that justice had not been seen to be done.

Weighing these frustrations of the courts against the undoubtedly greater competence of the minister in assessing the dictates of public interest, Lord Reid reached the following conclusion[27]:

> I would therefore propose that the House ought now to decide that courts have and are entitled to exercise a power and duty to hold a balance between the public interest, as expressed by a minister, to withhold certain documents or other evidence, and the public interest in ensuring the proper administration of justice. That does not mean that a court would reject a minister's view: full weight must be given to it in every case, and if the minister's reasons are of a character which judicial experience is not competent to weigh, then the minister's view must prevail. But experience has shown that reasons given for withholding whole classes of documents are often not of that character.

---

[26]    [1955] P 190. Much the same thing happened in *Gain* v *Gain* [1961] 1 WLR 1469 in respect of a medical report of a naval surgeon commander.
[27]    [1968] AC 910 at 952. This conclusion had been contended for in untested decisions of the Court of Appeal: see *Re Grosvenor Hotel, London (No. 2)* [1965] Ch 1210.

Lord Pearce said[28]:

> It is conceded that under the existing practice there can be no weighing of injustice in particular cases against the general public disadvantage of disclosure and its effect on candour. But it is argued that a judge, who is the only person who can properly weigh the former, is incapable of properly weighing the latter. I do not understand why he cannot do so, especially if the ministry gives some specific details of the type of document in question and some specific reasons why it is undesirable to allow production. It is a judge's constant task to weigh human behaviour and the points that tell for or against candour. He knows full well that in general a report will be less inhibited if it will never see the light of public scrutiny, and that in some cases and on some subjects this may be wholly desirable. He also knows that on many subjects this fact has little if any important effect. Against this he can consider whether the documents in question are of much or little weight in the litigation, whether their absence will result in a complete or partial denial of justice to one or other of the parties or perhaps to both, and what is the importance of the particular litigation to the parties and the public. All these are matters which should be considered if the court is to decide where the public interest lies.

### 10.4   By what criteria should claim to withhold be judged?

As the speech of Lord Reid in *Conway* v *Rimmer* makes clear, the process of weighing the competing claims to withhold and to compel disclosure is one of balancing the interests of all parties. However, even before this stage is reached, the party claiming that the documents should be disclosed must show that production of the documents is necessary for the purpose of fairly disposing of the case. Both matters must be considered. In addition, the courts have been troubled by the question of whether, and if so under what circumstances, the court should privately inspect the documents in order to make its determination. The court's approach to these questions may vary as between so-called 'class claims' and 'contents claims'.

#### 10.4.1   'Class' versus 'Contents' claims
A class claim is a claim to withhold all documents falling within a specifically described class, for example minutes of Cabinet meetings, or all documents pertaining to an inquiry under s. 49 of the Police Act 1964. In this kind of claim, the actual contents of the documents are irrelevant, and the claim is based on an invariable need for confidentiality of documents of the kind described in the claim. The courts have regarded class claims relatively unfavourably, because of the possibility of a blanket attempt to protect documents, many of which may be of a purely routine nature.

   A contents claim is based on the contents of an individual document, and is more favourably regarded because of the more specific justification provided to the court. In *Conway* v *Rimmer*,[29] Lord Reid said that in the case of a contents claim, the court would comparatively rarely be disposed to dissent from the view taken by the government,

---

[28]   Ibid at 987. The 'candour' argument in favour of withholding documents has never recovered from the blows dealt to it in *Conway* v *Rimmer*, and is demonstrably less valid than the similar, but distinct, argument in relation to informers; but see 10.4.1, post.

[29]   [1968] AC 910, 943. See also the speech of Lord Upjohn, ibid at 933.

because the responsible minister must usually be more competent than the court to assess the possible harm to the public interest that might result from disclosure. In the case of a class claim, it is more practicable for the court to form a judgment as to the cogency of the minister's claim.

The main justification for class claims was once the need to promote candour in those who wrote reports. It was suggested that, if it became known that confidential reports might be disclosed for the purposes of private litigation, the elements of frankness and candour in their preparation might be lost. However, in more recent cases, the courts have declined to hold that responsible public servants would forbear to be candid merely because of the possibility of some future disclosure. In *Science Research Council v Nassé* [1980] AC 1028, 1070, Lord Salmon rejected the argument entirely. In the same case, Lord Fraser (ibid at 1081) thought that the concern to prevent disclosure was not a matter of public policy at all, but a private interest of the individuals who prepared the documents, which must yield to the public interest in favour of disclosure. Subsequent cases appear to have held specifically that possible loss of candour is not, *per se*, a sufficient ground to support a class claim.[30] But the powerful dissent of Lord Wilberforce in *Burmah Oil Co. Ltd v Bank of England* [1980] AC 1090, 1112, should not be lightly dismissed. Speaking of the candour argument, Lord Wilberforce said:

It seems now rather fashionable to decry this, but if as a ground it may at one time have been exaggerated, it has now, in my opinion, received an excessive dose of cold water. I am certainly not prepared, against the view of the Minister, to discount the need, in the formation of such very controversial policy as that with which we are here involved, for frank and uninhibited advice from the Bank to the Government, from and between civil servants and between Ministers.

It is submitted that, with respect to certain classes of document, certainly those so involved with the formation of government policy, there should still be room for consideration of the need for candour. It may be that with 'lower level' documents, the need for candour will carry less weight, but it is submitted that this does not justify excluding the argument altogether.

In *Neilson v Laugharne* [1981] QB 736, the plaintiff commenced an action against a chief constable claiming damages for trespass, false imprisonment and assault arising from the search of the plaintiff's house during his absence and his detention at a police station. No charges were brought against him. He sought discovery of reports prepared for an inquiry by the chief constable under s. 49 of the Police Act 1964, which by statute had to be sent to the Director of Public Prosecutions and the Police Complaints Board. No criminal or disciplinary charges were brought by either against the police officers involved as a result of the inquiry. It was held that, if statements made in the course of such an inquiry were disclosed for the purpose of civil litigation, the statutory intent to promote full and frank cooperation in the inquiry would be impeded. The Court of Appeal was apparently unimpressed by the supposed demise of the 'candour doctrine', and expressly used that ground to hold that the public interest required non-disclosure. Oliver LJ pointed out that police officers who make statements in such an inquiry may be potential defendants in a subsequent action, or may have to report matters which are critical of officers of superior

---

[30] See, e.g., *Campbell v Tameside (MBC)* [1982] QB 1065, per Ackner LJ at 1077; *Williams v Home Office* [1981] 1 All ER 1151.

rank, under whom they must continue to serve. There would be no guarantee of candour in inquiries leading to possible criminal or disciplinary action (a very important and compelling public interest) if confidentiality were not respected.

Clearly, this kind of inquiry has some special aspects. The reasoning of the Court of Appeal would not be appropriate to every kind of report or document, but perhaps the decision serves to show the cogency of Lord Wilberforce's plea that the candour argument should not be abandoned altogether.

### 10.4.2   Necessity for fairly disposing of the case
By RSC, Ord. 24, r. 13(1):

> No order for the production of any documents for inspection or to the Court shall be made under any of the foregoing rules unless the Court is of opinion that the order is necessary either for disposing fairly of the cause or matter or for saving costs.

In *Burmah Oil Co. Ltd* v *Bank of England* [1980] AC 1090, the House of Lords (Lord Wilberforce dissenting) found that 10 of the documents in question were likely to reveal the attitude of the Bank of England to the transactions which were the subject of the action, and that consequently these were documents 'necessary for fairly disposing of the cause' within the meaning of Ord. 24, r. 13(1). The House further found that inspection of the documents by the House would not harm the public interest, and ordered the documents to be produced for that purpose. Having inspected the documents, however, the House held that the documents did not contain the 'necessary' material, and on that ground, upheld the government's objection to disclosure.

The party seeking disclosure must, therefore, demonstrate that the documents sought fall within Ord. 24, r. 13(1) before any question of balancing interests can arise. In *Air Canada and Others* v *Secretary of State for Trade and Another (No. 2)* [1983] 2 AC 394, a number of airlines sued the Secretary of State, alleging that he had acted ultra vires and unlawfully in directing the British Airports Authority to increase landing charges at Heathrow airport in an allegedly discriminatory manner. The government successfully objected to the requested production of communications between ministers, and memoranda prepared for the use of ministers, which related to the formulation of government policy as to the Authority and the limitation of public sector borrowing. The House of Lords found that the documents were not likely to be 'necessary' for the purposes of Ord. 24, r. 13(1) and on that ground refused to inspect them. The judge at first instance, Bingham J, had agreed to inspect the documents on the ground that they were likely to affect the outcome of the case 'one way or the other'. Both the Court of Appeal and the House of Lords held that this approach was incorrect. The test was not whether the documents would be in any way helpful, but whether they would help the party seeking disclosure. The opponent was entitled to withhold documents helpful to the opponent, if a supportable ground for withholding existed.

The party seeking disclosure has a two-part burden, the first to show that the documents are likely to be 'necessary' (which is sufficient to induce the court to inspect them) and the second (over which he has little or no control) to show on inspection that they are in fact 'necessary' (which will result in disclosure).

In *Science Research Council* v *Nassé* [1980] AC 1028, 1071, Lord Salmon posed the question of what 'necessary' in the present context means. He answered the question in the following way:

It, of course, includes the case where the party applying for an order for discovery and inspection of certain documents could not possibly succeed in the proceedings unless he obtained the order; but it is not confined to such cases. Suppose, for example, a man had a very slim chance of success without inspection of documents, but a very strong chance of success with inspection, surely the proceedings could not be regarded as being fairly disposed of, were he to be denied inspection.

It will be recalled that in *Conway v Rimmer* the probationer police officer was able to show that the reports in the custody of the chief constable were likely to be 'necessary' and that on inspection, the House found that they were in fact 'necessary'. More recently, in *Campbell v Tameside MBC* [1982] QB 1065, the plaintiff was a schoolteacher who had been attacked in the classroom by an unruly pupil and seriously injured. She sought preliminary discovery of reports maintained by the local education authority, which were believed to contain material which might reveal whether the authority had known of the pupil's propensity for violence, which was such that he should have been placed in a special school. The Court of Appeal agreed with the conclusion of the judge at first instance that there was 'a real risk of the plaintiff being the victim of a denial of justice if the documents were not disclosed', and so found that they were 'necessary'. The procedure for preliminary discovery (i.e. discovery before commencing an action) permitted under RSC, Ord. 24, r. 7A(1), is expressly designed to assist plaintiffs in cases where insufficient evidence to justify commencement of an action is available without discovery of documents in the possession of a proposed defendant. Such cases therefore fit aptly within Lord Salmon's definition of 'necessary'.

### 10.4.3 Balancing competing interests
If the documents sought appear 'necessary for disposing fairly of the cause', then the court must balance the public interest in the administration of justice, which requires disclosure of necessary evidence, against any asserted public interest in withholding the documents. The balancing process is well described in the quotation from the speech of Lord Reid in *Conway v Rimmer* ([1968] AC 910 at 952) set forth in 10.3, ante. Lord Reid added that the test was to be whether the withholding of the documents was 'really necessary for the proper functioning of the public service'.

In *Campbell v Tameside MBC* [1982] QB 1065, 1075-6, Ackner LJ stated a number of 'basic principles' relating to the balancing process, among which are:

1.   The exclusion of relevant evidence always calls for clear justification. All relevant documents, whether or not confidential, are subject to disclosure unless on some recognised ground, including the public interest, their non-disclosure is permissible.

2.   Since it has been accepted in this court that the documents for which the plaintiff seeks discovery are relevant to the contemplated litigation, there is a heavy burden on the education authority to justify withholding them from disclosure . . ..

5.   The proper approach where there is a question of public interest immunity is a weighing, on balance, of the two public interests, that of the nation or the public service in non-disclosure and that of justice in the production of the documents. Both in the 'class' objection and the 'contents' objection the courts retain the residual power to inspect and order disclosure . . ..

6.  A judge conducting the balancing exercise needs to know whether the documents in question are of much or little weight in the litigation, whether their absence will result in a complete or partial denial of justice to one or other of the parties or perhaps to both, and what is the importance of the particular litigation to the parties and the public. All these are matters which should be considered if the court is to decide where the public interest lies . . .

It is submitted that the emphasis in the judgment of Ackner LJ in favour of disclosure, and the burden of justification falling upon the entity seeking non-disclosure is to be welcomed. The more routine or 'low level' the documents, the more jealously should any claim to withhold be scrutinised. This principle comports not only with the principles laid down by Lord Reid in *Conway* v *Rimmer* but also with the spirit of the Rules of Court and the public interest in the free availability of relevant evidence.

### 10.4.4   *Should the court inspect the documents?*

The question of whether the court should privately inspect the documents as part of the balancing process has caused some division of opinion[31]. Since *Conway* v *Rimmer*, it has rarely been doubted that the court has power to do so, but the wisdom of exercising that power has been challenged, on the basis that the court cannot assess the possible harm to the public interest as competently as the minister seeking to withhold. In this regard, there is again a distinction between class claims and contents claims, the court being much less reluctant to inspect in the former than in the latter. So too, the court will be more ready to inspect in the case of lower level documents, such as the chief constable's reports in *Conway* v *Rimmer* itself, and the local education authority's documents in *Campbell* v *Tameside MBC*.

Both in *Burmah Oil Co. Ltd* v *Bank of England* and *Air Canada and Others* v *Secretary of State for Trade and Another* (ante) the House of Lords accepted that the court should inspect the documents, once it was shown that they were likely to be necessary for fairly disposing of the case, and it is submitted that this is plainly correct. In *Burmah Oil*, Lord Edmund Davies observed ([1980] AC 1090, 1129) that a judge may well feel that he cannot profitably embark on a balancing exercise without himself seeing the documents in question, and cited in support the dicta of Lord Reid and Lord Upjohn in *Conway* v *Rimmer* [1968] AC 910 at 953 and 995 respectively. This dictum was cited and followed by Ackner LJ in *Campbell* v *Thameside MBC* [1982] QB 1065, 1076 and is surely both sensible and correct.

No doubt there may be cases in which a contents claim is made for a document of high public interest, in an 'affairs of state' case or some comparable situation, where the court is in no position to question the minister's grounds of objection, in which inspection would be both fruitless and undesirable. The court has power to act accordingly. But it is submitted that in general, even in the case of the high level documents which the court was called upon to consider in the *Burmah Oil* and *Air Canada* cases, inspection should be the usual procedure. This would be in accordance with the spirit of the principles laid down in *Conway* v *Rimmer*, which form the basis of the present law.

---

[31]   In *Conway* v *Rimmer*, the House rejected the argument that inspection by the court without reference to the parties was contrary to the rules of natural justice, whether or not the Crown is a party. Lord Morris, more cautious, held that there was a power to inspect which should be exercised sparingly. To the same effect are the observations of Lord Wilberforce in *Burmah Oil Co. Ltd* v *Bank of England* (HL) [1980] AC 1090, 1116-7.

## 10.5   Governmental and administrative matters

Nothing in the authorities on affairs of state limits the area of governmental activity to the comparatively dramatic circumstances of the wartime cases, or to the lofty foreign-policy cases. Government policy is nowadays formulated and carried out in relation to a wide and ever-increasing sphere of activity, and the principles laid down in *Conway* v *Rimmer* apply over the whole spectrum. They apply to local as well as national government. It is no doubt true to say that the more mundane and essentially administrative the subject, the less likely it is that a class of documents will satisfy the test propounded by Lord Reid, or that the contents of any given document will be of sufficient delicacy and gravity to warrant its exclusion; but each case will be examined on its merits. The illustrations that follow are those areas in which the courts have been called upon most frequently to weigh the competing interests, and which seem to be the most critical in practice.

### 10.5.1   Economic and fiscal policy

A good illustration in modern times is that of documents relating to the government's economic policy. It was at one time doubted whether economic as opposed to political content would suffice to give rise to a claim based on public-policy immunity at all. Thus, in *Smith* v *East India Co.* (LC) (1841) 1 Ph 50, in what was essentially a commercial action, despite the fact that the company played a vital role in the political government of India, documents passing between the court of directors and the British Government Commissioners for India were held to be the subject of public-policy immunity, solely by virtue of their political content. But as it became more and more clear that it is an important function of government to regulate if not to participate in economic and commercial activity, the mood changed. In *M. Isaacs & Sons Ltd and Others* v *Cook*,[32] it was held that communications passing between the Prime Minister of Australia and the Australian High Commissioner in London, which were said to contain matter defamatory of the plaintiff, were to be withheld on the ground of public policy, even though the contents of such communications were plainly commercial in character, and had little political significance outside the commercial sphere.

In *Burmah Oil Co. Ltd* v *Bank of England*[33] the company sought a declaration against the Bank that a sale by the company to the Bank of certain stock at a price required by the Government, pursuant to an agreement made in 1975, was inequitable and unfair, and claimed an order for the transfer back of the stock at the 1975 price. The company had, at the time of the agreement, been in dire financial straits because of an international oil crisis, and the agreement had been designed to 'rescue' the company, under the very close control of the Government working through the Bank. The company sought discovery of all relevant documents. The Crown (which was not a party to the suit), intervened and objected to the production of some 62 documents, which for this purpose were divided into three categories. Categories A and B both related to the formulation of government economic policy, at ministerial level and at a lower level.[34] The majority of the Court of Appeal[35] were in favour of upholding the objection taken by the Crown. Lord

---

[32]   [1925] 2 KB 391. In a case of a commercial nature, there is no doubt that the court will scrutinise a claim based on public policy with great care: see, e.g., *Robinson* v *State of South Australia (No. 2)* (PC, South Australia) [1931] AC 704 at 715–6.
[33]   (CA) [1979] 1 WLR 473; affirmed (HL) [1980] AC 1090.
[34]   Category C was classified as 'confidential'. As to this, see 10.7 post.
[35]   Bridge and Templeman LJJ (Upholding Foster J at first instance).

Denning MR, dissenting, did not accept that the 'rescue' operation was a matter of policy. He said, [1979] 1 WLR at 486:

> Now I can understand that privilege in regard to high questions of state policy, such as those dealing with foreign affairs or the defence or security of the realm. But I do not think it should be extended to commercial transactions undertaken by the government or the Bank of England. This rescue operation of Burmah was *par excellence* a commercial transaction. Such as those which the City of London has undertaken many a time in recent years.

The House of Lords upheld the majority of the Court of Appeal. Lord Wilberforce saw no need to inspect the documents, in view of the clear and detailed certificate of the minister. The other Lords, having inspected the documents, held that none of them contained matter of such evidential value as to make an order for their disclosure necessary to dispose fairly of the case. Lord Scarman ([1980] AC at 1144) described the documents as ' "high level". They are concerned with the formulation of policy. They are part of the inner working of the government machine.'

Although *Burmah's* application was unsuccessful for the reasons stated, the case makes it clear that the formulation of policy in any area may be the basis of an objection to disclosure based on public-policy immunity. The court is no longer limited to consideration of what would formerly have been regarded as political in the sense of the highest affairs of state.

### 10.5.2   Other home affairs

For the same reason, any other functions of central government are now to be treated in the same way. We have seen that the courts have considered claims to public-policy immunity based on the government's policy as to the British Airports Authority (*Air Canada v Secretary of State for Trade*) and the need for confidentiality in inquiry into possible criminal and disciplinary breaches within police forces (*Neilson v Laugharne; Hehir v Commissioner of Police of the Metropolis*). In *Williams v Home Office* [1981] 1 All ER 1151, McNeill J considered, and in part overruled, an objection to the disclosure of communications between, and memoranda relating to meetings between, ministers and highly placed officials concerning a so-called prison 'control unit', based on the fact that such documents were intimately involved with the formulation of government policy. The plaintiff was a prisoner who claimed damages against the Home Office for alleged false imprisonment and ultra vires conduct in placing him in such a unit.

### 10.5.3   Local governmental, statutory and other bodies

Since much of the burden of government now devolves upon local government and a variety of statutory bodies, the same rules are now to be applied to documents in the custody of these entities. We have seen, for example, that in *Campbell v Tameside MBC* the court considered an application for public-policy immunity pertaining to the records of a local education authority. The application of the rules to entities under the level of central government was emphatically affirmed by the House of Lords in *D v NSPCC* [1978] AC 171, in which it was argued, *inter alia*, that the Society could not maintain a claim of public-policy immunity because it was not an organ of central government. The Society, a voluntary body incorporated by royal charter, had power under the Children and Young Persons Act 1969 to bring care proceedings in a juvenile court, although it was under no duty to do so. The Society sought help from members of the public in supplying it with information about children who might be ill-treated, and offered a guarantee of confidentiality to informants. Someone informed the Society that the plaintiff's daughter had been ill-treated, information which proved to be without foundation. The plaintiff brought an action for damages for negligence on the part of the Society, alleging that it had exercised insufficient care in investigating the complaint before sending an inspector to her home to see the child. The plaintiff sought discovery of, *inter alia*, the identity of the informant and the Society claimed that the identity ought to be withheld on the ground of public policy.

The Court of Appeal by a majority[36] held that the plaintiff was entitled to discovery of the identity, Scarman LJ and Sir John Pennycuick holding specifically that public-policy immunity was confined to matters of central government. The House of Lords reversed the ruling. The decision turned primarily on the analogy of the immunity accorded to police informers (see 10.6, post) but the House also disposed of the contention that the Society could not claim public-policy immunity because it was not an organ of central government. Lord Simon of Glaisdale, in the course of a careful refutation of any such requirement, observed ([1978] AC at 235–6):

> . . .'the state', cannot on any sensible political theory be restricted to the Crown and the departments of central government (which are, indeed, part of the Crown in constitutional law). The state is the whole organisation of the body politic for supreme civil rule and government — the whole political organisation which is the basis of civil government. As such it certainly extends to local — and, as I think, also statutory — bodies in so far as they are exercising autonomous rule. . . . There is a recurrent transfer of functions between central, local and statutory authorities. For example, near the heart of the issue before your Lordships, the Crown as parens patriae had traditionally a general jurisdiction over children; a residue is now exercised in the High Court, but the bulk has been devolved by statute on local authorities.

Although *D v NSPCC* was a case involving a voluntary body, it represents a fairly fruitful field of inquiry for the courts in relation to public-policy immunity. Matters concerning the welfare of children provide not only a substantial field of litigation, but also a wide variety of documentation compiled by those concerned with child welfare, some of it adverse to one or both parents, and almost all of it clearly relevant to the litigation. The reports made by local authority social workers dealing with the welfare of children have been sought by parents for the purposes of litigation of issues of custody, wardship and adoption. Such reports are confidential and contain a good deal of confidential material, yet they may represent a significant source of potential evidence. The courts have generally held such reports to be protected from disclosure, on the ground that there is an important public policy in keeping confidential the workings of social services departments and similar bodies.[37]

In *R v City of Birmingham DC, ex parte O* [1982] 2 All ER 356, a majority of the Court of

---

[36] Scarman LJ and Sir John Pennycuick, Lord Denning MR dissenting.
[37] See, e.g., *Official Solicitor v K* [1965] AC 201; *Re D (Infants)* [1970] 1 WLR 599. It should be noted, however, that it is not the practice to allow discovery in wardship cases, and it is difficult to tell how far these cases turn on that point, rather than public-policy immunity.

Appeal[38] went so far as to hold that the social services committee of a local authority and the authority's social services department, to which the authority, as required by statute, had delegated its social services functions, were entitled to withhold from a councillor its files relating to prospective adoptive parents. The councillor was not a member of the social services committee, but was concerned about the suitability of the proposed adoptive parents. She alleged, and the Court of Appeal appear to have accepted, that access to the files would assist her in properly discharging her duties as a councillor. However, the Court held that the need for confidentiality in such a sensitive area must prevail.

## 10.6   Information given for the detection of crime, etc.

It has long been a rule of English law that in any public prosecution, or information for fraud against the revenue laws, or in any civil proceedings arising from either of these, no question may be asked and no evidence may be given which would tend to reveal the identity of any person who has given information leading to the institution of the prosecution or information. There is said to be an overriding public interest in preserving the anonymity of informants, because of the obvious likelihood of sources of information drying up otherwise. A public prosecution is, in modern law, likely to include any case brought by or after investigation by the police, or any executive body having police powers for any purpose, and indeed the police informer is the classic example of the species. But the rule should, it is submitted, and might now well be held to, apply also to private prosecutions, there being no obvious ground of public policy for distinguishing private from public prosecutions for this purpose. The rule prevents any question, direct or indirect, which would tend to reveal the identity of an informant or the channel of information.

In *Marks* v *Beyfus* (CA) (1890) 25 QBD 494, the modern rule was stated by Lord Esher MR. The plaintiff, who had brought an action alleging a conspiracy to prosecute maliciously, sought to elicit from the Director of Public Prosecutions the name of his informant. The refusal of the Director to answer was upheld. But Lord Esher did recognise that there must be one exceptional case (ibid at 498):

> . . . if upon the trial of a prisoner the judge should be of opinion that the disclosure of the name of the informant is necessary or right in order to show the prisoner's innocence, then one public policy is in conflict with another public policy, and that which says that an innocent man is not to be condemned when his innocence can be proved is the policy that must prevail.

The police informer supplying information about crime is, of course, not the only source of information upon which public bodies may act and indeed depend for their ability to act. The identity of informers on matters involving possible frauds against the revenue laws has long been protected, and in a modern context this application of the rule

---

[38]   Lord Denning MR and Sir Sebag Shaw, Donaldson LJ dissenting. Donaldson LJ dissented primarily on the ground that, in his opinion, the authority had no right to keep its documents from an elected representative, even if she was not a member of the social services committee. The decision of the majority turned in part on the contrary proposition: cf. *R* v *Clerk to Lancashire Police Committee, ex parte Hook* [1980] QB 603.

was confirmed in *Alfred Crompton Amusement Machines Ltd v Commissioners of Customs & Excise (No. 2)* (HL) [1974] where the commissioners had obtained information from customers of the company and others, relevant to assessments of the company's liability for purchase tax, which were the subject of an intended arbitration. It was held that the commissioners were entitled to withhold documents which would reveal the sources of their information, since if it became known that sources of information could not be kept secret, the working of the legislation under which the commissioners' powers were exercised in relation to the tax would be harmed by a lack of information. Lord Cross of Chelsea, with whom the other members of the House, on this point, agreed, said[39]:

> Here . . . one can well see that the third parties who have supplied this information to the commissioners because of the existence of their statutory powers would very much resent its disclosure by the commissioners to the appellants and that it is not at all fanciful . . . to say that the knowledge that the commissioners cannot keep such information secret may be harmful to the efficient working of the Act. In a case where the considerations for and against disclosure appear to be fairly evenly balanced the courts should I think, uphold a claim to privilege on the ground of public interest and trust to the head of the department concerned to do whatever he can to mitigate the ill-effects of non-disclosure.

The obvious importance of a free supply of information to the working of various public bodies has been responsible for the extension of the informant rule to situations beyond, but analogous to the original example of the detection of crime. In *Rogers v Home Secretary; Gaming Board for Great Britain v Rogers* [1973] AC 388, the Gaming Board refused applications by Rogers for certificates of consent to the grant to him of licences under the Gaming Act 1968 to operate certain gaming establishments. The refusal followed a letter to the Board from the Assistant Chief Constable of Sussex concerning Rogers. In some unexplained way, Rogers obtained a copy of the letter, and laid an ·information against the Assistant Chief Constable, alleging criminal libel. The proceedings resulted from the issue by Rogers of witness summonses against the Chief Constable of Sussex and the secretary of the Board, to attend at the magistrates' court and produce documents, including copies of the letter. The House of Lords held that the witness summonses should be set aside. Lord Reid said (ibid at 401):

> I do not think that 'the public service' should be construed narrowly. Here the question is whether the withholding of this class of documents is really necessary to enable the board adequately to perform its statutory duties. If it is, then we are enabling the will of Parliament to be carried out.
> There are very unusual features about this case. The board require the fullest information they can get in order to identify and exclude persons of dubious character and reputation from the privilege of obtaining a licence to conduct a gaming establishment. There is no obligation on anyone to give any information to the board. No doubt many law-abiding citizens would tell what they know even if there was some risk of their identity becoming known, although many perfectly honourable people do not want to

---

[39] Ibid at 434. The remarks contained in the last sentence cited from the speech of Lord Cross on the 'burden of proof' point, should be read in conjunction with those of Lord Reid in *Conway v Rimmer* [1968] AC 910 at 952; see 10.3 ante.

be thought to be mixed up in such affairs. But it is obvious that the best source of information about dubious characters must often be persons of dubious character themselves. It has long been recognised that the identity of police informers must in the public interest be kept secret and the same considerations must apply to those who volunteer information to the board. Indeed, it is in evidence that many refuse to speak unless assured of absolute secrecy.

It is to be noticed that *Rogers's* case was a not inconsiderable extension of the rule as expounded in *Marks* v *Beyfus*, because not only did it involve applying the rule to administrative rather than judicial proceedings but it extended the rule to cover information which need not involve criminal or dishonest conduct at all, but could be general observations on character or reputation, based perhaps in part on opinion. It seems, therefore, that the doctrine may have been extended to cover information given secretly for the benefit of the suppression of undesirable behaviour generally, or the promotion of any necessary vigilance over the conduct of public affairs, if those objects are at least partly dependent on the free flow of information.

This impression is supported by the (obiter) remarks of Lord Widgery CJ on the subject of evidence and correspondence given and supplied to inspectors who carried out a statutory investigation into the affairs of a company.[40] It is convincingly confirmed by the decision of the House of Lords in *D* v *NSPCC* [1978] AC 171, the facts of which were examined in 10.5.3 ante. The House was perfectly prepared to draw an analogy between information supplied to the police, and that supplied to the Society for the purpose of enabling it to carry out its duties and to take decisions whether to exercise its powers to institute care proceedings. Lord Simon of Glaisdale said (ibid, at 241):

> I have already cited long-standing and approved authority to the effect that sources of police information are not subject to forensic investigation. This is because liability to general disclosure would cause those sources of information to dry up, so that police protection of the community would be impaired. Exactly the same argument applies in the instant case if for 'police' you read 'NSPCC' and for 'community' you read 'that part of the community which consists of children who may be in peril'. There can be no material distinction between police and/or local authorities on the one hand and the appellants on the other as regards protection of children. It follows that, on the strictest analogical approach and as a matter of legal rule, the appellants are bound to refuse to disclose their sources of information.

Lord Diplock, having observed engagingly, that (ibid at 218–9):

> My Lords, in [*Rogers* v *Home Secretary; Gaming Board for Great Britain* v *Rogers*] this House did not hesitate to extend to persons from whom the Gaming Board received information for the purposes of the exercise of their statutory functions under the Gaming Act 1968 immunity from disclosure of their identity analogous to that which the law had previously accorded to police informers. Your Lordships' sense of values might well be open to reproach if this House were to treat the confidentiality of information given to those who are authorised by statute to institute proceedings for the protection of neglected or ill-treated children as entitled to less favourable treatment in a court of law than information given to the Gaming Board . . .

---

[40]   *R* v *Cheltenham Justices, ex parte Secretary of State for Trade* (DC) [1977] 1 WLR 95 at 100.

saw the same analogy as Lord Simon:

> The anonymity of those who tell the police of their suspicions of neglect or ill-treatment of a child would be preserved without any extension of the existing law. To draw a distinction in this respect between information given to the police and that passed on directly to a local authority or to the NSPCC would seem much too irrational a consequence to have been within the contemplation of Parliament when enacting the Children and Young Persons Act 1969.

It is true that the neglect and ill-treatment of children may well amount to a criminal offence, but the information passed to the Society is not given primarily for this purpose, but in order to enable suitable steps to be taken on behalf of any children found to be neglected or ill-treated. It would appear that the way is now open for further extensions of the informant rule in suitable cases, along the lines which have been suggested.

One such extension was apparently made by Sir Robert Megarry V-C in *Buckley* v *Law Society* [1984] 3 All ER 313, when he held that the Society's duty under the Solicitors Act 1974 to intervene in the practice of a solicitor suspected of dishonesty, a power exercised in the public interest, entitled the Society to refuse to disclose the identity of persons who had supplied information about solicitors suspected of dishonesty.

## 10.7 Confidentiality

Where A supplies to B documents or information under some promise, express or implied, of confidentiality, the question whether B may subsequently be compelled to disclose or produce such documents or information has given rise to considerable debate. Attempts to avoid disclosure may be, and have been, asserted in two guises. First, it may be said that confidential information is in itself a separate ground of private privilege, which attaches to documents and information in certain circumstances and is subject to the usual rules of private privilege. As to this, it now seems to be established that, except: (a) in cases to which legal professional privilege or the limited, statutory 'journalistic' privilege applies; and (b) in cases where confidential information is imparted in the course of bona fide 'without-prejudice' negotiations (in which cases the material is privileged irrespective of any question of confidentiality as such), no privilege arises in respect of material imparted in confidence.[41]

Secondly, it may be said that imparting confidential information may involve questions of public policy, and may enable an objection to be taken upon that basis. This argument has met with rather more success. It is true that it cannot be in every case that the mere fact of confidentiality will outweigh the public interest in disclosure for the purposes of litigation, but in certain cases it may as part of the overall picture have that effect. In *Alfred Crompton Amusement Machines Ltd* v *Commissioners of Customs & Excise (No. 2)* [1974] AC 405, the House of Lords considered, and rejected, the argument for the commissioners that the fact of receipt of information from customers of the company relating to the company's liability for purchase tax, in circumstances obviously intended to be confidential, of itself entitled the commissioners (and indeed bound them) to withhold

---

[41] *Chantrey Martin & Co.* v *Martin* (CA) [1953] 2 QB 286. The separate privilege point was briefly revived by Lord Denning MR in the Court of Appeal in the *Alfred Crompton* case, [1972] 2 QB 102 at 134, once again tapping the stream of Equity. But it was laid to rest in the House of Lords in the same case: see [1974] AC 405 at 429, per Lord Cross of Chelsea.

that information on the ground of public policy. But Lord Cross of Chelsea said (ibid at 433–4):

> 'Confidentiality' is not a separate head of privilege, but it may be a very material consideration to bear in mind when privilege is claimed on the ground of public interest. What the court has to do is to weigh on the one hand the considerations which suggest that it is in the public interest that the documents in question should be disclosed and on the other hand those which suggest that it is in the public interest that they should not be disclosed and to balance one against the other.

This approach has been approved and followed in subsequent decisions.[42] Although the circumstances in which confidential information is imparted vary considerably from case to case, it is no doubt true, as Browne LJ observed in *Science Research Council v Nasse*[43] that 'the courts should and will do all they can to uphold the moral and social duty not to break confidences'. But unless there is some compelling public interest in the confidence, it will not prevail over the public interest in disclosure. A misleading impression is sometimes given by references in the context of confidentiality to such cases as *Rogers, Alfred Crompton* and *D v NSPCC*. Although it is true that the information given in those cases was given in confidence, and though the phrase was canvassed, the real ground of decision in each was that the information was necessary for the efficient running of some part of the public service, be it the collection of tax, the management of gaming establishments or the protection of neglected children, and that disclosure would be likely to result, not only in a breach of confidence, but in information not being given in future. Balancing the public interests, as Lord Cross of Chelsea proposed, led accordingly to a decision against disclosure, but to see such a decision as giving effect to confidentiality *per se* would be to miss the point.

The law relating to confidential reports was much discussed in the Court of Appeal and the House of Lords in *Science Research Council v Nassé; Leyland Cars (BL Cars Ltd) v Vyas* (CA) [1979] QB 144; (HL) [1980] AC 1028. These two appeals, which were heard together, concerned employees who alleged that refusal of promotion by their employers was motivated by unlawful discrimination. They wanted discovery of confidential reports by their employers concerning both themselves and the other employees who were considered for promotion at the same time.

The employers in each case did not object to disclosure of the reports relating to the applicants, but did object to discovery of those dealing with the rivals. Both the Court of Appeal and the House of Lords accepted Lord Cross of Chelsea's treatment of confidentiality as the correct one. It was argued for the applicants that the reports were necessary for disposing fairly of the case, and that once it was shown that they were relevant, no element of confidentiality could protect them from disclosure. The argument was rejected, and although much of the decision turned on the particular practice of discovery in industrial tribunals, both the Court of Appeal and the House of Lords were prepared to view the case in a wider context. The Court of Appeal, balancing the arguments for and against disclosure, came down against it on the facts of the cases before

---

[42]  See, e.g., *D v NSPCC* [1978] AC 171; *Science Research Council v Nassé* (HL) [1980] AC 1028. The view was not entirely new: see, e.g., *Wheeler v Le Marchant* (CA) (1881) 17 Ch D 675, per Sir George Jessel MR at 681.

[43]  (CA) [1979] QB 144 at 179, affirmed by the House of Lords [1980] AC 1028.

them. Lord Denning MR thought that the application for discovery went 'beyond what is necessary'. Lawton LJ, differing in terms of emphasis, said ([1979] QB at 177):

> In my judgment, when balancing the interest of the applicant against the desirability of preserving confidentiality, the judge or chairman must remember that Parliament has created new causes of action which it has enacted are to be tried like actions in tort. If among the defendants' documents there are some (albeit confidential ones) which will help the applicant to prove his case, he is entitled to see them.

But he also pointed out the interest of the public generally in, 'the maintenance of efficient and fair procedures for taking on and promoting employees, allotting places in universities and for the granting of housing accommodation and services', and added: 'I am satisfied that general orders for discovery such as are commonly made in the High Court are not necessary' ([1979] QB 144 at 177).

In the House of Lords, it was said, while upholding the actual decision of the Court of Appeal, that the tribunal should inspect the documents in order to determine whether discovery was necessary for disposing fairly of the case. While reiterating that confidentiality itself would be insufficient to create public-interest immunity, the House also rejected the notion that confidentiality should be ignored once the relevance of the documents was established. The true position was clearly stated by Lord Edmund Davies, who may have had in mind the observation of Browne LJ in the Court of Appeal on the duty of the courts to uphold the 'moral and social duty not to break confidences' ([1980] AC 1028 at 1074):

> Learned counsel for the appellants went so far as to submit that the confidential nature of the documents here in question is totally irrelevant to the matter of discovery, and that the tribunal or court should therefore wholly ignore the protests of third parties against the disclosure of information furnished by them in the belief that neither it nor its sources would ever be revealed. . . . But for myself I am wholly unable to spell out from the absence of [statutory provision] the conclusion that confidentiality is an irrelevance. It is true that it cannot of *itself* ensure protection from disclosure [his Lordship referred to the *Crompton* case and *D* v *NSPCC*], but confidentiality may nevertheless properly play a potent part in the way in which a tribunal or court exercises its discretion in the matter of discovery.
>
> There was ample evidence supporting the view expressed by the Court of Appeal that the disclosure to inspection of confidential reports could well create upsets and unrest which would have a general deleterious effect. And a court, mindful of that risk, may understandably – and properly – think it right to scrutinise with particular care a request for their inspection. That is not to say, however, that the fear of possible unrest should deter the court from ordering discovery where the demands of justice clearly require it, but it serves to counsel caution in such cases.

It may well be necessary to apply these principles in future to a large and varied number of problems in many fields. It is submitted that any balancing of the issues must in future comprehend: firstly, the nature of the documents themselves and their relevance to the proceedings; secondly, the nature of the confidence given in the particular case and the probable effects on the future supply of information of disclosure; and thirdly, in the light of those considerations, what the overall requirements of the interests of justice are.

### 10.7.1   Non-privileged but confidential relationships

The willingness of the courts to give effect to confidentiality, so far as they properly can in the overall exercise of their judgment, has been demonstrated by decisions in other areas in which confidentiality has played an important part. An important area comprises relationships which, although essentially confidential, enjoy no private privilege such as that attaching to the relationship of lawyer and client. Such relationships are those of doctor and patient, priest and penitent, probation officer or social worker and client. Such confidential information as changes hands in the proper working of these relationships is often imparted orally, rather than in documents, but this operates only to shift the battleground from discovery to examination in the witness-box. The courts recognise the public interest in the free exercise of confidential relationships, and will not lightly compel answers which may result in the damaging of an individual relationship, or of the standing of a professional man or his profession generally. In particular, the courts will not compel breaches of confidence when no good purpose would be served thereby.[44] The law on this subject was developed in part by important cases involving proceedings for contempt of court against journalists, and although Parliament has now provided a limited privilege for those responsible for publications with respect to their sources of information, these cases remain useful as indicating the approach the courts will take towards non-privileged confidential communications generally.[45] In *Attorney-General* v *Mulholland* [1963] 2 QB 477 at 492, Donovan LJ said:

> While the journalist has no privilege entitling him as of right to refuse to disclose the source, so I think the interrogator has no absolute right to require such disclosure. In the first place the question has to be relevant to be admissible at all: in the second place it ought to be one the answer to which will serve a useful purpose in relation to the proceedings in hand – I prefer that expression to the term 'necessary'. Both these matters are for the consideration and, if need be, the decision of the judge. And over and above these two requirements, there may be other considerations, impossible to define in advance, but arising out of the infinite variety of fact and circumstance which a court encounters, which may lead a judge to conclude that more harm than good would result from compelling a disclosure or punishing a refusal to answer.

These words are all the more striking for having been delivered in the course of a case in which Donovan LJ, like the other members of the Court of Appeal, found unhesitatingly that two journalists had been guilty of a grave contempt in refusing to answer questions properly put to them at a public inquiry dealing with matters of high national security. In another case arising from the same inquiry, *Attorney-General* v *Clough* [1963] 1 QB 773 at 792 Lord Parker CJ said that: '. . . it still . . . would remain open to this court to say in the special circumstances of any particular case that public policy did demand that the journalist should be immune'.

The effect of these views was summarised by Lord Denning MR in *Mulholland* in the following terms[46]:

---

[44]   See, e.g., *Attorney-General* v *Lundin* [1982] Crim LR 296.

[45]   See Contempt of Court Act 1981, s. 10. The present position of journalists and others responsible for publications, including the important cases of *British Steel Corporation* v *Granada Television Ltd* [1981] AC 1096 and *Secretary of State for Defence* v *Guardian Newspapers Ltd* [1984] 3 All ER 601, is considered in 10.11, post.

[46]   [1963] 2 QB 477 at 489. See also *Senior* v *Holdsworth, ex parte Independent Television News Ltd* (CA) [1976] QB 23.

Take the clergyman, the banker or the medical man. None of these is entitled to refuse to answer when directed by a judge. Let me not be mistaken. The judge will respect the confidences which each member of these honourable professions receives in the course of it, and will not direct him to answer unless not only it is relevant but also it is a proper and, indeed, necessary question in the course of justice to be put and answered. A judge is the person entrusted, on behalf of the community, to weigh these conflicting interests.

So, in cases of this kind also, there must be a balancing process, a weighing of the competing interests, and the interest of the public in confidences of the kind before the court is an important matter to be put into the balance.

## B: PRIVATE EVIDENTIAL PRIVILEGES

## 10.8 Self-incrimination

### 10.8.1 Judicial confessions: the need for privilege

In order to appreciate the need for privilege against self-incrimination, it is important to understand that a person who, in the course of giving evidence in judicial or quasi-judicial proceedings, gives an answer which may be construed as an admission of some offence or wrongdoing, is liable to have that answer used as evidence against him in subsequent proceedings in respect of the offence or wrongdoing. An answer which may be used in this way is sometimes described as a 'judicial confession'.

The simplest and most obvious form of judicial confession is when a defendant admits he is guilty of the offence for which he is being tried. This form is irrelevant to the subject of privilege, because no privilege exists which protects a party from questions directed to show that he is guilty of the offence or wrongdoing with which he is charged in the instant proceedings. If this were not so, no party could usefully be cross-examined by an opponent, and the need for freedom to establish one's case by cross-examination of the opponent has been recognised and enforced for as long as parties have been competent witnesses. Despite the heavy armour otherwise afforded to the defendant in a criminal case, s. 1(e) and (f)(i) of the Criminal Evidence Act 1898 specifically permits the Crown to take this course, and the defendant may be asked any question notwithstanding that it may incriminate him in the offence for which he is being tried.

What is more material for present purposes is putting to a witness any question, the truthful answer to which will or may incriminate him in respect of some offence with which he is *not* then charged. The answer itself may lead to his being charged, or, if the charge is already contemplated, may provide evidence against him to support it. In this case, too, the rule is that an answer given on oath will be admissible in the subsequent proceedings as a judicial confession. Thus in *R v Chapman* (1912) 29 TLR 117, when the defendant was before examining justices charged with unlawful carnal knowledge of a girl aged between 13 and 16, he admitted that he had had carnal knowledge of the girl while she was under 13, and that admission was received on a subsequent indictment for that offence. The precise nature of the proceedings is immaterial, provided that they are of a judicial or quasi-judicial kind, at which evidence is lawfully taken under oath. Thus, in addition to any civil or criminal proceedings, answers given at a coroner's inquest[47] or at a

---

[47] The importance of evidence given at inquests has diminished with the powers of the court, which is no longer able to take depositions or to return verdicts implicating named persons in an offence. See Criminal Law Act 1977, s. 56.

military tribunal of inquiry[48] will, equally, be admissible subsequently.

However, where evidence is being given at an inquiry or before a tribunal which is the creature of statute and therefore exercises purely statutory powers to receive evidence, the admissibility of answers given will depend principally upon the wording or apparent intention of the statute. Many such provisions deal with the question expressly[49] but where they do not, the general rule seems to be that answers will be admissible in subsequent proceedings, unless the witness was by the statute under compulsion to answer even incriminating questions. However, even where a statute provides for admissibility in subsequent proceedings, answers will be excluded if the questions put fall outside the scope of the statute and thus outside the power of the questioner.[50]

For various historical reasons, including, according to many writers, the dark memory of the compulsory examinations of the Star Chamber, the law has always leaned in favour of the rule that no one should be compelled to incriminate himself in an offence with which he is not charged, or to provide evidence against himself.[51] Thus, except in the cases where statute otherwise provides expressly, every witness is entitled to the privilege against self-incrimination.

### 10.8.2  Scope of the privilege

No witness is bound to answer any question if the answer thereto would, in the opinion of the judge, have a tendency to expose the witness to any criminal charge, penalty or, in a criminal case, forfeiture which the judge regards as reasonably likely to be preferred or sued for.

In practice, it is the exposure to possible criminal charges which is of importance. The rare and unimportant cases of liability to penalties and forfeiture seem to have had their origin in what are now remote and old rules of practice that equity would not, by discovery or interrogatories, aid either common informers or proceedings for forfeiture. The courts now have wide powers to give relief from forfeiture, and that part of the privilege has been abolished except in relation to criminal proceedings by s. 16(1)(*a*) of the Civil Evidence Act 1968.

There is no privilege with regard to questions the answer to which would tend to expose the witness to the risk of civil proceedings, even at the suit of the Crown[52] except in the rare instance of proceedings for a penalty. It was at one time thought that the common-law privilege included the right to refuse to answer a question tending to show that the witness had committed adultery. The view was never supported by any basis more substantial than that the ecclesiastical courts had some power, purely notional in modern history, to

---

[48]   *R* v *Colpus and Boorman; R* v *White* (CCA) [1917] 1 KB 574.

[49]   See, e.g., Bankruptcy Act 1914, s. 15, s. 166; Companies Act 1948, s. 167(4), s. 270(7); Companies Act 1967, s. 50. For statutory restrictions on the use of evidence given in certain ordinary proceedings see Theft Act 1968, s. 31; Criminal Damage Act 1971, s. 9. See also Civil Evidence Act 1968, s. 14(4), and 10.8.4, post. See also *London and County Securities Ltd and Others* v *Nicholson and Others* [1980] 1 WLR 948.

[50]   *Commissioners of Customs & Excise* v *Harz and Another* (HL) [1967] 1 AC 760; *Karak Rubber Co. Ltd* v *Burden and Others* [1971] 1 WLR 1748.

[51]   The use of breath-testing devices and subsequent blood or urine tests seems to be a notable modern exception. In the United States, the same memory led to the constitutional entrenchment of the privilege against self-incrimination in the Fifth Amendment — hence the celebrated expression 'to take the Fifth' but the American Fifth Amendment privilege against self-incrimination applies only to testimony and not to physical evidence: *Schmerber* v *California* 384 US 757 (1966).

[52]   Witnesses Act 1806.

impose forfeiture on lay offenders, and although the privilege was asserted as recently as 1891 by Bowen LJ in *Redfern v Redfern* [1891] P 139, it was demolished beyond recall as 'fanciful' by a more secularly inclined Court of Appeal in *Blunt v Park Lane Hotel Ltd and Briscoe* [1942] 2 KB 253. There was, indeed, a statutory privilege to the like effect, by virtue of s. 3 of the Evidence Further Amendment Act 1869, but it applied only to 'proceedings instituted in consequence of adultery' and was abolished for all purposes by s. 16(5) of the Civil Evidence Act 1968.[53]

Where the rule does apply, it permits the witness to refuse to answer, not only questions which may be incriminating directly, but also questions the answers to which are clearly capable of use in providing evidence against him. Thus, in *R v Slaney* (NP) (1832) 5 C & P 213, a witness in a prosecution for criminal libel, by advertisement in newspapers, stated in evidence that he knew who had written to a newspaper with an advertisement. He was permitted to refuse to answer a further question about the identity of this person, on the ground that the information could have enabled evidence of his own possible complicity to be obtained. And in principle, it seems that a party may invoke the privilege to avoid having to disclose evidence in response to a court order such as an Anton Pillar order.[54] This result was conceded, albeit with reluctance, by the House of Lords in *Rank Film Distributors Ltd v Video Information Centre* [1982] AC 380. In that case, compliance with the order, which had been obtained by the plaintiffs, might have provided evidence against the defendants that would have assisted a prosecution under s. 21 of the Copyright Act 1956. The actual result in this case would now be affected by statute[55] but the principle remains sound, since the power to make such orders is not restricted to cases involving intellectual property rights.[56]

But there is a judicial function of some importance of deciding whether the privilege should be allowed, or whether a witness must be compelled to answer an incriminating question. The judge must satisfy himself of two matters. First, by taking evidence in the absence of the jury and, if necessary, in camera, that the answer to the question would tend to expose the witness to a criminal charge. This is a process of legal inquiry, in the sense that the judge must look at the elements of the apprehended charge, and see whether the witness's fears are justified as a matter of law. Second, that the institution of the proceedings is not just 'a remote or insubstantial risk' but that there is a 'real and appreciable' danger to the witness, having regard to the ordinary operation of the law.[57]

This second requirement is sometimes far from easy. There are obvious cases where there would be clear evidence of a serious offence which in the ordinary way could not be overlooked. There are equally clear cases where no danger is involved, as in *Blunt v Park Lane Hotel Ltd and Briscoe* [1942] 2 KB 253, where the Court of Appeal saw not the remotest prospect of a witness being exposed, in 1942, to an ecclesiastical forfeiture in

---

[53]  So a witness may be asked or interrogated directly about his commission of adultery: *Nast v Nast and Walker* (CA) [1972] Fam 142.

[54]  An order made in ex parte proceedings to permit premises to be searched, with a view to finding tangible evidence, e.g., of infringement — a remedy much used in actions involving intellectual property rights, and named after *Anton Piller KG v Manufacturing Processes Ltd and Others* (CA) [1976] Ch 55.

[55]  See Supreme Court Act 1981, s. 72. See also *Universal City Studios Inc. and Others v Hubbard and Others* [1983] Ch 241.

[56]  See, e.g., *Emanuel v Emanuel* [1982] 2 All ER 342.

[57]  *Rio Tinto Zinc Corporation and Others v Westinghouse Electric Corporation* [1978] AC 547 per Lord Denning MR at 574.

respect of her adultery, and *R* v *Boyes* (1861) 1 B & S 311, 330, where although the defendant's possession of a royal pardon under the Great Seal would have been no answer to a prosecution by impeachment, it was unthinkable that such proceedings would be instituted against him. It was said in this last case that, once it appears that a witness is at risk, 'great latitude should be allowed to him in judging for himself of the effect of any particular question'. But this does not deprive the judge of the duty to rule on the privilege, and he must do so on the basis of what appear to be the practical realities of the situation.

It may be right to disallow the claim to privilege where the witness has already jeopardised himself by making a similar statement to the police, and is already in peril.[58] The judge can also take into account the apparent rarity of certain prosecutions, the trivial nature of the offence or the lapse of time since its commission, in assessing the likelihood of proceedings. But these matters must be weighed with great care.[59] The rarity of prosecutions seems to have influenced the argument in such cases as *Rio Tinto Zinc Corporation and Others* v *Westinghouse Electric Corporation* [1978] AC 547, where it was contended that because the European Commission had failed to impose fines (under art. 85 of the EEC Treaty) in respect of a cartel, of which it had knowledge, companies thought to be implicated in establishing or operating the cartel could be required to produce documents which might have the effect of incriminating them. Both the Court of Appeal and the House of Lords held that the argument was fallacious. Although there might be cases where such an inference could safely be drawn, in the present circumstances it was likely that production would increase the prospect of proceedings, by offering evidence upon which the Commission might be disposed, at last, to act. It would seem, therefore, that the judge should take into account an increase in the danger to the witness, which would result from making available evidence whose previous absence may have inhibited the institution of proceedings. Some limited forbearance on the part of an authority empowered to commence proceedings cannot necessarily be equated with inaction or unconcern.

Where a witness is wrongly compelled to answer a question in breach of the privilege against self-incrimination, his answer will be inadmissible in subsequent proceedings against him.[60] Herein lies, of course, the significance of the privilege in relation to judicial confessions.

### 10.8.3 Foreign law

Curiously, it was never decided at common law to what extent, if at all, the privilege may be claimed in response to a question which might have the effect of exposing the witness to some charge or penalty under the law of another country. There were dicta against the application of the privilege, unless the provisions of the relevant foreign law (a question of fact) were admitted on the pleadings, which suggests that it was felt inappropriate for the judge to attempt to assess the likelihood of proceedings being commenced in another jurisdiction.[61] There is clearly much force in this, as the judge must otherwise try to weigh, not only the substantive law but also the practice of the foreign court or prosecuting authority in order to assess whether the risk is real and appreciable.

In civil cases, a compromise formula has been laid down, and it is almost certain that the

---

58  *Brebner* v *Perry* [1961] SASR 177.
59  *Triplex Safety Glass Co. Ltd* v *Lancegaye Safety Glass (1934) Ltd* (CA) [1939] 2 KB 935.
60  *R* v *Garbett* (ExCh) (1847) 1 Den CC 236.
61  *USA* v *McRae* (LC) (1868) LR 3 Ch App 79.

common law would follow the same approach, were the matter to arise in a criminal case. By s. 14(1) of the Civil Evidence Act 1968:

> The right of a person in any legal proceedings other than criminal proceedings to refuse to answer any question or produce any document or thing if to do so would tend to expose that person to proceedings for an offence or for the recovery of a penalty—
>
> (a) shall apply only as regards criminal offences under the law of any part of the United Kingdom and penalties provided for by such law.

It should be noted that, by virtue of the European Communities Act 1972, the law of the EEC is a part of the law of England. Accordingly, in the *Westinghouse* case, it was not disputed in the House of Lords that fines which the European Commission could impose under art. 85, and which were recoverable by proceedings under English law, were, 'a penalty provided for by such law', within the meaning of the subsection.

While the subsection does extend the privilege to charges and penalties which may arise under law which is technically foreign, for instance the law of Scotland, it limits the sphere of operation territorially to that which an English judge is plainly competent to assess.

### 10.8.4 *Incrimination of spouses*

It was also never really clear at common law whether the privilege extended to refusal to answer questions which would tend to expose the spouse of the witness to some charge or penalty. There were dicta to the effect that it did extend thus far, but no further.[62] Again, statute has intervened in civil cases, and it must be assumed that the common law would now reach the same result in a criminal case: s. 14(1) of the Civil Evidence Act 1968 provides:

> The right of a person in any legal proceedings other than criminal proceedings to refuse to answer any question or produce any document or thing if to do so would tend to expose that person to proceedings for an offence or for the recovery of a penalty — . . .
>
> (b) shall include a like right to refuse to answer any question or produce any document or thing if to do so would tend to expose the husband or wife of that person to proceedings for any such criminal offence or for the recovery of any such penalty.

The intention of the Act is that the privilege of the witness and that of the witness's spouse shall be coextensive. That is the effect of the word 'like', and it is reinforced by the provisions of the remainder of the section. Section 14(2) applies the same immunity to statutory rights not to give self-incriminating answers in proceedings under statutory powers of inspection and investigation. Section 14(3) provides that where, by statute, a witness is compellable to answer even incriminating questions, such compulsion applies to answers which would incriminate the spouse as well as those which would incriminate the witness himself. And s. 14(4) provides that any statutory provision that answers given by a witness shall not be admissible against him in any given proceedings, shall be construed as providing also that such answers shall not be admissible in such proceedings against the spouse of the witness.

[62] *R v All Saints, Worcester (Inhabitants)* (1817) 6 M & S 194 per Bayley J at 201.

These provisions should be read together with those of s. 18(2) that references to the husband or wife of a person in the Act or in any amendment made by the Act do not include references to a person who is no longer married to that person.

## 10.9  Legal professional privilege

The relationship of lawyer and client and the preparation of materials for litigation enjoy at common law a special position in their entitlement to privilege. The term 'legal professional privilege', which is not entirely satisfactory, is used to comprehend two distinct rules. The first is the rule that communications between lawyer and client, made in the course of seeking and giving advice within the normal scope of legal practice, are privileged in all cases, at the instance of the client. The second is the rule that communications passing between a client or his legal adviser and third parties in contemplation of actual litigation are privileged, provided that use for the purpose of litigation is at least the dominant purpose of the communication; in this case too, the privilege is that of the client. In both cases, it is immaterial whether the communication is with advisers or third parties in England or elsewhere, or whether the contemplated litigation may take place in England or elsewhere.[63]

### 10.9.1  Lawyer and client

All communications passing between a legal adviser and his client, in the course of seeking and giving legal advice within the proper scope of the professional work of the legal adviser, are privileged at the instance of the client (not of the adviser). It is irrelevant in this case whether or not the advice is immediately connected with litigation then in contemplation, though it is probably true to say that all legal advice is concerned with a possible ultimate resort to litigation, even if (as is almost always the case) the advice is directed to avoiding it wherever possible.[64] The rule applies to solicitor and counsel alike, and so covers any advice given orally or in writing and any instructions given for the purposes of such advice. The rule applies also to advice sought of and given by salaried legal advisers, and it has been suggested, though not decided, that it may extend to the so-called 'McKenzie friend' who may appear to advise a layman in the presentation of a case, or to argue before a tribunal to which restrictions on rights of audience do not apply.[65] As we have seen, the law concedes little recognition to other confidential communications. Although statute has provided limited areas of privilege for those responsible for publications (Contempt of Court Act 1981, s. 10) and for patent agents (Civil Evidence Act 1968, s. 15)[66] no other confidential relationship enjoys the breadth of privilege accorded to that between lawyer and client.

The communications, if they are to be the subject of privilege, must have been made within the proper scope of the adviser's work, and during the continuance of the lawyer-client relationship, i.e. during the currency of the lawyer's professional retainer on behalf

---

[63]   *Re Duncan, Garfield* v *Fay* [1968] P 306. As to the privilege in investigative proceedings before the Commission of the European Communities, see *A M & S (Europe) Ltd* v *Commission of the European Communities (case 155/79)* [1983] QB 878.

[64]   See *Greenhough* v *Gaskell* (LC) (1833) 1 My & K 98.

[65]   *M. & W. Grazebrook Ltd* v *Wallens* (NIRC) [1973] ICR 256. In the case of a layman in such a position, the privilege may extend only to the conduct of the case itself. This is an increasingly important question, which requires clarification.

[66]   This does not extend to trademark agents: see *Dormeuil Freres SA* v *Dormeuil Menswear Ltd* [1983] LS Gaz 158.

of the client. This will, of course, include any communications necessary to bring the relationship into existence, such as an initial consultation or instructions. But no communication is privileged merely because one party to it is a lawyer, and where no professional relationship comes into being no privilege can arise. In *Minter v Priest* (HL) [1930] AC 558, where the defendant refused to act as a solicitor in a transaction relating to land, and was alleged to have defamed the plaintiff in the course of giving his reasons for so refusing, it was held that the relationship of solicitor and client had not been established, and that the communication, not being made for the purpose of establishing the relationship, was not privileged.

On the other hand, in any case where the relationship of lawyer and client clearly does exist, the privilege is not inhibited by the fact that the lawyer is advising professionally a body of persons of which he happens also to be a member, for example a tenants' association, voluntary organisation or board of trustees.[67]

By what might perhaps be described as an evidential application of the maxim, '*Nemo dat quod non habet*', it is clear law that a client who could himself maintain no privilege in respect of documents of a given class cannot better his position merely by handing them over to his solicitor. Thus, in *R v Peterborough Justices, ex parte Hicks* (DC)[1977] 1 WLR 1371, where the client could not have prevented the seizure by the police of a document, such seizure being properly made by virtue of a warrant under the Forgery Act 1913, his solicitors were in no better position to resist seizure of the document when in their hands, even though the defendant had placed it there in connection with the preparation of his defence. Where documents are delivered to a solicitor for his consideration and subsequent advice, such delivery may amount to a privileged communication. Indeed, this will surely be so wherever the documents are brought into existence for the purpose of obtaining advice. However, in *Frank Truman Export Ltd and Others v Commissioner of Police of the Metropolis* [1977] QB 952, Swanwick J held that pre-existing documents, which might have held some evidential value against the plaintiff as evidence of fraud, were privileged in the hands of the plaintiff's solicitor to whom they had been delivered for his consideration and advice in relation to likely criminal charges based on the apparent fraud. If this decision were correct, it would mean that by placing incriminating material in the hands of a solicitor at the crucial moment, a person may protect such material from an otherwise likely exposure by search warrant.[68] Such a course would certainly not be a proper means of avoiding discovery in a civil case.

It is to be hoped that the decision in the *Truman* case has effectively been overruled by the subsequent decision of the Court of Appeal in *R v King* [1983] 1 All ER 929, in which the holding referred to above was 'doubted'. The defendant, who was charged with conspiracy to defraud, sent certain papers to his solicitors, for transmission to a handwriting expert for his examination. The expert was not called as a witness by the defence, but at trial the prosecution served him with a *subpoena duces tecum* to produce the documents sent to him. The prosecution did not seek to elicit evidence of the instructions given to the expert by the defendant's solicitors, and wished only to establish what documents had been provided to him. The trial judge overruled a defence objection that the expert should not produce the documents because legal professional privilege attached

---

[67]   *O'Rourke v Darbishire* (HL) [1920] AC 581.

[68]   This result did not follow on the facts of the case, because the plaintiff's solicitor had voluntarily permitted the police to take the documents in question away, and on the issue whether an injunction would be granted against the police, this was conclusive: cf. *Butler v Board of Trade* [1971] Ch 680.

to them. The Court of Appeal held that the trial judge had been correct in his ruling. Pointing out that the observation of Swanwick J in *Truman* was 'not necessary for his decision', the Court held that the case provided no authority for any such rule. Since the documents were not brought into being for the purpose of the solicitor-client relationship, and were therefore not privileged in the defendant's hands, no privilege could attach to them in the hands of his solicitor, or those of the expert. Of course, the instructions given to the expert and his opinion rendered to the defendant and his solicitors would have been privileged (see 10.9.2, post).

No privilege will arise where the relationship of lawyer and client is in reality a front for the commission or furtherance of some fraudulent or dishonest act. It may be that the lawyer is an accomplice of the client, but the rule applies equally where the lawyer is made the innocent tool of the fraud. In *R* v *Jones* (CCR) (1846) 1 Den CC 166, the client deviously inserted a forged will into a bundle of documents relating to title, which he had delivered to an attorney, in the hope that the attorney would find and act on the forgery. The rule applies to any fraud or dishonesty which the client seeks to further under cover of legal advice, where the advice is intended by the client to assist or guide him in his dishonest designs.[69] It extends similarly to tortious acts involving deceit or conspiracy, which are later made the subject of civil actions, but not to other civil wrongs which cannot fairly be said to involve fraud or dishonesty. There must be at least a prima facie appearance of fraud or dishonesty before the judge questions an apparent case of legal professional privilege.[70]

If two or more clients jointly retain the professional services of a solicitor then it may be difficult to determine how the privilege should operate in subsequent litigation between the clients. A typical instance is that of the family solicitor who receives confidences from both husband and wife while helping them towards reconciliation or over some family arrangement. In later divorce proceedings, one party may wish to inquire about admissions made by the other to the solicitor. The rule appears to be a simple enough one, namely that matters arising in the course of and within the scope of a joint retainer must be disclosed to any of the joint clients. But if the solicitor acts or advises any one client outside the scope of the joint retainer, the usual privilege will attach. All that can be said within the ambit of the present work is that the task of distinguishing these areas is usually more difficult than that of stating the rule.[71]

### 10.9.2   Communications with third parties

Communications made between a party (or his legal adviser on his behalf) and a third party are privileged at the instance of the party if, but only if, they are made for the specific purpose of pending or contemplated litigation. This part of the rule is apt to cover communications with witnesses and their proofs of evidence, and is particularly important in relation to communications with potential expert witnesses, from whom it may be desired to obtain an opinion, but who are not legal advisers. Nothing in the provisions of RSC, Ord. 38, rr. 36–44, which impose certain obligations of disclosure of expert reports as a condition of calling the expert evidence concerned, affects the operation of the privilege; but a party may have to elect whether to disclose a report and

---

[69]   *R* v *Cox and Railton* (CCR) (1884) 14 QBD 153.
[70]   *Crescent Farm (Sidcup) Sports Ltd* v *Sterling Offices Ltd and Another* [1972] Ch 553. And see *Williams* v *Quebrada Railway, Land & Copper Co.* [1895] 2 Ch 751; *O'Rourke* v *Darbishire* (HL) [1920] AC 581.
[71]   See, e.g., *Harris* v *Harris* (DC) [1931] P 10.

call evidence of its contents, or to stand on the privilege, use the report for advisory and preparation purposes only and not adduce it as evidence.[72]

The requirement that the communication be made for the purposes of pending or contemplated litigation is one which limits very considerably the material which is so privileged, and represents an important distinction between this and the case of communications between client and legal adviser. In *Wheeler* v *Le Marchant* (CA) (1881) 17 ChD 675, the defendant was obliged to produce reports made to his solicitor by a surveyor, because although the reports related to the subject-matter of the litigation, they had been made at a time when no litigation was contemplated by the defendant.

There was at one time considerable uncertainty about whether the communication must have been made solely for the purposes of pending or contemplated litigation, whether it must have been a major, but need not have been the only purpose, or whether litigation need have been no more than one of a number of possible purposes. The debate which raged on this topic in the older cases, many of which seem very unsatisfactory[73] was resolved by the House of Lords in *Waugh* v *British Railways Board* [1980] AC 521. The plaintiff's husband, who was employed by the defendants, was killed in a collision between two trains, and she brought an action under the Fatal Accidents Act 1976 in respect of his death. The Board denied negligence and alleged contributory negligence on the part of the deceased. The plaintiff sought discovery of an internal report, prepared by the Board for submission to the railway inspectorate and the ministry. The report was also a valuable, and probably the best, source of evidence of the causes of the accident, containing as it did the statements of witnesses and a technical account of the collision. But the report was also designed, according to its heading, 'for the information of the Board's solicitor: this form is to be used by every person reporting an occurrence when litigation by or against the BRB is anticipated. It is . . . to be sent to the solicitor for the purpose of enabling him to advise the BRB in regard thereto.' The Board claimed that it was a privileged document. The House of Lords held that the public interest in the due administration of justice strongly required the disclosure of such a cogent piece of evidence, and that this requirement could be defeated only where preparation for the purposes of litigation was shown to be 'at least the dominant purpose' for which it was prepared. The fact that the report purported on the face of it to have been made for such a purpose, since litigation was clearly foreseeable after such an event, was not conclusive in itself of the dominant purpose of the document, and the court was entitled to look behind the claim made for itself by the document by its own wording. On the facts of the case, the House of Lords held that the report had other major purposes in relation to the safe running of the railways, and that submission to the solicitor was not shown to be the dominant purpose of preparation; the report must accordingly be disclosed.

### 10.9.3 Search warrants

In the context of search warrants, the Police and Criminal Evidence Act 1984 offers protection to 'items subject to legal privilege' against seizure pursuant to a search warrant issued under s. 8 of the Act. Although the seizure of items of evidence is only one aspect of the claiming of privilege, it is one which is of great importance in criminal cases, in which the police sometimes claim to be entitled to seize items of possible evidential significance

---

[72] For the detailed provisions of the rules and their operation, see 9.6, ante.
[73] See, e.g., *Jones* v *Great Central Railway Co.* (HL) [1910] AC 4; *Seabrook* v *British Transport Commission* [1959] 1 WLR 509.

from the defendant or his solicitors, pursuant to a search warrant. This causes considerable difficulties if material is on the premises to be searched which is in fact privileged, because if material is voluntarily handed over, the privilege may be lost, while if it is wrongly withheld, charges of obstruction may follow. Hopefully, a clear exclusion of certain material will assist. Section 10 defines 'items subject to legal privilege' as follows:

(1)   Subject to subsection (2) below, in this Act 'items subject to legal privilege' means —

(*a*)   communications between a professional legal adviser and his client or any person representing his client made in connection with the giving of legal advice to the client;
(*b*)   communications between a professional legal adviser and his client or any person representing his client or between such an adviser or his client or any such representative and any other person made in connection with or in contemplation of legal proceedings and for the purposes of such proceedings; and
(*c*)   items enclosed with or referred to in such communications and made —
   (i)   in connection with the giving of legal advice; or
   (ii)   in connection with or in contemplation of legal proceedings and for the purposes of such proceedings,

when they are in the possession of a person who is entitled to possession of them.

(2)   Items held with the intention of furthering a criminal purpose are not items subject to legal privilege.

The statutory definition follows closely the common-law position as to legal professional privilege. The Act excludes such items from the general power provided by s. 8 to seize items which are 'likely to be relevant evidence' pursuant to a search warrant, and therefore provides a proper ground for a legal adviser or third party assisting a defendant to withold such items in the event of a search. It is essential to appreciate that items subject to legal privilege are excluded absolutely from seizure, and are not subject to the 'special procedure' established by Sch. 1 to the Act (10.12, post).

**10.10   Matrimonial communications**

The privilege against compelled disclosure of communications between spouses made during the marriage (matrimonial communications) has now been abolished in all cases. Contrary to popular belief, the privilege recognised in English law was not a common-law privilege, but was created by statute to take account of the competence accorded to parties and their spouses by statute during the nineteenth century (see 11.3, post). It was enacted originally by s. 3 of the Evidence Amendment Act 1853 and re-affirmed in s. 1(*d*) of the Criminal Evidence Act 1898 to deal with the new competence of the defendant and the defendant's spouse in criminal cases. As the competence of the spouse as a prosecution witness became broader, similar privilege provisions continued to be enacted, for example in s. 39 of the Sexual Offences Act 1956 and s. 30 of the Theft Act 1968.

   Contrary to the feeling in other parts of the common-law world, but in accordance with the illiberal attitude of English law towards privileges, the privilege against compelled disclosure of matrimonial communications came to be thought of as anachronistic. It was abolished 'except in relation to criminal proceedings' by s. 16(3) of the Civil Evidence Act 1968. Section 16(4) likewise abolished a related privilege against compelled evidence of the occurrence or non-occurrence of marital intercourse, which existed pursuant to s. 43(1) of the Matrimonial Causes Act 1965. The Police and Criminal Evidence Act 1984, s. 80 created sweeping new rules governing the competence and compellability of the spouse in criminal cases. Until this time, Parliament was no doubt reluctant to abolish a privilege claimable in a criminal case, especially as the House of Lords had previously held that the witness spouse should not be a compellable prosecution witness.[74] But the new provisions provided the opportunity to do so, and both privileges referred to above were abolished by s. 80(9) of the Act.

### 10.11 Persons responsible for publications

As observed in 10.7 and 10.9, ante, the law has accorded relatively little formal recognition to the claims of confidential relationships to enjoy privilege. An aspect of professional confidence which troubled the courts on a number of occasions is that existing between persons responsible for publications and their sources of information.[75] At common law, no privilege existed for confidential communications passing between the two, and journalists were sometimes held to be guilty of contempt of court for refusing to disclose the identity of the source. This situation led to some disquiet. It was mitigated hardly at all by the obscure 'newspaper rule', which to a very limited degree protected newspapers and journalists from having to disclose their sources in answer to interrogatories or by pre-trial discovery. The rule applied to libel actions only, and offered protection only during the discovery stage. It was too limited, uncertain and anachronistic to afford any real protection.[76] The protection realistically available was limited to the reluctance of the courts to compel the disclosure of sources, unless some compelling reason of public policy demanded it: this we considered in 10.7, ante.

A valiant but unsuccessful attempt was made to assert a general journalistic immunity based on public policy in *British Steel Corporation* v *Granada Television Ltd* [1982] AC 1096. The impact of the arguments made in support of the immunity was, unfortunately, greatly reduced by the fact that, of all the judges who considered the case in its speedy passage to the House of Lords, only Lord Salmon, dissenting in the House, had any doubt that Granada had acted in a manner which would in any event have disqualified them from relief. During a national steel workers' strike in 1980, an unknown executive of BSC 'leaked' some 250 confidential documents belonging to BSC, which had the potential to embarrass the corporation in the light of its public posture about the strike. Granada promised the executive that his identity would be kept confidential, and used the documents in a current affairs programme on which the chairman of BSC appeared. Later, the documents were returned to BSC in a mulilated form, apparently to protect the

---

[74] See *Hoskyn* v *Commissioner of Police of the Metropolis* [1979] AC 474; and as to the competence and compellability of the spouse, 11.6, post.

[75] See, e.g., *Attorney-General* v *Mulholland* [1963] 2 QB 477; *Attorney-General* v *Clough* [1963] 1 QB 773.

[76] See generally RSC, Ord. 82, r. 6; *Hennessy* v *Wright (No. 2)* (1888) 24 QBD 445n; *Hope* v *Brash* [1897] 2 QB 188. For a modern acknowledgement that the rule was inadequate to support a general theory of immunity, see the speech of Lord Fraser in *British Steel Corporation* v *Granada Television Ltd* [1981] AC 1096 at 1197–1199.

identity of the executive. BSC commenced proceedings to compel Granada to disclose the name of the source, on the ground that it was relevant to their proceedings for breach of copyright and other wrongs which Granada conceded they had committed. Precedent for such relief was to be found in *Norwich Pharmaceutical Co.* v *Customs and Excise Commissioners* [1974] AC 133.

At first instance, Sir Robert Megarry V-C declined to find that the press was entitled to any especial immunity, and indeed felt that if anything, the authorities pointed the other way. The Court of Appeal proved somewhat more open to the idea. Lord Denning MR held that in general, the press would not be compelled to disclose sources, while emphasising that this did not mean that any privilege existed, merely that the courts would usually forbear to compel. Lord Denning also held that the court's forbearance would be lost if the press acted 'irresponsibly', a phrase which, as Lord Salmon pointed out in the House of Lords, is difficult to define. Lord Denning felt that Granada had behaved 'irresponsibly' in the context of the case at hand.

Watkins LJ shared Lord Denning's view as to the merits of Granada's conduct, but his judgment is nonetheless a remarkably strong assertion of public-policy immunity in the context of press sources. He said ([1981] AC at 1138–1139):

> It is, I believe, well founded on ample legal authority that newspapers and television and broadcasting authorities and their servants are in principle immune from disclosing their confidential sources of information. This principle has been applied in a number of cases before courts and tribunals, some of which have achieved public prominence. The public can be said to approve of it. It is in their interest to do so. It is, therefore, a public-interest immunity.

Watkins LJ added that no question of privilege was involved, but asserted that the importance of a free press amply justified a general immunity from disclosure of sources. Unfortunately, his Lordship cited no authority in support of his proposition, which for the reasons stated in the judgment of Sir Robert Megarry V-C and at 10.7, ante, appears not to have found support at common law. It may be that Watkins LJ intended only to describe the practice of the courts not to compel in the absence of some compelling reason.

In the House of Lords, Granada's conduct once more proved the undoing of the immunity argument. Only Lord Salmon, who considered Granada to have performed a public service, dissented. The other Lords agreed that, although the courts had an inherent wish to respect journalistic confidences, no public-policy immunity existed which would override the public policy of making relevant evidence available to the court and to litigants. Since BSC undoubtedly had a meritorious cause of action, they were entitled to disclosure. Lord Wilberforce disavowed the apparently contrary assertions in the judgments of the Court of Appeal. He said: ([1981] AC 1170–1171):

> All these authorities (and there is none the other way before this case) came down firmly against immunity for the press or for journalists. To contend that, in principle, journalists enjoy immunity from the obligation to disclose, which may however be withheld in exceptional cases, is, in my opinion a complete reversal of the rule so strongly affirmed . . . .
>
> The only support for reversal is to be found, at least by implication, in some passages in the judgments of the Court of Appeal in the present case. But these must be read in the light of their decision, on the whole matter, that disclosure should be ordered. I do not think that Lord Denning MR should be understood as departing from his judgment in [*Attorney-General* v *Mulholland* [1963] 2 QB 477] and from every reported case. Such

a reversal would place journalists (how defined?) in a favoured and unique position as compared with priest-confessors, doctors, bankers and other recipients of confidential information and would assimilate them to the police in relation to informers. I can find nothing to encourage such a departure even with the qualifications sought to be introduced to the general principle asserted.

Parliament chose to introduce the reversal referred to by Lord Wilberforce and took the most remarkable step of introducing what appears to be a new statutory privilege. Although earlier cases were argued on the basis of public-policy immunity, the wording of the section is in effect apt to create a privilege which will always operate, except in defined circumstances. Section 10 of the Contempt of Court Act 1981 provides:

> No court may require a person to disclose, nor is any person guilty of contempt of court for refusing to disclose, the source of information contained in a publication for which he is responsible, unless it be established to the satisfaction of the court that disclosure is necessary in the interests of justice or national security or for the prevention of disorder or crime.

For the purposes of this section, 'publication' includes 'any speech, writing, broadcast or other communication in whatever form, which is addressed to the public at large or any section of the public': see ss. 2(1); 19. The section does not define the phrase 'for which he is responsible', but it is submitted that the category of responsible persons must include the journalist or reporter, the owner and publisher of a newspaper or periodical, and those involved in a managerial or production capacity with a television or radio broadcast.

The application of the section fell to be considered in *Secretary of State for Defence* v *Guardian Newspapers Ltd* [1984] 3 All ER 601. A copy of a government memorandum, classified secret, was 'leaked' to the *Guardian* newspaper. The memorandum related to the handling of publicity over the installation of nuclear weapons at a Royal Air Force base, and had been circulated to the Prime Minister, senior Cabinet ministers and the Cabinet secretary. The *Guardian* published the memorandum, and the Crown subsequently claimed its return in order to attempt to identify the informant. The *Guardian* asserted that it was entitled to withhold its copy of the memorandum by virtue of s. 10. The House of Lords was unanimous in holding that s. 10 should be of 'wide and general application', and that accordingly, it was sufficient to attract the protection of s. 10 if the order for disclosure might, not necessarily would, have the effect of forcing the disclosure of a source of information. The House also held unanimously that the section must prevail unless one of the four specifically enumerated exceptions applied, and that the onus of establishing that an exception applied lay on the party seeking disclosure, and might be discharged by proof on a balance of probabilities.[77] The facts of the case, however, produced substantial disagreement. The judge at first instance, Scott J, and the Court of Appeal, held that the Crown had proved that disclosure was necessary in the interests of national security. In the House of Lords, the majority, Lords Diplock, Roskill and Bridge agreed with the courts below, despite powerful dissent by Lords Scarman and Fraser.[78]

[77] In view of the decision in *R* v *Ewing* [1983] QB 103 (3.7.3, ante) their Lordships' decision as to the standard of proof, which was unnecessary to the overall decision in the case, may have to be reconsidered.
[78] To those raised on conventional concepts of judicial functions, the prospect of the Lords dividing over the facts, in the face of unanimous factual agreement by the judge at first instance and the Court of Appeal, is not uninteresting.

In relation to the only point of import apparently decided by the House, Lord Fraser said (ibid at 612):

> The application of [s. 10] is, in my opinion, not limited to the case where a publisher of information is required in terms to disclose the source of information or to do something which *will* certainly disclose it, and refuses to do so. The provision extends also to a case such as the present, where the publisher is called on, and refuses, to do something which may or may not lead to disclosure of the source. The wider construction of the section which appealed to Griffiths LJ appears to me to be correct (see [1984] Ch 156 at 166).

Certainly, many points remain to be decided which were not germane to this case, but it is submitted that the willingness of the House to take a broad view of the provisions of s. 10 is to be welcomed.

**10.12   Search warrants**

In our discussion of legal professional privilege, we saw that the seizure of items of potential evidential significance represented an important aspect of the claiming of privilege in criminal cases, and that the Police and Criminal Evidence Act 1984 provides protection against the seizure, pursuant to search warrant, of items subject to that privilege (10.9.3, ante).

The Act does not exempt other confidential materials from seizure, but in the case of two kinds of materials, provides that access may be gained to them only by order of a circuit judge, and not pursuant to a search warrant issued by a justice of the peace under s. 8 of the Act. These two categories of materials are known respectively as 'excluded material' and 'special procedure material'. Schedule 1 to the Act provides a procedure for making application to a circuit judge for access to excluded and special procedure material, and specifies the conditions which must be satisfied before an order for access may be made. It is not proposed to explore the detail of these provisions here.

Excluded material and special material are defined by the Act (see ss. 11–14) at some length. For our purposes, it will suffice to note that both consist of materials brought into being or acquired pursuant to some relationship of confidence, including journalistic materials, personal medical, psychiatric and counselling records and business communications. In relation to both excluded material and special procedure material, a person holds material in confidence if he does so under either an express or implied undertaking or obligation. The further detail of these provisions is outside the scope of this work. As in the case of items subject to legal privilege, it is to be hoped that these specific provisions will clarify situations in which confidential materials may in future be withheld in the event of a search pursuant only to a search warrant, and in the absence of any order by a circuit judge.

**10.13   Without-prejudice negotiations**

Because of the obvious public interest in the proper compromise of civil litigation whenever this can be achieved, the law offers a measure of protection to communications designed to arrive at this result. The danger of making or responding to any offer in settlement of litigation is that the gesture may later be construed as some admission of liability. For this reason, communications with an opponent may be made 'without prejudice'. The effect of this is that they may not, at trial, be referred to on the issue of liability or willingness to settle. Without-prejudice negotiations (usually contained in correspondence) will not be ordered to be disclosed on discovery, and will not form part of the bundle of correspondence, referred to by way of contrast as 'open', which is placed before the court in the normal course of events.

The privilege attaching to without-prejudice correspondence covers all bona fide offers of settlement or compromise, whether the litigation is pending or contemplated. The words 'without prejudice' need not actually appear on a letter designed to have the effect described, but the practice of using them by way of heading is both usual and desirable. Conversely, the mere insertion of the words will not assist a letter which is not a bona fide approach within the scope of the rule. Once negotiations have commenced, the rule obviously protects not only offers of settlement, but also responses by way of acceptance or counter-offer.

Although without-prejudice negotiations are usually carried on by correspondence, there is nothing to preclude their conduct by other means, such as oral attempts at settlement by the parties or their advisers. In particular, in matrimonial cases, negotiations may have taken place through the good offices of a mediator or counsellor. Where this occurs, and offers and suggestions are relayed to the parties via a third party, it has been held that the substance of the negotiations is privileged as if they were made in correspondence. Thus, in *McTaggart* v *McTaggart*[79] where an interview between the spouses had been arranged by a probation officer on a 'without-prejudice' basis, either spouse was entitled to object to evidence of what had been said being received at trial. However, the privilege is that of the parties, so that the probation officer is not entitled to object, and where the privilege had been waived by the parties, the judge was bound to admit the evidence. In *Mole* v *Mole*[80] it was held that the principle applies equally where one party only is interviewed by the probation officer with a view to reconciliation, and that where any person acting in the same capacity arranges an interview which is in fact intended to be without prejudice, the same result obtains. However, it must be noted that without-prejudice negotiations can only be conducted where the parties or those acting on their behalf engage in discussions aimed at a settlement. Where, therefore, a case worker spoke to the respondent to affiliation proceedings with a view to possible adoption of the child, and was not acting as the agent of either party, the respondent's admissions to the worker of paternity were not privileged, and were admitted on the issue of paternity.[81]

Although without-prejudice correspondence is not admissible at trial on the issue of liability or willingness to settle, it may be admissible, the issue of liability having been determined, on other issues, for example on the question of costs where delay or unreasonable refusal to settle may be material. And since an agreement to compromise litigation is one made for good consideration and fully enforceable, without-prejudice correspondence is admissible to show that an agreement was reached and what the terms of such agreement were in any subsequent proceedings with reference to it. In *Calderbank*

---

[79]   (CA) [1949] P 94. See the judgment of Cohen LJ at 96.

[80]   (CA) [1951] P 21. The rule would also apply to communications made between the parties themselves for the same purpose; see *Theodoropoulas* v *Theodoropoulas* [1964] P 311. The suggestion in *Bostock* v *Bostock* [1950] P 154 that the rule does not apply to meetings between the parties and their solicitors can hardly be correct.

[81]   *R* v *Nottingham Justices, ex parte Bostock* (DC) [1970] 1 WLR 1117. In the case of industrial conciliators, Parliament has provided for a statutory privilege in the Employment Protection (Consolidation) Act 1978, s. 133(6).

332 Public Policy and Privilege

v *Calderbank*,[82] Cairns LJ suggested that a letter offering items of compromise in a matrimonial matter, and pointing out the possibility of its admissibility, might be produced to the judge on such an issue. In the Family Division, such letters have become known as 'Calderbank letters'. But more recently, it has been recognised that their use should not be confined to matrimonial cases. In *Computer Machinery Co. Ltd* v *Drescher and Others* [1983] 3 All ER 153, 156, Sir Robert Megarry V-C said:

> In my view, the principle in question is one of perfectly general application which is in no way confined to matrimonial cases. Whether an offer is made 'without prejudice' or 'without prejudice save as to costs', the courts ought to enforce the terms on which the offer was made as tending to encourage compromises and shorten litigation; and the latter form of offer has the added advantage of preventing the offer from being inadmissible on costs. . . . What I have been saying is as obiter as what Cairns LJ said (and Scarman LJ and Sir Gordon Willmer concurred with) in *Calderbank* v *Calderbank*; but I hope the attention of the profession (including authors and editors)[83] will be more generally directed to what seems to me to be a valuable procedural process that is too little used.

In *Cutts* v *Head and Another* [1984] 1 All ER 597, the Court of Appeal held that such a letter was an appropriate way to proceed in any case in which the procedure of a payment into court was inappropriate. Though where a payment into court is possible, a *Calderbank* letter should not be used as a substitute.

## 10.14 Questions for discussion

### 10.14.1 *R* v *Coke; R* v *Littleton*

1 Assume that Coke's solicitors, on his instructions, send samples of his handwriting to a handwriting expert for comparison with Exhibit GG1, and that the prosecution wish to make these samples available for trial. May Coke make any claim of privilege?

2 Would the position differ if these samples were seized by the police, acting under a search warrant, from the offices of Coke's solicitors?

3 May Littleton assert any privilege with regard to the tape-recorded conversation with his wife?

4 If Coke and Littleton testify in their defence at trial, may they assert the privilege against self-incrimination in cross-examination with respect to the offences charged against them?

### 10.14.2 *Blackstone* v *Coke*

1 May Coke assert any privilege to prevent Fr Wigmore from being compelled to testify about any confession Coke may have made to him?

2 May the local authority successfully object to Coke's application for production of their files, made with a view to showing that Margaret may have given the authority a different account of how she became pregnant?

---

[82] [1976] Fam 93, 105–6. See also *McDonnell* v *McDonnell* [1977] 1 WLR 34, 38.
[83] The Vice-Chancellor complains in his judgment that the texts have not dealt with *Calderbank*. Evidently, his Lordship was not referred to the first edition of this work at p. 296.

3  May Margaret make use of a copy of the letter of 20 February 1985, the original of which was inadvertently sent to her solicitors? Had Margaret's solicitors refused to return the original, what should Coke's solicitors have done?

# 11 Witnesses: Competence and Compellability; Oaths and Affirmations

## A: COMPETENCE AND COMPELLABILITY

### 11.1 General rule

Any treatment of the subject of the handling of witnesses must begin by considering whether there are any restrictions on who may be called to give evidence, and whether giving evidence should be regarded as an optional activity, in which the proposed witness may decline to engage, or as an obligation enforceable by the court. These questions are referred to respectively as those of competence and compellability. A witness is said to be competent if, by the existing rules of law, his evidence is receivable by the court in the proceedings concerned. A witness is said to be compellable if he is not only competent, but may lawfully be required by the court, under sanction of penalty as a contemnor, to give his evidence.[1]

These questions are, and must remain, quite distinct from that of whether individual pieces of evidence enjoy some privilege in the hands of the witness, a matter considered in the preceding chapter. We are now concerned with the evidence of the witness as a whole, and so with his competence and compellability concerning all the matters material to the case on which he could speak.

The general rule of English law is that all witnesses are both competent and compellable, a rule justified by the need to make available to the court, as far as possible, all relevant and admissible evidence which may assist it in the determination of the issues.[2] At common law, this consideration was counterbalanced, and probably more than counterbalanced, by the emergence of an important body of exceptional cases in which various witnesses were held not to be competent, for reasons which will be referred to in the next paragraph. The exceptions have gradually been reduced and simplified by a series of judicial and statutory reforms, but continue to play a significant role in the conduct, particularly, of criminal cases. Unfortunately, the piecemeal nature of the reform, which has occupied nearly two centuries, has left certain areas of ambiguity in a field which has no obvious need for complexity, and it is submitted that a comprehensive statutory statement of the rules would be both fairly simple and highly desirable.

---

[1] In appropriate cases, particularly where the witness is a party or has some interest in the outcome of the proceedings, a refusal to give evidence will lead to the drawing by the tribunal of fact of adverse inferences.

[2] The rule applies to all witnesses, including experts: *Harmony Shipping Co. SA* v *Saudi Europe Line Ltd and Others* (CA) [1979] 1 WLR 1380; *R* v *King* [1983] 1 All ER 929.

## 11.2 Exceptions

It is, happily, unnecessary to consider in detail the scope of the various historical exceptions which grew up at common law, although it is certainly instructive to understand and bear in mind the justification which the common law advanced for them, some of which continue to underlie the exceptions which survive. It is possible to identify two particular fears which led to the wholesale rejection of the evidence of certain potential witnesses, and it must be said that these fears were so seriously regarded, that very sound reasons for admitting the evidence, based on its obvious cogency and on clear considerations of convenience, were rejected out of hand. There can be no doubt that the fears blinded the law to many cases of grave injustice which resulted from incompetence imposed in these cases.

The first fear may be described broadly as a fear of manufactured or exaggerated evidence resulting from self-interest. This fear led to the rejection of the evidence of the parties to the proceedings and of that of their spouses, though curiously not of other relatives of the parties, and of the evidence of any proposed witness personally interested in the outcome of the proceedings. The second fear may be described broadly as a fear of the evidence of certain persons as such, because of personal characteristics which supposedly rendered of no account any evidence which they might give, in whatever circumstances. Into this category of incompetence fell children of tender years and persons of defective intellect, whose condition in life was thought to require incompetence; those convicted of 'infamous crimes' whose conduct was thought to disqualify them as acceptable witnesses; and, most extravagently of all in modern eyes, non-Christians, whose inability to be properly sworn was held to remove the essential sanction of the oath, without which evidence was not to be received.

The most exaggerated and unnecessary incompetences have long since gone, whittled away and finally removed by statute during the nineteenth century. Thus, although at common law the evidence of atheists and believers other than Christians could not be received, the rule was modified by the middle of the eighteenth century. In *Omychund* v *Barker* (LC) (1745) 1 Atk 21 the evidence of non-Christians who held a belief in the 'Governor of the Universe' was held to be receivable. The problem of atheists, who held no belief capable of providing a sanction against untruthfulness, caused greater concern, but they were rendered competent by the Evidence Further Amendment Act 1869. The incompetence of those convicted of infamous crimes was modified in 1828 to make the incompetence only coextensive with their period of sentence, and was abolished by the Evidence Act 1843. The same Act abolished incompetence stemming only from interest in the outcome of the proceedings.

The cases which, despite some measure of reform and simplification, still call for detailed attention are: the parties and their spouses (in which the difficulties are now confined to defendants in criminal cases and their spouses) and children of tender years. These matters will be fully examined in the paragraphs which follow, after which mention will be made of persons of defective intellect, an incompetence which survives in much modified form.

Where an issue arises as to the competence or incompetence of a witness, that question is one of law for the judge, and depending upon the circumstances, the judge may have to receive evidence of secondary facts in order to determine the issue. In a criminal case, any issue as to the competence or incompetence of a prosecution witness should be decided as a preliminary issue at the outset of the trial. If the defence dispute the competence of a prosecution witness, the prosecution bear the burden of proving the competence of the witness beyond reasonable doubt: *R* v *Yacoob* (1981) 72 Cr App R 313. In civil cases, the time of decision is, no doubt, a matter for the discretion of the judge. It is submitted that the burden of proving competence should lie upon the party asserting it, in accordance with the general rules governing the burden of proof of secondary issues.

## 11.3  Parties to the proceedings

The abolition of incompetence through interest in 1843 paved the way for abolishing the incompetence of the parties themselves, who are no doubt the most striking example of the species of interested persons. For civil proceedings, the abolition was effected by the Evidence Act 1851, with the exception of proceedings instituted in consequence of adultery and actions for breach of promise of marriage, in which cases the incompetence survived until the Evidence Further Amendment Act 1869. The result of the abolition was that the parties became competent witnesses in every case, and, following the general rule, compellable. This is the position in the present law, and it involves the proposition that a party to civil proceedings may both give evidence himself and, if he thinks it wise, subpoena any other party to give evidence also. The rule as it now stands is one of the obvious convenience.

The position in criminal cases was complicated by a variety of historical considerations. The issue was, of course, whether the defendant was to be regarded as a competent witness. Although it was, on the face of it, desirable that his position should be equated to that of a party to civil proceedings, the consequence of his being thereby rendered compellable gave rise to much heart-searching. Dark references abounded in the nineteenth century to a reversion to the inquisitorial practices of Star Chamber and the evil of defendants being compelled to provide evidence against themselves by being forced into the witness-box. In the United States, the Fifth Amendment to the Federal Constitution, itself inspired by the same historical considerations, offered the criminal defendant the right not to incriminate himself, a right which necessarily included the right not to be compelled to give evidence at his trial. There were also technical problems of reconciling the idea of a compellable defendant with the incidence of the burden of proof in criminal cases. In the end, the matter was resolved by compromise, in a series of statutory provisions culminating in the Criminal Evidence Act 1898. The compromise was, in essence, that the defendant was rendered competent only for the defence, and was expressly made non-compellable.[3] This unique deviation from the traditional rules rendered necessary a series of supplementary provisions dealing with evidence given by the defendant. The prosecution may not comment upon the failure of the defendant to give evidence in his defence pursuant to the Act.[4] If the defendant elects to give evidence,

---

[3]   Criminal Evidence Act 1898, s. 1 and proviso (*a*). The rule applies to all criminal cases, with the unimportant exception of prosecutions for public nuisance under the Evidence Act 1877 in which the defendant is both competent and compellable.

[4]   Criminal Evidence Act 1898, s. 1 proviso (*b*). The necessity for this provision has been doubted. Nothing in the Act prevents the judge or a co-defendant from commenting on the matter, but the judge must do so in a balanced way, and in particular must not suggest to the jury that they are entitled to infer guilt from the defendant's failure to give evidence. See *R* v *Rhodes* (CCR) [1899] 1 QB 77; *R* v *Mutch* (CA) [1973] 1 All ER 178; *R* v *Sparrow* (CA) [1973] 1 WLR 488. Stronger comment is permissible in some cases than in others, but great caution must be exercised see also *R* v *Brown and Routh* [1983] Crim LR 38.

although he may be asked any question tending to criminate him in the offence charged, he may not be cross-examined about his character or about any offences not charged, except in the limited circumstances prescribed by the Act.[5] The defendant is, unless otherwise ordered, to give his evidence from the witness-box.[6] This provision reflects the fact that if the defendant elects to give evidence, his evidence is evidence in the case for all purposes, even it if has the effect of incriminating him or a co-defendant,[7] and he is to be regarded in the same way as any other witness called for the prosecution or the defence.

## 11.4 A defendant in a criminal case

The position which resulted from the provisions of s. 1 of the Criminal Evidence Act 1898 must now be examined in detail. It will be convenient to look at the defendant as a potential witness (a) for the prosecution; (b) on his own behalf; and (c) for a co-defendant.

### 11.4.1 For the prosecution

The Act left unaffected the common-law rule of incompetence so far as the prosecution are concerned. The important consequence of this is to prevent the prosecution from calling a defendant to give evidence for the prosecution against a co-defendant. In *R v Grant and Others*[8] indictments were quashed where, in the course of committal proceedings, the prosecution called persons jointly charged, and others charged with offences intended to form part of the same indictment, to give evidence against their co-defendants. It follows, therefore, that if the prosecution think it desirable to call a person in such a position, they must first ensure that he ceases, before giving evidence, to be a defendant. This will be the case if he has already been acquitted of all the matters alleged against him, or if he has pleaded guilty to all the matters alleged against him in the indictment. If neither of these has happened before he is required as a witness, then the prosecution must either (a) offer no evidence against him (or enter a *nolle prosequi*) or (b) accept his plea of guilty to a part of the indictment to which it is offered, and agree to formal verdicts of not guilty, or to leave other charges on the file, as may be appropriate. The effect is that the former defendant is no longer a party to any proceedings before the jury, and is therefore both competent and compellable for the prosecution.[9]

The practice whereby former defendants give evidence for the prosecution, having pleaded guilty, in the hope of attracting a lenient sentence, is a common one. From time to time, the courts have laid down different rules of practice as to the sentencing of a defendant who pleads guilty and whom it is proposed to call as a prosecution witness. At one time, it was the fashion to prefer that one who 'turns Queen's evidence' should be sentenced before giving his evidence, so as to avoid the risk and the appearance of his giving evidence in a manner calculated to attract a lenient sentence.[10] This is contrary to the general rule of practice, whereby all defendants are sentenced together at the

---

[5]   Criminal Evidence Act 1898, s. 1 provisos (e) and (f). See Chapter 4, ante.
[6]   Criminal Evidence Act 1898, s. 1 proviso (g).
[7]   *R v Rudd* (CCA) (1948) 32 Cr App R 138.
[8]   (CCA) [1944] 2 All ER 311. See also *R v Sharrock and Others* [1948] 1 All ER 145. The actual result in *Grant* might be affected now by the rule that committals for trial are not bad merely because some inadmissible evidence is received, but the principle remains: *R v Norfolk Quarter Sessions, ex parte Brunson* (DC) [1953] 1 QB 503.
[9]   *R v Boal; R v Cordrey* (CCA) [1965] 1 QB 402 at 411. But since he is an accomplice, the jury must be warned of the danger of acting on his uncorroborated evidence. See 14.7.2 post.
[10]   *R v Payne* (CCA) [1950] 1 All ER 102.

conclusion of all the proceedings, when the judge has had the fullest possible opportunity to assess the respective involvement and culpability of all the defendants. In more recent time, the courts have shown a marked preference for adhering to this usual practice, even where a former defendant is to be called as a prosecution witness, though ultimately, the matter is one for the discretion of the trial judge, having regard to all the circumstances of the case before him.[11] There may well be cases in which the credibility of such a prosecution witness may be seriously compromised unless his sentence is known before he gives evidence, so that it appears that he has nothing to gain.

An accomplice, whether or not jointly charged, against whom proceedings are pending but who is not being tried in the instant proceedings, for example because the indictment has been ordered to be severed, should not be called for the prosecution unless an undertaking is given by the prosecution that proceedings will be discontinued against the accomplice.[12] This appears to be a rule of practice, rather than of law, because the accomplice is not a party to the proceedings before the jury. The purpose of the rule is to prevent the possibility of a conviction being obtained by the tactical use of separate trials when evidence would have been incompetent on a joint trial. In *R* v *Pipe*[12] it was held to be wholly irregular to call for the prosecution a receiver of stolen goods, who had been charged and against whom proceedings were about to start, to give evidence against the thief from whom he had received the stolen goods. But the matter appears, ultimately, to be a matter of judicial discretion.[13]

### 11.4.2   On his own behalf

As we have seen in outline, the Criminal Evidence Act 1898 provides that the defendant is to be a competent, but not compellable, witness for the defence. This is achieved by the following wording of s. 1:

Every person charged with an offence shall be a competent witness for the defence at every stage of the proceedings, whether the person so charged is charged solely or jointly with any other person. Provided as follows:-

(a) A person so charged shall not be called as a witness in pursuance of this Act except on his own application.

It has already been observed that the defendant, if called upon his own application, is to be treated in all respects as any other witness in the case, subject only to the remaining provisos to s. 1. The evidence which he gives must be considered by the jury and given such weight as they think fit. If the defendant elects to give evidence, he may be cross-examined freely to show his guilt, or that of any co-defendant, subject only to provisos *(e)* and *(f)*: his evidence is evidence in the case for all purposes. Even where his own evidence in chief is limited to an admission of his own guilt and does not advance his own case, he may be cross-examined to show the guilt of his co-defendant.[14] By s. 79 of the Police and Criminal Evidence Act 1984:

[11]   *R* v *Weekes* (1980) 74 Cr App R 161; *R* v *Coffey* (1976) 74 Cr App R 168. See the authorities set out in Archbold, 41st ed., para. 4–124.
[12]   *R* v *Pipe* (CA) (1966) 51 Cr App R 17.
[13]   *R* v *Pipe* (ante) and *R* v *Turner and others* (1975) 61 Cr App R 67, per Lord Parker CJ at 78-9. And see 11.4.3, post. The point is a lacuna in s. 1 as it now stands.
[14]   *R* v *Paul; R* v *McFarlane* (CCA) [1920] 2 KB 183; *R* v *Rudd* (CCA) (1948) 32 Cr App R 138.

If at the trial of any person for an offence—

*(a)* the defence intends to call two or more witnesses to the facts of the case; and,
*(b)* those witnesses include the accused,

the accused shall be called before the other witness or witnesses unless the court in its discretion otherwise directs.

The provision for competence 'at every stage of the proceedings' is wide enough to include evidence at the commital proceedings, at which the defendant is competent by virtue of the section.[15] It also comprehends not only evidence given in his defence before the jury, but evidence given by the defendant for any other purposes in the trial, for example on the trial of an issue of admissibility on the voir dire,[16] and during the course of mitigation. In *R* v *Wheeler* (CCA)[1917] 1 KB 283, it was argued that the defendant was not liable to be convicted of perjury in respect of his false evidence during mitigation, because a conviction for perjury is only possible if the defendant has been 'lawfully sworn', and the defendant was not a competent witness after conviction, the issue in the case having been determined. The argument was rejected. Mitigation is a 'stage of the proceedings'.

### 11.4.3 For a co-defendant

The circumstances will be rare indeed in which a defendant before the jury is called to give evidence for a co-defendant, where he does not propose to do so in his own defence, since he would thereby expose himself to cross-examination on his own case, and since, being a defendant, he is not compellable to give evidence at the instance of a co-defendant, any more than he is on his own behalf. There is no doubt, however, that the phrase 'for the defence' is wide enough to allow of his competence for a co-defendant, and there seems to be no reason why in a proper case, one defendant should not give evidence for another, for example on the voir dire. It may also be observed that if one defendant gives evidence in his own defence, he may be cross-examined on behalf of a co-defendant, even though he has not given evidence adverse to that co-defendant, for the purpose of eliciting any matters favourable to the case of the co-defendant.[17]

Of course, a person who ceases to be a defendant, before his co-defendant is called upon to make his defence, for example where the case against him has been withdrawn from the jury at the close of the prosecution case, becomes both competent and compellable for the co-defendant in accordance with the usual rule.[18] But what of the defendant whose trial is for some reason postponed until after the trial of others involved? Here, we find an even more serious illustration of the lacuna referred to in note 13, as may be seen from the decision of Lawton J at first instance in *R* v *Richardson and others* (1967) 51 Cr App R 381. H, M and others had originally been jointly charged, but at the outset of the trial, M succeeded in an application for a separate trial because of his bad health. H then applied for a witness summons to compel M to testify at trial on behalf of H. M was clearly a competent witness for H, but it was argued that he was not a compellable witness for H

---

[15] *R* v *Rhodes* (CCR) [1899] 1 QB 77.
[16] *R* v *Cowell* (CCA) [1940] 2 KB 49.
[17] *R* v *Hilton* (CA) [1972] 1 QB 421.
[18] *R* v *Boal; R* v *Cordrey* (CCA) [1965] 1 QB 402 at 411.

because of the protection afforded him by s. 1 of the Criminal Evidence Act 1898. Lawton J rejected this argument, and held that M was compellable since the word 'proceedings' in that section must be construed to mean 'a trial which is going on', and since M was not then on trial. It is, of course, true that M was not then a defendant before the jury, even though he was charged and to be tried later, and that the Act does not preclude the conclusion reached by the learned judge. However, the decision produces unsatisfactory results in practice, if only because the prosecution may be enabled to evade the intent of s. 1 of the Act, by having available for cross-examination as a defence witness a defendant ordered to be tried separately, in circumstances where the prosecution should not be permitted to compel that defendant on their own behalf. The decision was based in part on an analysis of the position at common law prior to 1898, but it is submitted that the pre-1898 authorities were, to say the least, ambiguous[19] and it seems unsatisfactory that the protection of one who will be a defendant should be made to depend on the largely procedural consideration of who wishes to compel him.[20] Nor is it clear why the pre-1898 position should have been thought significant, in view of the radical change in the law brought about by the Criminal Evidence Act 1898.

### 11.4.4   *R* v *Coke; R* v *Littleton*

It seems most unlikely that the prosecution would wish to seek to call either Coke or Littleton against the other, unless one voluntarily decides to plead guilty to the charge against him. Where serious charges are involved against both, it would not be right to think of dropping the case against either, and there is no real room for accepting pleas to lesser charges here. Thus, it follows that Coke and Littleton will remain incompetent witnesses for the prosecution, but will be competent (not of course compellable) in their own defence and in that of each other; in the circumstances of this case, the last possibility hardly arises. If either gives evidence in his defence, he may be freely cross-examined about both offences as a witness in the case for all purposes. The circumstances illustrate the advantage of being last on the indictment, and so being called upon last to make one's defence. Coke, being first on the indictment, must take his decision whether or not to give evidence before he knows what is likely to be said in evidence by Littleton, either in chief or in cross-examination. Littleton may hear Coke's evidence before deciding. If Coke elects not to give evidence, he has lost his chance of contradicting in evidence anything said against him subsequently by Littleton, though he may seek to repair the damage by cross-examination. The point has some relevance for the prosecution, in deciding the order in which to indict. It is best from their point of view to order the defendants so that those against whom the case seems weakest appear as early in the indictment as their involvement in the offences will properly allow, so that they cannot rely upon not having the case against them made stronger by the evidence of their co-defendants.

### 11.5   Spouses of parties

We have seen that the abolition of incompetence through interest by the Evidence Act 1843 paved the way for the competence of the parties themselves. For the same reason, the

---

[19]   *R* v *Payne* (CCA) (1872) LR 1 CCR 349; *R* v *Bradlaugh* (1883) 15 Cox CC 217, in neither of which can any firm rule at common law be fairly said to have been established.

[20]   It is, however, to be noticed that the witness will enjoy the privilege against self-incrimination, which as a defendant would not be available to him in respect of the offence charged because of proviso (*e*) to s. 1. In many cases, this may well render his evidence valueless to the party calling him.

competence of the spouses of parties was rendered inevitable. It was enacted for civil cases by the Evidence Amendment Act 1853, subject to the exceptions of proceedings instituted in consequence of adultery and breach of promise of marriage which the Act of 1851 had left in respect of parties, and these exceptions were likewise removed for spouses by the Evidence Further Amendment Act 1869. Consequently, in civil cases, the spouses of the parties are now both competent and compellable, in accordance with the general rule.

As with the parties themselves, very different considerations prevailed in relation to criminal cases. The issue here was the extent to which the defendant's spouse might be competent either for the prosecution or for the defence. The position at common law was far from satisfactory. On the one hand, there had always been felt a sense of natural repugnance at the thought of spouses giving evidence against each other[21] and of apprehension at the obvious dangers of perjured and exaggerated evidence. Coupled with these factors was the compelling influence of the legal fiction that husband and wife were one person in law, a fiction which died only with reluctance towards the end of the nineteenth century. Taken together with the privilege against self-incrimination, which because of the fiction was extended to the spouse, it provided a formidable barrier to competence.[22] But on the other hand, despite these powerful inducements to incompetence, it had been recognised as early as the seventeenth century, that the enforcement of the law demanded some degree of deviation from the strict rule. The precise limits of the deviation were never certain. However, as we shall see, it came to be recognised that a defendant's spouse might be a competent witness for the prosecution in some instances.

## 11.6  Spouse of a defendant in a criminal case

The common law had developed in an uncertain fashion, particularly with respect to the competence and compellability of the spouse as a witness for the prosecution. The Criminal Evidence Act 1898 and later statutes made piecemeal modifications to the supposed common law rules. As reflected in the first edition of this work and summarised below, these provisions and the decisions based on them left the law in a state of considerable complexity on the issue of competence, and with the issue of compellability apparently resolved against compellability in any case, even where the spouse might be a competent prosecution witness. Both the common law and the piecemeal statutory reforms have now been superseded by the relatively straightforward provisions of s.80 of the Police and Criminal Evidence Act 1984, which lay down comprehensive rules governing the competence and compellability of the spouse of the defendant in criminal cases. These will be examined below.

Two preliminary points should be made. The first is that in *R* v *Pitt* [1982] 3 All ER 63, a case decided before the coming into effect of the Police and Criminal Evidence Act 1984, it was held that where a wife was a competent, but not compellable witness for the

---

[21]  Such feeling of repugnance as has manifested itself in recent times has been directed generally to the idea of compelling spouses, rather than rendering them competent. But even as to this, repugnance has largely receded. See,e.g. the powerful dissenting speech of Lord Edmund-Davies in *Hoskyn* v *Commissioner of Police of the Metropolis* (HL) [1979] AC 474 at 501; Police and Criminal Evidence Act 1984, s. 80; 11.6, post.

[22]  '. . . it hath been resolved by the justices, that a wife cannot be produced either against or for her husband, *quia sunt duae animae in carne una*; and it might be a cause of implacable discord and dissention between the husband and the wife, and a means of great inconvenience'. Co. Litt. 6b.

prosecution against her husband, the choice open to the wife to testify or not to testify existed up to the moment she entered the witness-box, and was unaffected by the fact that she might previously have made a witness statement, or even given evidence at the committal proceedings. Once she is sworn, of course, she beomes an ordinary witness and must answer any proper questions put to her on behalf of any party, and may be treated as a hostile witness if appropriate. There appears to be no reason to depart from this decision for the purpose of the new rules laid down by the 1984 Act, by virtue of which the same situation can arise. The same choice faces the defendant himself.

The second is that by virtue of s.80(8) of the Police and Criminal Evidence Act 1984, which replaced a corresponding provision in s.1(b) of the Criminal Evidence Act 1898, the failure of the spouse of the defendant to give evidence shall not be made the subject of any comment by the prosecution. As in the case of the prohibition against comment on the failure of the defendant himself to give evidence, this prohibition affects only the prosecution, and does not restrict comment by a co-defendant, or, within proper and reasonable bounds, by the judge.

### 11.6.1 Pre-1984 law

It is helpful to an understanding of the provisions of s.80 of the Police and Criminal Evidence Act 1984, to consider briefly the state of the law which preceded them. As indicated above, the pre-existing law had the unfortunate characteristics of uncertain common-law rules modified by piecemeal statutory changes. The most important principles may be summarised as follows.

#### 11.6.1.1 The spouse as a prosecution witness.

At common law, the spouse of the defendant was generally incompetent as a prosecution witness. Permitting one spouse to testify against the other in breach of this principle resulted in a reversal of any conviction so obtained on appeal.[23] The rule grew up partly as a result of the legal fiction of the unity of husband and wife, and partly because of the policy of the law in preserving and upholding the integrity of the matrimonial relationship.[24] However, even at common law some exceptions were recognised. The problem was that the extent of the exceptions was never finally decided. Common-law commentators generally agreed that the spouse was competent on a charge of high treason, in which case public policy requiring conviction in the interests of the state overrode that requiring the preservation of the matrimonial relationship. But as to more mundane offences there were few clear rules. It was established that the spouse was a competent witness as to offences of violence committed against the spouse, because in such cases the spouse against whom the offence is committed is often the only available witness and without his or her testimony, the offence might go unpunished.[25] But there was no real agreement on the question of what offences were to be regarded as offences of violence against the spouse for this purpose.[26] There was also some suggestion that the spouse might be competent in the case of offences against minor members of the family, for the same reasons of policy, but this was never settled at

---

[23]  See *R* v *Deacon* [1973] 1 WLR 696; *R* v *Mount; R* v *Metcalfe* (1934) 24 Cr App R 135.

[24]  The question of the competence of a spouse must be carefully distinguished from that of the privilege of a spouse not to divulge during testimony communications made by the other spouse during the marriage. This privilege was abolished in civil cases by s. 16(3) of the Civil Evidence Act 1968 and in criminal cases by s. 80(9) of the Police and Criminal Evidence Act 1984. See Chapter 10.

[25]  *Lord Audley's Case* (1632) 3 St Tr 402.

[26]  See, e.g., *R* v *Yeo* [1951] 1 All ER 864n; *R* v *Verolla* [1963] 1 QB 285.

common law and was left to occasional statutory intervention.

The Criminal Evidence Act 1898 left untouched any 'case where the wife or husband of a person charged with an offence may at common law be called as a witness without the consent of that person'. But s.4(1) of the Act provided additionally that 'the wife or husband of a person charged with an offence under any enactment mentioned in the schedule to this Act may be called as a witness either for the prosecution or defence and without the consent of the person charged'. The offences enumerated were supplemented and varied from time to time, but in its final form the schedule incorporated most offences against the person and sexual offences against children and young persons, child destruction and persistent refusal or neglect to maintain. It was in many important respects superseded by later specific statutory competences, for example those relating to sexual offences contained in the Sexual Offences Act 1956.

The most far-reaching reform, however, was that contained in s.30(2) and (3) of the Theft Act 1968. Section 30(2) provided that a person should be entitled to bring proceedings against that person's spouse for any offence, as if they were not married, and should be a competent witness as to any such offence. Section 30 (3) provided that even in relation to proceedings not brought by the spouse, the spouse should be a competent witness as to any offence which was an offence 'with reference to that person's wife or husband or to property belonging to the wife or husband', and this whether the defendant was charged alone or jointly with any other person. Since these subsections were not confined to any particular type of offence, as long as the proceedings were brought by the witness spouse, or there was some connection with the person or property of the witness spouse, they made a substantial incursion on the common-law rules. Indeed, when considered in conjunction with earlier statutory provisions, they may well have effectively replaced the common-law rules in all but a few cases—a view adopted by most commentators and in the first edition of this work.

Curiously, the common-law position as to compellability of the spouse as a prosecution witness was settled very late and with significant dissent. It is true that the House of Lords had held in *Leach* v *R* [1912] AC 305 that where the spouse was competent by virtue of s.4 of and the schedule to the Criminal Evidence Act 1898, the spouse was nonetheless not compellable. But in *R* v *Lapworth* [1931] 1 KB 117, the Court of Criminal Appeal refused to follow that authority in deciding the corresponding question of compellability in a case where the spouse was competent at common law, holding that if the spouse was competent, then like any other witness at common law (except the defendant) the spouse was also compellable. In this confused and inconsistent state the law remained until the House of Lords (Lords Wilberforce, Dilhorne, Salmon and Keith of Kinkel, Lord Edmund Davies dissenting) resolved the matter by holding in *Hoskyn* v *Commissioner of Police of the Metropolis* [1979] AC 474 that even where the spouse was competent, by virtue of whatever common-law or statutory rule, he or she was nonetheless never compellable as a prosecution witness.

Both the reasoning of the majority of the House and that expressed in the powerful dissenting speech of Lord Edmund Davies had an important influence on the eventual statutory resolution of the law in s.80 of the Police and Criminal Evidence Act 1984. Lord Salmon (ibid at 495) pointed out that the competence of the (in this case) wife, in the case of an offence of violence committed against her by her husband, was allowed by the common law for the wife's protection, and should not be forced upon her where she was reluctant, on mature reflection, to testify against him because of forgiveness and reconciliation, and had no fear of further violence. Such compulsion could in some cases destroy the marriage. On the other hand, Lord Edmund Davies [27] pointed out that some offences are too grave to be compromised simply because the wife changes her mind about testifying , and that being compellable is a useful protection for a wife witness who is basically disposed to testify but it subject to intimidation or coercion if she does so voluntarily.

*11.6.1.2   The spouse as a defence witness.* The Criminal Evidence Act 1898 rendered the spouse a competent witness for the defence, whether the defendant was charged solely or jointly with any other person, and by s.1(c) (now repealed in consequence of s.80 of the 1984 Act) provided that:

> The wife or husband of the person charged shall not, save as in this Act mentioned, be called as a witness in pursuance of this Act except on the application of the person charged.

The phrase 'save as in this Act mentioned' referred to the exceptional cases provided for by s.4 and the schedule to the Act, which dispensed with the consent of the defendant in a case in which the spouse might be a competent prosecution witness. The importance of the necessity for the application of the defendant was simply that, save in the exceptional cases, the defendant to whom the witness spouse was married was entitled to exercise control over the calling of the witness spouse as a witness. This meant that the position of that defendant was different from that of other defendants jointly charged, who could not, save in the exceptional cases, call the witness spouse without the consent of the defendant spouse. This rule corresponded with the common-law rule,[28] and reflects the policy of the law that it is just as invidious to permit a co-defendant to call the spouse of a spouse defendant as to permit the prosecution to do so, so that only in the exceptional cases previously referred to might this be done.

The 1898 Act did not settle the compellability of the spouse witness for the defence. Although as a matter of practice, a defendant would probably think long and hard before calling a reluctant or hostile spouse to give evidence for the defence, the question might have been of importance. Subsequent statutes, notably the Sexual Offences Act 1956 and the Theft Act 1968, provided expressly that the spouse should not be compellable even when rendered competent, and even though these provisions were probably intended to refer primarily to competence for the prosecution (since the spouse was already generally competent as a defence witness under the 1898 Act), they were also capable of application to the spouse as a defence witness, for example in the exceptional cases in which a co-defendant was entitled to call the spouse without the consent of the defendant spouse. Taken together with *Leach* and *Hoskyn*, they probably indicated that the spouse was not a compellable witness for the defence prior to the Police and Criminal Evidence Act 1984, though the matter was by no means beyond argument. Policy would not necessarily dictate the same result as in the case of the spouse as a prosecution witness.

*11.6.2   The Police and Criminal Evidence Act 1984, s. 80*

This section has enacted a sweeping change in the law governing the competence and

---

[27]   Ibid at 499. See also the 11th Report of the Criminal Law Revision Committee, para. 149.
[28]   *R v Thompson* (CRR) (1872) LR 1 CCR 377.

compellability of the spouse of the defendant in a criminal case, adopting in part various of the policy considerations developed by the common law and in earlier statutory provisions. The substance of the new law (with the exception of the law relating to former spouses contained in s. 80(5) which will be considered in 11.7, post) is contained in s. 80(1)–(4). These subsections are as follows:

> (1)   In any proceedings the wife or husband of the accused shall be competent to give evidence—
> (a) subject to subsection (4) below, for the prosecution; and
> (b) on behalf of the accused or any person jointly charged with the accused.

> (2)   In any proceedings the wife or husband of the accused shall, subject to subsection (4) below, be compellable to give evidence on behalf of the accused.

> (3)   In any proceedings the wife or husband of the accused shall, subject to subsection (4) below, be compellable to give evidence for the prosecution or on behalf of any person jointly charged with the accused if and only if—
> (a) the offence charged involves an assault on, or injury or a threat of injury to, the wife or husband of the accused or a person who was at the material time under the age of sixteen; or
> (b) the offence charged is a sexual offence alleged to have been committed in respect of a person who was at the material time under that age; or
> (c) the offence charged consists of attempting or conspiring to commit, or of aiding, abetting, counselling, procuring or inciting the commission of, an offence falling within paragraph (a) or (b) above.

> (4)   Where a husband and wife are jointly charged with an offence neither spouse shall at the trial be competent or compellable by virtue of subsection (1) (a), (2) or (3) above to give evidence in respect of that offence unless that spouse is not, or is no longer, liable to be convicted of that offence at the trial as a result of pleading guilty or for any other reason.

Section 80(6) provides that where the age of a person is material by virtue of subsection (3), that age may be deemed to be, or to have been, that which appears to the court to be or to have been the age of that person at the material time. Section 80(7) provides that a 'sexual offence' for the purposes of subsection (3) means an offence under the Sexual Offences Act 1956, or under certain other statutes. Earlier statutory provisions affecting the competence and compellability of the spouse, including s. 1(c) and (d) of the Criminal Evidence Act 1898, s. 39 of the Sexual Offences Act 1956, and s. 30(3) of the Theft Act 1968, are repealed in consequence of this section.

The law as laid down by s. 80 may be stated in the following propositions.

*11.6.2.1   The spouse as a prosecution witness.* The spouse is always a competent prosecution witness, except as to an offence with which the witness spouse is charged jointly with the defendant spouse, and of which the witness spouse remains liable to be convicted at trial. As in the case of a co-defendant, the spouse may be rendered competent for the prosecution in such a case only where he or she is no longer liable to be convicted, either because he or she has pleaded guilty to that offence, or 'for any other reason', for example because the prosecution offer no evidence against the witness spouse on that charge. While this appears to be a radical departure from the common-law principles, in reality it is probably little more than a rationalisation of the trend ever since the Criminal Evidence Act 1898, culminating in s. 30 of the Theft Act 1968 which, as pointed out above, had already effectively repealed the common-law rule of general incompetence. The policy in favour of making evidence available wherever possible seems now to be firmly established.

The spouse is a compellable prosecution witness only where the charge falls under one of the categories listed in subsection (3), and is otherwise not compellable for the prosecution, even when competent. It will be noted that the offences listed in subsection (3) reflect the common-law concern with offences against the witness spouse, with respect to which the Act adopts the philosophy expressed by Lord Edmund Davies in his dissenting speech in *Hoskyn*. No doubt prosecuting authorities will take into account the gravity of the charge, the likelihood of reconciliation, the possibility of intimidation and other matters in deciding whether a reluctant spouse should be compelled to testify in any given case. The listed offences also reflect the concern of the common law and earlier statutes with offences, particularly sexual offences, against children and young persons. Like offences against the spouse, these have the characteristic that the evidence of the witness spouse is often the decisive, if not the only available prosecution evidence. It is clear that the children and young persons involved need not be children of either spouse. The subsection applies equally, for example, to the children of others lured to the home by one spouse for the purposes of sexual abuse.

*11.6.2.2 The spouse as a witness for the defendant spouse.* The witness spouse is always a competent witness on behalf of the defendant spouse. The witness spouse is also a compellable witness for the defendant spouse, except in the case previously referred to in which the spouses are jointly charged with an offence with respect to which the witness spouse remains liable to be convicted at trial.

*11.6.2.3 The spouse as a witness for a co-defendant.* The spouse is always a competent witness for a co-defendant. There is no requirement that the spouse be called on the application of the defendant spouse, as was formerly the general rule under s.1 of the Criminal Evidence Act 1898. However, the spouse is compellable by a co-defendant only where the charge is one of those listed in subsection (3).

*11.6.2.4 R v Coke; R v Littleton.* The above rules may be illustrated by considering Mrs Littleton's competence and compellability in the criminal trial of Coke and Littleton. Mrs Littleton is not charged with an offence, so that there is no question of any joint charge which would bring subsection (4) into play. Consequently, Mrs Littleton would be a competent prosecution witness. Furthermore, the offence of indecent assault on Angela Blackstone, with which Littleton is charged, is a sexual offence against a person under the age of 16, and is therefore an offence listed in subsection (3). Mrs Littleton is accordingly not only a competent, but also a compellable prosecution witness. She is, of course, both competent and compellable as a witness for Littleton.

## 11.7  Former spouses

At common law, the incompetence of a spouse survived the termination of the marriage, in respect of matters which occurred during the marriage. In *Monroe* v *Twistleton* (NP) (1802) Peace Add Cas 219, the plaintiff was held not to be entitled to call the divorced wife of the defendant in order to prove a contract allegedly made between the defendant and himself during the marriage. The rule was followed in *O'Connor* v *Marjoribanks* (1842) 4 Man G 435, in which personal representatives suing in respect of the alleged conversion of part of an estate were not permitted to call the widow of the deceased with a view to proving what instructions about the disposal of the estate had been given by the deceased during his lifetime. A former spouse was, of course, competent to give evidence concerning events that occurred after the termination of the marriage. Whether or not the incompetence of a former spouse related also to events which occurred prior to the marriage appears never to have been decided.

The termination of the marriage may be, and in the older cases more commonly was, effected by a decree of nullity. If a decree of nullity is based on a ground which renders the marriage voidable only, so that there has been a valid marriage up to the date of the decree, then it does not affect incompetence with respect to events before the decree.[29] However, a technical distinction was made in cases where the decree was based on a ground which rendered the 'marriage' void *ab initio*. In such a case, there had never been, in law, a valid marriage, and no rule of incompetence could therefore arise, let alone survive.[30]

The mere fact that the parties to a marriage are not cohabiting has no effect on the existence of incompetence due to the relationship of marriage. This applies whether the parties are living apart without any express arrangement, or pursuant to a separation agreement, or even pursuant to a decree of judicial separation or non-cohabitation order made by a court. In *Moss* v *Moss* [1963] 2 QB 799, the Divisional Court rejected an argument that the word 'coverture', used in the older cases to describe the duration of the incompetence, connoted cohabitation only, so as to render a spouse competent to give evidence of events which occurred after the spouses had ceased to cohabit. While the marriage endured, so did the 'coverture', and a spouse was incompetent in respect of matters occurring during such period.

The rule in *Monroe* v *Twistleton* has never been formally abrogated in civil cases, but its position has become exceedingly tenuous, and it might profitably be decently buried if and when the opportunity arises. Its main problem has been the intervention of statute all around it. In s. 1 of the Evidence Amendment Act 1853, which rendered competent the spouses of the parties in almost all civil cases, the words used to describe those so made competent were 'husband' and 'wife'. If the incompetence of former spouses survives, therefore, it must be because those words exclude former husbands and wives. This would produce the preposterous result that while existing spouses are competent and compellable in respect of events during the marriage, former spouses are not. For this reason alone, it has probably been assumed that the Act effectively abrogated *Monroe* v *Twistleton*, so far as civil cases are concerned. This convenient construction is, unfortunately, difficult to justify especially in view of *Shenton* v *Tyler* [1939] Ch 620, a decision on the identical words in s. 3 of the same Act relating to matrimonial privilege. In this case a strong Court of Appeal held, after an exhaustive review of the authorities that the words 'husband' and 'wife' could not be construed so as to include widowers and widows. The truth is that *Monroe* v *Twistleton* depends on a premise (the incompetence of

---

[29]  *R* v *Algar* (CCA) [1954] 1 QB 279.
[30]  *Wells* v *Fisher* (NP) (1831) 1 Mood & R 99.

spouses) which, in civil cases, is not longer valid.

In criminal cases, the history of the competence of former spouses took a very different course and *Monroe* v *Twistleton* enjoyed a more vigorous old age. In *R* v *Algar* [1954] 1 QB 279, the defendant was charged with the forgery of his wife's signature on cheques drawn on her bank account during 1947 and 1948. In 1949, the marriage was annulled because of the impotence of the defendant, a ground which rendered the marriage voidable only. The former wife was called at the defendant's trial in 1953. The Court of Criminal Appeal quashed the conviction, holding, following *Monroe* v *Twistleton*, that she remained incompetent with respect to the matters alleged in the indictment.

However, in keeping with the statutory provisions introduced by s. 80 of the Police and Criminal Evidence Act 1984, the rule in *Monroe* v *Twistleton* has been abolished in criminal cases. Section 80(5) of the Act now provides:

> In any proceedings a person who has been but is no longer married to the accused shall be competent and compellable to give evidence as if that person and the accused had never been married.

It is to be noted that the Act deals with all terminated marriages as the common law would have done if they had been declared void *ab initio*, and not declared voidable or terminated by death or dissolution. This is a very strong provision, which makes it clear that any incompetence which may remain in the spouse of the defendant endures only during the marriage and ends with the marriage, even with respect to matters which occurred during the marriage.

## 11.8 Children of tender years

The concern of the common law with regard to the competence of young children is based upon very different considerations to those discussed earlier in this chapter. The question here is one of reliability. It affects civil and criminal cases alike, and little or no difference is to be observed in the courts' approach to them.

The competence of a child of tender years is based entirely on the opinion of the judge, who must examine the child with a view to establishing whether or not he may be relied upon, in the sense that he understands the importance of telling the truth, and the consequences of falsehood. The judge has a positive duty to embark upon the inquiry, irrespective of the views of the parties. He must do so, even though, in a criminal case, the examining justices have taken a view that the child is competent,[31] and the inquiry must be held in open court in the presence of the jury and recorded for the transcript.[32]

There is no set age at which a child ceases to be 'of tender years' or becomes competent to give evidence. In the recent case of *R* v *Hayes* [1979] 1 WLR 234, 237, it was said by the Court of Appeal that 'the watershed dividing children who are normally considered old enough to take the oath and children normally considered too young to take the oath, probably falls between the ages of eight and ten'. But the range of ages of the children accepted or rejected by the court as competent witnesses, in the considerable number of reported cases, is greater than that, and little profit can be derived from accumulating statistics on the subject.[33] Indeed, to do so would be to miss the point. The question is not

---

[31]  *R* v *Surgenor* (CCA) [1940] 2 All ER 249.
[32]  *R* v *Khan* (1981) 73 Cr App R 190; *R* v *Reynolds* (CCA) [1950] 1 KB 606.
[33]  A selection of examples is given in Phipson, *Evidence,* 13th ed., para.31–09.

the precise age of the child, but whether the judge, after his inquiry, forms the view that the child has the necessary degree of intelligence and understanding. The Court of Appeal in *Hayes* observed (ibid at 237) that:

> We think it right also to approach the matter on the footing that this is very much a matter within the discretion of the trial judge and we think that this court, although having jurisdiction to interfere if clearly satisfied that the trial judge's discretion was wrongly exercised, should hesitate long before doing so. The judge sees and hears the boy or girl, which means very much more than the bare written word.

The important question is, on what basis the judge should make his assessment of the child's intelligence and understanding. Here, the newer cases diverge from the older. Originally, at common law, the main and overriding question was whether the child understood the oath. Unless he did, and showed appreciation of the nature of an oath and the divine sanction against falsehood, he was not to be regarded as competent. Competence and the taking of the oath went hand in hand.[34] Therefore, the questions posed by the judge to the child were primarily directed to his understanding of the oath itself. In *R* v *Brasier*,[35] which was formerly a leading authority, the judges having noted that evidence could lawfully be given only on oath, held that there was no 'precise or fixed rule' about age, and continued: '. . . their admissibility depends upon the sense and reason they entertain of the danger and impiety of falsehood, which is to be collected from their answers to questions propounded to them by the court'.

The difficulties of enforcing this requirement were considerable, and led to such extreme results as the interruption of trials to allow children to be instructed about the oath, or even, in certain instances, to receive some basic religious training, in order to give evidence. In due course, frustration with this manifestly unrealistic way of treating child witnesses led Parliament to enact that in criminal cases, children might, subject to proper inquiry concerning their intelligence, be permitted to give evidence unsworn. This avoided the equation of competence and oath by removing the child from the duty of being sworn altogether. By s. 38(1) of the Children and Young Persons Act 1933:

> Where, in any proceedings against any person for any offence, any child of tender years called as a witness does not in the opinion of the court understand the nature of an oath, his evidence may be received, though not given upon oath, if, in the opinion of the court, he is possessed of sufficient intelligence to justify the reception of the evidence, and understands the duty of speaking the truth.

The section, which succeeds earlier provisions, has the great advantage of pointing the court in a direction more calculated to further the ends of justice than that of inquiry into a child's religious state. It also had, however, the disadvantage that because of the absence of the oath, special provision had to be made to emulate the usual consequences of sworn evidence. Thus, a new offence akin to perjury was built by s. 38(2), because perjury itself required the defendant to have been 'lawfully sworn' in the proceedings. More

---

[34]   This equation was not at all restricted to children. At common law, atheists and 'infidels' were originally incompetent because of their inability to be properly sworn. The importance of the oath was very great, and was central to the competence of any witness.

[35]   (CCR) (1779) 1 Leach 199, 1 East PC 443. The child witness in the case is variously reported as having been 'five' and 'under seven'. Cf. *R* v *Wallwork* (CCA) (1958) 42 Cr App R 153.

significantly, whereas the common law had required the jury, as a matter of practice, to look for corroboration of the evidence of a child of tender years, a stricter requirement was made for unsworn evidence, and by the proviso to s. 38(1), where such unsworn evidence is given for the prosecution, the defendant, 'shall not be liable to be convicted of the offence unless that evidence is corroborated by some other material evidence in support thereof implicating him'.[36]

The two kinds of evidence receivable from children, sworn and unsworn, have continued to coexist somewhat uncomfortably because of these distinctions, and it has not been at all easy identify the frontiers of each. Happily, the criterion suggested to the courts by s. 38(1), based on the intelligence of the child and his understanding of the duty to speak the truth, has now been found to correspond with what the law sees as the true test of competence. In *R* v *Hayes* [1977] 1 WLR 234, the defendant was charged with inciting three boys to commit acts of gross indecency with him, and with committing such an act with one of the boys. At the time of the trial, the boys were aged twelve, eleven and nine respectively. The youngest boy gave unsworn evidence under s. 38(1). The judge, after an exchange of questions and answers, allowed the two older boys to be sworn. The appeal was based on certain answers which led to doubt about whether the oldest boy called had any belief in God, or in the divine sanction of an oath. The appeal raised, in effect, the question whether the view propounded in *Brasier* should continue to stand as a proper test of competence in modern law. The Court of Appeal, dismissing the application for leave to appeal, dealt with the matter thus (ibid at 236–7):

> The court is not convinced that that is really the essence of the court's duty in the difficult situation where the court has to determine whether a young person can or cannot properly be permitted to take an oath before giving evidence. It is unrealistic not to recognise that, in the present state of society, amongst the adult population the divine sanction of an oath is probably not generally recognised. The important consideration, we think, when a judge has to decide whether a child should properly be sworn, is whether the child has a sufficient appreciation of the solemnity of the occasion and the added responsibility to tell the truth, which is involved in taking an oath, over and above the duty to tell the truth which is an ordinary duty of normal social conduct.

It now appears that the test of competence is, in reality, not far removed from that laid down for the giving of unsworn evidence under s. 38(1). It is submitted that this is a healthy development in the law. It may be that there is an added maturity which comes with the advance of age, which enables a child to appreciate the solemnity of the proceedings and so be enabled to take the oath, but there can be no doubt that it is desirable that the reception of evidence should be based upon the test of intelligence and appreciation of the duty of telling the truth.

### 11.8.1 *R* v *Coke; R* v *Littleton*

It is, of course, far more satisfactory that a child should be sworn, wherever this course may properly be taken. In view of her age there seems little doubt that Angela Blackstone may give evidence on oath, although the judge must, briefly, establish this fact to his satisfaction, by framing questions suitable to elicit her view of the seriousness of the

---

[36] See 14.6 and 14.7, post.

proceedings, and attitude to speaking the truth, not just in a social context, but in the context of the proceedings.

## 11.9   Persons of defective intellect

There was, at common law, an undeveloped view that 'lunacy' was a bar to competence. The view probably resulted both from the dangers of unreliability and from doubtful capacity to appreciate the nature of an oath. It is, of course, a fairly modern tendency in the law to seek to recognise and accommodate the more sophisticated diagnosis and treatment of mental illness, and the law has not always kept pace with the consequences of the obsolescence of the generic classification of mental patients under the heading of lunacy.[37]

Although the position in contemporary law is largely unexplored, it seems that the court will take a pragmatic view, and accord competence to a person of defective intellect, which corresponds with the judge's view of his capacity to understand the nature of the proceedings and to speak the truth to the best of his ability. The question is whether the proposed witness is, at the time of being called, capable of giving proper evidence. If his lack of capacity is a temporary one, his evidence may be receivable after a suitable adjournment, as may be the case with a witness who arrives at court drunk. Incapacity will not be accepted if the witness's evidence can be taken with reasonably practicable precautions, particularly if the evidence may be important.[38]

The matter is, therefore, one for the judge, who should, if necessary, inquire into the capacity of the witness in open court and in the presence of the jury. If the witness is declared to be competent, he may give evidence on any relevant issue,[39] and is subject to the normal rules of evidence.

## 11.10   Miscellaneous exceptions to the rule of compellability

Apart from the defendant and the defendant's spouse in criminal cases, the general rule is that all competent witnesses are compellable to give evidence. There are a number of comparatively unimportant further exceptions, which are noted here, primarily for the sake of completeness.

The Sovereign and foreign heads of state, though competent, are not compellable. By various statutory provisions, certain persons who are accredited diplomats or officers of international organisations, enjoy a greater or lesser degree of immunity from compellability, according to their accredited status as such.[40]

By s. 6 of the Bankers' Books Evidence Act 1879:

A banker or officer of a bank shall not in any legal proceeding to which the bank is not a party, be compellable to produce any banker's book the contents of which can be

---

[37]   As witness the continued existence of the M'Naghten Rules.

[38]   Cf. *R* v *Hill* (CCR) (1851) 2 Den CC 254, where an inmate of an asylum, whose 'only delusion' (sic) was that spirits occasionally talked to him, was permitted to give evidence in a prosecution for manslaughter.

[39]   Including, it seems, that of his own sanity: *Hunter* v *Edney* (1885) 10 PD 93.

[40]   Diplomatic Privileges Act 1964: Consular Relations Act 1968; International Organisations Act 1968; Diplomatic and Other Privileges Act 1971; State Immunity Act 1978, s. 20.

proved under this Act, or to appear as a witness to prove the matters, transactions, and accounts therein recorded, unless by order of a judge made for special cause.

The purpose of the provision is to protect bankers and their officers from the onerous requirements which might otherwise follow from the frequent recourse of the courts to evidence contained in banker's books. The Act provides sufficient modes of proof of entries in such books, and a procedure for obtaining orders for their discovery and inspection. These are dealt with in 15.3.5, post.

## B: OATHS AND AFFIRMATIONS

### 11.11   The requirement of sworn evidence

We saw in the preceding section of this chapter that the ability to take the oath was, at common law, a central and probably the central element of competence as a witness. It was, historically, and is today a fundamental rule that evidence given to the court for any purpose shall be sworn, though more modern times have countenanced exceptional cases, which would not have been admitted in earlier days. Evidence is sworn if the witness is first required to take a lawful oath or affirmation, which carries with it the sanction of the law against false evidence.

Evidence given unsworn is, unless given in one of the cases recognised as exceptional, a nullity, and any conviction or judgment based on it will be set aside on appeal. In *R* v *Marsham, ex parte Pethick Lawrence* (DC) [1912] KB 362, where the magistrates' court, by error, conducted a case on the basis of unsworn evidence and thereafter re-heard the case in the proper manner on the same day, an appeal was brought on the ground that the defendant had stood in jeopardy twice because of the procedure adopted by the court. The appeal failed. The first hearing, based on unsworn evidence, had been a nullity, and the defendant had not then stood in jeopardy. And in *Birch* v *Somerville* (1852) 2 ICLR 253, where the Lord Lieutenant of Ireland was permitted (irregularly) to give evidence 'on my honour as a peer', it was held that, but for acquiescence at the time, the irregularity would have been sufficient ground for an order for a new trial.

Witnesses may be sworn either by taking the oath in a lawful form, or by affirming. The rules relating to both were formerly complex, but have happily been simplified and rationalised by the Oaths Act 1978. Both possibilities may now be considered shortly.

### 11.11.1   Oaths

By s. 1(1) of the Oaths Act 1978, any oath may be administered and taken by the witness holding the book in his uplifted hand, and repeating the words of the oath prescribed by law.[41] Section 1(2) goes on to provide that the oath shall be administered in this manner, unless the witness voluntarily objects thereto, or is physically incapable of taking the oath in the prescribed way. This is a significant provision, in that it places the onus on the witness to notify the court of any objections which he may have to being sworn in the prescribed manner, except in the case of physical incapacity. Formerly, the witness was

---

[41]   The forms of oath were at one time diverse. In 1927, the judges of the King's Bench Division approved by resolution the following form for all civil and criminal proceedings in the courts over which they presided, and it has now passed into universal usage: 'I swear by Almighty God that the evidence I shall give shall be the truth, the whole truth and nothing but the truth.'

asked his religion, and if, being neither a Christian nor a Jew, it was inappropriate to swear him on the New or Old Testament, the court embarked of its own motion upon an inquiry to find a suitable book, or determine whether the witness should affirm. If no objection is made, it now follows from s. 1 that the witness has been lawfully sworn.

The Act does, however, provide fully for proper objections by witnesses, and clearly it is right that a witness should be sworn in a manner which he regards as binding, wherever this may be done without undue delay or inconvenience. By s 1(3) of the Act: 'In the case of a person who is neither a Christian nor a Jew, the oath shall be administered in any lawful manner.'

The 'lawful manners' referred to are various,[42] and have grown up haphazardly over a period of time. Members of non-Christian religions (other than Jews) are permitted to be sworn upon a book regarded in their religion as holy, although the appropriateness of holy books has been judged, not always accurately, by the court's own view of the dictates of witnesses' beliefs. There are special forms of oath appropriate to Quakers and Moravians. The ancient practice of swearing by kissing the Testament is permitted, while the Scots practice of swearing by the uplifted hand is specifically preserved as a lawful form by s. 3 of the Act.

### 11.11.2 Affirmations
By the Oaths Act 1978, s. 5:

(1) Any person who objects to being sworn shall be permitted to make his solemn affirmation instead of taking the oath.[43]

(4) A solemn affirmation shall be of the same force and effect as an oath.

The section has the welcome result that any witness may choose to affirm, as a voluntary alternative to being sworn. Previously, the judge was required to be satisfied after inquiry, either that the witness had no religious belief, or that being sworn would be contrary to his religious belief, although the letter of the law was frequently ignored in practice.

In addition to those who object to being sworn, a person may be permitted to affirm if 'it is not reasonably practicable without inconvenience or delay to administer an oath in the manner appropriate to his religious belief' (s. 5(2)). This provision is designed to cater for oaths of an unusual nature which might find the court administration unprepared and ill-equipped. It happens that witnesses occasionally insist upon some form of unusual oath, for the purpose of embarrassing the court, or of seeking to avoid giving evidence, and in order to meet this possibility, s. 5(2) is made enforceable by s. 5(3): 'A person who may be permitted under subsection (2) . . . to make his solemn affirmation may also be required to do so.'

---

[42]  There is a fascinating compendium to be found in Phipson. *Evidence*, 12th ed., paras 1519–22 and 13th ed., paras 31–35 and 31–38.

[43]  The form of affirmation, which was provided by the Oaths Act 1888, s. 2 (now the Oaths Act 1978, 6(1), is as follows: 'I [full name] do solemnly, sincerely, and truly declare and affirm that the evidence I shall give shall be the truth, the whole truth and nothing but the truth.'

## 11.12   Effect of oaths and affirmations

In *R* v *Hayes*[44] the Court of Appeal observed that it would be unrealistic to suppose that in contemporary society, the divine sanction of an oath was generally recognised. The case was concerned with child witnesses, but the observation was directed also to adults and it can hardly be denied that more temporal sanctions probably have more effect in ensuring, so far as it can be ensured, that witnesses are under some influence to speak the truth.

The Oaths Act 1978 recognises the trend by implication, by providing that the formal taking of the oath in court is to be the binding and effective act, for legal purposes, rather than the belief or conscience which may or may not lie behind the oath in the case of any individual witness. In other words, a witness is not to be permitted to escape the consequences of having been sworn simply by claiming subsequently that the oath was not such as to bind him, having regard to his beliefs. Section 4 of the Act provides:

(1)   In any case in which an oath may lawfully be and has been administered to any person, if it has been adminstered in a form and manner other than that prescribed by law, he is bound by it if it has been administered in such form and with such ceremonies as he may have declared to be binding.

(2)   Where an oath has been duly administered and taken, the fact that the person to whom it was administered had, at the time of taking it, no religious belief, shall not for any purpose affect the validity of the oath.

The real sanction against false evidence given on oath is, of course, prosecution for perjury. By s. 1 of the Perjury Act 1911, perjury in a judicial proceeding is committed: '[i]f any person lawfully sworn as a witness . . . in a judicial proceeding wilfully makes a statement material in that proceeding, which he knows to be false or does not believe to be true'.[45] The importance of the lawful swearing of witnesses is clearly apparent, because this offence, providing the sanction, cannot be committed otherwise. But it would be sufficient if the oath were taken in the circumstances envisaged by s. 4 of the Oaths Acts 1978, and because, by s. 5(4) of the 1978 Act, an affirmation is 'of the same force and effect as an oath', false evidence on affirmation falls within the scope of perjury.

## 11.13   Exceptions to the requirement of sworn evidence

There are some minor exceptions to the rule requiring sworn testimony. These are described briefly below. Until comparatively recently, there also existed a major exception, or apparent exception, in the form of the unsworn statement from the dock in a criminal case. This occupied a substantial amount of space in the first edition of this work, but the abolition by statute of this venerable piece of legal history now requires nothing more than a short requiem. The exceptions are as follows:

(a)   The evidence of children of tender years may be received unsworn, where the provisions of s. 38(1) of the Children and Young Persons Act 1933 apply: see 11.8.ante.

(b)   The evidence of a witness called merely to produce a document may be received

---

[44]   [1977] 1 WLR 234. And see para. 11.8, ante.
[45]   As to the law concerning perjury generally, see Archbold, 41st ed., paras 24–54 et seq.

unsworn, provided that the document can be identified, or its identity is not in dispute.[46]

(c)   Where a judge or counsel is asked to explain some aspect of a case in which he has been judicially or professionally engaged, he may appear and speak unsworn from his proper place in court.[47]

(d)   On licensing applications, evidence may be received unsworn, although the court may refuse to accept unsworn evidence, if the application is opposed.[48]

(e)   In extradition cases, a statement made abroad, usually in the country seeking extradition of the defendant, may be admitted in evidence even if not made under oath and subject to the penalty of perjury, provided that it was made in circumstances of sufficient gravity and formal solemnity for the witness to appreciate fully the importance of telling the truth: see *R* v *Governor of Pentonville Prison, ex parte Passingham and another* [1982] 3 All ER 1012.

(f)   Unsworn statements made from the dock by the defendant in a criminal case were traditionally regarded as an exception to the requirement of sworn evidence, although this is rather misleading because such statements were not really 'evidence' in the true sense. The right of a defendant to make an unsworn statement grew up in the course of the nineteenth century, in order to compensate for his inability to give evidence in his defence (before 1898), and for his inability, in cases of felony, to be represented by counsel (before 1836).[49] The rule evolved that the defendant might put his case to the jury in his own words without being liable to cross-examination, and it seems to have been analogous to counsel's closing speech, rather than to the giving of evidence. However, it came to occupy a position in the order of trial which aligned it procedurally with the giving of evidence, namely as part of the case of the defendant, before the speeches of counsel. When the disabilities of the defendant were at length removed, it would have been logical, and probably wise, to abolish the practice as obsolete, at least in the case of a legally represented defendant. No doubt out of considerations of fairness to the defence, this was not done, and indeed the Criminal Evidence Act 1898, s. 1 proviso (*h*) specifically provided that: 'Nothing in this Act shall affect . . . any right of the person charged to make a statement without being sworn.'

The unsworn statement co-existed uneasily with the new right to give evidence, and with the closing speech of defence counsel. It was often regarded as an alternative to the giving of evidence, and in more recent criminal practice, formidable difficulties arose in terms of identifying exactly what effect the unsworn statement might have. Despite a battery of decisions by the appellate courts, these problems were never satisfactorily resolved.[50] In particular, it was never determined whether the unsworn statement had any, and if so what, evidential value, and if not, how the judge should direct the jury about it. In the end, the problems outweighed its utility. It was perceived as an unnecessary encumbrance on modern criminal procedure, a protection no longer needed by the defendant. It died of old age, complicated by statutory abolition: Criminal Justice Act 1982, s. 72.

---

[46]   *Perry* v *Gibson* (1834) 1 A & E 48.

[47]   The practice is one of last resort, for obvious reasons of avoiding embarrassment. The practice of the Court of Appeal, Criminal Division, is now to prefer evidence from counsel on affidavit, where necessary, dealing with his conduct of a case at trial.

[48]   *R* v *Sharman and Others, ex parte Denton* (DC) [1898] 1 QB 578.

[49]   A defendant was from an early date entitled to counsel in cases of misdemeanour, and in cases of treason, after 1695.

[50]   See, e.g., *R* v *George* (1978) 68 Cr App R 210; *R* v *Coughlan* (1976) 64 Cr App R 11; *R* v *Shimmin* (1882) 15 Cox CC 122; and generally, the first edition of this work, pp.322–324.

## 11.14    Questions for discussions: *R* v *Coke; R* v *Littleton*

1   In what circumstances might Coke and Littleton be competent witnesses (a) for the prosecution; (b) in their own defence; (c) for each other? Would they be compellable in any such case?

2   In what circumstances may Mrs Littleton be a competent witness (a) for the prosecution; (b) for her husband; (c) for Coke? Will she be compellable in any such case?

3   How should the competence of Angela Blackstone as a witness be determined? What options are open to the court with regard to her evidence, and what are their advantages or disadvantages to the prosecution and defence respectively?

# 12 Examination in Chief

## 12.1 Nature and conduct of examination in chief

Examination in chief is the process whereby a party, who has called a witness to give evidence on his behalf, elicits from that witness evidence relevant to the issues and favourable to the examiner's case. The examination can be conducted safely only on the basis of a signed proof of evidence supplied by the witness, dealing with the matters on which he can speak, but of course the examination need not be confined to the contents of the proof, and may range over any matters relevant to the issues which transpire to be within the competence of the witness. The proof of evidence should be taken by a solicitor, since it is improper in general for counsel to interview a witness, other than an expert.[1] In a criminal case, examination in chief of the prosecution witnesses is conducted on the basis of, but is not restricted to, the contents of the deposition or witness statement of the witness.

With the exception of the parties themselves, and of expert witnesses, who are never excluded from court, the judge may require that a witness withdraw from court until called to give evidence. In criminal cases, this is the general rule for all witnesses, although the police officer in charge of the case is usually permitted to remain in court, at least until the start of police evidence, in the absence of any specific objection to his presence. In civil cases, the witnesses are usually present, unless specifically ordered to withdraw upon the application of any party. The matter is one for the discretion of the judge, and no question of natural justice is involved. If a witness deliberately remains in court after being ordered to leave, his evidence may not be admitted, but a judge has no discretion to exclude evidence on the sole ground that the witness has been present in court before giving evidence.[2]

It is important that evidence in chief should be given in the words of the witness, not those of the examiner, and consequently leading questions are not permitted.[3] A leading question is one which puts words into the witness's mouth, or suggests directly the answer

---

[1]  The Senate of the Inns of Court and the Bar has now recognised that in cases in a magistrates' court, where counsel is not attended by a solicitor, it may be necessary and permissible for counsel to take a proof of evidence.

[2]  See generally *Moore v Registrar of Lambeth County Court* (CA) [1969] 1 WLR 141; *R v Briggs* (CCA) (1930) 22 Cr App R 68; *Tomlinson v Tomlinson* [1980] 1 WLR 323.

[3]  Evidence elicited in chief by leading questions is not inadmissible, but its weight is often very slight: *Moor v Moor* (CA) [1954] 1 WLR 927.

which the examiner expects of him.[4] It is however, permissible to lead the witness on the following matters:

(a)   On preliminary matters, preparatory to questions about the facts in issue. It is usual, for example to lead the witness's name and address.[5].

(b)   On any matters which are not in dispute.

(c)   Where a witness is called to deal with some fact already in evidence, he may be asked directly about that fact.

(d)   Where leave has been granted to treat the witness as hostile: see 12.4.post.

(e)   By agreement between all concerned. It is common and good practice for an advocate to indicate to his opponent over what area the opponent may lead a given witness without objection.

Every witness called is required to identify himself to the court by giving his name and address. In a case where disclosure of the name and address of the witness might endanger the witness, or where it is necessary to the proper administration of justice, the judge has power to allow the details to be written down.[6] There are statutory provisions to ensure the anonymity of complainants and defendants in rape offences, and of children and young persons in proceedings of any kind.[7]

The detailed procedural considerations of the calling of evidence are outside the scope of this work, and reference should be made to texts dealing with procedure. There are, however, three important matters of evidential significance, which arise commonly in the course of evidence in chief, and which must be treated in some depth. These are:

(a)   The use by witnesses of documents to refresh the memory, while giving evidence.

(b)   The admissibility of previous consistent, or self-serving statements made by the witness.

(c)   The treatment of adverse and hostile witnesses.

## 12.2   Refreshing the memory

All too often, a considerable time elapses between the occurrence of events relevant to proceedings, and the trial of the proceedings themselves. It would be unrealistic to expect that a witness will always be able to give accurate and reliable evidence about events unless he is able to refresh his memory by looking at some note or document. This is true particularly of witnesses such as police officers, who have to give evidence in many different cases. On the other hand, a document cannot refresh the memory accurately unless its own accuracy can be vouched for, a factor which in effect dictates the making of the document as soon as possible after the events with which it deals.

---

[4]   The avoidance of leading questions is not an easy technique to acquire. If, for example, it is sought to elicit that Littleton touched Angela Blackstone on the leg, it would be leading to ask; 'Did he touch you on the leg?' or even: 'Did he touch you?' The proper way would be: Q: 'Did Littleton do anything to you?' A: 'Yes.' Q: 'What was that?' or some formula to the same effect. For practical hints, see Murphy and Barnard, *Evidence and Advocacy*, p.121 et seq.

[5]   Unless the address is in itself relevant, e.g., to the question of jurisdiction in a divorce case.

[6]   *R v The Socialist Worker Printers & Publishers Ltd and Another, ex parte Attorney-General* (DC) [1975] QB 637.

[7]   See the Sexual Offences (Amendment) Act 1976, s. 4 and s. 6; Children and Young Persons Act 1933, s. 39.

The rule is that a witness may, while giving evidence, refresh his memory by reference to any document which was made or verified by the witness, contemporaneously with the events to which it relates. These limitations on the origin of the documents which may be referred to are treated seriously, and before a witness is permitted to refer, an application must be made to the judge, who should inquire of the witness whether the conditions are satisfied. The judge should satisfy himself of this, whether or not any objection is taken, and if the conditions are not fulfilled, should not allow the reference; if they are fulfilled, the witness is entitled to refer.[8]

It is worth emphasising that the conditions of reference apply only to the use by the witness of the document to refresh his memory while giving evidence in the witness-box. Before giving evidence, there is nothing to prevent a proposed witness from looking at any document available to him, whatever its origin. In *R v Richardson* [1971] 2 QB 484, it was argued that it was improper for a witness to look, outside court, at a document which could not be used in court because of its lack of contemporaneity, in this case a statement made to the police some time after the event. The Court of Appeal rejected the argument. Quite apart from the apparent reasonableness of the principle that any witness, whether for the prosecution or the defence, ought not to be denied access to a statement made by him for the purpose of the proceedings, to seek to deny such access would create a highly artificial situation. The Court pointed out that the view contended for would tend to turn the giving of evidence into a test more of memory than of reliability; that it would do nothing to deter the dishonest witness, because it would be effectively unenforceable, but it would place substantial difficulties in the way of an honest and conscientious witness. It is, therefore, perfectly proper, not only for a witness to look at his statement or proof of evidence outside court before giving evidence, but also for counsel to take steps to see that the witnesses on is side have access to such documents as will help them, and it seems that this should be done in a case where lapse of time may otherwise mar the evidence of a witness. Opinion differs on whether counsel has any duty to inform his opponent when his witnesses have, to his knowledge, seen their statements, but there appears to be no rule of law to this effect; such a course is desirable, because the weight to be attached to the evidence of the witness may well be affected.[9]

In whatever way the witness may assist his recollection before giving evidence, once he enters the witness-box, he is bound by the reference rule set forth above. We may now consider in more detail, firstly the conditions of reference to, and secondly, the treatment of, memory-refreshing documents, including such evidential value as they may have.

### 12.2.1 Qualities of memory-refreshing documents

*12.2.1.1 Made or verified by the witness.* The best and most reliable memory refresher is a note made at the time of the events referred to, and compiled for the express purpose of subsequent use in the witness-box. The archetype is, of course, the police officer's notebook. However, the requirement of law does not go so far. There is no rule that the document must have been compiled for any particular purpose. It need not even be in the

---

[8]  The question is one for the judge rather than the other side, although cross-examination on the origin of the document is permitted.

[9]  *Worley v Bentley* (DC) [1976] 2 All ER 449; *R v Westwell* (CA) [1976] 2 All ER 812. If there is any such duty, it is evidently one founded in professional etiquette, and no more. The safe course for any advocate is probably to assume that his opponent's witnesses have seen their statements or proofs outside court.

handwriting of the witness, or made by him personally; but he must at least have verified it while it was being compiled by another (or soon enough afterwards to make his verification contemporaneous: see 12.2.1.2, post, by checking its contents at that time and by acknowledging them to be accurate, while the events were still fresh in his memory. It is preferable that he should have recorded his verification, for example by signing the document. This is not a legal requirement, but renders more likely the judge's finding that the witness is entitled to refer. A good illustration of the making and verification of a document is *Anderson* v *Whalley* (1852) 3 Car & Kir 54, in which a ship's log-book, kept by the mate and later checked and authenticated by the captain, was said to be a document from which either was entitled to refresh his memory.

A memory-refreshing document is not required to be in any particular form, as long as it complies with the conditions. In *R* v *Mills; R* v *Rose* (CCA) [1962] 1 WLR 1152, a police officer was allowed to refresh his memory from a note which was, in effect, a partial transcription of a tape-recording of incriminating conversations which took place between the defendants while in custody at the police station. The tape-recording itself was not used in evidence, but the officer was able, relying partly on his own recollection and partly on the note, to give evidence of what was said in the conversation. Quite apart from the admissibility of the tape-recording as such, as a piece of real evidence, there is similarly no reason why D/I Glanvil should not give evidence from any contemporaneous note made by him from the recording of the conversation between Littleton and his wife. Because there is no requirement of form, a statement made to the police may be referred to, if it satisfies the requirement of contemporaneity.

Following *R* v *Mills; R* v *Rose,* it was until recently assumed that a witness who did not personally make a document and who later wishes to use it to refresh his memory, must, in order to be held to have properly verified the document, have seen, read and confirmed the document as accurate either while it was being made or at the first practicable opportunity thereafter, while its contents were fresh in his mind. However, in *R* v *Kelsey* (1981) 74 Cr App R 213, the Court of Appeal held that the witness need not actually see the document at all, as long as he sees that a document is being made, has it read back to him and confirms its accuracy, and these events occur contemporaneously within the meaning of the rule. The appellant argued that a prosecution witness had wrongly been permitted to refresh his memory about the registration number of a car, while giving evidence, by reference to a contemporaneous note made at the witness' dictation by a police officer. The witness had not seen the note at or near the time when it was made, but the officer had read it back to him and the witness had confirmed its accuracy. The cynical may perhaps term this process 'verification by hearsay', but the Court was undeterred by such theorectical problems. Taylor J said (ibid at 217):

> The question we have to decide is, therefore, whether witness A can verify a note he dictates to B only by reading it himself, or whether it is sufficient if the note is read back by B to A at the time for confirmation. In most cases we would expect the note to be read by A if it is made in his presence. But what of the instant case, or cases involving the blind or illiterate? In our view there is no magic in verifying by seeing as opposed to verifying by hearing. *Mills and Rose* illustrates this, and shows that Winn J's words were somewhat too restrictive. What must be shown is that witness A has verified in the sense of satisfying himself whilst the matters are fresh in his mind, (1) that a record has been made, and (2) that it is accurate.

It must, of course, be proved that the note produced at trial is in fact the one made at the time and read back to the witness, and in *Kelsey* the police officer was able to do this. Accordingly, the appellant's argument failed and the appeal was dismissed.

The making and verification of a document or note is proper and sufficient if effected by two or more witnesses pooling their recollections, in order to produce the best possible record of events. This is a standard practice of police officers and was specifically approved in *R v Bass* (CCA) [1953] 1 QB 680, as being the most efficient method of producing an accurate memory refresher. When delivering the judgment of the Court of Criminal Appeal, Byrne J said:

> This court has observed that police officers nearly always deny that they have collaborated in the making of notes, and we cannot help wondering why they are the only class of society who do not collaborate in such a matter.

The judge went on to observe that such collaboration was the most natural and best explanation for two identical notebooks made by officers dealing with the same events, a phenomenon which is, from time to time, treated with some suspicion in cross-examination of the officers. The practice of collaboration is natural and useful. To seek to forbid it would not deter the dishonest witness, but would place unnecessary difficulties in the way of the honest and conscientious. It matters not at all whether the result of the collaboration is the production of two or more notes made by the witnesses individually or one note made physically by one witness and verified by the others. Each is entitled to refer to the note which he has either made or verified. It would, therefore, be natural, rather than surprising, if at the trial of Coke and Littleton, the notebooks of D/I Glanvil and D/S Bracton are identical in their treatment of events which both officers witnessed. Since the officers would make use of their notebooks to make their witness statements, the same observation applies equally to the statements.

### 12.2.1.2 Contemporaneous with the events to which it relates.

The requirement of contemporaneity is the safest means of vouching for, at least, the substantial accuracy of the document. The word 'contemporaneous' is not, of course to be applied literally in every case, as many events provide no opportunity for a note to be made as they actually occur. In some instances, this is feasible, for example where a police officer makes a note during an interview taking place between the defendant and another officer, but in general the word is given an extended meaning, in order to make the rule workable in practice.

In order to be contemporaneous with the events to which it relates, a document should have been made at the first practicable opportunity, and if not made literally comtemporaneously, it must certainly have been made while the events were still fresh in the mind of the witness. In *R v Richardson* [1971] 2 QB 484, the Court of Appeal commented that 'this definition does provide a measure of elasticity and should not be taken to confine witnesses to an over-short period'. There is no set time beyond which a document cannot be a contemporaneous record; it is a matter of fact and degree for the judge in every case.[10] In *R v Langton* (CCR) (1876) 2 QBD 296, the defendant had compiled a document over a period of a fortnight, on the basis of which a witness had paid over sums of money to workmen at the end of the fortnight. The witness was allowed to look at the document in order to refresh his memory about what sums he had paid. But the

---

[10]   *R v Simmonds* (CA) [1969] 1 QB 685; *R v Richardson* (ante).

longer the period, the less the likelihood that the court will accept that the document is within the rule.[11]

The older rule was that the original contemporaneous document should be referred to, if in existence, and that where the witness had no independent recollection of the events and so was dependent upon being permitted to refresh his memory, the original alone might be used unless any copy available was itself contemporaneous.[12] However, in modern practice, there would seem to be no reason why a later copy should not be referred to, provided that it can be shown to be a true copy of the contemporaneous original. It would appear unnecessary and pedantic to apply to memory refreshers the rules relating to strict proof of the contents of documents as evidence in their own right. The question is of importance in the not uncommon circumstances which arose in *R* v *Cheng* (1976) 63 Cr App R 20. The defendant was arrested in February 1972 but subsequently absconded. The trial did not take place until March 1975 and in the intervening period of time, the police officer's notebook had been lost. The officer was allowed to refresh his memory by reference to his witness statement, upon it being shown to the court's satisfaction, firstly that the original (lost) notebook had been contemporaneous, and secondly, that the officer had made his statement by copying the relevant part of his notes. And where an officer makes, contemporaneously, rough notes of an interview, which he shortly afterwards incorporates into a full note, expanding them with the aid of his recollection, he should be allowed to refresh his memory from the full note and not just from the rough, even though the contents of the two are not identical.[13] It would be possible to extract from these cases the principle that where a contemporaneous original is made, the witness should be permitted to refresh his memory from a newer copy of, or derivation from, the original, provided that the copy or derivation is compiled exclusively from the contents of the original, the actual and fresh recollection of the witness, or a combination of the two.

### 12.2.2   Treatment of memory-refreshing documents

Reference by a witness to a document while giving evidence may have one of two results. It may revive or refresh his memory, so as to enable him to give oral evidence, from his refreshed recollection, of what he actually perceived or did. On the other hand, it may be that the memory of the witness is not assisted, and that consequently, he is unable to do more than say, 'I do not remember. But I can say that the document was made at the time, and that it is accurate.' It is vital to observe that, at the outset, a document used to refresh the memory is not evidence. Indeed, it will frequently, if not usually, be inadmissible hearsay, unless in a civil case it may be admitted under Part I of the Civil Evidence Act 1968. What is evidence is what the witness states from the witness-box by way of giving oral evidence.[14] American writers, particularly Wigmore, have pointed out that the fact that two results of showing the document to the witness are possible should perhaps be taken to indicate that two different approaches should be employed. The first, in the case

---

[11]   The matter is one very much for the discretion of the trial judge. Though periods much longer than *Langton* would be unlikely to satisfy the rule, there will always be exceptional cases, where the events will be assumed to have been fresh enough. In *R* v *Fotheringham* (CA) [1975] Crim LR 710, a witness who was an accomplice was allowed to refer to his statement to the police made some 22 days after the event. This must surely be close to the outer limit of the rule.

[12]   *R* v *Harvey* (1869) 11 Cox CC 546.

[13]   *Attorney-General's Reference (No. 3 of 1979)* (CA) (1979) 69 Cr App R 411.

[14]   There is no objection to a witness reading from a contemporaneous note when he himself has failed to recollect the incident concerned. However, evidence of that kind is unlikely to carry much weight.

of 'present recollection revived' where the document refreshes the memory of the witness, would involve holding simply that the oral evidence of the witness should be accepted and that the document should, at common law, have no evidential significance. The second, in the case of 'past recollection recorded', where the witness' recollection is not assisted, but the witness states that the document was accurate when made, would involve holding that the only available evidence is the document and that the document may be hearsay and inadmissible. American jurisdictions have generally created an exception to the rule against hearsay, which provides for the admissibility of such past recollection recorded, subject to certain foundational requirements designed to ensure reliability; see, e.g., Federal Rule of Evidence 803(5).

English law has perceived no need for such subtleties. At least since *Maugham v Hubbard* (1828) 8 B & C 14, it has been established that even in the case of past recollection recorded, which Professor Cross terms 'reconstruction' of the events (*Evidence*, 5th ed., p 233), the witness is treated as having personal knowledge of the events recorded in the document, provided that he can state that the document was made contemporaneously and was accurate when made. In *Maugham v Hubbard*, a witness was shown an acknowledgement of a payment, signed by him, and thereupon testified that, although the had no recollection of having been paid the sum stated in it, he had no doubt that such was the case. This evidence was held to be sufficient to prove the payment, even though the acknowledgement was unstamped and therefore could not be sufficient without the parole evidence of the witness that the payment had in fact been made.

Nonetheless, a memory-refreshing document may attain some evidential status, depending on the course taken in cross-examination, since cross-examination may lend relevance to and thus render admissible a piece of evidence, which would not otherwise have been admissible as part of the case of the party calling a witness.

The opposing party is entitled to inspect a document used by a witness either before testifying or while in the witness-box, for the purpose of refreshing his memory.[15] The opposing party may further cross-examine the witness with regard to any part of the document used by the witness to refresh his memory, without making the document evidence for the party calling the witness.[16] If, however, cross-examination takes place on other parts of the document, the rule is that the party calling the witness is entitled to put the document in evidence as part of his case.[17] The reason is that matters falling outside the use of the document as a memory refresher have been raised, the document has a new relevance and the jury are entitled to see the subject-matter of the cross-examination; whereas cross-examination restricted to the portions referred to by the witness amounts to no more than questioning on his oral evidence.

The putting of the document in evidence, where this occurs, involves its production for the inspection of the jury, or other tribunal of fact. The jury must, therefore, be directed as to the evidential use which they are entitled to make of the document, and its relationship

---

[15]    *Burgess* v *Bennett* (1872) 20 WR 720; *Owen* v *Edwards* (1983) 77 Cr App R 191. The inspection must be confined to matters relevant to the case, though it need not be confined to the parts used by the witness to refresh his memory.

[16]    This should not be confused with the rule that calling in cross-examination for a document in the possession of the opponent (not one used as a memory refresher) involves putting the document in evidence if called upon to do so. See 13.8 post, Contrast *Senat* v *Senat* [1965] P 172 with *Stroud* v *Stroud* [1965] 1 WLR 1080.

[17]    *Gregory* v *Tavernor* (NP) (1833) 6 C & P 280; *Senat* v *Senat* [1965] P 172; *Owen* v *Edwards* (1983) 77 Cr App R 191.

to the oral evidence given by the witness. Here there is a manifest divergence between the rule at common law, which continues to govern criminal cases, and the provisions of the Civil Evidence Act 1968 which have deliberately modified the position in civil cases.

At common law, where a memory-refreshing document is put in evidence, it is evidence only of the consistency of the witness, and goes only to his credit. In *R* v *Virgo* (1978) 67 Cr App R 323, the conviction was quashed where the trial judge directed the jury, by necessary implication, that the diary of a prosecution witness, used by the witness to refresh his memory, could be regarded as evidence of the truth of the facts contained in it. The witness had been cross-examined extensively on the document in a way which clearly justified its being put in evidence, on the issue of the credit of the witness; but it could have no other evidential value, and the jury were to try the case on the evidence before them, including the oral evidence of the witness. The point is that the jury's assessment of the weight to be accorded to the evidence of the witness may be affected by its consistency or otherwise with the document.

In civil cases, the position is governed by s. 3(2) of the Civil Evidence Act 1968 which is in the following terms:

> Nothing in this Act shall affect any of the rules of law relating to the circumstances in which, where a person called as a witness in any civil proceedings is cross-examined on a document used by him to refresh his memory, that document may be made evidence in those proceedings; and where a document or any part of a document is received in evidence in any such proceedings by virtue of any such rule of law, any statement made in that document or part by the person using the document to refresh his memory shall by virtue of this subsection be admissible as evidence of any fact stated therein of which direct oral evidence by him would be admissible.

The provision is part of the overall structure of Part I of the Act (dealt with in detail in Chapter 8, ante) the object of which is to transfer the emphasis of the rules of evidence from questions of admissibility to those of weight. It follows that in a civil case, the judge may always consider a memory-refreshing document as evidence of the facts contained therein, provided that oral evidence by the witness would be admissible of such facts by virtue of the rules of evidence generally. He may act on the facts revealed by the document for any proper purpose, although clearly it is not in every case that a memory-refreshing document would command any substantial weight. The judge may, of course, also use the document for the purpose of assessing the credit of the witness, but is not confined to this use of it, as would be the position at common law.

### 12.3 Previous consistent or self-serving statements

At common law, a witness may not give evidence that he has, on a previous occasion, made a statement consistent with his present evidence. Variously called the rule against previous consistent statements and the rule against self-serving statements, the rule is soundly based on the proposition that such a statement can have no improving effect on the evidence of the witness given on oath in court. Such statements are also objectionable as hearsay. At common law, they are excluded, subject to certain exceptions, both as evidence of consistency and as evidence of the truth of the facts stated.

Thus, in *R* v *Roberts* (CCA) [1942] 1 All ER 187, where the defendant was charged with murder, he was not permitted to state in evidence that two days after the killing, he had told his father that his defence would be one of accident, as it indeed was at the trial. The rule applies to statements in any form, including what might be termed indirect statements by conduct. In *Corke v Corke and Cook* (CA) [1958] P 93, a suit for divorce, the wife and co-respondent, who had been found together in compromising circumstances, but had denied adultery, were not permitted to give evidence that they had telephoned a doctor to ask for a medical examination (which did not take place), with a view to confirming their denial of adultery.

Before coming to the exceptional cases at common law, it will be convenient to observe that in this instance too, the Civil Evidence Act 1968 has radically altered the position in relation to civil cases. By s. 2(1):

> In any civil proceedings a statement made, whether orally or in a document or otherwise, by any person, whether called as a witness in those proceedings or not, shall be admissible as evidence of any fact stated therein of which direct or oral evidence by him would be admissible.

This appears to be quite wide enough to include previous consistent statements, and is generally accepted as having this effect.[18] Such evidence will be subject to the provisions of s. 2(2), relating to cases where the maker of a hearsay statement proposed to be tendered in evidence is called as a witness; so that the leave of the court will be required before evidence may be given of the previous consistent statement, and such evidence shall not be given before the conclusion of the evidence in chief of the witness, except in the cases stipulated by s. 2(2) (*b*)(*i*) and (*ii*). Such statements, where admitted, are by virtue of the section, evidence of the truth of the facts stated therein, provided that oral evidence by the witness would be admissible of such facts under the general rules of evidence. In many cases, if not the great majority, the admission of a previous consistent statement made by a witness called to give oral evidence will be of no, or no appreciable, value to a party. In such a case, the judge may refuse leave under s. 2(2), or treat the evidence as having some, probably slight, value as showing consistency and thus going to credit. But there are cases, for example those corresponding to the common-law exceptions by virtue of which it is admitted under the res gestae rule or to rebut a suggestion of recent fabrication, where a previous consistent statement may be of substantial value; so too where the recollection of the witness may legitimately be supposed to have suffered since the making of the statement, by reason of lapse of time, illness or some other such cause.

By s. 6(4) of the Act, a previous consistent statement admitted under s. 2 is incapable of corroborating the evidence of the maker. This result would also follow at common law, because of the absence of the essential requirement of an independent source (see 14.4, post).

At common law, previous consistent statements are admissible in the following exceptional cases, each of which, happily, may be justified by circumstances which lend to the statement a relevance which ordinarily, it would not enjoy.[19] As we have seen, in the

---

[18]  *Phipson* (13th ed., para.17—05) contends that s. 2 does not render admissible statements implied by conduct, as in *Corke v Corke and Cook* [1958] P 93. But the words 'orally or in a document or otherwise' do not, it is submitted, in themselves exclude the possibility, and admissibility is more in keeping with the policy of the Act.

[19]  No writer on the subject of previous consistent statements can fail to acknowledge his indebtedness to the seminal article on the subject by Mr R.N. Gooderson [1968] CLJ 64, which explores perceptively the various cases of admissiblity at common law.

ordinary case, a witness's story is not enhanced by the fact that is has been rehearsed out of court, prior to being given in evidence. The common-law rules are still in full force in criminal cases. The exceptions, which are considered in detail either here, or in an appropriate place in another chapter, are:

(a)   Where a statement is admissible by virtue of the res gestae rule.

(b)   Where a wholly or partially self-serving statement is made by the defendant, in relation to an offence charged, when questioned about the offence.

(c)   Where a witness gives evidence of a previous identification of the defendant.

(d)   Where a statement is admissible as a recent complaint in a sexual case.

(e)   Where a statement is admissible to rebut a suggestion of recent fabrication.

### 12.3.1   Statements admissible under the res gestae rule

The res gestae rule is one of the common-law exceptions to the rule against hearsay, and in effect allows evidence, otherwise objectionable as hearsay, to be given, where a statement is an integral part of the transaction to which it relates, and so ought to be given in evidence, so as to invest the evidence of the transaction with a completeness, in the absence of which the evidence might be ambiguous or misleading. The normal case is of a spontaneous statement made contemporaneously with the transaction by a participant or bystander. Habitually, therefore, the rule operates to admit what are in reality previous consistent statements, although they are also often given in evidence by other witnesses, who heard them being made. The subject of the res gestae rule is considered in detail in 6.11 ante.

### 12.3.2   Statements made by the defendant when questioned about the offence

Statements made by the defendant, concerning the offence charged, in response to questioning, occasion great difficulty. Such statements occupy, in their own right, the entirety of Chapter 7. The defendant may, of course, admit the offence charged; conversely, he may deny it in a manner consistent with his defence at trial, in which case the statement which he makes is self-serving within the meaning of the present rule. Very frequently, he makes a statement, which the jury may regard as partly incriminating and partly self-serving. It seems that, with the exception of statements of a self-serving nature made with the express intention of ensuring their inclusion in the evidence given for the prosecution, by way of 'infiltration' of the prosecution case, the jury ought to hear whatever the defendant may say about the allegation made against him, in order to determine whether the statement, read as a whole, amounts to a confession. It is true that the evidential value of a self-serving statement is materially less than that of a confession of guilt or an adverse admission, but the defendant's prior statements are admitted in evidence, both for the above reason, and as evidence of his reaction when charged with the offence and, if he gives evidence to the same effect, as evidence of consistency. See generally 7.13, ante.

### 12.3.3   Evidence of previous identification

Evidence of identification of the defendant, as the person who committed the offence charged, has been the subject of considerable controversy and anxiety. The danger of conviction on the basis of inaccurate evidence of identification has haunted the courts throughout modern criminal practice, particularly since the case of Adolf Beck, early in the century, and has found recent expression in the guidance provided for such cases turning on identification evidence in *R* v *Turnbull* (CA) [1977] QB 224. The subject must be approached both from the standpoint of admissibility, and from that of the treatment of identification evidence generally, and with regard to the factors affecting its weight.

*12.3.3.1 Admissibility of evidence of previous identification.* A witness may, of course, give evidence that he saw the defendant commit the offence charged, or that he saw the defendant in circumstances from which the jury would be entitled to draw that inference. This would be direct evidence implicating the defendant, albeit its treatment must be subject to the guidelines discussed in 12.3.3.2, post. But there are theoretical objections to evidence that the witness, on an occasion subsequent to the commission of the offence, but before giving evidence, made an out-of-court identification of the defendant (a 'previous identification'). If given by the person who made the previous identification, such evidence would appear to be self-serving when tendered in support of his evidence given at the trial identifying the defendant as the person who committed the offence. If given by any other person who witnessed the previous identification, for example a police officer who conducted an identification parade, it is exceptionable as hearsay. It is no answer to the objection to say that the use made of such evidence might be limited to that of consistency with the witness's identification evidence at trial. Nonetheless, there is no doubt that evidence of previous identifications is admissible both from the identifying witness and, unless the evidence would contradict that of the identifying witness directly, from another witness who perceived the identification being made.[20] Despite the observation of Lawton LJ in this case, that it would be wrong 'to set up artificial rules of evidence, which hinder the administration of justice'. it is manifest that the admission of evidence of this kind must be regarded as an exception to the general rule. It is, however, equally true that the exception is based upon cogent and important considerations.

Where a question of identification arises, it is obviously in the interests of the defendant, no less than that of the prosecution, that the matter should be investigated at the earliest possible moment after the offence, by allowing the prospective witness the opportunity, under properly controlled conditions, to confirm or repudiate any initial identification implicating the defendant, who is at that stage a suspect. The longer this process is delayed, the greater the risk of error, and to wait until trial would almost always increase the risk to unacceptable proportions. But while these considerations militate in favour of evidence of previous identifications being received, they do not assist on the question whether such evidence is to be admitted for the purpose of proving that the defendant is the person who committed the offence or only for the purpose of confirming evidence of identification given at the trial. This is a distinction which does not appear always to have been appreciated in the authorities.[21]

In *R* v *Christie* [1914] AC 545, the defendant was charged with indecent assault on a small boy. Shortly after the alleged offence, the boy, together with his mother and a police officer, approached the defendant, and the boy said, 'That is the man,' and went on to describe what had been done to him. The defendant said in reply, 'I am innocent,' and the issue was one of identification. The boy, giving evidence unsworn, identified the defendant in court. He was not asked about the identification at the time of the defendant's arrest, but evidence to that effect was elicited from the other witnesses. The House of Lords held that the evidence was admissible. Although the members of the

---

[20]  *R* v *Osbourne; R* v *Virtue* (CA) [1973] 1 QB 678.
[21]  See Libling [1977] Crim LR 268 et seq.

House were not *ad idem* in their reasons,[22] it is submitted that it is possible to extract from the various speeches that the evidence of what had taken place out of court was admissible for the purpose of confirming the evidence of the boy identifying the defendant as the man who had committed the offence. The objections of Viscount Haldane LC and Lord Moulton seem to have been based primarily on the failure of the prosecution to elicit the boy's words from the boy himself, an objection even then disavowed by Lord Atkinson and which would be unlikely to be heeded in modern times. And Lord Reading held that the evidence of the prior identification would have been admissible from the boy himself. The relevance of the evidence was indeed asserted by Viscount Haldane to be 'to show that the boy was able to identify at the time and to exclude the idea that the identification of the prisoner in the dock was an afterthought or a mistake' ([1914] AC at 551).

But the proposition that evidence of identification is admissible only for the purpose of confirming the identification made in court can only be tested against decisions in cases where the identifying witness is not available to give evidence at trial, or where such witness is called, but is unable or unwilling to identify the defendant (or anyone) as being the subject of the earlier identification. Although such cases are more properly dealt with as a problem of the rule against hearsay, because the previous identification can hardly be described as self-serving where there is no evidence for it to serve, it is instructive to mention the position here for the assistance it may offer as to the purpose of the admissibility of such evidence generally. In *R* v *Burke and Kelly* (1847) 2 Cox CC 295, a witness had previously identified a man as being one of two who had robbed him two days earlier, but was unable at trial to say that the defendant Kelly had been that man. The prosecution were permitted to call a police officer to give evidence that the witness had, on the previous occasion, identified Kelly. This was a case where the witness was able to say that he had identified someone, and another witness was called to supplement that evidence by plugging the gap in the first witness's memory of who had been identified. Even without making the obvious comment on the weight of such evidence,[23] the admissibility of the evidence of the police officer seems tenuous. If it was tendered merely to confirm that the witness had identified someone, a fact unlikely to be disputed in itself, then no mention of Kelly should have been made. Even if the witness were able to say at trial that, although now unable to say whom he had identified, he was sure that he had been correct at the time, it is difficult to say in what way the evidence of the officer could be said to 'confirm' this. It seems little different from allowing the officer to say, 'The witness told me it was Kelly,' and it is not easy to envisage any court admitting that as evidence of the truth of what the witness had said.

The Court of Appeal was prepared, however, to follow and even extend the principle in *R* v *Osbourne; R* v *Virtue*.[24] Both defendants had been picked out on identification parades, the defendant O by Mrs B, and the defendant V by Mrs H. At the trial, both witnesses failed to confirm their previous identification. Mrs B stated that she was unable

---

[22]   It is essential to bear in mind that the decision in *Christie* was concerned primarily with the admissibility of the boy's words as words spoken in the presence of the defendant, having regard to the defendant's reaction to them. Also that in 1914, the words were not admissible as a recent complaint in a case such as that charged, whereas they would now certainly be so.

[23]   The weight may not always be open to such comment. As Lawton LJ said in *Osbourne and Virtue*, 'if the experience of this court is anything to go by, accused persons often look much smarter in the dock than they do when they are first arrested' [1973] 1 QB 678, at 690.

[24]   [1973] 1 QB 678. It should be said, in fairness, that the word 'follow' in the text is subject to the observation that the court did not apparently hear any argument based on hearsay, and *Burke and Kelly* was not cited to them.

to remember having picked anyone out, while Mrs H's evidence was so unsatisfactory that it could not properly be regarded as an identification of V in court. Evidence from a police officer was then called for the prosecution, over an objection made on behalf of O, that the witnesses had previously identified O and V respectively. The Court of Appeal upheld the admission of the evidence, holding that the decision in *Christie* justified the rather tersely stated principle that: '. . . evidence of identification other than identification in the witness-box is admissible'. In the case of Mrs H, the matter was probably little different to that of *Burke and Kelly*. In the case of Mrs B, however, it was argued that the evidence of the officer was inadmissible, because it contradicted the evidence of Mrs B, who was not a hostile witness. The argument seems sound in principle, but was rejected on the actual substance of what Mrs B had said. Presumably, had she stated, wrongly, that she had picked out someone other than O, the result might have been different. The decision has been much criticised, and it is certainly unfortunate that the hearsay problem of the officer's evidence, and the purposes of its admissibility were not considered.[25]

It is submitted that the view taken by the Court of Appeal of *Christie* is simplistic and misleading, and that the true view of it is that evidence of previous identification is permitted, by way of an exception, because if it were not, the administration of justice would suffer the dual perils that the strength of a good identification would seep away with time, and that a bad identification would carry an ever-increasing risk to the defendant, perhaps culminating in an assumption by the witness that his poor memory is somehow confirmed by the mere fact that the defendant is in the dock charged with the offence. The true rule is surely that evidence of previous identification is to be restricted to the case where a witness is able to give evidence in court of the identity of the offender, and is admissible only for the purpose of confirming the evidence, in which role it has a cogency normally missing from self-serving statements. In addition, it may, subject to the not inconsiderable reservations to *Burke and Kelly* made earlier, be permissible to extend the rule to cases where the witness, although unable to state in evidence whom he identified previously, can say that he identified someone and that he was sure at the time that his identification was correct. As Libling [1977] Crim LR 268 at 277, points out, such evidence can be cross-examined on effectively as to accuracy at the time of the previous identification, and is free from the major danger inherent in hearsay evidence. In these cases, *Osbourne and Virtue* is surely correct in holding that evidence may be given by a witness who perceived the previous identification being made.

In *Sparks* v *R* [1964] AC 964, 981 Lord Morris of Borth-y-Gest observed that there is no rule that permits the giving of hearsay evidence, merely because it relates to a question of identity. The American Federal Rules of Evidence have adopted the expedient of declaring that evidence of a prior out-of-court identification shall be regarded as non-hearsay evidence (Rule 801 (d) (1)), but there is no authority for this sensibly pragmatic view in English law.

It may be doubted whether, in practice, a jury may be expected to exhibit any reaction to evidence of previous identification, other than to say, 'It must be the right man,' and certainly very careful guidance is required, if any extension to the original rule is to be

---

[25]   The court might also have been assisted by the observations of the Privy Council in *Sparks* v *R* [1964] AC 964, in which, dealing with evidence of identification which exculpated the defendant (in that the victim said that her attacker was coloured, while the defendant was white) Lord Morris of Borth-y-Gest said, at 981: 'There is no rule which permits the giving of hearsay evidence merely because it relates to identity.'

contemplated. It is submitted that the following words, taken from the speech of Lord Moulton in *Christie* [1914] AC at 558, are as forceful now as when they were first uttered:

Identification is an act of the mind, and the primary evidence of what was passing in the mind of a man is his own testimony, where it can be obtained. It would be very dangerous to allow evidence to be given of a man's words and actions, in order to show by this extrinsic evidence that he identified the prisoner, if he was capable of being called as a witness and was not called to prove by direct evidence that he had thus identfied him.

*12.3.3.2  Treatment of identification evidence.* Admissibility is only the first facet of evidence of identification, and has probably given rise to less concern than the vexed question of the weight and reliability of such evidence. Periodically, cases where some miscarriage of justice appears to have occurred because of mistaken evidence of identification reopen the problems of trying to ensure the detection of faulty evidence in a field more open to error than most. In *R v Turnbull*[26] a five-member Court of Appeal considered four separate appeals against conviction, and laid down guidelines for the treatment of cases which depend wholly or substantially on the correctness of one or more identifications of the defendant. The guidelines were said to 'involve only changes of practice, not law', but the Court also emphasised that failure to follow them is likely to lead to a conviction being quashed, and will do so where the failure results in the conviction being regarded by the Court of Appeal as unsafe or unsatisfactory. The guidelines may be summarised as follows:

(a)  The judge should always warn the jury of the special need for caution before convicting the accused in reliance upon the correctness of identification evidence, drawing their attention to the possibilities of error.

(b)  The judge should invite the attention of the jury to examine closely the circumstances in which the identification was made; the conditions under which and the length of time for which the observation took place. Was the defendant known to the witness, or was there any particular reason why the witness might be expected to remember the defendant? How soon after the event did the witness give a description to the police?

(c)  The judge should remind the jury specifically of any weaknesses which have appeared in the identification evidence.

(d)  If the prosecution have reason to believe that there is any material discrepancy between the description of the defendant given at first to the police, and his actual appearance, or in any case where the defence so request, they should supply the defence with particulars of the description first supplied to the police.

(e)  Where the quality of identification evidence is good, the jury may safely be left to assess it, and may convict on that basis. Conversely, where the quality of the evidence is poor, the judge should withdraw the case from the jury, and direct an acquittal, unless there is other evidence which goes to support the correctness of the identification. The judge should tell the jury what evidence there is which may support the identification.[27] In

---

[26]  [1977] QB 224, Lord Widgery CJ, Roskill and Lawton LJJ, Cusack and May JJ.
[27]  Such evidence need not amount technically to corroboration; for instance, it need not come from a source independent of the witness. See generally 14.8, post.

particular, he must direct them that the fact that the defendant elects not to give evidence, cannot of itself support it, although he may, of course, point out that the identification evidence is uncontradicted by evidence from the defendant. Where the defendant puts forward an alibi, a defence which is of course crucial to the correctness of identification evidence, the jury may regard its falsity as supporting the identification, but should only do so if they think that the false alibi was put forward for the purpose of deceiving them, and not, for example, out of stupidity or panic.

In addition to the guidelines laid down in *Turnbull* for the treatment of evidence actually before the court, there are rules for the guidance of the police, covering the conduct of identification parades and the use of photographs for the purpose of identifying suspects. The detailed provisions of these rules are outside the scope of the present work. Pursuant to s. 66 of the Police and Criminal Evidence Act 1984, Codes of Practice will, when adopted by Parliament, replace the present rules for the conduct of identification parades and the identification of suspects by means of photographs (see Archbold, 41st ed., para.14–3 et seq).[28]

Following the report of Lord Devlin's Committee on Evidence of Identification, the Attorney-General, in a written answer to the House of Commons, [29] stated that the Director of Public Prosecutions would attach very considerable importance to the proper working of the rules when deciding whether or not to institute proceedings. Moreover, in any committal proceedings or subsequent trial, the prosecution would not invite a witness to make a 'dock identification', where the witness had not previously identified the defendant at an identification parade. The importance of this statement of principle is very great, if only because it encourages identification in properly controlled circumstances, and discourages identification by means of one-to-one 'confrontation' or in court while the defendant is in the dock, because of the danger that the witness will feel that his identification is supported by the presence of a suspect at the police station, or as defendant in the dock.[30]

From similar considerations, the Director proposed that in cases where evidence of identification was involved, the identifying witnesses would be called at committal, and that the short-form procedure under s. 1 of the Criminal Justice Act 1967 (now s. 6(2) of the Magistrates' Courts Act 1980) whereby the committing justices may commit without consideration of the evidence, would not be followed in such cases. By this means it is hoped to evaluate the evidence at an early stage, and allow the presentation of an alibi, if the defence wish to put one forward.[31]

---

[28]   As to the use of photographs and video-tapes in the identification of suspects, see generally *R v Lamb* (1980) 71 Cr App R 198; *R v Fowden and White* [1982] Crim LR 588; *R v Dodson; R v Williams* [1984] Crim LR 489; and 15.5.5, post.

[29]   Although the answer relates strictly only to cases of which the Director has the conduct, the hope was expressed that other prosecuting authorities would follow his lead, and this seems to have been the case. Hansard, May 27, 1976. Vol 912, No. 115.

[30]   This principle may be departed from where it is impracticable to hold a proper identification parade, for example because the defendant is of very unusual physical appearance, *R v Hunter* (CA) [1969] Crim LR 262, or refuses to attend a parade or to take part, *R v John* (CA) [1973] Crim LR 113. The appellate courts have in the past quashed convictions where the method of obtaining identification evidence was irregular and unsafe; *R v Cartwright* (CCA) (1914) 10 Cr App R 219.

[31]   The practice has since been modified because of the pressure on the courts. Now s. 6(2) may be used by consent and with the approval of the court to avoid inordinate delay in committals or to spare, for example, child witnesses the ordeal of giving evidence twice where the defence do not require it.

### 12.3.4 Recent complaints in sexual cases

It must be confessed that, if ever there was some reasoned basis for the exception about to be discussed, it has become well hidden in the mists of time. Bracton tells us somewhat enigmatically that a woman who complains of rape should 'go to the next town and there make discovery to some credible persons of the injury she has suffered'.[32] The reason for this may lie in the suspicion which fell at common law on a woman who failed to complain within a short time of an outrage done to her, but almost certainly Oliver Wendell Holmes J is correct in his unkind stigmatisation of the recent complaint as 'a perverted survival of the ancient requirement that a woman should make hue and cry as a preliminary to an appeal of rape'.[33]

Whatever its origin, the phenomenon survives in modern law, and fits uneasily into the role of admissible evidence, though any requirement for a complaint as a prerequisite to conviction has long since perished. The exception is that in sexual cases, evidence may be given by the complainant and by any person to whom the complaint was made, of a complaint made voluntarily, and at the first opportunity reasonably afforded. The complaint is admissible only for either of two purposes: (a) to confirm the evidence of the complainant relating to the offence; and/or (b) to rebut or disprove consent on the part of the complainant, if that is an issue in the case.

With regard to the first purpose, it should be noted that a recent complaint, although it may confirm the complainant's evidence, is not capable of corroborating that evidence, and the corroboration which is to be looked for of the complainant's evidence in a sexual case as a matter of practice, must be sought elsewhere. This is because the complaint lacks the necessary element of an independent source.[34]

The exception applies only to sexual cases. From the older authorities, it is clear that it was for a long period doubtful whether there was a more general application to offences of violence, and there were certain cases in which the exception does appear to have been so applied. Thus, in *R v Wink* (NP) (1834) 6 CP 397, a complaint was admitted, apparently under this rule, in a case of robbery. And perhaps on a closer analogy, there was some suggestion that a recent complaint could be admitted in a matrimonial case, to support a charge of cruelty.[35] It must be remembered that recent complaints may at times overlap with statements made in the defendant's presence, with statements admissible under the res gestae rule, and with dying declarations, and the older cases do not always distinguish adequately between these various heads of admissibility, simply because the distinctions did not crystallise until comparatively modern times. But the older cases cannot really survive the decisions in *R v Lillyman* (CCR) [1896] 2 QB 167, and *R v Osborne* (CCR) [1905] 1 KB 551, which have, by necessary implication, restricted the rule to sexual cases.

For some time after these decisions, it was thought that the rule applied only to offences against females, but in *R v Camelleri* (CCA) [1922] 2 KB 122, it was held that recent complaints might be admitted in sexual cases generally, and in that case the exception was accordingly applied to a charge of indecent assault on a male.

The complaint may be admissible even it it was not made in the defendant's presence.

[32]  *DeCorona*, b.3. fol. 147; expounded in Blackstone's Commentaries, vol 4, c.15, 21.
[33]  *Commonwealth* v *Cleary* (1898) 172 Mass 175.
[34]  See e.g., *R* v *Lovell* (CCA) (1923) 17 Cr App R 163. See also 14.4, post.
[35]  *Berry* v *Berry and Carpenter* (1898) 78 LT 688. The attempt to establish this rule in this and other civil cases was probably due to the incompetence of the parties at that time. However, the question was raised as recently as *Fromhold* v *Fromhold* (CA) [1952] 1 TLR 1526. The possibility must be obsolete since the Civil Evidence Act 1968 came into force.

Indeed, if made in his presence, the complaint may well be admissible for other reasons, depending upon his reaction to it. Whether a complaint was 'recent' is a question of fact and degree in every case. Certainly it is not necessary that it was made within the comparatively short period required for admissibility under the res gestae rule. On the other hand, the complaint must have been made at the first opportunity which reasonably presented itself. Thus, it is not a question of the length of time *per se*. The availability of persons to whom the complainant might reasonably be expected to speak, her age, her emotional state and the nature of the offence may all be relevant, and it is a matter for the judge to rule on, having regard to all the circumstances.[36]

The 'recent' element is not only a safeguard against concocted self-serving complaints, but also some guarantee that the complaint has at least some value as evidence of the matters in respect of which it is admissible. For the same reason, it is a requirement that the complaint must have been voluntary and spontaneous. This does not rule out a complaint made in response to questioning, but if it is, in effect, dragged out of a reluctant complainant by leading or threatening questions or, even worse, by force, it will not be made voluntarily and is likely to be rejected. In *R v Osborne* [1905] 1 KB 551, where the owner of a fried-fish shop was alleged to have indecently assaulted a girl under 13 who had come to the shop with friends, a complaint was upheld where it was induced by a friend with the question, 'Why are you going home?'. It seems that non-leading questions, designed to inquire about the complainant's distress, will not offend against the rule, but the question for the judge is not who spoke first, but was it a voluntary and spontaneous complaint. It was succinctly stated by Ridley J in *Osborne* as follows (ibid at 556):

If the circumstances indicate that, but for the questioning there probably would have been no voluntary complaint, the answer is inadmissible. If the question merely anticipates a statement which the complainant was about to make, it is not rendered inadmissible by the fact that the questioner happens to speak first.

In earlier cases it was held, not without some logical force, that although the complainant might relate that she had made a recent complaint, for the purpose of confirming her evidence, she was not to be permitted to relate the details of what she had said. The distinction is an important one, in that if the substance of the complaint could be given, in addition to the fact of its having been made, then particulars of the offence, including the identity of the defendant, might be placed before the jury as confirmatory evidence, which would be wholly inadmissible to prove the truth of the facts stated. It might have been expected that the evidence would be restricted to the fact of the complaint being made, in the light of this difficulty, but in *R v Lillyman* [1896] 2 QB 167, the Court for Crown Cases Reserved came down firmly on the other side. The victim of an alleged indecent assault and attempted rape was held to be entitled to relate not only the fact that she had made a recent complaint to her mistress, but also the substance of what she had said.

The jury must, nonetheless, be directed that the only relevance of the complaint lies in its confirmatory value of the complainant's evidence, and in its value on the issue of consent, if that is in issue in the case, and that they are not entitled to regard the complaint as evidence of the truth of the matters stated by the complainant in it. It is one of those

---

[36] *R v Cummings* (CCA) [1948] 1 All ER 551. Some examples are collected in Archbold, 41st ed., para. 4–309, but no rule can be laid down based on the passage of time alone.

directions which juries must, to say the least, find very confusing, especially as they must also be told that even if it is confirmatory of the complainant's evidence in court, the complaint cannot in law corroborate that evidence. The dangers of admitting detailed evidence of a previous consistent statement are very great, particularly where identity is in issue, and it is certainly arguable that *Lillyman* is by no means a necessarily desirable decision.

It follows, of course, that if consent is not is issue, and the complainant does not give evidence, there is no ground upon which a recent complaint can be admitted. In *R v Wallwork* (CCA) (1958) 42 Cr App R 153, the defendant was charged with incest with his daughter, aged five. The little girl went into the witness-box, but proved unable to give evidence. Evidence was then admitted from the grandmother of a complaint made to her by the girl, in which she had stated that the defendant was the perpetrator of the act. It was held that the evidence was inadmissible, there being no function for it to perform. Consent was obviously not in issue, and there was no evidence which the complaint could confirm. Lord Goddard CJ suggested that in such a case, the fact of the complaint might be given, as opposed to its substance, but this seems contrary both to principle and authority, and has not found acceptance in other cases.

### 12.3.5   *R v Coke; R v Littleton*

The two exceptions which have just been discussed, relating to previous identifications and recent complaints, are likely to be of great importance to the case of Coke and Littleton. In the case of Margaret Blackstone, there is no difficulty of identification; Coke does not dispute it, and even if he did, where the witness is able to state that she knows the defendant personally, much of the danger inherent in evidence of identification is removed. In such a case, the judge would remind the jury of the fact, and the other circumstances of the identification, and would no doubt feel it to be quite safe to leave the matter to the jury. But Margaret's complaint to her mother is quite another matter. Although it was made shortly afterwards, it seems that Margaret did not take the first reasonably practicable opportunity to make it. This in itself would not conclude the matter, because account must obviously be taken of her age, and very distressed condition, arising not only from what had happened to her, but to her younger sister while in a sense under Margaret's protection. But it is more worrying that Margaret's mother found so much difficulty in extracting the story from her, and the judge would have to take account of the possibility that the complaint might have been devised to cover what might otherwise seem to be her lack of responsibility. It is clear that the judge has a very difficult task to perform. It may be that the evidence of both Mrs Blackstone and Dr Vesey of Margaret's extreme distress may tip the scales in favour of admission, provided that, following *Osborne*, the judge takes the view that a complaint would inevitably have been made.

Angela's case presents less of a problem, so far as her complaint is concerned. Clearly, it was voluntary and spontaneous, and made at the first practicable opportunity. No one would reasonably expect a young girl to complain to the first person she meets, and her waiting until her arrival home would not affect the issue. This will have the consequence that evidence both from Angela, and from her mother will be admissible both of the fact that a complaint was made, and of its substance, i.e. the detail of the offence which she gave. But there is a more difficult and crucial problem in the evidence of identification. The fact that Littleton's defence is one of mistaken identity, and an alibi, gives rise to very serious issues indeed. The circumstances of the identification are very similar to those in

*Christie*, where the boy's words, 'That is the man', were admitted as evidence of a previous identification. There was, however, a good deal of disagreement about whether the detail of the offence, related by the boy in the defendant's presence, formed part of the act of identification, as Lord Atkinson was prepared to hold, or whether the identification was limited to the words 'That is the man', as Viscount Haldane LC and Lord Moulton thought. It may well be that Lord Atkinson's view was based on the consideration that, at the time of *Christie*, the words could not be admitted as a recent complaint on the offence charged.

But it will be clear to the jury, if evidence of the identification is admitted, that Angela was identifying Littleton as the man who assaulted her, and evidence of the details will emerge from the recent complaint and from her evidence in court. It is, therefore, imperative for the judge to consider the nature of the evidence of identification, from the standpoint of the *Turnbull* guidelines, a matter with which the House of Lords in *Christie* was not, of course, concerned. The judge would also have to remind the jury that she gave no verbal description of her assailant, and of the fact that Angela's attention may have been focused as much on the music, and on her sister, as on Littleton himself. On the other hand, she had a fairly long time, with no physical obstruction and in good conditions, in which to observe him. It may be that one satisfactory step would be to ask Littleton to stand on an identification parade, to see whether Margaret can identify the man who assaulted her sister, as she suggests in her statement. This would be quite likely to be decisive one way or the other. Certainly, if Margaret picked out Littleton, the evidence of identification would appear to be formidable.

The jury would also be entitled to take into account, as confirming the evidence of identification, the conversation between Littleton and his wife, if they accept it as an adverse admission. The judge would be entitled, provided that a prima facie case exists at the close of the prosecution case, to direct the jury to consider any evidence given by Coke from the witness-box implicating Littleton, though not Coke's statement under caution, which is, of course, inadmissible against Littleton.

## 12.3.6 Rebuttal of suggestions of recent fabrication
Although the final exception to be considered is one which arises in cross-examination or re-examination, rather than examination in chief, it is convenient to deal with it in the present context as being a recognised exception to the rule against previous consistent statements. The exception is that where, in cross-examination it is suggested that the witness has fabricated his evidence within some ascertainable period of time, he may rebut the suggestion by showing that before that time, he had made a statement consistent with his evidence to another person. The relevance of the previous statement in such circumstances is readily apparent.

Where, therefore, a witness gave evidence that a will had been forged, and it was suggested to him that he had invented his evidence out of enmity towards the defendant, the witness was permitted to prove that he had made the same statement to a third person, at a time before the cause of the enmity arose.[37] And in *R v Oyesiku* (CA) (1971) 56 Cr App

---

[37]  *Flanagan v Fahy* [1918] 2 IR 361. The oft-cited case of *R v Coll* (CCR Ireland) (1889) 24 IR 522 appears to be rather an example of an explanation in re-examination of an apparent inconsistency exposed in cross-examination. The witness was asked why no reference had appeared in his statement to the defendant, when he had implicated the defendant in his evidence. He was allowed, having admitted that the statement made no such reference, to explain the inconsistency in terms of an omission, and to point out that an earlier statement made by him had referred to the defendant. See also *R v Benjamin* (CCA) (1913) 8 Cr App R 146.

R 240, where it was put to the defendant's wife that she had prepared her evidence in collusion with her husband, she was likewise allowed to prove that, after the defendant's arrest and before she had any opportunity to speak to him, she had made to his solicitor a statement to the same effect.

The suggestion must, however, be in the terms set out above. A general cross-examination designed to show that the evidence is unreliable, or even untruthful, will not let in a previous consistent statement. In *Fox* v *General Medical Council* (PC) [1960] 1 WLR 1017, a doctor was charged with infamous conduct, in relation to his adulterous association with a woman patient, who subsequently committed suicide. The Privy Council upheld the decision of the GMC that the evidence of a friend of the doctor, stating that the doctor had, after the patient's death, made to him a statement consistent with his case, was not admissible merely because the doctor's evidence was challenged as being generally untrue. Lord Radcliffe stated the rule in the following terms:

> If in cross-examination a witness's account of some incident or set of facts is challenged as being a recent invention, thus presenting a clear issue as to whether at some previous time he said or thought what he has been saying at the trial, he may support himself by evidence of earlier statements by him to the same effect. Plainly the rule that sets up the exception cannot be formulated with any great precision, since its application will depend on the nature of the challenge offered by the course of cross-examination and the relative cogency of the evidence tendered to repel it.

Lord Radcliffe then considered the nature of the cross-examination which had taken place, and concluded that it was directed to showing the general untruthfulness of the doctor's evidence and that his answers were consistent with either view of the case. His Lordship went on:

> Could it have made any contribution to the (Disciplinary Committee's) judgment on the veracity of his whole account for them to know that in such a situation he had told the old friend substantially the same story as to his innocence of the matters charged as he was now telling at the hearing? Their Lordships do not think that it could. In their view, the challenge to the appellant's evidence that was raised by the cross-examination was not of the order that could be affected by proof of statements made by him of that kind at that date. No tribunal that was not otherwise prepared to accept the appellant's general story could have been led to do so by hearing what he had told [the friend] on April 15. So regarded, the evidence rejected is no more than the previous assertion of the defence story told at the trial, which Humphreys J pointed out in *R* v *Roberts* is clearly inadmissible.

It seems that it must be possible for the court to detect a specific time at or after which it is suggested that the fabrication took place. This and this alone lends cogency to a statement made before that time, tending to negative the suggestion.

Because of the purpose for which the previous statement is admitted, at common law, its evidential effect is limited to the rebutting of the suggestion made of recent fabrication, and it cannot be used as evidence of the truth of what the witness then said. In this respect, it runs parallel to the general rule affecting admissible previous consistent statements, for example recent complaints, and for the same reason it may not amount to corroboration of the evidence of the witness. This is the position in criminal cases.

In civil cases, not for the first time, we must note that the position has been altered by statute. Section 3(1)(*b*) of the Civil Evidence Act 1968 provides that:

(1)   Where in any civil proceedings—

(*b*) a previous statement made by a person called as [a witness in those proceedings] is proved for the purpose of rebutting a suggestion that his evidence has been fabricated,

that statement shall by virtue of this subsection be admissible as evidence of any fact stated therein of which direct oral evidence by him would be admissible.

It may be doubted whether this provision is as radical a change as it appears to be. If the statement is consistent with the evidence given, then the judge will be unlikely to give more weight to it as evidence of the truth of the facts stated in it than he would be inclined to give to the evidence of the witness itself. The role of statements admitted for this purpose will continue to be one of rebuttal, in which, if properly admitted, they may of course be very cogent. Section 6(4) preserves the common-law position that statements admitted for the present purpose are incapable in law of corroborating the evidence of the maker.

### 12.4   Unfavourable and hostile witnesses

Witnesses who 'fail to come up to proof', in other words who are unfavourable in their evidence to the party calling them, or less favourable than might have been expected, are one of the hazards of litigation. It by no means follows that a witness in this position is dishonest, or motivated by malice towards the party calling him. It may be that his knowledge or recollection are not as great as was supposed, or as was once the case. The tenor of what he is able to say may have been misunderstood or exaggerated in the course of taking his proof of evidence. It may, however, be that the witness is dishonest or malicious, and he may actually set out to sabotage the case of the party calling him. Given that a party may not, generally, in evidence in chief put leading questions to his own witness, or in effect cross-examine him, what is that party entitled to do in order to repair any damage caused to his case? The answer involves consideration of two possible remedies, which are: (a) the acceptance of the evidence, combined with calling other admissible evidence in favour of the party's case: and (b) direct discrediting of the witness by reference to previous statements made by him inconsistent with his evidence.

### 12.4.1   Use of other evidence

Any party to litigation is entitled to call all the admissible evidence at his disposal which may assist him in proving his case. This principle is not affected by the fact that part of that evidence turns out to be unfavourable or insufficiently favourable. Consequently, the mere fact that a witness proves unfavourable does not prevent the calling of any other available evidence dealing with the matters which the witness was supposed to prove.[38] Indeed, if the rule were otherwise, the quantity of evidence which could be called would depend upon the accidental factor of whether the unfavourable witness was called first or last.

Within the category of other available evidence must now be counted, in civil cases,

---

[38]   *Ewer v Ambrose* (1825) 3 B & C 746, where the defendant had the misfortune to call a witness who proved the exact opposite of the proposition which he had been called to support.

admissible hearsay statements made by the witness himself. While nothing in the Civil Evidence Act 1968 operates to allow a party to discredit directly a witness who is not hostile, the wording of s. 2 undoubtedly permits the putting in evidence of hearsay statements, in addition to the oral evidence of the witness, and (subject to the provisions of s. 2(2)) for the purpose of supplementing the oral evidence given by the witness. The course suggested is possible only with leave, by virtue of s. 2(2), and the putting in of the statement must wait until the end of examination in chief, subject to the power of the judge to allow the statement to be narrated in chief 'on the ground that to prevent him from doing so would adversely affect the intelligibility of his evidence': s. 2(2)(*b*)(ii).

It is submitted that this course is appropriate to cases where a witness is unfavourable, or insufficiently favourable because of his inability properly to deal with the matters put to him as a result of failing recollection caused by age, illness or the lapse of time. Hearsay evidence would no doubt be an inappropriate subject of leave (and would anyway be devoid of weight) where it was sought to bolster up an inherently unreliable or reluctant witness. The use of hearsay evidence to supplement unfavourable evidence in proper cases was recognised even before the 1968 Act. In *Harvey* v *Smith-Wood* [1964] 2 QB 171, an elderly witness was called for the plaintiff on the trial of her action in March 1963. The witness was unable to deal, to the plaintiff's satisfaction, with certain crucial events, which had occurred in January 1951, by reason of his own age and the considerable lapse of time. Lawton J 'with some regret' acceded to an application to admit in evidence a written statement made by the witness in 1956, dealing with those events, under s. 1(1) of the Evidence Act 1938.[39] The regret expressed was 'because it seems to me that it is an unfortunate situation if counsel can call a witness and, when that witness does not come up to proof, counsel should be allowed to produce some earlier document which shows that on some other occasion the witness made a different statement'. Lawton J went on to say that counsel should hesitate to adopt such a course 'except in very special circumstances'.

It is submitted, with respect, that the reservations alluded to by Lawton J may more happily be applied to questions of weight, than to those of admissibility[40] and under the 1968 Act, subject always to questions of weight, it would seem proper to build up a case by the admission of all the available evidence. Where it is foreseeable that evidence may not be as favourable as might otherwise be expected, having regard to the characteristics of the witness and to the lapse of time, it would no doubt be wise to serve appropriate notices in compliance with RSC, Ord. 38, r. 21, but where the defect in the evidence arises *ex improviso* at the trial, the court may waive the requirement if no injustice is caused to the other side.[41]

### 12.4.2 Direct discrediting

English law regards it as embarrassing and undesirable that a party should be permitted to impeach directly the evidence of a witness whom he has tendered to the court as a witness of truth. And it is clear that he may do so only where the witness is not simply

---

[39]   This section differed in important respects from s. 2 of the 1968 Act, but it is necessary only to refer to the fact that, under the 1938 Act, the statement was admissible without leave on the facts of *Harvey* v *Smith-Wood*.

[40]   This view had received judicial support previously, e.g., in *Bearman's Ltd* v *Metropolitan Police District Receiver* (CA) [1961] 1 WLR 634 per Devlin LJ at 655. This case was cited to Lawton J and must have been in his mind, as he had himself appeared as counsel on that occasion, though it turned on a different point.

[41]   *Morris* v *Stratford-on-Avon RDC* (CA) [1973] 1 WLR 1059.

unfavourable, but is 'hostile' in the sense that he displays some hostile animus towards the party calling him, and evinces no desire to give evidence fairly or to tell the truth. Hostility may stem from malice, bribery, intimidation or a mere indisposition to cooperate. It is interesting to note that not all common-law jurisdictions find the 'voucher rule', whereby a party cannot impeach his own witness, necessary or even desirable. A majority of American jurisdictions now permit a party to impeach a witness he has called, on the ground that a party is not responsible to the court for his testimony merely because that party has called the witness in the hope of supporting his case. These jurisdictions provide accordingly that a witness may be impeached by any party, including the party calling him: see, e.g., Federal Rule of Evidence 607.

The position at common law was never developed to any satisfactory extent, beyond the principle stated above. The judge always enjoys a residual power to put any question which he thinks necessary in the interests of justice, even though such questioning may take the form of cross-examination.[42] But the real problem was whether a party could ever impeach a hostile witness called by him, by putting to the witness a statement previously made by him inconsistent with his evidence. There were dicta that this course was permissible, based mainly upon policy considerations of preventing bribery and other dishonest acts of interference with the administration of justice.[43] But it was left to Parliament to lay down a general rule to that effect, and the need grew in urgency with the growth of the practice of taking proofs of evidence in all forms of litigation.

The provision now in force is s. 3 of the Criminal Procedure Act 1865 which provides that:

> A party producing a witness shall not be allowed to impeach his credit by general evidence of bad character; but he may, in case the witness shall in the opinion of the judge prove adverse, contradict him by other evidence, or, by leave of the judge, prove that he has made at other times a statement inconsistent with his present testimony; but before such last-mentioned proof can be given the circumstances of the supposed statement, sufficient to designate the particular occasion, must be mentioned to the witness, and he must be asked whether or not he has made such statement.

The construction of this inelegantly worded enactment has caused great difficulty. It is clear enough that the section applies alike to civil and criminal proceedings, and that proof of a previous inconsistent statement requires leave of the judge.[44] But what is the meaning of 'adverse' which the judge is required to assess? It is unfortunate that the draftsmen of the 1865 Act did not heed the comments made in *Greenough* v *Eccles and Others*[45] when there fell to be construed the identically worded s. 22 of the Common Law

---

[42]   *Bastin* v *Carew* (NP) (1824) Ry & M 127.

[43]   *Melhuish* v *Collier* (1850) 15 QB 878 per Erle CJ at 890 is an example.

[44]   This is a question of pure discretion for the trial judge. The requirement of leave cannot be circumvented by reliance on s. 4 of the Act (13.6, post) which has been held not to apply to one's own hostile witnesses: *R* v *Booth* (1981) 74 Cr App R 123.

[45]   (1859) 5 CB (NS) 786 per Williams and Willes JJ. The section reduced Cockburn CJ to the anguished cry: 'The solution by my learned brothers is a solution of a difficulty, otherwise incapable of any solution, but I am not satisfied therewith, and without actually dissenting from their judgment, I do not altogether assent to it.' As reported in 28 LJCP 160 at 164. The section also causes problems over the words, 'Contradict him by other evidence', which at common law, might have been done in the case even of a merely unfavourable witness; the phrase is generally assumed to restate this right, which involves reading into the section the parenthesis, 'as he might have done heretofore, and also [to prove . . . . etc.]'. This is a drastic piece of construction, but it is difficult to make sense of it otherwise.

Procedure Act 1854. The court held that the word 'adverse' must be construed to mean 'hostile', on the somewhat desperate reasoning that, if the word signified no more than 'unfavourable', it was hard to see how the judge should be able to form any opinion on that matter; whereas hostility could be demonstrated to him by reference to the previous statement and the demeanour of the witness.

An application must be made in every case in which it is sought to treat a witness as hostile, and the judge must be shown the statement proposed to be proved.[46] In a criminal case, it is the duty of prosecuting counsel to show the statement to the judge in any case where the witness is clearly hostile, and to ask for leave to cross-examine the witness as hostile.[47] The treatment of a hostile witness must be confined to the courses permitted by the section, that is to say contradiction by other evidence (as might be done with an unfavourable witness) and (with leave) proof of a previous inconsistent statement, subject to the preliminary questions required by the section to establish authorship of such a statement. It is not permissible to attack the credit of a party's own witness by general evidence of bad character.

It seems that the Act has not, however, removed the power of the judge at common law to allow any question to be put which seems to him to be necessary in the interests of justice. In *R v Thompson* (1976) 64 Cr App R 96, the victim of an alleged offence of incest was called for the prosecution, but refused to give evidence. The trial judge permitted her to be treated as hostile. It was argued on appeal that this course was not open, at least in so far as the proof of her previous statement was concerned, because the witness having given no evidence, there was no 'present testimony' with which the previous statement could be said to be 'inconsistent', under s. 3. This attractive argument failed. The Court of Appeal held that, whatever the position might be under the statute, the judge retained a power at common law to satisfy the interests of justice by requiring the witness to answer any question directed to that end.

It remains to consider the evidential effect of a previous inconsistent statement proved by virtue of s. 3 of the Criminal Procedure Act 1865, and yet again, the picture is of a limited effect applicable to criminal cases at common law, modified for civil cases by statute. At common law, if the hostile witness, being shown his statement, admits that it is true, then his adoption of it becomes his evidence, and no separate question of the evidential value of the statement as such arises. But where the witness admits that he made the statement, but continues to give evidence inconsistent with it, the jury must be directed to try the case upon his evidence. They may use the statement only as evidence going to the credit of the witness, and it will be a serious misdirection to invite them to act upon the contents of the statement as evidence of guilt.[48] It is immaterial whether the inconsistent statement is an unsworn statement, or one such as a deposition, made on oath in other

---

[46]   Even where the witness is a party called by his opponent, there must be a ruling on hostility; *Price v Manning* (CA) (1889) 42 ChD 372.

[47]   *R v Fraser; R v Warren* (CCA) (1956) 40 Cr App R 160. Where a witness turns hostile at committal proceedings, the prosecution may wait until the trial before treating him as such: *R v Mann* (1972) 56 Cr App R 750.

[48]   *R v Golder and Others* (CCA) [1960] 1 WLR 1169. Though where the evidence is otherwise strong, the proviso to s. 2 of the Criminal Appeal Act 1968 may be applied; *R v Oliva* (CCA) [1965] 1 WLR 1028.

proceedings.[49] In *R* v *Harris*[50] the Court of Criminal Appeal said:

> . . . it was permissible to cross-examine this girl upon the assertions she had previously made, not for the purpose of substituting those unsworn assertions for her sworn testimony, but for the purpose of showing that her sworn testimony, in the light of those unsworn assertions, could not be regarded as being of importance.

In such a case, the jury must, therefore, assess the evidence of the witness in the light of the statement put to him, to show inconsistency, and if the inconsistency is substantial and is unexplained to their satisfaction, the statement may altogether destroy the effect of the evidence. Be that as it may, the jury cannot substitute the statement for the evidence.

In civil cases, the position is now governed by s. 3(1) of the Civil Evidence Act 1968:

> Where in any civil proceedings—
>
> (a) a previous inconsistent or contradictory statement made by a person called as a witness in those proceedings is proved by virtue of section 3 . . . of the Criminal Procedure Act 1865; . . .
>
> that statement shall by virtue of this subsection be admissible as evidence of any fact stated therein of which direct oral vidence by him would be admissible.

Unlike the corresponding provision under s. 3(1)(*b*), dealing with previous consistent statements admitted to rebut suggestions of recent fabrication, this does create a radical change in the use of previous statements. The judge in a civil case may now elect to act on the previous statement, sworn or unsworn, of the hostile witness, in preference to his evidence from the witness-box. It is submitted that this is a useful provision, which might well be extended in modified form to criminal cases, perhaps limited to cases where the previous statement is sworn (as it often is). Where a witness is hostile, it is not infrequently the case that he has been intimidated, or otherwise interfered with, and it is by no means unthinkable that a jury should be able to consider what he said on oath about the matter previously, at a time before his evidence was subjected to pressure, and perhaps accept it as evidence of the truth of what he then said.

## 12.5 Questions for discussion

### 12.5.1 *R* v *Coke; R* v *Littleton*

1 Devise a series of questions to take Margaret and Angela Blackstone through their evidence in chief, without leading them.

2 If D/I Glanvil and D/S Bracton apply to refresh their memories from their notebooks, what must the judge take into account before permitting this?

3 Under what circumstances may the officers' notebooks be put in evidence? What evidential value would they have?

---

[49]   *R* v *Birch* (CCA) (1924) 18 Cr App R 26; and *R* v *Golder and others* (CCA) [1960] 1 WLR 1169 were both concerned with sworn evidence at a magistrates' court in the committal proceedings.

[50]   (1927) 20 Cr App R 144, at 147. The helpful phrase forbidding 'substitution of the statement for the evidence' also appears in *R* v *White* (CCA) (1922) 17 Cr App R 60 at 64.

4  May Angela Blackstone, her mother or the officers give evidence of the identification of Littleton in the street? What considerations apply generally to the evidence of identification of Littleton?

5  May evidence be given of the accounts given to their mother by Margaret and Angela of what had happened at Coke's flat? If so, what evidence may be given, and to what effect?

6  If at the committal proceedings, Margaret refuses to give evidence, or asserts that she consented to the act of intercourse, what should counsel for the prosecution do?

### 12.5.2  *Blackstone* v *Coke*

1  Consider questions 3, 4 and 5 above in the context of *Blackstone* v *Coke*.

# 13 Cross-examination and Beyond

## 13.1 Introduction

Consideration of the course of evidence, following the discussion of examination in chief in the last chapter, must take into account both cross-examination by the party against whom a witness is called, and re-examination by the party calling the witness, where necessary in the light of cross-examination. But it will also be convenient to deal, in this chapter, with two subjects falling outside what might be termed the routine course of evidence. These are evidence called in rebuttal, and witnesses called by the judge of his own motion. These topics will each be examined in the sections which follow, and, as with examination in chief, we shall be concerned with their evidential rather than procedural aspects, although some comment on the latter will be helpful, and will be made where the practice of calling witnesses bears upon the evidential questions which arise.

*A: CROSS-EXAMINATION*

## 13.2 Liability to cross-examination

Any witness who has been sworn on behalf of any party is liable to be cross-examined on behalf of the other party to the proceedings. The liability does not depend upon whether the witness has given evidence adverse to the case of the cross-examining party, because it is perfectly proper for cross-examination to take place for the purpose of eliciting facts favourable to the cross-examiner's case, irrespective of the nature of the witness's evidence in chief. The right to cross-examine exists even where the witness has given no evidence in chief, either because counsel calling him decides, once he had been sworn, not to ask any questions of him,[1] or because, as frequently happens in the case of witnesses who exactly corroborate witnesses already called, he is sworn solely for the purpose of being tendered for cross-examination. The latter practice is common in the case of police officers whose evidence in chief will be identical, any one of whom can give the relevant evidence in chief, but all of whom may be required for cross-examination by the defence.

Cross-examination is, however, like any other questioning, subject to the rules of evidence, one of which is that the answers elicited must be directly relevant to an issue in the case, or indirectly so, as in the case of questions going to credit. Where it appears that a witness is unable to give relevant evidence, it would seem that no question of cross-examination can arise, and the same result obtains where examination in chief is stopped

---

[1]    *R v Brooke* (NP) (1819) 2 Stark (NP) 472. If a witness gives no evidence in chief then there can be no cross-examination concerning his credit because it cannot be relevant: *Hobbs v C.T. Tinling & Co. Ltd; Hobbs v Nottingham Journal Ltd* (CA) [1929] 2 KB 1.

by the judge for any reason properly within his power, before any relevant question has been put.[2]

It seems that where a witness, who has given evidence in chief, becomes unavailable to be cross-examined, his evidence in chief remains admissible, but is unlikely to carry very much weight.[3] If his absence from the witness-box is temporary, for instance because of illness, it is obviously desirable that an adjournment should be granted, wherever this can be done without undue inconvenience or delay, in order to allow cross-examination to take place. However, if a witness absconds with a view to avoiding cross-examination, an obvious inference is to be drawn by the tribunal of fact, which would be justified in rejecting the witness's evidence altogether.[4]

If a witness gives evidence unsworn (see 11.8 and 11.13, ante), he is liable to cross-examination, except, apparently, where a witness is called only to produce a document whose identity is otherwise proved, and where a judge or counsel speaks from his place in court about a case in which he has been judicially or professionally engaged.

### 13.3    Effect of omission to cross-examine

Failure to cross-examine a witness who has given relevant evidence for the other side is held technically to amount to an acceptance of the witness's evidence in chief. It is, therefore, not open to a party to impugn in a closing speech, or otherwise, the unchallenged evidence of a witness called by his opponent, or even to seek to explain to the tribunal of fact the reason for the failure to cross-examine. In *R v Bircham* (CA) [1972] Crim LR 430, for example, counsel for the defendant was not permitted to suggest to the jury that the co-defendant and a witness for the prosecution were the perpetrators of the offence charged, where that allegation had not been put to either in cross-examination. Accordingly, it is counsel's duty, in every case: (a) to challenge every part of a witness's evidence which runs contrary to his own instructions; (b) to put to the witness, in terms, any allegation against him which must be made in the proper conduct of the defence; and (c) to put to the witness counsel's own case, in so far as the witness is apparently able to assist with relevant matters, or would be so able, given the truth of counsel's case. The duty is, of course, not to be interpreted as a licence to introduce irrelevant matters, and is to be carried out with due regard to the undoubted discretion of counsel to omit reference to matters of an apparently trivial or minor significance in the context of the case as a whole. This paragraph should be read in conjunction with the observations made in 13.4, post, with regard to counsel's duty in the conduct of cross-examination.

The second consequence of failure to cross-examine is a tactical one, but no less important for that. Where a party's case has not been put to witnesses called for the other side, who might reasonably have been expected to be able to deal with it, that party himself will probably be asked in cross-examination why he is giving evidence about matters which were never put in cross-examination on his behalf. The implication of the question is that the party is fabricating evidence in the witness-box, because if he had ever mentioned the matters in question to his legal advisers, then they would have been put on his behalf at the proper time. The point is one much beloved of prosecuting counsel in

---

[2]    *Creevy* v *Carr* (NP) (1835) 7 C & P 64.
[3]    For example, where the witness dies after giving evidence in chief: see *R* v *Doolin* (1832) Jebb CC 123 (in which the witness fainted and was 'supposed by many to be dead').
[4]    *Shea* v *Green* (DN) (1866) 2 TLR 533.

criminal cases, though quite what weight juries attach to it, if they follow it at all, is unclear. However, there is some risk that the defendant's credit as a witness may be affected by failure to cross-examine fully on his behalf. If counsel has, by inadvertence, omitted to put some part of the case which should have been put, it is accordingly his duty, at the first possible moment, to mention that fact to the judge and apply for any necessary witness to be recalled for that purpose. The judge has a discretion in every case whether or not to allow any witness to be recalled for further cross-examination,[5] and will ordinarily permit this if it can be done without undue inconvenience, delay or injustice to another defendant.

The duty to cross-examine is habitually and sensibly dealt with by agreement between counsel that no adverse inference will be suggested, if counsel forbear from putting to corroborative witnesses, matters which have clearly been put to at least one witness, and where it is not to be expected that the corroborative witness will contradict the first. The device saves much time, and can be employed for yet more laudable purposes, where the putting of issues is confined to one witness, for the purpose of sparing children or other vulnerable witnesses the ordeal of dealing with delicate questions. Where the device is properly employed, no point will be taken on a failure to put every matter to every witness. However, counsel for a defendant must consider with great care how far he may properly refrain from cross-examination. Frequently the forbearance is confined to the corroborative evidence of police officers, whose evidence may safely be expected to correspond with their depositions, and even then often to relatively minor matters, unless it is clear that the witness intends to do more than reassert his evidence in chief, and to make no concession to the cross-examination.

## 13.4 Nature and conduct of cross-examination

Cross-examination is the process whereby a party seeks: (a) to test the veracity and accuracy of evidence in chief, given by a witness called for another party; and (b) to elicit from that witness any relevant facts which may be favourable to the case for the cross-examiner. Cross-examination designed solely to discredit the witness and to destroy or reduce his credibility, is sometimes known as 'impeachment' and is perfectly permissible.

A witness who has been sworn is compellable to answer any proper question put in cross-examination, whether directed to an issue in the case (i.e. to the substance of his evidence) or to his credit as a witness. With the exception of the defendant in a criminal case, whose position is governed by s. 1 of the Criminal Evidence Act 1898, a witness may be compelled to answer even questions directed to showing his bad character, for the purpose of impugning his credit as a witness. The credit of a witness depends upon the view which the tribunal of the fact ultimately takes of: (a) his knowledge f the facts; (b) his impartiality; (c) his truthfulness; and (d) his respect for his oath or affirmation. These qualities may, therefore, be attacked to the extent necessary to dissuade the tribunal from relying on the witness's evidence, but counsel has a duty not to exceed what is required, and the judge may restrain unnecessary cross-examination, even where some basis for the

---

[5]  In *R v Wilson* [1977] Crim LR 553, the Court of Appeal refused to interfere with the discretion of the trial judge, who had allowed the defendant to be recalled for the purpose of being cross-examined as to his previous convictions, where such course was proper, but had been inadvertently omitted. The court had some doubts, but inadvertence is a fact of life, especially in a complicated case, and should not be allowed to prevent a fair trial, if it can be avoided.

questions can be found as a matter of law.[6]

It should, however, be noted that in one important case, relating to imputations on character, there is now a statutory restriction on cross-examination concerning credit. By s. 2(1) of the Sexual Offences (Amendment) Act 1976:

> If at a trial any person is for the time being charged with a rape offence to which he pleads not guilty, then, except with the leave of the judge, no evidence and no question in cross-examination shall be adduced or asked at the trial, by or on behalf of any defendant at the trial, about any sexual experience of a complainant with a person other than the defendant.

Section 2(2) provides that the judge shall give leave only where on application being made to him, he is 'satisfied that it would be unfair' to the defendant not to do so. The meaning of this subsection was considered by the Court of Appeal in *R v Viola* [1982] 3 All ER 73. The only issue on the trial of the defendant for rape was whether the complainant had consented to the sexual intercourse with the defendant. The defendant had, at trial, sought, and been refused leave to cross-examine the complainant about her alleged sexual relations with other men shortly before and shortly after the alleged rape. It was held that the test should be: (1) whether the proposed cross-examination was relevant to the defendant's case according to the common-law rules of evidence; and (2) if so, whether the judge was satisfied that it was more likely than not that the cross-examination might reasonably lead the jury to take a different view of the complainant's evidence.[7] If the proposed cross-examination satisfies both parts of the test, then it should ordinarily be permitted. On the other hand, since the purpose of the section is to prevent evidence and questions which merely suggest the general bad character of the complainant, with a view to showing that because of such character she should not be believed on her oath, any evidence or questions which have no relevance apart from this should be rejected.

On the facts of the case, the Court of Appeal held that the cross-examination proposed should have been allowed, because it was relevant to the issue of consent, and because the jury might have taken a different view of the complainant's evidence. The Court pointed out that decisions whether to admit evidence in such circumstances are extremely difficult, and often borderline. The proximity in time of the alleged other acts to the occasion of the offence charged, the number of men allegedly involved and the fact that the complainant was alleged to have played an active role in initiating the sexual activity were instrumental in leading the Court to its decision. The point was that in the judgment of the Court, the jury might have found the evidence relevant to the issue of whether or not the complainant consented on the occasion of the offence charged. Had the questions done no more than suggest that the complainant consented on other occasions, or even that she was promiscuous, the result should , it is submitted, have been different. It might in some cases be relevant also to adduce evidence tending to show that someone other than the defendant was the source of semen or injury on the complainant's body.

It should be noted that the section does not restrict evidence or questions about the past

---

[6]   *R v Sweet-Escott* (1971) 55 Cr App R 316. Courts have also held various methods of cross-examination unfair; see, e.g., the now forbidden practice of cross-examining a defendant on his application for legal aid: *R v Stubbs* [1982] 1 All ER 424.

[7]   The second part of the test had already been established by the Court of Appeal in *R v Mills* (1978) 68 Cr App R 327, approving the earlier decision of May J in *R v Lawrence* [1977] Crim LR 492. But these decisions did not address the issue of relevance or offer guidance as specifically as did the Court in *Viola*.

sexual relationship of the complainant with the defendant, since such evidence and questions are relevant to the issue of consent. Obviously, the consent refers to consent with the defendant, and evidence of prior consensual sexual relations between the complainant and the defendant is far easier to justify than evidence of sexual relations between the complainant and other persons. The latter will often appear to be no more than an attempt to attack the complainant's general character.

In cross-examination there is less restriction on the form of questions than in examination in chief, and in particular, leading questions may be employed freely. It has been said that the questions put should not be in the nature of comment on the facts (the proper place for which is in counsel's closing speech) or such as to provoke argument between counsel and the witness. Forms which offend against this rule are said to be: 'I suggest that . . .;' 'Are you asking the jury to believe that . . .?' 'That's hardly consistent with . . . is it?' and the like.[8] It is also undesirable that counsel should draw to the attention of the witness what has been said in evidence by other witnesses, and invite his comment on such other evidence, or invite the witness to agree or to disagree with it.[9] It must be confessed, however, that the above forms are in regular use in practice and seem not to be restrained, unless obvious embarrassment is being caused, and of course it it not right that the flow of questioning should be interrupted for purely technical errors to be corrected.

The conduct of cross-examination is the subject of rules of professional conduct drawn up by the Bar Council, originally published in November 1950 and since modified. The detail of these rules is outside the scope of this work, but they are set out in *Archbold*[10] and should be studied in depth by every intending advocate. The essence of the rules may perhaps be expressed by saying that they impose upon counsel the duty fearlessly to represent his client, and to put in cross-examination every matter necessary for the proper presentation of the case.[11] At the same time, counsel must use his judgment and discretion to avoid making unnecessary allegations, particularly against absent third parties and in a public trial. The more grave the allegation to be put, the more it should be scrutinised in relation to its necessity to the case. These observations apply most strongly to allegations directed to credit only, and counsel should seek verification of such allegations from his

---

[8]   See the observations of Lord Hewart CJ in *R* v *Baldwin* (CCA) (1925) 18 Cr App R 185. Particular care must be taken when dealing with potentially sensitive matters affecting credit.

[9]   *North Australian Territory Co. Ltd* v *Goldsborough Mort & Co. Ltd* (CA) [1893] 2 Ch 381. However, there can normally be no objection to asking one expert witness for his comments on other expert evidence.

[10]   41st ed., para. 4–317 and Appendix C. The rules are not binding on the court. If a judge seeks to persuade counsel to fail to comply with them, counsel must either withdraw, or comply under protest and look for redress elsewhere; see *R* v *McFadden and Others* (CA) (1975) 62 Cr App R 187. But counsel cannot be criticised in terms of professional conduct if he observes the rules.

[11]   The vexed question of what counsel may properly do when representing a defendant who does not give evidence, seems at long last to be settled, in favour of the view that he must fully present his case in cross-examination, as in any other case. The decision whether to give evidence is that of the defendant, not counsel, and may be made at the very last possible moment. Of course, the failure of the defendant to give evidence, where grave allegations have been made on his behalf, may properly be made the subject of strong comment in the summing-up. Any other rule would subject counsel to intolerable and embarrassing decisions about whether he should present his case fully, or hold back in case the defendants elects not to give evidence subsequently. See *R* v *Brigden* (CA) [1973] Crim LR 579. The view that it is wrong for counsel to make grave allegations in cross-examination and then not call the defendant was voiced by Lord Goddard CJ in *R* v *O'Neill; R* v *Ackers* (CCA) (1950) 34 Cr App R 108, but may be regarded as abrogated. The view expressed in support of it by Waller LJ in *R* v *Callaghan* (CA) (1979) 69 Cr App R 88 was withdrawn by the learned Lord Justice in a statement reported at 70 Cr App R 232 after representations from the Bar.

instructing solicitor, or personally ascertain that there are reasonable grounds for believing such allegations to be true, so far as he is reasonably able to do so. Cross-examination should be as short as is consistent with a proper presentation of the case, and should in no case be conducted with a view to harassing, intimidating or browbeating the witness.

## 13.5   Application of the rules of evidence to cross-examination

The normal rules of evidence apply to matters elicited in cross-examination, as they do to matters elicited in chief. There is no licence to elicit evidence which is inadmissible merely because it arises in the course of cross-examination. Thus, in *R v Thomson* (CCA) [1912] 3 KB 19, where the defendant was charged with using an instrument on a woman (who had died) with intent to procure her miscarriage, the defendant's counsel was held to have been rightly prevented from asking a prosecution witness in cross-examination whether the deceased woman had not told her that she intended to procure her own miscarriage, and later, that she had in fact done so. The evidence was hearsay at any stage of the examination of the witness, and must be excluded. Similarly, where the judge has excluded an out-of-court statement, made by a defendant, as being inadmissible in law, it may not be referred to subsequently for any purpose, including that of cross-examination on behalf of a defendant.[12]

But it should be noted that the course taken in cross-examination may, of itself, render admissible evidence which would have been inadmissible from the witness in chief, and then the witness may deal with the evidence in cross-examination and re-examination. The point is that cross-examination may legitimately raise further issues, and therefore render admissible evidence which could not previously have been given. We saw in the last chapter that, where a witness is cross-examined upon the contents of a document from which he has refreshed his memory, if the cross-examination strays beyond those parts of the document actually used for that purpose, then the document becomes evidence where it certainly was not before, and may be referred to and asked about accordingly. Much the same will occur where a document is admitted in chief for the purpose, say, of identifying handwriting contained in it, and in cross-examination its contents are referred to. The contents are then made evidence by reason of the cross-examination. And where a witness is asked for the first time in cross-examination about acts done by him, or words spoken between him and a party to the proceedings, such acts and words thereupon become evidence, and may be dealt with accordingly. In the case of the words spoken the witness would be permitted, in cross-examination or re-examination, to state the whole of the conversation put to him.

We must now turn to look at three important evidential matters which arise in the course of cross-examination. These are: (a) cross-examination using previous inconsistent statements; (b) the rule that answers given on collateral matters are final; and (c) the consequences of cross-examination on documents.

## 13.6   Previous inconsistent statements

We saw in Chapter 12 that in the treatment of a hostile witness, the use of previous

[12]   *R v Treacy* (CCA) [1944] 2 All ER 229. Unless permitted under s. 76(4) of the Police and Criminal Evidence Act, 1984; see 7.7, ante.

statements made by the witness on other occasions, inconsistent with his evidence, is a crucial weapon available for the purpose of impeaching the witness. The same weapon is no less potent in the case of witnesses called for the other side, who are expected and taken to be hostile. At common law, it was open to a cross-examiner to put to a witness his previous inconsistent statements, but the rule was circumscribed by the requirements[13] that, if the statement put was in writing, the witness must be shown the document before he could be asked whether he had said something different on another occasion (which removed the element of surprise); and that if the statement was proved, having been denied by the witness, it must be made evidence as part of the cross-examiner's case (which inhibited the use of statements in many cases). While the first of these requirements was relaxed to some extent by s. 5 of the Criminal Procedure Act 1865, the second, by a curious quirk of fate, has in effect received statutory force for civil cases by virtue of s. 3(1)(a) of the Civil Evidence Act 1968.[14]

The use of previous inconsistent statements in cross-examination is now governed by s. 4 and s. 5 of the Criminal Procedure Act 1865, which complement the provision of s. 3 dealing with the use of such statements against a party's own hostile witnesses.[15] Section 4 provides:

> If a witness upon cross-examination as to a former statement made by him relative to the subject-matter of the indictment or proceeding and inconsistent with his present testimony, does not distinctly admit that he has made such statement, proof may be given that he did in fact make it; but before such proof can be given the circumstances of the supposed statement, sufficient to designate the particular occasion, must be mentioned to the witness, and he must be asked whether or not he has made such statement.

The section is not expressed to apply exclusively to oral or written statements, but it may be assumed that s. 4 is intended to apply to both written and oral statements. It is implicit in the section that the cross-examiner is entitled to ask the witness about the former statement, and the draftsman evidently considered that he was building upon that rule of common law. The right to prove any statement which is not 'distinctly admitted' not only deals with the possibility of ambivalent or evasive answers, when the witness is asked about the previous statement, but also precludes the objection that the proof of the previous statement, if denied, might offend against the rule of common law that answers in cross-examination which go only to collateral matters must be accepted as final.[16]

The section applies alike to statements made previously on oath, for example, a deposition made in committal proceedings, and those made previously unsworn in any circumstances, for example on being interviewed by the police.[17] The question whether

---

[13] Said to derive from *Queen Caroline's Case* (1820) 2 B & B 287, which itself is hardly compelling authority, but may well have reflected the contemporary position at common law.

[14] Regardless of whose case it may form part of, the use of previous statements in civil proceedings now involves the risk of the judge accepting the statement as evidence of facts stated in it. This may be desired in the case of one's own hostile witnesses, but in the case of the other side's, may involve a searching assessment of how much of the statement may be favourable to the other side, inconsistencies notwithstanding: cf. *R v Ford and Others* (1851) (CCR) 5 Cox CC 184.

[15] Like s. 3, s. 4 and s. 5 apply to civil and criminal proceedings alike, and succeed provisions of the Common Law Procedure Act 1854.

[16] See 13.7, post.

[17] *R v Hart* (CCA) (1957) 42 Cr App R 47: *R v O'Neill* (CA) [1969] Crim LR 260. In the latter, a defendant who gave evidence exculpating a co-defendant was rightly cross-examined on his oral statement to the police, in which he had said the opposite of his evidence.

such statement is 'relative to the subject-matter of the indictment or proceeding' appears to be one within the competence and discretion of the judge, and not one solely for the judgment of the cross-examiner, or the opinion of the witness.[18]

The words following the semi-colon correspond to those in s. 3, and require a fair and proper foundation to be laid before the statement may be proved.

Section 5 of the Act provides:

A witness may be cross-examined as to previous statements made by him in writing, or reduced into writing, relative to the subject-matter of the indictment or proceeding, without such writing being shown to him; but if it is intended to contradict such witness by the writing, his attention must, before such contradictory proof can be given, be called to those parts of the writing which are to be used for the purpose of so contradicting him: Provided always, that it shall be competent for the judge, at any time during the trial, to require the production of the writing for his inspection, and he may thereupon make such use of it for the purposes of the trial as he may think fit.

The section envisages two stages in the use of previous inconsistent statements made in, or reduced into, writing. The first part of the section permits the cross-examiner rather more scope for surprise than did the common-law rule, as applied in *Queen Caroline's Case*, and indeed was intended to abrogate the requirement of showing the witness the document before any questions were asked. The cross-examiner may show the document to the witness and ask questions while it is in the hands of the witness. But the use made of the statement must, in order to remain within the first part of the section, fall short of 'contradiction' of the witness. This seems to mean that the cross-examiner may ask the witness, first whether he has ever made a statement on another occasion inconsistent with his evidence, and second (showing him the document) whether, on seeing the statement, he wishes to adhere to the evidence he has given. If the answer is that the witness is prepared to alter his evidence materially, the damage to his credit is done. If he sticks to his evidence, the cross-examiner must choose whether to accept that answer, or whether to enter the second stage. If he chooses the latter course, he will proceed to contradict the witness by the document, in other words put to him that the relevant part of the document (identifying it to him) is a true account, and not the witness's evidence. At this point, but not before—another significant departure from the common-law rule—the document may be proved to contradict the witness, and must then be put in evidence, having of course been made relevant by the second stage of cross-examination.

The provision in s. 5 that the judge may require production of the document, and may make use of it for the purposes of the trial, means that the cross-examiner must have the document available in court even if it is never shown to the witness.[19] The proviso does not, however, allow the judge to treat the previous statement as evidence of the truth of the facts stated in it, in a criminal trial. The evidential value of a statement proved under s. 4 or s. 5 is, at common law, the same as one put to a hostile witness under s. 3, i.e. it goes to the consistency of the witness and, therefore, to the credit of the witness, but no further. In particular, the statement cannot be substituted for the evidence of the witness (see 12.4.2, ante). The contrary suggestion accordingly cannot be one of the 'purposes of the trial', for which the judge may make use of the statement.

---

[18]   *R* v *Bashir; R* v *Manzur* [1969] 1 WLR 1303, per Veale J at 1306.
[19]   *R* v *Anderson* (CCA) (1929) 21 Cr App R 178.

In civil cases, as we have seen, statute has altered the position, as it has in respect of hostile witnesses. We may now set out s. 3(1)(*a*) of the Civil Evidence Act 1968 in its entirety:

Where in any civil proceedings—

(*a*) a previous inconsistent or contradictory statement made by a person called as a witness in those proceedings is proved by virtue of section 3, 4 or 5 of the Criminal Procedure Act 1865; . . .

that statement shall by virtue of this subsection be admissible as evidence of any fact stated therein of which direct oral evidence by him would be admissible.

It is clear that special care is needed with regard to the use of previous statements in civil cases. Whereas in the case of a hostile witness it may be desirable, from the point of view of the party calling the witness, that the judge be persuaded to accept the previous statement as evidence of the facts stated in it, and so to substitute the statement for the witness's evidence, the same is far less likely to be true in the case of a witness called for the other side, to whom a statement is to be put under s. 4 or s. 5 of the 1865 Act. Indeed, even if there is some discrepancy, the overall impression of the statement may be favourable to the party calling the witness. In any event, the judge might give leave to admit the witness's previous statement under s. 2 of the 1968 Act, and we have seen that it is now quite proper for this to be done, merely for the purpose of supplementing the witness's recollection. Thus, cross-examination along these lines must be far more restrained, and may be less effective in civil cases than in criminal.

### 13.7 Finality of answers on collateral issues

Because cross-examination may be directed to matters going solely to the credit or the character of the witness, and because cross-examination may elicit evidence which was not elicited in chief, and even evidence that would not have been admissible in chief, it is apparent that the course of cross-examination may result in some proliferation of the issues aired before the court. If this were wholly unrestrained, the time and attention of the court might be devoted, in a measure disproportionate to their importance, to a series of facts not directly relevant to the issues between the parties in the proceedings. There is, therefore, a sensible rule, designed to avoid undue proliferation of side issues, that a cross-examiner must accept as final answers given in response to questions dealing with 'collateral' matters. Acceptance as final means that the cross-examiner cannot seek to contradict the answer by calling further evidence in rebuttal on his own behalf, and not that he himself cannot continue to challenge it in cross-examination, or is obliged to admit its truth.

The test of what is collateral is not always simple, but turns upon whether the content of the answer is of direct relevance to some issue which must be decided in order to resolve the proceedings in favour of one party or the other. If the matter is of such direct relevance, it is not collateral. Perhaps the most helpful statement of the rule was that made by Pollock CB in *Attorney-General v Hitchcock* (1847) 1 Exch 91 which was to the effect that if the answer given is a matter which would have been admissible in chief, as a piece of evidence called for the cross-examiner, because of its relevance to issues in the case, then the matter is not collateral, and may be rebutted. It would follow that cross-examination going solely to credit will lead to collateral answers. Thus, in *R* v *Burke* (1858) 8 Cox CC 44, an Irish witness, giving evidence through an interpreter, asserted that he was unable to speak English. He denied in cross-examination having spoken English to two persons in court. It was not permissible to call evidence in rebuttal to the effect that the witness had spoken in English, because the cross-examination was designed solely to attack the veracity of the witness. But the position would be quite different if the witness's command of the language had been relevant, e.g. to his alleged authorship of some material document, or his ability to make an alleged confession or adverse admission and so had gone to an issue in the case.

A useful illustration of the rule can be seen in rape cases. If, on behalf of Coke, it were to be suggested to Margaret Blackstone that she had had previous sexual experience with Coke, or had in some way deliberately provoked Coke to sexual activity with her, such questions would go to the root of the defence, in that they are clearly relevant to the issue of consent. Conversely, if, with leave of the judge,[20] it were to be suggested that Margaret had previously had sexual relations with Coke's mate, Kevin, that matter would be one going to credit only and would be final, as being collateral.[21]

There are exceptional cases in which the exploration of collateral issues cannot be avoided if a fair trial is to be secured, and in such cases an answer may be the subject of further evidence even if collateral. In this connection, we shall look at the statutory exception permitting the proof of previous convictions which have been denied, at the common-law exceptions of bias or partiality, reputation for untruthfulness and medical evidence affecting reliability, and at a statutory exception relating to the impeachment of admissible hearsay evidence in criminal cases.

### 13.7.1   *Previous convictions*
By s. 6 of the Criminal Procedure Act 1865:

> A witness may be questioned as to whether he has been convicted of any misdemeanour, and upon being so questioned, if he either denies or does not admit the fact, or refuses to answer, it shall be lawful for the cross-examining party to prove such conviction; . . .[22]

This provision must, of course, be read subject to those of s. 1(*e*) and (*f*) of the Criminal Evidence Act 1898, which govern and restrict the circumstances in which the defendant in a criminal case may be asked about his previous convictions (see 4.12 et seq., ante); and to those of the Rehabilitation of Offenders Act 1974 and of s. 16(2) of the Children and Young Persons Act 1963, governing and restricting the use of certain previous convictions to which those provisions refer (see 4.14, ante). In other words, s. 6 must be taken as meaning that, in cases where such questions may properly be put to a witness, the previous convictions may be proved, unless admitted. Of course, unlike more general allegations

---

[20]   Required because of s. 2 of the Sexual Offences (Amendment) Act 1976; see 13.4, ante.

[21]   See *R* v *Riley* (CCR) (1887) 18 QBD 481; *R* v *Holmes* (CCR) (1871) LR 1 CCR 334; *aliter*, where sexual relations with others is directly relevant, e.g. to the issue of paternity in affiliation proceedings.

[22]   The original wording referred to 'any felony or misdemeanour'; but by s. 1 of the Criminal Law Act 1967 the distinction was abolished, and the practice in all cases assimilated to that relating to misdemeanours. *Quaere*, whether the section applies to purely summary offences, whose status at common law was unclear.

affecting credit, character and other collateral matters, previous convictions may be proved easily and with precision, the more so as the keeping of records becomes increasingly systematic, and permits increasing ease of access. Previous convictions may be proved, pursuant to the section, by a certificate of the court of conviction, purporting to be properly signed by the appropriate officer and dealing with the substance and effect of the charge and the conviction recorded, coupled with evidence of the identity of the witness as the person so convicted.[23]

### 13.7.2 Bias or partiality

Any fact tending to suggest bias or partiality on the part of a witness may be cross-examined to, and may be proved in rebuttal, if denied. Although in a sense collateral, the matter is a vital one to be considered by any tribunal of fact. In *R* v *Mendy*[24] it was said that the rule of finality is not absolute, and that it is wrong to keep matters from the jury, which may suggest some attempt to interfere with the course of the trial in order to favour some bias or partiality. In that case the defendant's husband, who was to be called as a witness on her behalf, was waiting outside court (according to the usual practice in criminal cases) until his turn to give evidence. He denied later, in cross-examination, that while outside court he had spoken to a man who had been seen in the public gallery taking notes of other evidence. The implication was that the witness was prepared to inform himself illicitly of what was going on in court, prior to his being called, for the purpose of tailoring his evidence to the advantage of his wife. The prosecution were allowed to rebut the denial.

There are many ways in which bias or partiality may be manifested. In *R* v *Shaw* (1888) 16 Cox CC 503, a prosecution witness, who denied in cross-examination that he had quarrelled with the defendant and had threatened to take revenge on him, was allowed to be contradicted. In *R* v *Phillips* (1936) 26 Cr App R 17, the defendant was charged with incest with his daughter. His defence was that the daughter, and another daughter called to give evidence for the prosecution, had been 'schooled' in their evidence by their mother, and that the charge was a fabrication. In addition to this, it was suggested that the daughters had given similarly schooled evidence at a previous summary trial, at which the defendant had been bound over in respect of an alleged indecent assault on the same daughter. The girls denied in cross-examination that they were giving false evidence, and further denied having made admissions that their evidence at the summary trial had been schooled. It was held that the trial judge had erred in refusing to permit the defendant to call rebutting evidence from persons to whom the admissions were said to have been made. The Court of Criminal Appeal held that such evidence went 'to the very foundation of the appellant's answer to the charge', and not just to a question of credit.[25]

In *R* v *Busby* (1982) 75 Cr App R 79, it was held that where it was alleged that police officers had threatened a defence witness, in order to seek to deter him from testifying on

---

[23]    See now s. 73 of the Police and Criminal Evidence Act, 1984. For civil cases see the remaining provisions of s. 6 of the Criminal Procedure Act 1865 and s. 18 of the Prevention of Crimes Act 1871. The evidence of identity need only be such that the court can properly draw the inference that it has been established, and need not be conclusive; *Martin* v *White* [1910] 1 KB 665.

[24]    (CA) (1976) 64 Cr App R 4. And see *Attorney-General* v *Hitchcock* (1847) 1 Exch 91, per Pollock CB at 100.

[25]    The phrasing of the judgment is not, with respect, entirely happy. The foundation of the defence was that the charge was untrue, not that the girls were not to be believed because they had admitted fabricating evidence before. Nor is the court's view that the rebutting evidence could be treated as evidence of the truth of the facts stated, free from difficulty. However, the decision is clearly right on the facts.

behalf of the defendant, the officers' denial of that allegation was not a collateral issue, and that the witness had been wrongly prevented from giving evidence of the alleged threat. If true, the evidence would have shown that the officers were prepared to go such lengths in order to see the defendant convicted. Referring to *Phillips* and *Mendy*, the Court held that the evidence was such that the defendant had been entitled to have it given as part of his defence. It is interesting to note that the Court did not refer to, and may not have been referred to, the old case of *Harris* v *Tippett* (NP) (1811) 2 Camp 637, in which the decision was contrary to that in *Busby*, and which must presumably now be treated as overruled. It is submitted, however, that this development is to be welcomed, and that *Busby* is plainly to be preferred.

Bias or partiality may, in some circumstances, arise from the relationship between a witness and the party on whose behalf he is called, although there must be something over and above the relationship itself, suggestive of such quality, on the facts of the case. In *Thomas* v *David*[26] in an action on a promissory note, a witness called for the plaintiff denied a suggestion made to her in cross-examination that she was the mistress of the plaintiff, her employer. The defendant's case was that he was not the maker of the note: in effect that it was a forgery. Coleridge J held that the relationship was relevant to the facts, and that the witness might be contradicted. After further evidence, a verdict was entered for the defendant. Coleridge J said:

> Is it not material to the issue whether the principal witness who comes to support the plaintiff's case is his kept mistress? If the question had been whether the witness had walked the streets as a common prostitute, I think that that would have been collateral to the issue, and that, had the witness denied such a charge, she could not have been contradicted; but here, the question is, whether the witness had contracted such a relationship with the plaintiff, as might induce her the more readily to conspire with him to support a forgery.

A party may exhibit 'partiality' in relation to his own case, where he behaves in such a way as to suggest that his claim is false or exaggerated. For example, the plaintiff may have been heard to admit that he suffered injuries in a manner inconsistent with his cause of action against the defendant in respect of those injuries,[27] or there may be evidence that the plaintiff has suborned false witnesses.[28] These matters go beyond the question of credit, and are receivable in evidence as an admission adverse to the case of the party affected. If, therefore, such matters are put to a party called as a witness and are denied, they may be proved in rebuttal as relevant to the issues.

But the exception seems to apply only where there is alleged in cross-examination actual bias or partiality. The mere fact that a witness is alleged to have admitted some fact consistent with bias or partiality, for example that he has been offered a bribe in connection with his evidence in the case, will not suffice to defeat the finality rule, unless it is suggested that he in fact accepted a bribe, i.e., that he is actually biased or partial.[29] The

---

[26]   (NP) (1836) 7 C & P 350. The decision has not escaped criticism: see e.g. *R* v *Cargill* (CCA) [1913] 2 KB 271.
[27]   Cf. *Moriarty and Another* v *London, Chatham & Dover Railway Co.* (1870) LR 5 QB 314.
[28]   Cf. *Melhuish* v *Collier* (1850) 15 QB 878.
[29]   *Attorney-General* v *Hitchcock* (1847) 1 Exch 91.

fact that a witness has spoken of being offered or receiving a bribe may drastically affect his credit, but is nonetheless collateral to the issues in the case; a suggestion that he in fact accepted a bribe points to some actual defect in his evidence, which is directly relevant to the outcome of the case. In *Phillips*, the suggestion that the girls had admitted having given schooled evidence on a previous occasion, was secondary to the principal suggestions made to them, namely that their evidence at the instant trial was false and schooled, and it was to this point that the cross-examination was ultimately directed.

In *Attorney-General* v *Hitchcock* (1847) 1 Exch 91, the defendant, a maltster, was charged with using a cistern in breach of certain statutory requirements. His counsel asked a prosecution witness in cross-examination whether he had not previously said that he had been offered £20 by officers of the Crown, if he would state that the cistern had been so used. The witness denied the allegation. The question was whether the defence were entitled to call a witness of their own to state that the prosecution witness had said this. It was held that they could not. Pollock CB said (ibid at 101) that the reason was:

. . . that it is totally irrelevant to the matter in issue, that some person should have thought fit to offer a bribe to the witness to give an untrue account of a transaction, and it is of no importance whatever, if that bribe was not accepted. It is no disparagement to a man that a bribe is offered to him; it may be a disparagement to the person who makes the offer. If, therefore, the witness is asked the fact, and denies it, or if he is asked whether he said so and so, and denies it, he cannot be contradicted as to what he has said. *Lord Stafford's* case was totally different. There the witness himself had been implicated in offering a bribe to some other person. That immediately affected him, as proving that he had acted the part of a suborner for the purpose of perverting the truth.

### 13.7.3 Reputation for untruthfulness
A witness may be called to state his opinion that a witness called on the other side should not be believed, in that he is unworthy of belief on his oath. This form of evidence is little used, and almost devoid of modern authority, but did arise for consideration in *R* v *Richardson; R* v *Longman* [1969] 1 QB 299, in which the Court of Appeal took the opportunity of restating the extent of this exception to the rule of finality. It said that a witness may be asked whether he has knowledge of the reputation of the impugned witness on his oath. In the case under appeal the trial judge permitted evidence to be given thus far, but refused to allow a further question to be put in the form; 'From your personal knowledge of Mrs C, would you believe her on her oath?' It was held that this question should have been allowed also, and that the witness may state his own opinion in addition to his evidence of general reputation, provided always that his evidence is based upon his own personal knowledge. However, the Court of Appeal emphasised that a witness called for this purpose cannot, in chief, give his reasons for his opinion of the credibility on oath of the impugned witness. The inadmissibility of reasons in evidence in chief is an old rule, which at one time applied strictly to any evidence of opinion. It has almost certainly ceased to have effect, so far as expert-opinion evidence is concerned, and has been doubted increasingly in modern practice. But it is submitted that in the present context, it is of considerable value in preventing a multiplicity of side issues from arising, which the court could not hope to investigate satisfactorily. There is no power to prevent the witness being asked for his reasons in cross-examination, although the course would ordinarily be a perilous one, and the answers would have to be accepted as final.

### 13.7.4   Medical evidence affecting reliability

Medical evidence may be called to show that a witness suffers from some disease, defect or
abnormality of the mind, such as to affect the reliability of his evidence. The rule is akin to,
but more specialised than that just discussed concerning reputation and opinion. The
modern rule is to be gleaned from *Toohey* v *Commissioner of Police of the Metropolis*
[1965] AC 595. Toohey and two others were charged with assault with intent to rob. Their
defence was that the alleged victim had been drinking and was behaving very strangely,
and that while they were taking him home, he had become hysterical and had imagined
that he was going to be robbed. A police surgeon gave evidence for the defence and said
that when he examined the alleged victim there were no signs of injury on him, that he
smelt of alcohol, and that throughout the examination he was weeping and hysterical. The
appeal turned on the question whether the trial judge was correct in refusing to allow the
doctor to be asked his opinion of the part played by alcohol in the victim's hysteria, and
whether he was more prone to hysteria than a normal person. The House of Lords held
that the further questions should have been permitted, firstly because they sought to elicit
matters of direct relevance to the defence, and secondly, because the evidence was
admissible for the purpose of impeaching the victim's credit as a witness. The second of
these reasons involved overruling the decision of the Court of Criminal Appeal in *R* v
*Gunewardene* [1951] 2 KB 600, in which it had been held that the most that could be asked
of a medical witness was whether, from his knowledge, he would believe the impugned
witness on his oath; and that no reasons might be given in chief. This would have equated a
doctor with a witness called to deal with general reputation, or to give a lay opinion based
upon personal knowledge. Lord Pearce reviewed the older authorities, concluding that
'the older cases are concerned with lying as an aspect of bad character, and are of little help
in establishing any principle that will deal with modern scientific knowledge of mental
disease and its effect on the reliability of a witness'. Later in his speech with which the
other members of the House concurred, Lord Pearce observed (ibid at 608):

> Human evidence shares the frailties of those who give it. It is subject to many cross-
> currents such as partiality, prejudice, self-interest and above all, imagination and
> inaccuracy. Those are matters with which the jury, helped by cross-examination and
> common sense, must do their best. But when a witness through physical (in which I
> include mental) disease or abnormality is not capable of giving a true or reliable account
> to the jury, it must surely be allowed for medical science to reveal this vital hidden fact
> to them.

Lord Pearce concluded (ibid at 609):

> *Gunewardene's* case was, in my opinion, wrongly decided. Medical evidence is
> admissible to show that a witness suffers from some disease or defect or abnormality of
> mind that affects the reliability of his evidence. Such evidence is not confined to a
> general opinion of the unreliability of the witness but may give all the matters necessary
> to show, not only the foundation of and reasons for the diagnosis, but also the extent to
> which the credibility of the witness is affected.

It should be noted, however, that where the witness is mentally capable of giving reliable
evidence, medical evidence is not admissible on the weight of the evidence given by the
witness, even if this may be affected to some degree by his medical condition. The question

of whether or not a witness is in fact giving reliable evidence, as opposed to the question of whether or not he is capable of so doing, is one for the jury to decide, aided by argument from counsel and appropriate warnings by the judge: see *R v MacKenney and Others* (CA) (1981) 72 Cr App R 78. This is in accordance with the rules governing the use of expert testimony generally (see 9.4, ante.)

### 13.7.5 Impeachment of admissible hearsay evidence
The Police and Criminal Evidence Act 1984 makes provision for certain evidence to be given on collateral issues in criminal cases, with leave of the court, for the purpose of impeaching the supplier of information used to compile a record, where hearsay evidence of the record is admissible by virtue of s. 68 of the Act. The supplier of the information will usually not be called as a witness in such a case, and cross-examination will not be possible. This is dealt with further in 13.11.2, post.

## 13.8 Cross-examination on documents

We have already dealt with, and need not repeat, the rules relating to the use of previous written statements inconsistent with the present testimony of a witness, and cross-examination on documents used to refresh the memory (see 12.2.2, 12.4.2 and 13.6, ante). We saw that if a document is put in evidence as a result of cross-examination in these circumstances, then its evidential effect is limited in criminal cases following the rules of the common law, but that, by virtue of s. 3 of the Civil Evidence Act 1968, it may in a civil case be treated as evidence of any fact stated in it of which direct oral evidence would be admissible. We must now look at the use in cross-examination of documents which do not fall into those categories, and which stand or fall in their own right as pieces of evidence, according to the normal rules of admissibility. Such documents are obviously of an almost inifinitely various nature, and may be either in the possession of the cross-examiner or of the opponent of the cross-examiner.

A document in the possession of the cross-examiner is either admissible in itself, in which case it may be put in evidence and cross-examined upon in its own right, or inadmissible (usually on the ground of hearsay) in itself. We have seen that evidence cannot be made admissible just because it is used in cross-examination if it was inadmissible in chief, as in *R v Treacy* [1944] 2 All ER 229, where it was held improper to cross-examine upon the contents of a document which had been held to be inadmissible.[30] The most that can be done with an inadmissible document, therefore, is to ask the witness to look at the document and, without describing the nature or contents of the document to the court, to invite him to consider whether he wishes to give any further or different evidence.[31] If a witness, on being shown a document, asserts or admits that its contents are true, then those contents which he so adopts become part of his evidence. But the contents of an inadmissible document cannot be made evidence unless they are so adopted. In *R v Gillespie and Simpson* (CA) (1967) 51 Cr App R 172, the defendants were charged with offences of dishonesty in accounting to their employers for sums of money less than those

---

[30] Of course, the contents of an inadmissible document may be extremely useful in providing information from which questions in cross-examination may be framed. It is perfectly proper to make use of the contents for the purpose of framing the most effective questions, provided that the existence and contents of the document are not revealed to the court: *R v Rice and Others* (CCA) [1963] 1 QB 857.

[31] See *R v Yousry* (CCA) (1914) 11 Cr App R 13.

which, according to the documentation prepared by salesgirls, had been received from customers. The conviction was quashed, on the ground that the defendants had been asked in cross-examination to read aloud the documents prepared by the salesgirls, who had not been called. What the prosecution had done was to purport to make admissible the contents of documents which were inadmissible hearsay, merely by putting them to the defendants, when the defendants did not in any way adopt or acknowledge the truth of those contents.

Documents in the possession of the opponent of the cross-examiner are subject to a special rule. At common-law, if the cross-examiner calls for and inspects in court a document in the possession of his opponent or his opponent's witness, then the cross-examiner is bound to put the document in evidence as part of the cross-examiner's case. Thus in *Stroud* v *Stroud*[32] in the course of a defended suit for divorce, counsel for the husband cross-examined a doctor called on behalf of the wife, and called for and inspected in court certain medical reports prepared by other doctors concerning the wife, which the witness had with him. It was held that counsel for the wife was entitled to insist upon the reports being put in as part of the husband's case; and counsel for the husband having elected to put in some of them, counsel for the wife was entitled to have the remainder put in also. The rule is a curious one, and it is to be noted that it comes into operation even if cross-examination has not been concerned with the contents of the documents. The rule developed in the absence of a general process of discovery at common law, and it was argued before Wrangham J in *Stroud* v *Stroud* that the modern principle of disclosure of all relevant, non-privileged documents, had rendered the rule obsolete. The learned judge accepted that in the case of documents which had not, but ought to have been disclosed on discovery, the cross-examiner would be entitled to inspect them in court without being compelled to put them in evidence, as he would have been before the start of the trial, under the Rules of Court. But although the importance of the rule has undoubtedly diminished since the advent of a general principle of disclosure, Wrangham J pointed out that the rule may still be of significance in cases where there is no discovery, particularly in criminal cases: and indeed, it would seem still to apply to such cases.

One argument worthy of attention, which was not available at the time of *Stroud* v *Stroud* is that such documents can no longer be admitted in civil cases because of s. 1(1) of the Civil Evidence Act 1968, which provides that:

> In any civil proceedings a statement other than one made by a person while giving oral evidence in those proceedings shall be admissible as evidence of any fact stated therein to the extent that it is so admissible by virtue of any provision of this Part of this Act or by virtue of any other statutory provision or by agreement of the parties, but not otherwise.

This section may affect the rule in civil cases because of the clear limitation of the words 'but not otherwise', but only on the assumption that documents so put in evidence are admitted as evidence of the truth of the facts stated therein. Whether this is so appears never to have been decided in England,[33] but it is difficult to see any other basis, which

---

[32]   [1963] 1 WLR 1080. Contrast carefully the rule applying to documents used to refresh the memory, which is quite distinct: *Senat* v *Senat* [1965] P 172; see 12.2, ante.

[33]   The position appears to have been recognised as being so in Australia; see the authorities set out by Professor Cross, *Evidence*, 5th ed., p. 262.

would apply equally to all cases, on which documents could be admitted if called for and inspected. It is strange that the point has never been decided in a criminal case, where s. 1 could not interfere with the admission of such documents. It may be that the courts would hesitate long before admitting hearsay in such circumstances, and would opt for some lesser evidential purpose according to the nature of the document in any given case. This would inevitably involve some difficulty, because no obvious evidential purpose presents itself (for example, consistency) which could be applied uniformly to all documents admitted under the rule. If the rule is to survive, some statutory clarification would not be unwelcome.

## B: BEYOND CROSS-EXAMINATION

### 13.9 Re-examination

Very little need be said about re-examination. It is the process whereby a party calling a witness may seek to explain or clarify any points that arose in cross-examination and appear to be unfavourable to his case. Re-examination is, therefore, possible only where there has been cross-examination and is limited to matters raised in cross-examination: it is not an opportunity to adduce further evidence in chief. Thus, in *Prince* v *Samo* (1838) 7 A&E 627, where cross-examination took place of a witness for the plaintiff about part of a hearsay statement, which would have been wholly inadmissible in chief, the plaintiff was entitled to re-examine on any matter arising from the portion of the statement referred to in cross-examination, but was not entitled to elicit any other portion. However, the re-examiner may deal with all matters relevant to those raised in cross-examination, even if not dealt with expressly by the cross-examiner.

A witness is entitled to explain any apparent contradiction or ambiguity in his evidence or damage to his credit arising rom cross-examination, and this may involve reference to facts which have not previously been given in evidence, if they are properly relevant in order to deal with the points put in cross-examination. Where, therefore, a witness was asked in cross-examination why his evidence was that the defendant was one of a number of persons who attacked a deceased, when he had made a statement in which he did not refer to the defendant at all, he was allowed to be asked in re-examination whether he had made an earlier statement, in which he had referred to the defendant.[34] In this case, the re-examination was directed to re-establishing the credit of the witness but the principle is the same where it is sought to clear up some question of fact. And evidence admitted in re-examination can, therefore, be powerful and dangerous. The effect of cross-examination in letting in further evidence must be carefully considered before it is embarked upon. If, for example, it is suggested in cross-examination of a police officer that the officer followed the defendant because of a determination to be vindictive against him, the officer may be re-examined to elicit his true reasons for following him. The resulting evidence, which would have been wholly inadmissible in chief, is potentially devastating.

Leading questions are not permitted in re-examination, for the same reason as in the case of examination in chief.

### 13.10 Evidence in rebuttal

The general rule of practice, in both criminal and civil cases, is that every party must call

---

[34] *R* v *Coll* (CCR, Ireland) (1889) 24 IR 522.

all the evidence on which he proposes to rely during the presentation of his case, and before closing his case. This involves the proposition that the parties should foresee, during their preparations for trial, what the issues will be, and what evidence is available and necessary in order to deal with those issues. The definition of the issues in a civil case by exchange of pleadings, and in a criminal case (to a far more limited extent) by service of the prosecution statements and the settling of an indictment,[35] is designed to enable this to be done wherever possible.

It must, however, be recognised that in some cases, it will not be possible to foresee every piece of evidence which may be required, because proceedings have a habit of taking courses which occasion surprise and sometimes embarrassment to one or more of the parties. It has long been the rule that the judge may permit evidence to be called by a party who has been taken by surprise by some development at the trial, in order to 'rebut' evidence given against him by the other side, after that party's case has been formally closed.[36] The circumstances in which this discretion will be exercised have not always been so clear.

It is certain that the power will not be exercised in order to aid a careless or inadvertent party, who has simply failed to take the trouble to prepare his case adequately. And it would be carelessness or inadvertence to fail to foresee that the other side will bring evidence designed to contradict and disprove one's case. The test was originally that laid down by Tindal CJ in *R v Frost*, [37] in fairly restrictive terms:

> The Crown . . . cannot afterwards support their case by calling fresh witnesses, because they are met by certain evidence that contradicts it. They stand or fall by the evidence they have given . . . but if any matter arises *ex improviso* which no human ingenuity can foresee . . . there seems to me no reason why the matter which so arose *ex improviso* may not be answered by contrary evidence on the part of the Crown.

In more modern times, it has been felt that the test propounded by Tindal CJ is unduly narrow, and ought to be restated to allow the trial judge more discretion to further the interests of justice, [38] and it is pertinent to note that the competence of the defendant as a witness since 1898, coupled with his right in most cases to withhold his defence until trial, has made the task of prosecution more difficult. It may be, although *R v Frost* has not been overruled, that the test is now one of reasonable foreseeability, and that if the course of the trial takes a party into uncharted waters, which could not have been anticipated before trial on a sensible and alert view of the case, further evidence ought to be permitted to deal

---

[35]   The defence are not obliged to reveal the nature of the defence before trial, except where they are required to serve notice of alibi, and even then the judge has a discretion to permit evidence of alibi to be given, notwithstanding that no notice has been served: Criminal Justice Act 1967, s. 11.

[36]   But in a case tried with a jury, no evidence may be given after the retirement of the jury. In a criminal case, any breach of this rule will lead to the conviction being quashed: *R v Owen* (CCA) [1952] 2 QB 362; even where the evidence is apparently irrelevant: *R v Wilson* (CCA) (1957) 41 Cr App R 226; and even where the defence consent; *R v Corless* (CA) (1972) 56 Cr App R 341. Though the Court of Criminal Appeal has approved the admission of evidence for the defence, where a witness arrived at court during the summing-up (and so was not being recalled) and the judge summed up his evidence subsequently: *R v Sanderson* [1953] 1 WLR 392. As to the position in Magistrates' Courts, see *Webb v Leadbetter* (DC) [1966] 1 WLR 245.

[37]   (1840) 9 C & P 129 as reported in 4 St Tr NS 85 at 386.

[38]   See, e.g., *R v Crippen* (CCA) [1911] 1 KB 149.

with the matters which have occasioned surprise.[39] Certainly, it would seem wrong for the court to be deprived of material evidence in such circumstances, which might be the case on the basis of an unbending interpretation of the words, 'which no human ingenuity can foresee'.

But on either test, the rule will not cover evidence which was clearly reasonably foreseeable, and ought to have been adduced as a proper and necessary part of the prosecution case. In *R* v *Day* (CCA) [1940] 1 All ER 402, a conviction was quashed where the prosecution were permitted to call a handwriting expert, not only after the close of their own case, but after the defendant had given evidence, and where it was obvious from the outset that the evidence might well be required.

In civil cases, evidence in rebuttal has been permitted in cases where evidence has been given, or issues raised, which could not have been foreseen on the pleadings and which have accordingly taken a party by surprise; or where a party has been misled about the true nature of the claim or defence. But in a civil action, the judge may equally decline to entertain any unpleaded issue, and will usually do so if the departure from the pleaded issues is a serious one, going to the very nature of the claim or defence. This consideration indeed reflects the true objection to evidence in rebuttal, which is that the contrary case will already have been presented, to an end and in a way which does not correspond with the actuality, and the prejudice which can arise if a party is allowed to alter his case, after the case against him has been presented, is obvious.

Evidence in rebuttal is not permissible of collateral matters except in certain cases (see 13.7, ante) or where it would simply be confirmatory of the party's case as already put.[40]

### 13.11 Impeachment of admissible hearsay evidence

The major objection to the admission of hearsay evidence is that it cannot effectively be cross-examined to, and in particular, it may be observed that it is difficult, if it is possible at all, to impugn effectively the credibility of the maker of a hearsay statement, who is not called as a witness. Nonetheless, in both civil and criminal cases, certain hearsay statements are now admissible, as evidence of the facts stated in them.[41]

*13.11.1 Civil cases*
Part 1 of the Civil Evidence Act 1968, which provides for the general admissibility of such statements in civil cases seeks to offer at least some compensation for the inability of an opponent to cross-examine the maker of a statement who is not called as a witness. Section 7 provides:

(1) . . . where in any civil proceedings a statement made by a person who is not called as a witness in those proceedings is given in evidence by virtue of s. 2 of this Act—

(*a*) any evidence which, if that person had been so called, would be admissible for the purpose of destroying or supporting his credibility as a witness shall be admissible for

---

[39] Cf. *R* v *Owen* (CCA) [1952] 2 QB 362, per Lord Goddard CJ at 366; *R* v *Milliken* (CA) (1969) 53 Cr App R 330 at 333.
[40] *Jacobs* v *Tarleton* (1848) 11 QB 421.
[41] See Chapter 8, ante.

that purpose in those proceedings; and

(*b*)   evidence tending to prove that, whether before or after he made that statement, that person made (whether orally or in a document or otherwise) another statement inconsistent therewith shall be admissible for the purpose of showing that that person has contradicted himself . . .

The section, therefore, simulates the cross-examiner's weapons of cross-examination concerning credit, and the use of previous inconsistent statements. Although in the absence of the maker, the weapons provided by s. 7 are obviously less potent than in a case where cross-examination is possible, there are disadvantages also for the party putting in the evidence, who may be unable to restore the credit of the maker, or to explain any apparent ambiguity or inconsistency in his statements.

The same limits on the exploration of collateral matters are prescribed as would be the case in cross-examination. The proviso to s. 7(1) reads:

Provided that nothing in this subsection shall enable evidence to be given of any matter of which, if the person in question had been called as a witness and had denied that matter in cross-examination, evidence could not have been adduced by the cross-examining party.

The section also equates the evidential effect of previous inconsistent statements proved by virtue of s. 7(1)(*b*) with that of such statements put to a witness under s. 4 or s. 5 of the Criminal Procedure Act 1865. Although the primary purpose of such statements, reflected in s. 7(1)(*b*) itself, is to show the inconsistency of the maker, in a civil case the statements put may also be used as evidence of the admissible facts stated in them, by virtue of s. 3(1)(*a*) of the Act. Accordingly, by s. 7(3), the provisions of s. 3(1)(*a*) are expressly applied to statements admitted under s. 7(1)(*b*), so that these statements also may be treated as evidence of any fact stated in them, of which direct oral evidence by their maker would be admissible.

Section 7(2) extends the operation of s. 7(1) to persons who originally supply information from which a record, admissible by virtue of s. 4, is compiled, and such a person may, therefore, be treated in all respects as if he were the maker of a hearsay statement admissible by virtue of s. 2.

### 13.11.2   *Criminal cases*
The Police and Criminal Evidence Act 1984 makes similar provision for the impeachment of admissible hearsay evidence admitted pursuant to s. 68 of the Act. Paragraph 3 of sch. 3 to the Act provides:

Where in any proceedings a statement based on information supplied by any person is given in evidence by virtue of section 68 . . .—

(*a*)   any evidence which, if that person had been called as a witness, would have been admissible as relevant to his credibility as a witness shall be admissible for that purpose in those proceedings;

(*b*)   evidence may, with the leave of the court, be given of any matter which, if that person had been called as a witness, could have been put to him in cross-examination as relevant to his credibility as a witness but of which evidence could not have been adduced by the cross-examining party; and

(c)   evidence tending to prove that that person, whether before or after supplying the information, made a statement (whether oral or not) which is inconsistent with it shall be admissible for the purpose of showing that he has contradicted himself.

'Proceedings' in this paragraph, as in the Act generally, means criminal proceedings: see s. 72(1). Comment is necessary on sub-paragraphs (b) and (c).

Sub-paragraph (b) is, essentially, a new statutory exception to the rule of finality on collateral issues (see 13.7, ante). Where a witness testifies, he may be cross-examined about collateral issues relevant only to credit, but save in the exceptional cases discussed in 13.7, no evidence may be adduced by the cross-examiner to contradict his denials. Section 68 of the 1984 Act requires that, if hearsay evidence is to be admissible, one of the statutory conditions relating to the person who supplied the information should be fulfilled. In most cases, this will mean that he is not before the court as a witness, and cannot be cross-examined. The Act therefore provides that, notwithstanding the general rule, evidence may be adduced (subject to leave) on a collateral issue. If this were not so, the opponent would frequently be deprived of all opportunity to impeach the supplier of the information. It is submitted that the granting or refusal of leave should depend on whether or not the evidence is likely to affect the jury's view of the credibility of the information supplied. This provision is notably different from that of the Civil Evidence Act 1968, which in an analogous situation expressly precludes such evidence: see the proviso to s. 7(1) of the Civil Evidence Act 1968 set forth above.

Sub-paragraph (c) preserves the right to impeach by reference to previous inconsistent statements, but now the statement will be inconsistent with the information supplied, rather than with testimony at trial, again because usually the supplier will not be called as a witness.

It should be noted that these provisions do not affect the common-law rules as to the evidential value of the evidence described. Thus, evidence admissible under sub-paragraph (c) that the supplier of the information contradicted the information supplied is admissible to show that the supplier contradicted himself, but the inconsistent statement is not evidence of the truth of any fact stated therein. Similar observations may be made, in so far as appropriate, on evidence admissible under sub-paragraphs (a) and (b).

### 13.12   Judge's power to call witnesses

Ordinarily, the working of the adversarial system in litigation requires that the judge should not interfere with the decision of the parties to call or not to call certain evidence. In a civil case, where the judge has the duty of finding the facts, as well as that of presiding over the conduct of the trial, he is entitled to draw any proper inferences about the strength or weakness of a party's case from failure to call what appears to be relevant and available evidence. In a criminal trial, however, somewhat different considerations apply, because of the incidence of the burden and standard of proof, and because of the judge's particular duty to ensure a fair trial of the issue of guilt or innocence.

It has long been recognised that the judge has power, in a criminal trial, to call of his own motion any witness who has not been called either for the prosecution or the defence, if in his opinion it is necessary to do so in the interests of justice.[42] The power must be

---

[42]   *R v Chapman* (1838) 8 C & P 558.

exercised with great care, bearing in mind that it is the duty of the prosecution to call all the witnesses who can give relevant evidence, unless they appear to be incapable of belief, even where they may give evidence inconsistent with the prosecution case. If the prosecution fail to call a witness who on the face of it ought to be called, it is open to the judge to invite the prosecution to call him.[43] If neither side calls a witness, the judge should assume that there is a good reason for such a course, especially where neither side makes any application to him in the matter. It has often been said that the judge's power to call a witness should be exercised rarely and sparingly.[44] Like any other evidence, the witness must be called before the retirement of the jury, and there is no doubt that it must be even rarer than suggested above, that he should be called after the defence case has been closed.

In *R* v *Cleghorn* [1967] 2 QB 584, a conviction was quashed where, on a charge of rape, the trial judge called a witness who had not been called by either side. The witness was called after the defence case had been closed, and the case thereafter assumed a different aspect. Although no rule applicable to all cases can be laid down, it has been helpfully suggested[45] that the calling of witnesses by the judge should generally be confined to cases where analogous to the case of *R* v *Frost*,[46] a matter has arisen '*ex improviso*, which no human ingenuity can foresee'.One proper use of the power is a case where the judge concludes that the prosecution are wrongly declining to call a witness, who ought to be called in the interests of a fair trial. It is not always an answer to say that the defence can call the witness, because they should be in a position to cross-examine and not be obliged to call him as their witness in chief.[47] It may also be proper for the judge to call a witness who seems hostile to both sides, but whose evidence may nonetheless be material.

A witness called by the judge may be cross-examined by either side only with leave,[48] although if his evidence affects adversely the case for either side, it is inconceivable that leave should be refused.

### 13.13   Questions for discussion

#### 13.13.1   *R* v *Coke; R* v *Littleton*
1   May counsel for Coke cross-examine Margaret Blackstone as to:

(a)   The fact that she consented to have sexual intercourse with Coke on 8 July 1979?

(b)   The fact that she had led him to believe on other occasions that she was prepared to have sexual intercourse with him?

(c)   The fact that Margaret is promiscuous?

(d)   The fact that Margaret has had sexual intercourse with Coke's mate, Kevin?

(e)   The fact that Margaret threatened to accuse Kevin of raping her?

(f)   The fact that Margaret has previous convictions for theft?

---

[43]   *R* v *Oliva* [1965] 1 WLR 1028.
[44]   See e.g., *R* v *Edwards and Others* (1848) 3 Cox CC 82; *R* v *Cleghorn* [1967] 2 QB 584.
[45]   In *R* v *Harris* (CCA) [1927] 2 KB 587.
[46]   (1840) 9 C & P 129 as reported in 4 St Tr NS 85 at 386. See 13.10, ante.
[47]   Cf. *R* v *Tregear* (CA) [1967] 2 QB 574. The prosecution's duty must be exercised so as to further the cause of justice, which must involve consideration of the consequences of the defence calling a witness in chief. But if the evidence of a witness would form part of the defence case then the prosecution are not obliged to call him, particularly if doing so would merely confuse the jury: *R* v *Nugent* [1977] 1 WLR 789.
[48]   *Coulson* v *Disborough* (CA) [1894] 2 QB 316.

2   In relation to any of these matters on which cross-examination is possible, would the defence be entitled to call evidence in rebuttal if Margaret denies them in cross-examination?

3   If Margaret's evidence in chief varies materially from the contents of her statement to the police, what steps may Coke's counsel take? What results will any such course have, and what must counsel bear in mind before embarking on it?

4   If Margaret has a known history of lying, what evidence might be called on behalf of Coke to deal with this?

### 13.13.2   Blackstone v Coke

1   Consider question 3 above in the context of *Blackstone* v *Coke*.

2   If Coke is permitted to adduce the hearsay statement of Anthony Henneky, what steps might Margaret take to discredit it?

# 14  Corroboration

## 14.1  Meaning of corroboration

The word 'corroboration' connotes support or confirmation, and indicates, in relation to the law of evidence, that certain evidence (the evidence to be corroborated) is confirmed in its tenor and effect by other admissible and independent evidence (the corroborating evidence). In any case where one piece of evidence confirms and supports another, corroboration therefore takes place if both pieces of evidence are accepted by the tribunal of fact.[1] Although, as an obvious truism, any case is stronger if evidence in its support is corroborated than it would otherwise be, this elementary proposition of weight is not what most concerns us in the law of evidence. The law must perceive and resolve the fundamental question of whether the court should ever be permitted to act, for the purpose of giving judgment in favour of a party, upon the uncorroborated evidence of a single witness or document, tendered alone and unsupported in proof of that party's case; or whether, conversely, there is any need to insist upon corroboration of evidence, so that the unsupported evidence of a single witness or document will always be sufficient, if accepted by the court; or whether, to take a middle view, there are certain cases (and if so, what cases) in which corroboration of the evidence of a single witness or document should be required before a case can be found to be proved.

Both extreme views present problems. A complete disregard for the desirability of corroboration may indicate a lack of sensitivity to the inherent unreliability of certain types of evidence, and may render some decisions unsafe. On the other hand, a rigid insistence upon corroboration may unnecessarily damn many a perfectly sound case which has the misfortune to have been witnessed by only one person.

## 14.2  The rule at common law

In contrast to systems of law based on Roman law, in which there is a general requirement of corroboration, the common law holds that in the absence of some specific rule to the contrary, the court may for any purpose act upon the uncorroborated evidence of a single

---

[1] 'There is nothing technical in the idea of corroboration. When in the ordinary affairs of life one is doubtful whether or not to believe a particular statement one naturally looks to see whether it fits in with other statements or circumstances relating to the particular matter; the better it fits in, the more one is inclined to believe it.' *DPP* v *Kilbourne* [1973] AC 729 per Lord Reid at 750.

[2] Despite the apparent divergence, the rules of Roman and common law probably produce little significant difference in practice, there being a wide measure of agreement about the kinds of evidence which are reliable and those that are prone to be unreliable. The difference is that in one system, the

witness or document.[2] The rule applies both to civil and criminal cases[3] and regardless of whether the evidence in support of the case is agreed or disputed. It need hardly be emphasised that, quite apart from any question of requirement, any party is at liberty to adduce whatever evidence he sees fit by way of corroboration of other evidence in his favour, subject to the rules of admissibility.

The common-law rule has been modified by two groups of exceptions in which a requirement of corroboration has been recognised, either by statute or by the practice of the common law itself. With the exception of affiliation cases, requirements for corroboration now apply only to evidence tendered by the prosecution in a criminal case, and the law in this area has been developed almost exclusively by such cases. The two groups differ considerably in nature and operation, and must be kept entirely distinct. Nonetheless, they share a common and cogent justification for not acting on the uncorroborated evidence of a single witness. In some cases, the justification is to be found in the gravity of the subject-matter of the case itself, but more frequently it lies in the inherent danger of unreliability of certain classes of evidence. Such danger may arise from the personal characteristics of a witness, from some personal interest in the outcome of a case or in the acceptance of his evidence, from some personal motive for giving evidence against a party, or simply from the nature of the evidence itself. The groups of exceptions comprise:

(a) Cases where corroboration is required as a matter of law. In these cases, certain kinds of evidence are required as a matter of law to be corroborated, before any conviction or judgment may be based upon them. The requirement is provided for by statute and is mandatory, so that if there is no evidence capable of amounting to corroboration, the judge must withdraw the case from the jury, or dismiss the claim, as the case may be. A conviction or judgment obtained in breach of the requirement will be set aside on appeal.

(b) Cases where corroboration is to be looked for as a matter of practice. In these cases, the common law has recognised the undesirability of a tribunal of fact acting on certain kinds of uncorroborated evidence, without warning itself of the danger of so doing. What is mandatory in these cases is an appropriate warning, usually conveyed by judge to jury in the course of summing-up, of the danger involved. The absence of such warning will be a ground of appeal, and despite the use of the term, 'a matter of practice', the requirement of a warning is in effect a rule of law and is mandatory.[4] The important difference between these cases and the cases in which corroboration is a statutory requirement is that here, provided the jury are properly warned, they may if they wish act on the uncorroborated evidence in question, for the purpose of convicting, and if they do so, no appeal will lie for that reason.[5]

---

result is arrived at by applying 'the general rule' and in the other by applying 'an exception to the general rule', according to the circumstances.

[3]   Corroboration is of greatest importance in relation to criminal cases, the critical authorities being concerned with directions by judge to jury on the subject. Appellate courts are frequently apt to quash convictions on appeal for misdirection. In civil cases, appellate courts are slow to intervene unless it is shown that the trial judge simply did not advert to the question, and express references are not usually essential in the judgment, provided that the judge was alive to the dangers, if any, inherent in the evidence. It cannot be assumed so safely that juries will appreciate the problem.

[4]   *R v Baskerville* (CCA) [1916] 2 KB 658; *Davies v DPP* (HL) [1954] AC 378.

[5]   *R v Baskerville* (CCA) [1916] 2 KB 658.

These two groups of exception must be examined in detail, but it will first be useful to consider the respective roles of judge and jury in the treatment of corroboration, and the legal qualities which evidence must possess, in order to be held capable of corroborating other evidence. These considerations underlie the rules applicable to the exceptional cases.

## 14.3 Functions of judge and jury

The assessment of corroboration falls into two parts, which are respectively a question of law and a question of fact. Whether evidence is capable in law of constituting corroboration is a question of law for the judge. In deciding the question, the judge must consider whether the evidence said to be capable of corroboration fulfils the requirements dealt with in 14.4 below. In the light of his conclusions, the judge must then either withdraw the case from the jury, if corroboration is required as a matter of law and none is available, or give the jury the necessary warning, if the jury are required to look for corroboration as a matter of practice. The direction must, of course, include appropriate guidance on what parts of the available evidence the jury are entitled to regard as corroborative, or, if it be the case, that there is no such evidence.[6] There is a real possibility that a jury may be confused by a direction couched in technical legal terms, and the judge should state the requirements using everyday language. It is unnecessary to use the word 'corroboration' itself, and indeed, it may be preferable to avoid it and employ some synonym such as 'support' or 'confirmation'.[7] However, the question whether evidence capable of corroborating other evidence does in fact do so is one of fact for the jury, like any other question of the acceptance, rejection or weight of evidence.[8]

## 14.4 Necessary qualities of corroborative evidence

In order to be capable in law of constituting corroboration, evidence must be: (a) admissible in itself; (b) from a source independent of the evidence requiring to be corroborated; and (c) such as to tend to show, by confirmation of some material particular, not only that the offence charged was committed, but also that it was committed by the defendant. In *R* v *Baskerville*[9] Lord Reading CJ expressed the requirements in the following terms:

> . . . evidence in corroboration must be independent testimony which affects the accused by connecting or tending to connect him with the crime. In other words, it must be evidence which implicates him, that is, which confirms in some material particular not only the evidence that the crime has been committed, but also that the prisoner committed it. The test applicable to determine the nature and extent of the

[6]   *R* v *Beck* [1982] 1 All ER 807; see also *R* v *Cullinane* [1984] Crim LR 420; *R* v *Reeves* [1979] 68 Cr App R 331; *R* v *Charles and Others* (CA) (1976) 68 Cr App R 334n.

[7]   *DPP* v *Kilbourne* (HL) [1973] AC 729 per Lord Hailsham of St Marylebone at 740; *DPP* v *Hester* (HL)[1973] AC 296 per Lord Diplock at 327.

[8]   The jury of course will not act for any purpose, including corroboration, on evidence which they reject. See *DPP* v *Hester* (HL) [1973] AC 296 per Lord Morris of Borth-y-Gest at 315; *DPP* v *Kilbourne* (HL) [1973] AC 729 per Lord Hailsham of St Marylebone at 746.

[9]   (CCA) [1916] 2 KB 658 at 667. See also *DPP* v *Kilbourne* [1973] AC 729 per Lord Hailsham of St Marylebone at 741.

corroboration is thus the same whether the case falls within the rule of practice at common law or within that class of offences for which corroboration is required by statute.[10]

### 14.4.1 Admissible
This means, of course, that the evidence must conform in itself to the general rules of admissibility and so be capable of being received for the purpose of proving guilt as charged.

### 14.4.2 Independent
It is obvious that confirmation of the evidence of a witness is worthless coming from the witness himself, or for that matter, from one with whom the witness has been in collusion.[11] In *R* v *Whitehead*,[12] where the defendant was charged with unlawful sexual intercourse with a girl under sixteen, it was suggested that the girl's recent complaint made to her mother was capable of constituting the necessary corroboration of her evidence. Lord Hewart CJ pointed out that if this were the case, 'it is only necessary for her to repeat her story some twenty-five times in order to get twenty-five corroborations of it'. Thus, even where at common law a previous statement made by the witness is admissible, as in the case of a recent complaint, it cannot amount to corroboration of the witness's evidence.

However, a somewhat different rule has developed in regard to the visible distress of the complainant, which is witnessed independently. This has been held to be evidence capable of amounting to corroboration of the complainant's evidence, subject to the two conditions that it must be independently observed, and that it must appear to the court to be genuine and unfeigned. In *R* v *Chauhan* (1981) 73 Cr App R 232, the defendant was charged with indecent assault on a woman. The complainant extricated herself and ran to a lavatory, where she was observed by a fellow employee, who had heard her cries. The defendant admitted that he had been with the complainant, but denied any wrongdoing, and said that the complainant had been behaving normally. The trial judge left the complainant's distress to the jury as potentially corroborative of her evidence. On appeal against conviction, the Court of Appeal went out of its way to praise the clarity of the judge's summing-up in this regard, and held that he had been right to permit the jury to consider the complainant's visible distress, about which the fellow employee (independent observer) had testified, with a clear warning to regard it as corroboration only if they were sure that the distress was genuine and unfeigned.

In *R* v *Redpath* (1962) 46 Cr App R 319, 321 Lord Parker CJ pointed out that in some cases, for example where the distress is no more than part and parcel of a recent complaint made by a girl to her mother, the jury should be directed to attach little or no weight to it. Indeed, it is submitted that in such a case, even where the distress is witnessed by an independent person, the evidence lacks the quality of independence necessary for potentially corroborative evidence, and should not be left to the jury as such. In the later

---

[10]   The same principles appear to apply to civil cases in which corroboration is to be looked for: *Alli* v *Alli* (DC) [1965] 3 All ER 480.

[11]   A rule which is not avoided even by the ingenious suggestion made through the mouth of Jack Point in Gilbert and Sullivan's *Yeomen of the Guard* that the evidence of one of his eyes was corroborated by that of the other!

[12]   (CCA) [1929] 1 KB 99. See also *R* v *Christie* (HL) [1914] AC 545.

case of *R* v *Knight* [1966] 1 WLR 230, Lord Parker CJ commented further on what he had said in *Redpath*:

> Despite what was said in that judgment, there has been a tendency since then for judges to leave to the jury almost every case where a complainant is seen to be in a distressed condition, and in several cases since *R* v *Redpath*, and in particular *R* v *Okoye* [[1964] Crim LR 416] and *Luisi* [[1964] Crim LR 605], I endeavoured to stress that the distress shown by a complainant must not be over-emphasised in the sense that juries should be warned that except in special circumstances little weight ought to be given to that evidence.

It is submitted that, because of the inevitable doubt as to independence and genuineness, Lord Parker's words should be scrupulously heeded.[13]

At common law, previous consistent statements, put in cross-examination, or documents used to refresh the memory admitted as a result of cross-examination, are admissible only exceptionally and even then are not evidence of the truth of facts stated therein; so that they lack both admissibility and independence, when assessed as possible corroborative evidence.[14] In civil cases, however, previous statements made by a witness are now, by statute, not only admissible but admissible as evidence of the truth of facts stated therein, subject to the provisions of ss. 2, 3 and 4 of the Civil Evidence Act 1968 (see Chapter 8, ante). It was accordingly thought necessary to deal expressly with the status of such statements for the purposes of corroboration, and the Act confirms that the lack of independence precludes their use for this purpose. Section 6(4) of the Act provides:

> For the purpose of any enactment or rule of law or practice requiring evidence to be corroborated or regulating the matter in which uncorroborated evidence is to be treated—
>
> (a) a statement which is admissible in evidence by virtue of section 2 or 3 of this Act shall not be capable of corroborating evidence given by the maker of the statement; and
> (b) a statement which is admissible in evidence by virtue of section 4 of this Act shall not be capable of corroborating evidence given by the person who originally supplied the information from which the record containing the statement was supplied.

For the same reasons, para. 4 of sch.3 to the Police and Criminal Evidence Act 1984 provides that a hearsay statement contained in a record, and admissible in criminal proceedings by virtue of s. 68 of the Act, shall not be capable of corroborating evidence given by the person who supplied the information on which the statement is based.

### 14.4.3   *R* v *Coke; R* v *Littleton*

It is clear, therefore, that whatever other corroboration may be available of the evidence

---

[13]   See also *R* v *Dowley* [1983] Crim LR 168. The thoughtful and interesting commentary to this case in the *Criminal Law Review* points out that, unlike *Redpath* and *Chauhan*, the evidence of distress in *Dowley* corroborated only the complainant's account of a rape by someone, and in no way implicated the defendant. Since the defendant was still legally married to the complainant (a decree nisi had been granted, but not made absolute) and since the facts were somewhat bizarre, the danger was particularly significant.

[14]   See Chapter 12, ante; and *R* v *Virgo* (CA) (1978) 67 Cr App R 323.

of Margaret Blackstone of the alleged rape by Coke, corroboration may not be found in her complaint to her mother, even if the complaint is admissible. It makes no difference whether evidence of the complaint is given by Margaret, her mother or both, because it is the source of the statement which lacks independence. It is, however, possible that corroboration may be found in the evidence of Margaret's distressed condition given by her mother and Dr Vesey, for the reasons stated above.

*14.4.4 Confirmation of material particular tending to show not only commission of the offence but also its commission by the defendant*
This condition is the most restrictive and limiting of the legal requirements for corroboration. The extent to which evidence needs to be corroborated is a question almost as fundamental as that of whether it should be required at all. Little reflection is needed to see that it cannot be required that evidence should be corroborated in every point, because the demands of such a rule would be too onerous, and because the evidence requiring to be corroborated would then become almost superfluous. On the other hand, confirmation of some minor or peripheral detail in an item of evidence would not be enough to increase confidence in it to the desired degree. The rule, therefore, is that the corroborating evidence must confirm the evidence requiring corroboration in at least one particular which is directly relevant to the issues in the case, in that it tends to suggest not only that the offence charged has been committed, but also that it has been committed by the defendant. It does not matter that the evidence may be circumstantial rather than direct, as long as the jury would be entitled to draw from it an inference, which, if drawn, would have the effect of implicating the defendant in the offence charged.

*Cracknell* v *Smith* [1960] 1 WLR 1239 was an affiliation case, in which the evidence of the complainant required to be corroborated as a matter of law. The complainant gave evidence of having had sexual intercourse with the defendant at about the likely time of conception. It was suggested that the evidence of her mother to the effect that the defendant had visited her home to see the complainant at about the relevant period, and had met the complainant at the corner of the street on various occasions, might amount to corroboration. The argument was rejected on appeal by the Divisional Court. The evidence amounted to no more than evidence of opportunity, and did not either directly or by any permissible inference implicate the defendant in an act of sexual intercourse with the complainant. And in *James* v *R*[15] on a charge of rape, it was held that medical evidence showing that the complainant had had sexual intercourse at about a time consistent with her allegation, was incapable of affording corroboration of her evidence of the rape, because it did not confirm any more than an act of sexual intercourse and in particular did not offer any confirmation of the identity of the man involved or of the alleged lack of consent.

*14.4.4.1 R* v *Coke; R* v *Littleton.* This authority is of direct relevance to the case of Coke, in so far as the evidence of Dr Vesey and Dr Espinasse goes only to show sexual intercourse, which is not in dispute, and does not confirm Margaret's evidence of lack of consent. Had the medical evidence gone further, and demonstrated some injury consistent with forcible intercourse, the position would be very different, and such evidence would, no doubt, be capable of corroborating Margaret's evidence.

The above rules apply in every case where corroboration is required as a matter of law

---

[15] (PC, Jamaica) (1970) 55 Cr App R 299; see also *R* v *West* (1983) 79 Cr App R 45.

or is to be looked for as a matter of practice, as Lord Reading CJ pointed out in *R* v *Baskerville*, though it might be strictly more accurate to say that they apply to every such case, subject to any express modification suggested by the wording of the statute in the former class of case. As we shall see, the wording of the sections within this class is not uniform, but in practice, the actual requirement seems to vary very little.

### 14.5 Cumulative corroboration

There may, of course, be several pieces of evidence that are independently capable of corroborating evidence that requires corroboration. In such a case, the judge should in his summing-up identify all such evidence, and leave the jury to assess the respective weight of each piece of evidence. But a distinct question has been identified, of whether several pieces of evidence, which are individually incapable of constituting corroboration, may together be capable of constituting corroboration because of their cumulative effect—a situation which the author may perhaps be forgiven for terming 'gang corroboration'.

As to the legitimacy of this approach to the evidence, there are two views. The first view states that the sum total of a number of pieces of evidence, the value of each of which as corroboration is nil, must also be nil. This is, superficially, an attractive proposition. However, a second view is that evidence cannot be considered in such abstract mathematical terms. It is well recognised in the context of permissible areas of proof, and the rule against hearsay, and expressed in the res gestae principle, that a fact or event must be considered as a whole, and with due regard to all surrounding circumstances, including facts related in time and place. Professor Cross (*Evidence*, 5th ed., p.207) has cogently argued that the whole picture surrounding, say, a rape, may be such as to corroborate the complainant's evidence abundantly, even though any one of the pieces of evidence which go to make up that picture, taken individually, may be insufficient because, for example, it does not implicate the defendant. It is submitted that the jury should be invited to consider the whole picture. Of course, it may be that in some cases, the whole picture is in fact no better than the parts taken individually, and in such a case, that must be accepted. But if the jigsaw puzzle is composed of pieces which, when fitted together, are suggestive not only of rape, but of rape by the defendant, why should the jury not look at the whole picture for their corroboration?

The question of cumulative corroboration was discussed at length, with a remarkable degree of judicial disagreement, in *Thomas* v *Jones* (QBD) [1920] 2 KB 399, (CA) [1921] 1 KB 22. The appellant was charged on complaint before the Radnor Justices with being the father of a bastard child born to his housekeeper, the respondent, and was adjudged to be the father. The evidence showed that the appellant was a bachelor farmer, and that the respondent had resided in his house; that on the morning of the birth, when the respondent was in labour, the appellant (who had no other female servant) lit a fire for her and took her tea and brandy; that the appellant sent for a doctor; that after the birth, he permitted the respondent and the child to reside in his house for five weeks; and that when the respondent subsequently wrote to him, enquiring whether he meant to pay for the child, the appellant did not reply to her letter. The Divisional Court (the Earl of Reading CJ and Roche J, Avory J dissenting) held that although none of the above facts, taken singly, was capable of amounting to the required corroboration of the respondent's evidence, their cumulative effect might do so. The Earl of Reading CJ said ([1920] 2 KB at 406):

In this case I come to the conclusion that there is, in law, evidence upon which the justices could decide that the respondent's testimony was corroborated in some material particular by other evidence. Each fact found by the justices as tending to corroborate the respondent's evidence may by itself be insufficient as corroboration; but the cumulative effect of the evidence, regarded not separately but collectively, may be, and I think in this case is, sufficient. I am not unmindful of the argument that this evidence is equally consistent with action dictated by kind and humane considerations; but I think the circumstances proved, taken in conjunction with the omission to answer the letter, are sufficient to justify the magistrates' decision. The question is one rather of the right inference of fact than one of law.

Avory J dissented on the ground that, in his opinion, the pieces of evidence, taken together, were perfectly consistent with the actions of a humane employer towards a female servant who was in trouble and had nowhere to go. It would, therefore, be dangerous to permit them to be regarded as potentially corroborative, because whether taken singly or together, they did not implicate the appellant in the paternity. This view is not inconsistent with the view of the majority that cumulative corroboration might be permissible on the right facts.

In the Court of Appeal, the case produced another division. Scrutton LJ agreed with the majority in the Divisional Court, on the ground that he could not say that the magistrates, with their local knowledge, had been wrong to regard the cumulative facts as corroborative, even if the learned Lord Justice might personally have taken a different view. But the majority (Bankes and Atkin LJJ) held that the appeal must be allowed. Bankes LJ agreed substantially with Avory J in the Divisional Court. Atkin LJ, however, dealt a blow to the view advanced by the Earl of Reading CJ ([1921] 1 KB at 48):

> There was a suggestion in the court below that, although each one of these facts in itself was insufficient, yet the accumulation of them might make them sufficient . . . It may be that light may be thrown upon something, which in itself is innocent and irrelevant, by some other circumstance which though not itself conclusive may yet be illuminating. But, apart from that, it appears to me impossible, when dealing with the question of corroboration, that the accumulation of pieces of evidence, each of which by itself is not admissible as corroborative evidence, can amount in whole to corroboration. *Ex nihilo nihil fit.* That appears to me to be different from circumstantial evidence, where evidence of independent facts, each in itself insufficient to prove the main fact, may yet, either by their cumulative weight or still more by their connection one with the other as links in a chain, prove the principal fact to be established.

Professor Cross (loc.cit.) points out that Atkin LJ gives no reason for his distinction between potentially corroborative evidence and other circumstantial evidence but adds that it can be justified by the fact that the former must be directed specifically to a material particular. One might add further that it must implicate the defendant in the matter complained of.

All the judges who participated in *Thomas v Jones*, and who constituted two very powerful courts, were aware of the danger that the justices had before them what might have been no more than evidence of compassionate conduct on the part of the appellant, and it was this feeling which ultimately prevailed. But in all probability, as suggested by

Professor Cross, a court considering the question of corroboration in a case involving more orthodox facts might well now leave the whole picture to the tribunal of fact as potential corroboration, if that picture seemed to implicate the defendant in a material particular, and regard the question more as one of weight for the tribunal of fact.

### 14.6 Corroboration required as a matter of law

We have already noted that the exceptions within this category are statutory cases, and that the absence of evidence capable of amounting to the necessary corroboration will be fatal to the conviction or judgment. It must also follow that if the jury reject all the evidence capable of amounting to such corroboration, no conviction is possible, and the jury should be directed in those terms. The terms and extent of the corroboration required in each case are provided for by the statute itself, and except as so provided no further corroboration is necessary as a matter of law. It may, of course, happen that the evidence in a particular case may be such as to bring the case also within one of the practice exceptions, so that the corroboration necessary to such cases will have to be looked for, but this will be coincidental, and in general only the requirement of the statute need be observed.

The principal cases are as follows:

#### 14.6.1   Treason
In a prosecution for High Treason by compassing the death or restraint of the Sovereign or the heirs of the Sovereign, it is provided by s. 1 of the Treason Act 1795 that there should be no conviction without 'the oaths of two lawful and credible witnesses'. The use of the word 'credible' must presumably be taken to import that the jury must accept the evidence of both or all such witnesses, and be prepared to act on the evidence of each taken individually.

#### 14.6.2   Perjury
Perjury was the one exception known to the common law, in which the evidence of one witness was insufficient for a conviction. However, the position is now governed by s. 13 of the Perjury Act 1911, which provides that a person shall not be convicted of any offence against the Act, or of any other statutory offence of perjury or subornation of perjury, 'solely upon the evidence of one witness as to the falsity of any statement alleged to be false'. It will be observed that the statute prescribes the element of the offence for which corroboration is required, that is to say the falsity of the statement, and no requirement is imposed in respect of other elements of the offence. The corroborative evidence must, therefore, be directed to that issue.

#### 14.6.3   Personation at elections
A person charged with personation at any general or municipal election shall not be convicted summarily or committed for trial for such offence 'except on the evidence of not less than two credible witnesses': Representation of the People Act 1949, s. 147 (5).

#### 14.6.4   Speeding
Under s. 78A(2) of the Road Traffic Regulation Act 1967 (added to s. 203 of the Road Traffic Act 1972) a person charged with an offence of exceeding the speed limit 'shall not be liable to be convicted solely on the evidence of one witness to the effect that in the

opinion of the witness the person prosecuted was driving the vehicle at a speed exceeding a specified limit'. The purpose of this provision is to provide a safeguard against the possible unreliability of such evidence of opinion, because of the likelihood of error in relating an impression of the speed of a vehicle to a precise speed limit. The corroboration must go to the observation of the witness.[16] However, the evidence of the reading of a speedometer or other measuring device is evidence of fact, so that readings of such instruments are not within the section, and indeed may themselves be corroborative of opinion evidence of observation.[17]

### 14.6.5 *Sexual Offences Act 1956, ss. 2, 3, 4, 22 and 23*

These specific offences, which deal with procuring the defilement of women and girls by various means, and with procuring women and girls for the purpose of prostitution, are subject to a proviso in these terms: 'A person shall not be convicted on the evidence of one witness only unless the witness is corroborated in some material particular by evidence implicating the accused'. The extent of the corroboration required in these cases is equated by the statute with that looked for at common law in the practice exceptions, under the rule in *Baskerville*.

### 14.6.6 *Affiliation cases*

By s. 4(2) of the Affiliation Proceedings Act 1957, as amended, it is provided that: '. . . the court may adjudge the defendant to be the putative father of the child, but shall not do so, in a case where evidence is given by the mother, unless her evidence is corroborated in some material particular by other evidence to the court's satisfaction'. There is clearly some reason for caution in affiliation cases, where the complainant is not only, in a sense, the complainant in the 'sexual case', but also has an obvious interest in the acceptance of her evidence, and this is no doubt the reason for the requirement of corroboration. What is less clear is the provision that the evidence of the complainant must be corroborated 'to the court's satisfaction'. It is, of course, true that the magistrates are the judges both of the law and of the facts, and must address their minds both to the evidence capable of amounting to corroboration, and to the weight which they are prepared to give to the evidence available. Nonetheless, just as in the case of a jury, it is always necessary that the evidence be accepted by the tribunal of fact before corroboration can occur, and it is doubtful whether the words in question actually add anything to the requirement of the section.

### 14.6.7 *Unsworn evidence of children*

It has been observed in 11.8 ante, that in any criminal case, a child of tender years who does not understand the nature of an oath, may give evidence unsworn 'if, in the opinion of the court, he is possessed of sufficient intelligence to justify the reception of the evidence, and understands the duty of speaking the truth': Children and Young Persons Act 1933, s. 38(1). Because of the obvious danger of such a course, which may be gauged by the fact that the common law looks for corroboration as a matter of practice even where the child is sworn, the section contains a proviso that: 'where evidence admitted by virtue of this section is given on behalf of the prosecution the accused shall not be liable to be convicted of the offence unless that evidence is corroborated by some other material evidence in support thereof implicating him'.

---

[16] *Brighty* v *Pearson* (DC) [1938] 4 All ER 127.
[17] *Nicholas* v *Penny* (DC) [1950] 2 KB 466: *Swain* v *Gillett* (DC) [1974] RTR 446.

The position of unsworn evidence given by virtue of s. 38(1) in relation to corroboration was comprehensively examined by the House of Lords in *DPP v Hester* [1973] AC 296. The defendant was charged with indecent asssault on a girl of 12, who gave evidence about the alleged offence on oath. Her sister, aged nine, gave unsworn evidence for the prosecution under s. 38(1). The question which fell to be decided by the House was whether the unsworn evidence of the sister could, in law, be capable of corroborating the sworn evidence of the complainant.[18] It was argued that the requirement of corroboration as a matter of law contained in s. 38(1) precluded the use of unsworn evidence for the purpose of corroborating other evidence. This argument derived from the earlier decision in *R v Manser* (1934) 25 Cr App R 18, in which it was held that the unsworn evidence of a child given under s. 38(1) 'was not to be accepted as evidence at all' unless it was corroborated. *Manser* is open to some doubt simply because the report fails to make clear whether or not the complainant gave evidence on oath or unsworn,[19] but is open also to the far more fundamental criticism that the decision appears to have been based on a wrong interpretation of the proviso to s. 38(1), which requires, not that the unsworn evidence shall be corroborated for the purpose of being admissible, but that the unsworn evidence shall not be sufficient for a conviction unless it is corroborated. The House of Lords in *Hester* corrected this view, holding that unsworn evidence, being admissible, is capable of corroborating other evidence in the case against the defendant. The House also considered in some depth the converse question of how the unsworn evidence of the sister could be corroborated, and held that such corroboration might be found in the sworn evidence of the complainant. The result was that the two girls were capable in law or corroborating each other (mutual corroboration) where one was sworn and one unsworn, and that the requirement of the proviso to s. 38(1) was satisfied by such corroboration of the unsworn evidence by the sworn.

The House of Lords further held, however, that the unsworn evidence of a child given under s. 38(1) could not corroborate or be corroborated by other unsworn evidence given under s. 38(1). Although obiter on the facts of *Hester*, it is submitted that this view is demonstrably correct. It may be based soundly upon the very wording of s. 38(1), which calls for 'some other material evidence in support thereof', which is apt to refer to evidence other than evidence admitted under the section. The same view was also expressed, equally obiter, in *R v Campbell*[20] by Lord Goddard CJ, who regarded *Manser* as authority for the proposition and intended to approve it in the course of a general review of the principles relating to the evidence of children.

### 14.6.7.1  *R v Coke; R v Littleton.*   These rules will be of importance if Angela Blackstone is thought by the court to be a child of tender years, who falls within the ambit of s. 38(1) on the principles discussed in Chapter 11. Her unsworn evidence will require to be corroborated, before Littleton may be convicted of indecently assaulting her. Such corroboration may be supplied by the sworn evidence of Margaret, provided that she can implicate Littleton in the commission of the offence, as it seems she can. Angela's unsworn

---

[18]   The complainant's evidence fell into a category of case where corroboration was to be looked for as a matter of practice; see 14.7, post.

[19]   The Lords in *Hester* took the view that she had probably been sworn. In *R v Campbell* (CCA) [1956] 2 QB 432, Lord Goddard CJ favoured the alternative construction of events.

[20]   [1956] 2 QB 432. The witnesses in *Campbell* were all sworn, but the court expressed its intention of reviewing the question of children's evidence generally, so as to offer some guidance over the field as a whole.

evidence, thus corroborated, may reciprocate by supplying corroboration of Margaret's evidence, which is to be looked for as a matter of practice because she is the complainant in a sexual case (14.7, post). Although it may be thought that corroborative evidence is not in short supply in the case of Coke and Littleton, the implications of *Hester* are frequently of considerable importance in practice. For example, it is obviously significantly better for the prosecution if at least one of a number of children is found to be capable of taking the oath. Even though the jury may not find the evidence of a child significantly more compelling just because he or she is sworn, the fact may very well prevent the prosecution case from being held to be technically defective at its close, because the proviso to s. 38(1) cannot be complied with.

## 14.7 Corroboration to be looked for as a matter of practice

We have already seen that the common law recognised certain cases in which, because of some inherent risk of unreliability, the judge must warn the jury of the dangers of acting on uncorroborated evidence of the sort in question; that the requirement for the warning is one of law, the omission of which will be a ground of appeal[21]; and that if the warning is properly given, the jury may if they see fit convict on the uncorroborated evidence.[22]

The common law identified certain cases in which the apparent dangers of evidence justified a requirement for a corroboration warning, and these are dealt with individually below. It cannot be said that the categories are closed, or that the law will not identify new areas of suspect evidence. However, the courts have, in recent decisions, concentrated more on the problems raised by individual witnesses, rather than the idea that the categories of suspect witness should be extended. It seems that the trial judge may, and should, give the jury a warning as to the danger of convicting on uncorroborated evidence, in any case where the danger appears to be great enough to warrant it. In *R* v *Bagshaw* [1984] 1 All ER 971, the defendants, who were nurses at Rampton Hospital, a secure hospital for patients suffering from serious mental disorders, were charged with ill-treating patients. They were convicted, based in large part on the testimony of patients. The trial judge warned the jury to treat this evidence with the greatest caution, but did not give a full corroboration warning, namely that it would be dangerous to convict on the basis of their uncorroborated evidence. The Court of Appeal allowed the appeal against conviction, on the ground that the full warning had been required. The Court said (ibid at 977):

> Patients in hospital under the 1959 Act are not a category like accomplices or complainants in sexual cases, nor would we wish to make them into an additional category. Patients detained in a special hospital after conviction for an offence or offences, even if they are not a category, may well fulfil to a very high degree the criteria which justify the requirement of the full warning in respect of witnesses within accepted categories. It seems to us that in such cases nothing short of the full warning that it is dangerous to convict on the uncorroborated evidence of the witness will suffice.

---

[21] The appeal will almost always be allowed, the application of the proviso rarely being thought justifiable. See generally *Davies* v *DPP* (HL) [1954] AC 378.

[22] See *R* v *Henry and Manning* (CA) (1968) 53 Cr App R 150. In *R* v *Thorne and Others* [1977] 66 Cr App R 6, the Court of Appeal confirmed the point in vivid terms, holding that 'the evidence of villains . . . can be admitted and that convictions based on such evidence can stand'.

No doubt the characteristics of any witness may, in the circumstances of a given case, justify the extension of this general principle, which is, it is submitted, a sound one.

There has been considerable dispute as to the need for a warning in a case where a prosecution witness has any personal interest in the outcome of the proceedings, apart from that which he may have as an accomplice or complainant in a sexual case, for which the law already provides. It now appears that the judge may in his discretion give a full corroboration warning to the jury, but that there is no rule of law requiring such a warning. The desirability of such a warning was suggested by Edmund Davies J in *R v Prater* [1960] 2 QB 464, 466:

> This court, in the circumstances of the present appeal, is content to found itself on the view which it expresses that it is desirable that, in cases where a person may be regarded as having some purpose of his own to serve, the warning against uncorroborated evidence should be given.

Such a course was also approved by Lord Hailsham of St Marylebone in his speech in *DPP v Kilbourne* [1973] AC 729, 740. Subsequent cases, however, have shown the courts to be unwilling to adopt any general rule requiring a corroboration warning in the case of the witness with an axe to grind. In *R v Stannard* [1965] 2 QB 1,14, Winn J said that, 'The rule, if it be a rule, enunciated in *R v Prater* is no more than a rule of practice.' The court in *R v Whitaker* (1976) 63 Cr App R 193, described *Prater* as a 'qualified decision'. At the same time, there was a general agreement that a trial judge should advise some degree of caution with respect to the evidence of any witness who appeared to have an axe to grind, even if a full corroboration warning were not required.

In the first edition of this work, it was suggested that further elucidation from the Bench would be welcome, and in *R v Beck*[23] the authorities were reviewed by the Court of Appeal. One of the grounds of appeal advanced was that the judge had failed to give a corroboration warning regarding witnesses who 'had a purpose of their own to serve in giving evidence'. Delivering the judgment of the Court, Ackner LJ said ([1982] 1 WLR at 467):

> [Counsel for the appellant] accepts that an accomplice direction cannot be required whenever a witness may be regarded as having some purpose of his own to serve. Merely because there is some material to justify the suggestion that a witness is giving unfavourable evidence, for example out of spite, ill-will, to level some old score, to obtain some financial advantage, cannot, counsel for the appellant concedes, in every case necessitate the accomplice warning, if there is no material to suggest that the witness may be an accomplice. But, submits counsel for the appellant, even though there is no material to suggest any involvement by the witness in the crime, if he has a 'substantial interest' of his own for giving false evidence, then the accomplice direction must be given. Where one draws the line, he submits, is a question of degree, but once the boundary is crossed the obligation to give the accomplice warning is not a matter of discretion. We cannot accept this contention. In many trials today, the burden on the trial judge of the summing-up is a heavy one. It would be a totally unjustifiable addition to require him, not only fairly to put before the jury the defence's contention that a

---

[23]   [1982] 1 WLR 461. See also *R v Stainton* [1983] Crim LR 171.

witness was suspect, because he had an axe to grind, but also to evaluate the weight of that axe and oblige him, where the weight is 'substantial', to give an accomplice warning with the appropriate direction as to the meaning of corroboration together with the identification of the potential corroborative material.

We take the view that if and in so far as *R v Prater* . . . was not a decision on its own particular facts, it in no way extended the law as laid down in [*Davies v DPP* [1954] AC 378] . . .

While we in no way wish to detract from the obligation on a judge to advise a jury to proceed with caution when there is material to suggest that a witness' evidence may be tainted by an improper motive, and the strength of that advice must vary according to the facts of the case, we cannot accept that there is any obligation to give the accomplice warning with all that entails, when it is common ground that there is no basis for suggesting that the witness is a participant or in any way involved in the crime the subject-matter of the trial.

Clearly, there is some force in the propostion that it would be very difficult in practice to draw any satisfactory line between those witnesses as to whom a corroboration warning might be required, and those as to whom it would not, since in almost every case there will be found some witness who has, arguably, some interest of his own to serve in having his evidence accepted by the tribunal of fact. It may safely be anticipated that a general rule requiring a corroboration warning would produce a multiplicity of appeals and little certainty. But, as *Beck* makes clear, the judge should, in the course of his ordinary duty to present the defence fully to the jury, point out any substantial reason for treating the evidence of such a witness with caution. Unlike the rules governing corroboration, which apply only to prosecution witnesses, this applies also to witnesses called by one defendant whose evidence adversely affects a co-defendant.

In *Nembhard v R* [1982] 1 All ER 183, the Privy Council declined to find that there was any general rule requiring a corroboration warning where the only evidence implicating the defendant on a charge of murder was a dying declaration made by the deceased. Again, however, it was emphasised that the trial judge has a duty to leave the jury with a clear consciousness of the need for care in assessing the significance of such a declaration.

### 14.7.1 Sworn evidence of children

Quite apart from the specific danger of unsworn evidence admitted under s. 38(1) of the Children and Young Persons Act 1933 (see 14.6.7,ante) the common law recognised in the sworn evidence of children of tender years both the risk of unreliability inherent in the age of a young witness, and the danger of childish imagination and collusion. There are obvious dangers in the uncorroborated evidence of one child, and, where there is a likelihood of collusion, of more than one child to the same effect. The rule, therefore, is that the judge must always warn the jury of the danger of acting on the uncorroborated evidence of children of tender years, and, if there is a realistic possibility of collusion, of that possibility.[24]

It has been seen in Chapter 11 that there is no prescribed age at which a child must be regarded as being, or as having ceased to be, one of tender years. And for the same reason, there is no defined age at which a child ceases to be a proper subject of a corroboration

---

[24] *R v Campbell* [1956] 2 QB 432; *R v Morgan* (CA) [1978] 1 WLR 735.

warning. The matter is one for the discretion of the judge. In *R* v *Morgan*[25] the defendant was charged with indecent assault on a boy of 11. The victim, his brother aged 12 and a youth who at the time of the incident, some 12 months before the trial, was aged 16, gave evidence on oath for the prosecution. The trial judge warned the jury about the evidence of the victim, but gave no warning about the evidence of the brother or the youth. The court of Appeal held that that judge had erred in his omission in the case of the brother, but that on the facts of the case, no warning had been required in the case of the youth. Roskill LJ said, ibid at 739:

> We do not think it possible to state as a general proposition what the age is above which is becomes unnecessary for a judge to give a warning such as I have already mentioned. This is an example of a situation where the trial judge is much better placed to consider the matter than any appellate court can be. The judge will, in those circumstances, obviously apply his mind to the problem and ask himself the question whether, having seen this boy in the witness-box, he was of an age which made it desirable to give this warning.

It is clear from *Campbell* and *Hester* that sworn evidence of a child is capable of corroborating both other sworn evidence in the case, and the unsworn evidence of another child admitted under s. 38(1) of the Children and Young Persons Act 1933. It may, therefore, be said that the evidence of different children is capable of being mutually corroborative, except in the case where all the evidence is given unsworn under s. 38(1). In *DPP* v *Kilbourne* [1973] AC 729 a logical and important extension of the principle was recognised. The defendant was charged with offences of buggery, attempted buggery and indecent assault on two groups of boys. Counts 1—4 comprised offences committed in 1970 against group 1; and counts 5—7 related to offences committed in 1971 against group 2. Evidence of the offences in each group was admissible both directly to prove the offences in that group and, under the similar-fact principle, to prove those in the other group. The House of Lords upheld the direction given by the trial judge that the evidence of the children in either group concerning any particular offence was capable of being corroborated by that of children in the other group, being evidence of admissible, similar conduct by the defendant. The decision depends, of course, on the principle of mutual admissibility under the similar-fact rule; if the evidence of children dealing with other offences is admissible to prove guilt as charged, then there is no reason why it should not be capable of affording corroboration, as implicating the defendant in the commission of the offence charged. But where different offences do not fall within the similar-fact principle, evidence given on one would not be admissible to prove another, and would therefore be incapable of affording corroboration of evidence relating to the other.

### 14.7.2 Evidence of accomplices

In common parlance, the term 'accomplice' describes one who has in some way been

---

[25] [1978] 1 WLR 735. The appeal was dismissed because the evidence was so overwhelming that no miscarriage of justice could have occurred. The court recognised also the necessity of drawing to the jury's attention the possiblity of collusion, and held that on the facts this had been adequately done. The question of collusion is probably no more than one aspect of the truism that the jury will not act for any purpose, including that of corroboration, on evidence which they do not accept as truthful; see the observations of Lord Hailsham of St. Marylebone in *DPP* v *Kilbourne* [1973] AC 729 at 746.

involved culpably in the wrongdoing in question. In criminal cases, such persons are sometimes called for the prosecution to give evidence against a defendant. Frequently, they are persons who were originally charged jointly with the defendant, and are therefore competent witnesses for the prosecution only because they have pleaded guilty or have had proceedings against them discontinued or for whatever reason have ceased to be defendants in the proceedings. Habitually, they agree to give evidence for the prosecution in return for not being prosecuted, or for having their plea of guilty to a lesser offence accepted by the prosecution, or in the hope of attracting leniency in sentence. In other cases, the evidence given discloses that a witness may be implicated in the offence charged, and so stand in peril of being prosecuted subsequently. In all such cases, the common law recognised an obvious danger, arising from the motive of avoiding or minimising the witness's own involvement in the offence charged, and of emphasising, or it may be, fabricating, that of the defendant. A warning must accordingly be given to the jury that the evidence of an accomplice is dangerous to act upon, in the absence of corroboration.

The question of what persons are to be regarded as accomplices for the purpose of the law relating to corroboration was settled in modern times by the House of Lords in *Davies v DPP* [1954] AC 378. Davies and one Lawson were members of a group of youths, who attacked and fought with another group. A member of the other group was stabbed, and died. Lawson was charged with his murder, and acquitted. Subsequently, the defendant was charged with the murder and Lawson gave evidence for the prosecution. There was no evidence that Lawson knew that the defendant was carrying a knife. The House of Lords upheld the trial judge's decision not to treat Lawson as an accomplice to murder. In the course of his speech, Lord Simonds LC declared that an accomplice is one who, when called to give evidence for the prosecution, falls into any one of the following three categories:

(a) Participants in the offence charged, whether as principals or aiders and abettors. This class, often referred to as *'participes criminis'* was described by Lord Simonds as the 'natural and primary meaning of the term "accomplice" '.[26]

(b) Participants in offences held to be admissible as probative of the offence charged, under the similar-fact principle. These are, as it were, *participes criminis* by extension.

(c) On a trial for theft, handlers receiving stolen goods from the thief are accomplices of the thief.[27]

---

[26] The question whether a witness falls into this class is usually, but not always, a straightforward one. One example of difficulty is the case of affray, in which the various participants may have no contact with each other in the fight. In such a case, they will not be regarded as accomplices, although it has been said that the jury should be warned that if the witness was not acting in self-defence, then he was committing an offence identical to that charged: *R v Sidhu; R v Singh; R v Singh* (CA) (1976) 63 Cr App R 24. The same problem may arise with conspirators who engage in entirely separate acts in furtherance of the conspiracy.

[27] At the time of the decision in *Davies*, the offence was receiving, under the Larceny Act 1916. It appears to have been assumed that the rule carries over to the offence of dishonest handling under the Theft Act 1968; see e.g. Archbold, 41st ed.,para.16–16. There may, however, be cases where a person who handles other than by receiving has no real connection with the thief. It is also curious that Lord Simonds did not postulate the converse proposition that the thief is an accomplice on the trial of the receiver. Interestingly, Professor Cross comments that there are cases where a lack of connection would prevent the relationship from arising (*Evidence*, 5th ed., p. 199) as may be the case in Lord Simond's category. There is some authority that the rule should apply both ways; *R v Crane* (CCA) (1912) 7 Cr App R 113; *R v Vernon* (CCA) [1962] Crim LR 35.

Lord Simonds added that these categories were settled law, and should not be varied judicially.

The accomplice rule applies only to witnesses called for the prosecution. A defendant who gives evidence in his own defence is not an accomplice for the purpose of making his evidence subject to the requirement of a corroboration warning, even though that evidence may implicate a co-defendant in the offence charged.[28] However, there is authority that the trial judge should give the jury a direction to treat such evidence with care, in so far as it implicates a co-defendant in the offence charged, since the testifying defendant has an interest of his own to serve.[29] No doubt the same observation would apply to a witness called for a defendant whose evidence implicated a co-defendant, and if that witness appeared to be implicated in the offence charged, it might be appropriate to give a corroboration warning, even though the witness is not called by the prosecution. It is submitted that a direction in the case of a defendant giving evidence in his own defence should not be strongly worded. While the court must be mindful of the protection of the implicated defendant, it must surely also be mindful of the right of the testifying defendant to present his case from the witness-box without the automatic taint of a corroboration warning. It appears that it has not yet been fully argued that it may actually be improper for the judge to appear to undermine the evidence of a defendant in this way, and it is submitted that the argument might properly be made in a meritorious case. Such a case must present differences from those which involve the evidence of prosecution witnesses.

A police officer or an informer or other agent acting as an entrapper or *agent provocateur* appear not to be accomplices for the purposes of the rule, even though they may, in a sense, participate in the offence, for the purpose of detection or obtaining evidence against the defendant. In *Sneddon v Stevenson* [1967] 1 WLR 1051, a police officer drove his car in such a way to attract the attention of a known prostitute, and when she approached, arrested her for soliciting. The argument that the officer was an accomplice was rejected, primarily on the basis that the rationale for the rule is absent in a case where the activity of the witness is carried on in the course of law enforcement. It may be, however, that the rule would be too widely expressed, if it were held in all cases to exclude an extrapper, investigator or *agent provocateur*. Certainly, there are cases where such a person acts for reward or out of some personal motive, in which case a warning ought to be given for the reasons given at the beginning of 14.7. It is submitted that there may well be cases where the officer or agent deliberately or inadvertently becomes too involved in the commission or planning of an offence, and becomes to that extent an accomplice in the sense that he has some motive for concealing or minimising his involvement, possibly at the expense of the defendant.

Whether a witness is an accomplice is a question of fact for the jury, and the judge should direct the jury as to any witness who is in law capable of being so regarded (see *R* v *Riley* (1980) 70 Cr App R 1). In most cases, the witness's status is hardly in doubt, because he will be one who has pleaded guilty to the offence charged or to a lesser offence arising from the same facts, or will admit his complicity in his evidence in chief. There are, however, some cases where a witness may deny complicity in the offence, suggested to him in cross-examination, in which event the jury must determine his status according to their view of the evidence. There must be evidence from which the jury could properly infer that

---

[28]   *R* v *Barnes; R* v *Richards* (CCA) [1940] 2 All ER 229.

[29]   *R* v *Loveridge and Loveridge* (1982) 76 Cr App R 125; *R* v *Knowlden and Knowlden* (1981) 77 Cr App R 94 (decided before, but reported after *Loveridge); R* v *Bagley* [1980] Crim LR 572.

a witness is an accomplice, and this may arise from cross-examination, or from any other evidence, but the mere fact that complicity is suggested to the witness in cross-examination does not make him an accomplice if he does not accept it.

The judge must exercise his discretion on giving or withholding a warning where a witness who may be an accomplice gives evidence which is of no or of marginal relevance to the guilt of the defendant. In such a case, it would seem unnecessary and sometimes undesirable to give a warning which may suggest undue prominence to the jury in their consideration of the evidence, but the point has been left open by the Court of Appeal.[30] More difficult is the case where the witness gives evidence relevant to the issue, but favourable to the defendant. In *R* v *Peach* [1979] Crim LR 245, it was held that the judge, although not required to give a warning, might do so, even where the effect of the evidence was to exculpate the defendant, because the witness might have his own motives for giving such evidence. Nonetheless, it is submitted that the true rationale is missing where the evidence does not materially increase the chances of conviction, and the judge should not impeach a witness for the prosecution who does not come up to proof. It is submitted that a preferable approach is that suggested in *R* v *Royce-Bentley* [1974] 1 WLR 535, where a witness for the prosecution, who on his own admission was an accomplice by participation in the offence charged, gave evidence mainly favourable to the defendant, but in part supporting the case for the prosecution. The Court of Appeal held that the trial judge had acted correctly in consulting counsel on whether a direction should be given, and thereafter taking the course which appeared to him to be more favourable to the defence.

### 14.7.2.1 *R* v *Coke; R* v *Littleton.*

If Coke were to plead guilty to raping Margaret Blackstone, and thereafter give evidence for the prosecution against Littleton on the charge of indecently assaulting Angela, some question might arise of whether he should be regarded as an accomplice. On his own evidence, to the effect that he neither knew what Littleton was doing, nor played any part in that offence at any stage, he would not be so. If, however, the jury formed the view on the evidence before them that Coke played his part in luring both girls to his flat for indecent purposes, knowing Angela to be under the age at which she could legally consent, then they might well take such a view of him, and it would seem that the judge ought to give a warning. Conversely, if Littleton pleaded guilty and gave evidence against Coke, he could not be regarded as an accomplice merely because he may have co-operated with Coke in arranging the meeting with Margaret, but might well be so if he knew that Coke was prepared to use force in order to have sexual intercourse with her, if necessary. As we have observed, if Coke and Littleton are jointly tried, having pleaded not guilty, they should not be accomplices if they give evidence in their defence.

### 14.7.3 *Evidence of complainants of sexual misconduct*

### 14.7.3.1 *In criminal cases.*

Quite apart from the specific statutory provisions of the sections of the Sexual Offences Act 1956 which require corroboration as a matter of law (14.6.5), the jury should as a matter of practice look for corroboration of the evidence of

---

[30]   In *R* v *Meechan* (CA) [1977] Crim LR 350.

the complainant in any case of a sexual offence, and they must be given a warning accordingly. The complainant for present purposes is the victim of the offence. Although the terminology suggests hostile action by the defendant, this is not necessarily the case, and in certain sexual offences, for example incest or buggery, the 'victim' may be a willing participant in the act charged. In such a case, the 'victim's' evidence may well fall within the accomplice rule, in addition to that now under consideration.[31] In any event, however, the rule respecting complainants is distinct from that concerning accomplices, and founded upon different considerations. The justification for the rule is the inherent danger arising from the fact that sexual allegations are simple and often tempting to make, but difficult to refute, and from the characteristic possibility of hysterical or malicious invention or simply the instinct for preservation of the complainant's reputation or material interests. Of course, particular care is needed where the complainant is also a child.

The rule applicable to complainants has developed with considerable force, and applies somewhat inflexibly to all sexual offences, regardless of the age or sex of the complainant and of the nature of the issues in the case. It applies, therefore, even where the evidence of the complainant has no or only marginal significance in implicating the defendant in the offence charged. Thus, in *R* v *Midwinter* (1971) 55 Cr App R 523, the omission of a corroboration warning in relation to the complainant's evidence was held to be fatal to the conviction, even though the complainant had not identified the defendant, and the case turned solely upon an alleged confession by the defendant. And in *R* v *Marks* [1963] Crim LR 370, the absence of a warning was similarly fatal to a conviction for unlawful sexual intercourse with a girl under 16, where the only issue was the age of the complainant at the material time.

Curiously, however, it has been held that the evidence of the complainant of a sexual offence does not require corroboration if it is admitted under the similar-fact principle in a trial concerning another offence, even though corroboration is required of the complainant's evidence of the offence charged.[32] It is submitted that this decision, which conflicts with the rule in the analogous cases of children and accomplices, is difficult to justify and should be reversed. The danger, in a case where similar-fact evidence consists of as yet unproved allegations, must surely be considerable. There is presumably no doubt that the two complainants are capable of corroborating each other in such a case.

In *R* v *Longstaff* [1977] Crim LR 216, the question was left open by the Court of Appeal (the appeal being allowed for other reasons) whether a police officer, to whom indecent overtures were made in a public lavatory, was 'the complainant' on a resulting charge of attempted indecency. It seems probable, by analogy with the authority on police officers alleged to be accomplices[33] that the answer should be in the negative. Certainly, wherever the officer was acting in his professional capacity, the rationale of the rule would be absent.

### 14.7.3.2  *R* v *Coke; R* v *Littleton.*

It follows from what has been said above that Margaret and Angela Blackstone, each of whom was the complainant in relation to the alleged offence against her, must be the subject of a warning, quite apart, in Angela's case,

---

[31]  Mere submission to a sexual act will not, it seems, render the complainant an accomplice in the absence of the necessary knowledge and intent; *R* v *Dimes* (CCA) (1911) 7 Cr App R 43.

[32]  *R* v *Sanders* (CMAC) (1961) 46 Cr App R 60.

[33]  Cf. *Sneddon* v *Stevenson* (DC) [1967] 1 WLR 1051.

from considerations of age. Nor does it matter that the issues in the two cases differ, that is to say that in Coke's case the issue is solely one of consent, whereas in Littleton's case, the defence will be a complete denial coupled with an alibi. There is, of course, no reason in law why the evidence of Margaret and Angela should not be mutually corroborative and it may be left to the jury on that basis to say whether it is in fact corroborative or not.

*14.7.3.3 In matrimonial cases.* The question of corroboration in civil cases generally is, as has been indicated, of less significance than in criminal matters, because of the greater likelihood of a judge directing his mind correctly to the inherent dangers of certain kinds of evidence. In matrimonial cases, the new approach to such cases dating from the Divorce Reform Act 1969, by virtue of which contested cases are discouraged, has greatly diminished the importance of a number of evidential matters, of which corroboration is one. In affiliation cases, where the incidence of contested cases remains high and the dangers of uncorroborated evidence substantial, corroboration is required as a matter of law. There remains, however, a residual rule, applicable alike to proceedings in the High Court, the county court and magistrates' courts in the matrimonial jurisdiction, and its extent was, for modern purposes, defined by Divisional Court in *Alli* v *Alli* [1965] 3 All ER 480. The principles may be stated as follows:

(a)   In considering any alleged matrimonial offence, the court should, as a matter of practice, look for corroboration of the evidence of the complainant, and should normally require it if available on the facts of the case. This applies, not only to allegations of sexual misconduct, but to matrimonial offences generally.

(b)   Whereas an appellate court may always interfere with a finding, if it appears clearly that the court of trial has proceeded oblivious of the dangers of uncorroborated evidence, the court will intervene on appeal in cases where sexual misconduct is alleged, or where evidence of adultery is that of a willing participant, unless the court of trial has warned itself expressly. In any such case, it is of course open to the court of trial, after a proper warning, to act on the uncorroborated evidence of the complainant, and in *Alli* the decision of the justices to do so was upheld on the facts. There is, nonetheless, in the decision of the Divisional Court, an obvious equation of sexual allegations and evidence of willing participants, with the analogous cases of complainants and accomplices in criminal cases.

*14.7.4   Claimants to the property of deceased persons*
The court will look, as a matter of practice, for corroboration of the evidence of persons within this class. There is, however, no requirement as a matter of law.[34]

**14.8   A note on identification cases**

Cases which turn wholly or substantially upon evidence of visual identification have, in recent times, given rise to considerable anxiety. In the leading case of *R* v *Turnbull*[35] Lord Widgery CJ, in the course of laying down guidelines of practice for dealing with such cases, held that where the quality of identifying evidence is poor, the trial judge should

[34]   *Re Hodgson, Beckett* v *Ramsdale* (CA) (1885) 31 ChD 177; *Re Cummins, Cummins* v *Thompson* (CA) [1972] Ch 62.
[35]   (CA) [1977] QB 224. See also 12.3.3, ante.

withdraw the case from the jury, and direct an acquittal, 'unless there is other evidence which goes to support the correctness of the identification'. Lord Widgery continued:

> This may be corroboration in the sense lawyers use that word; but it need not be so if its effect is to make the jury sure that there has been no mistaken identification. The judge should point out to the jury evidence capable of supporting the identification, and also any evidence which the jury might mistakenly think to be so capable, for example the defendant's decision not to give evidence.

It is to be observed that the Lord Chief Justice was not seeking to define a new area of corroboration, and indeed, he emphasised that his judgment was laying down, not new rules of law, but changes in practice. It seems, however, that there is at least an indication that a quasi-corroborative rule has developed, which differs from the formal corroborative rules discussed above, in that: (a) there is no technical limitation on the nature of the evidence suitable for this purpose, so that it may be found in any evidence admissible in the case, whether capable of amounting to corroboration or not; (b) the requirement arises only when the judge makes a value judgment of the quality of the evidence to be corroborated, so that there is no general rule applicable to evidence of visual identification as such; and (c) if, but only if, the evidence is poor in quality, the judge should withdraw the case from the jury if it is unsupported.

**14.9   Mutual corroboration**

By mutual corroboration is meant the use of the evidence of two or more witnesses, each of whom require as a matter of law or practice to be corroborated, for the purpose of affording corroboration *inter se* and so satisfying the requirement in each case, irrespective of any evidence from other sources capable of affording corroboration. The rule is that, except in two cases, mutual corroboration is always permissible and is in law sufficient to satisfy the requirement in respect of each witness. The two exceptions are:

(a)   The unsworn evidence of two or more children.[36]

(b)   The evidence of two or more accomplices, being *participes criminis* in the offence charged. The restriction does not affect the evidence of accomplices within the other two categories laid down by Lord Simonds in *Davies* v *DPP*.[37]

**14.10   Corroboration afforded by the defendant himself**

Cases where corroboration of the evidence of a prosecution witness is sought in the conduct of the defendant or statements made by the defendant, including his evidence at trial, have occasioned some difficulty. Two distinct situations must be addressed, the first relating to the defendant's out-of-court conduct and statements, the second to the defendant's evidence at trial.

*14.10.1   The defendant's out-of-court conduct and statements*
Corroboration of the evidence of prosecution witnesses is sought primarily in other

---

[36]   *DPP* v *Hester* (HL) [1973] AC 296. See 14.6.7, ante
[37]   (HL) [1954]. See 14.7, ante.

evidence adduced by the prosecution. This may include evidence called by the prosecution of the conduct or statements of the defendant, and these, may, of course, have the effect of confirming the evidence to be corrorborated in a material particular, implicating the defendant in the offence charged. There is no doubt that such evidence may, in law, constitute corroboration of other prosecution evidence. Typical of such a case is that in which the defendant, when questioned, gives the police a story which he subsequently admits to be false, or which is subsequently proved to be false. In *Credland* v *Knowler*[38] the defendant at first denied having left his home and having accompanied children to a spot where it was alleged he committed an indecent assault. Later, he acknowledged this account to be false and admitted that he had accompanied the children to the place in question, but maintained his denial that he had committed any offence. It was held that the defendant's admission of having given an untrue statement was capable in law of corroborating the evidence of the children.

We have also seen that, where evidence of the defendant's behaviour on other occasions is admissible to prove his guilt as charged, because it is relevant to that issue, evidence of such previous behaviour is capable in law of corroborating other evidence given for the prosecution as to the offence charged.[39]

It is, however, important that the judge direct the jury to consider the reasons underlying the defendant's previous conduct or statements. Such a direction is particularly crucial where the prosecution rely on lies told by the defendant as corroboration. Although the lies may, in law, be capable of constituting corroboration, the jury should be made clearly aware that they need not be accepted as such. If it is apparent that the defendant's motive for lying was to evade detection or to fabricate a defence, then it may well be permissible for the jury to accept the lies as corroborating other prosecution evidence and as implicating the defendant in the offence charged, but if the motive is unrelated to any such intent, there is an obvious risk of injustice. In *R* v *Lucas* [1981] QB 720, 724 Lord Lane CJ, delivering the judgment of the Court of Appeal, enumerated four factors to be considered in assessing an out-of-court lie as corroboration:

> To be capable of amounting to corroboration the lie told out-of-court must first of all be deliberate. Secondly it must relate to a material issue. Thirdly the motive for the lie must be a realisation of guilt and a fear of the truth. The jury should in appropriate cases be reminded that people sometimes lie, for example, in an attempt to bolster up a just cause, or out of shame or out of a wish to conceal disgraceful behaviour from their family. Fourthly the statement must be clearly shown to be a lie by evidence other than than of an accomplice who is to be corroborated, that is to say by admission or by evidence from an independent witness.

In *R* v *Dowley*[40] the defendant was convicted of the rape of a woman to whom his marriage was in the process of being dissolved, a decree nisi of divorce having been pronounced but not yet made absolute. The complainant's evidence clearly amounted to evidence of rape,

---

[38]  (DC)(1951) 35 Cr App R 48. In cases where the defendant's silence in response to an allegation may be held against him, it seems that such silence may amount to corroboration. See *R* v *Cramp* (1880) 14 Cox CC 390 (the point was not considered on appeal); *R* v *Chandler* (CA) [1976] 1 WLR 585. Such cases are very limited; see 7.14, ante.

[39]  *DPP* v *Kilbourne* [1973] AC 729. See 14.7, ante. For examples, see *R* v *Hartley* (CCA) [1941] 1 KB 5; *R* v *Mitchell* (CCA) (1952) 36 Cr App R 79.

[40]  [1983] Crim LR 168. See also *R* v *West* (1983) 79 Cr App R 45.

and required a corroboration warning, for the reasons stated earlier in this chapter. The defendant at first denied having seen the complainant on the relevant occasion, but later admitted that he had seen her, had driven with her out of town, and that some sex-play had taken place between them. The defendant maintained, however, that no rape had occurred and that he had lied only because he was afraid that another woman he had been seeing since the break-up of his marriage might be offended by what had happened. The trial judge failed adequately to draw to the jury's attention the possibility that the motive for the defendant's lies might be something other than guilt and a fear of the truth. The appeal against conviction was allowed, since it was not clear that the jury should have accepted the out-of-court lie as corroboration of the complainant's evidence, and the jury's decision to acquit the defendant on a related charge of kidnapping arising from the same incident showed that the jury were not entirely satisfied with the complainant's evidence.

By s. 62(10) of the Police and Criminal Evidence Act 1984 it is specifically provided that:

Where the appropriate consent to the taking of an intimate sample from a person was refused without good cause, in any proceedings against that person for an offence—

(*a*)   the court in determining—
   (i)   whether to commit that person for trial; or
   (ii)   whether there is a case to answer; and
(*b*)   the court or jury, in determining whether that person is guilty of the offence charged,

may draw such inferences from the refusal as appear proper; and the refusal may, on the basis of such inferences, be treated as, or as capable of amounting to, corroboration of any evidence against the person in relation to which the refusal is material.

No corresponding provision is made for a refusal to consent to the taking of an non-intimate sample, as provided by s. 63 of the Act, but there is a provision for a non-intimate sample to be taken without the consent of the suspect under certain circumstances specified in the section. The inference and corroboration provision of s. 62(10) is no doubt intended to compensate for the inability of the police to require an intimate sample without the consent of the suspect. Intimate and non-intimate samples are defined by s. 65 of the Act.

### 14.10.2   The defendant's evidence

Different questions arise with regard to the defendant's evidence from the witness-box in his defence on the trial of the offence charged. Here, a distinction of some importance must be drawn between the substance of the defendant's evidence (i.e., the facts to which he testifies) in which corroboration may be sought, and the mere fact that the jury may choose to disbelieve the defendant's evidence, which cannot amount to corroboration. In *R v Chapman; R v Baldwin*[41] the Court of Appeal held that the judge had been in error in

---

[41]   [1973] QB 774. Of course, if the jury disbelieve the defendant, they may be more inclined to convict on uncorroborated prosecution evidence, if that course is open to them. It has been suggested that *Chapman* would not apply in every case; see e.g. *R v Boardman* in the Court of Appeal, [1975] AC 421 per Orr LJ at 428-9. But it is submitted that *Chapman* must be correct in the overwhelming majority of cases.

directing the jury that if they rejected the defendant's evidence, that rejection of itself might be regarded as corroborative of the evidence for the prosecution. Roskill LJ said: 'Mere rejection of evidence is not affirmative proof of the contrary of the evidence which has been rejected'.[42] On the other hand, as Lord MacDermott said in *Tumahole Bereng v R*[43]: 'Corroboration may well be found in the evidence of an accused person; but that is a different matter, for there confirmation comes, if at all, from what is said, and not from the falsity of what is said,' Thus, in *R v Dossi*,[44] the defendant's admission in evidence that he had fondled a child was capable of amounting to corroboration of the child's evidence, since it confirmed what the child said in a material particular, even though the defendant maintained that his fondling had been platonic, whereas the child said that it was in circumstances amounting to an indecent assault. Presumably, the evidence of a defendant, which is evidence in the case generally, is capable of corroborating prosecution evidence against a co-defendant.

In *R v Lucas* [1981] QB 720, to which reference has already been made, Lord Lane CJ expressed the opinion that, subject to the same four safeguards as he required as a condition of out-of-court lies being acceptable as corroboration, a lie told by the defendant during his evidence at trial might also be regarded as potentially corroborative of evidence called for the prosecution. However, Lord Lane made it clear that he did not intend to question the decision in *R v Chapman; R v Baldwin* on its own facts, but that 'properly understood, it is not authority for the proposition that in no circumstances can lies told by a defendant in court provide material corroboration of an accomplice'. Lord Lane added that the Court was in agreement on this point with the Court of Appeal in *R v Boardman* (see note 42). Although Lord Lane's observations may seem to weaken the distinction between the fact of being disbelieved by the jury per se, and the content of a defendant's evidence, it would seem from his approval of the passage from the speech of Lord MacDermott in *Tumahole Bereng v R* cited above, and from his disapproval of a direction that would invite the jury 'without more, to use their disbelief of the defendant as corroboration of the accomplice', that Lord Lane did not intend to depart from the previously well established rules. Indeed, the Court specifically held that the fact that the jury may prefer the evidence of an accomplice to that of the defendant does not, of itself, provide corroboration of the accomplice's otherwise uncorroborated evidence.

It seems that a party who does not bear the legal burden of proof may decline to give evidence without running the risk of that decision being regarded as corroboration. In particular, in a criminal case, the defendant's failure to give evidence is not capable of affording corroboration of evidence given for the prosecution.[45]

## 14.11 Questions for discussion: *R v Coke; R v Littleton*

1  What requirements of corroboration arise in relation to the evidence of (a) Margaret, and (b) Angela Blackstone?
2  What evidence is to be found in the papers which would be capable in law of corroborating the evidence of each girl?
3  If either Coke or Littleton pleads guilty and gives evidence for the prosecution

---

42  Ibid at 780. The distinction is described as 'clear' (at 783). See also *R v Lucas* [1981] QB 720.
43  (PC, Basutoland) [1949] AC 253 at 270.
44  (CCA) (1918) 13 Cr App R 158. See also *Corfield v Hodgson* (DC) [1966] 1 WLR 590.
45  *R v Jackson* (CCA) (1953) 37 Cr App R 43. And see *Cracknell v Smith* (DC) [1960] 1 WLR 1239.

against the other, what requirements of corroboration may arise? How would the position differ from that where each pleaded not guilty and gave evidence in his defence implicating the other?

4   What are the respective functions of the judge and jury in relation to the requirements of corroboration?

# 15 Documentary and Real Evidence

## A: DOCUMENTARY EVIDENCE

### 15.1 Documentary evidence generally

Thus far, this part of this book has considered the mechanics of adducing evidence by calling witnesses to testify on oath. Evidence may also be given by the production to the court of documents that are admissible in evidence, as evidence of their own contents. An important distinction must be drawn between documents whose contents are admissible in their own right as direct evidence, and documents which contain admissible hearsay, which are admissible, if at all, only to the extent of the hearsay statements contained in them. For example, a lease or a written contract will be admissible in its own right as direct evidence of the existence and terms of the lease or contract, whereas a record compiled by a person acting under a duty, admissible by virtue of s. 4 of the Civil Evidence Act 1968, will be admissible only for the purpose of adducing the admissible statements contained in the record. Another way of expressing the distinction is to say that the contents of the lease constitute direct evidence of the lease itself; whereas the contents of the record constitute only evidence of other facts contained in statements made in the record. The admissibility of hearsay contained in documents was considered in Chapters 6, 7 and 8. This chapter will deal with documents the contents of which are admissible as direct evidence in their own right, and will be concerned with the rule requiring proof of such documents by what is termed 'primary evidence', and the requirements for proof of due execution.

It should also be noted that this chapter is concerned with private, as opposed to public documents. We have considered the admissibility of public documents, both at common law and by statute in Chapter 6 (6.13, ante). Private documents are that vast majority of documents which have not been compiled by public officials, and which fall accordingly outside the public domain and the rules of admissibility governing documents in the public domain.

It is worth observing at the outset that documentary evidence is subject to the rules of evidence generally. The admissibility of a private document is subject to the same rules, subject only to statutory modification, as is that of oral evidence. A document may, therefore, be objected to on the ground that its contents are inadmissible, for example because they are hearsay and do not fall within any recognised exception to the rule against hearsay.[1] Documents used as evidence must also be distinguished carefully from documents used to refresh the memory of a witness while giving evidence orally. The latter are not evidence in themselves, unless they are made so by the conduct of cross-

---

[1] See, e.g., *Myers* v *DPP* (HL) [1965] AC 1001; 6.2, ante.

examination, and even then are evidence of facts stated therein only by statute and only in civil cases.[2]

The question of what exactly may constitute a 'document' is far fom easy to answer, and appears not to be capable of being answered uniformly for all purposes. It is clear that the prime characteristic of a document is that it should contain and convey information. It seems also that the word implies writing or other inscription, though in modern times, the storing of information in diagrammatic form or in a computer, or the audio or video recording of information is probably equally acceptable for many purposes. The form of a document, and the materials of which it is composed, are probably of limited contemporary importance. In *R* v *Daye* [1908] 2 K B 333, Darling J pointed out that paper itself had been preceded by parchment, stone, marble, clay and metal. He went on to say that an object may be regarded as a document, whatever its material, 'provided it is writing or printing and capable of being evidence'. In more recent times, a tape-recording of a conversation has been held to be a document which, if referred to in a party's pleading, must be produced for inspection on notice, under RSC, Ord. 24, r. 10(1): *Grant and Another* v *Southwestern & County Properties Ltd and Another* [1975] Ch 185. And the majority view of the Court of Appeal in *Senior* v *Holdsworth, ex parte Independent Television News Ltd*[3] has probably discredited the older view that film (and presumably videotape) were not to be regarded as documents.

The courts have been disposed to recognise successive technological developments in the storage and reproduction of information, by treating as documents for most purposes anything which is the functional equivalent of the traditional paper document. Happily, however, the courts have at the same time exhibited a reluctance to burden the new documents with the restrictive rule requiring proof by primary evidence. For example, in *Kajala* v *Noble* (1982) 75 Cr App R 149, it was held that that rule was 'limited and confined to written documents in the strict sense of the term, and has no relevance to tapes or films'. No doubt the very different realities of producing copies of the new technological documents abundantly justifies a departure from a rule conceived in an age when the only form of copying was handwritten reproduction. This does not indicate that film, tape, videotape, microfilm, microfiche and the like are not to be regarded as documents for general purposes.

The following statutory definitions, dealing with the use of the word 'document' in the statutes to which they relate, have in any case, for important evidential purposes considerably widened the more traditional definitions. For the purpose of the now general admission of hearsay evidence in civil proceedings, by virtue of Part 1 of the Civil Evidence Act 1968, the word 'document', as defined by s. 10(1) of the Act:

. . . includes, in addition to a document in writing—

(*a*)   any map, plan, graph or drawing;
(*b*)   any photograph;
(*c*)   any disc, tape, sound track or other device in which sounds or other data (not being visual images) are embodied so as to be capable (with or without the aid of some other equipment) of being reproduced therefrom; and

---

[2]   See *R* v *Virgo* (CA) (1978) 67 Cr App R 323; Civil Evidence Act 1968 s. 3(2); and generally 12.2.2, ante.
[3]   [1976] QB 23. For the older view, see *Glyn* v *Western Feature Film Co.* (1915) 85 LJ Ch 261.

(*d*) any film, negative, tape or other device in which one or more visual images are embodied so as to be capable (as aforesaid) of being reproduced therefrom.

In criminal cases the Criminal Evidence Act 1965, which permitted a limited use of documentary hearsay evidence in criminal cases, provided simply that a 'document' for the purposes of that Act was 'any device by means of which information is recorded or stored' (ibid s. 1(4)). The Police and Criminal Evidence Act 1984 has considerably widened the scope of admissibility of documentary hearsay in criminal cases (see 8.3, ante). Section 118(1) of the 1984 Act adopts the same definition of a 'document' for the purpose of the Act as that set forth in Part 1 of the Civil Evidence Act 1968, which has been cited above. The definition is now, therefore, the same in relation to the admissibility of documentary hearsay in civil and criminal cases.

Having observed that private documents are subject to the ordinary rules of admissibility, including any statutory modifications, it remains only to consider whether there are any special additional rules applicable to documents as such. In this connection, three matters arise: the proof of the contents of a document; the proof of due execution of documents, where required to be proved; the admissibility of extrinsic evidence for the purpose of explaining, contradicting, or varying the contents of a document.

Of these three considerations, the third is of contemporary importance only in relation to contracts, in the form of the 'parol evidence rule'. This is a rule of specialised application, and is outside the scope of the present work.[4] The first two considerations will now be examined.

### 15.2 Proof of contents: the primary evidence rule

It is an ancient, albeit much neglected rule of the common law that a party who wishes to rely on the contents of a private document as direct evidence, must adduce 'primary' (as opposed to 'secondary') evidence of the contents of that document. The meaning of these terms is considered below. It may be observed that the usual meaning of the term 'primary evidence' is the production of the original document. Various reasons have been advanced for the rule. It is certainly the last outpost of the 'best-evidence' rule, discussed in Chapter 1 (1.7, ante): see *Kajala* v *Noble* (1982) 75 Cr App R 149; *Garton* v *Hunter* [1969] 2 QB 37. It would be surprising if it were not connected with an anxiety to give effect to the terms of the document with as much accuracy and certainty as possible. The rule arose, of course, in an age where the only method of producing copies was by handwriting, and the possibilities of fraud or error were legion.

The rule requiring primary evidence applies to all cases in which a party seeks to rely upon the contents of a document as direct evidence, or as evidence proving the document itself. In *Augustien* v *Challis* (1847) 1 Exch 279, the plaintiff sued a sheriff for negligence in withdrawing a writ of *fieri facias* (a method of executing on a judgment) in the plaintiff's favour. The sheriff's defence was that another creditor, the debtor's landlord, was entitled to receive rent from the debtor, and that this entitlement enjoyed priority over the judgment debt to the plaintiff. Proof of the priority depended upon proof that the rent was indeed due to the debtor's landlord under the terms of the lease. Since the existence and terms of the lease were to be proved, the rule required the production of the original lease as primary evidence. The landlord failed to produce the lease, and his evidence that rent

---

[4] See Cross, *Evidence*, 5th ed., p. 608; Phipson, *Evidence*, 12th ed., para. 1871 et seq.

was due under the lease was held to be inadmissible secondary evidence. And in *MacDonnell* v *Evans* (1852) 11 CB 930, the court disallowed a question sought to be put to a witness for the plaintiff in cross-examination, the object of which was to elicit the reaction of the witness to a letter written to him accusing him of forgery. Since the existence and terms of the letter were to be proved, the contents of the letter should have been proved by primary evidence, and the question was disallowed because this had not been done.

Conversely, where there is no intent to prove the contents of the document as direct evidence, and the document is used for some other purpose only, the rule requiring primary evidence does not apply. If, for example, a party wishes to prove that the relationship of landlord and tenant existed and no more, and is not concerned to prove the existence or terms of any particular lease, there is no need to adduce primary evidence of the lease. Secondary evidence, such as the oral evidence of one of the parties, may be adduced to prove the relationship: *R* v *Holy Trinity, Kingston-upon-Hull (Inhabitants)* (1827) 7 B & C 611. Similarly, a document may be identified by a copy, if no reliance is placed on its contents as evidence: *Boyle* v *Wiseman* (1855) 11 Exch 360. In *R* v *Elworthy* (1867) LR 1 CCR 103, a solicitor was prosecuted for perjury, it being alleged that he had wilfully and falsely denied having prepared a draft of a statutory declaration. The prosecution adduced secondary evidence to show, firstly that the draft in fact existed and was in the possession of the defendant, and secondly that certain alterations had been made to its contents. The defendant's conviction was quashed on appeal. Although the secondary evidence was perfectly proper for the first purpose, it was inadmissible for the second, since the prosecution then wished not merely to prove the existence and location of the document, but to rely upon its contents as direct evidence of the alleged forgery. For this purpose, primary evidence was required.

As noted above, the courts have declined to extend the rule to documents consisting of film, tape and the like. There is little reason to burden these categories with a restrictive and formalistic rule conceived in the days before technology had begun to spawn new forms of storing information which give a new meaning to the term 'original'. The American Federal Rule of Evidence 1001, by sub-rules (3) and (4), seeks to deal with the necessarily expanded concept of an original, by offering the following definitions of the terms 'original' and 'duplicate'. (A subsequent rule holds that a duplicate, as thus defined, is generally admissible to the same extent as an original.)

(3) Original. An 'original' of a writing or recording is the writing or recording itself or any counterpart intended to have the same effect by a person executing or issuing it. An 'original' of a photograph includes the negative or any print therefrom. If data are stored in a computer or similar device, any printout or other output readable by sight, shown to reflect the data accurately, is an 'original'.

(4) A 'duplicate' is a counterpart produced by the same impression as the original, or from the same matrix, or by means of photography, including enlargements and miniatures, or by mechanical or electronic re-recording, or by chemical reproduction, or by other equivalent techniques which accurately reproduce the original.

In *Kajala* v *Noble* (1982) 75 Cr App R 149, a prosecution witness, by viewing a BBC news film, identified the defendant as a member of a group of persons who had caused a serious public disturbance. The original film was retained by the BBC, and at trial the prosecution relied on a video-cassette, which the court was satisfied was an authentic copy of the original film. On appeal against conviction, it was argued for the defendant that since the prosecution had relied upon the contents of the film, and since the film should be regarded as a document, primary evidence should have been required. The Court declined to extend the rule beyond 'written documents in the strict sense of the term' and held that it had no application to tapes or films. This is in accordance with the abandonment of the best-evidence rule generally, and it is fairly safe to say that the rule requiring primary evidence will remain so limited.

In criminal proceedings the Police and Criminal Evidence Act 1984, s. 71 provides the following specific exception to the rule in criminal cases:

In any proceedings the contents of a document may (whether or not the document is still in existence) be proved by the production of a microfilm copy of that document or of the material part of it, authenticated in such manner as the court may approve.

The rule requiring primary evidence has not been applied to documents admitted because they contain admissible hearsay statements and not as direct evidence in their own right. Rather, express statutory provisions have been made for proof of such documents (dealt with in Chapter 8).

### 15.2.1 Kinds of primary evidence
The following kinds of evidence of the contents of documents are primary, within the meaning of the rule discussed above.

### 15.2.1.1 The original.
This is of course the most obvious and most satisfactory kind of primary evidence. It is usually possible to identify the original document with certainty, but difficult cases do arise. If a deed is executed by various parties in a number of duplicates, each such duplicate is 'the original' and all must be produced.[5] Similarly, counterparts of a lease, one signed by the lessor only and the other by the lessee only, are each 'the original', so far as the party signing is concerned.[6]

These cases result, of course, from the fact that duplicates and counterparts of the kind mentioned are not in any sense copies, but together represent the deed executed by the parties. Whether a document is a counterpart or a duplicate is essentially a question of intent, rather than of the means by which the document is generated. Ideally, a document intended to be a counterpart should be produced to look like an original, but it is the originality of the execution of the document by signature or other means that really matters. Even if produced by means such as a photocopier, a document can be the original or a counterpart original, if executed as such by the necessary parties. However, if a document is executed and then photocopied, it is likely to be regarded as a copy, unless there is clear evidence that it was nonetheless intended to have effect as an original or a counterpart. Duplicates are traditionally produced by one and the same impression, for example where successive carbons are created by one signature, but as Federal Rule of Evidence 1001(4) indicates (see above) it will probably be necessary for the courts to re-define the term to keep pace with modern technology.

---

[5] *Forbes v Samuel* [1913] 3 KB 706.
[6] *Roe d West v Davis* (1806) 7 East 363.

*15.2.1.2   Copies of enrolled documents.*   Where the original private document is one which is, by law, required to be enrolled in a court or other public office, the copy officially issued by such court or office is treated as the original. Thus, the probate copy of a will is conclusive evidence of the words of the will. However, the court is entitled to look at the original enrolled will when considering any question of construction of the will, for example to look at erasures apparent in the original but not in the probate copy.[7]

*15.2.1.3   Admissions of contents.*   A party may adduce as primary evidence of the contents of a private document an admission made by his opponent with respect to such contents. The rule applies both to formal and informal admissions, and to oral as well as written admissions. In *Slatterie* v *Pooley* (1840) 6 M & W 664, the plaintiff sued on a covenant, which had the effect of creating an indemnity in respect of certain debts. The debts covered by the indemnity were contained in the schedule to a deed, which was inadmissible in evidence. The inclusion of the debt in the schedule was allowed to be proved by an oral admission, binding on the defendant, to that effect.

**15.3   Admissibility of secondary evidence**

A party who wishes to rely upon the contents of a document must, as we have seen, adduce primary evidence of the contents. Only in the exceptional cases enumerated below will secondary (i.e., non-primary) evidence be admissible. However, if secondary evidence is admissible, it may be adduced in any form in which it may be available, whether by production of a copy, of a copy of a copy, by oral evidence of the contents or in any other form. It is often said that 'there are no degrees of secondary evidence'. The secondary evidence must be authenticated by foundational evidence that the alleged copy is in fact a true copy of the original.[8]

Secondary evidence is admissible to prove the contents of a document in the following exceptional cases:

(a)   If a party fails, after notice, to produce the original.
(b)   If a stranger to proceedings refuses to produce the original.
(c)   If the original is lost.
(d)   If it is impossible to produce the original.
(e)   If the document is or forms part of a banker's book.

It should be emphasised that the exceptions to the rule requiring primary evidence are designed to provide relief in a case where a party is genuinely unable to produce the original through no fault of that party. If the proponent of the document has the original in his possession or it is within his power to obtain and produce it, he may not rely on the exceptions, even where his failure to produce the original is innocent, in the sense that it is not a deliberate concealment: cf. *R* v *Wayte* (1982) 76 Cr App R 110.

*15.3.1   Failure to produce after notice*
Nor would it be right for a party to be able to prevent his opponent using a document in evidence by withholding the original. Accordingly, where a document is in the possession

---

[7]   *Re Battie-Wrightson, Cecil* v *Battie-Wrightson* [1920] 2 Ch 330.
[8]   *R* v *Collins* (CCA) (1960) 44 Cr App R 170.

of one party, an opponent may serve notice to produce the document.[9] The notice to produce does not compel the production of the original, but if the original is not produced, its contents may be proved by secondary evidence. This means that, unlike a *subpoena duces tecum*, a notice to produce may be served even on the defendant in a criminal case, because in the absence of compulsion, there is no violation of the defendant's privilege against self-incrimination. If the notice is not complied with, not only may the document be proved by secondary evidence, but the party failing to comply will not be allowed to rely upon the original, if it should be inconsistent with the secondary evidence.[10]

In certain cases, service of notice is unnecessary. Most importantly, by RSC, Ord. 27, r. 4(3):

> A party to a cause or matter by whom a list of documents is served on any other party . . . shall be deemed to have been served by that other party with a notice requiring him to produce at the trial of the cause of matter such of the documents specified in the list as are in his possession, custody or power.

For this purpose, therefore, notice will not be necessary in respect of documents in the immediate control of the opponent which are, following the usual procedure, disclosed by list after close of pleadings.

Notice need not be served if the document sought is itself a notice, for example a notice to produce or a notice to rely on previous convictions for the purpose of s. 27(3) of the Theft Act 1968. Notice is not required where production of a document is required by necessary implication by the nature of the proceedings, for example a charge of theft of the document; or where the document is admitted to have been lost or destroyed.

### 15.3.2 *Lawful refusal of stranger to produce*

If a document is in the possession or custody of a stranger to the proceedings, its contents may be proved by secondary evidence in any case where the stranger is lawfully entitled to refuse to produce it, for example because it is privileged in his hands, or he is beyond the jurisdiction of the court. If, however, the refusal is unlawful, secondary evidence will not be admissible, because production of the original may be compelled. Refusal to produce by the stranger in such a case may be punishable by proceedings for contempt or by making him liable in respect of any resulting loss.[11]

An excellent example of the proper working of this exception is *R* v *Nowaz* [1976] Crim LR 510, where documents which the prosecution wished to prove were protected by diplomatic immunity, so that production of the originals could not be compelled. It was held that the prosecution were entitled to give secondary evidence of the contents of the documents by calling a police officer to testify. In *Kajala* v *Noble* (1982) 75 Cr App R 149, to which we have already referred, it appears to have been assumed that the policy of the BBC in insisting on retaining the originals of their films precluded production of the original, so as to render the video-cassette copy admissible as secondary evidence. It does

---

[9]  Such notice is habitually served together with notice to admit any documents in the possession of the server; these documents will then be taken to be admitted unless objected to in response to the notice.

[10]  *Doe d Thompson* v *Hodgson* (1840) 12 A & E 135.

[11]  *R* v *Llanfaethly (Inhabitants)* (1853) 2 E & B 940.

not appear to have been argued that the original might not have been beyond compulsion. It is right to say that the case was not decided on this basis, because the Court felt that the rule requiring primary evidence should not be applied to films. However, the argument proposed might have strengthened the defendant's argument at least to some extent.

### 15.3.3   Original lost

Where the original document cannot be found or identified after due search, its contents may be proved by secondary evidence. It is for the party seeking to rely on the document to show that all reasonable steps by way of search have been taken.

### 15.3.4   Production of original impossible

Secondary evidence will be admissible where the actual production of the original is impossible, for example where the document takes the form of an inscription on a tombstone or a wall. In *Owner* v *Bee Hive Spinning Co. Ltd* [1914] 1 KB 105, the same principle was applied to a notice giving particulars of mealtimes in a factory, which by statute was obliged to remain affixed to the wall of a particular place, and so was 'legally impossible' to produce.

It is interesting to compare, in this respect, the question of production of public documents. Although such documents would rarely, if ever, be impossible to produce, the production of the original would almost always be a matter of very great inconvenience and difficulty. Such a difficulty faced Alderson B in *Mortimer* v *M'Callan* (1840) 6 M & W 58, where it was suggested that the original books of the Bank of England ought to be produced for the purpose of proving their contents. It was held that the resulting inconvenience amounted to impossibility of production. The proof of most public documents is now governed by statute, and it may be noted that in many cases, the production of a certified or sealed copy will suffice (Evidence Act 1845, s. 1), and that in the absence of any specific provision, a public document produced from proper custody may be proved by a certified or examined copy (Evidence Act 1851, s. 14).

### 15.3.5   Bankers' books

Bankers' books are relevant to a considerable variety of cases. With the exception of the books of the Bank of England, they are private documents, and so in theory should be proved by primary evidence. Because of the obvious inconvenience of the rule to banks, whose records of customers' accounts are often required in litigation, special provisions were enacted by the Bankers' Books Evidence Act 1879. By s. 3 of the Act:

> Subject to the provisions of this Act, a copy of an entry in a bankers' book shall in all legal proceedings be received as prima facie evidence of such entry, and of the matters, transactions, and accounts therein recorded.

The provision is subject to two conditions set forth in subsequent sections:

> 4.   A copy of an entry in a bankers' book shall not be received in evidence under this Act unless it be first proved that the book was at the time of the making of the entry one of the ordinary books of the bank, and that the entry was made in the usual and ordinary course of business, and that the book is in the custody or control of the bank

> 5.   A copy of an entry in a bankers' book shall not be received in evidence under this

Act unless if be further proved that the copy has been examined with the original entry and is correct . . .

Section 6 provides that where the contents of a bankers' book may be proved under the Act, a banker or officer of the bank shall not be compellable to produce the original or to appear as a witness to prove the contents 'unless by order of a judge made for special cause'.

A most important provision for the conduct of many kinds of litigation, in particular prosecutions for offences of dishonesty, in contained in s. 7 of the Act, which provides:

On the application of any party to a legal proceeding a court or judge may order that such party be at liberty to inspect and take copies of any entries in a bankers' book for any of the purposes of such proceedings. An order under this section may be made either with or without summoning the bank or any other party, and shall be served on the bank three clear days before the same is to be obeyed, unless the court or judge otherwise directs.

By s. 9 of the Act as originally enacted, the expression 'bankers' books' included 'ledgers, day books, cash books, account books, and all other books used in the ordinary business of the bank'. In *Barker v Wilson* [1980] 2 All ER 81, it was argued that records kept on microfilm were not 'bankers' books' for the purposes of s. 9. The Divisional Court, however, saw no reason why the rules enacted for the bankers of 1879 should cease to apply merely because the bankers of 1980 enjoyed greater technological advantages in maintaining their records, and held that microfilm records fell within the terms of s. 9. Recognising the wisdom of the principle expressed in *Barker v Wilson*, Parliament, by sch. 6 to the Banking Act 1979, substituted an amended s. 9, which provides by its second subsection that:

Expressions in this Act relating to 'bankers' books' include ledgers, day books, cash books, account books and other records used in the ordinary business of the bank, whether those records are in written form or are kept on microfilm, magnetic tape or any other form of mechanical or electronic data retrieval mechanism.

But regardless of the manner in which bankers' books are compiled and maintained, the Act permits the use of secondary evidence only in the case of documents that fall within the definition given in the revised s. 9. In *R v Dadson* (1983) 77 Cr App R 91, the defendant was charged with various offences arising from the alleged misuse of his cheque card. At trial, copies of letters from the bank's correspondence file, written to the defendant by the bank, were admitted in evidence in reliance on s. 9. Quashing the conviction, the Court of Appeal held that the correspondence did not consitute 'bankers' books'. It simply fell outside the statutory definition. Moreover, the file in which the letters were maintained was not one of the ordinary books of the bank and the letters were not entries made in the ordinary course of banking business. The copies, had, therefore, been wrongly admitted and in view of the stress laid upon them in the summing-up of the trial judge as evidence that the defendant knew that he had no overdraft facility, the appeal was allowed.

The amended s. 9 also provides that the expressions 'bank' and 'banker' refer to any recognised bank, licensed institution or municipal bank within the meaning of the Banking Act 1979, the Trustee Savings Bank, the National Savings Bank and to the Post

Office in the exercise of its powers to provide banking services. In *R* v *Grossman* (1981) 73 Cr App R 302, the question arose whether the court had jurisdiction to make an order under the Act directed to the London head office of a bank, but actually designed to have effect in relation to the books of a related bank established under the laws of a foreign jurisdiction. The Commissioners of Inland Revenue sought and were granted an order for the inspection of bankers' books, which it was thought might provide evidence useful in the prosecution of the defendant for alleged fraud against the Revenue. The bank account in question was held at Savings and Investment Bank in Douglas, Isle of Man, a company established under Manx law. This bank had no place of business in England, but was licensed to operate as a bank under Manx law and collected cheques through the medium of Barclays Bank in the Isle of Man. An application was made to the Deemster in the Isle of Man for an order for inspection under the corresponding provisions of the Manx Bankers' Books Evidence Act 1935, but this application was refused, since the Manx Act applied only to proceedings within the Isle of Man. In order to avoid this problem, the Commissioners sought an order against Barclays Bank in London, and not the Douglas branch of Barclays. The order was granted at first instance. Although Barclays took a 'neutral stance' in the matter, Savings and Investment Bank challenged the order,and prevailed in the Court of Appeal. Lord Denning MR pointed out that the Manx banks were subject to a separate legal system, and were separate entities from Barclays of London. It would not be right to compel them to open their books in support of proceedings in England and Wales. Shaw and Oliver LJJ agreed, the latter holding that, while such an order might be made in appropriate circumstances, a very strong showing would be required, no doubt to overcome the natural hesitancy of any court in making an order directed to a foreign jurisdiction. It is submitted that such an order might be appropriate, notwithstanding the difference in jurisdictions, where two banks have a more direct connection than did Barclays and Savings and Investment Bank in this case, though obvious problems of enforcement arise if no books are physically kept within the jurisdiction.

The s. 7 provision is a drastic one, applying to civil and criminal proceedings alike and for a great variety of purposes. It has rightly been held that it is a substantial interference with liberty, which should be countenanced only after serious consideration: *Williams and Others* v *Summerfield* [1972] 2 QB 513. This case appears to be the first reported decision dealing with the application of the Act to a criminal case. It had been thought well established, that in civil cases the matter should be resolved primarily by discovery, and that matters not discoverable should not be revealed by a side-wind, by means of an application under the Act.[12] In *Williams* v *Summerfield*, Lord Widgery CJ recognised that the discovery approach could not be applied to criminal cases. The learned Lord Chief Justice indicated that magistrates faced with an application for an order under the Act should approach such applications in the same way as an application for a search warrant, the grant of which is, the Lord Chief Justice said, 'a very serious interference with the liberty of the subject, and a step which would be taken only after the most mature, careful consideration of all the facts of the case'. In some cases, magistrates might decline to exercise their jurisdiction, on the ground that the case was one more suitable for the High Court. Another court has echoed, more recently, Lord Widgery CJ's further observation that the order for inspection should be granted to strengthen an existing case, and not to

---

[12]   See generally *Waterhouse* v *Barker* [1942] 2 KB 759; *Re Bankers' Books Evidence Act 1879, R* v *Bono* (1913) 29 TLR 635.

create a case which does not already exist, i.e. only when the application for an order is not, effectively, a fishing expedition: *R* v *Nottingham Justices, ex parte Lynn* [1984] Crim LR 554.

The serious nature of the order is amply demonstrated by the fact that it may be applied for on an ex parte basis, without notice to the person affected, and may be made against a person who is not a party to the case.[13] In *R* v *Grossman* (1981) 71 Cr App R 302, 309, the facts of which have been dealt with above, Oliver LJ made the following observation about the making of orders under such circumstances:

> I am bound to say that I think the practice of making orders ex parte in respect of the accounts of persons who are genuinely third parties unconnected with the proceedings (save that they may perhaps be in possession of some evidence) is a most undesireable one. The Act provides no machinery for going back to the judge once the order has been made; so that the party affected, if he wishes to object, must apply (as in this case) to be joined and then appeal to this Court. That strikes me as a profoundly unsatisfactory situation; and speaking for myself, I would like to see it become a regular practice that in cases where third parties are involved the order should either not be made until the account owner has been informed and given an opportunity to be heard or should be made in the form of an order nisi, allowing a period for the person affected to come before the court and show cause why the order should not be effective.

Although, in civil cases, the question of production of copies of entries in bank accounts will, no doubt, continue to be dealt with on discovery, it remains to be seen whether, as held in the older cases, an affidavit to the effect that disclosure would incriminate the person affected will prevent an order under the Act, as it would an order for further discovery. After *Williams* v *Summerfied*, it seems clear that no such privilege applies in a criminal case, at least as to the offences charged or which are charged as a result of matters discovered by the inspection ordered.

### 15.4 Proof of due execution

In the case of public documents, the mere production of an admissible copy is generally sufficient to satisfy any requirement of proof of due execution of the document, in accordance with the maxim, *Omnia praesumuntur rite et solemniter esse acta*. The presumption is, of course, rebuttable, although not without difficulty. In the case of private documents, due execution must be proved by evidence, except where the document is more than 20 years old and comes from proper custody, in which case there arises a presumption of due execution and so of formal validity.

Due execution is proved by evidence of the signature of the person by whom the document purports to be signed and by evidence of attestation, if required for the document in question. Due execution may be admitted in criminal proceedings by virtue of s. 10 of the Criminal Justice Act 1967, and in civil proceedings when the admission is deemed to have been made for the purposes of the rules: RSC, Ord. 27, r. 1 and r. 2. Proof of due execution is dispensed with where an opponent refuses to produce a document after notice to do so.[14]

---

[13]   See, e.g., *R* v *Andover Justices, ex parte Rhodes* [1980] Crim LR 644.
[14]   *Cooke* v *Tanswell* (1818) 8 Taunt 450.

The means of proof of due execution, where required, are: (a) evidence of handwriting; (b) evidence of attestation; and (c) by an applicable presumption.

### 15.4.1 Evidence of handwriting

There is an obvious relevance in evidence which proves the authenticity of the handwriting of the person purporting to be the signer or executer of the document. Handwriting may be proved in any of the following ways.

*15.4.1.1 Direct evidence.* The evidence of the signer himself or of a witness who perceived the execution of the document is admissible and sufficient evidence of due execution. The proof of signature by such means will suffice to identify the signer, as well as to establish the name signed, unless the evidence reveals circumstances which call for further investigation, for example where the signature is not distinctive and the name signed is a common one.[15]

*15.4.1.2 Opinion.* Non-expert witnesses who are familiar with the signature of the purported signer, or who have on other occasions received documents bearing the purported signature or made in the purported handwriting of the purported signer, may state their opinion that the document is signed by the person by whom it purports to be signed. The weight of such evidence may, of course, vary very considerably according to the circumstances of the case.

*15.4.1.3 Comparison.* The comparison of disputed writings with known writings by scientific means is a well established subject of expert-opinion evidence. The basis for such evidence is contained in s. 8 of the Criminal Procedure Act 1865 which applied to criminal proceedings, a provision which had been available in civil cases since the enactment of the Common Law Procedure Act 1854. The section provides that:

> Comparison of a disputed writing with any writing proved to the satisfaction of the judge to be genuine shall be permitted to be made by witnesses; and such writings, and the evidence of witnesses respecting the same, may be submitted to the court and jury as evidence of the genuineness or otherwise of the writing in dispute.

The phrase 'to the satisfaction of the judge' leaves unresolved the question of the standard to which the 'genuineness' of the writing to be compared with the disputed writing must be proved. It was at one time thought that even in a criminal case, the standard of proof required on such a secondary issue was no higher than the preponderance of probabilities: see *R* v *Angeli* [1979] 1 WLR 26. However, in *R* v *Ewing* [1983] QB 1039, it was held that the standard required in a criminal case was proof beyond reasonable doubt. This is discussed in detail in 3.7.3, ante.

Possibly because s. 8 pre-dates the general recognition of the scientific study and comparison of handwriting, it is not expressly provided that the comparison should be made by a witness qualified as an expert. Nonetheless, it is unlikely that the evidence would command real weight if made by a 'lay' witness, unless giving evidence of his opinion based on personal familiarity. Scientific comparison of samples of handwriting is a matter for experts. The jury may, and inevitably will where it is relevant to do so,

---

[15]  *Jones* v *Jones* (!) (1841) 9 M & W 75.

compare the appearance of various documents produced to them, but they should not be invited to make a comparison of handwriting without the help of expert evidence. In *R v Tilley; R v Tilley* [1961] 1 WLR 1309 the prosecution obtained in the course of cross-examination samples of the handwriting of the defendants, with a view to comparing the samples with handwriting on a receipt said to be in respect of a car which the defendants were charged with stealing. No expert was called concerning the handwriting, and the point was not pursued by the prosecution. However, the conviction was quashed on appeal because the jury were supplied with photographs and a magnifying glass, and were invited by the comments of the judge in summing-up, to form their own unaided comparison of handwriting. It follows, therefore, that where the jury are not being invited to make any such comparison, but have in their possession documents which may lead them to seek to do so, they should be warned specifically against such a course. This done, the jury may of course make other proper use of the documents placed before them in evidence.[16]

The ultimate question of whether the handwriting on the known specimen is also that on the disputed writing, or the document whose due execution is to be proved, is of course a question of fact for the jury or other tribunal of fact. It follows that the handwriting expert should, technically, limit his evidence to a statement of the comparison made by him, and his resulting opinion should technically be confined to relevant similarities or differences.[17] Nonetheless, the modern practice is for the witness to be permitted to state his opinion about authorship, and in civil cases this would seem to follow from the provisions of s. 3(1) and (3) of the Civil Evidence Act 1972.[18]

### 15.4.2 Evidence of attestation

Due execution of documents which require attestation may be proved by the evidence of the attesting witnesses, or one of them. At one time, a document requiring attestation could be proved to have been duly executed only in this way, but it was provided by s. 3 of the Evidence Act 1938 that in both civil and criminal cases, it might be proved as if no attesting witness were alive. This means that either of the other methods of proof suggested in this section may be employed, although the most satisfactory way will be to prove the handwriting of an attesting witness, where possible.

The older rule still applies to wills, and these must be proved by evidence of attestation, unless it is shown that all the attesting witnesses are dead, insane, beyond the jurisdiction or unable to be traced. However, the practice is not to insist on the strict application of the rule where probate is granted in common form.

An attesting witness is called as the witness of the court. So he may be cross-examined by any party, including the party seeking to prove the document.[19] If an attesting witness proves hostile or unreliable, then he may be contradicted by other evidence by any party.[20] An attesting witness may not claim legal professional privilege.[21]

---

[16]   *R v O'Sullivan* [1969] 1 WLR 497.
[17]   *Wakeford v Bishop of Lincoln* (PC, Consistory Court of Lincoln) as reported in 90 LJ PC 174.
[18]   For the scope of expert opinion evidence generally, including the expression of opinions on ultimate issues, see Chapter 9, 9.4.1, ante.
[19]   *Oakes v Uzzell* [1932] P 19.
[20]   *Bowman v Hodgson* (1867) LR 1 P & D 362.
[21]   *In the Estate of Fuld (No. 2), Hartley v Fuld* [1965] P 405.

### 15.4.3   Presumptions

It is presumed:

(a)   That a document which is proved or purports to be more than 20 years old, and which is produced from proper custody, was duly executed. 'Proper custody' means only that the document is shown to have been kept in a place, or in the care of a person who might reasonably and naturally be expected to have possession of it, having regard to the nature of the document and the circumstances of the case.

(b)   That a document was executed on the date which it bears.

(c)   That in the case of a deed other than a will, any alterations thereto were made before execution, but in the case of will, conversely, that any alterations were made after execution.

## B: REAL EVIDENCE

## 15.5   Nature of real evidence

Real evidence is the name usually given to quite diverse forms of evidence which have in common the characteristic that the tribunal of fact is invited to observe and draw conclusions from things, persons, places or circumstances; and so to act on its own perception for any necessary evidential purposes. Real evidence may, therefore, rank among the most cogent kinds of evidence, but also among the most difficult to assess in terms of weight, at least before the event. The forms of real evidence in common use are the following.

### 15.5.1   Material objects

The court may look at and draw any proper conclusions from its visual observation of any relevant material object produced before it. The material object may itself be the subject-matter of the case, as where the court looks at the fit of a suit of which the quality is disputed. It may be an object ancillary to the issue but nonetheless relevant to it, as for example where the court looks at an object alleged to be an offensive weapon, by reason of having been adapted for causing injury to the person. The tribunal of fact is entitled to act on the results of its own perception, even where this conflicts with other evidence given about the object, although in a case where the true nature or characteristics of the object cannot be assessed by mere visual observations, without the assistance of expert evidence, the jury must be warned not to rely upon unaided visual opinion. This would be the case in looking at objects bearing examples of handwriting, comparisons of which should not be made without assistance[22] although the jury may obviously make use of their observation for any purpose short of comparison. And it has been held to be wrong to direct a jury to feel entirely free to form their own view about the presence and age of blood stains on an object, in the face of categoric scientific evidence on that subject.[23] If expert evidence called on behalf of the parties differs in its conclusions about the object, and the tribunal of fact has, therefore, to choose what evidence to accept, it may, no doubt use its powers of observation in making such choice.

---

22   See 15.4.1.3, ante.
23   *Anderson v R* (PC, Jamaica) [1972] AC 100. See generally Chapter 9 and 9.4.1, ante.

### 15.5.2 Appearance of persons or animals

The physical characteristics of a person or animal may be observed for any relevant purpose. Thus, the height or other personal features may be ascertained by observation, and the nature and extent of any injuries examined. The court may also take into account any characteristics apparent to it on observing the person or animal, even if not intended to be conveyed, such as a tendency to left-handedness, defects in hearing or vision, or the propensity of an animal to be ferocious.

### 15.5.3 Demeanour of witnesses

In considering the credit of a witness and the weight to be given to his evidence, the court may consider not only what is said, but the way in which it is said. This includes the attitude of the witness to the court, his general demeanour, his apparent frankness, evasiveness or other reaction to questioning (particularly hostile, in cross-examination) and his apparent power or lack of power of recollection.

### 15.5.4 Views

A view is an inspection, out of court, of the *locus in quo*, or other place relevant to the case, or of some object, person or animal which cannot conveniently be brought to court. The view may involve any appropriate test or demonstration, as if made in court. A view can be a difficult event to control. It is important that all interested parties, their legal representatives and the tribunal of fact should, as far as can be arranged, have the same sight and opportunity to observe. They must also be protected against exposure to extraneous and irrelevant matters. With a jury, the problems are particularly acute, and it is essential that each member of the jury should attend and be enabled to form an individual impression. Where one member of the jury, who lived close to the *locus in quo*, was 'deputed' to view it and 'report back' to the others, who accordingly had no such opportunity, the conviction was quashed.[24] It is equally essential, if the view is attended by witnesses, in order to explain relevant matters or to give some demonstration, that the witness should speak or demonstrate only at the direction of the judge, in the presence of all concerned, and for the purpose only of the necessary demonstration or explanation.[25] In a matter tried by a judge alone, the same rules should be followed, although the dangers to be·guarded against are less acute, and the extent of the view may be widened. In the *Ocean Island case*[26] Sir Robert Megarry VC personally visited and spent a considerable time on the island and drew numerous conclusions from his lengthy and detailed observation of its characteristics; though the litigation was, on any basis, exceptional.

### 15.5.5 Tapes, photographs, film, etc.

Although in modern law visual and audio recordings may be regarded as documents, at least for some purposes (see 15.1, ante) they have a further, important potential to supply matter of evidential value, because of the possibility of direct perception. A tape or film may yield detail and nuances over and above the mere text of the matters recorded therein. Some detail of the circumstances of the recording, some visible characteristic, some inflexion of the voice may put a different complexion on the recorded matter, as compared

---

[24] *R v Gurney* (CA) [1976] Crim LR 567. See also Juries Act 1974, s. 14.
[25] *Karamat v R* (PC, British Guiana) [1956] AC 256. See also *R v Martin* (CCR) (1872) LR 1 CCR 378.
[26] *Tito and Others v Waddell and Others (No. 2)* [1977] 2 WLR 496.

with a mere transcript of the words spoken or the things done. The sound, accent of a voice, the physical appearance of a thing or person may resolve some ambiguity or clothe with meaning some unexplained passage in the text. The recordings are, therefore, to that extent real evidence and often have an effect similar to a view or the production of a material object. To the extent that recordings are admissible as real evidence, it is no objection to admissibility that the evidence is meant to, and does in fact, convey information because it is offered for direct observation by the court, and not as a species of hearsay.

Thus, in *The Statue of Liberty* [1968] 1 WLR 739, Sir Jocelyn Simon P admitted in evidence a record made on cinematograph film of the radar echoes, recorded mechanically without human intervention, of the vessels involved in a collision. The recording was the equivalent of a photograph or series of photographs, from which the court could, by observation, gain information about the courses of the vessels at material times. This decision represents an uncomfortable interface between the common-law hearsay rule and the potential of modern technology. Clearly, Sir Jocelyn Simon P's categorisation of the evidence tendered as real evidence cannot disguise the fact that the information produced by the radar device was tendered with a view to showing that the facts stated by the record of the radar echoes were, in fact, true. At common law, there would be a powerful argument for excluding such evidence as hearsay. At the time when *The Statue of Liberty* was decided, the Civil Evidence Act 1968 was not yet in force, and the Evidence Act 1938 did not assist the admissibility of the evidence. There is no doubt that, in some civil cases, comparable evidence produced by a computer might now be admitted under s. 5 of the 1968 Act, but bearing in mind the definition of a 'computer' given in s. 5, referring to devices for 'storing and processing information', it is by no means clear that a machine which 'sees' and records events as they occur is to be treated as being a 'computer'. A further problem arises with regard to the possible admissibility of such evidence under s. 4 of the Act, because of the requirement of personal knowledge. This problem was acknowledged in relation to corresponding wording of the Criminal Evidence Act 1965 by the Court of Appeal in *R* v *Pettigrew* (1980) 71 Cr App R 39, and is to be anticipated as arising again under the new provisions of ss. 68 and 69 of the Police and Criminal Evidence Act 1984. These matters are dealt with more fully in Chapters 6 and 8, ante.

Whatever the ultimate impact of these technological problems on the rule against hearsay, the reasoning of Sir Jocelyn Simon P has been employed in a number of subsequent cases. In *R* v *Wood* (1982) 76 Cr App R 23, it was held that where a computer was used only as a calculator, the information used to programme the computer being within the personal knowledge of persons available as witnesses, the print-out which represented the result of the computer's calculations was not hearsay, but was admissible at common law as a piece of real evidence. And in *Castle* v *Cross* [1984] Crim LR 682, it was held that a police officer was entitled to give evidence of the reading of an 'Intoximeter 3000' device, which was admitted to be efficient to the required degree, and where there was no suggestion that the machine was not working properly. The reading was admitted as a piece of real evidence.

The court must, before admitting recordings as evidence, be satisfied that the evidence which may be yielded is relevant and that the recording produced is authentic and original.[27]

---

[27]   *R* v *Maqsud Ali; R* v *Ashiq Hussain* (CCA) [1966] 1 QB 688.

The requirement of proof of originality is met by evidence sufficient to raise a prima facie case, in that the provenance and history of the recording up to the moment of production in court, are properly accounted for.[28] If there is any real possibility that the recording might have been interfered with, and is not original, it should be excluded.[29]

It may be that where a recording is of such poor quality that it would be wrong to expect the jury to form a fair assessment of the contents, it should be excluded.[50]

The above principles apply to the use of films produced by hidden, automatic security cameras installed in banks and elsewhere for the purpose of recording robberies and other incidents. The jury are entitled to consider the film as identification evidence of the persons recorded on it, subject to the foundational requirements stated above. See, e.g., *R v Dodson; R v Williams* [1984] Crim LR 489.

## 15.6 Questions for discussion

### 15.6.1 *R v Coke; R v Littleton*

1  By what evidence should the contents of the writing found in Coke's flat (exhibit GG1) be proved?

2  By what evidence should it be proved, if possible, that the writing on exhibit GG1 is that of Coke?

3  What direction, if any, should the jury be given about their use of exhibits GG1 and GG3?

4  What is the evidential significance of the tape-recording of the conversation between Littleton and his wife, made by D/I Glanvil?

5  What matters must be established before the tape-recording can be admitted in evidence, and what matters, if established by the defence, might prevent its admission?

### 15.6.2 *Blackstone v Coke*

1  Review the letter sent to Coke by his solicitors dated 20 February 1985. If Margaret Blackstone's solicitors obtain this letter and wish to cross-examine Coke on it at trial, how should the letter be proved? (Ignore questions of privilege.)

---

[28]  *R v Robson; R v Harris* [1972] 1 WLR 651. For a detailed treatment of this matter, see 3.7.3, ante.

[29]  *R v Stevenson; R v Hulse; R v Whitney* [1971] 1 WLR 1.

[30]  *R v Robson; R v Harris* [1972] 1 WLR 651.

# 16   Proof Without Evidence

## 16.1   When evidence may not be required

In view of the observations made in the early pages of the first chapter of this book about the importance of evidence to establish a charge, claim or defence, the title of this chapter may occasion some surprise. But there are some circumstances in which a court will, or may, find facts in issue or relevant facts established wihout requiring proof by means of evidence. This short chapter will examine these convenient techniques, which often permit considerable savings of judicial time and of costs.

The cases to be considered are those in which: (a) facts are formally admitted for the purpose of the proceedings; (b) notorious or readily demonstrable facts are noticed judicially by the court; and (c) where facts are presumed in favour of the party asserting them. Only the subject of presumptions have been considered previously in this book (3.3, ante) and then only briefly for their effect on the burden of proof.

## 16.2   Formal admissions

Proof may be dispensed with altogether where a fact is formally admitted for the purposes of the proceedings, and so ceases to be in dispute between the parties. Before the coming into force of s. 10 of the Criminal Justice Act 1967 formal admissions were possible only in civil cases, but now may be made also in criminal cases.

### 16.2.1   Civil cases
In civil cases, formal admissions may be made in various ways. If a fact is in issue, it may be admitted on the pleadings, and if so admitted, the fact is almost invariably deemed to be conclusively established against the admitting party unless the admission is deleted by amendment.[1] Formal admissions may also be made in response to a notice to admit or to interrogatories, or at any stage by agreement between the parties before or at trial. In the latter event, the admissions should be in written form and signed by or on behalf of each party concerned.

The effect of the admission is such that a party may rely on any fact admitted, which is in his favour, for any purpose (including the signing of judgment, if the admission extends to

---

[1]   An admission may also be made by default of pleading, or by failing in certain cases to traverse a fact by a pleading; see RSC, Ord. 27, r. 1; Ord. 18, r. 13 and r. 14. For the practice in the county court see CCR, Ord. 9, rr. 1–3; Ord. 20. An admission in a pleading which is amended to delete it may sometimes be relied upon as an informal admission: see 7.1, ante.

all the facts in issue). Evidence concerning a fact admitted is neither needed nor admissible. Care must be taken not to rely solely on admissions, where some further inference falls to be drawn from the facts admitted before judgment can follow; the court will act upon admitted facts, but will require evidence on any further facts necessary for success in the case. When a formal admission is made in civil proceedings it is binding only for the purpose of those proceedings, but in such proceedings is conclusive of the facts admitted.

## 16.2.2 Criminal cases
By s. 10 of the Criminal Justice Act 1967:

(1) Subject to the provisions of this section, any fact of which oral evidence may be given in any criminal proceedings may be admitted for the purpose of those proceedings by or on behalf of the prosecutor or defendant, and the admission by any party of any such fact under this section shall as against that party be conclusive evidence in those proceedings of the fact admitted.

(2) An admission under this section—

(a) may be made before or at the proceedings;
(b) if made otherwise than in court, shall be in writing;
(c) if made in writing by an individual, shall purport to be signed by the person making it . . .;
(d) if made on behalf of a defendant who is an individual, shall be made by his counsel or solicitor;
(e) if made at any stage before the trial by a defendant who is an individual, must be approved by his counsel or solicitor (whether at the time it was made or subsequently) before or at the proceedings in question.

(3) An admission under this section for the purpose of proceedings relating to any matter shall be treated as an admission for the purpose of any subsequent criminal proceedings relating to that matter (including any appeal or retrial).

(4) An admission under this section may with the leave of the court be withdrawn in the proceedings for the purpose of which it is made or any subsequent criminal proceedings relating to the same matter.

This section provides a self-contained code for formal admissions in criminal cases which had previously not been possible. The major differences between the statutory practice in criminal cases and the common-law practice in civil cases are the requirements in s. 10(2) concerning form and approval in certain circumstances and the possibility of withdrawal of the admission with leave of the court under s. 10(4). Unless withdrawn, however, the admission is similarly conclusive and presumably leave should be granted only where there is a real and appreciable risk that an admission has been made inadvisedly, or is for any reason suspect. There is no objection in principle to a formal admission by the defence of all the facts alleged by the prosecution, where these are not in dispute and the defence turns on other matters, but care must be taken to ensure that the jury appreciate the significance of what is being done, and can distinguish the facts as admitted from any argument addressed to them.[2] The admissions should, and sometimes must be, in writing, but if they are not, should at least be in a form capable of being accurately recorded in the shorthand note.[3]

Two general matters merit observation, with respect to both civil and criminal proceedings. The first is that formal admissions must be distinguished carefully from the informal admissions and confessions dealt with in Chapter 7, Sections A and B, ante. The latter are merely pieces of evidence tendered among others as constituting evidence against a party supplied by his own acts and words, and may be rejected by the court as inadmissible or of negligible weight, or be made the subject of evidence to contradict or discredit them; they are in no sense formal admissions and are most certainly not conclusive. The second is that in both civil and criminal cases, it is the duty of legal advisers to consider what formal admissions, if any, can and should properly be made on behalf of their clients for the purposes of any proceedings in which they are engaged. Of course, care must be taken not to make unjustified admissions, but failure to admit facts which are not really disputed wastes time and costs, and the latter may be visited on the client.

### 16.3 Judicial notice

By a rule applicable both to civil and criminal cases generally, no evidence is required of a fact of which the court will take judicial notice, that is to say a fact of which the court will acknowledge the truth without the necessity for proof. Facts which will be judicially noticed are those which are notorious, or which are readily demonstrable by reference to proper sources. If the fact is not one which will be judicially noticed, it must be proved by evidence. There are obviously very many facts which will be judicially noticed, and the process is capable of saving a great deal of time which would otherwise be spent in calling the substantial volumes of evidence often curiously necessary to prove the most self-evident facts. As Professor Cross has demonstrated,[4] the process of judicial notice is carried on habitually in almost every case which comes before the courts, often without being recognised as such, because of numerous tacit assumptions; the relevance of the defendant's possession of a jemmy to a charge of burglary against him is based on an assumption of fact that a jemmy is frequently employed for the purposes of burglary. We must look, however, principally at judicial notice in the sense of conscious application of the judicial mind to the facts concerned. This in turn involves consideration of (a) notice of notorious facts, (b) notice after reference to sources. In addition there are some cases where judicial notice is to be taken by statute, generally of seals and their authenticating or official devices; these need not be considered specifically here.

### 16.3.1 Effect of judicial notice

Judicial notice differs from formal admissions in that the fact judicially noticed is established, not by concession of a party but at the behest of one party and, if necessary over the objection of the opponent. In a civil case, this is hardly significant, since if the judge is prepared to notice a fact judicially, he would no doubt reach the same conclusion if evidence of the same fact were to be adduced. In a criminal case, however, a problem

[2] *R v Lewis* (CA) [1971] Crim LR 414.
[3] *R v Lennard* (CA) [1973] 1WLR 483. Magistrates' Courts Rules 1981, r. 71
[4] *Evidence*, 5th ed., pp. 161–2.

might be perceived as to how the jury should be directed as to the noticed fact, once the judge has noticed it judicially. The jury, as the tribunal of fact, must of course be directed as to the effect of the judicial notice.

In the United States, a distinction is made between criminal and civil cases as to the direction to be given (juries being commonly used in both kinds of case). This is well illustrated by Federal Rule of Evidence 201(g) which provides:

> Instructing jury. In a civil action or proceeding, the court shall instruct the jury to accept as conclusive any fact judicially noticed. In a criminal case, the court shall instruct the jury that it may, but is not required to accept as conclusive any fact judicially noticed.

This distinction is attributable principally to the constitutional rule that in a criminal case, no directed verdict can be given against the defendant: *Ross* v *United States* 374 F2d 97 (8th Circ 1967). Directing the jury to accept a judicially noticed fact is regarded as the equivalent of a direction to find proved a part of the prosecution case, and therefore of a partial directed verdict against the defendant. In England, it appears to be accepted that, where a fact is judicially noticed, the jury must be directed to accept such fact as proved. For example, in *R* v *Simpson* [1983] 3 All ER 789, the Court of Appeal held that, since a flick-knife is an article within the meaning of s. 1(4) of the Prevention of Crime Act 1953 and is therefore an offensive weapon *per se*, the judge should take judicial notice that a flick-knife is an offensive weapon, and direct the jury accordingly.

It seems that the question of whether or not a flick-knife is an offensive weapon remains one of fact, and not one of law, and it has been argued powerfully that all questions of fact are to be decided by the jury (cf. *Gibson* v *Wales* [1983] 1 WLR 393; *R* v *Williamson* (1977) 67 Cr App R 35). The American position, therefore, has a certain obvious degree of appeal, although the same argument could be made in a civil case. That position tends to preserve the role of the jury as the tribunal of fact, and thereby serves an important constitutional interest. However, the English rule also has attractions. Perhaps the most important of these is the need for uniformity in areas which are not subject to reasonable dispute, and which are therefore proper areas for judicial notice. Although the American rule is founded primarily on constitutional considerations, it may be that the point made by Federal Rule of Evidence 201 (g) is not beyond argument in England.

### 16.3.2 Notorious facts

Matters of common knowledge, which are too notorious to be capable of serious dispute or debate will be judicially noticed without reference to any source. There are so many instances in the decided cases, and so many more potential subjects of such notice that any attempt at compilation would be pointless, but it would seem that Professor Cross's category of tacit notice would probably fall under this head. The flavour of the subject will be sufficiently apparent by reference to a few examples, and those most beloved of textbook writers include the facts that a fortnight is too short a period for human gestation,[5] that cats are normally kept for domestic purposes,[6] that criminals have unhappy lives[7] and that the advancement of learning is among the purposes for which the

---

[5] *R* v *Luffe* (1807) 8 East 193. But not curiously, that 360 days is too long: see *Preston-Jones* v *Preston-Jones* (HL) [1951] AC 391.
[6] *Nye* v *Niblett and Others* (DC) [1918] 1 KB 23.
[7] *Burns* v *Edman* [1970] 2 QB 541.

University of Oxford exists.[8] The imagination will readily supply a fund of similarly notorious facts in circumstances of all kinds, but those given also serve to suggest the difficulties of proof by evidence which are surmounted by judicial notice in relation to apparently obvious facts.

### 16.3.3 Notice after reference

This type of notice, while undoubtedly well established, creates one or two problems of a kind which are by no means purely theoretical, in that it explores very keenly the dividing line between the taking of judicial notice and the reception of evidence. The actual differences between the two processes are clear. Judicial notice involves a finding of fact by the judge, after which the jury (if there is one) should be directed on the basis that the fact is established. It involves the proposition that no evidence should be admissible to contradict directly the fact judicially noticed. Judicial notice creates a precedent in law, at any rate coterminous with the demonstrability of the truth of the fact noticed; judicial notice that camels are domestic animals may be taken as a universal truth affecting camels generally,[9] whereas the status of a particular foreign sovereign may be noticeable only until the next *coup d'etat*, and must be established anew by reference in each case. But the taking of evidence has none of these characteristics. Matters sought to be established by evidence are questions of fact for the jury. Save in the rare case of legally conclusive evidence, evidence may always be contradicted and explained by contrary evidence. Evidence has effect for the purposes of the instant proceedings only, and (save for the very limited possibility of estoppel) has no effect to prove facts in any other proceedings. Despite these distinctions, however, the two processes come very close where the judge makes reference to sources for the purpose of informing himself, and thereafter taking judicial notice.

It seems clear that the judge should take judicial notice, whether or not he refers to any source, only of facts which appear to him, in the light of his information, to be either sufficiently notorious or to be readily demonstrable. In *Brune v Thompson* (1842) 2 QB 789, it was held that judicial notice could not be taken that part of the Tower of London lay within the City of London, it being equally notorious that part of it lay in the county of Middlesex. It is for the party inviting judicial notice to provide any necessary source of reference, and the judge may refuse to notice any fact for which a proper reference is not provided, a course adopted by Lord Ellenborough in *Van Omeron v Dowick* (NP) (1809) 2 Camp 42, when declining to notice a royal proclamation in the absence of the official *Gazette* containing it. It is obviously desirable that all those facts which in reality require evidence should be left to be proved by evidence, and not short-circuited by the taking of judicial notice.

Judicial notice after reference is taken of the following matters, which are briefly stated here[10]:

(a) Of the existence and contents of public statutes and of the law of England (including now, the law of the European Communities); of the procedure and privileges of

---

[8]   *Oxford Poor Rate Case* (1857) 8 E & B 184; at the present author's university, this decision was generally regarded as a common-law exception based on the obvious difficulty of proving such a proposition by evidence.

[9]   *McQuaker v Goddard* (CA) [1940] 1 KB 687.

[10]   The detail of these matters is comprehensively set out, together with the relevant authorities, in Phipson, *Evidence*, 13th ed., paras 2–11 et seq.

both Houses of Parliament; and of the jurisdiction and rules of each division of the High Court.

(b) Of customs which have been settled by judicial decision, or certified to and recorded in any division of the High Court, such as those of the City of London certified by the Recorder of London. Recent customs must have been recognised more than once by judicial decision, but there is no other requirement concerning frequency of recognition, and the courts incline against requiring proof by evidence over and over of apparently well established customs.[11]

(c) Of professional practice, for example that of the Ordnance Survey[12] or of conveyancers[13] in interpreting references on maps or conveyancing documents.

(d) Of political matters and affairs of state, or the view of the government on such matters including the status and recognition of foreign governments. The practice in such cases is to obtain and act upon the certificate of the Secretary of State, which is for this purpose a source from which the facts contained in it are readily demonstrable, and authoritatively stated.[14]

(e) Readily demonstrable public facts, for example historical or geogaphical facts, or the meaning of words in common usage. For these purposes, reference may be made to apparently objective and authoritative public works, such as histories, maps and dictionaries.

The matters referred to in (d) and (e) above pose a problem of demarcation as between evidence and judicial notice, inasmuch as facts of public concern, stated in public documents, may be proved by evidence of the contents of those documents. The rule is one of common law, but in civil cases now enjoys the statutory authority of s. 9 of the Civil Evidence Act 1968 in the cases there referred to.[15] So far as the matters in (e) are concerned, it may be that the use of such works before taking judicial notice must be confined to what Phipson[16] calls 'refreshing the memory of the judge', in the sense that only notorious or readily demonstrable facts so ascertained may be noticed, any others being a proper subject for evidence. The matters in (d) are more easily reconciled. In practice a certificate of the Secretary of State is invariably regarded as conclusive evidence of the truth of any statement it makes concerning foreign affairs, the status of foreign sovereigns and governments, relations with or between foreign powers and so on. Whether its contents are regarded as matters of conclusive evidence or of judicial notice makes little real difference, despite the varying pronouncements on the subject.[17]

There is no such easy solution, however, to two far more formidable and practically significant problems. These arise: where the court takes judicial notice after receiving evidence on the fact noticed; and where the process of judicial notice is bound up with personal knowledge on the part of the judge.

[11]   *Brandao v Barnett* (HL) (1846) 12 Cl & F 787; *George v Davies* (DC) [1911] 2 KB 445.
[12]   *Davey v Harrow Corporation* (CA) [1958] 1 QB 60 at 69.
[13]   *Re Rosher* (1884) 26 ChD 801.
[14]   The court regards itself as incompetent to judge such matters, and will defer to the view of the responsible minister on behalf of the government: *Duff Development Co. Ltd* v *Government of Kelantan* (HL) [1924] AC 797; *The Parlement Belge* (CA) (1880) 5 PD 197; *Mighell v Sultan of Johore* (CA) [1894] 1 QB 149.
[15]   See generally 6.8, ante.
[16]   *Evidence*, 13th ed., para. 2–22.
[17]   In *Duff Development Co. Ltd* v *Government of Kelantan* (HL) [1924] AC 797, Lords Finlay and Sumner seem to contradict each other on the point, see at 813 and 824.

### 16.3.4 *Judicial notice after evidence*

There seems to be no doubt that a judge may inform himself by hearing evidence, as well as by reference to works, on matters which he is invited to notice judicially. The *locus classicus* is *McQuaker* v *Goddard* [1940] 1 KB 687. Branson J, faced with the problem of deciding whether a camel was a wild or domestic animal for the purpose of the common-law rules governing liability for animals, not only heard a great deal of conflicting expert evidence about the behaviour of camels, but himself consulted books on the subject. Having done so, the learned judge took judicial notice of the fact that the camel was a domestic animal. Both the trial judge, and Clauson LJ in the Court of Appeal, which upheld the decision, made it clear that the process was one of judicial notice, and that the evidence was directed only at assisting the judge to come to his view. Although it may be conducive to the peace of mind of camels and their owners to have a view of them embedded in precedent, it is by no means easy to see how a fact could properly be described as either 'notorious' or 'readily demonstrable', while attracting such a difference of expert opinion, and if the same process could be applied to any such case, the function of a tribunal of fact in assessing evidence might be seriously eroded. The fact that a judge (or jury) forms a view of evidence given in one case cannot generally assist another tribunal of fact in a subsequent case. But it is submitted that this use of judicial notice is proper, provided that it is restricted to the notice of constant facts (such as the nature of camels) which are not dependent upon the facts of any given case.

### 16.3.5 *Personal knowledge*

The question of the extent to which a judge may make use of any personal knowledge which he may have of the facts canvassed before him, is an unresolved one. It seems clear that any person involved in a case as a member of a tribunal of fact may not act on his personal knowledge of the particular facts of a case, in the sense of supplementing the evidence from fortuitous personal knowledge.[18] But in a more general sense, it has been held that, 'properly and within reasonable limits', a judge may apply such general knowledge as he may have of the subject-matter to the process of understanding and evaluating the evidence.[19] Outside such limits, a judge should exclude from his mind such personal knowledge as he has, and it would seem wrong for him either to act evidentially on such knowledge, or to use that knowledge in the process of judicial notice. Justices and jurors have been held to be entitled to make use of such local or general knowledge as they may have. In *Ingram* v *Percival* (DC) [1969] 1 QB 548 it was held that justices had acted properly in making use of their local knowledge of tidal conditions. But in *Wetherall* v *Harrison* (DC) [1976] QB 773, while holding that the Bench had been entitled to take into account the professional knowledge of one of their number in evaluating medical evidence called for the prosecution, and to draw on their own wartime experience of innoculations, the Divisional Court stressed that such knowledge might be drawn on only to evaluate evidence given, and not used as evidence in itself. So far as justices (and jurors) are concerned, the court accepted that they must be free to draw on such knowledge, if only

---

[18]   If a member of the tribunal of fact has such particular knowledge then he should be sworn and give evidence but play no further part judicially in the case: *R (Giant's Causeway etc. Tramway Co.)* v *Antrim Justices* [1895] 2 IR 603; of *R* v *Antrim Justices* [1901] 2 IR 133.

[19]   *Chesson* v *Jordan* [1981] Crim LR 333; but cf. *Reynolds* v *Llanelly Associated Tinplate Co. Ltd* (CA) [1948] 1 All ER 140 (trial judge wrong to make use of personal knowledge in evaluating prospects of a workman with certain skills and of certain age).

because they are not trained judicially to exclude extraneous matters from their minds, but the rule is anyway one of common sense given that one has local benches and juries.

In a sense, the use of such knowledge may be said to be a form of subjective judicial notice, but it is obvious from the above observations that it is qualitively very different from true judicial notice, and it is probably best regarded as one means open to the judge of testing the weight of the evidence before him. Certainly the preponderance of authority would not extend the taking of judicial notice to facts within the personal knowledge of a judge or magistrate, simply because personal knowledge does not make a fact either notorious or readily demonstrable; only common or readily ascertainable knowledge would appear to have that effect. This is not to say that a court should sit with its mind switched off, merely that there must be a judicial exercise of the mind to keep the available information in its proper place.[20]

## 16.4 Presumptions

Presumptions have already been considered in relation to their effect on the burden of proof (see 3.3, ante). We also saw at that time that, as in the case of judicial notice, American courts, while permitting the use of presumptions against the defendant in a criminal case, do not permit the judge to instruct the jury that they must (as opposed to may) find proved the presumed fact on proof of the primary fact. We must now consider the detailed operation of presumptions in general, bearing in mind always the requirements for rebuttal which flow from the effect produced by the presumption upon the burden of proof. We shall also consider the more important individual presumptions to which these principles apply.

A presumption is a rule of law by virtue of which, where a party proves one fact (the primary fact) a second fact (the presumed fact) will also be taken to have been proved, in the absence of evidence to the contrary. A party who adduces evidence sufficient to overcome the effect of the presumption is said to rebut the presumption. The theoretical basis for recognising presumptions is that the presumed fact would, in the usual course of events, flow naturally from the existence of the primary fact, so that there is a rational connection between the two so strong that it is unnecessary to require evidence of the presumed fact in the absence of unusual circumstances. Where a presumption operates to establish the presumed fact, the judge will, in a civil case, find the presumed fact proved or, in a criminal case, direct the jury to find the presumed fact proved. No evidence is then required to establish the presumed fact. Where a presumption is of the 'persuasive' kind, the opponent may rebut the presumption only by disproving the presumed fact to the appropriate standard of proof; if it is of the 'evidential' kind, the opponent may rebut the presumption by introducing evidence against the presumed fact sufficient to amount to a prima facie case, whereupon the presumed fact will be decided according to the applicable rules as to the burden and standard of proof, as any other fact in the case.

It would be comforting to suppose that presumed facts have some common feature, but the recognised presumptions are in fact diverse, and beyond some form of rational connection between the primary and presumed facts (the cogency of which is also rather

---

[20] Where a tribunal sits as a specialist body, for example an industrial tribunal, it may make much freer use of its expertise, and act on its own view: *Dugdale* v *Kraft Foods Ltd* [1976] (EAT) 1 WLR 1288; but the rule appears to extend only to such specialist bodies carrying out a specialist statutory function.

variable) no common feature of significance can be discerned. Indeed, presumptions have defied attempts at classification, and such attempts have generated more academic fury than almost any other subject within the law of evidence. For present purposes, it will be accepted that the law recognises a number of different presumptions which have distinct characteristics, and which therefore must be examined individually.

As we have seen, a presumption requires two things: (a) that a certain primary fact shall be proved; and (b) that on proof of the primary fact, a presumed fact shall thereupon be taken to have been proved, in the absence of evidence to the contrary. If these requirements were universally insisted upon by the courts and by writers, there would be a great deal less confusion about presumptions than there in fact is. A rule of law that has the two requirements set forth above may properly be termed a true presumption. Unfortunately, the term 'presumption' is also frequently applied to rules of law which are in reality quite distinct from presumptions, and for the purpose of distinguishing these false presumptions, true presumptions are then unnecessarily referred to as 'rebuttable presumptions of law'. The three most commonly encountered false presumptions are as follows:

(a)   Rules of law which provide that some fact shall be taken in all cases to be true, without proof of any primary fact, until the contrary is proved. Into this category fall the 'presumptions' of innocence and sanity. These are really no more than expressions of the incidence of the burden of proof in such cases. In one sense, any fact may be said to be true unless somebody proves the contrary, but in reality, such facts fall to be proved in accordance with the normal rules of evidence, including the burden of proof; this is dealt with in Chapter 3.

(b)   Rules of law which preclude the assertion of some necessary fact, without which cases of a certain sort cannot be maintained. Such are the rules that a child under the age of ten cannot be guilty of a criminal offence, and that a boy under fourteen cannot be guilty of rape. It is now almost universally agreed that such rules are rules of substantive law, and have nothing to do with the rules of evidence. Though sometimes termed 'irrebuttable' or 'conclusive' presumptions, they are clearly not presumptions at all. An irrebuttable presumption is a contradiction in terms.

(c)   Inferences of fact, which a tribunal of fact may, but need not, draw, are sometimes known as 'presumptions of fact'. The phrase fully justifies Phipson's stricture that, 'in reality it is no more than a slightly grandiose term for the ordinary process of judicial reasoning about facts'.[21] The phrase expresses the relationship between pieces of circumstantial evidence, and facts in issue or relevant facts in the case. Where a defendant is found in possession of recently stolen goods, or is caught in the act of destroying some item of evidence, then obviously it is open to a jury to draw the inference that he knew or believed the goods to be stolen, or that the evidence was unfavourable to him, as the case may be. To speak of a presumption is unnecessary and misleading, because the jury are not in any circumstances bound to draw that inference, even if no evidence is called for the defence. Much of the difficulty arises because of inexact usage, both judicial and extra-judicial. The high-water mark of the inexactitude led the House of Lords in *DPP* v *Smith* [1961] AC 290 to seek to elevate into a principle of law, effectively into a true presumption, the fairly obvious proposition of common sense that a man apparently in normal control of his faculties should be taken to have intended the natural and probable consequences of his act. In the course of his speech, with which the other Lords agreed, Viscount Kilmuir

---

[21]   *Evidence*, 13th ed., para. 41–04.

went so far as it say that it did not matter whether one called it a presumption of law or of fact. By s. 8 of the Criminal Justice Act 1967, Parliament put the matter back where it belonged—in the area of fact for the jury. The section is worth citing in full, because it expresses very well how such inferences operate:

A court or jury, in determining whether a person has committed an offence,—

(a)   shall not be bound in law to infer that he intended or foresaw a result of his actions by reason only of its being a natural and probable consequence of those actions; but
(b)   shall decide whether he did intend or foresee that result by reference to all the evidence, drawing such inferences from the evidence as appear proper in the circumstances.

Thus reduced into real terms, the misuse of the word 'presumption', lacking as it does any legal force in this context, is exposed. None of this makes it any less likely that a jury will act on such evidence in appropriate cases.

The three misuses of the word 'presumption' described above will not be further considered, and we shall now turn to the most important true presumptions, rebuttable presumptions of law, in relation to which on proof of some primary fact or facts, the court will find proved a presumed fact, in the absence of evidence to the contrary. It is not proposed to consider the presumptions arising from possession of or title to land, or the maxim *res ipsa loquitur*, for which reference should be made elsewhere in works dealing with the substantive law. The law relating to the statutory presumptions arising under s. 11 and s. 12 of the Civil Evidence Act 1968 is dealt with in 9.13, and that relating to certain presumptions about the due execution of documents in 15.4.3, ante.

### 16.4.1   Presumption of legitimacy

It will be presumed that a child is the legitimate child of a husband and wife, and accordingly that access took place between them resulting in conception of the child, on proof of the following primary facts: (a) that the child was born to the wife; (b) that it was born during lawful wedlock or within the normal period of gestation after wedlock has ended; and (c) that the husband was alive at the date of conception.

This presumption is hedged about with historical considerations, principally the concern of the common law not to permit proceedings to bastardise children and so subject them to the once considerable stigma of illegitimacy. The presumption itself remains useful, although its force has been somewhat weakened by the provision now embodied in s. 48(1) of the Matrimonial Causes Act 1973 that the evidence of a husband or wife is admissible in any proceedings to prove that intercourse did or did not take place between them during any period. Furthermore, both spouses are now compellable to give evidence of these matters: Civil Evidence Act 1968, s. 16(4); Police and Criminal Evidence Act 1984 s. 80(9). See 11.5, ante.

Proof of the primary facts must be properly made. But conversely the mere fact of voluntary separation during the marriage[22] or the mere fact that divorce proceedings have been commenced or a decree nisi granted,[23] or even that at the time of the birth the mother

---

[22]   *Ettenfield* v *Ettenfield* (CA) [1940] P 96.
[23]   *Knowles* v *Knowles* [1962] P 161.

has remarried following decree absolute[24] will not affect the operation of the presumption, if they are so proved. However, where the separation is by virtue of a court order, not only will the presumption cease to apply, but there will arise a contrary presumption of illegitimacy based on the assumed absence of sexual intercourse between husband and wife in such circumstances, though this presumption may be rebutted by evidence that sexual intercourse did in fact take place between them during the period of ordered separation: *Hetherington* v *Hetherington* (1887) 12 PD 112. Accordingly, where the child is born more than nine months after the making of the order for separation, the child will be presumed to be illegitimate.

At common law, there was originally a rule of law precluding proceedings to bastardise a child if, at the time of conception, the husband was 'within the four seas', so that lawful access could have taken place. This rule of law was abrogated, but left in its wake considerable uncertainty as to what evidence was required to rebut the presumption of legitimacy. Because of the once considerable stigma attaching to illegitimacy, there was some feeling that the presumption should be rebuttable only by evidence that proved illegitimacy beyond reasonable doubt, and despite the gradual erosion of rules which applied that standard to issues of status and conduct in family law cases generally, the position was left unresolved by the decisions of the House of Lords in *Preston-Jones* v *Preston-Jones* [1951] AC 391 and *Blyth* v *Blyth* [1966] AC 643. Eventually, the matter was resolved by statute, s. 26 of the Family Law Reform Act 1969, which provides that:

> Any presumption of law as to the legitimacy or illegitimacy of any person may in any civil proceedings be rebutted by evidence which shows that it is more probable than not that that person is illegitimate or legitimate, as the case may be, and it shall not be necessary to prove that fact beyond reasonable doubt in order to rebut the presumption.

The presumption is unlikely to arise in a criminal case, but it is submitted that, if this should occur, the standard of proof on rebuttal would vary according to whether the rebuttal was being attempted by the prosecution or the defence. Only in the former case would a standard beyond reasonable doubt be required.

In civil cases, the section has laid to rest a number of older authorities which explored the kinds of evidence which might be admissible to rebut the presumption. Any relevant and admissible evidence, whether in the form of evidence of sexual intercourse between the wife and a man other than the husband, the impotence or absence of the husband at the time of conception, evidence derived from blood tests or any other such evidence, may be introduced. Furthermore, it has been held that even relatively slight evidence may be sufficient to rebut the presumption. In *S* v *S* Lord Reid said, referring to s. 26[25]:

> That means that the presumption of legitimacy now merely determines the onus of proof. Once evidence has been led it must be weighed without using the presumption as

---

[24]   *Maturin* v *Attorney-General* [1938] 2 All ER 214; *Re Overbury. Sheppard* v *Matthews and Others* [1955] Ch 122.

[25]   [1972] AC 24, 41. That the point made in the text about Lord Reid's speech in this case is not entirely academic is shown by the decision of Rees J in *T(H)* v *T(E)* [1971] 1 WLR 429, a case which demonstrates how critical questions of the presumption and the burden of proof can be in a close case.

a make-weight in the scale for legitimacy. So even weak evidence against legitimacy must prevail if there is not other evidence to counterbalance it. The presumption will only come in at that stage in the very rare case of the evidence being so evenly balanced that the court is unable to reach a decision on it. I cannot recollect ever having seen or heard of a case of any kind where the court could not reach a decision on the evidence before it.

It is submitted that this statement of the effect of s. 26 is not entirely satisfactory. The implication of Lord Reid's words is that the presumption is only evidential, so that when evidence sufficient to constitute a prima facie against the presumed fact is adduced, the presumption disappears, leaving the issue to be determined without it. Yet the section appears to call for disproof of the presumed fact to the usual standard of proof in a civil case, which is consistent with Parliament's intention that the presumption should be persuasive, even though disproof need not be made to the criminal standard of proof. The matter stands in need of further clarification. Certainly, it may be true that the court will no longer require any unusually cogent proof, merely because the issue of legitimacy is involved, but this affects the weight of the evidence adduced rather than the burden of proof itself.

### 16.4.2 Presumption of marriage

It will be presumed that a man and woman are or were validly married on proof of either of the alternative primary facts: (a) that they went through a ceremony of marriage; or (b) that they have cohabited together. The presumption extends to include the necessary presumption of formal capacity to marry.

In *Piers and Another* v *Piers* (HL) (1849) 2 HL Cas 331, where the marriage had been celebrated in a private house and there was no evidence that the necessary special licence had been obtained, the presumption was held nevertheless to apply. And where cohabitation is shown, the presumption is not rebutted merely because it is shown that such cohabitation preceded any ceremony between the parties[26] or even by evidence that the marriage, if celebrated, took place under a system of law which required registration of it, and that no entry appeared in the relevant register.[27]

The effect is that the presumption is a strong one, although its importance has naturally declined somewhat with the advent of modern records, which are admissible in evidence. The presumption may not be employed to prove the validity of an alleged existing marriage in a prosecution for bigamy; in such a case, the existing valid marriage must be proved by direct evidence that the defendant was a party to a ceremony which resulted in a valid marriage, though apart from the identity of the defendant, this may be proved by production of a certified copy of the entry in the relevant register.[28]

It is clear that strong evidence is needed to rebut the presumption, where it applies. In *Piers and Another* v *Piers* Lord Cottenham LC, citing with approval words from older authority said[29]: 'The presumption of law is not lightly to be repelled. It is not to be broken

---

[26] *Hill* v *Hill* (PC, Barbados) [1959] 1 WLR 127.

[27] *Re Taplin, Watson* v *Tate* [1937] 3 All ER 105.

[28] *R* v *Kay* (1887) 16 Cox CC 292; in *R* v *Shaw* (1943) 60 TLR 344, where evidence was given of a ceremony and the defendant did not give evidence, the Court of Criminal Appeal held the evidence to be sufficient. The prior marriage may sometimes be proved by admission by the defendant; but see 7.3, ante.

[29] 2 HL Cas 331 at 362, citing *Morris (otherwise Williams)* v *Davies and Another* (1837)(HL) 5 Cl & F 163 at 265, per Lord Lyndhurst.

in upon or shaken by a mere balance of probability. The evidence for the purpose of repelling it must be strong, distinct, satisfactory and conclusive.' The word 'conclusive' has been rightly criticised as begging the issue, but it is true that strong evidence is necessary. In *Mahadervan v Mahadervan* [1964] P 233, the Divisional Court held that the presumption might be rebutted only by evidence which satisfied the court beyond any reasonable doubt that the marriage was not a valid one, though today it might well be held that the ordinary civil standard of proof applies (see 3.9, ante). The evidence must nonetheless be cogent. Evidence of incapacity[30] or of a valid prior marriage [31] will suffice, but not where the prior marriage is of doubtful validity.[32]

In *Mahadervan* v *Mahadervan*, it was argued that the presumption did not apply in favour of a foreign marriage, at least where such marriage, if proved, would invalidate an English one celebrated subsequently. Of this argument, Sir Jocelyn Simon P said ([1964] P 233 at 247):

> To accept it would give expression to a legal chauvinism that has no place in any rational system of private international law. Our courts in my view apply exactly the same weight of presumption in favour of a foreign marriage as of an English one, and the nationality of any later marriage brought into question is quite immaterial.

### 16.4.3   Presumption of death

A person will be presumed to have died on proof of the following primary facts: (a) that there is no acceptable evidence that the subject has been alive at some time during a continuous period of seven years or more; (b) that there are persons likely to have heard of him, had he been alive, who have not heard of him during that period; and (c) that all due inquiries have been made with a view to locating the subject, without success.[33]

The existence of a person likely to have heard of the subject appears to be a necessary requirement, and was so treated by Sachs J in his judgment in the leading modern case of *Chard* v *Chard*. The learned judge refused to presume a wife to be dead, even though there was no evidence that she had been alive since 1918. The issue was whether she was alive in 1933 (when she would have been aged 43) in which year the husband had gone through a ceremony of marriage with the petitioner, who now sought a decree of nullity based on its bigamous character. The husband had spent most of the intervening period in prison, and there was no reason to suppose that he was likely to have heard of his first wife between 1918 and 1933. Since there was no person likely to have heard of the first wife during this time, Sachs J held that the presumption of death could not apply, and granted the decree. There is some authority for saying that the absence of a person likely to have heard may be remedied by the making of all reasonable inquiries,[34] but the better view seems to be that the two primary facts are separate, and that each is necessary. What amounts to the making of reasonable inquiries, and what amounts to the absence of acceptable evidence that the subject is alive during the period, are questions of fact in every case.

The presumption is only that the subject died at some time during the period; his death on any particular day will not be presumed, and must be proved by evidence if in issue. In

30   *Tweney* v *Tweney* [1946] P 180.
31   *Gatty and Gatty* v *Attorney-General* [1951] P 444.
32   *Taylor* v *Taylor* [1967] P 25.
33   *Chard* v *Chard* [1956] P 259, per Sachs J at 272.
34   *Doe d France* v *Andrews* (1850) 15 QB 756, per Alderson B.

*Re Phene's Trusts* (1870) 5 Ch App 139, the court, while prepared to presume that a nephew of the testator was dead in 1868, he having last been heard of as a deserter from the United States Navy in 1860, would not presume that he survived the testator, who had died in January 1861. Indeed, strictly, the presumption is only that the subject is dead at the date of trial, although in a number of decisions it appears to have been applied retrospectively. In *Chipchase* v *Chipchase* [1939] P 391 the wife married H1 in 1915, and having heard nothing of him after 1916 went through a ceremony of marriage with H2 in 1928. When the wife applied for a maintenance order against H2 in 1939, it was successfully objected that the 1928 marrriage was not shown to be valid, there being no evidence that H1 was dead in that year. The Divisional Court remitted the case to the magistrates to consider whether there was any evidence to rebut the presumption of death, although strictly the presumption should have been only that H1 was dead at the date of the trial in 1939, and not in 1928. More significantly, the same more liberal view has been taken in cases of succession,[35] so as to permit the distribution of property along the lines dictated by a presumption that the testator died within a given period before the trial, and it may be said with some caution that this view is likely to be adopted in the future.

The period of seven years is, however, strictly insisted upon, and it is often pointed out that, though the rule is to some extent illogical, a period of six years and 364 days is not enough. Nor is there any presumption that the subject died from any particular cause, died childless or died celibate, though these matters may be capable of inference on the evidence, as a question of fact.[36] It should be remembered that it is always open to the court to infer death (or that someone is alive) as a matter of fact, as it is to make any other proper inferences from the evidence.[37] No question of the presumption arises in such a case; it is a matter of circumstantial evidence. What is sometimes called the 'presumption of continuance'—an instance of which is that if a person is shown to be alive at a certain time, his continuing life may be inferred—is no more than an example of such an inference, and will yield to the presumption of death where the latter applies.

The following statutory provisions should be noted in connection with presumptions of death:

(a)  By s. 184 of the Law of Property Act 1925, if commorientes die after 1925, and it is to be decided who died first, it shall be presumed that they died in order of seniority, and consequently that the younger was the survivor.[38] This rule does not apply to cases where A is proved to have died at a certain time, and B has not been heard of for seven years or more prior to A's death, when the presumption is that A survived B.

(b)  By s. 19(3) of the Matrimonial Causes Act 1973, on a petition for presumption of death and dissolution of marriage:

In any proceedings under this section the fact that for a period of seven years or more the other party to the marriage has been continually absent from the petitioner and the

---

[35]  *Re Aldersey, Gibson* v *Hall* [1905] 2 Ch 181; though a contrary view was taken in other cases, e.g. *Re Rhodes, Rhodes* v *Rhodes* (1887) 36 ChD 586.

[36]  *Re Jackson, Jackson* v *Ward* [1907] 2 Ch 354.

[37]  As in *Re Watkins, Watkins* v *Watkins* [1953] 1 WLR 1323, where despite the absence of inquiries, which precluded reliance on the presumption, the court inferred death from the circumstantial evidence, including a very long absence.

[38]  The rule does not apply to all cases. See, in respect of spouses, one of whom dies intestate, the modification introduced by the Intestates' Estates Act 1952, s.1(4). See also the Cestui que Vie Act 1666.

petitioner has no reason to believe that the other party has been living within that time shall be evidence that the other party is dead until the contrary is proved.

For the purpose of assessing whether or not the petitioner has had reason to believe that the other party has been living, only events during the period of seven years are relevant.[39]

(c)   By the proviso to s. 57 of the Offences against the Person Act 1861 (which defines the offence of bigamy):

Provided, that nothing in this section contained shall extend to . . . any person marrying a second time whose husband or wife shall have been continually absent from such person for the space of seven years then last past, and shall not have been known by such person to be living within that time.

Despite sometimes inconsistent authority, it seems that the defendant bears an evidential burden of raising by evidence the issue of absence for seven years, whereupon the prosecution must prove beyond reasonable doubt (in discharge of their legal burden of proof) that he did know the spouse to be living during that period of time.[40]

### 16.4.4   Presumption of regularity

The 'presumption of regularity', often expressed in the Latin tag, *omnia praesumuntur rite et solemniter esse acta*, really embodies three separate presumptions, which may be described as follows:

(a)   On proof of the primary fact that some official or public act has been performed or that a person acted in an official or public capacity, it is presumed that the act done complied with any necessary formalities, or that the person so acting was properly appointed for the purpose, as the case may be. This presumption applies to judicial acts in the sense that it is presumed that a person presiding over an inferior court or a tribunal, was validly appointed to do so.[41] It applies to a great variety of other official acts, such as those performed by constables or justices of the peace,[42] and even to acts of divine service performed in a building, which were presumed to have been performed after due consecration.[43]

It is sometimes said that this presumption cannot be relied on to establish an ingredient of a criminal offence, if the substance of the act or appointment is disputed at the trial.[44] But there is authority that such dispute must be made by way of challenge by evidence, which if correct, weakens the authority of the rule.[45] It may be that the presumption ought to apply, even in such cases, because it may be rebutted by very slight evidence of irregularity, and saves much specious dispute.

[39]   *Thompson* v *Thompson* [1956] P 414, per Sachs J at 425.
[40]   *R* v *Curgerwen* (CCR) (1865) LR 1 CCR 1.
[41]   *R* v *Roberts* (CCR) (1878) 14 Cox CC 101. But there is no presumption that the court or tribunal had jurisdiction in any particular matter: *Christopher Brown Ltd* v *Genossenschaft Oesterreichischer Waldbesitzer Holzwirtschaftsbetriebe Registrierte Genossenschaft mbH* [1954] 1 QB 8, per Devlin J at 13.
[42]   *Berryman* v *Wise* (1791) 4 TR 366.
[43]   *R* v *Cresswell* (CCR) (1873) 1 QBD 446.
[44]   *Scott* v *Baker* DC [1969] 1 QB 659.
[45]   *Campbell* v *Wallsend Slipway & Engineering Co. Ltd* (DC) [1978] ICR 1015.

(b)   On proof of the primary fact that a mechanical instrument is usually in order and working correctly, it will be presumed that it was so working and in order when used on a relevant occasion. Automatic traffic signals are a good example[46] and numerous other devices, for example the speedometer of a police vehicle proved to have been recently checked for accuracy, are treated in the same way.

(c)   On proof that necessary business transactions have been carried out, which require to be effected in a certain order, it will be presumed that they were effected in that order.[47]

### 16.4.5   Conflicting presumptions

Complex questions may arise when two conflicting presumptions act upon the same fact. Such problems arise principally in relation to the validity of successive marriages, on which may depend questions of legitimacy and of the power of the court to grant matrimonial relief. They also seem to arise in cases where it is uncertain whether a person is dead or alive. However, the conflict is usually illusory as a legal problem in these latter cases, because although the law recognises certain presumptions of death, continuing life is merely an inference which the tribunal of fact may draw from the absence of evidence of death. The inference in favour of continuing life may or may not be able to be drawn, depending upon whether a presumption of death operates on the facts of the case, and if so, upon whether there is evidence to rebut that presumption.

In *R* v *Willshire* (1881) 6 QBD 366, the defendant was convicted of bigamy, in that he had married W2 in 1868, during the lifetime of W1, to whom he had been married in 1864. In 1879, the defendant married W3 and during W3's lifetime in 1880, married W4 and was again charged with bigamy. The defendant's conviction was quashed because of the failure of the trial judge to leave to the jury the issue of whether W1 was alive at the time of the marriage to W3. If she was, then the marriage to W3 would have been invalid, and since the charge of bigamy in marrying W4 depended on proof that W3 was the defendant's spouse at the time of the marriage to W4, the defendant would have been entitled to a somewhat unmeritorious acquittal.

With the exception of Lord Coleridge CJ, all the members of the court (Lindley, Hawkins, Lopes and Bowen JJ) dealt with the issue presented as one simply of the burden of proof in a criminal case. Since the defendant had raised the issue of whether W1 was still alive at the time of the marriage to W3, that issue should have been left to the jury and the prosecution had to rebut the defendant's allegation beyond reasonable doubt. Lord Coleridge CJ, while dealing with the case as one concerned with the burden of proof, also suggested that the facts gave rise to conflicting presumptions, arising from the presumed validity of the marriages to W1 and W3 respectively. (Lord Coleridge CJ also thought that there was a presumption that W1 was still alive in 1879, because there was no evidence to show that she had died since 1864, but for the reasons stated above, this was actually no more than one possible inference from the facts. The jury could have inferred from the facts that W1 was alive in 1879, if the evidence appeared to warrant such an inference.) Lord Coleridge suggests that where there are conflicting presumptions, the presumptions cancel each other out, leaving the presumed facts to be decided on the whole of the evidence.

In criminal cases, this may be a convenient way of analysing the position, and because

---

[46]   *Tingle Jacobs & Co.* v *Kennedy* (CA) [1964] 1 WLR 638n. So too with breath-test devices, chronometers, radar equipment and many other instances.

[47]   *Eaglehill Ltd* v *J Needham (Builders) Ltd* (HL) [1973] AC 992.

the prosecution will always bear the burden of proving the defendant's guilt, little harm can result from it. However, in a civil case, cancellation out of conflicting presumptions may do no more than deny effect to one of the presumptions. In *Gatty and Gatty* v *Attorney-General*[48] the petitioner in a legitimacy suit had been born in 1901. His parents had gone through a ceremony of marriage in 1897, after his father had obtained a decree of divorce in the state of North Dakota earlier in the same year. For various reasons of law, there was some doubt as to whether the North Dakota decree was valid. It was held that because of the presumption that the father's first marriage was valid, the petitioner must prove all the facts necessary to show that the North Dakota decree was valid. In such a case, to speak of conflicting presumptions as to the respective validity of the father's first and second marriages would tend to deny the effect of the first in time. Therefore, if there is no evidence tending to cast doubt on the validity of an earlier marriage or to show that the earlier marriage was terminated by death or dissolution, evidence of the earlier marriage should overcome the presumption of validity of the later.

In *Taylor* v *Taylor* [1965] 1 All ER 872, Cairns J had before him a case of great factual complexity. In essence, the petitioner sought a decree of divorce with respect to her marriage with the respondent, which was contracted in 1942. Whether this marriage was valid depended upon the validity of the petitioner's earlier marriage contracted in 1928. Cairns J found as a fact that there was no decisive evidence that the 1928 marriage was invalid, and that a doubtful earlier marriage was insufficient to overcome the presumption of validity of the later marriage. Although the learned judge expressed himself to be following *Gatty*, and rejecting an argument that the conflicting presumptions cancelled each other out, his decision effectively denied the potency of the presumption in favour of the earlier marriage. The petitioner bore the burden of proving the validity of the second marriage, which must have been invalid if the earlier marriage were both valid and undissolved. If the evidence failed to establish the status of the earlier marriage decisively, the presumption in favour of the earlier marriage should probably have been held to overcome the presumption in favour of the validity of the later marriage.

It is submitted that, at least in a civil case, the facts should be analysed to see whether the party who bears the burden of proof has overcome any presumption earlier in time to an apparently conflicting presumption on which that party intends to rely. While it may be possible to question his application of the principle to the complex facts before him. Cairns J was surely correct in *Taylor* in holding that where the conflicting presumptions relate to two different events (here, the two marriages) the validity of the former must be tested first, in which case no 'cancellation' is required, and the validity of the second will depend on the validity of the first. If a case can exist in which two presumptions conflict in relation to the same fact, it would seem that such presumptions must cancel each other out. However, excluding the case of an issue of whether a person is alive or dead (to which only one presumption can apply) it is difficult to envisage a case in which this would occur.

## 16.5   Questions for discussion

The following questions apply to both *R* v *Coke; R* v *Littleton* and to *Blackstone* v *Coke*.

1   Prepare a list of facts which might properly be admitted formally for the purpose of the proceedings. Explain why those facts should be admitted.

---

    [48]   [1951] P 444. See also *MacDarmaid* v *Attorney-General* [1950] P 218; *Russell* v *Attorney-General* [1949] P 391.

2   What procedural steps should be taken to put the formal admissions before the court? What effect will the formal admissions have at trial?

3   Are there any matters which the judge may notice judicially? How should these matter be presented to the judge for this purpose, and what effect will the facts judicially noticed have at trial?

The following question applies only to *Blackstone* v *Coke*, but assume that the evidence in the earlier criminal case is also available for consideration.

4   Assume hypothetically that Parliament has passed the following statutory provision, which is applicable to these cases:

Where the paternity of any child is disputed, and a male person over the age of fourteen years admits, orally or in writing or otherwise, that he had sexual intercourse with the mother of the child at or near the time of conception, such male person shall be presumed to be the father of the child unless he proves the contrary.

Discuss the effect of this presumption on the issues to be resolved at the trial, having regard to the statements made both by Henry Coke and Anthony Henneky.

# Index